PHYSICAL EDUCATION AND THE STUDY OF SPORT

SECOND EDITION

Dr Bob Davis
Lecturer in Physical Education, Manchester Metropolitan University, Crewe & Alsager Faculty;
Chief Examiner (1986–93), Reviser and Practical Moderator 'A' Level Physical Education

Ros Bull, BEd (Hons) MSc
Principal Lecturer in Physical Education, Liverpool John Moores University;
Former Chief Moderator, 'A' Level Physical Education and Sports Studies (AEB) (1988–93)

Jan Roscoe, BEd (Hons) MSc
Teacher of 'A' Level Physical Education and Human Biology, Widnes Sixth Form College;
Anatomy and Physiology Consultant for 'A' Level Physical Education (AEB)

Dr Dennis Roscoe
Head of School of Maths and Sciences, Knowsley Community College;
Biomechanics Consultant and Assistant Examiner for 'A' Level Physical Education (1989–93)

Mosby
London Baltimore Bogotá Boston Buenos Aires Caracas Carlsbad, CA Chicago Madrid Mexico City Milan Naples, FL
New York Philadelphia St. Louis Sydney Tokyo Toronto Wiesbaden

Published in 1994 by Mosby, an imprint of Times Mirror International Publishers Limited

Reprinted 1996

Printed in Spain by Grafos S.A. Arte sobre papel, Barcelona, Spain

ISBN 0 7234 1972 8

For full details of all Times Mirror International Publishers Limited titles please write to Times Mirror International Publishers Limited, Lynton House, 7–12 Tavistock Square, London WC1H 9LB, England.

A CIP catalogue record for this book is available from the British Library.

Library of Congress Cataloging-in-Publication Data has been applied for.

Contents

Preface to Second Edition 5
Preface to First Edition 5
Acknowledgements 6

Part One: The Performer in Action **7**

1. *The Anatomy of Physical Performance* *8*
    1.1 The Human Skeleton in Action 8
    1.2 Joints in Action 19
    1.3 Muscles in Action 24
    1.4 Types of Muscular Contraction 33
    1.5 A Typical Muscle and its Structure from Gross to Molecular Detail 37
    1.6 How Coordinated Movement is Produced 42
2. *Cardio-Respiratory Systems* *49*
    2.1 The Heart 49
    2.2 The Vascular System 59
    2.3 Blood Flow in Muscles 64
    2.4 Respiratory Factors in Physical Performance 70
    2.5 Gas Exchange in the Lungs 77
    2.6 Lung Volumes and Physical Activity 82
3. *Energy for Exercise* *88*
    3.1 Energy and Work 88
    3.2 Energy Creation and Release within Muscle 93
    3.3 The Recovery Process after Exercise 100
    3.4 Oxygen Uptake/Oxygen Consumption 105
    3.5 Nutrition for Exercise 111
4. *Training for Physical Performance* *115*
    4.1 Physical Fitness and Fitness Testing 115
    4.2 Training 126
5. *Fitness for Life* *157*
    5.1 Obesity 157
    5.2 Cardiovascular Diseases 163
6. *Biomechanics: Linear Motion* *170*
7. *The Nature and Application of Force* *179*
    7.1 Force as a Vector 179
    7.2 Internal Forces 207
8. *Rotating Systems* *215*

Part Two: The Performer as a Person **229**

9. *The Nature and Classification of Skill* *230*
    9.1 Skill Defined 230
    9.2 Skill Classified 232
    9.3 Skill and Ability 235
10. *Information Processing in Perceptual-motor Performance* *237*
    10.1 Sensory Input 239
    10.2 Perception 242
    10.3 Decision Making 248
    10.4 Motor Output and Feedback 254
11. *Individual Differences* *259*
    11.1 Fundamental Movement Patterns 259
    11.2 Psychomotor Abilities 263

12 .*Principles of Learning and Teaching* 270
12.1 Learning 271
12.2 Teaching 279
13. *Psychology of Sport* 286
13.1 Personality 287
13.2 The Self Concept 292
13.3 Social Influences 296
13.4 Motivation 306
13.5 Optimizing Performance 316

Part Three: The Performer in a Social Setting **327**
14. *Important Concepts in Physical Education and Sport* 328
14.1 Towards a Concept of Leisure 333
14.2 Towards a Concept of Play 339
14.3 Towards a Concept of Recreation 342
14.4 What do we mean by Physical Recreation? 343
14.5 Towards a Concept of Sport 347
14.6 What is Physical Education? 353
15. *The Social Setting of Physical Education and Sport in Four Countries* 359
15.1 Geographical Influences on Physical Education and Sport 359
15.2 Historical Influences on Sport and Physical Education 362
15.3 Socio-Economic Factors Influencing Sport and Physical Education 366
16. *The Administration of Physical Education and Sport in Four Countries* 378
16.1 Administration of Physical Education 378
16.2 The Administration of Sport 398
16.3 The Organization of Outdoor Recreation and Outdoor Education 413
17. *Sociological Considerations of Physical Education and Sport* 426
17.1 Towards an Understanding of Sports Sociology 426
17.2 Society, Culture and Sport 430
17.3 Group Dynamics in Sporting Situations 439
17.4 Roles in Sport and Physical Education 445
18. *Some Contemporary Issues in Physical Education and Sport* 449
18.1 Societal: Excellence in Sport 450
18.2 Institutional: Outdoor Education 455
18.3 Subcultural: Women in Sport 460
19. *Historical Perceptives and Popular Recreation* 465
19.1 Historical Perspectives 465
19.2 Factors Underlying the Origins of Sport 468
19.3 The Pattern of Popular Recreation in Great Britain 469
20. *Athleticism in Nineteenth-Century English Public Schools* 488
20.1 Background to Public School Development 488
20.2 The Structural Basis of the English Public School System 489
20.3 The Technical Development of Sports in the Public Schools 492
20.4 Athleticism and Character Development 498
20.5 The Influence of Public School Athleticism on Sport in Society 500
21. *The Pattern of Rational Recreation in Nineteenth-Century Britain* 503
22. *Transitions in English Elementary Schools* 515
22.1 Nineteenth-Century Drill and Gymnastics 515
22.2 The 1902 Model Course 516
22.3 Early Syllabuses of Physical Training 518
22.4 The Effects of the Second World War (1939–45) 523

Index 527

Preface to Second Edition

The second edition of this book has involved a careful review and update of content and a radical redesign. The popular response of teachers and pupils to the first edition reflected an appreciation of a presentational style that was both academically stimulating and user-friendly.

The need for changes arose from the progress made in teaching 'A' level P.E. over a period of 6 years. These changes are reflected not only in the amazing uptake of the syllabus from 15 to 450 centres but also in the enthusiastic way teachers have attended in-service programmes, reviewed sections of the syllabus and investigated pro-active teaching styles.

The parallel development of the Sports Studies 'A' level and the recognition of the book as a basic undergraduate text has led to an extension of the scientific aspects to accommodate a broader readership.

Sport Psychology has been enhanced to include sections on aggression and attitudes in sport.

Finally, the authors have felt it necessary to rethink certain aspects and recognize recent societal changes associated with the reforms in the former Soviet Union and the end of apartheid in South Africa.

It is hoped that these changes will increase the quality of the content of the book and that the new design will improve its presentational appeal.

Bob Davis

Preface to First Edition

We are a team of four, all professionally involved in teaching physical education and sports studies in schools and in colleges of further and higher education. Our expertise ranges from physiology and biomechanics, through psychological dimensions to socio-cultural studies involving contemporary, historical and comparative perspectives. We are also experienced coaches and are engaged either in the teaching or the examining of formal physical education examination programmes.

Since the Second World War, physical education has changed dramatically from a physical training experience of therapeutics and sports skills to an educational medium as much concerned with personal development as with physical performance. This has led our subject to become increasingly reflective as well as active, where there is a desire to experience physical activity but also to understand and justify it.

In Britain the major step in this direction was the acceptance of physical education as a graduate subject and today we are following the American tradition by producing a wide range of first degrees, an increasing number at masters level and, at last, a number of doctorates.

For many years graduates had little opportunity to use their theoretical expertise in schools. However, this has changed with the introduction of physical education in the formal examination of 16- and 18-year-olds and with the recognition of such examinations as qualifications for higher education.

We were concerned by the absence of theoretical source material suitable for this age group. Higher education texts are often presented at too high a level and they are invariably specialized. We felt a need for a general text which would be interesting and readily understandable to young people.

Every attempt has been made to present a task-oriented book which will give students an introduction to the varied perspectives of our subject and help them to synthesize theory and practice. We have no doubts that the centre of our interest is in the physical experience of human movement, but we also believe that if we know more about the performer in action, the performer as a person, and the performer in society, we will be better equipped to study our field in the 1990s.

This book may be used as a basic textbook for students of all ages. It should be a useful text for teachers and should be valuable for sports coaches and youth leaders. Similarly, every attempt has been made to give this work an international perspective. Physical educationists in Europe, America and Australasia will find that most of the content applies to them as much as to the British and that the presentation style will appeal to them as a first-level text for their own assessment programmes. Finally, for those interested in comparative studies, this book should give an accurate picture of the level of understanding expected of a British 18-year-old with professional aspirations in physical education.

Bob Davis

Acknowledgements

We would like to acknowledge Shirley Doolan, John Helms, Peter Cullen and Rosemary Watts for their art-work; and Ken Travis for the photographs in Part Two.

Acknowledgements are also due to the Associated Examining Board for taking the initiative in creating two worthwhile Advanced level courses in physical education.

We would like to thank Pamela Baxby, Derek Benning, Janet Chapman, Derek Cocup, Robert Davis, John Honeybourne, David Kellett, Peter Morris, Gary Pullan, Jean Sivori, Kevin Sykes, Carol Taylor, Peter Walder for their patience and helpful comments on the four manuscripts which have been compiled together within this edition.

Further acknowledgement is due to the Macmillan Company of Australia Pty Ltd. for their permission to use material from *Physical Education: Theory and Practice* by Davis *et al.* in Part Two.

Finally, we would like to acknowledge James Watkins for his kind permission to adapt the following illustrations, from Watkins J., *An Introduction to the Mechanics of Human Movement,* MTP Press, 1983: Figures 7.9(c), 7.12(a) and (b), 7.14(c), 7.20(a), 7.44(a) and (b), 7.50, and 8.2.

Part One:

The Performer in Action

If we are to understand the **performer in action** we need to know how the body is put together, how it functions, how it moves, and how it applies forces to itself and other bodies with which it comes into contact.

Two main sections have been combined within Part One. These are the application of **human anatomy** and **physiology** (Chapters 1–5), and **biomechanics** (Chapters 6–8) to the study of physical education and sport.

The aim of **'The Performer in Action'** is to develop, very simply, and by no means completely, some of the concepts in these areas of study in the mind of the student, in as relevant and as practical a manner as possible. It will therefore be essential for the student to look at other texts on intermediate level Human Anatomy, Physiology, Biomechanics and Physics to search out more detail than is provided here, or to progress the concepts further as interest takes him or her.

The results tables included in this text are available for students to copy and use.

A short bibliography of texts whose reading would extend understanding and knowledge of relevant concepts is to be found, where appropriate, at the end of each chapter and at the end of both sections.

For the teacher, **'The Performer in Action'** will provide a series of practical activities which should help the non-scientific student to understand the essentials of anatomical, physiological and biomechanical concepts without the need for a detailed programme of specialist lessons. **A Teacher's Guide and Answer Book** to Part One is available from the authors. For details write to: Jan Roscoe, Holyrood, 23 Stockswell Road, Widnes, Cheshire WA8 9PJ.

Chapter 1
The Anatomy of Physical Performance

Athletic activity in all its forms of movement is made possible by the arrangement and functioning of bodily systems. The aim of this section is to discover how we move.

1.1 The Human Skeleton in Action

KEY WORDS AND CONCEPTS

Skeleton	**Hyaline or articular cartilage**	**Ossification .**
Axial skeleton	**White fibrocartilage**	**Diaphysis**
Appendicular skeleton	**Compact bone**	**Epiphyseal plate**
Articular	**Cancellous bone**	**Osteoblast**
Long bone	**Haversian system**	**Osteoclast**
Short bone	**Bony features**	**Osteocyte**
Flat bone	**Protrusions**	**Intramembranous ossification**
Irregular bone	**Depressions**	**Endochondral ossification**
Cartilage	**Epiphysis**	
Yellow elastic cartilage		

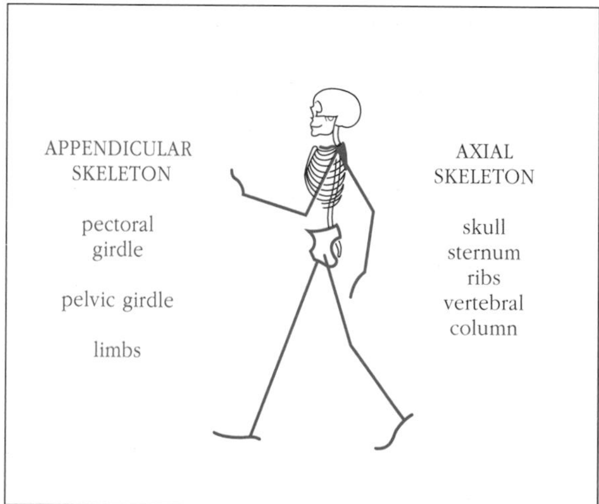

Figure 1.1 The 206 bones are divided into the appendicular and axial skeleton.

The human skeleton consists of 206 bones (Figure 1.1), many of which move or hinge at joints and which, in combination with over 600 skeletal muscles, enable the human body to achieve a variety of actions. such as running, throwing, striking, jumping, pulling and pushing.

Joints are covered with compressible **articular** (articular is a word which describes surfaces which move or hinge) or **hyaline cartilage** which serves to cushion the impact of large forces on bone ends. Joint movements are varied and complex. For example, the **shoulder joint** is constructed to permit swinging, throwing, striking and supporting movements. The **foot** is designed to support the body weight, to act as a shock absorber and to provide great flexibility of movement. All these skeletal bones and joints enable the body to carry out a vast range of complex movements demanded by a variety of differing physical and sporting situations.This section will help you to identify skeletal bones, skeletal connective tissues and their functions, to understand bone development with relation to a variety of physical activities and the influence of exercise on the developing skeleton.

The **human skeleton** has been created by evolution to perform the following functions:

1. To provide a lever system against which muscles can pull.
2. To provide a large surface area for the attachment of muscles.
3. To protect delicate organs (for example, the cranium protects the brain).
4. To provide shape to the body.
5. To provide support to the body (for example, the firm construction of the thorax which permits breathing).
6. To manufacture red blood cells and to store fat, calcium and phosphate.

Investigation 1.1 : Types of skeletons

Using the information in this section, work out the functions specific to the **appendicular** and **axial** skeletons.

TYPES OF BONES

The shape and size of bones are designed according to their specific functions. They can be **long**, **short**, **flat** or **irregular** (see Figure 1.2).

A long bone

A long bone consists of a hollow cylindrical shaft formed of compact bone with cancellous bone located at the knobbly ends of the shaft (see Figure 1.9). The **tibia** is an example of a long bone.

A short bone

A short bone consists of entirely cancellous bone surrounded by a thin layer of compact bone. The **carpals** in the wrist are examples of short bones.

Flat and irregular bones

Flat and irregular bones consist of two outer layers of compact bone with cancellous bone between them. The **cranium** is an example of a flat bone. Examples of irregular bones include the **vertebrae, the patella** or **sesamoid** bone (sited in the patella knee tendon) and wormian bones, which are small irregular bones sometimes formed in cranial sutures.

Irregular bones have no definite shape. The **vertebral column,** which is part of the axial skeleton, is composed of 24 unfused vertebrae, 5 fused sacral vertebrae attached to 4 fused coccygeal vertebrae, making a total of 26 bones.

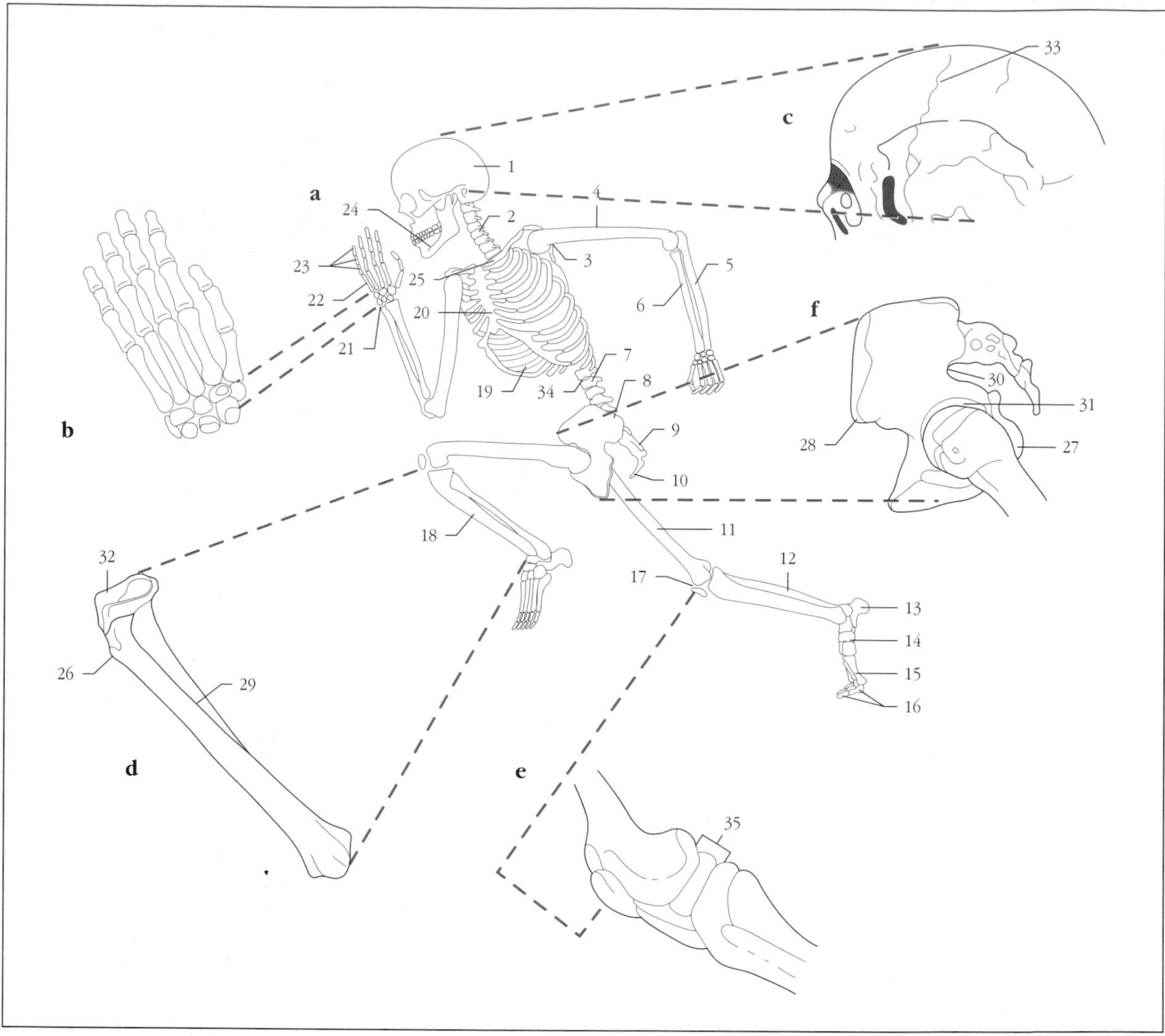

Figure 1.2 The human skeleton in action.

a The human skeleton

Examples and types of bones

- b Short
- c Flat
- d Long
- e Irregular
- f Flat

Some examples of bony features

- 26 Tuberosity
- 27 Tubercle
- 28 Spine
- 29 Ridge
- 30 Notch
- 31 Fossa
- 32 Condyle

Types of joints

- 33 Fibrous joint – suture
- 34 Cartilaginous joint – intervertebral disc
- 35 Synovial joint – knee

Investigation 1.2 : Identification of skeleton bones

Materials: skeleton. Figure 1.2, posters.

Task One

Refer to the skeleton drawing (Figure 1.2a) and identify the bones numbered 1–25.

Task Two

Using a skeletal model and Figures 1.1 and 1.2a, identify the major bones which make up the axial and appendicular skeletons.

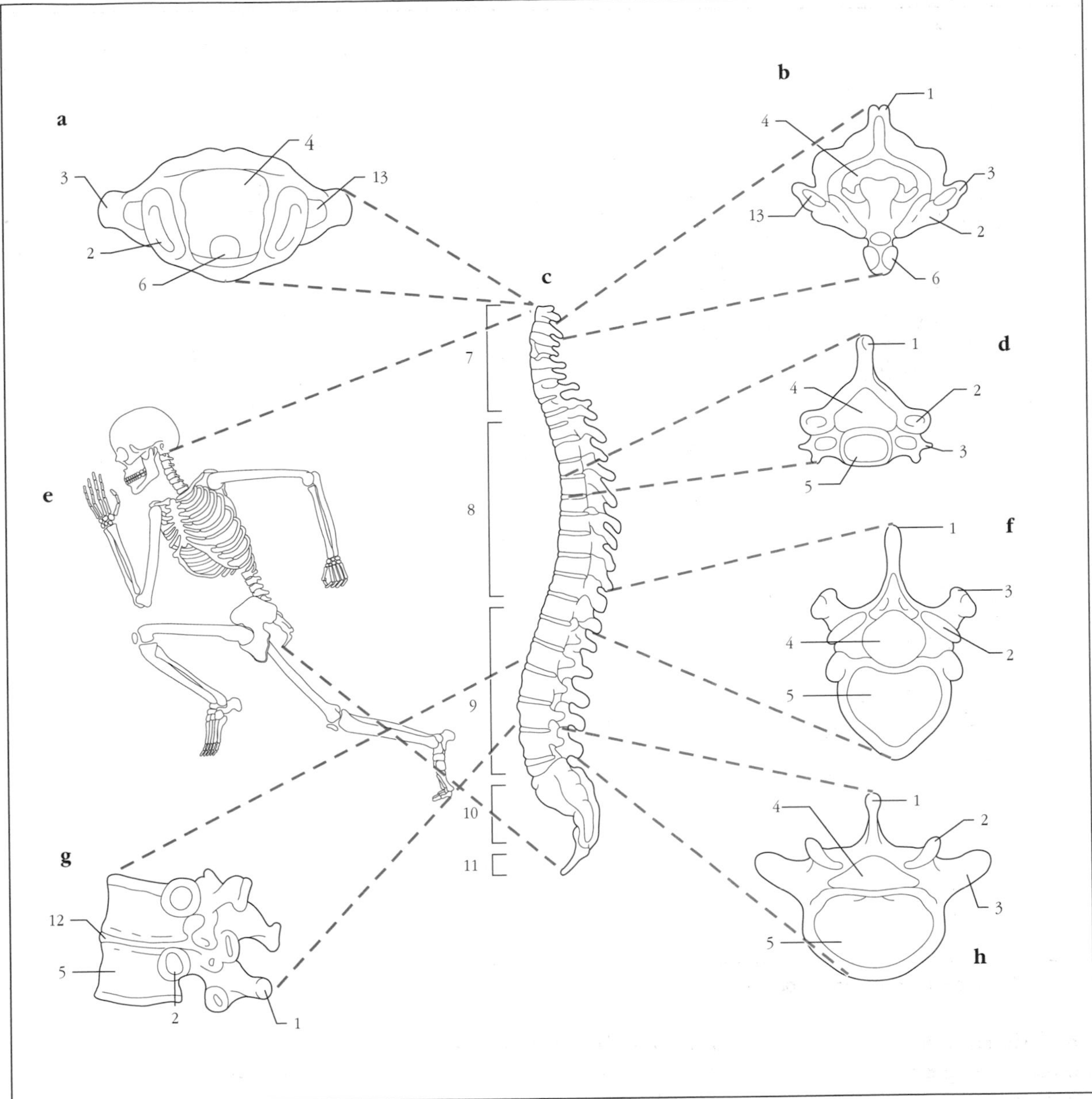

Figure 1.3 Vertebral column.

a. Atlas, superior view
b. Axis, superior view
c. Vertebral column, lateral view
d. Cervical vertebra, superior view
e. Human skeleton
f. Thoracic vertebra, superior view
g. Two lumbar vertebrae
h. Lumbar vertebra, superior view

1. Spinal process for attachment of back muscles
2. Articulating surface connection for ribs and other vertebrae
3. Transverse processes provide attachment for muscles and ligaments
4. Spinal canal through which spinal cord runs
5. Centrum or body of the vertebra which bears the body weight
6. Odontoid process of axis
7. Cervical vertebrae (7)
8. Thoracic vertebrae (12)
9. Lumbar vertebrae (5)
10. Sacrum (fused)
11. Coccyx
12. Intervertebral disc (cartilaginous joint)
13. Foramen for vertebral artery

Investigation 1.3

Task One (use the information in Figure 1.3)

1. Identify those structural features common to all unfused vertebrae.
2. Identify the five main regions of the vertebral column, numbered 7-11.
3. How is the basic plan of vertebrae modified in different regions of the vertebral column to perform different skeletal functions?
4. Identify the **axis and atlas** vertebrae. State the principal function for both vertebrae.

Task Two

Using the information in Figure 1.2, identify the labelled sesamoid bone. What is its function in relation to physical activity?

Task Three

Complete the following exercise in which you are asked to match the bone type to example and specific function. For example, join the linked types, examples and functions as shown for the femur.

Bone type	Example in the body	Specific function
flat	femur	gives strength
long bone	tarsal	protective
short	axis	acts as a lever
irregular	sternum	large surface area for muscle attachment

Task Four

Using a skeletal model and Figure 1.2, classify other examples for each of these four types of bones.

Task Five

Bend down and touch your toes. Explain what joints and bones are involved and what movement is brought about.

Investigation 1.4 : The identification of bony features

Materials: Figure 1.2, and skeletal bones.

Your task is to identify various bony features from the collection of bones supplied for this investigation and diagrams of the skeletal bones in this text or elsewhere.

Task One

Run your fingers along different types of long, short, flat and irregular bones. Feel for bumps and dents on the surface of these bones. These bony features are called **protrusions** and **depressions**, respectively.

Identify the following types of **depression:**

1. A **fossa,** which is a rounded depression—e.g. the **acetabular fossa**.
2. A **groove**—e.g. the deep **bicipital groove** near to the head of the humerus, which is occupied by one of the tendons of the biceps muscle.
3. A **notch**—e.g. the **sciatic notch**.

Protrusions are classified into the following types:

1. A **tuberosity,** which is a broad, rough, uneven bump—e.g. the **tibial tuberosity**.
2. A **tubercle** is a smaller version of a tuberosity—e.g. the **tubercle** of the iliac crest.
3. A **spine,** which is a sharp pointed feature—e.g. the **iliac spine**.
4. A **ridge, crest** or **line** runs along the shaft of a bone—e.g. along the **tibial crest**.

Protrusions that form part of a joint are called **condyles and epicondyles**. For example, the rounded condyles and the adjacent epicondyles of the femur that form part of the knee joint.

Task Two

Identify other examples of protrusions and depressions on a skeleton.

Task Three

What do you think is the function of these bony features?

Investigation 1.5 : A comparison of bone measurements

Materials: tape measures, skeletal poster.

Task One

Using a tape measure, on a partner or yourself, measure the circumference of bones at the wrist, elbow, ankle and knee.

1. Make a results table in which it is possible to compare measurements between males and females in the class or group.
2. Is the circumference (which is directly related to thickness of bone) an indication of maturity and strength of bones?

Task Two

Bones of males are more dense than those of females and the bones of an Afro-Caribbean skeleton are denser than those of the Caucasian skeleton. What effect would this information have when planning physical activity programmes?

Task Three

1. Identify the positions of the bones of the elbow joint (**humerus, radius, ulna**) and shoulder joint (**clavicle, scapula, humerus**) on a partner and relate the positioning of these bones to a skeletal chart and/or Figure 1.2a.
2. Discuss and list the joint types and ranges of movement of the elbow and shoulder joints (see Table 1 for details on joint types and movement patterns).

Task Four

1. Identify the **acromion** process of the scapula, **olecranon** process at the elbow end of the ulna and **styloid** process at the wrist end of the ulna.
2. Using a tape measure, measure the distance from the:
   a. acromion process to the styloid process;
   b. acromion process to olecranon process;
   c. olecranon process to the styloid process.
3. Identify the **head** of the **femur**, **femoral condyle** of the knee joint and **lateral malleolus** of the fibula.
4. Measure the distance from the:
   a. head of femur to the femoral condyle;
   b. femoral condyle to the lateral malleolus.
5. Record the results in a table for each individual. Include gender, skeletal height, bone measurement data from above and major sporting activity.
6. Collect data from males and females and record on bar charts the distribution of measurements from all individuals for each category of measurement.
7. Discuss and comment on the distribution of results obtained from different sporting groups, and males as opposed to females.

Task Five

Eight new events (handball, basketball and six rowing events) were introduced for women in the Olympic Games at Montreal in 1976. The data on heights of 186 medallists from these newly introduced events are shown superimposed on the height distribution of women aged 18–24 in the United States, which were used as a reference population. (Volleyball statistics have been included to give a complete set of women's team games in these Olympic Games. Reference source data adapted from Khosla, 1983.)

This information is represented on the graph (Figure 1.4). Note that the mean for the general population is 162 cm, and for the medallists 174 cm.

1. Using the information in Figure 1.4, discuss the proposition that there is an overwhelming bias in favour of the very tall in many team contests.
2. From the graph, work out the approximate proportion of the general population with height above 174 cm. What are the implications of this for selection of National Squads from groups of ordinary sportspeople?
3. Give other examples from sports where tallness, specific limb dimensions and shortness would be beneficial to performance.

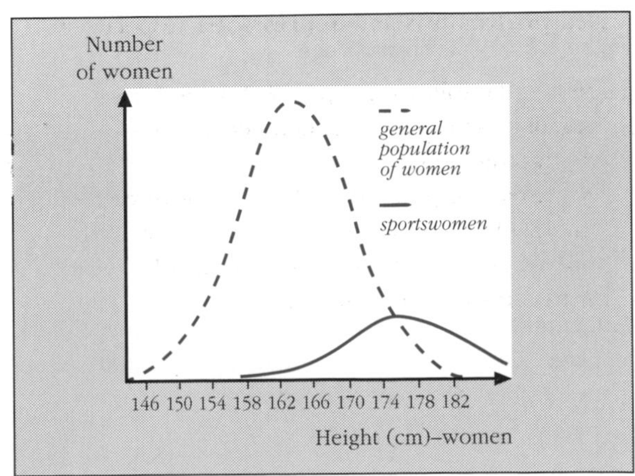

Figure 1.4 Height distributions of female Olympic medallists compared to those of women aged 18–24 in USA. (Adapted from Khosla, 1983.)

TYPES OF SKELETAL CONNECTIVE TISSUE

There are two types of **skeletal connective tissue**: namely, **cartilage** and **bone**.

Cartilage

Cartilage is a soft, slightly elastic tissue which consists of a matrix of **chondrin** (a gelatinous protein) which is secreted by specialized cells called **chondrocytes.** These cells position themselves in tiny cavities called **lacunae,** and are nourished by nutrients which diffuse across from the capillary network outside the cartilaginous tissue. There are three types of cartilage found in the human body:

a) **Yellow elastic cartilage** (Figure 1.5), which consists of yellow elastic fibres running through a solid matrix, with cells lying between the fibres. The pinna or ear lobe and epiglottis are examples of this tissue.

b) **Hyaline** or **articular cartilage** (Figure 1.6), which appears as a smooth bluish-white matrix tissue. The matrix is solid, smooth, firm and yet resilient and the cells appear in groups forming a cell nest. This type of cartilage is located on the surfaces of bones which form joints; it forms the costal cartilages which attach the ribs to the sternum and is also found in the larynx, trachea and bronchi.

c) **White fibrocartilage** (Figure 1.7), which consists of a dense mass of white fibres in a solid matrix, with the cells spread thinly among the fibres. It is a tough, slightly flexible tissue and it is found between the bodies of the vertebrae (called intervertebral discs, refer to Figure 1.3g), semi-lunar cartilages in the knee joint, and it surrounds the rim of the bony sockets of the hip and shoulder joints.

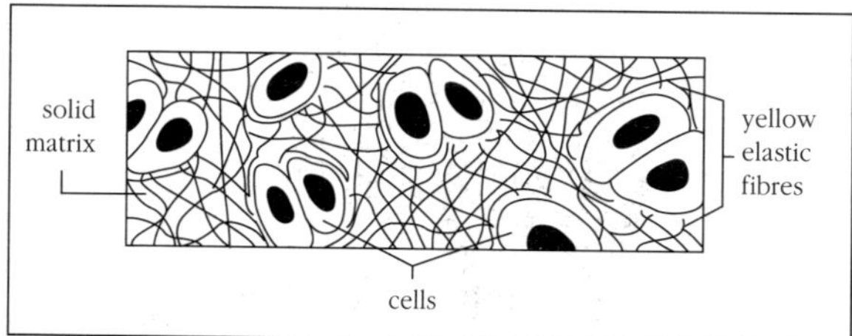

Figure 1.5 Yellow elastic cartilage.

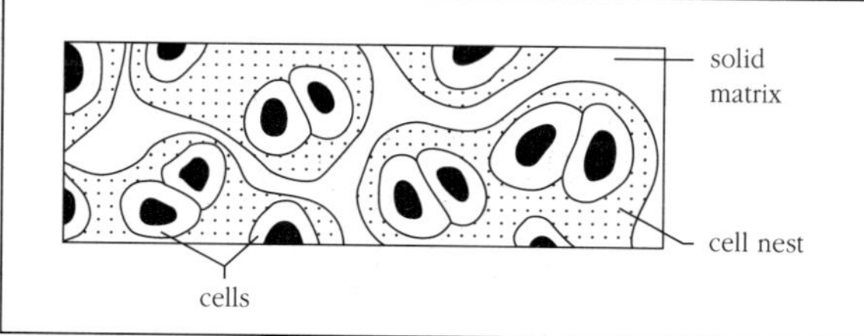

Figure 1.6 Hyaline or articular cartilage.

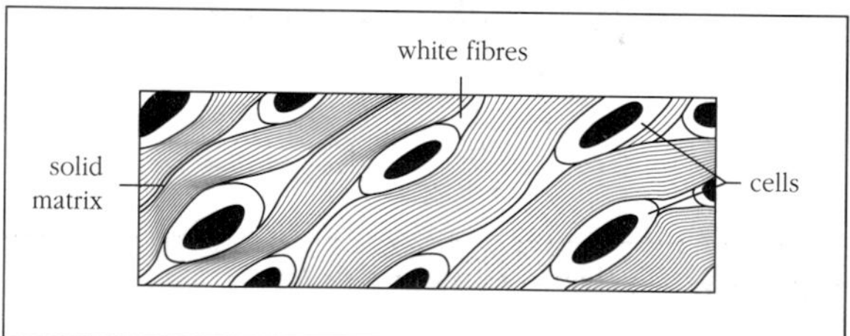

Figure 1.7 White fibrocartilage.

Investigation 1.6 : To examine cartilaginous tissue

Materials: projector slides/diagrams of cartilagenous tissue.

1. Examine the slides and/or diagrams of types of cartilage. For each type of cartilage, give a brief description of its specific function.
2. Why do you think cartilaginous tissue contains no blood vessels?
3. Explain the importance of cartilaginous tissue during physical activity.

Bone

Bone is classified as either **hard** (or **compact**) **bone** or **spongy** (or **cancellate**) **bone**. It is the hardest connective tissue in the human body and it is composed of water, organic material (mainly **collagen**, a structural fibrous protein which supports many body tissues) and inorganic salts, namely calcium phosphate, carbonate and fluoride salts.

Compact bone

Compact bone consists of thousands of collagen-based structures called **Haversian systems** (0.5 mm in diameter) which consist of a central canal surrounded by concentric ring-shaped calcium-based plates called lamellae. Figure 1.8 shows the microscopic detail of an Haversian system.

Spongy or cancellate bone (see Figures 1.9 and 1.10)

Spongy or **cancellate** bone has a honeycomb appearance which consists of a thin criss-cross matrix of bone tissue called **trabeculae** (a general term describing connective tissue which supports other tissues), with red bone marrow filling the tiny spaces.

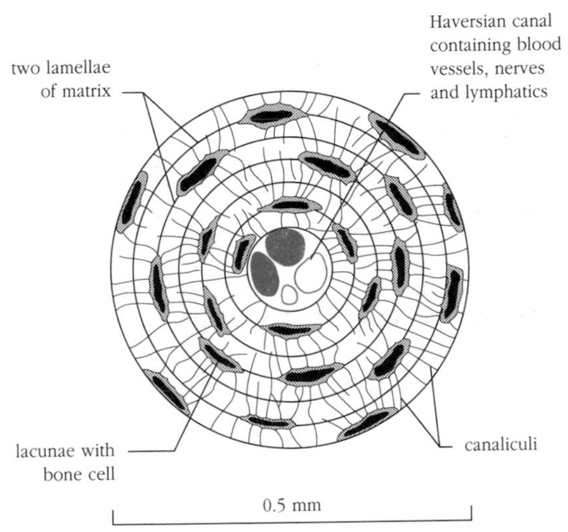

Figure 1.8 A microscopic Haversian system.

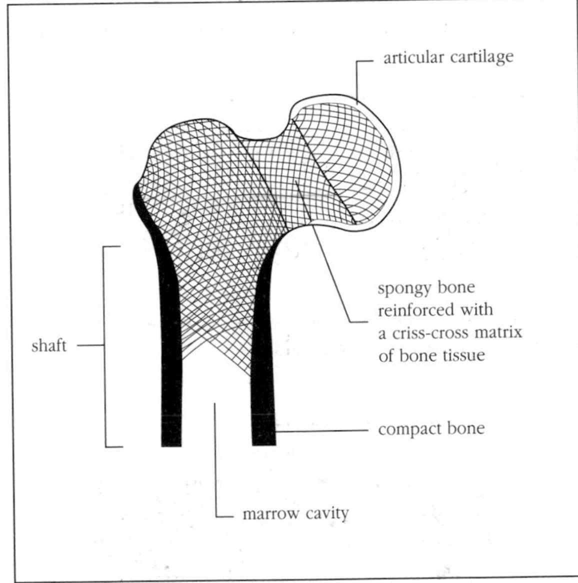

Figure 1.9 The head of the femur.

Investigation 1.7 : To examine the structure of bone

Task One

Consider the labelled structures in Figure 1.8 and/or projector slides if available and relate these structures to the following description:

> *'The bone cells are located in spaces called* ***lacunae*** *(which contain lymph) and they are arranged concentrically around a canal containing blood vessels, nerves and lymphatics (the Haversian canal). These bone cells run into a system of fine channels or* ***canaliculi****. It is the lymph in these channels which is responsible for carrying food and oxygen to the bone and for removing waste products.'*

Compact bone is surrounded by a tough, vascular tissue (tissue that contains vessels containing blood) called the **periosteum.**

Task Two

If you cut a long bone in half down the middle, you would be able to observe the structures shown in Figure 1.10.

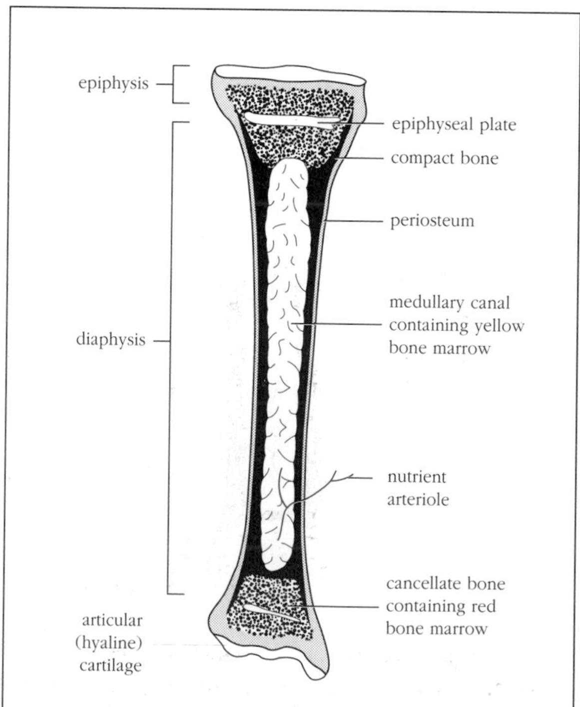

Figure 1.10 Longitudinal section of a long bone.

Using the information in Figures 1.9 and 1.10 and from specialist Human Biology texts, answer the following questions:

1. Where in a long bone is spongy bone located?
2. Why do you think red bone marrow is present in spongy bone?
3. Suggest reasons why long bones are hollow.
4. What is the function of the **yellow bone marrow** located in the **diaphysis**?
5. The surface of bones, except for articular surfaces, is covered by the **periosteum,** which attaches itself to the bone via tiny roots. What do you think are the principal functions of the **periosteum**?
6. Why is it important for the ends of bones to be reinforced with a criss-cross matrix of bone tissue as shown in Figure 1.9?
7. Observe and comment on the positioning of the compact bone in Figure 1.9.
8. Observe and comment on the positioning of the articular cartilage.

THE DEVELOPMENT OF BONES

Ossification is the process of bone formation or the conversion of fibrous tissue or cartilage into bone.

Within the developing foetus the short and long bones are formed as a result of **indirect ossification**, since the foetal cartilage is replaced by bone. This process is called **endochondral ossification**.

Figure 1.11 Endochondral ossification in a long bone.

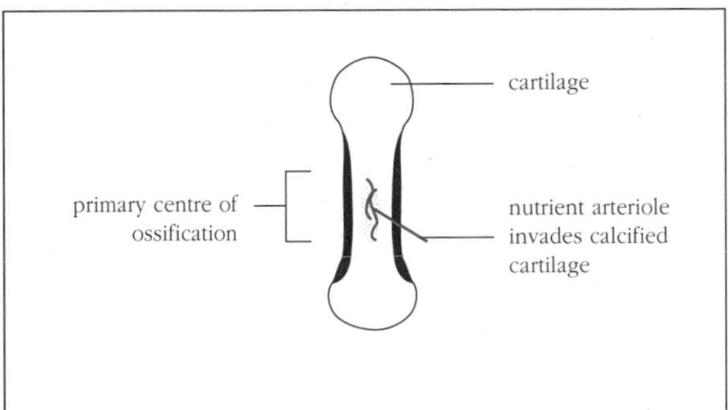

a) Bone-forming cells called **osteoblasts** *(os* means bone and *blast* means immature cell) first appear in the centre of the **diaphysis** (the primary centre of ossification), and surround themselves with calcium and phosphate ions supplied by the blood. Blood vessels invade the calcified cartilage and a cavity begins to form once the cartilage is replaced by bone. When the **osteoblast** becomes embedded in the **lacuna** of the bone matrix it becomes an **osteocyte.**

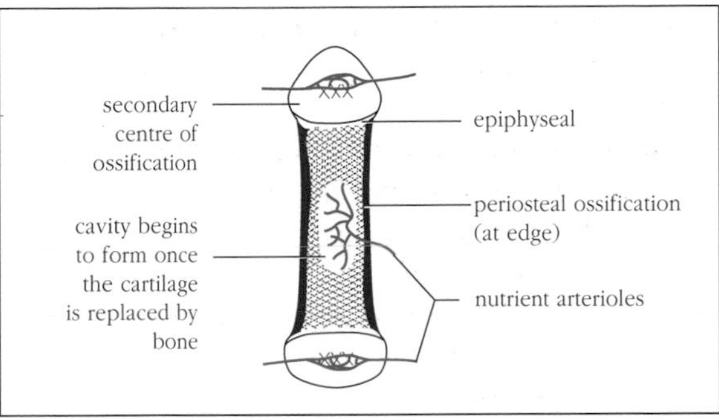

b) At birth most of the **diaphysis** consists of bone, and bone has started to appear in the **epiphysis** (the secondary centre of ossification). On the exterior, **periosteal ossification** continues.

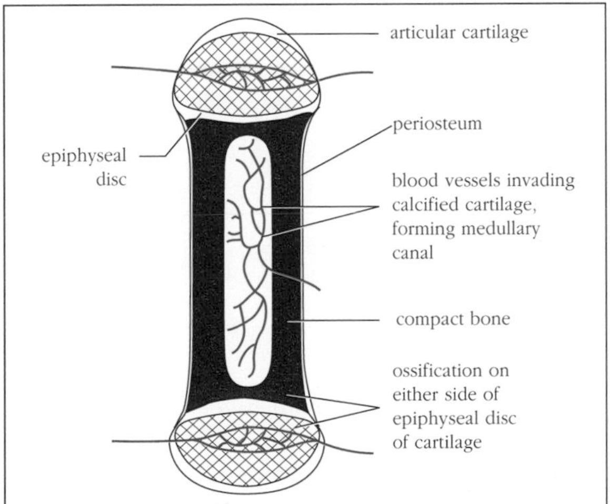

c) A disc of cartilage separates the bone at the **diaphysis** from the bone at the **epiphysis.** This disc is called the **epiphyseal disc** or growth disc because it is the only place where an increase in the length of the bone can take place. As the young child grows, increase in the length of the long bone can occur only at the **epiphyseal discs**.

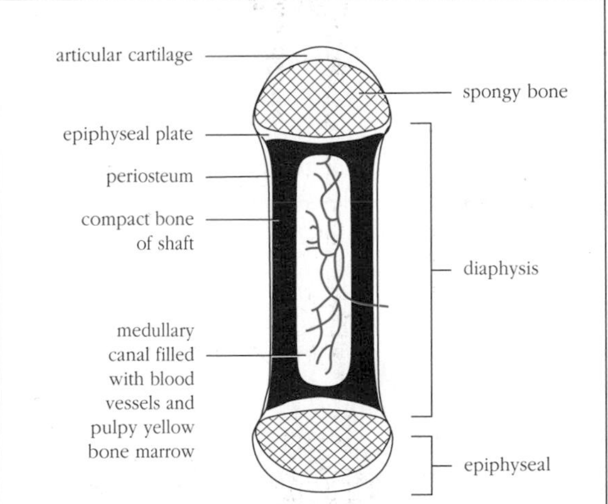

d) When the growth ceases the bony **diaphysis** is united with the **epiphysis** and the line of fusion is marked by a dense layer of bone. The age at which this fusion occurs varies, but long bones normally cease growing in late adolescence.

Throughout the development of the long bone, parts of the bone are re-absorbed so that unnecessary calcium phosphate is removed and structures such as the **medullary canal** are created. Specialized cells called **osteoclasts** carry out this job.

In addition, the bone becomes wider as a result of the **osteoblasts** laying down new layers of bone tissue in the deeper layers of the **periosteum**.

The process of **ossification** in a short bone takes place from the centre of the bone and radiates outwards.

Flat and irregular bones are developed in one stage directly from connective tissue. This process is called **intramembranous ossification.** At ossification centres, within the membrane, osteoblasts produce bone tissue along the membrane fibres to form cancellous bone. Beneath the periosteum, osteoblasts lay down compact bone to form the outer surface of the bone. The sutures of the skull gradually ossify during the development of a young child into adulthood as do the clavicle, scapula and pelvis.

As a result of **ossification,** the two types of bone tissue described earlier are formed, namely **cancellous** and **compact bone.** It is only at the joint sites that cartilage remains to form the edges where bones meet.

REVIEW QUESTIONS

1. What considerations, with respect to skeletal development, must a coach make in the planning of a training programme for a growing adolescent?

2. What beneficial effects does exercise have on the skeletal system?

Summary

1. You should be able to classify and identify skeletal bones in the axial and appendicular skeletons.
2. You should be able to classify and recognize the specific functions of bones according to their shape.
3. You should be able to recognize bony features and understand their functioning within the human body.
4. You should be able to appreciate variations of bone thickness, density and length in relation to sporting activities.
5. You should be able to identify the two types of skeletal tissue and be able to write briefly about their structure and function within the human body.
6. You should be able to describe the process of ossification in the different types of bones.
7. You should be able to understand the influence of exercise on the developing skeleton.

FURTHER READING

Donnelly J.E. *Living Anatomy* 2e, Human Kinetics, 1990.

Khosla T. Sport for tall, *British Medical Journal,* 1983.

Klausen K., Hemmingsen I. and Rasmussen B. *Basic Sport Science,* McNaughton and Gunn, 1982.

McMinn R.M.H. *et al. The Human Skeleton,* Wolfe, 1987.

Ross J.S. and Wilson K.J. *Foundations of Anatomy and Physiology,* Churchill Livingstone, 1981.

Rowett H.G.Q. *Basic Anatomy and Physiology,* Murray, 1984.

Seeley R.R., Stephens T.D.and Tate P. *Anatomy and Physiology* ISE 2e, Mosby–Year Book, 1992.

Thompson C.W. *Manual of Structural Kinesiology* 2e, Mosby–Year Book, 1994.

Wirhed R. *Athletic Ability and the Anatomy of Motion,* Wolfe, 1984.

1.2 Joints in Action

KEY WORDS AND CONCEPTS

joint feature:	movement patterns:	synovial joints:
fibrous joint	**flexion**	**ball and socket**
synovial joint	**extension**	**hinge**
ligaments	**abduction**	**condyloid**
pads of fat	**adduction**	**saddle**
synovial fluid	**circumduction**	**pivot**
menisci	**external rotation**	**gliding**
cartilaginous joint	**internal rotation**	
capsule	**supination**	
synovial membrane	**pronation**	
bursae	**dorsi flexion**	
pads of fat	**plantar flexion**	

So far our investigation into how we move has been concerned with a understanding and identification of the main bones and bony tissues in the human body. This next section will help you to understand how bones are connected to each other in order to achieve movement.

A **joint** is a site in the body where two or more bones come together, and joints are classified according to the amount of movement there is between the articulating surfaces.

TYPES OF JOINT

1. A **fibrous** or a **fixed joint** has no movement at all. Tough fibrous tissue lies between the ends of the bone, which are dovetailed together. Examples in the human body are the sutures in the skull, as illustrated in Figure 1.12 (also refer to Figure 1.2c).

2. A **cartilaginous joint** allows some slight movement. The ends of bones, which are covered in **articular** or **hyaline cartilage,** are separated by pads of **white fibrocartilage** and slight movement is made possible only because the pads of cartilage compress. In addition, the pads of cartilage act as shock absorbers. The intervertebral discs are examples of this type of joint, as illustrated in Figures 1.13 and 1.3g.

3. A **synovial joint** (Figure 1.14) is a freely moving joint, and is characterized by the presence of a **joint capsule** and **cavity.** This type of joint is subdivided according to movement possibilities, which are dictated as a result of the bony surfaces which actually form the joint (the knee joint is an example of this type of joint, which is illustrated in Figure 1.15).

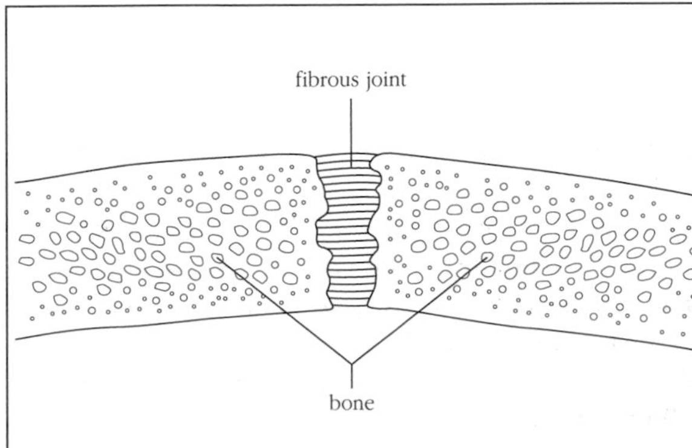

Figure I.12 Fibrous joint.

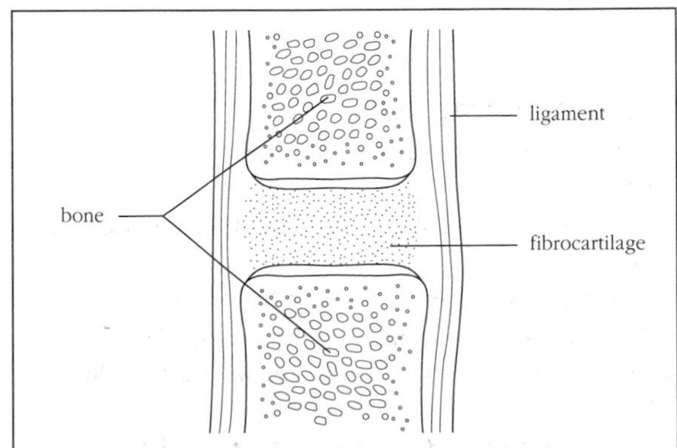

Figure 1.13 Cartilaginous joint.

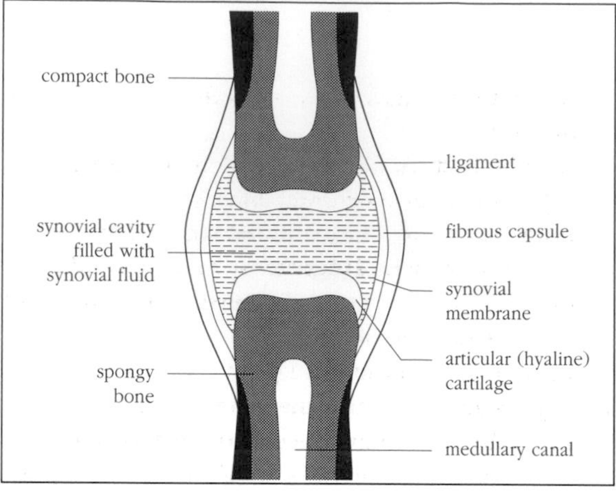

Figure I.14 Synovial joint.

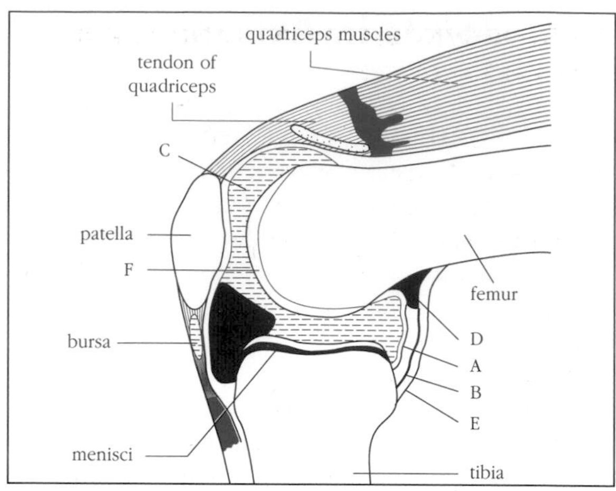

Figure 1.15 Synovial joint: the knee.

Investigation 1.8 : To consider the structure and function of the main types of joints

Materials: Human skeleton, skeletal/joint posters.

Task One

Identify the three types of joint classified so far. Locate the positioning of examples for each of these three types of joint on your own body.

Task Two

a. Jump off a box.

b. Run and bound.

c. Rotate your upper trunk against your lower body.

Explain the role of cartilaginous joints in these movements.

Investigation 1.9 : To examine the structures of a synovial joint

Task One

Using the synovial joint illustrated in Figure 1.15, match each letter to one of the structures listed below and explain the function of each structure by using appropriate reference books.

For example:

Structure:

1. **Articular or hyaline cartilage**—a smooth, shiny cartilage which covers the ends of bones and absorbs synovial fluid.
   Answer: F.
   Function: to prevent friction between bones; it is thought that when the joint is exercised, synovial fluid is squeezed out of the articular cartilage at the point of contact (McCutchen's Weeping Lubrication Theory).
2. **Joint capsule**—a sleeve of fibrous tissue surrounding the joint.
3. **Ligament**—a sleeve of tough, fibrous connective tissue, which is an extension of the joint capsule.
4. **Synovial membrane**—a sheet of epithelial cells inside the joint capsule.
5. **Synovial fluid**—the fluid enclosed in a joint, some of which is absorbed by hyaline cartilage during exercise.
6. **Pad of fat**—pads of fat which occupy the gaps in and around the joint.

Task Two

Two other features, **bursae** and **menisci**, appear in synovial joints. **Bursae** are little sacs of synovial fluid, and **menisci** are extra layers of fibrocartilage located at the articulating surfaces of joints. Suggest the functions of these special joint features and give examples from the human body.

Task Three

Identify the intracapsular ligaments.

Task Four

Sketch a diagram of a named **ball** and **socket** type of joint, labelling all the structures which provide joint strength and mobility.

Task Five

The effect of long-term training on hyaline cartilage is to causes a permanent cartilaginous thickening as a result of the laying down of additional cartilaginous cells.

Suggest reasons why you think an increase in hyaline cartilage thickness would be beneficial to an athlete.

TYPES OF SYNOVIAL JOINTS AND THEIR MOVEMENT RANGE

As the title suggests, all synovial joints are characterized by the presence of synovial fluid.

The possible ranges of movements within a synovial joint vary according to the shape of the articulating surfaces and therefore according to the joint type (this information is contained in Table l). In addition, specific movement patterns are briefly described in the following summary:

1. **Flexion** or bending.
2. **Extension** or straightening.
3. **Plantar flexion** or pointing the toes.
4. **Dorsiflexion** or bringing the toes towards the tibia.
5. **Adduction** or movement towards the midline of the body.
6. **Abduction** or movement away from the midline of the body.
7. **Circumduction** or a combination of flexion, extension, abduction and adduction.
8. **Rotation** or movement around the long axis of a bone (this may be **internal**—rotation inwards towards the body axis, or **external**—rotation away from the body axis).
9. **Pronation** or turning the palm downwards.
10. **Supination** or turning the palm upwards.
11. **Inversion** or turning the sole of the foot inwards.
12. **Eversion** or turning the sole of the foot outwards.

A full-page illustration of these different types of synovial joint and the type of movement allowed by them can be found on page 13, Figures 14–19, of Wirhed.

Table 1 : Types of synovial joint

Joint type	Shape of joint	Movement range	e.g. in the body
ball and socket	ball-shaped bone fits into a cup-shaped socket	3 axes – flexion and extension, abduction and adduction, rotation, circumduction	hip
hinge	convex and concave surfaces fitting together	1 axis – flexion and extension	distal joints of phalanges
pivot	ring-shaped, surrounding a cone	1 axis – rotation	radioulnar joint below elbow
condyloid and saddle	2 oval-curved bones fitting into a shallow depression	2 axes – flexion and extension, abduction and adduction, giving circumduction	metacarpophalangeal joints of the fingers, carpometacarpal joint of the thumb
gliding	2 flat gliding surfaces	a little movement in all directions.	joint between the clavicle and sternum

Investigation 1.10 : To associate movement patterns with types of synovial joint

Task One

Identify other examples of synovial joints located in the human body.

Task Two

Using the specific terms that are given to describe the basic movement categories, identify the possible movement patterns at your selected joints.

Investigation 1.11 : Joints in action

Observe the action pictures in Figure 1.16.

Figure I.16

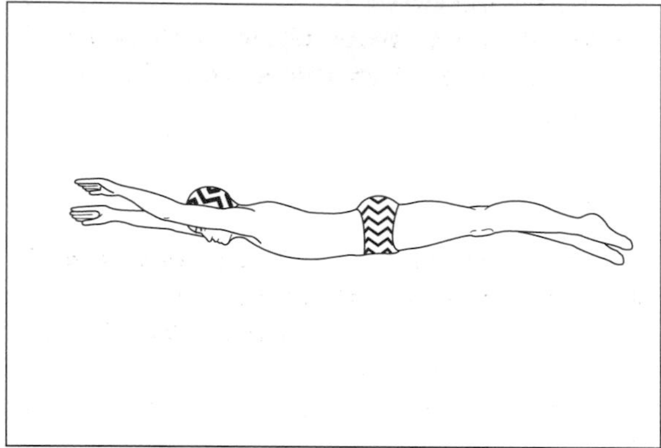

a

b

Task One

Name the types of synovial joint located at the knee and hip of the swimmer and basketball player. Analyse the movement patterns happening at these joints.

You may wish to select your own action pictures and answer the same questions.

Task Two

Choose a selection of flexibility exercises that are part of your normal warm-up (refer to p. 151 onwards for ideas). In groups compare the ranges of flexibility at selected joint sites. You may wish to use the idea of the mobility assessment test which is described in Chapter 4.

Task Three

During most physical activity, the knee joint plays a vital role in movement.

a. Describe how the anatomical structures of the knee joint protect and stabilize the joint.
b. Describe how the anatomical structures of the knee joint make movement possible.
c. In many sports, the knee joint is often injured as a result of impacts (with other sportspeople or objects) or excessive forces (as in weightlifting, throwing or jumping) or overuse. Make a list of the common injuries that occur in the knee joint. (You may wish to extend this line of investigation to other joint sites.)
d. Describe some of the ways you could prevent such injuries from occurring.

REVIEW QUESTIONS

1. What differences in their joints produce the differences in mobility between the hip joint and the elbow joint?

2. List the bones that articulate in the following joints:

a. knee
b. elbow
c. shoulder
d. thoracic vertebrae
e. hip

3. Identify the movement patterns performed at the joint sites listed for the following physical activities:

a. Pushing hockey ball: knees, elbows, wrists.
b. Sit and reach test (Task 5 described in Investigation 4.1): trunk, hip.
c. Step up onto a bench (Task 3 described in Investigation 4.1): knees, hip.
d. Basketball shooting: wrists, elbow, shoulders.
e. Vertical jump (Task 1(2) described in Investigation 4.1): ankles, knees, hip.

Summary

1. You should be able to classify joints into fibrous, cartilaginous and synovial joints.
2. You should to be able to identify and describe the features of the different types of synovial joint.
3. You should be able to appreciate how joint structure allows for a variety of different skeletal movements.
4. You should be able to describe briefly some of the common joint injuries and methods of prevention.

FURTHER READING

Donnelly J.E. *Living Anatomy* 2e, Human Kinetics, 1990.

Hay G.H. Reid J.G. *Anatomy Mechanics and Human Motion* 2e, Prentice Hall, 1988.

Klausen K. Hemmingsen I. and Rasmussen B. *Basic Sport Science,* McNaughton and Gunn, 1982.

Rowett H.G.Q. *Basic Anatomy and Physiology,* Murray, 1988.

Seeley R.R., Stephens T.D. and Tate P. *Anatomy and Physiology* ISE 2e, Mosby–Year Book, 1992.

Thompson C.W. *Manual of Structural Kinesiology* 2e, Mosby–Year Book, 1994.

Wirhed R. *Athletic Ability and the Anatomy of Motion,* Wolfe, 1984.

1.3 Muscles in Action

KEY WORDS AND CONCEPTS

skeletal muscle	**ligaments**	**muscle group**
fusiform	**origin**	**antagonistic muscle action**
pennate	**insertion**	**antagonist**
fibre types:	**tendon**	**agonist**
type I,	**aponeuroses**	**fixator**
IIa (FOG),	**periosteum**	**synergist**
IIb (FTG)	**fascia**	

One of the important functions of the human skeleton is to enable movement. Physical activity is achieved as a result of the action of over 600 muscles which contract or shorten, thereby facilitating the movement of the skeleton across its joints.

Muscles are the converters of energy, since they change chemical energy into mechanical energy. This is achieved as a result of the contraction of hundreds of muscle fibres within the connective tissue of each muscle.

During muscular contraction a muscle tightens to produce a state of tension which is adequate to meet the demands of the activity. The effect of regular physical activity is to develop and sustain local muscle strength and endurance. Some skeletal muscles, for example, the soleus muscle, are very fatigue resistant (this is because they consist of a high proportion of **slow twitch** fibres), whilst other muscles, for example, the biceps and gastrocnemius muscles, fatigue more quickly because they are essentially **fast twitch** (the details of slow and fast twitch muscle fibres are described later in this section). The effects of training in adapting muscle tissue to stress demands are discussed in Chapter 4. However, all muscles will contract *only* when stimulated by nerve impulses.

This section will help you to identify muscles, understand muscle structure and tension, how muscles are arranged in groups, how they are attached to bones so that movement can be produced and how muscular action can be analysed by performing simple motor tasks.

SHAPES OF MUSCLES (Figure 1.17b-e)

Skeletal muscles vary in shape and function. Each muscle shape, its origins, insertions and positioning, has been evolved specifically to deal with its unique functioning.

1. Fusiform

Fusiform means **spindle-shaped,** since the muscle fibres run the length of the muscle belly to converge at each end. This strap-like, round shape enables the muscle to perform a large range of movement fluidly.

2. Pennate

Pennate means **featherlike**. A pennate muscle is a flat muscle in which fibres are arranged around a central tendon, like barbs of a feather.

The major types of pennate muscles are grouped according to the way in which the fibres are arranged around the central tendon:

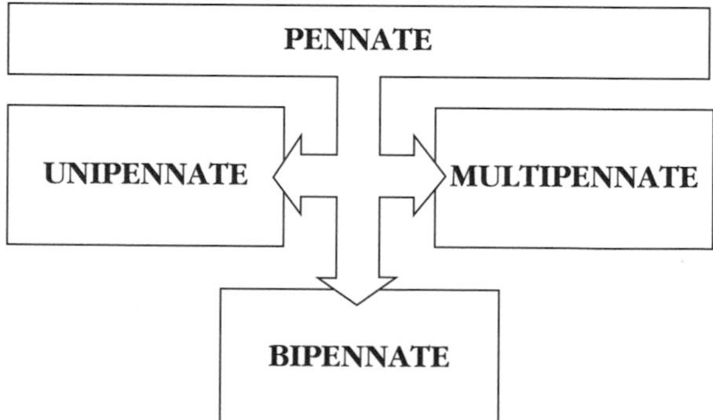

Pennate muscles have a very limited range of movement, but are very strong and powerful.

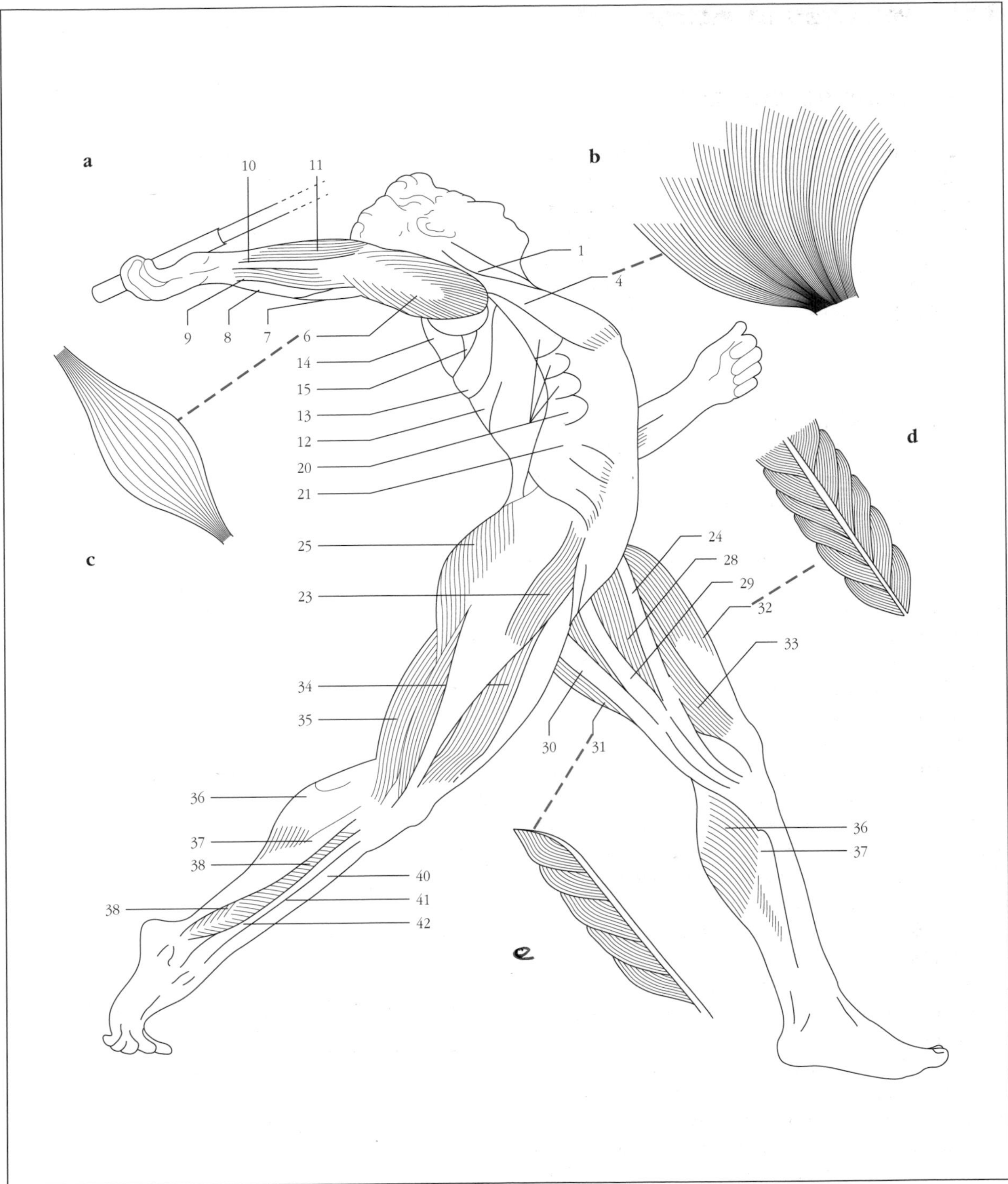

Figure 1.17 Muscles in action

a.Superficial muscles of the human body (1–42)

Muscle shapes:

b. Multipennate

c. Fusiform

d. Bipennate

e. Unipennate

Investigation 1.12 : Identification of muscle shapes and the relationship of muscle shape to its functioning

1. Give an example for each type of fusiform and pennate muscle shape illustrated in Figure 1.17.

2. Describe how the three types of **pennate** muscle shape are designed for efficient functioning within the human body.

Investigation 1.13 : Identification of muscles and their movement patterns

Materials: Figure 1.17 and muscle chart/slides.

Task One

Identify and label the muscles numbered 1-42 in Figure 1.17.

Task Two

Using the labelled muscles from Figure 1.17, and other reference material, identify the groups of muscles of the upper leg, their origins and insertions and classify them into functional categories: that is, flexors, extensors, adductors, abductors and rotators. For example:

Table 2 : Flexors—bending of the knee

Muscle	Origin	Insertion
Group		
HAMSTRINGS Biceps femoris	**Long head**-ischial tuberosity **Short head**-linea aspera of femur	Head of fibula & lateral condyle of tibia
Semimembranosus	Ischial tuberosity	Medial condyle of tibia
Semitendinosus	Ischial tuberosity	Below medial condyle of tibia

Task Three

Identify the groups of muscles of the shoulder and upper arm into functional categories.

Task Four

Identify the groups of muscles of the trunk into functional categories.

You may wish to extend this investigation by identifying the origins and insertions of other major muscles on skeletal bones.

Investigation 1.14 : To identify muscles in relation to simple motor tasks and to relate muscle size to performance

Materials: tape measures, muscle chart.

Task One: A standing long jump (see Figure 1.18)

Perform a standing long jump and measure the distance covered from the start line to the nearest point of landing. Record the best of three trials.

Figure 1.18 A standing long jump.

Task Two

By appropriate use of the muscle chart and by palpation, identify the muscles on the front of the thigh:

a. What is this group of muscles commonly called?

b. Name each main muscle located within this group.

Task Three

Stand normally, feet slightly apart. Using the tape, your partner measures (in cm) the circumference of your contracted thigh at its maximum girth or mid-distance from the hip to the knee joint, for both left and right legs. Record these measurements in the table provided.

Table 3 : Results table—the relationship of muscle size to performance

	Performance and measurements of class members				
	Self	1	2	3	4
Standing long jump distance in metres					
Thigh girths left thigh in cm right thigh in cm					

Task four

1. Compare within small groups the relationship between standing long jump and maximum thigh girths. Plot a graph of performances from the standing long jump (*x*-axis) against the maximum thigh girths (*y*-axis) of as many of your colleagues as possible. What does your graph show?
2. Are there differences in left and right thigh girths?

You may wish to extend this investigation by using other muscle groups such as those of the trunk and shoulder regions of the body.

TYPES OF MUSCLE FIBRE

Muscle tissue is composed of muscle fibres which contain **two main fibre types** which contract at different speeds; namely, **fast twitch fibres** or **type II** and **slow twitch fibres** or **type I.**

Within an individual, there are different proportions of these fibre types to be found in different muscles, and evidence supports the view that fibre type distribution is inherited.

All muscle contains a mixture of **slow** and **fast twitch fibres**. The major differences between the two types are related to:

1. **Speed of contraction**—slow twitch muscle fibres contract at a rate of about 20 per cent when compared with fast twitch muscle fibres.
2. **Muscle fibre force**—fast twitch fibres are bigger in size than slow twitch fibres, have larger motor neurons and therefore can generate high force rapidly.
3. **Muscle endurance**—slow twitch fibres are capable of resisting fatigue whereas fast twitch fibres are easily fatigued.

More recently, it has been discovered that type II is subdivided into type IIa and type IIb. Type IIa, otherwise known as **FOG** (**Fast** twitch high **Oxidative Glycolytic**), have a greater resistance to fatigue when compared with type IIb (**Fast Twitch Glycolytic—FTG**). The fatigue resistant nature of type IIa is entirely due to muscle adaptation in response to endurance training.

A summary of comparisons of these three types of muscle fibres is list below in Table 4.

Table 4 : Characteristics of fibre types

	Slow twitch	Fast twitch	
Characteristic	**type I**	**FOG type IIa**	**FTG type IIb**
Size	midway	small	large
Colour	red	midway	white
Aerobic			
Myoglobin content	high	high	low
Capillary density	high	midway/high	low
Oxidative enzymes	high	midway/high	low
Mitochondrial density	high	midway	small
Myosin ATPase activity	high	midway	low
Activity during low intensity exercise	high	midway	low
Anaerobic			
Glycogen stores	low	high	high
Phosphocreatine content	low	midway	high
Fatigue level	low	midway	high
Contractile time	slow	midway	fast
Relaxation time	slow	midway	fast
Activity during high intensity exercise	low	high	high

(Some of the terms used to describe the characteristics of fibre types may be unfamiliar, but you should be able to understand them once you have referred to relevant sections within this text.)

Investigation 1.15 : To consider some of the characteristics of fibre types

Task One

1. It can be deduced from the information summarised in Table 4 that slow twitch fibres are best suited to **aerobic** (performed with a full and adequate supply of oxygen) types of exercise, whereas fast twitch are specifically adapted for high intensity and mainly **anaerobic** (performed without sufficient oxygen to cope with the energy demand) types of exercise. Describe some of the characteristics which support this deduction.
2. The effects of specialized training can alter the metabolic functioning of fast twitch type IIb fibres so that they take on some of the characteristics of type I cells and become type IIa cells. Describe the ways in which metabolic functioning of type IIa cells will change as a result of specialist aerobic training.
3. In which sporting activities would the adaptation of fast twitch (type IIb) fibres to type IIa cells be relevant to a sportsperson?
4. What types of training would cause the adaptation of fast twitch fibres to type IIa cells?

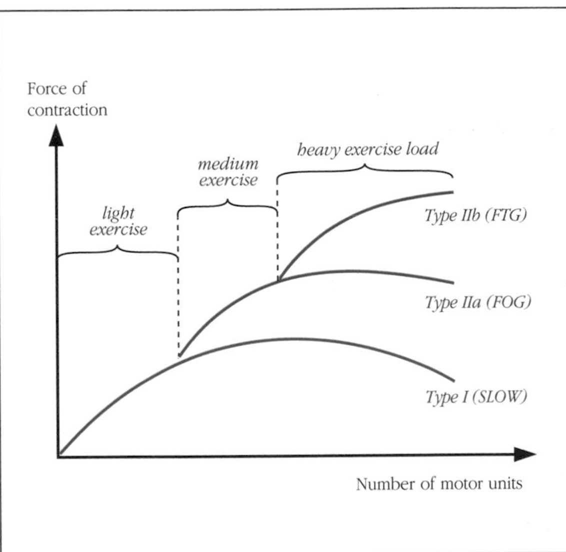

Figure 1.19

Task Two

Using the information in Figure 1.19, describe the order in which fibre types are recruited as the number of motor units increases.

Task Three

Another interesting study is the relationship between distribution of fibre type and different sporting activities.

Two diagrams illustrating this concept are found in *Sports Physiology* by Bowers/Fox (third edition), pages 128 and 129, Figures 6–17a and b (see Further Reading). Basically, the more explosive and intense the demands of a sport, the more likely it is that successful sportspeople will have a higher proportion of fast twitch muscle fibres in their muscles.

1. Using the information from this reference, comment on the the distribution of fibre type (for males and females) with respect to different sporting activities.
2. Do all athletes who are involved in power events have a higher percentage of fast twitch fibres in the muscles involved in the action? Suggest reasons for your answer.

HOW SKELETAL MUSCLE WORKS

Muscles and bones have specialized skeletal structures, such as **tendons** and the **periosteum** *(peri*—around + *oste*—bone) of a bone, which generally transmit muscular forces to bones or, in the case of **ligaments**, attach bone to bone (**ligaments** limit the range of movement of joints). These structures are commonly known as **musculo-skeletal attachments.**

Tendons

Muscles are attached to bones by **tendons** which pass over joints. Tendons are strong and inelastic and vary in length and structure from one to another. Small tendons, such as those to the muscles which control eye movement, have no nerve and blood supply; whereas large tendons, such as the Achilles tendon, are connected to the **central nervous system** and the **circulatory system** and therefore have nerves and a blood supply both of which are substantially less prolific and effective than in the actual muscles. In some cases the tendinous attachment to bone is a more flattened or ribbon-shaped connection, called an **aponeuroses.** This type of tendon is without nerves. An example is the aponeuroses of the internal oblique muscles (which tilt and rotate the trunk relative to the hip girdle).

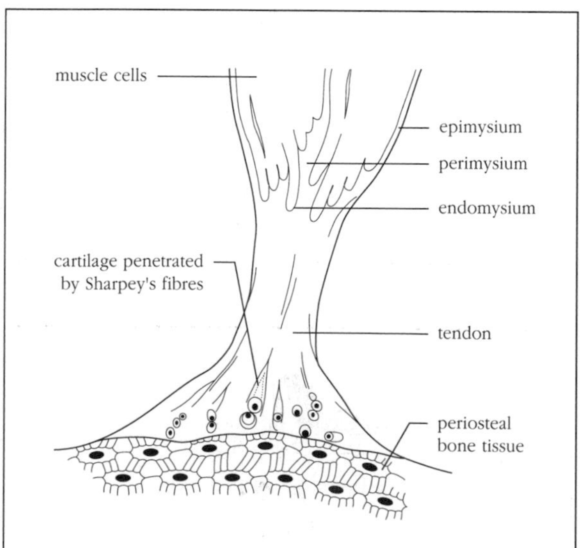

Figure 1.20 How a tendon connects muscle to bone. *(After Soloman and Davies, 1983.)*

Tendons are rigidly cemented to the **periosteum,** as illustrated in Figure 1.20.

Where the tendon fastens on to the periosteum, structures called **Sharpey's fibres** firmly attach tendon tissue on to periosteal tissue.

The **periosteum** is tough connective tissue whose function is to attach muscle tendons to bone, and to assist bone growth.

Other connective tissue

Fascia is a general form of connective tissue which overlays or underlines many body structures. A specialist example of this is the **epimysium** which is the name for the sheath or membrane which envelopes muscle systems (shown in Figure 1.20 as discussed in more detail later in this chapter).

Superficial fascia underlines the skin and forms the connective link between the skin and **deep fascia** of muscle.

The origin and insertion of muscles

The tendon at the static end of the muscle is called the **origin**, and the tendon at the end of the muscle closest to the joint that moves is called the **insertion** of that muscle.

The arrangement of muscles

Muscles which cause joints to bend are called **flexors**, whilst those muscle which straighten a joint are called **extensors.**

Skeletal muscles are normally arranged in pairs so that as one muscle is contracting the other is relaxing, thus producing co-ordinated movement.

The muscle that actually shortens to move the joint is called the **prime mover** or **agonist**, whereas the muscle that relaxes in opposition to the agonist is called the **antagonist**. Muscles which are prime movers for one movement act as antagonists for the opposite movement. For example, the **biceps** (agonist) contracts whilst the **triceps** (antagonist) relaxes (Figure 1.21a). This combined action causes the elbow to flex. When the elbow straightens the reverse occurs: the **triceps** (agonist) contracts whilst the **biceps** (antagonist) relaxes (Figure 1.21b). The action of muscles working in pairs is called **antagonistic muscle action**. Antagonistic muscle action limits and control movements, especially when there are groups of muscles acting together.

In addition, there are muscles which stabilize the origin to the prime move so that only the bone to which it is inserted will move. These are called **fixators** and **synergists**. **Fixator** muscles hold joints in position and are sited so that the origin and insertion are on opposite sides of a stabilized joint. **Synergists** are muscles which hold body position to enable the agonist to operate (*syn*—together + *ergon*—work). Note that the term 'fixator and synergist' could be applied to the same muscle.

a

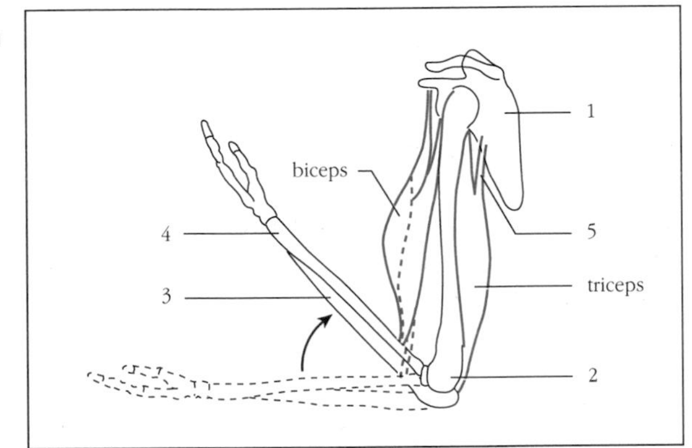

b

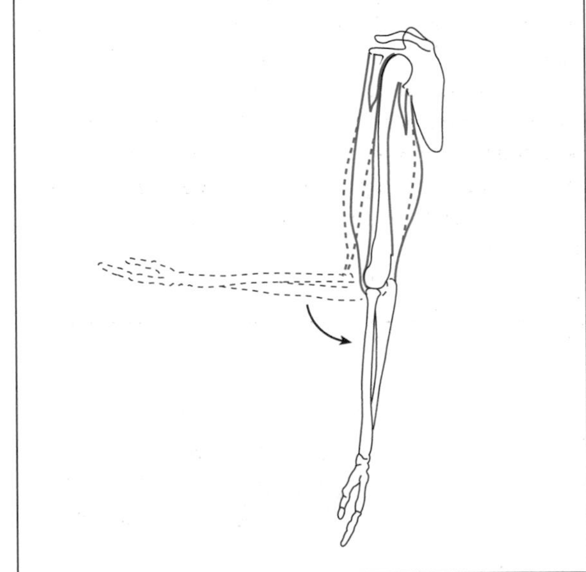

Figure 1.21

a. Flexion of the elbow.
b. Extension of the elbow.

a

b

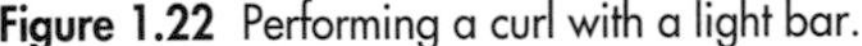

Figure 1.22 Performing a curl with a light bar.

Investigation 1.16 : An analysis of limb movement

Materials: bar with secured discs, Figures 1.21 and 1.22.

Task One

1. Perform a curl with a light bar (see Figure 1.22: make sure that your teacher shows you the correct technique).
2. Identify the bones numbered 1-4 in Figure 1.21a.
3. Identify the structure numbered 5 in Figure 1.21a.
4. Using an example from one of the muscles shown on Figure 1.21a explain what is meant by origin and insertion.
5. Identify and classify the muscles which are used in the action of curling a bar into the functional categories of **agonist** (or prime mover) and **antagonist**.
6. Using your own musculature and Figure 1.17, identify those muscles which act as **fixators** and **synergists** in the action of curling a bar.

Task Two

List the main agonists active in:

a. The legs whilst cycling.
b. The leg action of a swimmer during breast stroke.
c. The shoulder, arm and forearm whilst performing a push up.
d. Work out the muscles which are relaxing in opposition to the agonist muscles in a, b and c.

REVIEW QUESTIONS

1. What is the function of tendons?
2. What is the function of ligaments?
3. What are the functions of periosteal layers?
4. Identify the agonists that are active in:
   a. Elevating the shoulders.
   b. Hyper-extending the back.
   c. Abducting the hip.
   d. Dorsiflexing the ankle.
   e. Flexing the knee.
5. Work out the muscles which are relaxing in opposition to the agonist muscles of 4a–e .
6. Identify the agonist muscles that are active in:
   a. A pull up.
   b. Hitting a stationary hockey ball.
   c. A sit up.
   d. A vertical jump.
   e. Shooting in basketball.

Summary

1. You should be able to classify and identify skeletal muscle according to its shape and group.
2. You should be able to discuss the relationship between muscle size and performance.
3. You should be able to understand the role of fibre types with respect to sporting situations.
4. You should understand the role of musculoskeletal attachments in limb movement and analyse movements in terms of muscle action.
5. You should understand what is meant by origin and insertion and antagonistic muscle action.

FURTHER READING

Bowers R.W. and Fox E.L. *Sports Physiology* 3e, Wm C. Brown 1992.

Donnelly J.E. *Living Anatomy* 2e, Human Kinetics,1990.

Fisher G.A. and Jenson C.R. *Scientific Basis of Athletic Conditioning* 3e, Lea & Febiger, 1990.

Hay G.H. and Reid J.G. *Anatomy Mechanics and Human Motion* 2e, Prentice Hall, 1988.

Klausen K., Hemmingsen I. and Rasmussen B. *Basic Sport Science,* McNaughton and Gunn, 1982.

Seeley R.R., Stephens T.D. and Tate P. *Anatomy and Physiology* ISE 2e, Mosby–Year Book, 1992.

Solomon E.P. and Davis W.P. *Human Anatomy and Physiology,* The Dryden Press, 1987.

Thompson C.W. *Manual of Structural Kinesiology* 2e, Mosby–Year Book, 1994.

Wirhed R. *Athletic Ability and the Anatomy of Motion,* Wolfe, 1984.

1.4 Types of muscular contraction

KEY WORDS AND CONCEPTS

muscular contraction	**isokinetic mc**	**isotonic mc**
dynamic	**eccentric**	**concentric**
isometric muscle contraction (mc)	**ballistic**	**plyometrics**
	static	

In Investigation 1.16 you flexed or contracted the biceps muscle in your upper arm. This action was brought about by a changing state of contraction within the muscle tissue.

Muscular contractions can vary in speed, force and duration. For example, in cycling the action is cyclical and rhythmical, involving the interplay of agonist and antagonist, whereas the action of a boxer throwing a punch is ballistic in nature since the arm is moved fluidly by a short, fast contraction of the agonist, and the movement is stopped as a result of the antagonist brake action.

During muscular contraction, a muscle may shorten, lengthen or stay the same. Where a muscle changes length the contraction is classified as **dynamic**. When a muscle remains the same length, a **static** contraction occurs.

1. Static contractions—isometric muscle contraction

Another name for a static muscular contraction is an isometric contraction. (*Iso* means same and *metric* means length, hence same length.) This concept can be expressed as in Figure 1.23 or as:

$$\frac{\text{force of muscle}}{\text{contraction}} = \frac{\text{force expressed}}{\text{by resistance}}$$

The result is that the muscle length and tension in the arm wrestling contest remain static. It is found that pushing or pulling **without moving** can produce a strength gain in the muscles used. In a training situation this is done by exerting the maximum possible force in a fixed position for sets of 10 seconds, with a 60 second recovery interval. Its advantage is that a large amount of strength training can be done in a short time. Another advantage of **isometric training** is that it needs no special place or equipment and it can be done any time throughout the day. However, isometric training does little for cardiovascular fitness.

2. Concentric contractions—isotonic and isokinetic muscle contraction

The sort of exercise in which muscles are used in a normal **dynamic** way, and muscles contract at a speed controlled by the sportsperson in whatever activity is being done, is called **isotonic.** In this case, the work is labelled **concentric** or positive because the resulting tension causes the muscle to create movement by shortening its length. The advantage of this type of exercise is that it stimulates **real** sporting use of the musculature. One of the adaptations produced by this type of training or exercise is to increase the capillarization of both skeletal and cardiac muscle and to enable these muscles to become more resistant to the onset of fatigue. Therefore, it is most likely to lead to improvement in sporting performance.

In **isokinetic** exercise the point at which force acts moves at constant speed. For example, in a squat the shoulders move upwards at a constant speed regardless of the effort put into the exercise. Special machines are needed for isokinetics (the nearest usually available is a hydraulic exercise machine). Isokinetic exercises (concentric and eccentric) are used in special strength training programmes and human movement research.

Figure 1.23

The advantage of isokinetic training is that it removes from the exercise the differences between forces exerted at different angles of limbs at a joint (refer to Investigation 7.5, task 7, for a discussion on the effect of joint angle on forces applied by muscle systems). Like isotonic exercise, isokinetic training improves muscle strength and endurance, and cardio-vascular fitness as well.

3. Eccentric contractions—plyometrics

It is found that if maximum effort is put into an exercise **while a muscle group is lengthening,** then the muscle exerts a bigger force than in any of the other types of exercise mentioned above. In this case the work is labelled **eccentric** or negative.

This is the effect of the stimulus trying to prevent muscle lengthening, and it produces the biggest overload possible in a muscle, thereby enhancing its development as far as strength is concerned.

The chief practical use of this is in **plyometrics**, in which the sportsperson jumps down from a box and immediately jumps back over a bar or hurdle (Figure 1.24), or in fact performs any jumping exercise in which a landing followed by a jump occurs. You may wish to try some of these examples! (For a detailed discussion on the adaptations produced by training refer to Chapter 4.)

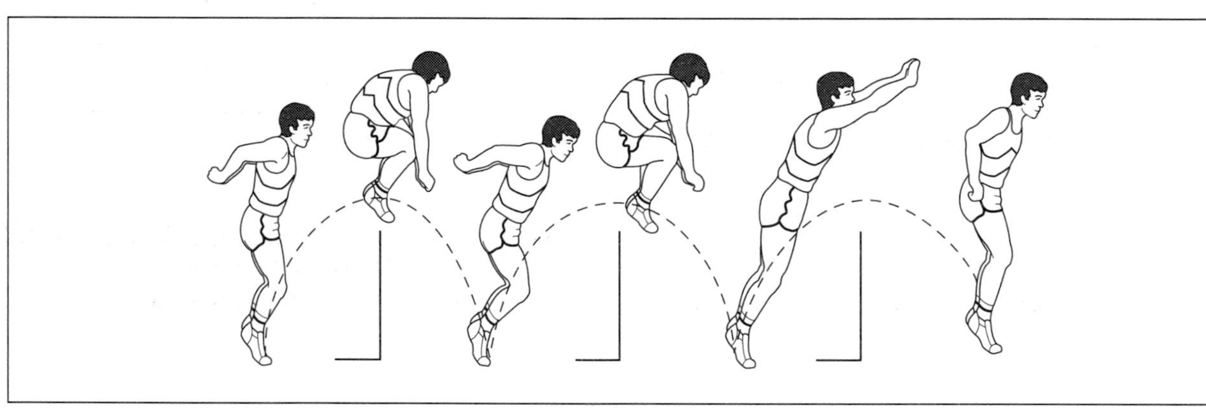

Figure 1.24 Examples of plyometric exercises.

Investigation 1.17 : Types of muscular contraction in relation to physical activity

Materials: chinning bar

Task One

a. Hang from a bar, as shown in Figure 1.25a, holding a 90° angle in the elbow joint.

b. From the bent arm position pull yourself up, as shown in Figure 1.25b .

c. When you have completed the chin-up, lower yourself slowly down to an arms extended position, as shown in Figure 1.25c.

Task Two

With the aid of the diagrams, work out the agonist muscles used for each exercise, their origins and insertions and the type of muscular contraction being used. Write your answers in the results table provided.

Figure 1.25

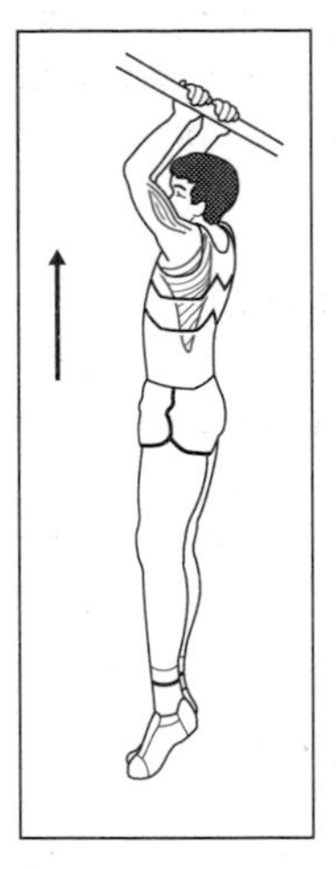

a.

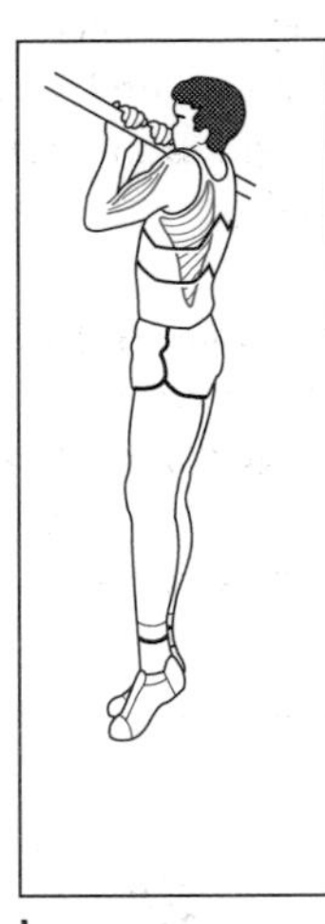

b.

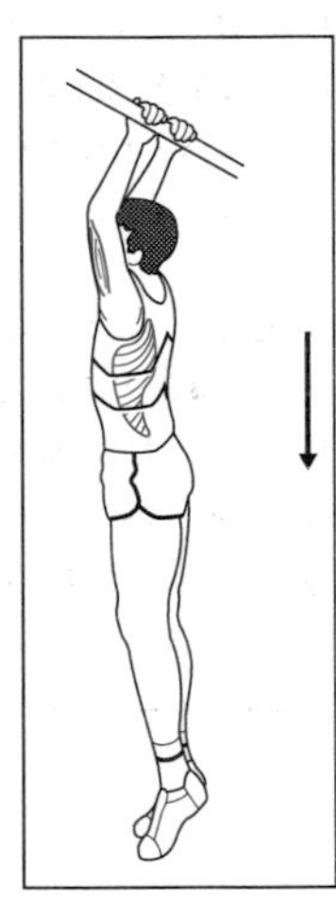

c.

Table 5 : Results

	Agonist muscles	Origin	Insertion	Type of contraction
a.				
b.				
c.				

Task Three

Figure 1.26 shows four different actions from different sports. The muscles indicated in the figures are the active ones used in the position or movements.

Make a table similar to Table 5 and complete the task of identifying the active muscles, their origins and insertions, and the types of muscle contraction. (Adapted from *Basic Sport Science* by Klaus Klausen.)

Figure 1.26

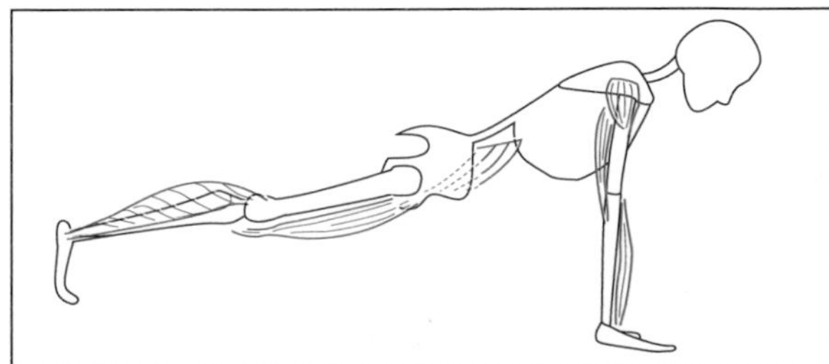

a. The push-up position.

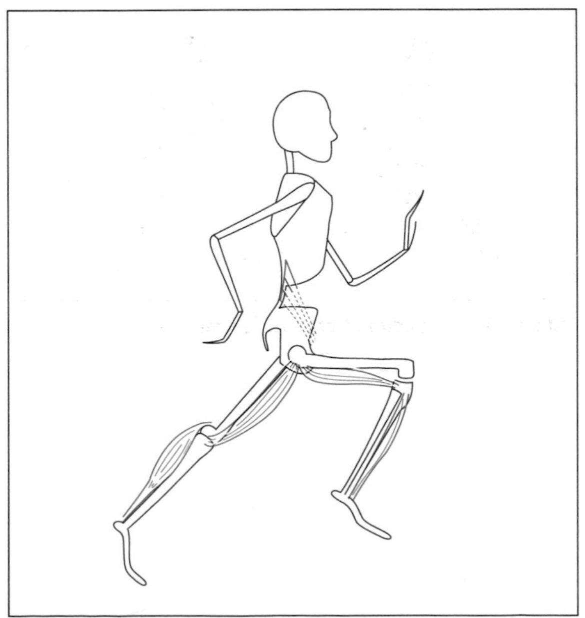

b. Sprinting.

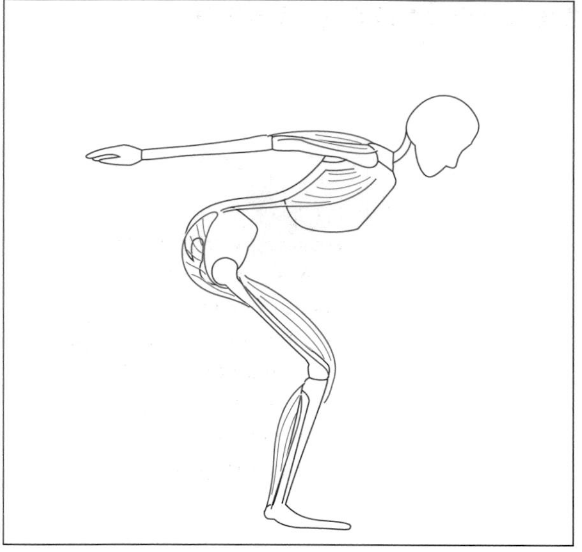

c. Starting position for swimming.

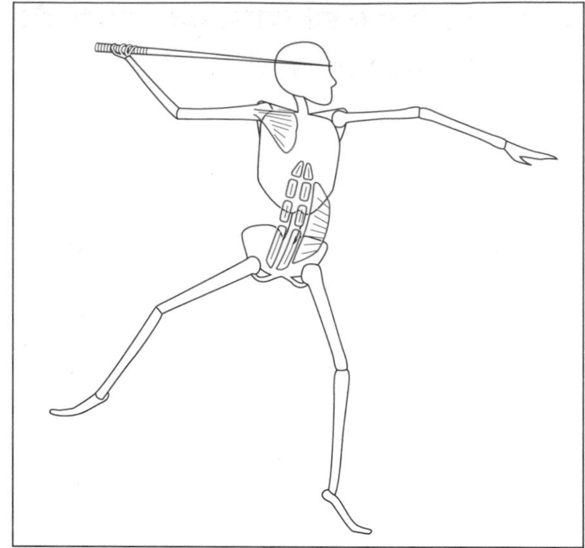

d. Throwing the javelin.

REVIEW QUESTION

Discuss the advantages and disadvantages of isometric, isokinetic and isotonic muscle contraction.

Summary

1. You should understand the concepts and the advantages and disadvantages of dynamic (isotonic and isokinetic) and static (isometric) contraction.
2. You should understand the concepts of concentric and eccentric contractions.
3. You should the able to identify types of muscle contraction in relation to practical situations, cojointly with agonist muscle identification.

FURTHER READING

Bowers R.W. and Fox E.L. *Sports Physiology* 3e, Wm C. Brown, 1992.

Chu D.A. *Jumping into Plyometrics*, Human Kinetics, 1992.

Donnelly J.E. *Living Anatomy* 2e, Human Kinetics, 1990.

Fisher G.A., Jenson C.R. *Scientific Basis of Athletic Conditioning* 3e, Lea & Febiger, 1990.

Hay G.H. and Reid J.G. *Anatomy Mechanics and Human Motion* 2e, Prentice Hall, 1988.

Klausen K., Hemmingsen I. and Rasmussen B. *Basic Sport Science,* McNaughton and Gunn, 1982.

Noble B.J. *Physiology of Exercise and Sport,* Mosby–Year Book, 1986.

Prentice W. *Fitness for College and Life* 4e, Mosby–Year Book, 1994.

Thompson C.W. *Manual of Structural Kinesiology* 2e, Mosby–Year Book, 1994.

1.5 A typical muscle and its structure from gross to molecular detail

KEY WORDS AND CONCEPTS

striated muscle	**muscle fibre**	**filaments—actin and myosin**
perimysium	**myofibril**	**ratchet mechanism**
epimysium	**sarcolemma**	**Huxley's theory of muscle contraction**
endomysium	**sarcoplasm**	**cross bridges**
red muscle	**sarcomere**	**triad vesicles**
white muscle	**myoglobin**	**nervous impulse**

To understand how a muscle converts chemical energy into mechanical energy, we need to understand the structural detail of voluntary muscle and what makes it contract.

Voluntary muscle is often referred to as **skeletal** muscle because it normally moves bones. Other descriptions include **striped** or **striated,** which derive their names as a result of the striped microscopic appearance of the muscle cells.

A typical muscle is the **gastrocnemius** or calf muscle which has its origin on the lateral and medial condyles of the femur and its insertion through the achilles tendon on the calcaneum or heel hone.

Figure 1.27c shows that the entire muscle is surrounded by a layer of connective tissue called the **epimysium**, which consists mainly of collagen fibres. The function of the epimysium is to provide a smooth surface against which other muscles can glide, and to give the muscle its form. The epimysium is the total envelope surrounding and connecting the muscle to the outer **fascia**.

Within the muscle are large bundles of muscle fibres or **fasciculi** which are surrounded by the **perimysium** (middle layer) consisting of collagen and elastic fibres. This information is illustrated in Figures 1.27c and d.

Within each bundle or fasiculus, are **muscle cells** or **fibres** each individually wrapped by a very thin layer of connective tissue or **endomysium** (*endo* final, *mysium*–muscle). Refer to Figure 1.27d.

All three connective tissue layers (epimysium, perimysium and endomysium) are connected to each other so that when the muscle fibres contract, they are ultimately linked to the tendons which are attached to bones across joints, thus creating voluntary movement (refer back to section on how skeletal muscle works (p. 30).

The muscle cell (see Fig. 1.27e)
Each cell consists of a multinucleate (multinucleate means containing many nuclei) fibre and is highly specialized for contraction. Although the diameter of the muscle cell is very small (10–100 μm—microns), its length can be extremely long (up to 0.5 m) depending on the length of the whole muscle. Therefore, it is important that the muscle cell can transmit its nerve impulses throughout the entire length of the fibre. As a consequence, skeletal muscle is a good conductor of electricity. The cell membrane or **sarcolemma** is very thin, which is important to allow efficient diffusion of oxygen and glucose into the cell, and carbon dioxide out of the cell. Positioned just inside the sarcolemma are numerous nuclei, hence the term 'multinucleate'. (The **nucleus** is the control centre of a cell.)

The **sarcoplasm** inside the cell is a specialized cytoplasm containing **sarcoplasmic reticula**, **'T' (triad) vesicles**, **enzymes** and **mitochondria**.

The **sarcoplasmic reticulum** is a network of internal membranes that run throughout the sarcoplasm and is responsible for the transportation of materials within the cell. The **'T' vesicle** is a sac which contains cellular secretions, such as calcium ions needed to initiate muscle contraction. **Enzymes** are the organic catalysts in that they regulate all chemical reactions within the cell (for example, ATPase is

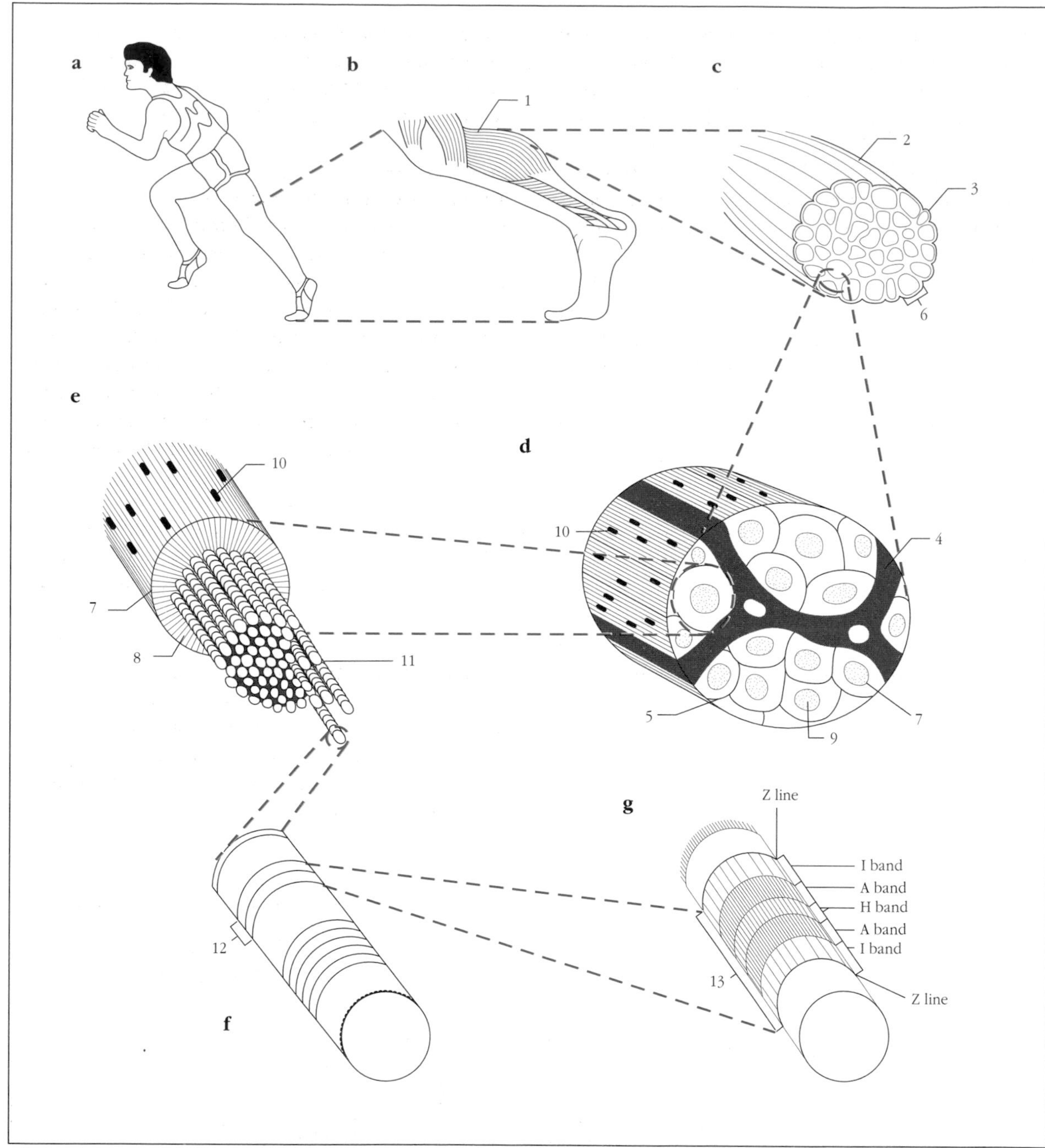

Figure 1.27 The structure of skeletal muscle from gross to molecular detail.

a. Sprinter in action.
b. Lower part of leg showing positioning of the gastrocnemius muscle
c. Cross-section through the gastrocnemius muscle.
c., d. Sections of the fasciculi.
e. Muscle cell.
f., g. Myofibril

1. gastrocnemius muscle.
2. belly of muscle
3. epimysium
4. perimysium
5. endomysium
6. muscle bundle or fasciculus
7. sarcolemma
8. sarcoplasm
9. muscle cell
10. nucleus
11. myofibril
12. banding pattern of myofibril
13. sarcomere with labelled banding pattern

needed to activate ATP which provides the energy needed for muscular contraction). **Mitochondria** are often referred to as the **power plants** of the cell, because most of the reactions of cellular respiration and hence energy release take place within them.

Figure 1.28 shows the distribution of mitochondria within slow twitch, type I muscle fibres. Those mitochondria positioned beneath the sarcolemma provide energy for the transport of ions and metabolites across the sarcolemma. Those mitochondria positioned deep within the muscle fibres provide energy for muscle contraction via ATP regeneration (refer to page 96 for additional information on the role of mitochondria within skeletal muscle tissue).

Some muscle fibres contain more sarcoplasm than others and these appear darker due to the presence of **myoglobin** (a form of haemoglobin that occurs in muscle cells). This type of muscle is called **red muscle** and it is best suited for long-term powerful contractions as in the postural extensor muscles (such as the rectus abdominus or erector spinae muscles, which tend to hold the body upright). **White muscle** contains less sarcoplasm and myoglobin, but more ATPase (the enzyme needed to assist energy release from ATP—see Section 3.2 for a discussion on energy generation and ATP). Therefore white muscle is best suited for speed. Flexor muscles, such as vastus medialis or biceps muscles, which can move limbs quickly, are examples of white muscle. Red and white muscle are also described as slow and fast twitch muscle, respectively. The properties of these different types of muscle cells or fibres were discussed in detail in the section on types of muscle fibre (p. 28).

Muscle myoglobin

Muscle myoglobin (a similar molecule to haemoglobin) has a temporary, but **greater** affinity for oxygen than haemoglobin. Therefore, muscle myoglobin will capture oxygen from saturated haemoglobin, thereby transferring oxygen **into** the muscle cell structure. Since myoglobin is present throughout the cell, oxygen is transferred from myoglobin molecule to myoglobin molecule **until** it reaches the mitochondria (where it is needed for energy producing reactions). This process is **in addition** to the **diffusion** of oxygen between capillaries (from the haemoglobin of red blood cells) and muscle cells, caused by the larger concentration (or partial pressure) of oxygen in haemoglobin than in the muscle cells. (See Chapter 2, p. 77–78, for a discussion about gas diffusion into muscle cells).

Muscle cell structure (see Fig. 1.27g)

Running longitudinally within the sarcoplasm are long, slender, light and dark structures called **myofibrils** (3 μm in diameter), which therefore create a striated appearance. Each myofibril consists of numerous units called **sarcomeres**.

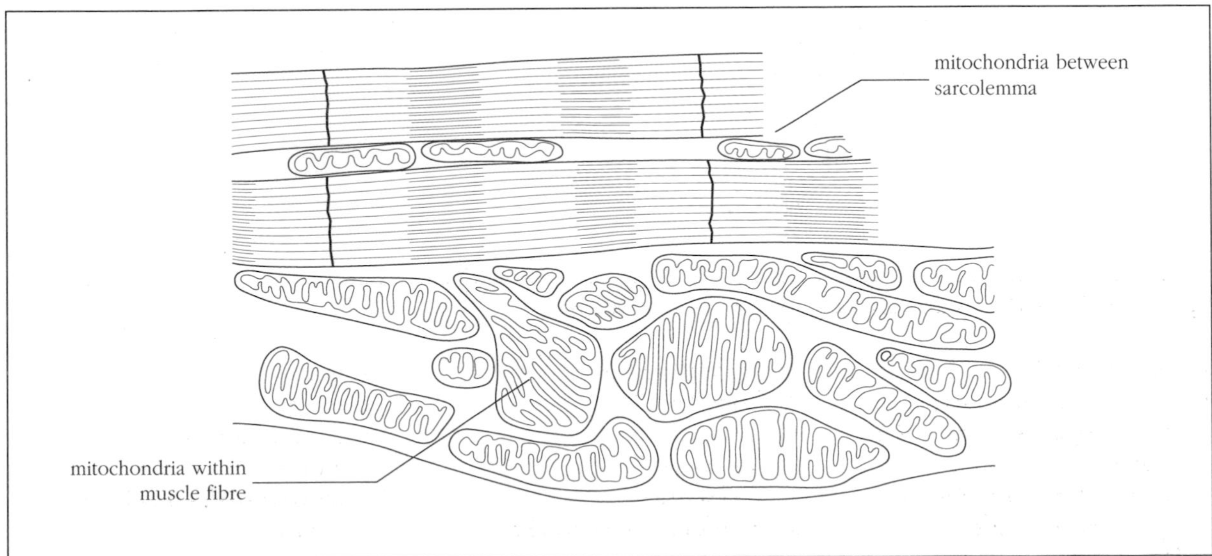

Figure 1.28 Mitochondrial density within slow twitch muscle fibres.

The sarcomere (see Figs 1.27g and 1.29)
Each sarcomere is the functional basic unit of a myofibril and there are thousands of sarcomeres forming a long chain within each myofibril. The **Z** membrane indicates the boundary from one sarcomere to the next.

The reason for this light and dark striated banding pattern (hence the name '**striped muscle**') is that it is composed of two types of longitudinal protein filaments:

Thick filaments of myosin—confined to the dark **A** band and **H** zone in the middle which has only thick myosin filaments.

Thin filaments of actin—which are found in the light **I** band and between myosin at the ends of the dark **A** band.

The **A** bands are positioned in the centre section of the sarcomere and consist of thick and thin filaments separated by an **H** zone which has only thick filaments. The **I** band is positioned at both ends of the sarcomere and consists exclusively of thin filaments.

The thin filaments connect the **Z** membrane and the inner edge of the nearer **A** band at each end of the sarcomere. The thick filaments join the outer edges of both **A** bands and therefore overlap the thin filaments in the **A** band. This arrangement is illustrated in Figure 1.29.

What happens when the muscle contracts?
The theory of muscle contraction is based on **Huxley's sliding filament theory of muscle contraction**.

In the relaxed muscle all the bands are visible, whereas in the contracted muscle the light **I** band narrows then disappears, since the thin actin filaments are being drawn further in between the thick myosin filaments (refer to Figure 1.29 to observe these differences between relaxed and contracted muscle).

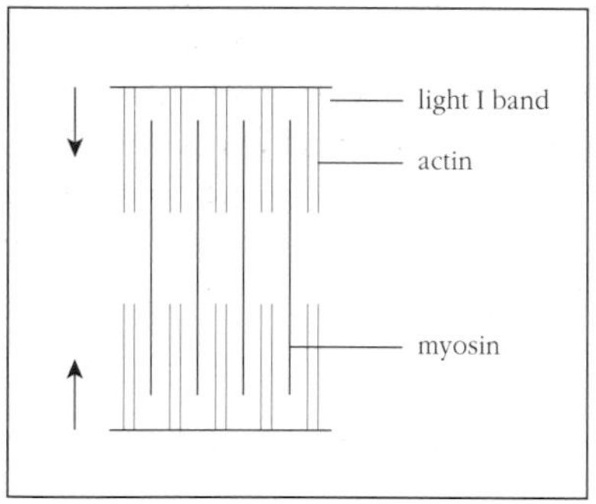

a.

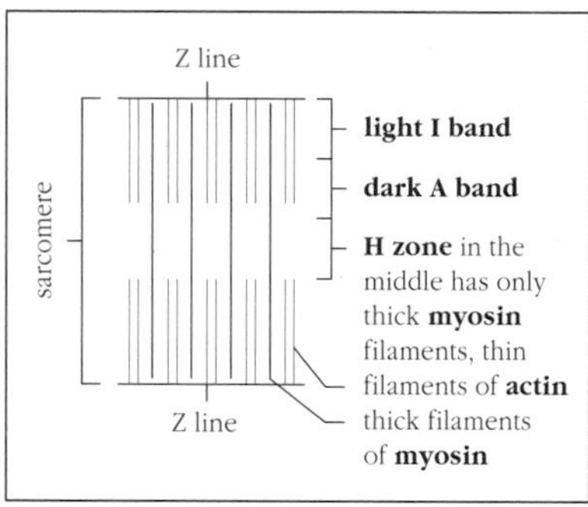

b.

Figure 1.29 Diagrammatic detail of a sarcomere a. relaxed and b. contracted *(After Huxley).*
a. Relaxed muscle
b. Contracted muscle
In muscle contraction light **I** band narrows then disappears as actin filaments are drawn further and further between filaments of myosin.

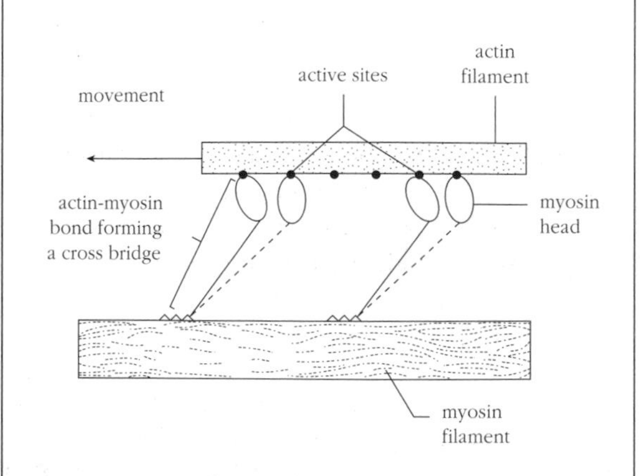

Figure 1.30 Sliding filament theory: actin-myosin bonds.

How do the two sets of filaments move between each other?

The key to the process of muscle contraction lies in the **overlapping** of the thick myosin and thin actin filaments, as seen in Figure 1.29.

When the nervous impulse reaches the muscle cell, it initiates the release of calcium ions (Ca^{++}) from special storage 'T' vesicles in the sarcoplasmic reticulum. The calcium ions stimulate the contraction of the muscle by exposing the active sites on the actin filaments (when the calcium is reabsorbed and nervous stimulation withdrawn, the muscle relaxes).

At the same time the heads of the myosin filaments become activated by adenosine triphosphate (ATP) which, when broken down into ADP and P_i, releases large amounts of energy. The myosin heads attach themselves to selected sites on nearby actin filaments to form **actin-myosin** bonds, usually called **cross bridges**. This process is illustrated in Figure 1.30. This is immediately followed by the detachment of the cross bridges and the reattachment of the myosin heads to the next actin sites and so on. The whole effect is to pull the actin filaments past the myosin filaments so that they form a bigger overlap (than in the resting state) and therefore shorten the sarcomere. The attachment, detachment and reattachment of cross bridges is called the **ratchet mechanism**.

With many thousands of thin filaments pulling past thick filaments in a single cell, and many thousands of muscle cells contracting in this way in the gastrocnemius and other voluntary muscles, skeletal muscle can quickly respond to the demands of ballistic activity, such as in a flat out 100 metre swim or sprint.

The strength of the muscular contraction is proportional to the number of cross bridges in harness, so that a muscle in a full state of contraction has a greater region within each cell of actin-myosin overlap, and hence a greater number of cross bridges in harness. There is no slippage within the cross bridges because of the non-aligned or offset attachments of the actin-myosin bonds.

Types of muscular contraction

When the muscle fibre is held at a certain point of stretching simultaneous with the actin-myosin bonding occurring, the result will be an isometric contraction (although what happens in this sort of contraction is that different fibres alternate in contraction). When the muscle fibre is stretched outwards at the same time as the actin-myosin bonding, an eccentric contraction will occur. The contraction becomes concentric when the actin filaments slide in between the myosin filaments.

Energy used for muscle contraction is derived from glucose and free fatty acids which are converted in the mitochondria into ATP which is then delivered to the contractile filaments.

REVIEW QUESTIONS

1. An understanding of the functional structure of muscle cells is an important basis for an understanding of physical activity. Discuss this statement.
2. List the proteins involved in muscle contraction and describe the role of each one.
3. Comment on the number and distribution of mitochondria with respect to muscle fibre types.

Summary

1. You should be able to describe the gross and microscopic structural detail of striated muscle cells.
2. You should be able to understand the mechanisms involved in striated muscle contraction.
3. You should be able to relate tension to types of exercise and muscular contraction.

FURTHER READING

Ackermann U. *Essentials of Human Physiology*, Mosby–Year Book, 1992.

Bowers R.W., Fox E.L. *Sports Physiology* 3e, Wm C. Brown, 1992.

Fisher G.A. and Jenson C.R. *Scientific Basis of Athletic Conditioning* 3e, Lea & Febiger, 1990.

Klausen K., Hemmingsen I. and Rasmussen B. *Basic Sport Science*, McNaughton and Gunn, 1982.

McArdle W.D. *Exercise Physiology – Energy, Nutrition and Human Performance* 3e, Lea & Febiger.

Prentice W. *Fitness for College and Life* 4e, Mosby–Year Book, 1994.

Seeley R.R., Stephens T.D. and Tate P. *Anatomy and Physiology* ISE 2e, Mosby–Year Book, 1992.

Simpkins J. and Williams J.I. *Advanced Human Biology*, Unwin Hyman, 1987.

1.6 How Co-ordinated Movement is Produced

KEY WORDS AND CONCEPTS

central nervous system	**golgi tendon apparatus**	**cerebellum**
peripheral nervous system	**muscle spindle apparatus**	**action potential**
sensory neurone	**muscle twitch**	**depolarization**
motor neurone	**gradation of contraction**	**hyperpolarization**
synapse	**spatial summation**	**potassium/sodium pump**
motor end-plate	**wave summation**	**saltatory conduction**
reflexive movement	**tetanic contraction**	**all-or-none law**
motor neurone pool	**voluntary movement**	**repolarization**

Muscle can contract only when a nerve ending is stimulated by outgoing impulses from the **central nervous system** (CNS), which consists of the brain and spinal cord. The contractile system for muscles is organized into a number of distinct parts, each of which is controlled by a single **motor neurone**, and each motor neurone will control a large number of muscle fibres. A group of fibres and its neurone is called a **motor unit** (refer back to the study of types of muscle fibre at the beginning of this chapter).

Figure 1.31 shows a typical motor neurone which divides into several branches as it reaches the muscle bed. These branches connect the motor neurone to the muscle fibres by specialized structures known as **motor end-plates.**

The transmission of neural messages along a neurone is an electrochemical proccess. When a neurone is not conducting an impulse it has a **resting potential** brought about by the outward diffusion of potassium (K^+ ions) along a concentration gradient and a negatively charged inside cell membrane when compared with the outside of the cell membrane.

An **action potential** (Figure 1.32) occurs at the point along the axon where the neural impulse is being propagated. It is initiated when sufficient numbers of sodium ions (Na^+ ions) are allowed to diffuse into the neurone. This **depolarizes** the axon to a critical threshold level. Action potentials occur in an **all-or-none** fashion. If an action potential occurs at all it is of the same magnitude and duration no matter how strong the stimulus.

Repolarization is the return of the membrane potential towards the resting membrane potential because of K^+ ion movement out of the cell and

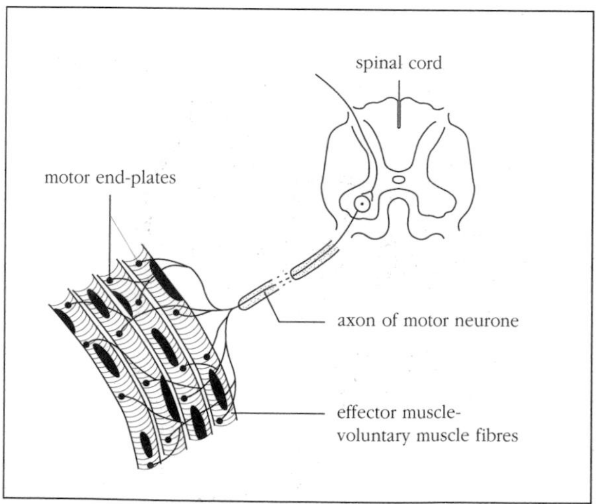

Figure 1.31 A motor unit.

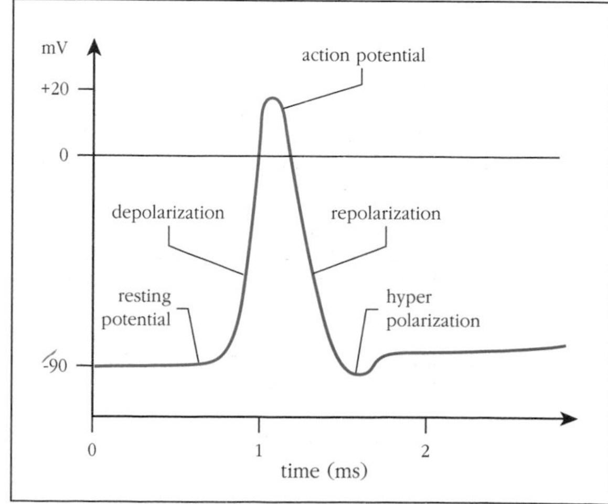

Figure 1.32 An action potential.

because Na^+ ion movement into the cell slows to resting levels. The after potential is a short period of **hyperpolarization**. The resting potential is restored by the sodium/potassium pump which establishes ion concentrations to their resting values.

An action potential initiated in one part of the cell membrane stimulates action potentials in adjacent parts of the membrane and so on. The speed of propagation along neurones varies greatly from cell to cell. Neurones that have large diameter myelinated axons conduct action potentials faster than small diameter unmyelinated axons. A myelin sheath (Figure 1.33—Conduction of an action potential in a myelinated axon) offers increased conduction velocity as a result of the action potential jumping from node to node. This process is called **saltatory conduction** and is less costly in terms of ion 'run down' since ion exchange occurs only at the Nodes of Ranvier.

Transmission of an impulse between neurones or from a neurone to an effector occurs at specialized junctions called **synapses** (Figure 1.34—A synapse). The wave of depolarization is unable to jump across the synaptic cleft; however, the problem is solved by the release of transmitter substances, such as acetylcholine, from the synaptic knobs. The transmitter substance diffuses across the synaptic cleft to bind with postsynaptic receptors. The sodium gates in the membrane open, allowing sodium to enter the axon and initiate the action potential. The electrical impulse can now pass directly from one cell to another.

The electrical impulse travels down the spinal cord and motor neurone to the **effector muscle** (the active muscle) in the way described above. The function of the **motor end plates** is to transfer the impulses from the small branching motor neurones to large muscle fibres (in all directions). This is achieved when the nerve action potential is followed by a muscle action potential. There is a delay of 0.5 milliseconds due to the time needed for the release of acetycholine from the synaptic knobs. An area of depolarization travels down the muscle cell, passing the entrances to the 'T' vesicles which secrete Ca^{++} ions needed to initiate muscle contraction (see page 37 for the subsequent reactions within the muscle cell). Each different fibre type is innervated by a different kind of motor neurone. When an electrical impulse reaches the muscle fibres of a **single motor unit**, the muscle cells contract simultaneously since they receive the same impulse from a single cell body of a motor neurone.

Each whole muscle consists of a large number of motor units. In muscles such as those in a leg or arm, there are about a thousand muscle fibres serviced by one motor unit; whereas, on smaller more sensitive muscles such as those in fingers, there are fewer fibres per motor unit. The nerve cell bodies of all the motor units are, for a given muscle, bound together at an appropriate level of the spinal cord to give the nearest access point to that specific muscle, and arrive as a concentrated bundle at the anterior horn of the spinal cord. These concentrated bundles or patches are called **motor neurone pools,** and there is a motor neurone pool for each muscle in the body.

The nature of the stimuli received at the muscle bed will determine the type of muscular response.

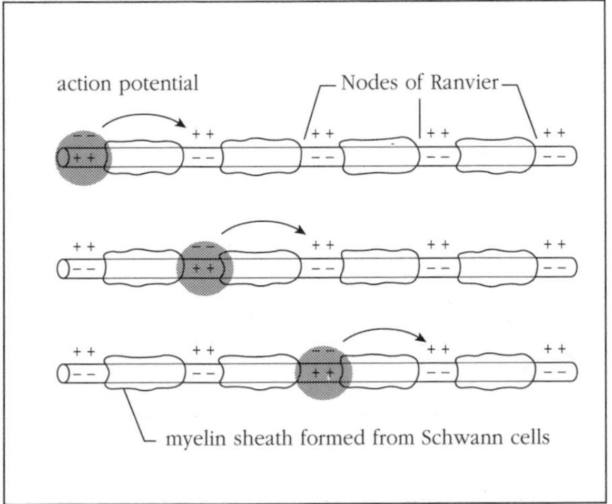

Figure 1.33 A myelin sheath. Conduction of an action potential.

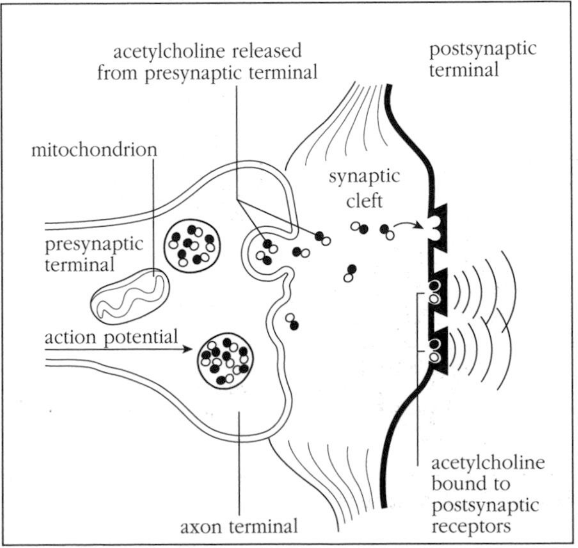

Figure 1.34 A synapse.

MOTOR-NEURAL FIRING PATTERNS

A muscle twitch (see Figure 1.35)

Stimuli received by the motor neurone pools are transmitted to the different motor units, which do not necessarily work in unison. The strength of the stimulus must be sufficient to activate at least one motor unit to produce any contraction at all. Once activated, **all** the muscle fibres in that motor unit will contract maximally by giving a **muscle twitch** lasting a fraction of a second. This is known as the ALL-OR-NONE LAW.

The contractile time of fast twitch fibres is much quicker than in slow twitch fibres. Therefore, fast twitch fibres produce greater contractile forces sooner.

Region A of Figure 1.35 shows the approximate time scale for a single motor unit muscle twitch.

Wave summation

The strength of a muscle can be increased in another way. If a second impulse is received at the motor neurone pool very quickly after the first one there will not have been time for relaxation to be completed before the next contraction begins. Therefore, the total contraction is increased. This adding on of contractions to produce a stronger effect due to increase in rate of stimulation is known as **wave summation.**

This is shown in region B of Figure 1.35, a stimulus (marked S on the graph) arrives **before** the motor unit has fully relaxed after the previous contraction.

Tetanic contraction

When impulses fire off so fast that there is no time for any relaxation at all, a state of absolute contraction is produced called **tetanic contraction.** Region C of Figure 1.35 shows this effect.

Gradation of contraction

Muscles can of course be contracted for longer than a fraction of a second. This is performed by a stronger stimulus activating many motor neurones in succession (different motor units will be involved, not necessarily the same ones in succession). This enables a muscle to exert forces of **graded** strengths, whose efforts will range from fine delicate precision controlled movements to strong dynamic powerful movements. This is called **gradation of contraction.**

Spatial summation (see Figure 1.36)

The term **spatial summation** refers to the fact that any given stimulus will cause motor units to be successively activated **over the volume** of muscle, i.e. different motor units are involved throughout the muscle. The advantage of **different** muscle fibres being activated throughout a muscle is that ATP consumption (the energy producing reaction) is shared throughout the muscle instead of being confined to single motor units, and therefore fatigue is spread throughout the muscle instead of being confined to small groups of fibres.

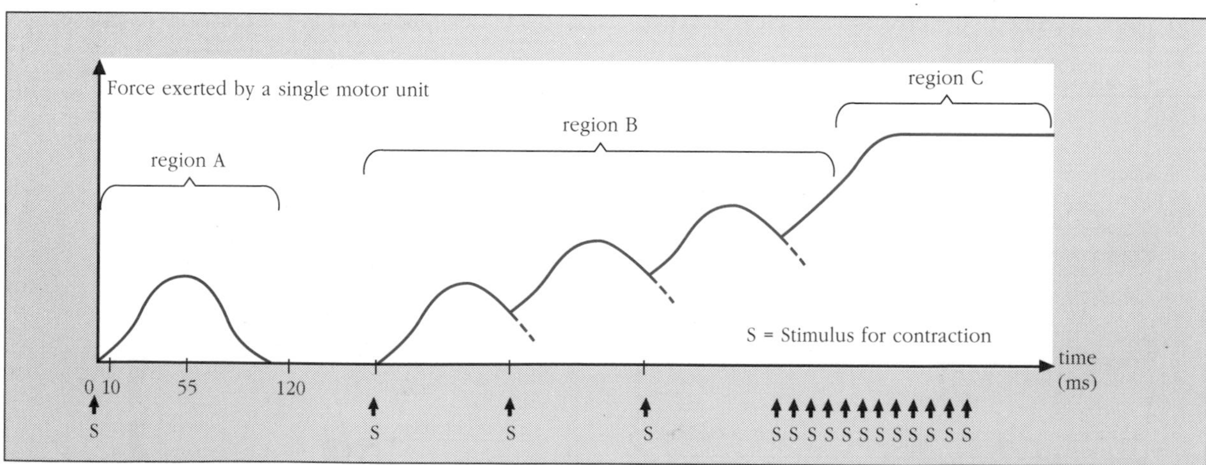

Figure 1.35 Muscle twitch.

Spatial summation is shown in Figure 1.36 in which the effects of five **different** motor units add up to produce a **resultant** whole muscle contraction.

This slight **out of step** action of motor units is a very important factor in maintaining **sustained** contraction at any strength. If some motor units are contracting while others are relaxing, and if this is **staggered** throughout the muscle, quite long periods of sustained contraction can be achieved, depending on the load being moved, or, in the case of **isometric contraction**, the tension being produced. All muscular action has to develop sufficient isometric tension in order to apply sufficient force to begin movement.

All the above ways of varying the strength of contraction depend on the size of stimulus, and normally they are used together to produce co-ordinated movement patterns which may vary from finely graded strengths to maximal contractions.

In addition to the action of motor units, co-ordinated movements are adjusted by **sensory feedback.** Within physical performance, the sportsperson is aware of pressure, pain, joint angles, muscle tension and speed of actions as a result of specialized proprioceptors such as **Golgi tendons** and **muscle spindles**. The Golgi tendon apparatus provides proprioceptive information associated with tendon movement. The muscle spindle apparatus detects and monitors muscle activity (Figure 1.37). When muscle fibres contract, ends of the muscle spindle come closer together, stimulating the sensory or afferent nerves which relay electrical impulses to the spindle cord. Motor or efferent nerves then relay electrical impulses to the muscle bed, followed by an adjustment in the state of muscle tension required for the execution of the physical task. This involuntary stretch reflex provides information such as state of muscle tension, length, position and rate of change of muscle length. Muscle spindles are important in the control and tone of postural muscles. Information from such proprioceptors is used as a basis for **decision making.** This sensory aspect of physical activity is included in the area 'The Performer as a Person', and provides the initial source of information which enables the muscle system to operate **stretch reflexes.**

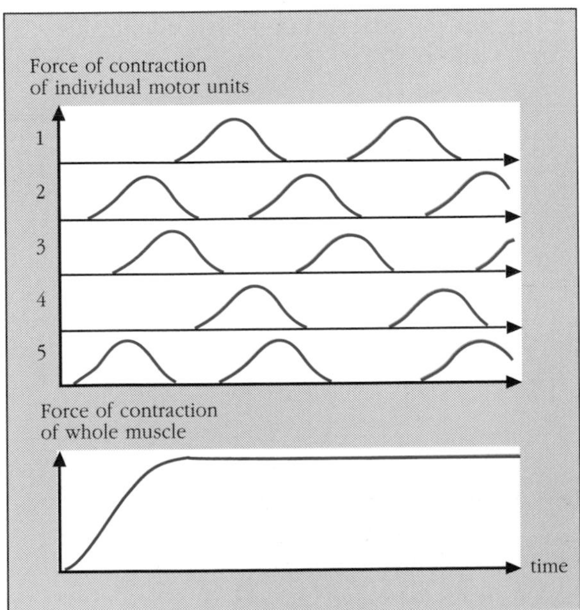

Figure 1.36 Spatial summation.

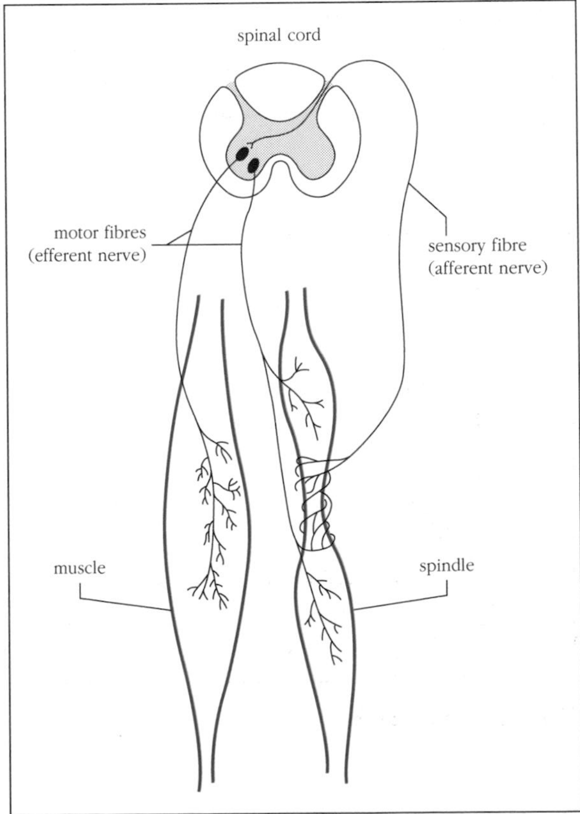

Figure 1.37 Muscle spindle apparatus.

THE ROLE OF REFLEXES IN CO-ORDINATED MOVEMENT

Reflexes play an important role in all forms of movement. The two types of reflex which originate from the CNS are:

a) **Voluntary reflexes**: where impulses originate in the voluntary motor cortex.
b) **Involuntary reflexes**: which originate from the stimulation of sense organs which produce electrical impulses in sensory neurones.

The **reflex arc** is the pathway along which unlearned and automatic learned responses travel.

How reflexes work

Figure 1.38 shows the unlearned reflex are for the knee jerk reflex.

The hammer strikes the knee, and the impulses travel up the sensory neurone into the spinal cord, through the connector neurone, and out via the motor neurone to the quadriceps muscle, which responds by contracting quickly.

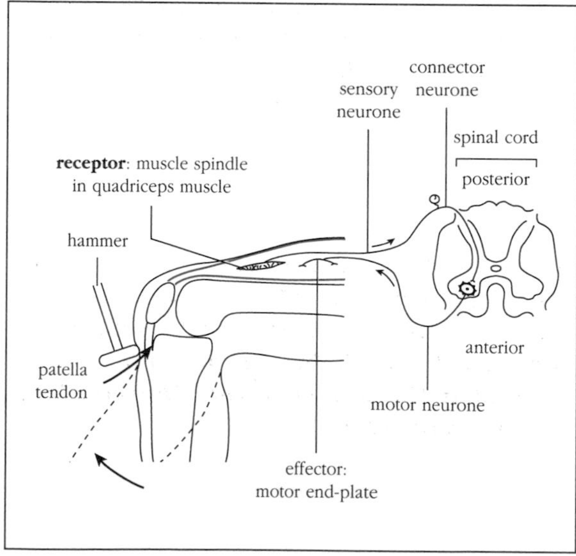

Figure 1.38 Knee jerk reflex.

Modification of movements

The self regulation of rhythmical movements between one muscle group and its antagonist is called **reciprocal innervation**. This concept explains how sensory information (from the muscle to the spinal cord) is linked by a connector neurone (within the grey matter of the spinal cord) to the motor neurone of the antagonistic muscle, to provide the necessary feedback for the continual adjustments of tension between muscle groups.

Modification of all muscular actions is under the control of the **cerebellum** of the brain. The cerebellum is rather like a final sorting section of a computer being fed continuously with information from all the sense organs, giving position of limbs, state of muscles (whether contracting or relaxing) and so on. It helps to create fine co-ordination and ensures that physical activity is carried out smoothly.

Investigation 1.18 : The reflex arc

Task One

Work in pairs. One of you sits with legs crossed in a relaxed position. Your partner firmly taps your patella tendon using a patella hammer or ruler (the patella tendon is positioned just below the knee cap). Describe and record the response of the knee to the tap. How can you tell that this response was a reflex action?

Task Two

Give an example of a skill you have learned which has become an automatic response to a stimulus.

Task Three

Distinguish between an automatic (reflex response) and fast reactions. Use examples from sporting situations to illustrate your answer.

REVIEW QUESTIONS

1. What is a motor unit?
2. Describe some of the factors which determine muscle speed and tension characteristics.
3. Explain the role of motor units in controlling the strength of muscular contractions in sports movements (AEB Sports Studies question 1991).

Summary

1. You should have a brief understanding of the structures and functions of the nervous system necessary for the production of co-ordinated movements in the human body.
2. You should be able to describe how co-ordinated movement is produced in relation to strength of stimulus, gradation of contraction, spatial summation and wave summation.
3. You should be able to describe how an action potential is propagated along a cell's membrane.
4. You should be able to understand the origins of voluntary and involuntary movements and describe the reflex arc.

FURTHER READING

Ackermann U. *Essentials of Human Physiology*, Mosby–Year Book, 1992.

Bowers R.W. and Fox E.L. *Sports Physiology* 3e, Wm C. Brown, 1992

Fisher G.A. and Jenson C.R. *Scientific Basis of Athletic Conditioning* 3e, Lea & Febiger, 1990.

McNaught A.B. and Callander R. *Illustrated Physiology*, Churchill Livingstone, 1981.

Seeley R.R., Stephens T.D. and Tate P. *Anatomy and Physiology* ISE 2e, Mosby–Year Book, 1992.

Simpkin J. and Williams J.I. *Advanced Human Biology*, Unwin Hyman, 1987.

Chapter 2
Cardio-Respiratory Systems

Athletic activity in events such as hockey, tennis, middle- and long-distance running, and cross-country skiing, requires the body to have the ability to endure tremendous physical and physiological demands.

This ability is commonly known as **staying power** or **endurance** and it is limited by the capacity of the **cardiovascular system,** comprising of the **heart** (its job is to pump blood around the body) and the vascular system, which consists of **blood** and **circulatory vessels** (which transport nutrients, waste products, hormones and other essential chemical compounds throughout the body and which link all other systems within the body), and the **respiratory** or **breathing system** (lungs) where the exchange of oxygen and carbon dioxide takes place.

These two systems work together to ensure that adequate amounts of oxygen are delivered to muscle and other tissue cells to meet the demands of exercise.

The capacity at which the **cardio-respiratory systems** operate will depend on the intensity, duration and type of muscular contraction being performed. For example, the longer and lighter the activity, the more the body will be limited by the capacity of the **aerobic energy system**; the shorter and higher the intensity of exercise, the more the body will be limited by the capacity of the **anaerobic energy system.** (See Section 3.2 for a detailed explanation on these two energy systems.)

The effect of exercise, particularly aerobic endurance training, is to improve cardio-respiratory functioning, especially that of the heart. (Cardiac functioning is used as a criterion to assess **physical fitness** levels.)

This chapter will help you to understand the structure, actions and adaptations of the **cardio-respiratory** systems in response to physical activity and exercise stress.

2.1 The Heart

KEY WORDS AND CONCEPTS

atrioventricular valve	**pulmonary arteries**	**heart rate**
atrium	**vena cavae**	**cardiac cycle**
ventricle	**aorta**	**systole**
cardiac	**cardiac impulse**	**diastole**
endocardium	**sino-atrial node**	**heart sounds**
myocardium	**atrioventricular node**	**radial artery**
pericardium	**fibres of Purkinje**	**carotid artery**
semilunar valves	**sympathetic nervous system**	**cardiac output**
mitral valves	**parasympathetic nervous system**	**stroke volume**
tricuspid valves	**bundle of His**	**Starling's Law of the Heart**
striped cardiac tissue		**pulse**
pulmonary veins		**adrenaline**

The heart is a pear-shaped organ located in the thoracic (chest) cavity. It lies just underneath the sternum between the lungs, with its apex positioned slightly to the left of centre of the body.

The heart consists of three layers:

a) The **pericardium** is an outer, double layered bag or **serous membrane** containing a thin film of fluid, the pericardial fluid (serum is a watery liquid which consists of plasma minus fibrinogen—a blood protein used in the clotting mechanism). The function of the pericardium is to reduce friction (with the other contents of the thoracic cavity and the cavity wall itself) and maintain heart shape.

b) The **myocardium** (Figures 2.1e and f) or **cardiac striped muscle tissue** forms the largest part of the heart wall. Cardiac muscle contracts in the same way as skeletal muscle. Each cell, with one nucleus positioned towards the cell centre, branches to unite with other cells. It is separated from adjacent cells by an **intercalated disc** which offers very little resistance to the neural impulse. Therefore, the cardiac impulse is transmitted throughout the myocardium. The whole effect is to create a united sheet of muscle.

The heart has a **pacemaker** (see Figure 2.2) which sends impulses throughout the myocardium and which is independent of the **central nervous system** (CNS) (since the heart generates its own impulses it is said to be **myogenic**). Because of its united structure, all cells forming the entire myocardium muscle sheet contract together producing a heartbeat. This is an application of the ALL-OR-NONE LAW.

c) The **endocardium** is a smooth, glistening **inner serous membrane** consisting of flattened epithelium which lines the heart cavities. Its function is to prevent friction between the heart muscle and flowing blood.

Investigation 2.1: To examine the structure of the heart

Materials: Heart model, heart and circulatory posters, fresh hearts (pig/sheep), dissection materials.
The following tasks assume availability of animal hearts for dissection. If this is not possible, then appropriate use of models and charts can be substituted.

Task One—external features

1. Work out the ventral (the front surface) and dorsal (the rear surface) sides of the heart.
2. Identify the external features of the heart which are labelled in Figure 2.1b.
3. Observe and identify the narrow vessels branching over the surface of the ventricles. These blood vessels supply the heart with food and oxygen, and transport carbon dioxide and other waste products away from the heart.
4. What happens if one of the main arteries to the myocardium becomes blocked with fatty lesions or a blood clot?

Task Two—heart valves (Figures 2.lc and d)

1. Cut a small opening in the right atrium and look down into the atrioventricular opening (this opening is between the top and bottom chambers of the heart). Pour a small amount of water into the atrium and observe the action of the valve as the bottom chamber fills. Write down your observations.
2. Now squeeze the bottom chamber containing the water. Observe and identify the vessel from which the water emerges.
3. Repeat this task on the left side of the heart.
4. Identify the valves located between the top and bottom chambers on both sides of the heart.
5. How are these valves supported?
6. Identify the heart valves sited in the vessels leaving the bottom chambers.
7. What is the function of heart valves?

Task Three—heart muscle (Figures 2.1c–f)

1. Cut the heart open longitudinally into two equal halves. Observe that the heart is divided into a four-chambered muscular bag.
2. Identify and name the structure which separates the left and right sides.
3. Name the top and bottom chambers.
4. Describe how the top chambers differ in their shape and thickness when compared with the bottom chambers. Suggest reasons for the functional significance of these differences.
5. Observe the walls of both bottom chambers. What type of tissue are these walls made of?
6. Notice, in Figure 2.1f, that each cardiac muscle fibre is connected by specialized junctions called **intercalated discs.** Explain the physiological reason for these structures.
7. The left bottom chamber has got a thicker wall than the right bottom chamber. What is the functional significance of this difference?

Task Four—vessels attached to the heart

Observe and identify the large vessels attached to the heart.

REVIEW QUESTIONS

1. The pathway of blood through the heart may be traced from the **superior** and **inferior vena cavae**, which empty deoxygenated blood into the right atrium. With the aid of Figures 2.1c and 2.3a–d, trace the pathway of blood from these large veins until it reaches the aorta. In your account, briefly mention the structure and function of the heart chambers, valves and blood vessels through which the blood flows.
2. How is the heart's structure suited to its function as a dual action pump?

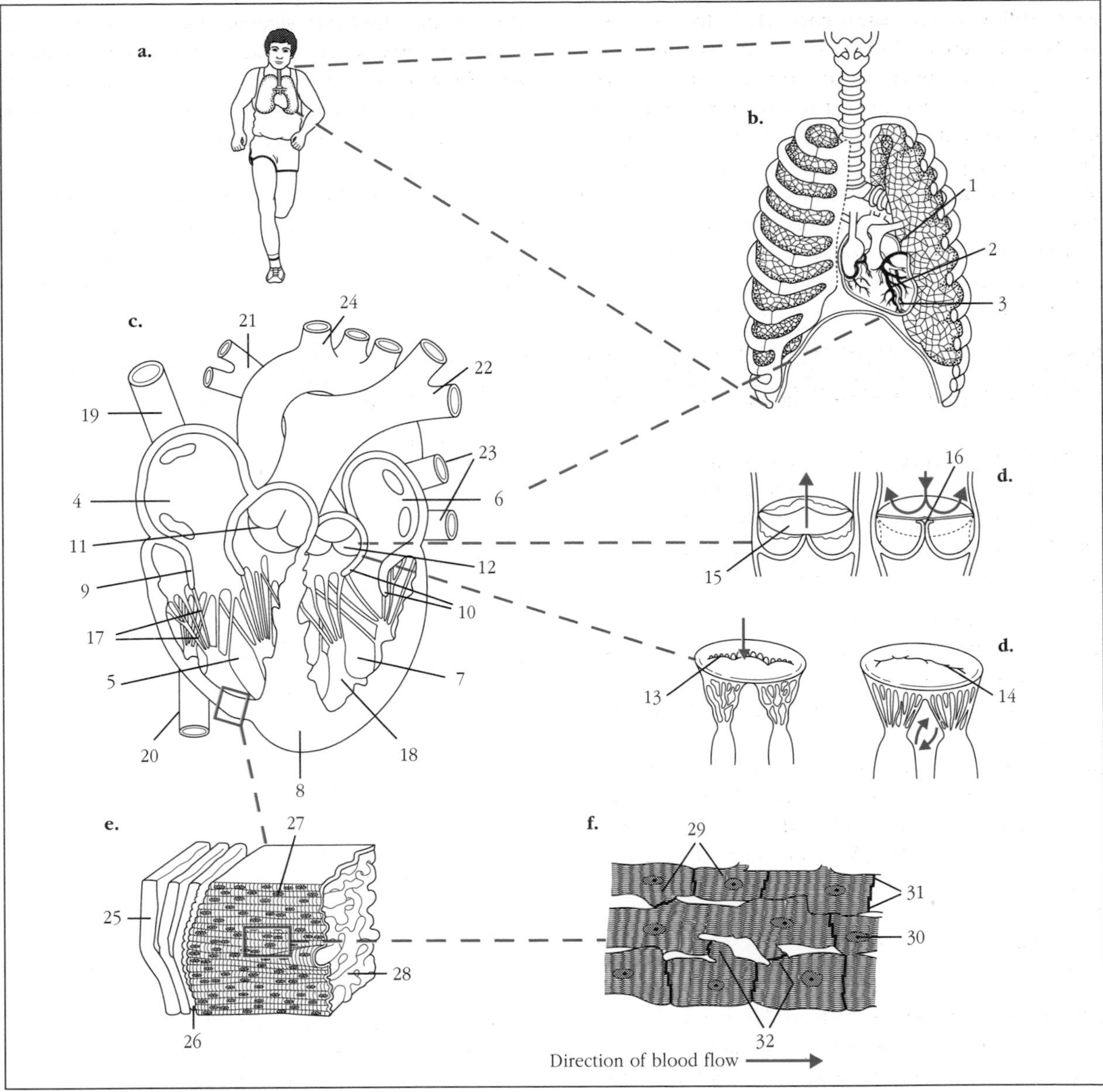

Figure 2.1 Cardiac anatomy.

a. Position of the heart within the body
b. Position of the heart within the thorax
c. Longitudinal section of the heart
d. Heart valves
e. Heart wall
f. Microscopic detail of myocardium

1 Pericardium
2 Coronary artery
3 Coronary vein
4 Right atrium
5 Right ventricle
6 Left atrium
7 Left ventricle
8 Septum

Atrioventricular valves:
9 Tricuspid valve
10 Mitral valve

Semi-lunar valves:
11 Pulmonary valve
12 Aortic valve
13 Mitral valve open
14 Mitral valve closed
15 Semi lunar valve open
16 Semi lunar valve closed by cusps
17 Chordae tendinae
18 Papillary muscle
19 Superior vena cava
20 Inferior vena cava
21 Right pulmomary artery
22 Left pulmonary artery
23 Left pulmonary veins
24 Aortic arch
25 Parietal pericardium
26 Visceral pericardium
27 Myocardium
28 Endocardium
29 Striations made up of myofibrils
30 Nucleus
31 Step-like intercalated discs
32 Connecting branches

HOW THE HEART WORKS

The dynamic action of the heart is that of a dual-action pump in that both sides of the heart contract simultaneously, even though the functions of the two sides are entirely different.

The cardiac impulse (see Figure 2.2)

Cardiac contractions are initiated by an electrical impulse (the **cardiac impulse**) which originates from the **pacemaker** or **sino-atrial node** (SA node). The electrical impulse travels down the atrial myocardium until it reaches the **atrioventricular node** (AV node) situated in the wall of the atrial septum. There is a slight delay so that the **atrial systole** (described below) is completed. The impulse then spreads into a specialized tissue, known as the Bundle of His, which connects the AV node to the septum and which has branches called **Purkinje fibres** within the septum and the ventricle walls. The Purkinje fibres are connected to ordinary cardiac muscle fibres. As a result of this branching network the impulse spreads throughout the ventricular walls, causing the ventricles to contract. This contraction is called **ventricular systole,** described below.

The heart's conducting system regulates the sequence of events which make up the **cardiac cycle.**

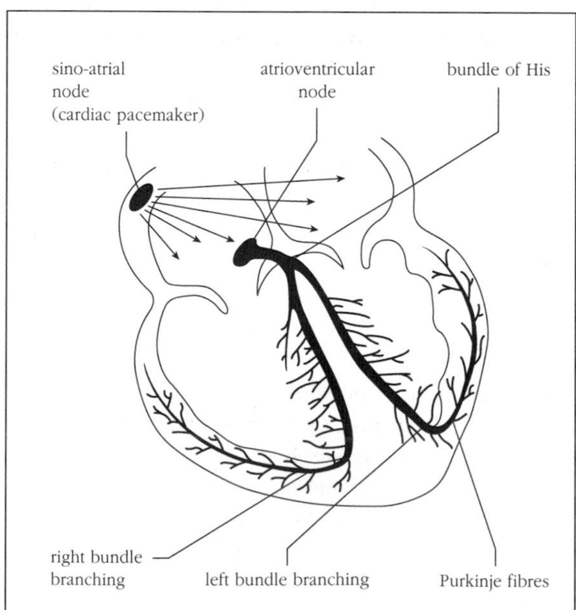

Figure 2.2 The cardiac impulse.

The cardiac cycle (see Figure 2.3)

The **cardiac cycle** is a sequence of events which make up one heartbeat and lasts for about 0.8 seconds. It thus occurs about 72 times per minute, depending on one's state of fitness. **Heart rate** is defined as the number of heart contractions per minute.

The cardiac cycle consists of a period of relaxation of the heart muscle, known as **diastole** (0.5 seconds) followed by a period of contraction of the heart muscle, known as **systole** (0.3 seconds), during which time the electrical impulse from the SA node is initiated in a set timed sequence.

Cardiac diastole

During **cardiac diastole** the heart relaxes for 0.5 seconds, during which time the sequence of events shown in Figures 2.3a and b occurs.

Figure 2.3 The cardiac cycle.

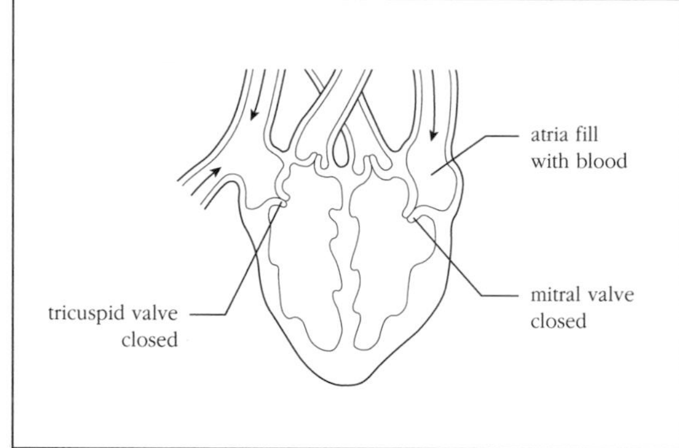

a. The atria fill with blood whilst the atrioventricular (mitral and tricuspid) valves are closed.

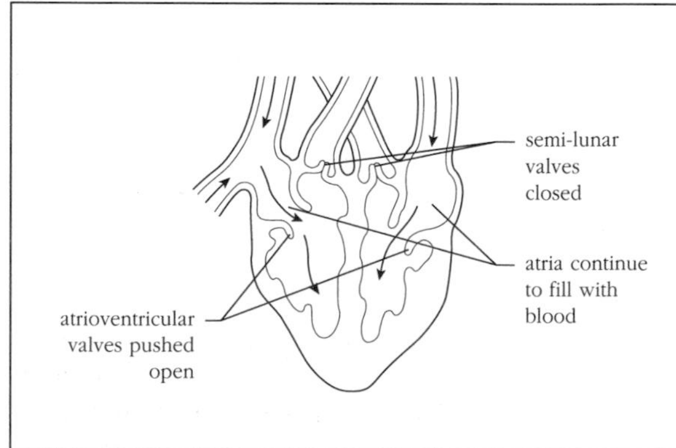

b. The atrioventricular valves are pushed open by rising atrial pressure and the ventricles start to fill with blood. During this time, the semi-lunar (or aortic and pulmonary) valves are closed.

Cardiac systole

During the 0.3 second contraction called **systole** the following sequence of events occurs:

Atrial systole *(Figure 2.3c)*

First, the SA node initiates an impulse causing a wave-like contraction across the myocardium of each atrium. The effect is for all the blood to be pushed past the atrioventricular valves into the lower chambers. The semi-lunar valves are closed during this activity.

Ventricular systole *(Figure 2.3d)*

This wave reaches the AV node, then a second contraction spreads across the ventricular walls and the atrioventricular valves close (these are the tricuspid and bicuspid or mitral valves). Pressure inside the ventricles continues to rise. The ventricles continue to contract until the continued increase in pressure pushes open the pulmonary valve on the right side of the heart and the aortic valve on the left side. The result is that blood flows into the pulmonary (lungs) and systemic (around the body) circulatory systems, respectively.

The cycle then begins again.

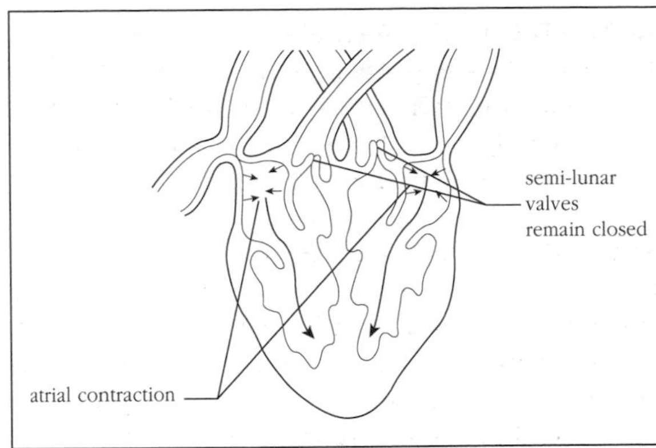

c. The atria contract. forcing blood into the ventricles.

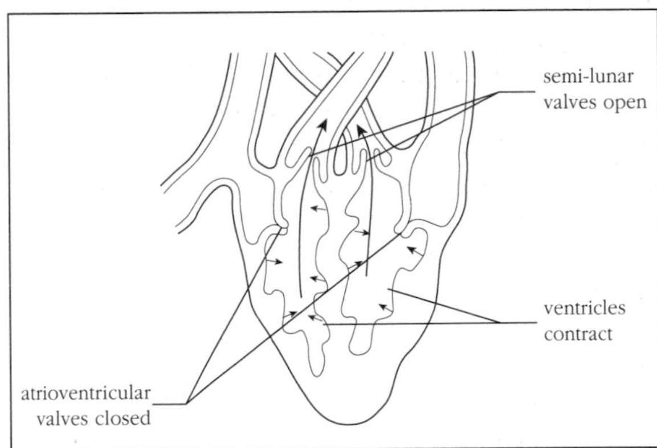

d. The ventricles contract and the atrioventricular valves close. Ventricular contraction forces open the semi-lunar valves, so that blood is ejected into the pulmonary artery and aorta.

Heart sounds

Heart sounds heard through the stethoscope are described as **'lub-dup'** and they are produced each time the heart valves close. The 'lub' sound is heard at the beginning of ventricular systole and is caused by the closure of the mitral and tricuspid valves. The 'dup' sound is heard at the beginning of ventricular diastole and is caused by the closure of the semi-lunar valves.

Cardiac output

When the ventricles contract, about 70–90 cm^3 of blood is ejected into the pulmonary artery and aorta. This volume is called the **stroke volume.** Stroke volume is regulated by venous return and stimulation from the **sympathetic nervous system.**

Cardiac output ($\dot{Q}$) is defined as the volume of blood pumped by each ventricle in one minute. At rest this is approximately 5 litres per minute. During vigorous exercise cardiac output may increase up to 30 litres per minute.

The following formula links cardiac output to stroke volume and heart rate:

$$\text{cardiac output} = \text{stroke volume} \times \text{heart rate}$$
$$\text{or} \quad \dot{Q} = SV \times HR$$

For example, if a person has a stroke volume of 75 cm^3 and a heart rate of 70 beats per minute (bpm), the cardiac output would be:

$$\dot{Q} = 75 \times 70$$
$$= 5250 \text{ cm}^3$$
$$= 5.25 \text{ litres per minute.}$$

Starling's Law of the heart

Cardiac output is dependent on the amount of venous blood returning to the right-hand side of the heart, otherwise known as **venous return.** During exercise, venous return increases and therefore cardiac output increases. This is caused by the myocardium being stretched, resulting in the myocardium contracting with greater force. Therefore, the stimulus which causes greater force of contraction is the stretching of the muscle fibres themselves. This relationship is known as **Starling's Law of the heart.**

The pulse

The **pulse** is a peristaltic wave produced in an artery. It is due to the contraction of the left ventricle forcing out 70–90 cm^3 of blood (stroke volume) into an already full aorta. The frequency of waves represents the number of heartbeats per minute.

Heart rate can be measured by **palpation**, **heart rate telemetry** – or by using an **electrocardiogram** (ECG), which is a graphic record showing the electrical activity of the heart (for further information, refer to a specialist physiology text, such as McNaught and Callender, see page 86).

Heart rate taken during or immediately after exercise can be used to indicate cardio-respiratory or **aerobic fitness.**

Regulation of heart rate

The continual adjustment of heart rate is controlled by the **sympathetic** and **parasympathetic nervous systems**, as illustrated in Figure 2.4.

These two nervous systems originate in the **cardiac centre** in the **medulla oblongata** and they work antagonistically. The effect of exercise is to speed up heart rate, and this is achieved by the sympathetic nerves transmitting impulses to the SA node and the release of **norepinephrine,** a transmitter substance produced by the adrenal medulla (glands situated at the top of each kidney) and released by the sympathetic neurones.

On the other hand, circulatory messages initiated by **baroreceptors** located in the aorta and carotid arteries, which respond to high blood pressure, are received by the cardiac centre, which responds by sending out impulses via the **vagus nerve** (parasympathetic nerves) to the SA node and heart rate slows down. This is an example of **negative feedback control, important** in maintaining **homeostasis** within the body (a term described in Chapter 4 when looking at control of body temperature).

Other factors such as elevated temperature and hormones such as adrenaline increase heart rate. For example, just prior to a competitive situation, the hormone **adrenaline** (fright, fight and flight) is released, which prepares the body for action. Adrenaline is released by the adrenal medulla (sited above the kidneys) in response to stimulation by the sympathetic nervous system. This hormone targets itself on the heart, blood vessels, liver and fat cells. The release of adrenaline stimulates glycogenolysis (the process of breaking down glycogen to liberate glucose), intracellular metabolism of glucose in skeletal muscle cells, and the breakdown of fats and proteins to form glucose.

The release of adrenaline results in a reduced blood flow and activity to organs such as the gut, skin and kidneys not essential for physical activity and increases blood flow to those organs such as skeletal muscle, lungs and cardiac muscle that participate in physical activity (see Figure 2.17, page 67). The effect of adrenaline lasts but a few minutes because it is rapidly metabolized, excreted or taken up by other tissues.

On the other hand, excessive potassium intake can slow down heart rate. In addition, gender and age also influence heart rate. It is found that females tend to have slightly higher heart rates than males and that heart rate generally slows down with age.

Ultimately, heart rate is dependent on a fine balance between the sympathetic and parasympathetic nerves which continually adjust to changing conditions.

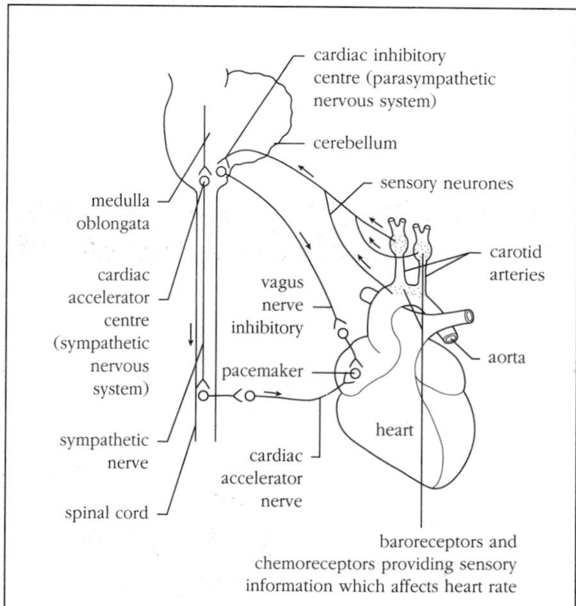

Figure 2.4 Nervous control of the heart beat.

Investigation 2.2 : Measuring heart rate

Materials: stop-watch or stop-clocks, heart and circulatory chart.

It is suggested that you work in mixed groups of five or six people.

Task One

1. Monitor your resting heart rate by palpation at the **carotid artery** and **radial artery** (the pulse can be located by pressing softly at the carotid artery, alongside the trachea in the neck, and across the wrist—the radial artery, when the arm is in a supine position). Count for six seconds, remembering that the count starts at zero. Then calculate your resting heart rate in beats per minute.
2. Repeat at each site using 10-second and 15-second counting periods. Do these counts in three positions:
   a. sitting
   b. lying down
   c. standing.

Task Two

Collate your group results using a table like Table 6.

Task Three

1. Are there any differences between heart rate taken at the radial and carotid arteries? Suggest reasons for your answer.
2. Many factors affect resting heart rate. Consider the differences in heart rate within your group and give reasons for these differences.
3. How does body position affect resting heart rate? Suggest reasons for variation of resting heart rate in the sitting, lying and standing positions.
4. What is being measured when you measure heart rate?

Table 6 : Results table A – sitting

	Heartbeat/min Radial Artery			**Heartbeat/min Carotid Artery**		
NAME	6	10	15	6	10	15
Self						

Investigation 2.3 : To listen to heart rate using a stethoscope

Materials: stethoscope.

1. Place the stethoscope upon the chest wall in the centre of the chest at the 5th intercostal space, as illustrated in Figure 2.5.

2. Describe what you can hear and which parts and actions of the heart are causing these sounds.

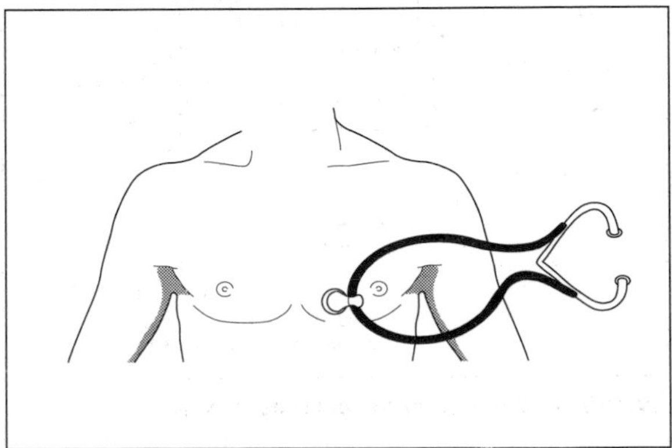

Figure 2.5 Listening to heart rate using a stethoscope.

Investigation 2.4 : To measure heart rate response to varying intensities of workload

Materials: select EITHER the step test OR cycle ergometer test described below for this investigation. Stop-watch or stop-clock. (Work in a mixed group so that you can compare your results.)

Task One

This investigation is best achieved with a heart rate monitor. If one is not available, work in pairs and get the passive partner to take and record heart rate values.

1. Note your heart rate at the beginning of the lesson for a 10-second count.
2. Record your heart rate immediately before the exercise commences for a 10-second count.
3. Commence exercising by either riding the bike or stepping on and off a bench at a low intensity work rate, for a period of three minutes (for the cycle ergometer test this could be achieved without resistance, and in the case of the step test with the aid of a metronome which establishes a low fixed rate of stepping).
4. Take heart rate values for a 10-second pulse count:
   a. One minute after the start of the exercise.
   b. Two minutes after the start of the exercise.
   c. At the end of the three minutes of exercise.
   d. Repeat the pulse count measurements every minute during the recovery phase until your heart rate has returned to its resting value prior to exercise.

Figure 2.6

5. Once your heart rate has returned to its resting value, and then repeat the same investigation but increase the workload. This can be achieved by increasing the frequency or resistance. (A weighted rucksack would be one way of increasing the resistance for the step test or alternatively one could increase the rate of stepping which is an increase in the frequency of muscle contraction. Resistance or frequency could also be increased for the cycle ergometer investigation.)
6. Repeat this investigation once more at a workload just under maximal effort, again by increasing the workload or frequency of exercise.

Task Two

1. Collate your results in table form (Table 7).

Table 7 : Results table – Heart Rate

Intensity of workload	HR at start of class	HR prior to exercise	HR 1 min after start of exercise	HR 2 min after start of exercise	HR at end of exercise (3 min)	HR during recovery (min) 1 2 3 4 etc.
low						
medium						
high						

2. Convert heart rate values into beats per minute. Draw a graph of your own results, with time in minutes on the *x*-axis (from heart rate prior to exercise to full recovery period) and heart rate in beats per minute on the *y*-axis, for the three different workloads.

Task Three

1. Account for any differences between your heart rate counts at the start of the lesson and just prior to exercise.
2. Using your own results, describe the relationship between heart rate and low, medium and high intensity workloads.
3. Suggest physiological reasons for increased heart rate values as workload intensifies.
4. Suggest physiological reasons for the differing patterns of recovery to the stress of the exercise.
5. A low heart rate during exercise and a small increase in heart rate as the intensity of the work increases generally reflect a high level of cardiovascular fitness. Compare your own results with your group members. Discuss your results in relation to gender, size, weight and levels of fitness.
6. Heart rate is increased and decreased as a result of the **sympathetic** and **parasympathetic nervous systems**, respectively. Using the information in the text, describe some of the factors that can influence heart rate.

Task Four

1. How reliable are the results of your investigation?
2. Does your investigation test what you set out to test?
3. Does your investigation produce a consistent pattern of results?

The answers to these questions will outline the concepts of **reliability** and **validity** in scientific investigations.

REVIEW QUESTIONS

1. Describe the relationship between stroke volume and submaximal and maximal exercise illustrated in Figure 2.7. Suggest reasons why maximal values for stroke volume are reached very early on in submaximal exercise.
2. Compare and suggest reasons for the trends shown in Figure 2.9, between cardiac output (bottom), stroke volume (top) and heart rate (middle) during rest, exercise and recovery.
3. Trained athletes often have resting heart rates of less than 60 beats per minute. This condition is known as '**bradycardia**' (*brady* meaning slow). Using the information in Figure 2.8, compare and contrast the hearts of a trained athlete and untrained person.

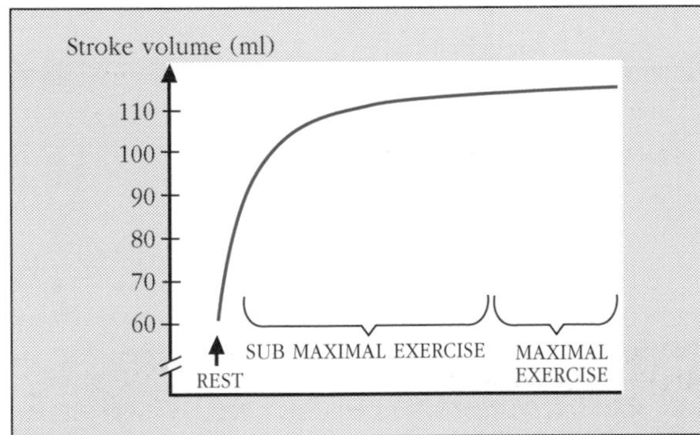

Figure 2.7

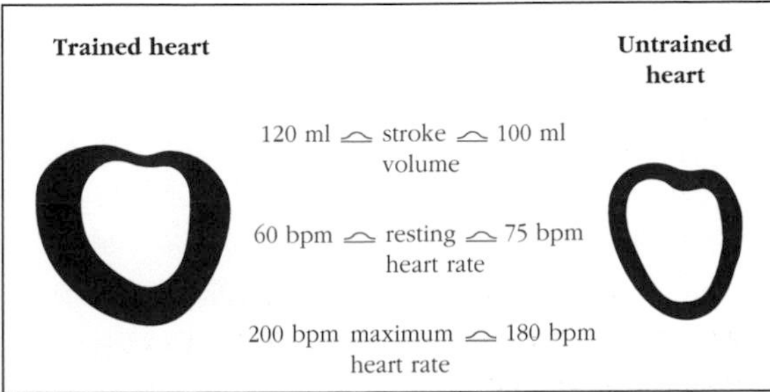

Figure 2.8

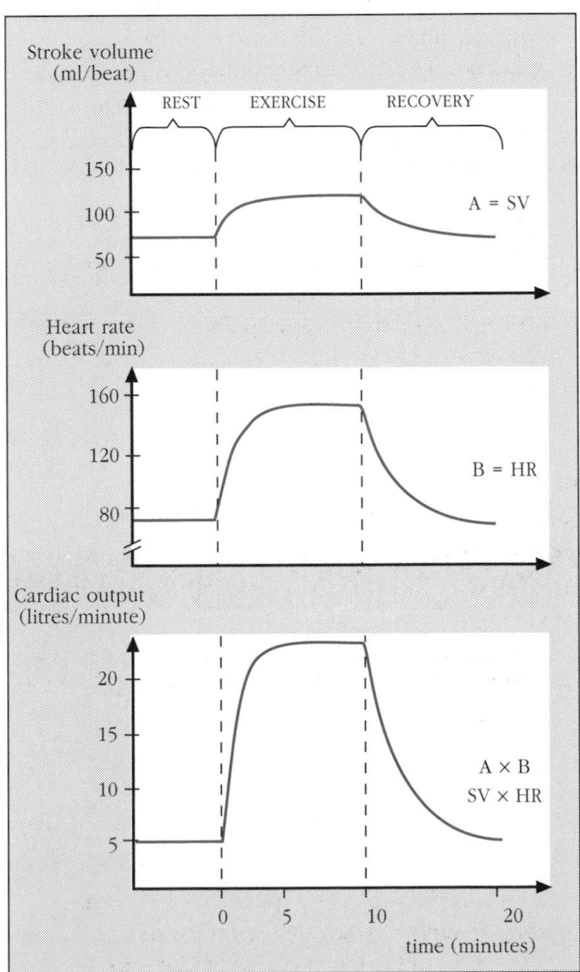

Figure 2.9

Summary

1. You should be familiar with the functions of the coronary arteries and veins.
2. You should be able to identify and understand the structure of heart tissue in relation to its functioning.
3. You should understand the concepts of cardiac impulse, cardiac cycle, cardiac output, Starling's Law of the Heart and pulse, and be able to describe the events of the cardiac cycle.
4. You should understand that the heart is myogenic since it initiates its own electrical impulse.
5. You should understand that the changing rate of heartbeat is controlled by two sets of nerves: the sympathetic and parasympathetic nerves, and that factors such as hormones and temperature affect heart rate.
6. By using investigational methods, you should be able to describe the effects of changing the body position on resting heart rate.
7. You should be able to identify the factors that affect stroke volume, and understand heart rate response to varying workloads.
8. You should be able to interpret data on cardiac dynamics.

FURTHER READING

Ackermann U. *Essentials of Human Physiology*, Mosby–Year Book, 1992.

Bowers R.W. and Fox E.L., *Sports Physiology* 3e, Wm C. Brown, 1992.

Klausen K., Hemmingsen I. and Rasmussen B. *Basic Sport Science,* McNaughton and Gunn, 1982.

McNaught A. and Callender R. *Illustrated Physiology,* Churchill Livingstone, 1981.

McArdle W.D., Katch F.I. and Katch V.L. *Essentials of Exercise Physiology,* Lea & Febiger, 1994.

Ross J.S. and Wilson K.J.W. *Foundations of Anatomy and Physiology,* Churchill Livingstone, 1981.

Rowett H.G.Q. *Basic Anatomy and Physiology,* Murray, 1988.

Seeley R.R., Stephens T.D.and Tate P. *Anatomy and Physiology* 2e, Mosby–Year Book, 1992.

2.2 The Vascular System

KEY WORDS AND CONCEPTS

plasma	**pulmonary circulatory system**	**precapillary sphincter**
corpuscles	**artery**	**venomotor tone**
red blood cells	**systemic circulatory system**	**constituents of blood**
white blood cells	**vein**	**pocket valves**
platelets	**arteriole**	**smooth muscle**
circulatory system	**venule**	**vasomotor control**

The key role of the **vascular system**, which is comprised of **blood** and **circulatory vessels**, is one of **transportation.** The effect of athletic activity is to increase the demand from body cells for nutrients from the digestive system and oxygen from the lungs, and to produce additional waste which needs carrying from body cells to the lungs and kidneys.

Blood is the specialized fluid tissue which carries out these functions within a closed system of vessels.

BLOOD

Blood is made up of 55% **plasma** and 45% **corpuscles.** In addition to the functions described above, it is involved in clotting, helps regulate body temperature, and transports hormones such as adrenaline around the body.

Plasma is a straw-coloured fluid which contains approximately 90% water, 8% blood proteins, 1% salts, 0.5% food substances. 0.04% waste products, gases such as oxygen and carbon dioxide, enzymes, hormones, antibodies and antitoxins.

(You may wish to find out more about each of these constituents of blood. For example, the plasma and red blood cell proportions can be determined using a technique for measurement called a haematocrit; see Green, *An Introduction to Human Physiology,* page 5.)

Investigation 2.5 : To examine blood cells

Materials: slides of blood cells, microscopes.

Task One—structure and function of red blood cells

1. Using Figure 2.10, identify, draw and label a red blood cell.
2. What is unusual about the structure of a red blood cell? How does the structure affect its life span?
3. Name the red pigment in red blood cells. What is its function? Explain how this function is carried out.
4. Where are red cells formed and how many occur per mm^3 of blood?
5. What effect does exercise have on the manufacture and the destruction of red blood cells?

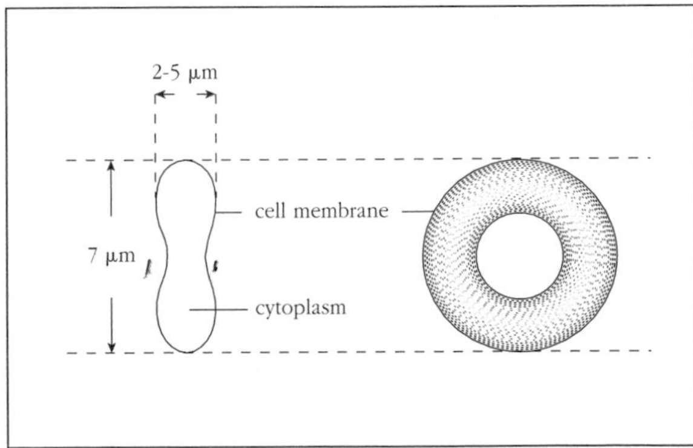

Figure 2.10 Red blood cell.

Task Two—structure and function of white blood cells

1. Identify, draw and label two types of white blood cell: one granulocyte and one non-granulocyte, giving the percentage of each found in blood.
2. What are the functions of these two types of cells?
3. Where are white cells formed and how many occur per mm^3 of blood?
4. Of what relevance are white blood cells to the active sportsperson?

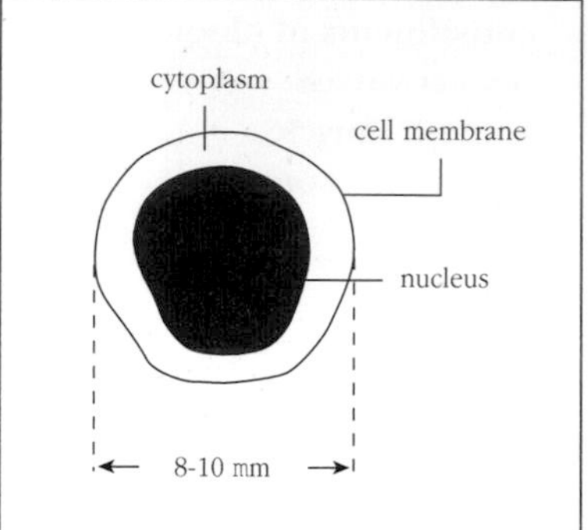

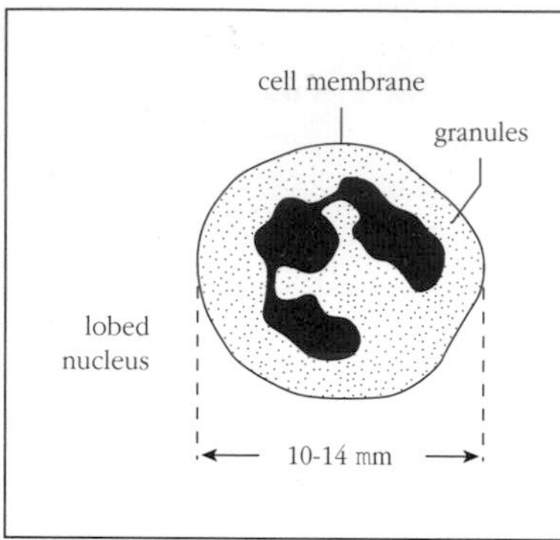

Figure 2.11 White blood cells.

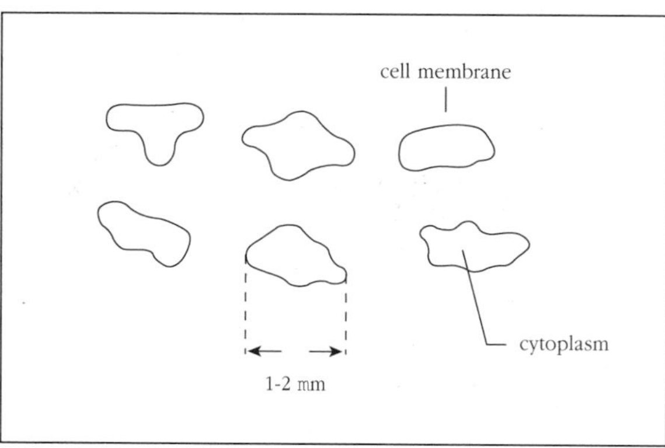

Task Three—structure and function of platelets

1. Identify and draw a platelet.
2. Where are platelets formed?
3. What is their function, and how many occur per mm^3 of blood?

Figure 2.12 Platelets.

BLOOD CIRCULATION (see Figure 2.13)

As a result of the dual pumping action of the heart, there are about 5.5 litres of blood continually circulating throughout the body.

The closed system of vessels containing circulating blood flows within two major circulatory systems:

1. **Pulmonary circulatory system**
2. **Systemic circulatory system**

These two systems are illustrated on the diagrammatic plan of Figure 2.13b.

Investigation 2.6 : To consider the two circulatory systems and the principal types of blood vessels

Materials: T.S. of blood vessels, microscopes, poster of the circulatory system.

Task One—blood circulation

1. Using Figure 2.13b, describe in your own words the course of blood from the time it enters the right atrium (then passes through the heart and the two circulatory systems) until it eventually returns to the right atrium again. Describe the changes in the composition of blood during this double circulation and name the heart chambers, organs and vessels it flows through.
2. The effect of exercise is to speed up heart rate. What effect will an increased heart rate have on blood circulation?

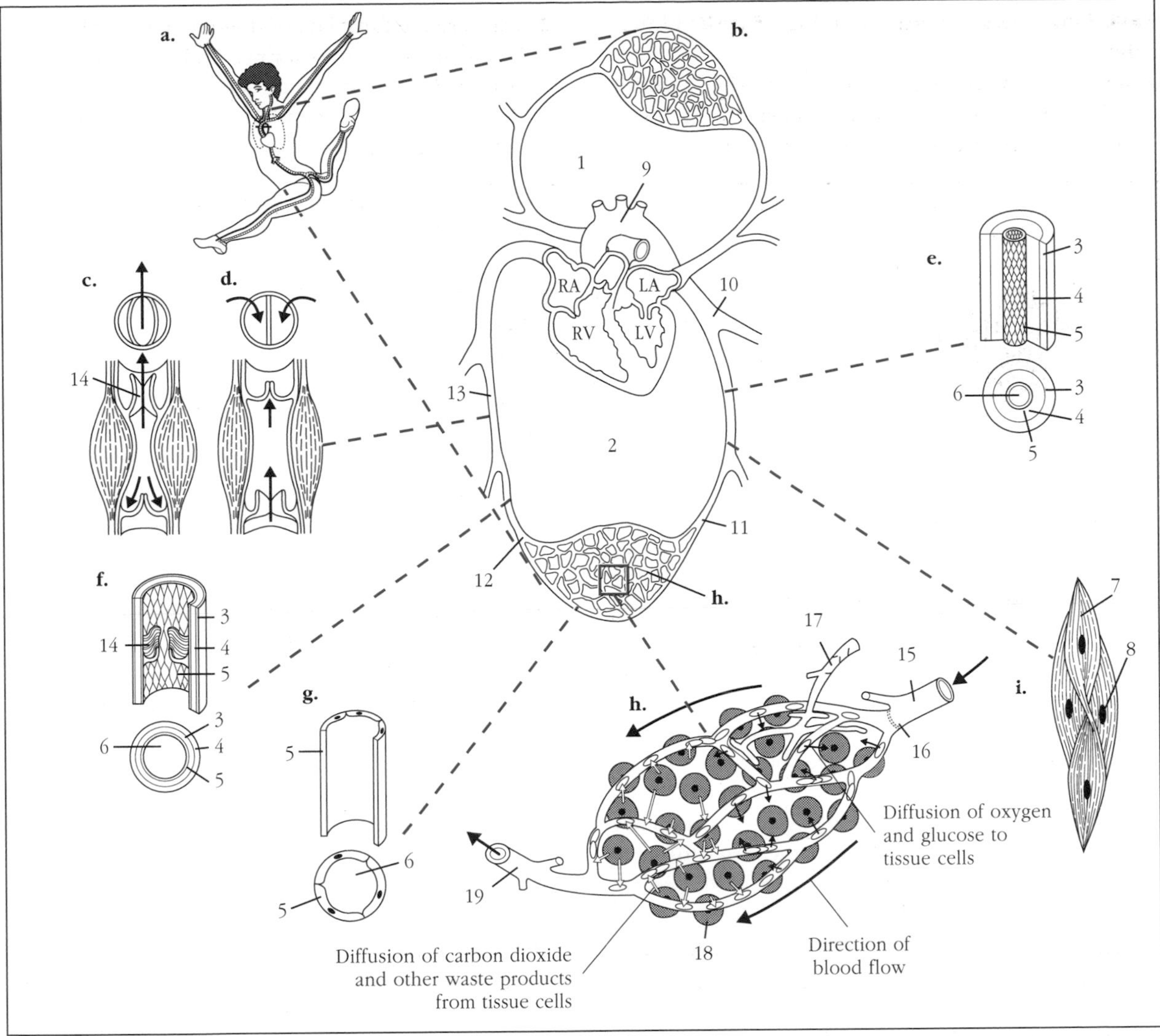

Figure 2.13 Blood circulation.

a. The human circulatory system.
b. Diagrammatic plan of circulatory system.
c. Skeletal muscle contracts: upper valve opened, lower valve closed.
d. Skeletal muscle relaxes: upper valve closed, lower valve opened.

e-g. Longitudinal and transverse section through:
- e. artery
- f. vein
- g. capillary

h. Capillary bed for gaseous exchange.
i. Involuntary or smooth muscle in walls of blood vessels.

1. Pulmonary circulatory system.
2. Systemic circulatory system.
3. Tunica externa (fibrous collagen layer).
4. Tunica media (smooth muscle and elastic fibrous layer).
5. Tunica intima (endothelial layer).
6. Lumen.
7. Smooth muscle (spindle-shaped).
8. Centrally positioned nucleus.
9. Aortic arch (leading to aorta).
10. Artery.
11. Arteriole.
12. Venule.
13. Vein.
14. Pocket valve.
15. Arteriole end of capillary bed (high pressure—oxygenated blood).
16. Precapillary sphincter.
17. Lymph vessel.
18. Tissue cell.
19. Venule end of capillary bed (low pressure—deoxygenated blood).

Task Two—blood vessels

Blood vessels vary in thickness and structural composition of their walls, diameter and overall length, according to their specific function.

1. Using the information in Figure 2.13e-g and prepared slides of blood vessels, identify an artery, a vein and a capillary network.
2. Observe the three layers of tissue which make up the walls of an artery and vein.
3. With the aid of diagrams, describe the structure of an artery, vein and capillary.
4. How is the structure of these three types of blood vessel suited to their specific function?

Arteries and veins

The walls of arteries and veins consist of smooth or involuntary muscle. Figure 2.13i illustrates the spindle-shaped muscle fibre structures, with each muscle fibre containing one centrally positioned nucleus. Unlike skeletal and cardiac muscle, its fibres lack striations, hence the name 'smooth'. The function of smooth muscle in arteries and arterioles (see below) is to vary the diameter of these vessels, thereby controlling blood supply to a region in the body.

Arteries subdivide into arterioles

Arterioles have the same structure as arteries but they are much narrower. In the **tunica media** region of the arteriole there is less elastic tissue, but it has a comparatively thick muscular coat. The function of arterioles is to control the inflow of blood to the **capillary bed.** This is achieved as a result of **vasomotor control** (described on p. 64) and the action of the precapillary sphincter, which is located at a point where the arteriole meets the capillary bed, as illustrated in Figure 2.13h.

Capillaries

Arterioles subdivide into **capillaries** which are the smallest blood vessels in the body, and which pass near to most muscle and other tissue cells.

The term **capillary bed** describes the total capillary structure within a muscle or other body organ. A capillary bed may contain thousands of **capillaries** for a given muscle, and it is found that the number of capillaries passing through a muscle can be increased by exercise, so that oxygen and other nutrients can be more efficiently carried to individual muscle cells.

Also, note that the large number of capillaries which eventually open out from the original artery, have a much larger **total** cross-sectional area than the artery (see Figure 2.14). This means that blood slows down dramatically as it enters the capillary system and speeds up again as it leaves. This affects, and is affected by, the blood pressure in the venous and arterial systems as explained below.

Capillary walls consist of a single layer of endothelium tissue, shown in Figure 2.13g (a simple tissue which lines all blood vessels). Their function is to be an exchange tissue, whereby dissolved materials diffuse in and out of the surrounding cells.

As blood passes through a muscle (or other) capillary system, it gradually gives up oxygen and nutrients and collects carbon dioxide and other waste products (as illustrated in Figure 2.13h). On leaving the capillary bed (the venous end of the capillary bed) the blood enters **venules** (refer to Figure 2.13b) which transport blood to the larger veins.

Veins

Veins have muscular coats which receive electrical stimulation. Alterations in the **venomotor tone** (explained on p. 64) produce changes in the capacity of circulation without affecting the veins' resistance to blood flow, since they are large diameter vessels.

With the exception of the **venae cavae**, all veins contain valves.

Investigation 2.7 : Blood vessels

Task One—arterioles

Dilate means to widen and constrict means to narrow. Why is it physiologically important for an arteriole to dilate and constrict, and therefore allow blood to flow or prevent blood from flowing?

Task Two—capillaries

Using the information in Figure 2.13h, explain how capillaries act as exchange beds.

Task Three—veins

1. How do these pocket valves operate?
2. Why are veins situated between muscles? (Refer to Figure 2.13c and d.)

REVIEW QUESTIONS

1. Construct a table which lists the different types of blood vessels and their structural and functional details.
2. In some ways heart muscle is similar to skeletal and smooth muscle. In other ways these three types of tissue are different. Make a list of the similarities and differences between these three types of muscle tissue.

Summary

1. You should be able to describe the characteristics of blood, and identify blood cells and their functions.
2. You should be able to identify the two major circulatory systems and the main blood vessels within them, and be able to trace the pathway of a blood cell through the heart and the two circulatory systems.
3. You should to be able to compare and contrast the structure and function of arteries, veins and capillaries, venules and veins.
4. You should to be able to compare and contrast the structure and function of cardiac, smooth and skeletal muscle.

FURTHER READING

Ackermann U. *Essentials of Human Physiology*, Mosby–Year Book, 1992.

Bowers R.W. and Fox E.L. *Sports Physiology* 3e, Wm C. Brown, 1992.

Green J.H. *An Introduction to Human Physiology*, Oxford Press, 1986.

McArdle W.D., Katch F.I. and Katch V.L. *Essentials of Exercise Physiology*, Lea & Febiger, 1994.

McNaught A.B. and Callender B. *Illustrated Physiology*, Churchill Livingstone, 1981.

Ross J.S. and Wilson K.J.W. *Foundations of Anatomy and Physiology*, Churchill Livingstone, 1981.

Seeley R.R., Stephens T.D. and Tate P. *Anatomy and Physiology* 2e, Mosby–Year Book, 1992.

2.3 Blood Flow in Muscles

KEY WORDS AND CONCEPTS

blood pressure	**respiratory pump**	**vasomotor control**
resistance	**vasodilation**	**muscle pump**
baroreceptors	**tissue fluid**	**venous return mechanism**
systolic blood pressure	**blood flow**	**vasoconstriction**
diastolic blood pressure	**peripheral resistance**	**lymph**
sphygomomanometer	**venomotor control**	

The rate at which blood circulates around the body depends on the needs of the body. During physical activity, working muscles may increase their oxygen consumption twenty fold when compared with the body's needs at rest. This section will help you to understand how and why the rate of blood flow changes as a result of physical activity.

The rate of blood flow depends on cardiac output and circulation ($\dot{Q}$ = SV × HR). Furthermore, any changes in cardiac output will result in changes in blood pressure.

BLOOD PRESSURE = BLOOD FLOW × RESISTANCE

The **resistance** to blood flow is produced by blood vessels **vasodilating** (or widening) and **vasoconstricting** (or narrowing) between working muscles. This is known as **peripheral resistance** caused by **blood viscosity** (viscosity is a term describing resistance to flow of any fluid, in this case a steady flow of blood through the vessels) and the changing shape of arterioles. Arteries are elastic vessels with a narrower diameter **lumen** (or central space) than veins, where pressures remain high. However, it is in the arterioles that pressure can change by the dilation and constriction of their muscular walls and precapillary sphincters (the tiny rings of muscle between arteriole and capillary vessels). This action is under the control of the **vasomotor** and **venomotor centres.**

VASOMOTOR AND VENOMOTOR CONTROL

Both control centres are located in the medulla oblongata (in the brain) and are regulated by the sympathetic and parasympathetic nervous systems (refer to Figure 2.4).

Vasomotor control

At rest a fall in blood pressure reduces the stimulation to the **baroreceptors** (Figure 2.4) in the aortic arch and carotid arteries. This reduction in stimulation is received in the vasomotor centre which acts by sending out nerve impulses to the arterioles, causing them to vasoconstrict and hence increase the blood pressure and speed up the heart rate. Exercise increases blood pressure which increases the stimulation to the baroreceptors. This increase in stimulation is received by the vasomotor centre which acts by sending out nerve impulses to the arterioles causing them to vasodilate, and hence blood pressure is reduced.

Venomotor control

Veins can change their shape. This is the result of venomotor tone, whereby the vein's muscular coat receives stimulation from the sympathetic and parasympathetic nervous systems.

Investigation 2.8 : To consider blood pressure

Using the information in Figure 2.14 answer the following questions:

Task One

1. Suggest reasons why systolic and diastolic blood pressure drops as the blood travels away from the left ventricle.
2. How does peripheral resistance vary from the aorta to the venae cavae?
3. As blood flows through the capillaries, there is a negligible effect of the pulse on the blood flow. Compare the pressures in the arteries, capillaries and veins. Why is the pressure in veins so low?
4. The total cross-sectional area of the aorta is smaller than the arteries which branch from it, the cross-sectional area of the arterioles is greater than that of the arteries, the total cross-sectional area of the capillaries is greater than that of the arterioles.
   a. What will be the effect on blood flow as it travels from the aorta to arteries to arterioles to capillaries?
   b. Describe the changes in cross-sectional area from the capillaries to the venae cavae and the effect of these changes on blood flow.
5. What would be the effect of exercise on:
   a. rate of flow of blood within the systemic circulatory system?
   b. blood pressure?

Task Two

Blood pressure rises and falls in relation to the cardiac cycle. Sketch a graph of the relationship of blood pressure (y-axis) to points of time on the cardiac cycle (x-axis).

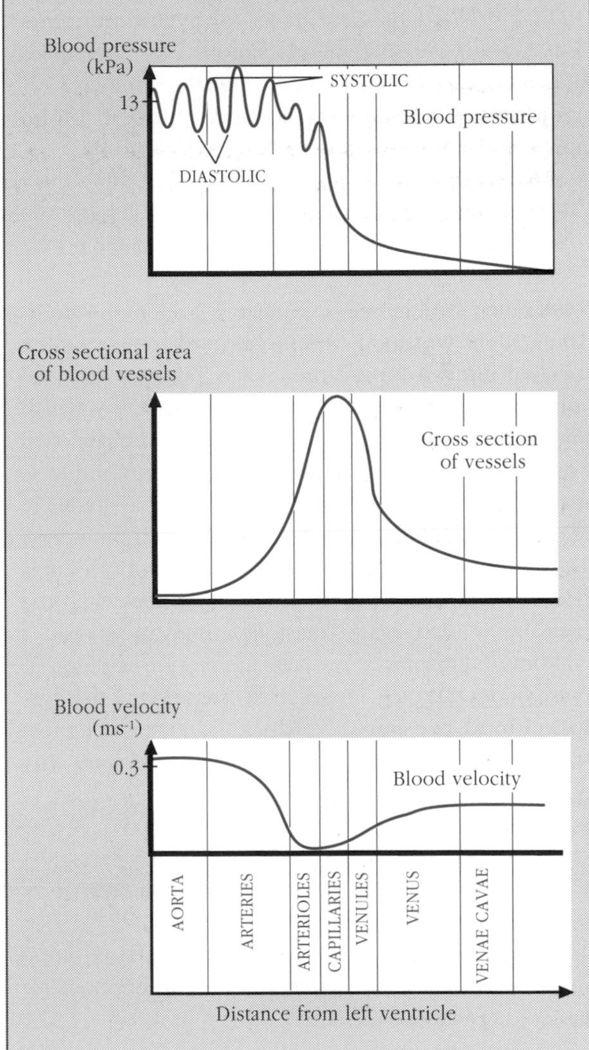

Figure 2.14 Changes as blood flows through the systemic system.

Investigation 2.9 : To record blood pressure at rest

Materials: blood pressure meter (**sphygmomanometer**). (Blood pressure meters supplied by companies such as Griffin and George give digitalized values.)
A **sphygmomanometer** is used to record blood pressure. The recording is written as:

$$\frac{120\text{ mmHg}}{80\text{ mmHg}} \quad \text{or} \quad \frac{15.8\text{ kPa}}{10.5\text{ kPa}} \quad \begin{matrix}\text{(systolic b.p.)}\\ \text{(diastolic b.p.)}\end{matrix}$$

Task One

The cuff is wrapped around the arm covering the brachial artery (upper arm). Air is pumped into the cuff to **no more** than 180 mmHg (24 kPa) by which time the cuff will feel tight around the arm and will compress the brachial artery so that no pulse is recorded. The air pressure inside the cuff is gradually released until the blood is felt spurting into the artery. The pressure (systolic) is now read, and more air is released until the artery is completely open when the pressure is read again (diastolic). Both these values will now be displayed on your monitor, in addition to pulse count. The top line recorded represents **the systolic blood pressure**, which is the maximum pressure produced by the left ventricle during systole. The bottom line is the **diastolic blood pressure** or pressure in the artery at the end of diastole.

Figure 2.15 Blood pressure cut off on arm.

- *It is important that you follow your teacher's instructions carefully when using the blood pressure meter.*

Task Two

1. Measure and record your own blood pressure.
2. Compare and account for differing blood pressures within your class members.

Investigation 2.10 : The effects of exercise on blood pressure, heart rate and blood flow

Materials: equipment for selected activity, blood pressure and pulse meter, graph paper, strip thermometer (a liquid crystal thermometer).

Task One

1. Work in mixed groups and select a demanding physical activity that all your group can manage. You may wish to choose a static and/or dynamic type of exercise. Make sure that you warm up prior to exercising.
2. Record your heart rate (HR), blood pressure (BP) and skin temperature (ST) prior to exercise.
3. Exercise flat out for a one minute period, then retake your blood pressure, heart rate and skin temperature immediately after the exercise has stopped.

Figure 2.16

Task Two

Record your results in Table 8.

Table 8 : Results Table

SELECTED EXERCISE ______________________

	prior to exercise	at the end of exercise
HR		
BP		
ST		

Task Three—analysis of results

1. Plot your results on a graph paper using the same *x*-axis for direct comparison.

Graph A: Arterial BP (mmHg) (*y*-axis) against time (min) (*x*-axis).
Graph B: Heart rate (beats/min) (*y*-axis) against time (min) (*x*-axis).
Graph C: Skin temperature (°C) (*y*-axis) against time (min) (*x*-axis).

2. Compare the relationships between blood pressure, heart rate and skin temperature.
3. What is the effect of dynamic and/or static exercise on systolic and diastolic blood pressure?
4. A small increase in skin temperature indicates that there has been a shift of blood flow to the skin. Where has the blood come from and why does this happen?
5. Which part of the brain is responsible for detecting blood temperature?

Task Four

The chart in Figure 2.17 shows how the percentage distribution of blood flow between different body systems changes when exercise is taken. Note that in the example the **total** blood flow is increased by **five times** during exercise compared to blood flow when a sportsperson is resting. This means that the heart muscle, for example, takes 5% of 5 litres/min at rest (i.e. 0.25 litres/min) whereas it takes 4% of 25 litres/min during exercise (i.e. 1 litre/min), an increase of four times the actual blood flow to the heart. **Total** blood flow will depend on the intensity of exercise, and it is possible to increase blood flow by up to ten times the resting value. (The estimated blood flow to fatty tissue, up to 10% at rest and about 1% during exercise, is not included in the graph.)

1. Using the information in Figure 2.17, describe the proportion of total blood flow going to different organs or body systems during rest and during exercise.
2. Suggest physiological reasons which explain how blood flow is redistributed.

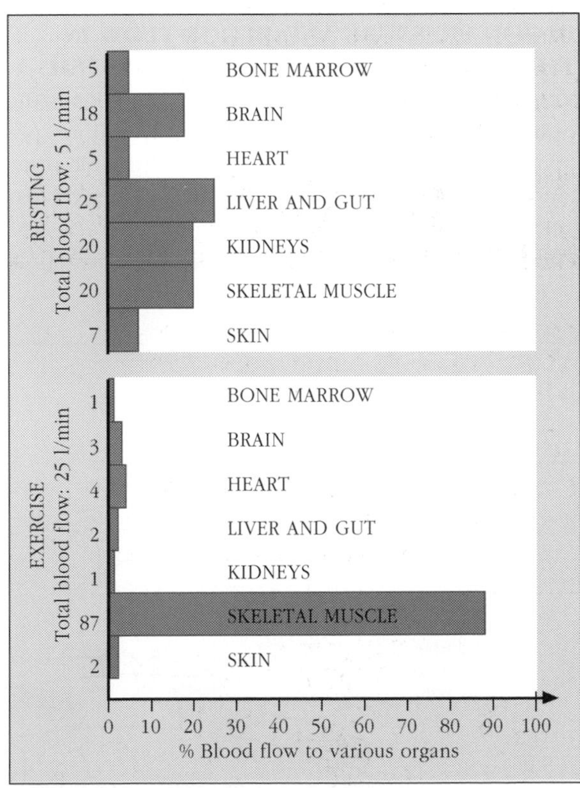

Figure 2.17 Change in percentage distribution of blood flow to various organs when exercise is taken.

Task Five

The effect of exercise on the heart muscle is to increase blood flow to the myocardium by up to five times the resting value. Explain possible reasons for this increase.

THE VENOUS RETURN MECHANISM

The volume of blood leaving the heart depends directly upon the pumping action of the heart. This also results in an increase in blood flow in the veins (see Figure 2.13c and d), known **as the venous return mechanism.**

At any one time veins contain three-fifths of circulating blood. This volume is significant, since venous return must be in excess of the rest of the circulating blood. Veins offer little **resistance** to blood flow and they can alter their shape as a result of venomotor control.

During exercise, skeletal muscle contracts and relaxes, thus squeezing sections of veins, thereby increasing venal return (see Figure 2.13c and d). This phenomenon is called the **muscle pump.**

During exercise, mean atrial pressures drop to around -16 mmHg (2.1 kPa) on inspiration. This reduction in atrial pressure improves venous return and is called the **respiratory pump.** Stroke volume increases until it plateaus off prior to maximal effort being achieved.

BLOOD PRESSURE AND BLOOD FLOW IN THE PULMONARY CIRCULATORY SYSTEM

Venous blood leaves the right ventricle and enters the pulmonary artery at a rate of about five litres per minute. The pulmonary blood vessels offer little resistance to blood flow (since they contain much less smooth muscle than systemic arteries, there is less energy stored in them during systole). The whole effect is to reduce peripheral resistance to blood flow.

Once the blood reaches the vast surface area of the pulmonary capillaries, it picks up oxygen by **gaseous exchange** from the alveoli. Then venules and veins stretch to accommodate the oxygenated blood and decreased blood flow as it travels to the left atrium of the heart.

TISSUE FLUID FORMATION AND DRAINAGE DURING EXERCISE (Figure 2.18)

At the arteriole end of the capillary bed, high blood pressure forces fluid (containing oxygen and glucose) through the capillary wall (Figure 2.18). This fluid permeates the spaces between the cells of all living tissues to become tissue fluid. Tissue cells extract the oxygen and glucose needed for tissue respiration, and excrete waste material such as carbon dioxide and urea at the venous end of the capillary bed where blood pressure is low and where most of the tissue fluid returns into the capillary vessels.

Excess tissue fluid enters the surrounding lymph vessels and eventually returns to the blood via the lymphatic system.

One of the effects of exercise is to increase systolic blood pressure and hence to increase the formation of tissue fluid so that more nutrients are made available for tissue cell respiration. During exercise lymph is returned to the blood more quickly due to the combined action of the muscle and respiratory pumps. These pumps contract and compress more forcibly on lymph vessels, thereby speeding up lymph flow.

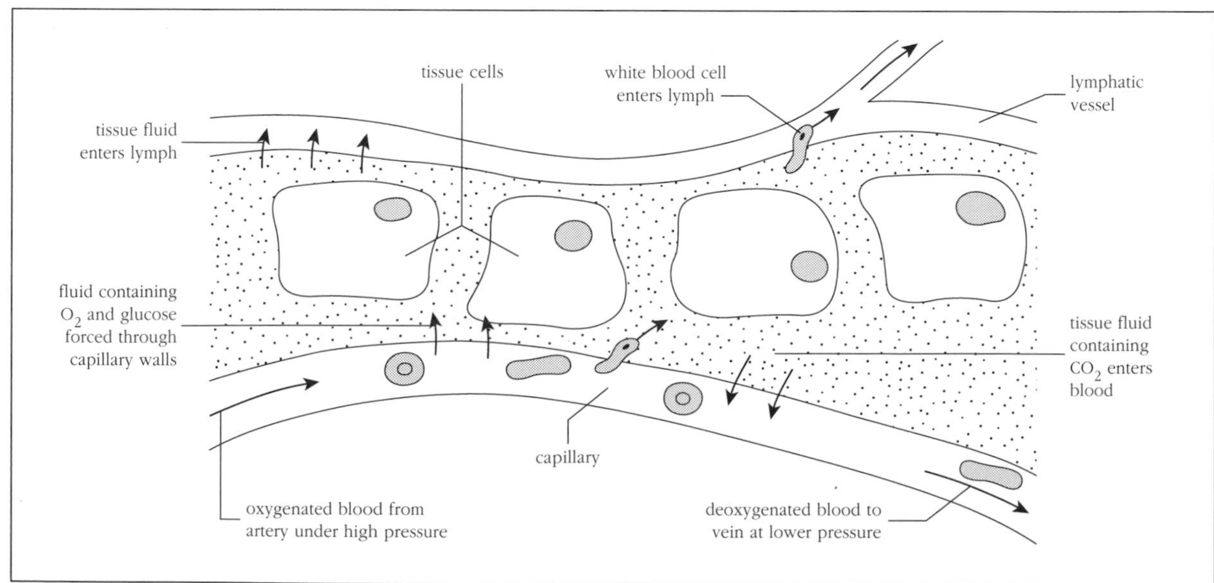

Figure 2.18

REVIEW QUESTIONS

1. What is the specialized structure in veins which prevents excessive distension and backflow of blood?
2. What effect will an increase in stroke volume have on venous return?
3. Why is it important that pressure and flow are low in the pulmonary circulatory system when compared with the systemic circulatory system?
4. Explain how arterioles affect blood pressure.
5. How does venous blood manage to return to the heart, despite the fact that it is travelling against gravity?
6. Explain which is more important in determining arterial blood pressure during rhythmical exercise: changes in vascular resistance or changes in cardiac output?
7. What factors are involved in the maintenance of blood pressure? Explain what they do.

Summary

1. You should be able to define blood pressure and describe the relationship between blood flow and peripheral resistance.
2. You should understand what is meant by vasomotor and venomotor control.
3. You should be able to compare blood pressure in different blood vessels and describe the effects of exercise on blood pressure and blood flow.
4. You should understand what is meant by the venous return mechanism, and the phenomena 'muscle pump' and 'respiratory pump'.
5. You should be able to explain the significance of a lower blood pressure in the pulmonary circulatory system when compared with the blood pressure in the systemic circulatory system.
6. You should be able to describe how tissue fluid is formed and drained away and explain the changes in flow that occur during exercise.

FURTHER READING

Ackermann U. *Essentials of Human Physiology,* Mosby–Year Book, 1992.

Bowers R.W. and Fox E.L. *Sports Physiology,* Wm C. Brown, 1992.

Fox E.L., Bowers R.W.and Foss M.L. *The Physiological Basis for Exercise and Sport* 5e, Wm C. Brown, 1993.

Green J.H. *An Introduction to Human Physiology,* Churchill Livingstone, 1986.

Lamb D.R. *Physiology of Exercise,* Macmillan, 1983.

McArdle W.D., Katch F.I. and Katch V.L. *Essentials of Exercise Physiology,* Lea & Febiger, 1994.

Seeley R.R., Stephens T.D.and Tate P. *Anatomy and Physiology* 2e, Mosby–Year Book, 1992.

2.4 Respiratory Factors in Physical Performance

KEY WORDS AND CONCEPTS

breathing	**larynx**	**phrenic nerves**
tissue respiration	**epiglottis**	**intercostal nerves**
gaseous exchange	**glottis**	**muscles used in inspiration**
pulmonary ventilation	**trachea**	**muscles used in expiration**
alveoli	**bronchi**	**chemoreceptors**
pulmonary pleura	**bronchioles**	**baroreceptors**
parietal membrane	**respiratory bronchioles**	**proprioceptors**
visceral membrane	**alveolar ducts**	**respiratory centre**
pleural cavity	**medulla oblongata**	**blood acidity**
pleural fluid	**pneumotaxic centre**	**vasomotor centre**
nasal cavity	**inspiration**	**Hering-Breuer reflex**
pharynx	**expiration**	**carotid arteries**

Running fast and breathing rapidly go hand in hand. As with the increase in heart rate, there is a corresponding increase in rate and depth of breathing. This is brought about by the actions of the **breathing system**, which is the mechanism whereby the gases, oxygen and carbon dioxide, are exchanged between the atmosphere and the blood vessels in the lungs during **gaseous exchange**.

This section will help you to understand the structure of the breathing system, the mechanics involved and the ventilatory responses to exercise.

Tissue respiration is the process by which cells use oxygen in order to release energy.

Pulmonary ventilation is the process of supplying fresh air to the **alveoli** which make up the lung tissue.

THE STRUCTURE OF THE LUNGS

Figure 2.19b illustrates the anatomy of the breathing system. Each lung is covered by serous membranes called **pulmonary pleura**. They are arranged like a double skin bag in which the outer membrane, called the **parietal membrane**, lines the chest cavity, and the inner membrane, called the **visceral membrane**, lines each lung, as illustrated in Figure 2.19b. In between the two membranes is the **pleural cavity** containing **pleural fluid.** The function of this lubricating fluid is to reduce friction between the two membranes during the dynamics of **breathing**. The pressure of this fluid is lower than the atmospheric pressure of air in the lungs. Atmospheric air pressure forces the pleural membranes against the inside of the thoracic cavity when it expands during inspiration (breathing in), thus causing the lungs to move with the chest during the breathing action.

The route by which air reaches our lungs

Air enters the breathing system through the nose (consisting of two nostrils and a nasal cavity) and mouth. The nose is lined with a dense blood capillary network and a ciliated mucous membrane. The air is warmed, filtered and moistened by this lining.

Incoming air proceeds into the **pharynx** (which is involved in both respiratory and digestive systems). The incoming air is warmed and moistened as it passes through the pharynx.

Next, the air passes through the **larynx** (the voice box situated at the top of the trachea), where it is further warmed, filtered and moistened. The larynx contains a semi-cartilaginous flap called the **epiglottis** which, when closed over the **glottis**, prevents food from entering the **trachea** (breathing stops when food is swallowed). The trachea is a single airway extending from the larynx to the two dividing bronchi.

Air then passes down the trachea which, approximately level with the fifth thoracic vertebra, divides into two short branching **bronchi** (one bronchus going to each lung). The bronchi further subdivide into smaller branches called **bronchioles**. The **epithelium** (a general term used to describe the type of tissue lining inner body cavities) which lines the trachea, bronchi and bronchioles contains goblet mucus cells and cilia (Figure 2.19c). Cilia carry the mucus, with trapped dust and pathogens, to the back of the throat where it is swallowed.

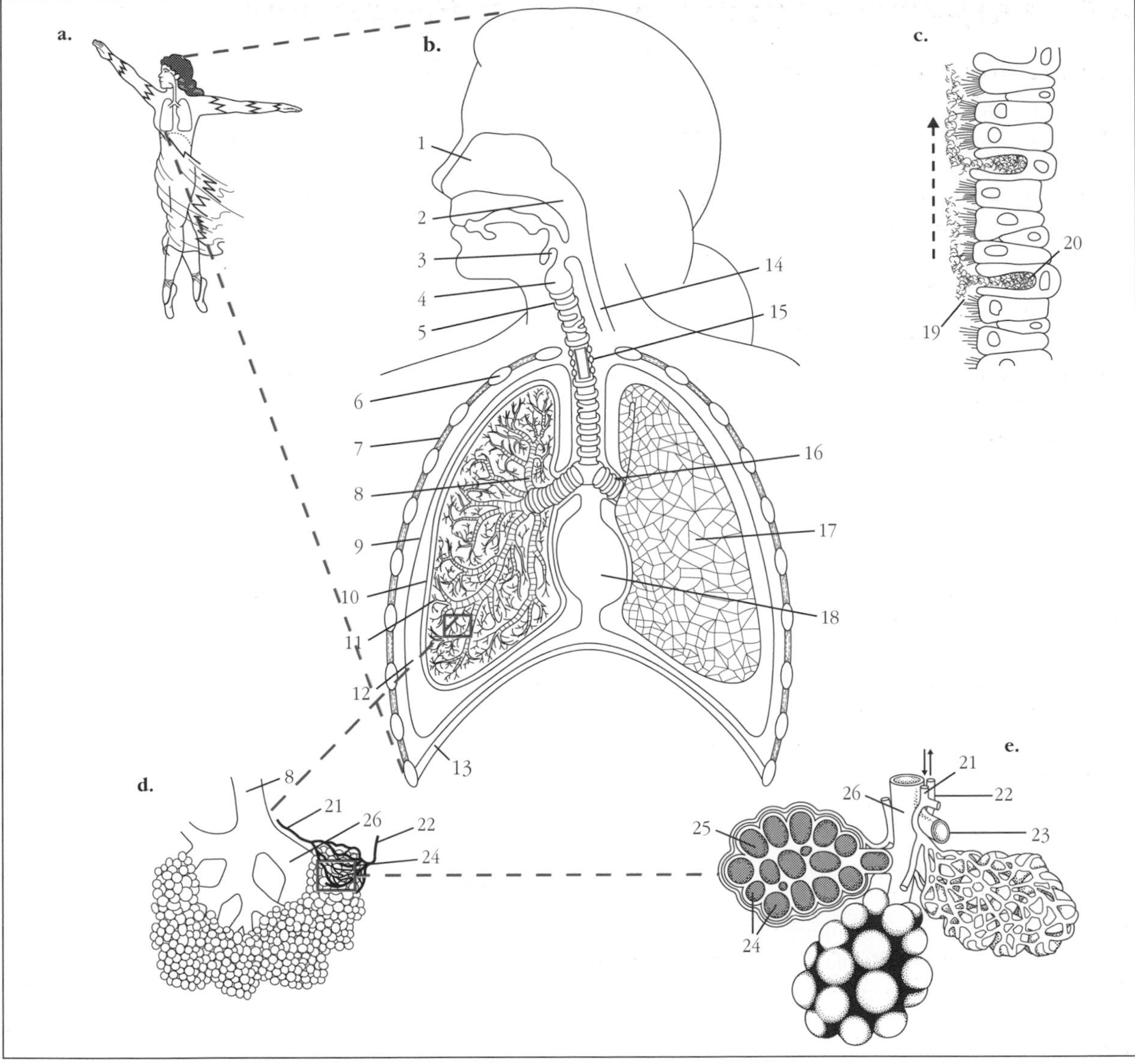

Figure 2.19 The anatomy of the breathing system.

a. The human breathing system.
b. Section of head and thorax: left lung, surface view; right lung, section.
c. Epithelial lining of cilia and goblet cells (found in structures 1, 2, 4, 8, 15 and 16).
d. Respiratory bronchioles leading to alveoli.
e. Alveoli.

- - - - - - - - - - - - ►
Flow of mucus and trapped pathogens and dust

———————►
Direction of blood flow

1. Nasal cavity.
2. Pharynx.
3. Epiglottis
4. Larynx.
5. Incomplete ring of cartilage.
6. Rib.
7. Intercostal muscle.
8. Bronchiole.
9. Parietal membrane.
10. Visceral membrane.
11. Right lung.
12. Pleural cavity containing pleural fluid.
13. Diaphragm.
14. Oesophagus.
15. Trachea, section.
16. Bronchus.
17. Left lung.
18. Position of heart.
19. Cilia.
20. Goblet mucus cell.
21. Branch of pulmonary artery (poor in O_2).
22. Branch of pulmonary vein (rich in O_2).
23. Alveolar duct.
24. Alveoli surrounded by capillary network.
25. Alveolus, section.
26. Respiratory bronchiole.

The bronchioles further subdivide into **respiratory bronchioles** which lead to **alveolar ducts.** Finally, the incoming air reaches millions of thin-walled air sacs or **alveoli** inside the lungs. **Gaseous exchange** takes place between the surface of the alveoli and the pulmonary capillaries which are separated only by the single walls of both systems. The surface area of the alveoli is estimated to be that of the size of a tennis court (Figure 2.19d and e).

The alveoli contain **macrophage cells** which are involved in the lung's defence mechanism. These cells engulf pathogens and transport them to the bronchioles. The pathogens are subsequently dealt with by the cleaning mechanism of the lungs, as described above.

Investigation 2.11 : To understand the structure and functioning of the respiratory organs

Task One—to examine the structure of the trachea

Materials: transverse section (TS) slide of a trachea.

1. The trachea has walls supported by curved hoops (incomplete rings of cartilage). Feel the cartilaginous rings through the skin of your own neck just below the larynx. What is the function of these rings of cartilage?
2. Why are these rings of cartilage incomplete?
3. Make a drawing showing the TS of the trachea. Indicate on it where you think the oesophagus is positioned.

Task Two—to examine the structure of animal lungs

Materials: lung model, fresh animal lungs, rubber tubing and disinfectant, suitable charts and diagrams.

(The following task assumes the availability of fresh animal lungs—if they are not available, charts or models should be substituted.)

1. How many lobes has each lung?
2. Press the lung tissue with your fingers. Describe what it feels like.
3. Identify the larynx, trachea and bronchi.
4. Using a piece of tubing, fill the lungs with water from the tap. Alternatively, use an electrical air pump. Describe what happens to the lungs and explain your observations.
5. Empty out the water, then cut through a small section of lung tissue below one of the bronchi. Identify the smaller branching bronchioles, arterioles and venules.

Task Three—to examine the structure of alveoli

Materials: TS slide of lung tissue, microscope.

1. Examine the prepared slide of a section of lung tissue.
2. Describe the structure of an alveolus. Figure 2.19e may assist you to observe some of the structures.
3. Why does the connective tissue below the epithelium lining the alveolus contain elastic tissue?
4. There are approximately three million alveoli in a pair of human lungs, varying in diameter between 70 and 300 microns (μm—a millionth of a metre or 10^{-6} m). Why is it important to have such a vast surface area of alveoli?
5. The alveoli are surrounded by an extensive vascular (blood) capillary network (shown in Figure 2.19e). Why is this necessary?
6. What effect does physical activity have upon size. structure and functioning of the alveoli?

REVIEW QUESTIONS

1. Beginning with atmospheric air entering the nasal cavities, trace the pathway of an oxygen molecule until it reaches an alveolar duct, identifying all the respiratory structures it passes on the way.
2. Using the information in Figure 2.19 and in the text above, work through the pathway of outgoing air.
3. How would breathing cold air affect the capability to perform exercise?

THE MECHANICS OF BREATHING

The actual mechanism of breathing is brought about as a result of the changes in air pressure (intrapulmonary pressure) in the lungs, relative to atmospheric air pressure. The latter changes are in turn brought about by the muscular action of the **intercostal** muscles and **diaphragm.**

The respiratory muscles

1. The intercostal muscles

The 11 pairs of intercostal muscles (which are arranged in two layers) occupy the spaces between the 12 pairs of ribs. The layers nearest to the lungs are called the **internal intercostal muscle fibres**. These fibres extend in a downward and backward direction from the lower margin of the rib above, to the upper margin of the rib below, with the upper attachment nearer to the sternum. The **external intercostal muscle fibres** lie on top of the internal intercostal muscles and extend in a downward and forward direction, with the lower attachment nearer to the sternum, in opposition to the internal intercostal muscles.

The first rib is a fixed rib and so when the **external** intercostal muscles contract, the other ribs are pulled towards this fixed rib, which results in an upward and outward movement of the thoracic cage during the process of **breathing in.** During quiet breathing the internal intercostal muscles remain passive.

The intercostal nerves, which originate from the **medulla oblongata,** located in the brain, stimulate the intercostal muscles.

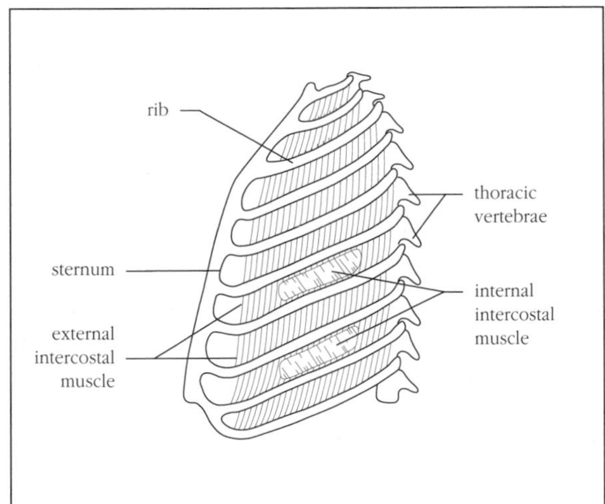

Figure 2.20 Lateral view of rib cage to show intercostal muscles.

2. The diaphragm (*Figure 2.21*)

The diaphragm is a dome-shaped sheet of muscle forming the floor of the thoracic cavity. It is attached to the vertebral column, lower ribs and sternum and radiates from a central tendon. It separates the thoracic from the abdominal cavity and it is innovated by the phrenic nerves whose nerve impulses originate from the medulla oblongata.

When the diaphragm contracts, its muscle fibres shorten and the central tendon is pulled downwards. The effect is to increase the depth of the thoracic cavity (and therefore assist in the intake of air).

The breathing mechanism at rest

During inspiration

The external intercostal muscles contract, whilst the internal intercostal muscles relax. This action causes the ribs and sternum to move upward and outward, thereby increasing the chest width from side to side and from back to back. In the meantime, pressure between the pleural membranes is reduced from –2 mmHg (–0.26 kPa) to –6 mmHg (–0.79 kPa). This negative pressure relative to gas pressure in the lungs allows the pressure of air in the lungs to stretch the elastic pulmonary tissue, which therefore expands in contact with the chest cavity. At the same time the diaphragm contracts, which causes this dome-shaped sheet of muscle to descend by approximately 1.5 cm (the effect is to increase the depth of the thoracic cavity). Stimulation of the phrenic and intercostal nerves causes the contraction of these breathing muscles.

The combined effect of the contraction of the external intercostal muscles and of the diaphragm, is to increase the volume occupied by the lungs. Therefore, the air pressure inside the lungs reduces. This results in atmospheric air being forced into the lungs via the nasal passages, trachea, bronchi and bronchioles, until air reaches the alveoli, and air pressure inside the lungs is equal to atmospheric pressure.

During expiration

The diaphragm and external intercostal muscles relax and return to their original positions. The ribs and diaphragm press on the pleural fluid. The relative pressure between the pleural surfaces increases from –6 mmHg (or –0.79 kPa) to –2 mmHg (or –0.26 kPa). The effect is to reduce the lung volume, thereby increasing air pressure inside the lungs so that it is now above atmospheric pressure, and so air is forced out via the respiratory passages. This is aided by the elastic recoil of alveolar tissue (from the stretched state of full lung expansion) until the lungs deflate to their original volume.

Figure 2.21 The breathing mechanism.

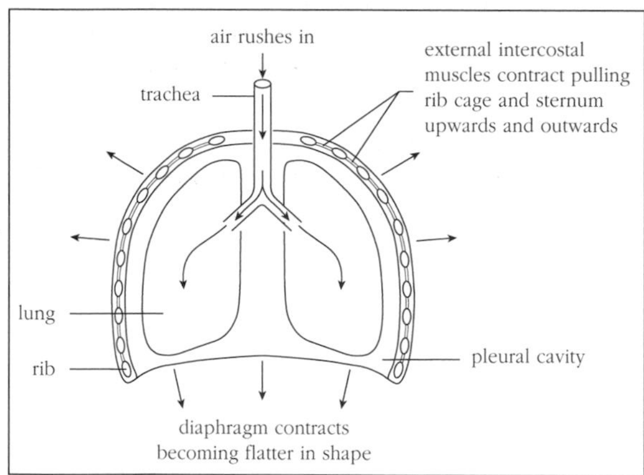

a Breathing in.

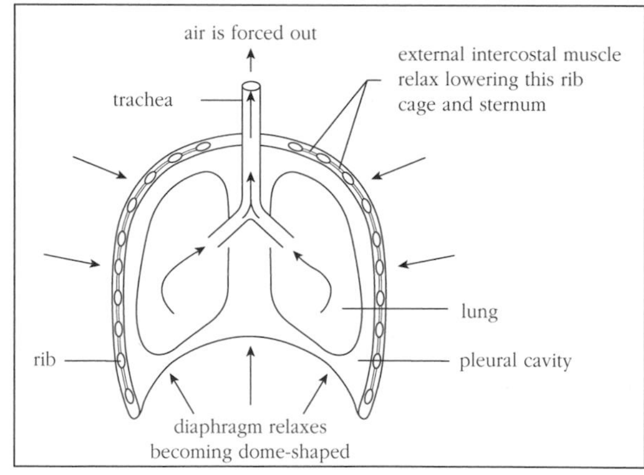

b Breathing out.

The breathing mechanism during exercise

During inspiration

A much larger volume of inspired air is achieved by the contraction of accessory inspiratory muscles.

In addition to the external intercostal muscles and diaphragm muscles contracting, **scaleni** and **sternocleidomastoids** contract. The effect is to raise the first and second ribs and sternum, respectively. During maximum efforts, the **trapezius** and **back** and **neck extensors** also contract and increase the size of the thorax even more.

During expiration

The combined contraction of the **internal intercostal** and **abdominal** muscles forces air out of the lungs (when the internal intercostal muscles shorten, the rib cage is actively moved downwards and the abdominal muscles force the diaphragm upwards).

Nervous and chemical regulators of the breathing mechanism

The rate of breathing is controlled subconsciously by the **medulla oblongata,** which regulates inspiration, and by the **pneumotaxic centre** in the **pons varolii,** which regulates expiration. Both these control centres are located in the **respiratory centre** in the brain stem.

During exercise

Increases in respiratory rates are brought about as a direct result of increases of carbon dioxide and increases in blood acidity levels. Blood acidity increases as a result of dissolved carbon dioxide forming carbonic acid (H_2CO_3) and the presence of lactic acid, resulting from anaerobic energy processes in working muscles.

In addition, the walls of the arch of the **aorta** and **carotid arteries** contain groups of sensitive cells called **chemoreceptors,** which respond to chemical changes in the blood (their main action is that of increasing respiration rates when the oxygen content in arterial blood drops), and **baroreceptors** which respond to changes in blood pressure, by sending messages to the vasomotor centre in the medulla (refer to Figure 2.4).

Both the respiratory centre and chemoreceptors are stimulated by an increase in the partial pressure of carbon dioxide concentration which raises the concentration of hydrogen ions in the blood via:

$$H_2CO_3 \rightarrow H^+ + HCO_3^-$$

thereby lowering blood pH. This causes an increase in both depth and rate of breathing.

Proprioceptors (sensors which feed information to the brain about joint angles, muscle stretch and body balance—see page 45) in joints and muscles and psychological factors such as anxiety and alertness are also responsible for increased ventilation rates. Stretch receptors located in the bronchi and bronchioles are stimulated by overstretching, experienced in hyperventilation. Impulses travel via the vagus nerve to the respiratory centre where inspiration is inhibited and expiration is stimulated. This mechanism is called the **Hering-Breuer reflex.**

The effects of exercise stress on the breathing system are to increase depth and rate of breathing, which are regulated by the muscular, neural and chemical mechanisms summarized in Figure 2.22.

During recovery

The rate of breathing is controlled by the medulla and pons varolii as a direct result of the change in carbon dioxide concentration and factors listed above. During the recovery phase, the carbon dioxide concentration falls and consequently there is a reduction in the stimulation of the phrenic and intercostal nerves. Therefore ventilation rates decrease. This reduction is rapid at first and then tails off until the breathing rate returns to normal.

The effect of exercise stress and recovery is that of a **continual** balance between **excitory** (positive) and **inhibitory** (negative) factors, some of which are shown in Figure 2.22.

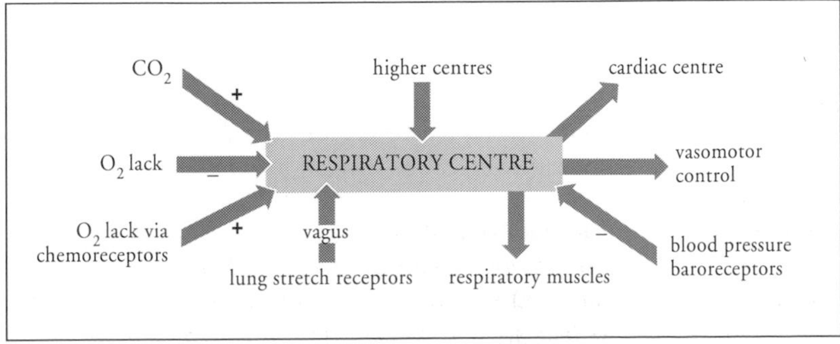

Figure 2.22 Factors affecting the activity of the respiratory centre. (After Green, 1986.)

REVIEW QUESTIONS

1. Complete Table 9, which investigates the muscles that are involved in breathing at rest and during exercise.

Table 9

Respiratory Phase	Muscle acting	Action
e.g. *Inspiration* **at rest** **during exercise**	diaphragm	flattens
Expiration **at rest** **during exercise**		

2. What do you think will be the long term effects of a training programme on the respiratory muscles and lung volumes? (You might be interested in counting ventilation at rest and during exercise to observe the mechanical effects described within this unit).

3. During exercise, ventilation rates may increase tenfold. How is this achieved?

Summary

1. You should be able to describe the structure and function of the nasal cavity, pharynx, trachea, bronchi, bronchioles, terminal respiratory units and alveoli, in the role of transportation of atmospheric air in and out of the lungs.
2. You should understand the process by which air moves in and out of the lungs (**pulmonary ventilation**), and how this process is achieved by the action of muscles at rest and during exercise.
3. You should have an understanding of the nervous and chemical regulators of breathing and how they affect ventilation rates.
4. You should have an understanding of the effects of training on improving pulmonary function.

FURTHER READING

Ackermann U. *Essentials of Human Physiology* 2e, Mosby–Year Book, 1992.

Fisher G.A.and Jensen C.R. *Scientific Basis of Athletic Conditioning* 3e, Lea & Febiger, 1990.

Green J.H. *An Introduction to Human Physiology*, Oxford, 1986.

McArdle W.D., Katch F.I. and Katch V.L. *Essentials of Exercise Physiology*, Lea & Febiger, 1994.

McNaught A.B. and Callender R. *Illustrated Physiology*, Churchill Livingstone, 1981.

Rowett H.G.Q *Basic Anatomy and Physiology*, Murray, 1987.

Seeley R.R., Stephens T.D.and Tate P. *Anatomy and Physiology* 2e, Mosby–Year Book, 1992.

Shephard R.J. *Exercise Physiology*, B.C. Decker, 1987.

Simpkins J. and Williams J.I. *Advanced Human Biology*, Unwin Hyman, 1987.

2.5 Gas Exchange in the Lungs

KEY WORDS AND CONCEPTS

gaseous exchange	**carbonic acid**	**diffusion gradient**
tissue respiration	**haemoglobinic acid**	**oxygen dissociation curve**
driving pressure	**haemoglobin**	**ventilation rate**
diffusion capacity	**myoglobin**	**respiratory frequency**
inhaled air	**oxyhaemoglobin**	**quiet breathing**
exhaled air	**carbaminohaemoglobin**	**hyperventilation**

One of the main functions of the breathing system is to operate in conjunction with the vascular system in the process of **gaseous exchange.**

This section will help you understand how it is possible for a two-way traffic to exist, whereby **oxygen** is transported in one direction from lung alveoli to tissue cell site, for the intracellular use of oxygen in the **mitochondria** (during **tissue respiration**), whilst **carbon dioxide** is travelling at the same time and in the same place in the opposite direction.

How gaseous exchange is achieved

During inspiration, alveolar pressure is lower than atmospheric pressure; therefore, air rushes in via the respiratory tract until the gas pressures are equalized. During expiration, the opposite occurs.

Also, despite a dense pulmonary capillary network, some alveoli have a poor or even non-exist blood supply. How do the lungs overcome this problem? At rest, inspired air goes to the alveoli with a good capillary network. The effect of regular exercise is to improve the capillary bed surrounding the alveoli and therefore increase the surface area available for gaseous exchange.

The movement of gases in and out of the circulatory system occurs by the process of **diffusion** (gas molecules moving from a region of high concentration to a region of low concentration) across the **epithelium** (membrane) separating alveoli from lung circulatory capillaries. This is due to differences in **partial pressures** of carbon dioxide and oxygen in the pulmonary systems.

Partial pressures

The **partial pressure** of a gas refers to its actual pressure as it exists within a mixture of gases. The **partial pressure** of oxygen in the atmosphere is about 20 kPa, which therefore means that oxygen contributes about 20% of the gas pressure in atmospheric air, the total pressure of which is 100 kPa. An oxygen partial pressure of 20 kPa represents a **concentration** of gas molecules equivalent to its normal atmosphere concentration. The partial pressure of oxygen in **alveolar air** is about 13 kPa, and from Figure 2.23 you will see that this oxygen pressure will force about 98% of haemoglobin in blood passing through the alveolar capillary bed to become oxygenated.

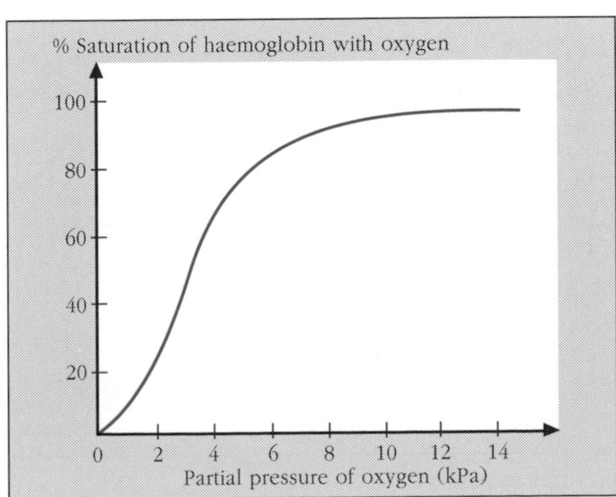

Figure 2.23 Haemoglobin–oxygen dissociation curve.

Standard conditions: 37°C, CO_2 = 5.26 kPa, pH = 7.4.

Oxygenation of haemoglobin (Figure 2.24a)

As blood is pumped through the pulmonary capillaries by blood pressure created by the heart, the red corpuscles are squeezed out of shape. This is the effect of the pressure of blood trying to force tiny corpuscles through tiny capillaries. This has the effect of forcing greater surface contact of the corpuscles with the capillary walls, which means that the oxygen diffusing across from the alveoli can more readily reach the haemoglobin in the red corpuscles.

Exercise increases the rate of expiration of air ($\dot{V}E$, the volume of expired air per minute is increased) tenfold, which means that up to ten times the resting amount of oxygen is exchanged. This is done by the heart increasing **pulmonary blood pressure** (the **driving pressure of blood** in the lung/alveoli transport system) by a small amount which is, however, sufficient to cause much bigger distortion of the red corpuscles in the pulmonary capillaries, and thus a much more rapid take up by the haemoglobin in the corpuscles.

Oxygen attaches to haemoglobin in red corpuscles in the following manner:

Hb	+	O_2	→	HbO_2
haemoglobin		oxygen		oxyhaemoglobin

Blood then carries oxyhaemoglobin to the tissue sites where the oxygen is released:

$$HbO_2 \rightarrow Hb + O_2$$

and used in the process known as tissue respiration.

TISSUE RESPIRATION

When oxyhaemoglobin reaches tissue cells where the oxygen is required for energy release, the process of **diffusion** of **oxygen** across the tissue capillary walls **into** the tissue cells occurs (as illustrated in Figures 2.13h and 2.24b).

The diffusion process is helped by a low oxygen molecular concentration in the tissue cells (because of energy creation using up oxygen stored in the cells) and a relatively high molecular concentration in the haemoglobin in the capillary.

Muscle cells contain a substance called **myoglobin** (a molecule similar to haemoglobin but which has a greater affinity for oxygen) which is depleted of oxygen by energy creating processes in the cells. Oxygen therefore diffuses via the myoglobin across muscle cells to the cell **mitochondria**, where it is used to produce the ATP needed for muscle contraction (see section 3.2 for a description of this aerobic process).

As energy is released in muscle cells, **carbon dioxide** is produced, so that the concentration of carbon dioxide in the muscle cells is higher than in the blood flowing through adjacent capillaries. Therefore, carbon dioxide **diffuses** across cell and capillary walls **into** the blood (see Figures 2.13h and 2.24b). Blood carbon dioxide loading will increase as the blood reaches the venous end of the capillary bed.

There are three ways in which carbon dioxide can be carried by the blood:

1. About 8% is carried as dissolved carbon dioxide in the blood plasma.

Figure 2.24

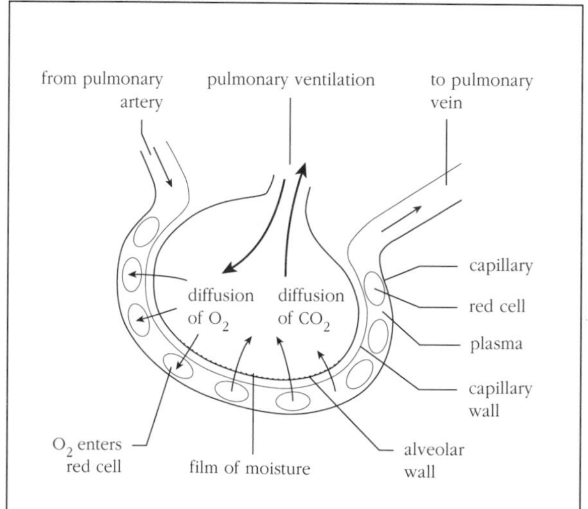

a. Oxygenation of haemoglobin.

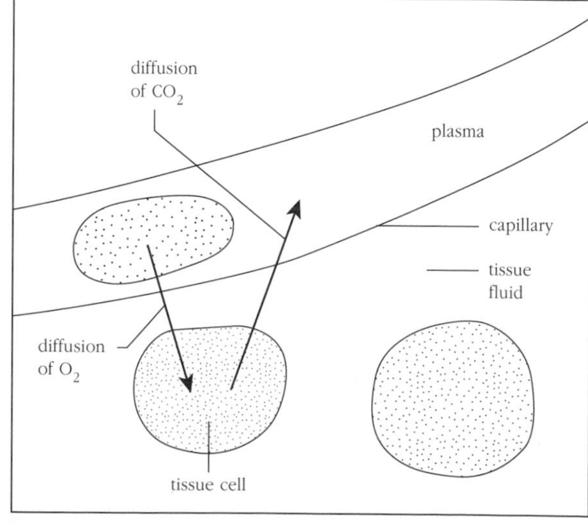

b. Tissue respiration.

2. More than 86% is converted to carbonic acid (H_2CO_3) within the red cell, assisted by the enzyme carbonic anhydrase as catalyst. The H_2CO_3 partially dissociates to produce H+ and HCO_3^- ions, thereby lowering the pH of venous blood. The H+ ions react with oxygenated haemoglobin (HbO_2) to produce haemoglobinic acid and release some oxygen for tissue respiration:

Step 1: $H_2O + CO_2 \rightarrow H_2CO_3 \rightarrow H^+ + HCO_3^-$
(carbonic anhydrase catalyst) (leaves RBC)

Step 2: $H^+ + HbO_2 \rightarrow HHb + O_2$
H^+ (remains in RBC); HHb (haemoglobinic acid); O_2 (for tissue respiration)

This is one of the mechanisms by which increased carbon dioxide in the blood causes the release of oxygen from haemoglobin. A further drop in pH caused by lactic acid accumulation during intense exercise will additionally stimulate oxygen release by the same process.

3. Less than 7% chemically combines with haemoglobin, once the haemoglobin has released its oxygen at the tissue site.

$$CO_2 + HbO_2 \rightarrow HbCO_2 + O_2$$
$HbCO_2$ (carbaminohaemoglobin)

The carbon dioxide is **not** absorbed at the same molecular site as oxygen, but still stimulates the release of oxygen for further tissue respiration.

These processes are in effect reversible when conditions of carbon dioxide and oxygen partial pressures are changed. For example, when venous blood carrying carbon dioxide reaches pulmonary capillaries in contact with oxygenated alveoli, pulmonary blood carbon dioxide partial pressure is higher than in the alveoli; therefore, carbon dioxide from the blood diffuses into the alveoli and is expired out of the lungs (Figure 2.24a).

Efficiency of gas process

Steep diffusion gradients of oxygen and carbon dioxide are maintained by:

a. good lung ventilation.
b. the vast surface area of alveoli.
c. the very short distance between alveolar lining and blood (only 0.5 μm in thickness).
d. constant blood flow.
e. the large amount of red corpuscles and muscle myoglobin.
f. moist lining.

At rest, approximately 250 cm^3 of oxygen diffuse per minute. The effects of exercise can increase this to around 2–2.5 litres per minute. One of the effects of training is to increase this capacity by increasing the surface area of alveoli available for diffusion, and strengthening the musculature involved in breathing so that lung capacity is larger and rates of breathing are higher.

Investigation 2.12 : Differences between inhaled & exhaled air

Task One

Consider the information in Table 10. What conclusions can you draw from the figures given in this table?

Table 10 : Proportion of O_2 and CO_2 breathed during exercise, compared to at rest

	Inhaled air	Exhaled air during quiet breathing	Exhaled air during exercise
% O_2	21	17	15
% CO_2	0.03	3	6

Task Two—The oxygen dissociation curve (data Table 11)

Exercise displaces the oxygen dissociation curve to the right as blood pH falls due to increased carbon dioxide pressure (concentration), and temperature increases.

1. Plot both sets of data in the same way as the oxygen dissociation curve. On the *y*-axis plot % saturation of haemoglobin with oxygen, and oxygen partial pressure on the *x*-axis.
2. Draw a vertical line at a spot on the *x*-axis where the oxygen partial pressure is at 5kPa and follow the line up through the curves. What do you notice about the saturation of haemoglobin with oxygen for the two curves?
3. What effect does the increased CO_2pp in venous blood, as it passes through muscle tissue, have on the release of oxygen from haemoglobin into muscle cell tissue? (Note that O_2pp is about 5kPa in venous haemoglobin.)

Table 11

Partial pressure of O_2 (kPa)	% saturation of haemoglobin with oxygen for CO_2pp 5.3 kPa	CO_2pp 9.3 kPa
1.3	7	4
2.6	27	15
3.9	53	35
5.3	70	58
6.6	79	71
7.9	85	82
9.3	90	88
10.5	95	94
11.8	98	98
13.0	100	100

4. On leaving the lungs, blood again has an oxygen partial pressure of 13 kPa. Trace the passage of the blood from this point through the circulatory system (see Table 12), highlighting:
   a. Oxygen partial pressure
   b. Carbon dioxide partial pressure
   c. Haemoglobin oxygen saturation until the blood returns through the complete circuit

Table 12

Position of blood	O_2pp (kPa)	CO_2pp (kPa)	% Hb O_2 Saturation
leaving lungs	13	5.3	100
entering muscle tissue	13	5.3	100
leaving muscle tissue-venous	5	9.3	35
venous blood arriving at lungs	5	9.3	35

REVIEW QUESTIONS

1. The lungs have no skeletal tissue so how do they increase in size on breathing in?
2. Describe how alveolar ventilation changes during exercise.
3. What three factors affect oxygen dissociation during exercise? How?

Summary

1. You should be able to understand the function of the breathing system in respect of gaseous exchange with the blood.
2. You should be able to describe how the breathing system adapts as a result of physical activity.
3. You should be able to summarize the concept of the partial pressures of gases and how the partial pressure of oxygen and carbon dioxide affects the oxygen carrying capacity of haemoglobin.
4. You should be able to appreciate how changes in carbon dioxide partial pressure in blood enables delivery of oxygen from haemoglobin to tissue sites.

FURTHER READING

Ackermann U. *Essentials of Human Physiology*, Mosby–Year Book, 1992.
Bower R.W. and Fox E.L. *Sports Physiology* 3e, Wm C. Brown, 1992.
Fisher G.A. and Jensen C.R. *Scientific Basis of Athletic Conditioning* 3e, Lea & Febiger, 1990.
Green J.H. *An Introduction to Human Physiology*, Oxford, 1986.
McArdle W.D., Katch F.I. and Katch V.L. *Essentials of Exercise Physiology*, Lea & Febiger, 1994.
Seeley R.R., Stephens T.D. and Tate P. *Anatomy and Physiology* 2e, Mosby–Year Book, 1992.
Simpkins J. and Williams J.I. *Advanced Human Biology*, Unwin Hyman, 1987.

2.6 Lung Volumes and Physical Activity

KEY WORDS AND CONCEPTS

pulmonary ventilation
quiet breathing
tidal volume
minute ventilation: $\dot{V}E$ and $\dot{V}I$
inspiratory reserve volume or inspiratory capacity
expiratory reserve volume or expiratory capacity
residual volume or functional residual capacity
vital capacity
total lung volume
spirometer

During quiet breathing, we exchange about 0.5 litres of air per breath (the **tidal volume** or TV) of which 350 cm^3 is alveolar ventilation and 150 cm^3 is **dead space** air (dead space represents the volume of the trachea, bronchi and other structures which do not take part in gas exchange). The **tidal volume** is the volume of air inspired or expired per breath.

Minute ventilation or minute volume is the amount of air inspired or expired in one minute. Minute ventilation is expressed as:

$$\dot{V}E = \text{volume of air expired in a minute}$$

or

$$\dot{V}I = \text{volume of air inspired in a minute}$$

The **inspiratory reserve volume** (IRV) is the volume of air that can be forcibly inspired after a normal quiet breath. Similarly, the **expiratory reserve volume** (ERV) is that volume of air that can be forcibly expired over and above resting tidal volume. **Residual volume** (RV) is the volume of air remaining in the lungs after maximum expiration. These lung volumes are illustrated in Figure 2.25.

Vital capacity (VC) is the maximal volume of air that can forcefully be expired after maximal inspiration in one breath. **Total lung capacity** (TLC) is the volume of air in the lungs after maximal inspiration and can be between four and eight litres in healthy adults. **Inspiratory capacity** (IC) is the tidal volume plus inspiratory reserve volume, **expiratory capacity** (EC) is the tidal volume plus expiratory reserve volume and the **functional residual capacity** (FRC) is a combination of the expiratory reserve volume and the residual volume.

Lung volumes and capacities can be measured by using a **spirometer** to produce a trace as illustrated in Figure 2.25. Notice in this trace how tidal volume increases during exercise.

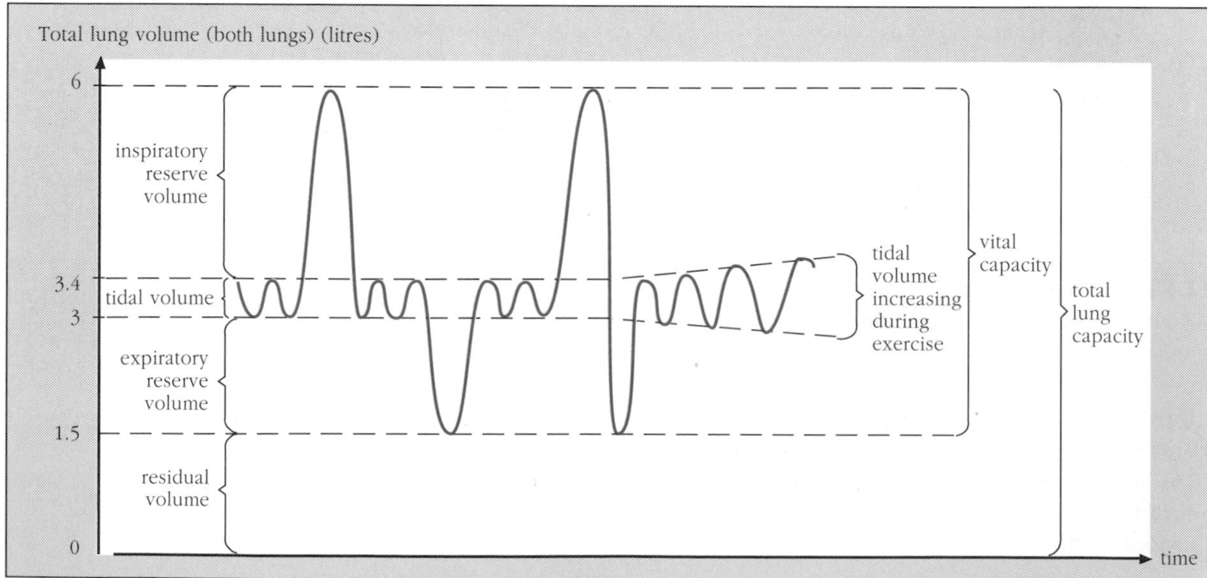

Figure 2.25 Spirometer trace showing lung volumes and capacities.

Investigation 2.13 : To determine lung volumes using a spirometer

Materials: spirometer with graph paper attached, wide-bore flexible tube, mouthpiece and noseclip, scales and tape-measure, disinfectant.

Task One

1. Weigh yourself and measure your height.
2. Sitting down, clip on the noseclip and insert a freshly disinfected mouthpiece. Breathe normally and set the cylinder in motion so that you are inspiring and expiring into the spirometer.
3. Now take a maximal breath in and out. Repeat three normal breaths followed again by maximal inspiration/expiration.

   (The rotating cylinder records the different lung volumes described earlier; however, unless the rotating cylinder is suitably calibrated, the printout is only qualitative.)
4. Remove the graph paper and, using the descriptions on lung volumes, mark on your TV, IRV, ERV, and VC.

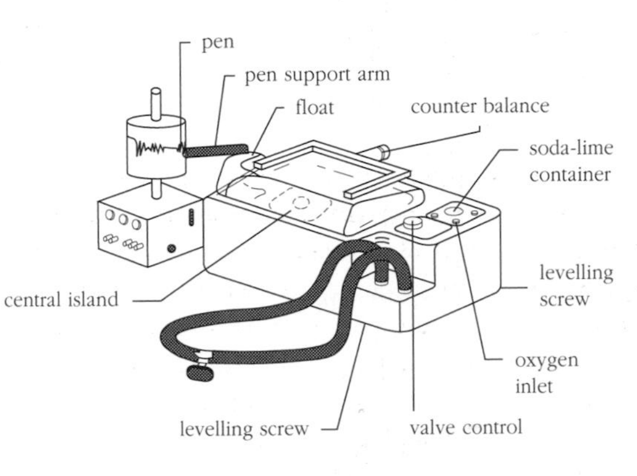

Figure 2.26 Spirometer.

Task Two

1. Assuming that your tidal volume in quiet breathing is 0.5 litres, work out your IRV and ERV.
2. Calculate your VC using the following equation:
   VC = TV (at rest) + IRV + ERV

Task Three—collation of results

1. Record your results in the table provided.
2. Collate the results of other students in your class.

Table 13 : Results Table

NAME OF SUBJECT	Height (metres)	Weight (kg.)	TV (litres)	IRV (litres)	ERV (litres)	VC (litres)
Self						

Task Four—analysis of results

1. Comment on the differing vital capacities. Discuss the relationship between vital capacity and height, weight, and gender.
2. Describe two experimental errors which could have affected the results.
3. What volume of gas remains in the lungs at the end of maximal expiration?

Investigation 2.14 : The measurement of lung volumes

Materials: a five-litre calibrated plastic bottle, rubber tubing, disinfectant.

A simple method of determining **vital capacity** and **tidal volume** is to use a calibrated plastic bottle, illustrated in Figure 2.27.

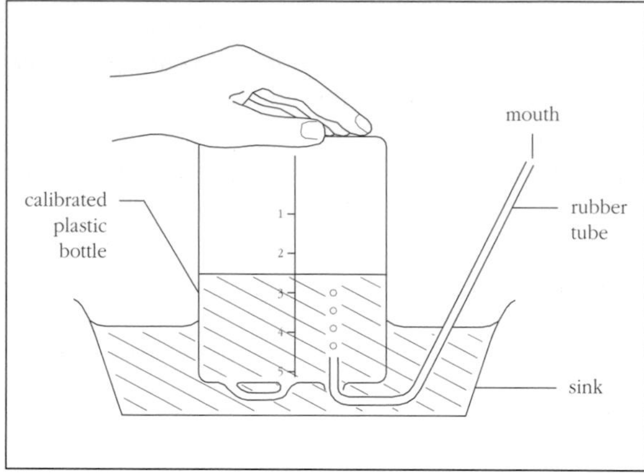

Figure 2.27 Measurement of lung volumes.

Task One

1. Calibrate a large plastic bottle up to 5 litres by filling it with water, one litre at a time, marking the levels.
2. Fill a sink with water and invert the bottle (full of water up to the 5 litre mark) into the sink.
3. Insert one end of the rubber tube into the neck of the bottle.
4. Take a deep breath and then exhale as hard as you can through the disinfected tubing so that the exhaled air displaces the water in the bottle.
5. The level of the water left in the bottle will give you your **vital capacity.**

Task Two

1. Push the rubber tubing half way up inside the bottle, making sure that it is clear of the waterline.
2. Breath in and out normally through the rubber tubing. The rise and fall in the water line with each breath accounts for the volume of air that is exchanged during quiet breathing. This volume is known as **tidal volume.**

Investigation 2.15 : To consider minute ventilation ($\dot{V}E$), tidal volume (TV) and frequency of breaths (f) during quiet breathing

This investigation is best done in groups with each member having a specific job.

Materials: Douglas bag, gasmeter, mouthpiece, tubing, noseclip and stop-clock, disinfectant.

Task One

1. Evacuate the **Douglas bag**, connect a freshly disinfected mouthpiece to the Douglas bag via the rubber tubing.
2. Sit quietly and insert the mouthpiece in your mouth and fit the noseclip.
3. Start the stop-clock and collect expired air in the Douglas bag for a 5 minute period, counting the number of breaths (f) taken for each minute.
4. Evacuate the Douglas bag into the gasmeter and determine the volume of air expired in 5 minutes.
5. Work out the minute volume:

$$\dot{V}E = \frac{\text{volume of air in 5 minutes}}{5}$$

6. Work out the tidal volume at rest:

$$TV = \frac{\dot{V}E}{f}$$

Task Two—collation of results

Record your results, and those other students in your class, in Table 14.

Task Three—analysis of results

Compare the group's results. Explain any differences in $\dot{V}E$ and TV between members of your group.

Table 14 : Results Table

Name	f (litres)	$\dot{V}E$ (litres)	TV (litres)
self			

Investigation 2.16 : To determine minute ventilation, respiratory frequency and tidal volume during a progressivley hard exercise test

(*This investigation is best achieved in a group, with each group member allocated a specific job.*)

Materials: as for 2.15, plus cycle ergometer.

Task One

1. The subject is seated on the bike and, while he/she is resting, one minute of expired air is collected in an evacuated Douglas bag. The number of breaths taken is also counted.
2. The volume of expired air passing through the gasmeter is measured and recorded.

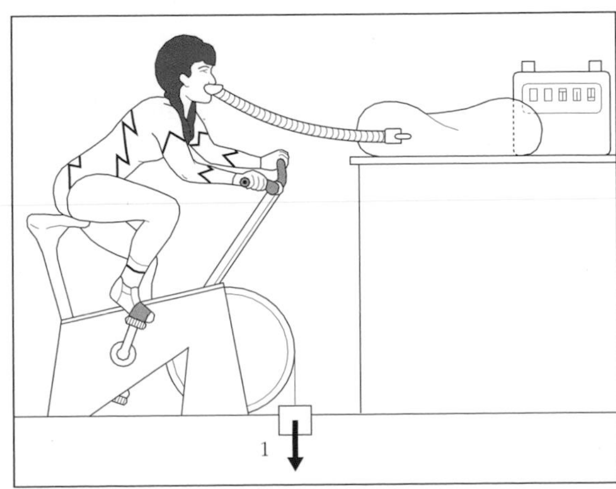

Figure 2.28

3. The same subject begins to ride the cycle ergometer at a low work intensity. After two minutes, the subject's air is collected in an evacuated Douglas bag for a one minute period. During this time the number of expirations is counted, and the volume of expired air passing through the gasmeter is measured and recorded.
4. In the meantime the subject continues to ride for a further three minutes at an increased medium work intensity. During the sixth minute of the investigation (i.e. the third of the three minutes at this workload) a further minute of air is collected and measured and the number of breaths counted.
5. This is repeated at a final maximal workload.

Note that work intensities need to be calculated prior to the investigation. This could be achieved by using a heart rate valve e.g. low intensity 130 bpm, medium intensity 160 bpm and high intensity in excess of 190 bpm.

Task Two

Record the results in Table 15. Work out the minute volume for each stage of the investigation:

$$\dot{V}E = TV \times f$$

Table 15 : Results

Work Intensity	$\dot{V}E$ (litres)	f	TV (litres)
1. Sitting on a bike			
2. light intensity			
3. medium intensity			
4. high intensity			

Task Three—analysis of results

1. On a piece of graph paper, draw curves of:
   a. minute ventilation ($\dot{V}E$)
   b. respiratory frequency (f)
   c. tidal volume (TV) on the *y*-axis, against work intensity on the *x*-axis. (Divide your graph paper into thirds and plot one graph under the next.)
2. Discuss the relationships between work intensity and minute ventilation ($\dot{V}E$), respiration frequency (f) and tidal volume (TV).
3. Compare tidal volume (during maximum work intensity) and the subject's vital capacity. Account for these differences.
4. Identify the muscles acting during inspiration and expiration when you are exercising to your maximal workload.
5. How reliable are the results of your investigation? Does your investigation test what you set out to test? Does your investigation produce a consistent pattern of figures?

The answers to these questions will outline the **reliability** and **validity** of your scientific investigations.

Task Four

Sketch a graph showing a spirometer trace, comparing lung volumes at rest of untrained and trained subjects. Show clearly the changes in the lung factors: inspiratory reserve volume, tidal volume, expiratory reserve volume, vital capacity and residual volume.

REVIEW QUESTIONS

1. What are the important respiratory volume indices and how do they change during exercise?
2. Describe and account for some of the long term effects of regular exercise on the respiratory volumes.
3. What three factors affect oxygen dissociation during exercise? How?

Summary

1. You should be familiar with the concepts of, and be able to measure, lung volumes and capacities.
2. You should understand the concepts of minute ventilation, tidal volume and ventilation rates during quiet breathing and during exercise.
3. You should be able to account for the differences in lung volumes and capacities between untrained and trained sportspersons.

FURTHER READING

Ackermann U. *Essentials of Human Physiology*, Mosby–Year Book, 1992.

Bowers R.W. and Fox E.L. *Sports Physiology* 3e, Wm C. Brown, 1992.

Fisher G.A. and Jensen C.R. *Scientific Basis of Athletic Conditioning* 3e, Lea & Febiger, 1990.

Klausen K., Hemmingsen I. and Rasmussen B. *Basic Sport Science*, McNaughton and Gunn, 1982.

McArdle W.D., Katch F.I. and Katch V.L. *Essentials of Exercise Physiology*, Lea & Febiger, 1994.

McNaught A.B. and Callender R. *Illustrated Physiology*, Churchill Livingstone, 1981.

Seeley R.R., Stephens T.D.and Tate P. *Anatomy and Physiology* 2e, Mosby–Year Book, 1992.

Shepherd R.J. *Exercise Physiology*, B.C. Decker, 1987.

Chapter 3
Energy for Exercise

3.1 Energy and Work

KEY WORDS AND CONCEPTS

work	**chemical energy**	**indirect energy measurement**
energy	**weight**	**energy expenditure**
power	**gravitational field strength**	**net oxygen cost**
joule	**direct energy measurement**	
watt	**efficiency**	

In scientific terms, energy and work mean the same thing and are interchangeable as concepts, energy being the capacity or ability of a system to do work.

The definition of **work** is:

work = force × distance moved (by the system acted upon by the force) in the direction of the force.

The unit of **work** and therefore of **energy** is the **joule** (J), which is defined as the work done (or energy used) when a force of **one newton** (N) acts through a distance of **one metre** (m).

This formula can be used to measure human energy output or work done—this will be illustrated by one of the following two investigations.

Investigation 3.1 : Energy output of a person running upstairs

This investigation uses the **weight** of the athlete as the **force** used, and the **vertical height** moved as the **distance** through which the force is applied. Here the energy output by the body will equal the work done in climbing the stairs and will be an approximate value not taking into account the motion of the student's body.

Task One—the experiment

1. The student should find his/her **weight** in **newtons** using bathroom scales.
   To convert from kilograms: multiply by 10 to obtain weight in newtons. (This is because the Earth pulls down with a force of 10 N for every kilogram mass—the force of gravity is called the **weight.** Refer to page 182) for a further discussion about weight and mass.)
2. Measure the **height** of the stairs to be climbed in **metres.**
3. The student should run up the stairs as fast as possible—the **time in seconds** being recorded for this activity.

Task Two—analysis of results

Calculate the energy output of the student using:

energy	=	**force**	×	**distance**
	=	**weight**	×	**height**
	=	mg	×	h

(The answer will be in **joules**.)

Task Three—calculation of power output

1. **power** is defined as:

   Energy (or **work**) used per **second**

2. The values from task two are therefore placed in the equation:

$$\textbf{power} = \frac{\textbf{energy}\ \text{(joules)}}{\textbf{time}\ \text{(seconds)}}$$

The answer will be in **watts,** where **one watt** is defined as the power produced when **one joule** of energy is used per **second.**

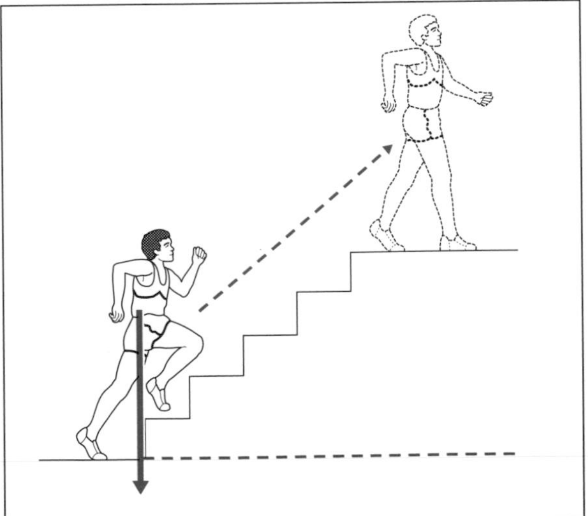

Figure 3.1 Running upstairs.

Investigation 3.2 : energy output of a person operating a bicycle ergometer

Task One—the activity

1. The **force** setting on the bike (load on bike wheel—marked L in Figure 3.2) is noted and the distance (milometer) set to zero.

   If the force setting is in kilograms, this needs converting to **newtons** using the information that the weight of one kilogram mass is 10 N.
2. The student then pedals as fast as possible for 30 seconds, and the **distance** travelled in metres (as recorded on the milometer) is noted.

   If the machine has no milometer, the distance travelled by the outer rim of the bike wheel as it turns past the friction belt is measured. This can be calculated by multiplying the circumference of the wheel by the number of revolutions done by the wheel in the time of the experiment.

   (Remember the answer to this should be in metres.)

Task Two—analysis of results

Energy output is now calculated using the formula:

$$\textbf{energy} = \textbf{force} \times \textbf{distance}$$

(The answer will be in **joules**.)

Task Three—calculation of power output

Using the definition of **power** in the investigation of energy output of a person running upstairs, this can be calculated using the formula:

$$\textbf{power} = \frac{\textbf{energy} \quad \text{(joules)}}{\textbf{time taken} \quad \text{(seconds)}}$$

(Answer in **watts**.)

Extension of investigation

With more sophisticated apparatus, the speed of the bike wheel can be monitored by a computer sensor, and a full profile of power output with time obtained. Alternatively, power measurements can be made over 10 seconds, 20 seconds and 30 seconds by using the bicycle ergometer method above. It is then possible to observe maximal power output, and how the power output changes as the athlete becomes more fatigued. This can be related to anaerobic power as discussed on page 108.

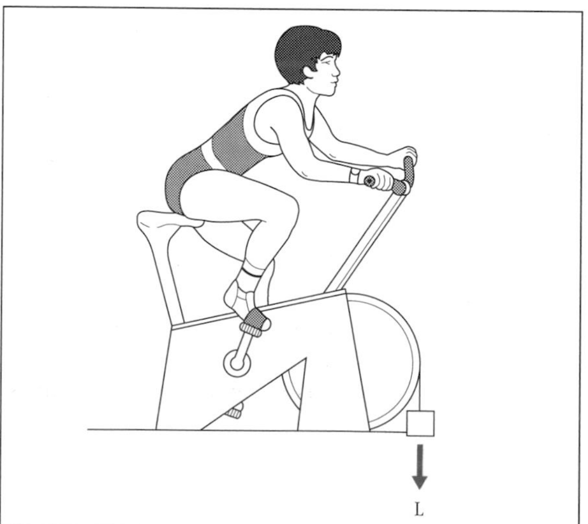

Figure 3.2 A bicycle ergometer.

CHEMICAL ENERGY

The question of where this energy comes from now arises, and it is fairly obvious that the original source of the energy is the food eaten by the person doing the exercise.

In fact, the energy is produced by a complex series of **chemical reactions** (to be discussed in detail below) and is then made available for contraction of muscles and other body functions.

This type of energy is called **chemical energy** since the energy is produced by chemical reactions, and is converted into **work** by the contraction of muscle.

If we were able to calculate the full energy value of all food eaten by a person and compare this with measured energy output (as in the investigations above), we would find that only a small proportion of this energy is converted into useful work.

The power needs of sporting activity

From the definition of power in the investigations above, we have:

$$\text{power} = \frac{\text{energy}}{\text{time}} = \frac{\text{force} \times \text{distance}}{\text{time}}$$

But $\frac{\text{distance}}{\text{time}}$ is a definition of speed; therefore

$$\text{power} = \text{force} \times \frac{\text{distance}}{\text{time}} = \text{force} \times \text{speed}$$

or, if the direction of the speed is fully taken into consideration:

$$\text{power} = \text{force} \times \text{velocity}$$

So it can be seen that power is a measure of force being applied at speed, and therefore is the appropriate concept in the bulk of sports requiring fast dynamic movements, such as jumping, throwing, sprinting, weight-lifting and most games.

It is suggested that another convenient activity (highly correlated with the two activities in Investigations 3.1 and 3.2) which would assess athletic power would be a timed 30 m sprint. Each of the three activities would assess a slightly different athletic **capability**, but would be a measure of the individual's **power.**

Measurement of chemical energy stored in food as fuel

There are two ways of measuring the amounts of chemical energy stored in food (which would then be available for conversion into useful forms of energy—such as mechanical energy—by the person who eats the food). The chemical process which releases the stored energy amounts to that of combination with oxygen—a process identical to the burning of food fuel in air.

The first method (called the **direct** method, since it directly measures energy produced by combination of the food with oxygen) therefore involves the burning of the food in a controlled way, and measuring the heat energy produced. This heat energy is measured by observing the rise in temperature of a quantity of water heated by the burning food.

(This method is described fully in standard texts on biology, for example Roberts' *Biology for Life* or the Nuffield GCSE Biology Texts.)

The second method is called the **indirect** method, since it uses the fact that every atom of carbon in the food combines with a molecule of oxygen during the chemical reaction, to produce one molecule of carbon dioxide and release a definite and constant amount of energy. Similarly, two hydrogen atoms in the food combine with one atom of oxygen to produce one molecule of water and release a different but also constant amount of energy. The method involves the measurement of the **amount of oxygen** consumed—which can therefore be related to the amount of energy released by the food.

For example, 134.4 litres of oxygen will oxidize 180 grams of glycogen to release 2867 kJ of heat energy

(1 kJ = 1 kilojoule = 1000 joules).

Therefore, for all food fuels, one litre of oxygen produces 22kJ of heat energy.

(For a detailed discussion on **oxygen consumption** see Section 3.4.)

THE EFFICIENCY OF THE HUMAN MACHINE

The human body is a machine performing work, but all machines use more fuel energy than they need for the task. The **mechanical efficiency** of any machine, including the human body, can be defined as:

$$\textbf{\% efficiency} = \frac{\textbf{useful work done} \times 100}{\textbf{energy used doing that work}}$$

Energy expenditure refers to the amount of energy required to perform an activity measured by oxygen consumption in the way outlined above.

The difference between the total oxygen consumed during the exercise (and subsequent recovery) and the resting oxygen consumption for the period of time involved (of exercise plus recovery) gives the **net oxygen cost** of the exercise—and hence the energy used performing the exercise at 22 kJ per litre of oxygen consumed.

With respect to the investigations above, in which amounts of **useful work done** are measured for students running up stairs or cycling on a bicycle ergometer, if net oxygen cost is measured it would be possible to compute the efficiency of the exercise process.

The percentage efficiency is usually within the range of 12 to 25 per cent for the human body. This means, that for every movement made, only 25 per cent of the energy consumed is used doing the actual movement (above that which is needed for the basal metabolic rate) and the other 75 per cent is converted into heat energy. Part of this heat energy is used to keep the body temperature above that of the surroundings (and stable at about 37°C) and the rest is lost to the surroundings. This means that whenever exercise is taken, a lot of heat energy is produced which can be used to raise body temperature. This is why shivering occurs (muscles contract involuntarily as a response to low temperatures) and why people clap their hands and stamp their feet when cold.

In activities such as walking or running the efficiency level is around 20–25 per cent. In swimming it is around two per cent.

A study of stair climbing has shown that the maximum efficiency (lowest energy costs) occurs at a speed of 50 steps per minute. As soon as this rate increases, efficiency is reduced. One can say that running even a fraction faster up the stairs means big increases in energy expenditure and rapid exhaustion. Conversely, tiny increases in efficiency, as a result of changes in technique or improved skill, will bring big reductions in energy expenditure. Therefore, improving skill levels is a much more profitable approach to improving performance than a simple increase in muscle strength.

Summary

1. You should be familiar with the concepts of work and energy, and particularly the definition:

   work = force × distance
   = weight × height

   and should be aware of the joule as the unit of measurement of work and energy. 1 kilojoule (kJ) = 1000 joules.
2. You should understand the concept of power as defined by:

   $$\text{power} = \frac{\text{energy used or work done}}{\text{time taken}} = \text{force} \times \text{velocity}$$

   and that the watt is the unit of power.
3. You should be familiar with the concept of chemical energy in respect of the energy store in muscles, and its relationship to actual food consumption and oxygen consumption.
4. You should be aware of the concept of efficiency defined by:

   $$\text{\% efficiency} = \frac{\text{useful work done} \times 100}{\text{energy used doing that work}}$$
5. You should appreciate that gains in skill development rather than strength development are more likely to improve efficiency of the human machine.

3.2 Energy Creation and Release Within Muscle

KEY WORDS AND CONCEPTS

tissue respiration
adenosine triphosphate (ATP)
adenosine diphosphate (ADP)
metabolism
alactic anaerobic system
lactic acid anaerobic system
aerobic system
glycolysis
Kreb's cycle
glycogen
electron transport chain
phosphocreatine
coupled reaction
pyruvic acid
mitochondria
oxidation of hydrogen atoms
sarcoplasm

Adenosine triphosphate (ATP) is the means of energy generation in **all** cells, but its supply is limited by the intensity and duration of the physical activity.

The human body has developed three distinct mechanisms for the transfer of food to energy within muscle. These mechanisms are commonly known as **energy systems**:

1. In the first few seconds of physical activity, energy is freed **anaerobically (anaerobic** means **without oxygen)** from the energy bonds in phosphates stored in muscles.

2. Glucose is **anaerobically** split to release energy within the muscle.

3. Energy is released **aerobically (aerobic** means **with oxygen)** from the oxidation of glucose and fatty acids, achieved as a result of oxygen being transferred to the muscle via the cardio-respiratory systems.

This chapter will help you to understand how these three mechanisms function to create and supply energy within muscle.

All chemical reactions either give out energy (exothermic) or take in energy (endothermic). This energy is what is referred to as **chemical energy** in the discussion above. The clever way that the biological system works is to **take in** energy (endothermic) with a series of chemical reactions from food and fuel, and **give out** the same energy (exothermic) with a **different** series of chemical reactions in order to provide energy for muscular contractions and other bodily functions. As a result **chemical energy** is converted into **mechanical** energy.

The endothermic reactions of acquiring energy and forming complex molecules within the system, such as glucose, are described in Section 3.5. This section describes the exothermic half of the energy system.

TISSUE RESPIRATION AND ENERGY RELEASE

The chemical reaction taking place inside tissue cell sites such as **sarcoplasm** and **mitochondria** can he expressed using the chemical equation:

$$\underset{\text{glucose}}{C_6H_{12}O_6} + \underset{\text{oxygen}}{6O_2} \rightarrow \underset{\text{carbon dioxide}}{6CO_2} + \underset{\text{water}}{6H_2O} + \text{Energy}$$

(This chemical reaction summarizes **aerobic respiration**. Note the energy released is always constant for a given quantity of glucose.)

The chemical energy released in tissue respiration is stored in the chemical bonds of **ATP** until it is required for **metabolism** (the term metabolism is used to describe all the chemical reactions that take place inside the body). This means that every time a muscle contracts, whether it be voluntary or involuntary muscle tissue, it uses energy which is derived from ATP:

$$ATP \rightarrow ADP + P_i + \text{energy}$$

ADP = **adenosine diphosphate**
P_i = **free phosphate**

THE PROCESS OF ENERGY RELEASE IN MUSCLE TISSUE CELLS

The clever way that chemical energy is converted into mechanical energy is achieved by the delivery of free energy from the ATP reactions above to the muscle proteins actin and myosin, to enable the cross bridges (in Huxley's Theory of Muscle Contraction) to connect and reconnect. This enables the actin (thin) filaments to slide over the myosin (thick) filaments during muscle contraction (refer to the discussion on muscle contraction in Chapter 1, p. 40).

Muscles have only a limited supply of ATP, which lasts a couple of seconds. As ATP is converted into **ADP** and **P_i**, energy is released. This is expressed using the chemical equation:

$$ATP \rightarrow ADP + P_i + energy$$

Later ATP **is recreated** via one of the three different mechanisms, called **energy systems**:

1. The alactic anaerobic system
2. The lactic acid anaerobic system
3. The aerobic system.

Energy from one of these systems is used in the reverse reaction of that above:

$$energy + ADP + P_i \rightarrow ATP$$

1. The alactic anaerobic system

In activity which lasts longer than a couple of seconds, the resynthesis of ATP relies on a substance called **phosphocreatine** (PC), which is also stored in our muscles. The amount of phosphagens stored (a general term referring to phosphates like ADP, ATP, and PC) is small, and therefore this system has a limited capacity of under ten seconds for a maximum workload.

Within this mechanism two immediate consecutive reactions occur within muscle cell sarcoplasm:

Step 1. $PC \rightarrow P_i + C + energy$

Step 2. $energy + ADP + P_i \rightarrow ATP$

The net effect of these reactions is:

$$PC + ADP \rightarrow ATP + C$$

You can see that the chemical bond between the P and the C in PC holds energy which is released when the phosphate (P) is combined with ADP to form ATP. This energy is then re-stored in the extra P_i bond in the ATP. The process is known as a **coupled reaction** since the energy released from PC is coupled with the energy demands of ADP to form ATP. The breakdown of PC is achieved **anaerobically** (without oxygen). Creatine (C) remains available for subsequent involvement in these reactions.

During flat out exercise, such as sprinting, jumping and weight-lifting, which last under ten seconds, ATP is replenished by this system. Since no oxygen is used, nor is there any lactic acid formed, this system is called the **alactic anaerobic system.** The main use of this system—usually abbreviated to ATP–PC system, is that it provides an immediate source of energy.

When hard physical activity exceeds the time limit or **threshold** up to which the ATP–PC system operates (i.e. all the PC is used up) ATP is replenished from carbohydrates and fats. This system is known as **the lactic acid system.**

One of the major problems facing speed endurance athletes is the development of their alactic/lactic threshold by training, so that muscle cell sarcoplasm is adapted to contain more ATP/creatine stores so that the ATP–PC system provides energy for longer periods of time at the highest possible rate.

2. The lactic acid system

The **lactic acid system** depends on a chemical process known as **glycolysis**—the break down of sugar (Figure 3.3).

Carbohydrate is stored in the muscle as **glycogen.** Like the ATP–PC system, these stores are high in power but low in capacity because not much glycogen is stored in muscle. It is the breakdown of glycogen that provides the energy to rebuild ADP into ATP.

Since there is no oxygen present, **anaerobic metabolism** takes place. **Pyruvic acid**, formed during glycolysis, is converted by the enzyme lactate dehydrogenase (LDH) to **lactic acid.** As the lactic acid

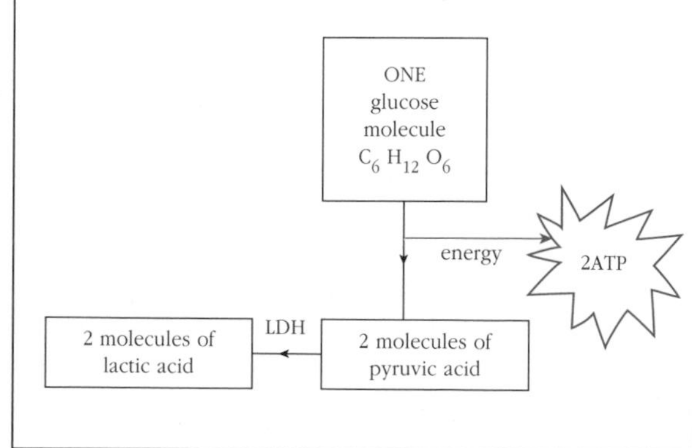

Figure 3.3 The lactic acid system.

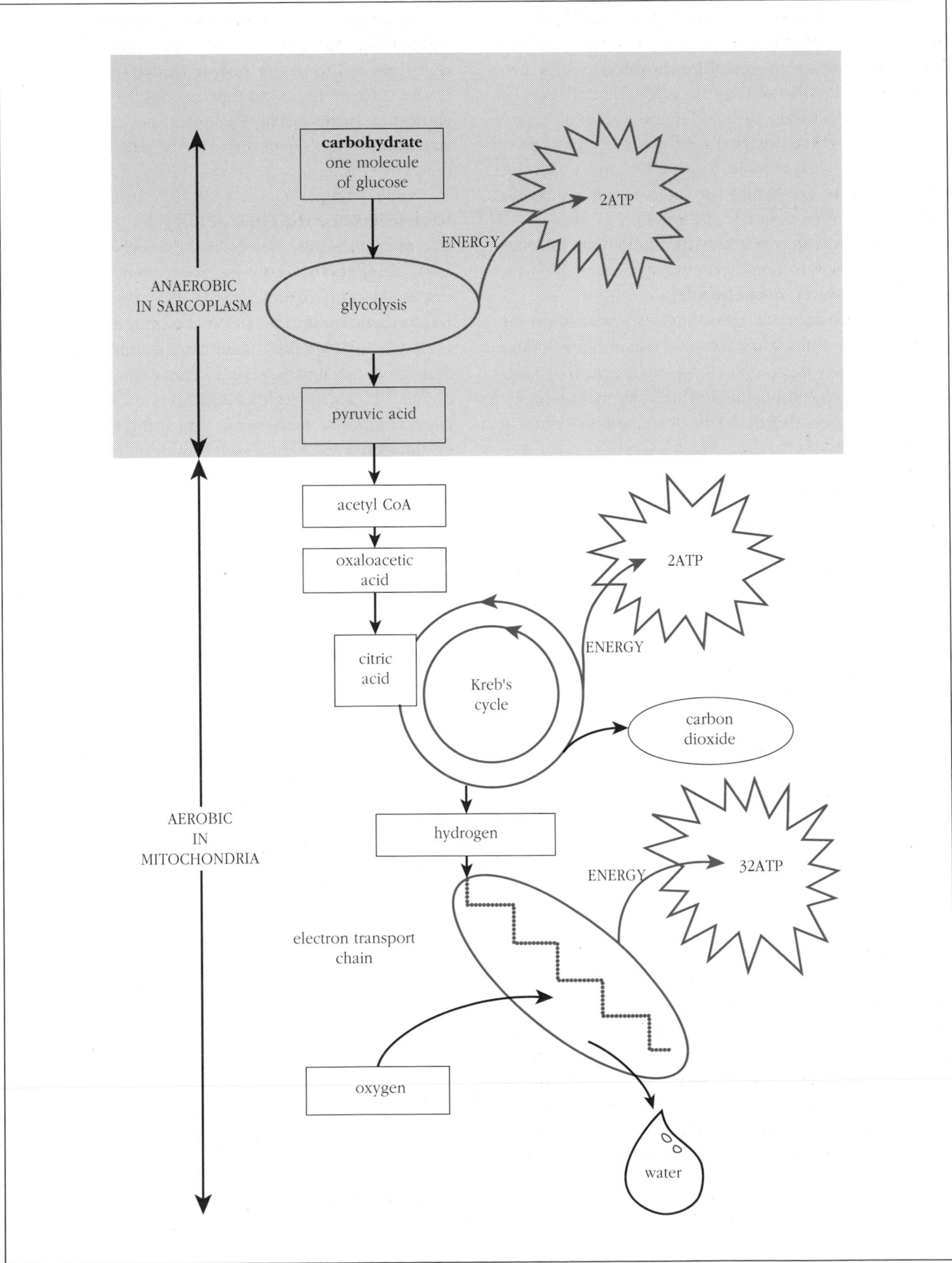

Figure 3.4 The aerobic system.

accumulates, muscle fatigue and pain occur. This is because the resultant low pH within the cell inhibits **enzyme** action in the cell **mitochondria**, which normally promotes the change of glycogen into energy. Hence the effect of lactic acid fatigue is to inhibit muscle action so that physical performance deteriorates (the enzymes responsible for aerobic and anaerobic energy release are located in mitochondria—muscle cells contain the largest concentration of these). All anaerobic processes happen throughout in the **sarcoplasm**, whereas aerobic processes occur within the confines of the cell **mitochondria**.

Events such as a 400 metre race rely heavily on the lactic acid system. After exercise has stopped extra oxygen is taken in to remove the lactic acid by changing it back into pyruvic acid. This is known as repaying the **oxygen debt** and is described in detail in Section 3.3.

3. The aerobic system

The aerobic system (Figure 3.4) relies on the presence of oxygen to break down completely carbohydrates and fats to carbon dioxide, water and energy. The energy yield is high, one molecule of glucose yields 36 molecules of ATP (in the lactic acid process the yield is 2 molecules of ATP!).

The first stage of the **aerobic** process is the same as that occurring in the anaerobic lactic acid system: **glycolysis**, i.e. the conversion of glycogen into two molecules of pyruvic acid (Figure 3.3), two ATP molecules and a number of **hydrogen atoms**. This process occurs via a series of about ten chemical reactions in the cell **sarcoplasm.**

From now on, all chemical reactions involved in the aerobic system take place within the muscle cell **mitochondria** (see page 39). The mitochondrion is often referred to as the **power house** of the cell, as it is the site of most energy production. Figure 3.5 shows the microscopic detail of a mitochondrion. The structures labelled in Figure 3.5 will be discussed below.

Kreb's cycle or the citric acid cycle

The two molecules of pyruvic acid are converted to a form of **acetyl CoA** (a 2-carbon compound) which enters the citric acid cycle by combining with **oxaloacetic acid** (a 6-carbon compound).

This process takes place in the inner fluid-filled matrix of the mitochondrion, containing the enzymes of the citric acid cycle. Within this cycle there are a large number of reactions in which the two molecules go through a series of changes until they are degraded to pairs of hydrogen atoms and carbon dioxide. Fatty acids are taken up by the cycle at this point. The total energy release from acetyl CoA, as a result of fat metabolism. is 34 ATP.

The electron transport chain

Oxygen is given off from the muscle myoglobin or made available from blood haemoglobin and is taken in by the **mitochondria** to be used to oxidize the hydrogens:

$$H \rightarrow H^+ + e^-$$

(hydrogen atom) (hydrogen ion) (electron)

length ≏ 2.5 μm
diameter 1.0 μm
cristae (electron transport chain)
inner fluid-filled matrix (Kreb's cycle)
outer smooth membrane

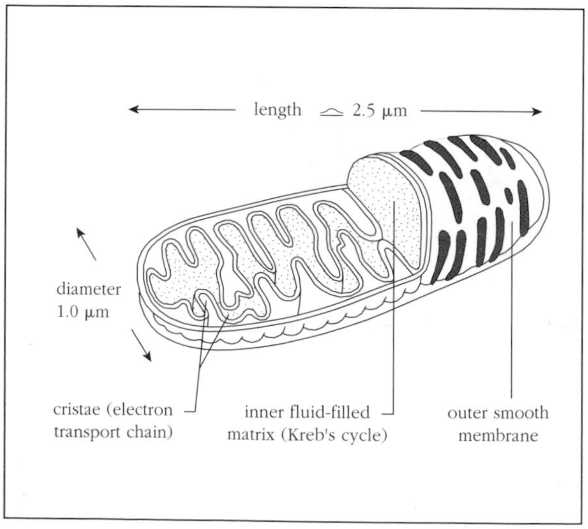

Figure 3.5 The mitochondrion — the organelle of respiration.

The hydrogen ions and electrons are charged with potential energy. The electron transport chain consists of a chain of hydrogen ion-electron pairs, linked to the folds of the inner membrane (cristae) of the cell mitochondria. Energy is released in a controlled step by step manner (each reaction is exothermic). For each pair of hydrogen atoms that enter this pathway, the net effect is the production of three molecules of ATP (endothermic) and one molecule of water. This is an **aerobic process**, with the final pair being accepted by molecular oxygen which combines with H^+ to produce water.

The total possible yield produced by aerobic metabolism is 36 or 38 molecules of ATP—the total energy yield is dependant on the biochemical pathway taken by the food fuel. This is the maximum possible from the complete oxidation of one molecule of glucose, but more, probably, than *per* molecule of glucose. ATP yield varies as this process is more or less complete. The overall equation expressing **aerobic respiration** is:

$$C_6H_{12}O_6 + 36ADP + 36P_i + 6O_2 \rightarrow 6CO_2 + 36\ ATP + 6H_2O$$

The aerobic route is 18 or 19 times more efficient than the anaerobic route, depending on the food fuel biochemical pathway.

Provided there is an adequate supply of oxygen to the working muscles, glucose and free fatty acids can be metabolized to produce ATP. The major advantage of fat fuels is that there is a much larger supply available to sustain steady state endurance activities such as marathon running.

Investigation 3.3 : To determine the energy sources for practical activities

(The material for this investigation was devised by Kevin Sykes. Principal Lecturer at Chester College of Higher Education, as part of an AEB A' level course.)

Materials: tape measure and stop-watch.

Task One—a standing long jump
Crouch down low with flexed knees and prepare to take off from both feet. Spring forward as far as possible and measure the distance achieved. The distance is measured between the front of the toes at take off, and the rear of the heels on landing. Record the maximum distance from three attempts.

Figure 3.6 A standing long jump.

Task Two
Identify the two baselines of a badminton court in your gym or sportshall. Start at one end and on the command 'GO' sprint as fast as you can to the far baseline and back three times altogether. making a total of six shuttle sprints. Get a partner to record your time.

Figure 3.7 A shuttle sprint.

Task Three—shuttle runs
Using the same baselines, perform a 30 length shuttle run at a steady pace. Get a partner to record your split times at 5, 10, 15, 20, 25 and 30 lengths. Record your split times in table 16 overleaf.

Task Four

1. Comment on the split times in your run.
2. How did you feel at various stages of the run and at the finish?
3. Roughly how long did it take you to recover?
4. Which of the energy systems is dominant in each of the three tasks?

Task Five—collation of results

Collate your own results and those of five other students in your class in Table 16 provided.

Task Six—analysis of results

1. Discuss your group results in relation to gender, height, weight and sporting interests.
2. Discuss the meaningfulness of these results and the limitations of such measurements.
3. How would these results differ as you get fitter? Explain your answer.

Table 16 : Results table

Name	standing broad jump (metres)	shuttle sprint (seconds)	shuttle runs (split times min/sec) 5 10 15 20 25 30
self			

REVIEW QUESTIONS

1. Write an equation which summarizes:
a) aerobic respiration
b) anaerobic respiration.
2. What role does ATP play in energy release?
3. Describe the special role mitochondria play in energy release.
4. During any event of low or high intensity, all three energy systems are used. However, the physical demands of the event will determine the relative proportions of the energy system(s) being used.
Complete the gaps in Table 17, identifying the major energy systems and examples in sporting activities in relation to performance time.

Table 17

Area	Performance time	Major energy system(s)	Examples of type of activity
1	less than 30 secs	ATP–PC	100 metres gym vault
2	30 secs–$1\frac{1}{2}$ mins		
3	$1\frac{1}{2}$–3 mins		
4	greater than 3 mins		

5. Describe the **predominant** energy system being used in the following activities (remember this will be related to the time of the activity and the effort involved):
   shotput, marathon, 200 metres breaststroke, a game of hockey, 100 metres hurdles race, gymnastics vault, modern pentathlon, a brisk walk.
6. Figure 3.8 represents the energy systems used during the following athletic events:
   100 metres, 400 metres, 1500 metres and marathon, but not necessarily in that order.
   a) Identify each event with an energy block and comment briefly on the reasons for your choice.
   b) Using the same key, complete a block to show the approximate proportions of aerobic/anaerobic work during a basketball game.

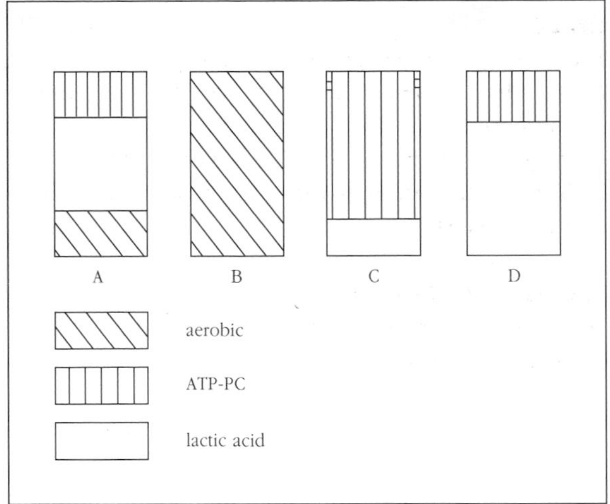

Figure 3.8 Energy blocks.

7. The energy sources for a 1500 metres race are very specific. During the first ten seconds the ATP-PC system is used, followed by a transition to the lactic acid system during the next minute. The pace settles into a short aerobic phase, followed by a return to the lactic acid system during the final sprint for the line.
   Using the same format, analyse the energy sources used in a game of hockey.
8. Select a sport with which you are familiar and describe the energy systems used in your selected sport. How can a knowledge of the three energy systems assist you in devising a training programme for your selected sport?

Summary

1. You should be able to understand how energy is stored as chemical energy in ATP within muscle.
2. You should be able to understand how energy is released and ATP is used for muscle contraction.
3. You should be able to understand that glycolysis is common to both anaerobic and aerobic energy release.
4. You should be able to understand that energy is released to recreate ATP via three sets of mechanisms—alactic anaerobic, lactic acid anaerobic and aerobic systems, and how each system works.
5. You should be able to apply the concept of energy systems to practical situations.

FURTHER READING

Bowers R.W. and Fox E.L. *Sports Physiology,* Wm C. Brown, 1992.

Fisher G.A., Jensen C.R. *Scientific Basis of Ahletic Conditioning* 3e, Lea & Febiger, 1990.

Fox E.L., Bowers R.W. and Foss M.C. *The Physiological Basis for Exercise and Sport* 5e, Wm C. Brown, 1992.

McArdle W.D., Katch F.I. and Katch V.L. *Essentials of Exercise Physiology,* Lea & Febiger, 1994.

Wootton S. *Nutrition for Sport,* Simon and Schuster, 1988.

3.3 The Recovery Process after Exercise

KEY WORDS AND CONCEPTS

oxygen debt or oxygen recovery	**alactacid oxygen debt component**	**oxygenated myoglobin**
phosphagen restoration	**lactacid oxygen debt component**	**muscle soreness**
		muscle glycogen stores

Normally, provided the effort or duration of exercise has not been too large, breathing and pulse rates rise as the need for oxygen rises to levels which enable ATP to be regenerated in muscles at the same rate as it is consumed. This is a continuous process which varies according to the work or energy performed by muscles during a sportsperson's day.

Initially, as exercise begins, ATP is consumed directly, then replaced via the ATP–PC anaerobic energy system, **as well as** glycolysis and aerobic conversion of carbohydrates to provide energy for ATP manufacture. The important point to note is that **all three mechanisms** of ATP manufacture occur continuously, but the **proportion** produced by the mechanisms changes as the exercise continues.

If exercise is intense enough, the cells rapidly run out of PC (so replacement of ATP by the ATP–PC mechanism stops: the alactic lactic threshold), not enough ATP is produced by aerobic processes, so **glycolysis** takes over as the predominant method of supply of ATP, with its production of lactic acid and rapid depletion of muscle glycogen (and oxygenated myoglobin, which is a further way in which oxygen is provided to muscle cells to generate energy aerobically).

Eventually, both ATP and glycogen will be used up, and exercise must stop, or the sportsperson will collapse!

Again, the important issue to stress is that **all mechanisms for manufacture of ATP are continuous**, and of course will continue when exercise stops—the evolutionary aim of the mechanisms being then to replace ATP and glycogen as quickly as possible—so that further exercise is possible.

LACTIC ACID AND THE OXYGEN DEBT

After every strenuous exercise, therefore, there are four tasks which need to be completed before the exhausted muscle can operate at full efficiency again:

a. replacement of ATP
b. removal of lactic acid
c. replenishment of myoglobin with oxygen
d. replacement of glycogen.

The first three of these require oxygen in substantial quantities—hence the need for rapid breathing and high pulse rate to carry oxygen to the muscle cells. This need for oxygen rapidly to replace ATP and

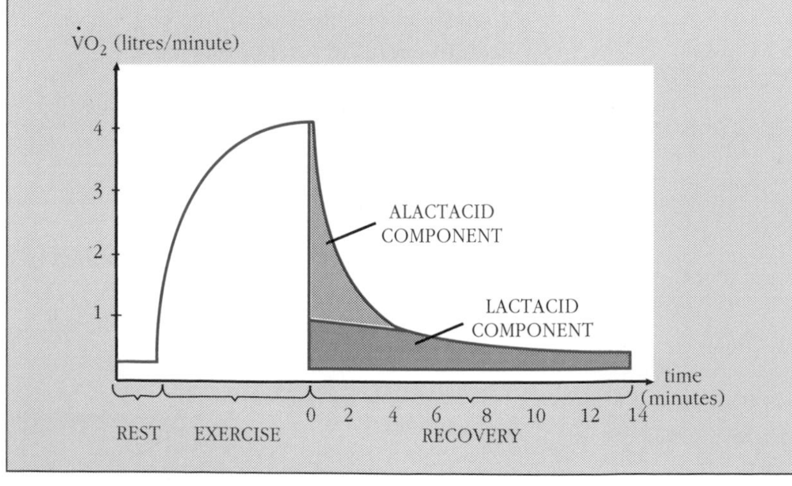

Figure 3.9 The relationship between O_2 consumption, and the time before, during and after maximal exercise.

remove lactic acid is known as the **oxygen debt**—or **oxygen recovery**.

Item d (replacement of glycogen) is a long term process which can take between 24–48 hours depending on the fitness level, diet of the sport's person and the intensity and duration of the exercise.

There are many other processes involved in oxygen recovery. For example, restoration of cardiac/pulmonary functioning to resting values, reversal of the high phosphate breakdown, return of body temperature to normal. All these processes will need additional oxygen (although substantially less than ATP manufacture and lactic acid removal) and therefore add time to paying back the oxygen deficit to the pre-exercise level.

Figure 3.9 shows how the need for oxygen falls following cessation of exercise. Obviously the more rapidly this process is complete, the quicker the sportsperson can resume exercise.

The two major components of oxygen recovery are:

1. **Alactacid oxygen debt**
2. **Lactacid oxygen debt.**

The contribution made by each to the overall process of oxygen recovery is marked on the graph, but note that both processes will occur initially, even though the alactic process is more rapid and is completed more quickly.

ALACTACID OXYGEN DEBT COMPONENT

Alactacid oxygen debt recovery is a rapid process involving the conversion of ADP back into PC and ATP, both of which will have been almost completely exhausted in the muscle cell sarcoplasm during intense exercise. This is achieved mainly by using the aerobic energy system, during which ATP and PC stores are refilled. This process is commonly known as **the restoration of muscle phosphagen stores** and its main function is to restore ATP, and provide normal levels of PC in the muscle (which is used in the coupled reaction which restores ATP via the ATP–PC mechanism). Three mechanisms contribute to this:

a. Energy from aerobic conversion of carbohydrate into carbon dioxide and water is used to manufacture ATP from ADP and P_i (the products of ATP consumption).

b. Some of this ATP is immediately utilized to create PC using the coupled reactions:

$$\text{ATP} \rightarrow \text{ADP} + P_i + \text{energy}$$
$$\text{energy} + P_i + \text{C} \rightarrow \text{PC}$$

c. A very small percentage of ATP is remanufactured via glycolysis to produce small quantities of lactic acid.

The size of the alactacid oxygen debt

The size of the alactacid oxygen debt is within a range of 2 to 3.5 litres, depending on the intensity of the exercise and the fitness of the sportsperson. Some of the adaptations produced by intense anaerobic training are an increase in ATP and PC stores in muscle cells, the ability to provide oxygen rapidly by improved capillarization, **and** an improved cardio-respiratory system which will provide the muscles with oxygenated blood more rapidly. These adaptations will increase the possible size of the oxygen debt in the fitter sportsperson, and reduce the recovery time.

Investigation 3.4 : Phosphagen restoration

This investigation asks the student to plot and interpret data relevant to the alactic oxygen recovery.

Task One
Consider Table 18 of results of experiments on phosphagen recovery.

Plot a graph of these data with recovery time on the *x*-axis and percentage phosphagen restored on the *y*-axis.

a. What would be the effect of restarting exercise after 30 seconds?
b. What resting interval would you recommend for full recovery?

Task Two—implications for interval training
Assuming that it takes about 30 seconds to deplete ATP and PC stores by 50% in a particular muscle group doing flat out exercise:

a. Sketch a graph showing levels of muscle phosphagen (ATP and PC content) against time (*x*-axis) for this exercise period, followed by a full recovery.
b. Sketch a similar graph for three periods of exercise, each of 30 seconds followed by 60 seconds rest. What happens to the level of phosphagen store just at the end of the third exercise period (i.e. after 210 seconds from the start of the session)?
(Ref. Bowers and Fox: *Sports Physiology*, 1992, p. 80, Fig. 5–3.)

Table 18 : Phosphagen recovery

Recovery time (seconds)	Muscle phosphagen restored
10	10%
30	50%
60	75%
90	87%
120	93%
150	97%
180	99%
210	101%
240	102%

THE FUNCTION OF OXYGEN-MYOGLOBIN IN PURGING OXYGEN DEBT

Part of the recovery mechanism after anaerobic exercise involves **myoglobin**, whose presence in muscle cells (particularly slow twitch red muscle) is discussed in the section on muscle cells on p. 39. The function of myoglobin is to facilitate the transport of oxygen into the muscle cell. During recovery after heavy exercise, the absence of sufficient oxygen to continue the provision of energy in muscles means that myoglobin becomes an important, if small-scale, carrier of oxygen from blood haemoglobin to the cell mitochondria—a process more rapid than natural diffusion of molecular oxygen.

Complete re-saturation of muscle myoglobin with oxygen is thought to be completed within the time period of the oxygen debt.

LACTACID OXYGEN DEBT COMPONENT

As intensity of exercise increases, so an increasing proportion of ATP replacement has to be provided by the lactic anaerobic mechanism, glycolysis, whose product is lactic acid. Eventually, glycogen in the muscles is used up by this process (taking about 45 seconds) if the exercise is hard enough. At this moment the capacity for manufacture of ATP ceases apart from a relatively low rate of production by aerobic mechanisms.

This means that when exercise stops, oxygen will be required to remove the lactic acid, and begin to restore muscle and liver glycogen—this is called **lactacid oxygen recovery**, which is a relatively slow process (compared with alactic phosphagen replacement) and which can last for minutes or hours depending on the severity of the exercise.

Again it should be stressed that this process will

begin as soon as lactic acid appears in muscle cell sites (i.e. as soon as exercise begins), and will continue utilizing breathed oxygen until recovery is complete, as indicated in Figure 3.9.

Table 19 shows what happens to the lactic acid during lactacid oxygen recovery.

The normal amount of lactic acid circulating in the blood is about 1–2 millimoles of lactic acid per litre of blood (mmol/l). In aerobic exercise this amount remains the same. However, in medium intensity workouts, such as a 30 minute run, this amount doubles to 4 mmol/l of blood. This latter amount represents the anaerobic threshold or the value of blood lactic acid concentrations above which an oxygen debt is acquired. During high intensity training, such as a 300 metre flat out run, lactic acid levels can reach up to 15–20 times resting values.

Most research into the speed of lactic acid removal suggests that at least one hour is required, although 50% of the debt is repaid in the first 15 minutes after exercise (Bowers and Fox, 1992; Karlsson, 1971). Secondly, the effects of active recovery, such as jogging or walking between runs or light swimming between high intensity swims, speed up the removal of lactic acid, as does a cool-down at the end of a training session (ref. Bowers and Fox *Sports Physiology*, p. 94, Fig. 5-13a).

Muscle Soreness

During intense exercise it has been found that the pH level of the blood is very low due to the accumulation of **lactic acid.** Muscle soreness is often associated with lactic acid build-up and it is thought that this is due to the effects of low pH (acidity) acting upon the pain receptors. As stated above, a cool-down will reduce the effects of muscle soreness after strenuous exercise by keeping blood capillaries dilated, and flushing oxygenated blood through muscles thereby increasing the possibility of oxidizing the lactic acid and removing it from muscle cells.

Regular repetition of an exercise will also increase capillarization within a muscle, which will additionally allow oxygenated blood to reach the lactic acid in muscle cells. This means that the fitter sportsperson should suffer less muscle soreness.

RESTORATION OF MUSCLE GLYCOGEN STORES

There are about 350 grams of glycogen in the body, some stored as muscle glycogen, the remainder in the liver. During strenuous exercise, blood glucose increases as the liver metabolizes its glycogen stores and the amount of glycogen (stored within muscles) will be metabolized to glucose within the muscle tissue. Depletion of muscle glycogen stores appears to be a significant factor in muscular fatigue.

In short-distance, high intensity exercise, such as an 800 metre race, muscle glycogen stores are replenished within a couple of hours.

In long-distance endurance activities, such as marathon racing, a **glycogen-loaded diet** prior to the competition increases muscle and liver glycogen levels. However, during prolonged exercise muscle and liver glycogen levels fall until a state of exhaustion is reached (ref. Fox *et al.*, 1993. p. 32, Fig. 2.17).

Complete restoration of muscle and liver glycogen stores is speeded up by a high carbohydrate diet. It has been found that replenishment of muscle glycogen stores is most rapid during the first few hours and then can take several days to complete.

Another factor which may account for the speed of recovery of muscle glycogen stores, during high intensity exercise compared with low intensity exercise, is that restoration of muscle glycogen is quicker in fast twitch fibres than slow twitch fibres.

The factors discussed so far in relation to the replenishment of muscle glycogen are important to sportspersons and coaches alike. They must understand the need to plan their training sessions and competitions or games so that recovery has occurred in time for the next bout of high intensity exercise.

Table 19 : Lactic acid utilization during lactacid oxygen recovery

Destination	Approximate % lactic acid involved
oxidation into carbon dioxide and water	65
conversion into glycogen — then stored in muscles or liver	20
conversion into protein	10
conversion into glucose	5

REVIEW QUESTIONS

1. a) How could the information on lactic acid removal be of use to an athlete and coach in the design of training sessions?
   b) Explain the importance of cool-down in assistance of lactacid oxygen recovery, and avoidance of muscle soreness.
2. Using the information in the sections on energy systems and oxygen recovery, complete the spaces in Table 20 with the major characteristics of the three energy systems in relation to the speed of running (ref. Bowers and Fox, p. 30, Table 2.2).

Table 20

ATP-PC (Phosphagen) System	Lactic Acid System	Oxygen System
	Anaerobic	Aerobic
Very rapid		
Chemical fuel: PC	Food fuel:	Food fuel:
	Limited ATP production	
Muscular stores limited	By-product, lactic acid causes muscular pain	
Used with sprint or any high-power, short-duration work up to 10 sec		Used with endurance or long-duration activities over 2–3 min duration

(After Bowers and Fox, 1992.)

Summary

1. You should understand what is meant by **oxygen debt** or **oxygen recovery**, including the two oxygen debt components—**alactacid** and **lactacid**.
2. You should understand the importance of cool-down in the removal of lactic acid and in the reduction of muscle soreness.
3. You should understand the role of oxygenated myoglobin during recovery from intensive exercise.
4. You should understand the significance of the time factor and the effects of diet on the restoration of muscle phosphagen and muscle and liver glycogen levels.
5. You should understand the application of energy concepts to sporting activities.

FURTHER READING

Bowers R.W. and Fox E.L. *Sports Physiology,* Wm. C. Brown, 1992.

de Vries H.A. *Physiology of Exercise* 5e, Wm. C. Brown, 1994.

Fox E.L., Bowers R.W. and Foss M.C. *The Physiological Basis for Exercise and Sport* 5e, Wm. C. Brown, 1993.

Karlsson J. Lactate and phosphagen concentrations in working muscles of man, *Acta Physiologica,* Scandinavia 358, 1971.

McArdle W.D., Katch F.I. and Katch V.L. *Essentials of Exercise Physiology,* Lea & Febiger, 1994.

Newsholme E. and Leech T. Fatigue stops play, *New Scientist,* 22 Sept. 1988.

3.4 Oxygen Uptake/Oxygen Consumption

KEY WORDS AND CONCEPTS

oxygen consumption
aerobic power
anaerobic power
$\dot{V}O_2$max.
Harvard step test
Wingate anaerobic power test
peak anaerobic power
minimum anaerobic power
fatigue index
lactacid capacity
alactacid capacity

Oxygen uptake or **oxygen consumption** is defined as the amount of oxygen a person consumes per unit of time (usually one minute). This concept is expressed as $\dot{V}O_2$, where V is volume, O_2 is oxygen and the dot over the V means *per unit of time*.

The oxidation of fuel foods requires a definite amount of oxygen per unit mass of fuel (1 kg), which can be measured indirectly by collecting expired air and comparing it with the composition of inspired air (i.e. by measuring the amount of **oxygen** that has been removed from the atmosphere and the amount of **carbon dioxide** that has been produced by the body).

At rest, oxygen uptake varies between 0.2 and 0.3 litres per minute. However, once an individual starts to exercise, the total body oxygen uptake increases proportionally with the intensity of the exercise, until a maximal work rate is reached. The highest $\dot{V}O_2$ achieved is expressed as **$\dot{V}O_2$max.** This concept of **maximum oxygen uptake** ($\dot{V}O_2$max.) is also known as **aerobic power.**

$\dot{V}O_2$max. can therefore be quantitively represented as the maximum amount of oxygen that a person can consume per minute during a progressive exercise test to exhaustion. This highest value represents the individual's maximal physiological capacity to transport and use oxygen.

A mean value of $\dot{V}O_2$max. for male students is about 3.5 litres/minute and for females is about 2.7 litres/minute. Endurance athletes, such as those who participate regularly in middle- and long-distance running, rowing and cross-country skiing, may reach 4–6 litres per minute. However, $\dot{V}O_2$max. depends on body mass as well as physical fitness, and it is therefore sometimes expressed in millilitres per kilogram of body mass per minute (ml/kg/min).

FACTORS AFFECTING MAXIMUM AEROBIC POWER

The availability of oxygen in the tissues is the limiting factor in any exercise. The physical limitations which restrict the rate at which energy can be released aerobically are dependent upon the chemical ability of the **muscular cellular tissue system** to use oxygen in breaking down fuels, and the combined ability of **cardiovascular** and **pulmonary systems** to transport oxygen to the muscular tissue system.

SIMPLE AEROBIC TESTS

Aerobic tests which are used as indicators of aerobic fitness include the Physical Work Capacity Test (PWC 170), the Cooper Run Test, the NCF Multistage Shuttle Run, the Fitech Step Test and the Queen's College Step Test.

Investigation 3.5—To measure maximum aerobic power

THE QUEEN'S COLLEGE STEP TEST

This investigation is a very simple method of determining maximum aerobic power. The data used to predict $\dot{V}O_2$max. (ml/kg/min) have been based on the results of male and female college students at Queen's College in New York, who had their $\dot{V}O_2$max. measured (using a treadmill test procedure) and then plotted in relation to the corresponding recovery heart rate scores obtained on the step test, to produce predicted maximal oxygen uptake scores as shown in Table 21.

Materials: stepping bench (41 cm high) stop-watch, metronome.

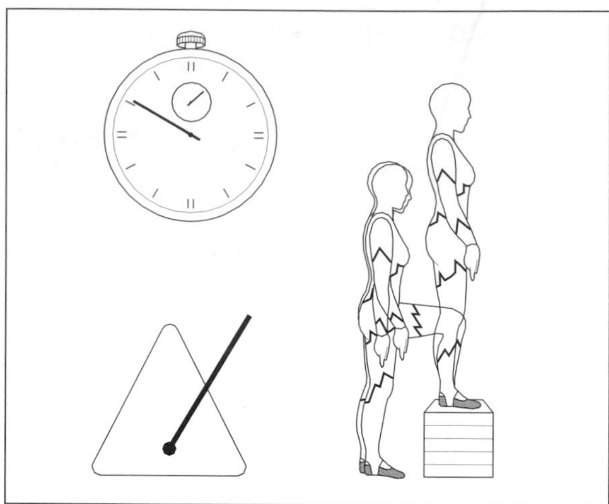

Figure 3.10 The Queen's College Step Test.

Table 21

Percentile ranking	Recovery HR, female (ml/kg/min)	Predicted $\dot{V}O_2$max.	Recovery HR, male (ml/kg/min)	Predicted $\dot{V}O_2$max.
100	128	42.2	120	60.9
95	140	40.0	124	59.3
90	148	38.5	128	57.6
85	152	37.7	136	54.2
80	156	37.0	140	52.5
75	158	36.6	144	50.9
70	160	36.3	148	49.2
65	162	35.9	149	48.8
60	163	35.7	152	47.5
55	164	35.5	154	46.7
50	166	35.1	156	45.8
45	168	34.8	160	44.1
40	170	34.4	162	43.3
35	171	34.2	164	42.5
30	172	34.0	166	41.6
25	176	33.3	168	40.8
20	180	32.6	172	39.1
15	182	32.2	176	37.4
10	184	31.8	178	36.6
5	196	29.6	184	34.1

Task One

1. Establish the step cadence: for females set the metronome at 88 beats per minute, for males at 96 beats per minute. Practise the step rhythm to adjust to the cadence of the metronome. The sequence is left up/right up/left down/right down—each element to a single metronome beat.
2. Take a rest and when you are ready begin to step for three minutes at the set step cadence.
3. At the end of the exercise period remain standing for five seconds. Then take your pulse count at the carotid artery for a 15 second count. Multiply by four to give the heart rate score in beats per minute (bpm).
4. Using the information in Table 21, work out your predicted $\dot{V}O_2$max. and percentile ranking, based on your recovery heart rate value.

Task Two—collation of results

1. Record in Table 22 your results and those of male and female students in your class.
2. Compare group results. Are there any differences within your group? Account for these differences.
3. Work out your predicted $\dot{V}O_2$max./min. for your total body mass by multiplying $\dot{V}O_2$max. (ml/kg/min) by your body weight in kgs. How does this value relate to the values given earlier in this unit?

Table 22 : Results Table

Name	Percentile Ranking	Recovery HR	Predicted $\dot{V}O_2$max. (ml/kg/min)
Self			

Task Three

1. Describe the two main factors which limit aerobic power.
2. Describe some of the ways in which aerobic capacity could be improved.
3. Which muscle fibre type is used predominantly in aerobic work?
4. Discuss the purpose of testing aerobic power with respect to endurance events.
5. Describe the energy systems used during the step test.

Task Four

Figure 3.11 shows how oxygen consumption changes as an athlete runs at a constant pace up a series of hills increasing in slope.

1. Describe and account for the pattern of oxygen consumption from the level ground until the end of the third hill.
2. Why does oxygen consumption begin to level off after the third hill?
3. The athlete is only just able to run up the final sixth hill where he/she achieves his/her $\dot{V}O_2$max. Explain what this concept means and why the athlete is unable to continue running at the set pace.
4. How would this pattern of oxygen consumption change if the athlete trained regularly over this terrain? Suggest possible reasons in your answer.

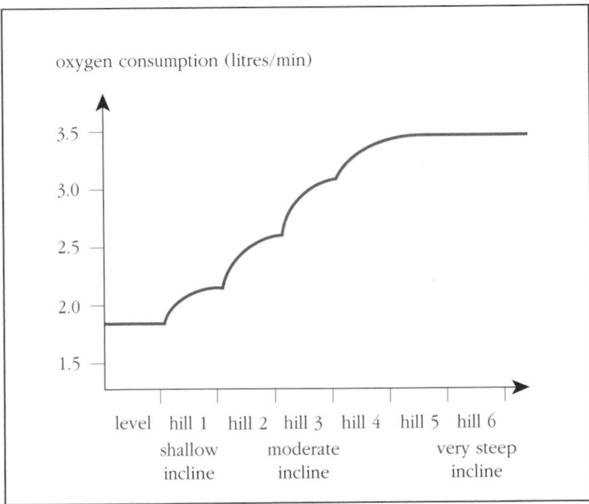

Figure 3.11 Change in oxygen consumption as an athlete runs, at a constant pace, up a series of hills increasing in slope.

Task Five

1. Sketch a graph which illustrates the amount of oxygen consumed in litres per minute (on the *y*-axis) against time (on the *x*-axis), for a jogger who at rest consumes 0.3 litres per minute, and who then starts to run at a steady pace for 20 minutes, having reached a 'steady state' of oxygen consumption at 1.75 litres per minute, 5 minutes into the run.
2. Label on your graph the part of the curve which is referred to as 'steady state' and explain what this concept means.

OXYGEN CONSUMPTION AS AN INDIRECT WAY OF MEASURING ENERGY COSTS—A HYPOTHETICAL EXAMPLE

Consider the following calculation as an example of how to go about estimating energy costs indirectly.

First, work out the **net oxygen cost** (the oxygen consumed during exercise above that which is needed at rest) from the resting and exercise rates of consumption. In our example these values are 0.4 litres per minute and 2.15 litres per minute, respectively, thereby giving a net oxygen cost total of 1.75 litres per minute.

Next, let us assume that the person undertaking the exercise works for a 10 minute period at this rate. The net oxygen cost for the 10 minutes will be $10 \times 1.75 = 17.5$ litres. As one litre of oxygen produces 22kJ of heat energy by combination with food fuel in the body, the energy cost of the exercise will be:

$$22 \times 17.5 = 385 \text{ kJ}$$

In practice the net oxygen cost will always be greater than that calculated for the duration of exercise, as the net oxygen cost continues after exercise stops, until oxygen consumption reaches its resting value.

You may wish to work out your own hypothetical example.

ANAEROBIC CAPACITY

In addition to the assessment of aerobic fitness, the measurement of **anaerobic capacity** (the ability to do physical work which is dependent upon the anaerobic mechanisms of energy supply) may also be of interest to those of you who are interested in short, explosive physical activities.

Investigation 3.6 : Measurement of alactacid anaerobic capacity and lactacid capacity

Figure 3.12 The cycle ergometer.

The **Wingate Anaerobic Cycling Test** was devised at the Wingate Institute in Israel. This test is a 30 second all out cycling test which is used to determine **maximal anaerobic power**. Anaerobic power **is the ability to produce energy by the ATP–PC system** (adenosine triphosphate-phosphocreatine system).

Task One

1. The subject warms up for a 2–3 minute cycling period to achieve a heart rate of 150 bpm.
2. The **work load** – or bike resistance mass, is worked out using the following information:
   a) **Aged under 15**: 35g per kg (grams of bike resistance mass per kilogram) of body weight.
   b) **Adult**: 45g per kg of body weight for the Fleisch ergometer. 75g per kg of body weight for the Monark ergometer. Set the cycle ergometer at the prescribed work load expressed in kg.
3. On the command '*go*' the subject pedals flat out for a period of **30 seconds**. During the first two seconds the resistance is adjusted and the timed flat-out cycling commences. For each five seconds of the investigation, a member of the group counts the number of pedal revolutions. Usually, the flywheel turns too quickly to count revolutions by eye. In this case a video recording or photo cell may assist the flywheel counting operation.
4. The subject pedals at a light load during a cool-down period.
5. The results for each five-second period are recorded in watts according to the following equation:

$$\text{Power (watts)} = \text{loadmass (kg)} \times \text{revolutions of flywheel in 5 seconds} \times \text{radius of flywheel (metres)} \times 12.33. \left(12.33 = \frac{2 \times 9.81 \times \pi}{5}\right)$$

6. Record your results in Table 23.

Table 23 : Results table

Time (sec)	No. of revolutions of flywheel	Power (watts)	Power/kg of body mass
0-2			
2-7			
7-12			
12-17			
17-22			
22-27			
27-32			

Task Two—analysis of results

1. Plot a graph of power (watts) (y-axis) against time in seconds (x-axis).
2. Identify the **alactacid capacity** or the maximal power per kilogram of body mass achieved in a 5-second period (watt/kg). This power is called **peak anaerobic power** and represents the power created by the ATP–PC system.
3. Work out the least **anaerobic power** during the test, i.e. the minimum power recorded and the time at which this happens.
4. At what times in the investigation were peak and minimum anaerobic power attained?
5. **Power decline** is a measure of fatigue which can be calculated as a percentage of the peak power using this formula:

$$\text{Power decline} = \frac{(\text{peak power} - \text{minimum power}) \times 100}{\text{peak power}}$$

For example:
Peak power = 1000 W/kg
Minimum power = 500 W/kg

$$\text{Power decline would be: } \frac{100 \times (1000 - 500)}{1000} = 50\%$$

6. A further interesting concept is the **fatigue index**. It can be calculated by using the formula:

$$\text{fatigue index} = \frac{\text{power decline}}{\text{time interval between peak and min. power (sec)}}$$

Work out the subject's **fatigue index.**

7. Identify the **lactacid capacity** or the average power over the 30-second period in **watts** per kilogram of body mass. This will be the area under the graph of power against time (in seconds) for the 30 seconds of the test divided by the time of the test (30 seconds).

Task Three

1. What do you think will be the effects on **anaerobic power** of:
   a) sprint interval training
   b) weight training
   c) jogging?
2. Which muscle fibre type is predominantly used during anaerobic exercise?
3. Give examples of three sporting activities which depend on anaerobic energy sources.

Other examples of anaerobic capacity tests include the stair climb described in Investigation 3.1 (Figure 3.1), short sprints such as a 30 metre sprint, the number of repetitions achieved in exercises such as squat-thrusts, press-ups, squat-jumps, dips or pull-ups.

Alternatively, you could use static tests such as holding a weight at a fixed angle, as illustrated in the Strongest Men in the World competitions.

Figure 3.13

Figure 3.14

REVIEW QUESTIONS

1. Explain what is meant by $\dot{V}O_2$max. and **anaerobic capacity**.
2. List three examples of physical activities which rely predominantly on aerobic metabolism for their energy supply.
3. List three examples of physical activities which rely predominantly on anaerobic metabolism for their energy supply.
4. Briefly describe a test which can be used to evaluate one's capacity when performing:
   a) aerobic work
   b) anaerobic work.
   Comment on the advantages and disadvantages of the tests you have described.

Summary

1. You should be able to understand which energy mechanisms predominate in practical activities.
2. You should understand what is meant by oxygen uptake, aerobic power, $\dot{V}O_2$max., anaerobic power and anaerobic capacity.
3. You should be able to describe the factors affecting aerobic power.
4. You should be able to discuss the purpose of testing aerobic power in relation to endurance activities.
5. You should be able to discuss the purpose of testing anaerobic power in relation to explosive exercise activities.

FURTHER READING

Bowers R.W. and Fox E.L. *Sports Physiology* 3e, Wm. C. Brown, 1992

deVries H.A. *Physiology of Exercise* 5e, Wm. C. Brown, 1994.

Fox E.L., Bowers R.W. and Foss M.L. *The Physiological Basis for Exercise and Sport* 5e, Wm. C. Brown, 1993.

Katch F.I. and McArdle W.D. *Introduction and Nutrition, Exercise and Health*, Lea & Febiger, 1993.

Klausen K., Hemmingsen I. and Rasmussen B. *Basic Sport Science*, McNaughton & Gunn, 1982.

Lamb D.R. *Physiology of Exercise*, Macmillan, 1983.

McArdle W.D., Katch F.I. and Katch V.L. *Essentials of Exercise Physiology*, Lea & Febiger, 1994.

Sharkey B.J. *New Dimensions in Aerobic Fitness*, Human Kinetics, 1991.

3.5 Nutrition for Exercise

KEY WORDS AND CONCEPTS

carbohydrates	**lipids**	**fatty acids and glycerol**
fats	**glucose**	**triglyceride**
proteins	**glycogen**	

The food and drink a sportsperson consumes daily provide the energy, from carbohydrates and fats, to maintain bodily functions, in addition to providing all the energy needed for training and competition. Food also contains other nutrients, namely proteins, minerals, vitamins, water and roughage.

This section will help you to understand how these nutrients are vital to life processes and how carbohydrates and fats are the main energy providers for physical activity.

A **balanced diet** containing proportions of carbohydrates, fats and proteins, together with minerals, vitamins, water and roughage, is important to an individual, whether active in sport or not, in order to maintain good health.

PROTEINS

Protein is present in most foods and is present in large quantities in meat, eggs and milk. It is needed for growth and body building. For example, protein is used to increase the strength of muscle fibres, described in Chapter 1 (p. 28). Damaged tissues (resulting from fracture, dislocations, sprains, muscle strains and bruising, often incurred during physical activity) need proteins to repair injury sites. Proteins are also essential to make enzymes required for metabolic functioning, **but** they are used as an energy source only when our body is depleted of all carbohydrates and fat sources.

MINERALS

Minerals are essential because they contain elements or small groups of elements needed to form part of the molecular structure of chemicals required by the body for life processes. For example, haemoglobin and muscle myoglobin contain an **iron** atom without which synthesis of haemoglobin would be impossible (lack of haemoglobin causes anaemia).

VITAMINS

Vitamins perform a similar role except that complex organic **radicals** are provided which are needed for the synthesis of molecules participating in life processes. Such radicals cannot be manufactured by the body, and therefore have to be ingested as part of the nutrition process (a radical is a stable group of atoms

Figure 3.15 A balanced diet.

which forms part of a complex molecule). For example, ascorbic acid, otherwise known as vitamin C, contains the radical **ascorbate** which is needed as part of the physiological **process** which prevents scurvy.

(See a specialist text on nutrition for a full list of vitamins and their effects on human health, such as Simpkin and Williams, 1987; or the *Nutrition and Sports Performance Resource Pack*, prepared by Dr Steve Wootten and published by the NCF.)

WATER

Water accounts for two-thirds of body weight. It is an essential ingredient in a daily diet because it dissolves more substances than anything else. As a result nearly all chemical reactions essential to life take place in a watery medium. It also allows materials to move from one place of the body to another. For example, blood plasma consists of 90 per cent water and transports a variety of substances, such as glucose, all around the body.

Water is very important as a heat regulator (heat is released as a result of tissue respiration). For example, blood plasma is able to take up heat and transport it to the body surface where it can be radiated away from the body. Another method of losing heat energy from the body surface involves water being excreted through the skin (sweating). As the water evaporates, the energy necessary to do this is extracted from the skin itself, thereby causing the skin to cool. Water is also lost as water vapour during expiration.

ROUGHAGE

Roughage or dietary fibre, found in cereals, provides bulk needed for the functioning of the large intestine.

CARBOHYDRATES AND FATS—THE ENERGY GIVERS

The bulk of chemical energy released by the chemical reactions involved in tissue respiration comes from carbohydrates and fats. Carbohydrates are the body's principal fuel, yielding 75 per cent of our energy requirements and fats the remainder.

Carbohydrates

Carbohydrates include sugar, starch and cellulose. The sugars can be either **simple sugars** or **monosaccharides** (e.g. glucose and fructose, both having the chemical formula $C_6H_{12}O_6$), or **complex sugars** or **disaccharides** (e.g. sucrose, maltose and lactose, all having the chemical formula $C_{12}H_{22}O_{11}$). Starch, found in food sources such as rice and potatoes, and cellulose are **polysaccharides**, since their molecular structures are chain-like multiples of glucose, and have the formula $(C_6H_{10}O_5)n$ where n represents the number of glucose units in the molecule. This number varies between 100 and 1000 depending on the biological origin of the starch. Most of the carbohydrates we ingest are in the form of starch and cellulose.

Cellulose does not provide energy, but is dietary fibre important in peristalsis in the large intestine. Peristalsis is a chain of muscular contractions which drives food along, thus preventing constipation.

Within the digestive tract, polysaccharides are hydrolysed to glucose and are stored as glycogen in both liver and muscle cells (the liver also has the function of converting glycogen into glucose when it is needed for tissue respiration).

One gram of carbohydrate provides 17 kJ of energy.

FATS

Fats are found in both animal and vegetable sources and should provide about 25 per cent of energy requirements. Foods such as butter and bacon are examples of those foods containing animal fats, with nuts and soya beans containing vegetable fats.

Within the digestive system, fats or **lipids** are converted by the enzyme **lipase** into **fatty acids** and **glycerol.**

Fats provide twice the energy yield of carbohydrates at 39 kJ per gram.

In the bloodstream, glucose (derived from fats and carbohydrates) can be sent directly to muscles for energy release by direct involvement in the ADP to ATP conversion reaction or the PC coupled reaction for the creation of ATP. Otherwise surplus glucose, not needed by these reactions, is converted (by the actions of the hormone **insulin**) into glycogen. This is stored in the liver (as **liver glycogen**) or in the muscle cell sarcoplasm (as **muscle glycogen**). If the body does not need the glucose, it enters the **fat metabolic system**, where it is converted to fatty acids and glycerol and is stored in the body as **triglycerides** (body fat) in adipose tissue and skeletal muscle. When energy is required from fat fuels, the contents of each individual adipose cell or muscle triglyceride are broken down into glycerol and free fatty acids. These are then transported by the circulatory system to the liver, where conversion to glucose takes place.

Other hormones taking part in the conversion of fat into carbohydrate are **glucagon** and **adrenaline** (insulin and glucagon are secreted by the Islets of Langerhans in the pancreas, and adrenaline is secreted from the adrenal glands situated on the top of each kidney).

The layer of fat formed under the skin (adipose tissue) acts as a heat insulator and can be formed as adaptation to cold conditions (and by the eating of suitably large amounts of carbohydrates) in a sporting context such as long-distance swimming.

ENERGY METABOLISM

The total intake of food must be sufficient to supply enough energy to keep cells alive, their systems working, and to meet the demands of any activity that the body undertakes. The **basal metabolic rate** is the body's basic cost of living and the **total metabolic rate** is the sum of the basal metabolic costs plus all the energy needed to carry out all daily activities. The energy requirements of an individual vary according to age, size, metabolic rate, gender, environment, and life style, and they are discussed in Chapter 5.

Fuel foods for action

Both carbohydrates and fats are used to supply **glycogen** necessary for all forms of physical activity. However, the utilization of carbohydrates and fats as nutrient fuels for muscle contraction during physical activity depends on the types of muscular activity; whether the work is intermittent, prolonged, light or heavy—in other words, the **exercise duration** and **exercise intensity**. Table 24 describes these relationships.

Table 24

Exercise intensity	Exercise duration	Fuel used
maximal sprint	short	carbohydrate
low to moderate	moderate up to 2 hours e.g. jogging	carbohydrate and fat equally
severe	prolonged e.g. cycling	less carbohydrate more fat

Training and fuel use

The influence of endurance training on metabolic mixture and rate of energy utilization is illustrated in Figure 3.16. This graph shows that untrained sportspersons who exercise at a low intensity will obtain the majority of their energy requirements from carbohydrates (column A). But if they continue to exercise long term at the same intensity, their metabolic systems will adapt by using more fat from the diet (and therefore less carbohydrate proportionately, column B). This means that more carbohydrate is available for the energy needed for increased effort during aerobic exercise (column C). Therefore, the total energy available to the adapted metabolism from both fats and carbohydrates increases, and the sportsperson becomes fitter and capable of more exercise.

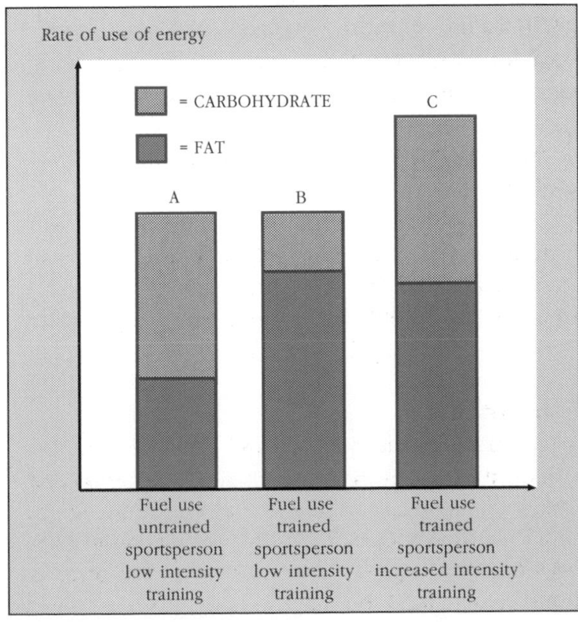

Figure 3.16

You may wish to extend this area of study. For example, it is possible to measure the rate of respiration using simple respirometers, and calculate respiratory quotients for proteins, fats and carbohydrates:

$$RQ = \frac{\text{volume of } CO_2 \text{ given off}}{\text{volume of } O_2 \text{ taken up}}$$

(See Simpkin and Williams, 1987, p. 80 onwards.)

REVIEW QUESTIONS

1. What are the purposes of each of the three basic groups of food?
2. How can high-carbohydrate diets influence metabolism?
3. How do you think different types of exercise could alter food intake?
4. Select two physical activities, one of short duration and high intensity and one of long duration and low intensity.
   a) Describe with the aid of a bar chart, the relative contributions of carbohydrates and fats as fuel foods for your two chosen activities.
   b) Account for the differences between fuel usage for your two chosen activities.
   c) Sketch a graph to illustrate the relationship between short, high intensity exercise and prolonged low intensity exercise and food fuel usage (ref. Bowers and Fox, *Sports Physiology*, Fig. 4.1, p. 57).

Summary

1. You should understand the functions of carbohydrates, fats, proteins, minerals, vitamins, roughage and water in the context of a balanced diet.
2. You should be able to appreciate the role of carbohydrates and fats in relation to intensity and duration of the exercise period.

FURTHER READING

Bowers R.W. and Fox E.L. *Sports Physiology* 3e, Wm.C. Brown, 1992

Katch F.I. *Introduction to Nutrition, Exercise and Health* 4e, Lea & Febiger, 1993.

McArdle W.D., Katch F.I. and Katch V.L. *Essentials of Exercise Physiology*, Lea & Febiger, 1994.

Simpkin J. and Williams J.I. *Advanced Human Biology*, Unwin Hyman, 1987.

Wootton S. *Nutrition For Sport*, Simon and Schuster, 1988.

Wootten S. *Nutrition and Sports Performance Resource Pack*, NCF, 1985.

Chapter 4
Training for Physical Performance

4.1 Physical Fitness and Fitness Testing

KEY WORDS AND CONCEPTS

fitness	**flexibility**	**speed**
motor fitness	**balance**	**power**
physical fitness	**body composition**	**construct validation**
agility	**co-ordination**	**reaction time**

Physical fitness is one of the basic requirements of life. Broadly speaking, it means the ability to carry out our daily tasks without undue fatigue. In the sporting context it is difficult to define since it can refer to psychological, physiological or anatomical states of the body. To most physical education teachers it is seen as a concept obtained by measuring and evaluating a person's state of fitness by using a battery of tests.

This section will help you to understand those aspects of **fitness** which are important to physical performance and good health.

TYPES OF FITNESS TEST

1. **Motor fitness tests** aim to look at neuromuscular components of fitness and therefore consider skill-related exercises and the capacity of the individual to repeat a particular exercise.
2. **Physical fitness tests** aim to look at anatomical and physiological components which determine a person's physical performance capacity. These tests make direct measurements of physiological parameters such as heart rate, oxygen uptake and flexibility.

The ability of a person to perform successfully at a particular game may not be an indicator of physical fitness, but an assessment of the motor fitness of the individual to perform the specific skills relevant to the game. Motor fitness refers to the **efficiency** of movements and, although including the **power** component, is mostly about **balance**, **agility** and **co-ordination**.

PHYSICAL FITNESS

The concept of **physical fitness**, in general athletic terms, means the capability of the individual to meet the varied physical and physiological demands made by a sporting activity, without reducing the person to an excessively fatigued state. Such a state would be one in which he/she can no longer perform the skills of the activity accurately and successfully.

The components of physical fitness are defined in Figure 4.1.

Strength is defined as the force exerted by muscle groups during a single maximal muscle contraction. (Refer to Chapter 1, which describes different types of muscle contractions.)

Endurance is the capacity to sustain movement or effort over a period of time. **Local muscle endurance** is the ability of the muscles to repeat movements without undue fatigue, while **cardiovascular endurance** is the ability of the cardiovascular system to transport oxygen to muscles during sustained exercise.

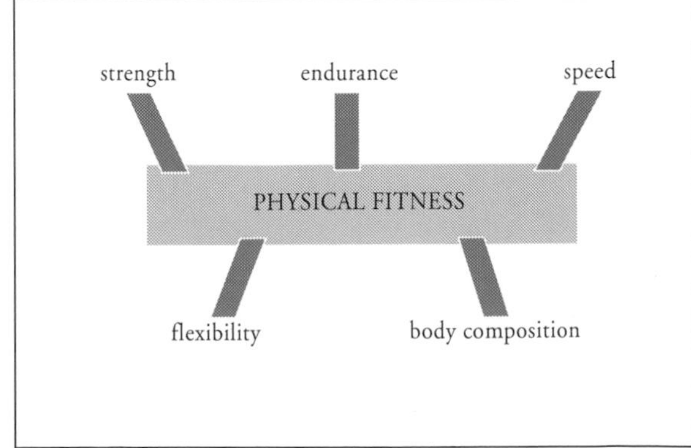

Figure 4.1

Speed is the maximum rate at which a person is able to move his/her body over a specific distance. In physical performance terms it refers to the speed of co-ordinated joint actions and whole body movements.

Flexibility is the range of movement possible at a joint. It is affected by the type of joint and muscle attachment.

Body composition is the concept describing the relative percentage of muscle, fat and bone. Body composition analysis is a suitable tool for the assessment of a person's state of fitness.

MOTOR FITNESS

Motor fitness refers to the ability of a person to perform successfully at a **particular** game or activity. Although there is an overlap in the components essential to both physical fitness and motor fitness, there are specific components, identified in Figure 4.2, which enable a person to perform a skill successfully and which are more directly relevant to motor fitness.

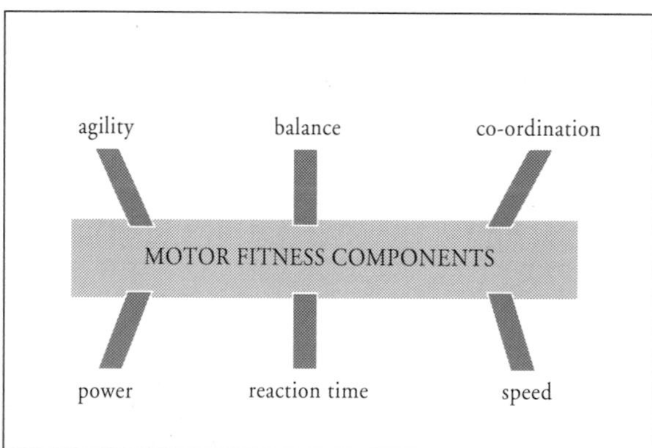

Figure 4.2

Agility is the physical ability which enables a person rapidly to change body position and direction in a precise manner.

Balance is the ability to retain the centre of mass of the body above the base of support. It is the awareness of the body's position in space and depends upon co-ordination between ears, brain, skeleton and muscles. **Static balance** is the ability to hold a balance in a stationary position, **dynamic balance** is the ability to maintain balance under changing conditions of body movement, shape and orientation.

Co-ordination is the ability to perform smooth and accurate motor tasks often involving the use of the senses and a series of correlated muscular contractions affecting a range of joints and therefore relative limb and body positions.

Power is a combination of **strength** and **speed** previously described as a component of physical fitness.

Reaction time is the interval of time between the presentation of a stimulus and the initiation of the muscular response to that stimulus.

Investigation 4.1 : The measurement of Fitness components

You are going to measure a number of indicators of your physical and motor fitness. The fitness ratings for each task are based on national norms for 16–19-year-olds. Results and scores for each test should be recorded in Table 35.

Before commencing this practical work make sure that you warm up thoroughly.

Task One —self-evaluation of body strength

1. Grip strength: to test grip strength.

Materials: hand grip dynanometer.

Use a hand grip dynanometer to **measure** grip strength. Record the maximum reading from three attempts from your dominant hand. and grip rating.

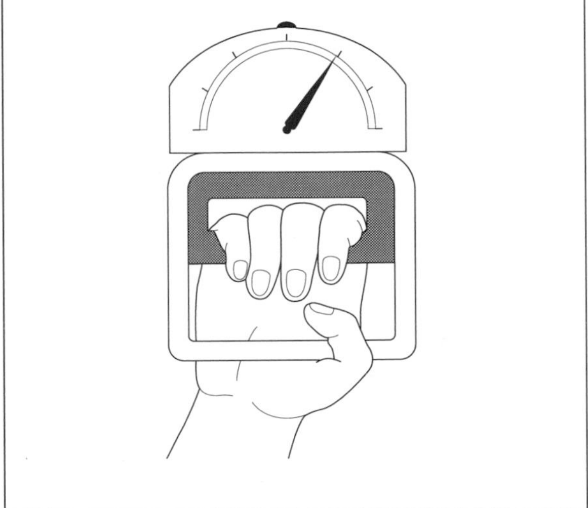

Figure 4.3 Hand grip dynanometer.

Table 25 : Grip rating

Dynamometer (kg) males	females	Rating
> 56	> 36	excellent
51-56	31-36	good
45-50	25-30	average
39-44	19-24	fair
< 39	< 19	poor

2. Vertical jump: to test the leg power vertically upwards.

Materials: vertical jump board.

Adjust the vertical jump board so that its lower edge touches your finger tips as both arms are held overhead at full body stretch with feet flat on the floor. Prepare to take off from both feet, flex your knees and then jump as high as you can, touching the calibrated scale with the finger tips of one hand. Record the maximum height from three attempts.

Table 26 : Vertical jump rating

Vertical jump (cm) males	females	Rating
> 65	> 58	excellent
50-65	47-58	good
40-49	36-46	average
30-39	26-35	fair
< 30	< 26	poor

Figure 4.4 Vertical jump.

Task Two—self-evaluation of local muscular endurance

1. Chins: to test strength and muscular endurance of the arm and shoulder muscles.

Materials: chinning bar.

Hang from a bar with your palms facing away from your body. Pull up until your chin is level with the bar. Repeat as many chins as possible ensuring that your arms reach a straight position between each effort. Record the number of chins achieved and the chin rating.

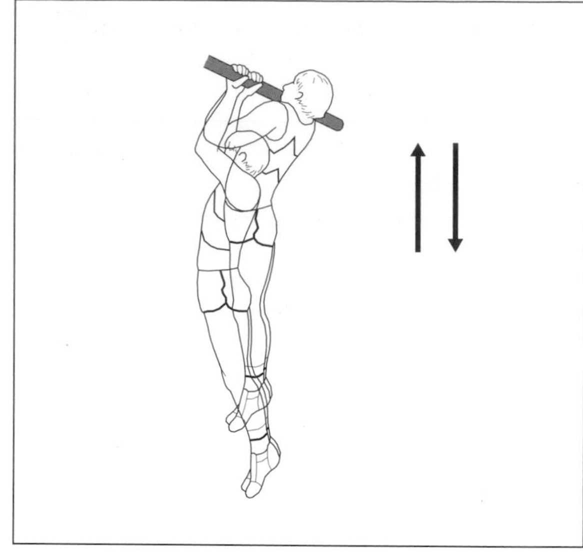

Figure 4.5 Chinning bar.

Table 27 : Chin rating

Number of chins: males	Number of chins: females	Rating
> 13	> 6	excellent
9-12	5-6	good
6-8	3-4	average
3-5	1-2	fair
< 3	0	poor

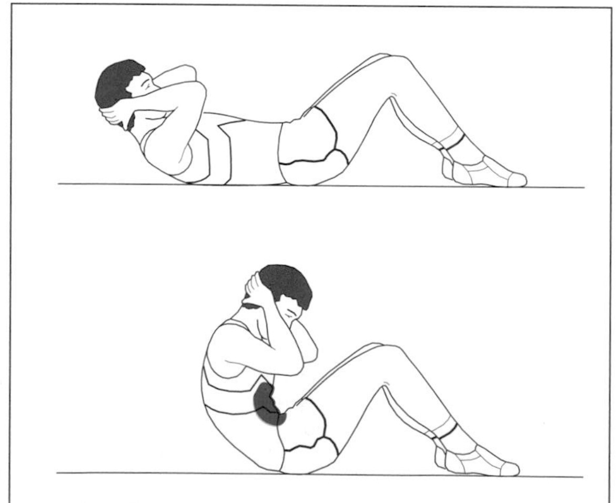

Figure 4.6 Sit-ups.

2. Sit-ups: to test the strength and muscular endurance of the abdominal muscles.

Lie down on a mat with your knees flexed at right angles. Get a partner to hold your feet and, on a signal, perform as many sit-ups (between your shoulders touching the ground and elbows touching your knees) as you can in 30 seconds. Get your partner to count the number of sit-ups achieved at 30 seconds. Record the number achieved and sit-up rating.

Table 28 : Sit-up rating

Number of sit ups in 30 sec: males	Number of sit ups in 30 sec: females	Rating
> 30	> 25	excellent
26-30	21-25	good
20-25	15-20	average
17-19	9-14	fair
< 16	< 8	poor

Task Three—self-evaluation of cardiovascular endurance

The Queen's College Step Test: to test cardiovascular endurance.

Materials: stepping bench (41 cm high), stop-watch, metronome.

This test for cardiovascular fitness is described in detail in Investigation 3.5, p. 106. The results have been extrapolated from the percentile rankings for recovery heart rate and predicted maximal oxygen consumption.

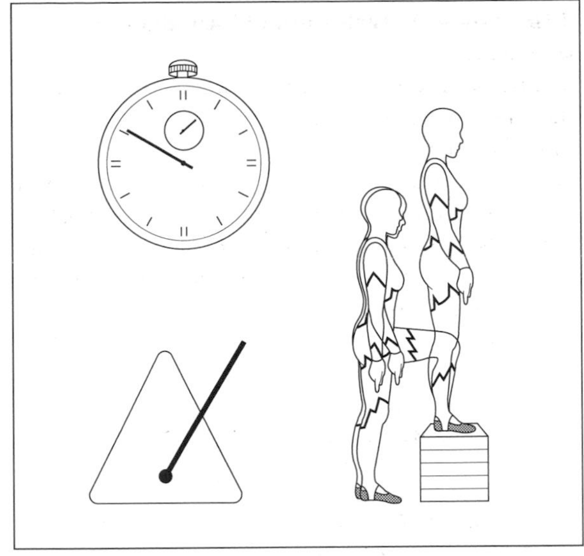

Figure 4.7 Step test.

Table 29 : Step test rating

Heart rate in bpm males	females	Rating
< 120	< 128	excellent
148-121	158-129	good
156-149	166-159	average
162-157	170-167	fair
> 162	> 170	poor

Task Four—self-evaluation of speed

30 metres sprint: to test the speed of a performer over 30 metres.

Materials: 50 metre tape-measure, stop-clock.

Mark out 30 m on your selected running surface. Using a flying start, sprint as hard as you can between the marked areas. Make sure that your sprint is timed by a partner from the start to the finish line, and record your time and speed rating.

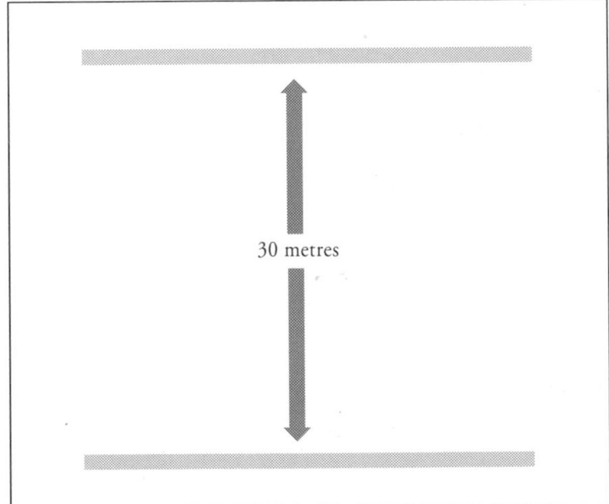

Figure 4.8 Speed test.

Table 30 : Speed rating

Time for 30m sprint males	females	Rating
< 4.0	< 4.5	excellent
4.2-4.0	4.6-4.5	good
4.4-4.3	4.8-4.7	average
4.6-4.5	5.0-4.9	fair
>4.6	>5.0	poor

Task Five—self evaluation of flexibility

Sit and reach test: to test the flexibility of the hips.

Materials: gymnastics bench, metre ruler.

Turn a gymnastics bench on its side and sit on the floor with your legs straight and feet flat against the side of the secured bench. Place a ruler on the upturned bench so that it extends 15 cm over the end of the bench, with the zero end extending towards you. Reach slowly forward as far as you can go and hold. Get a partner to read off the distance, in cm, past your heels to the stretched distance that your finger-tips have reached on the ruler. Record this distance and your flexibility rating.

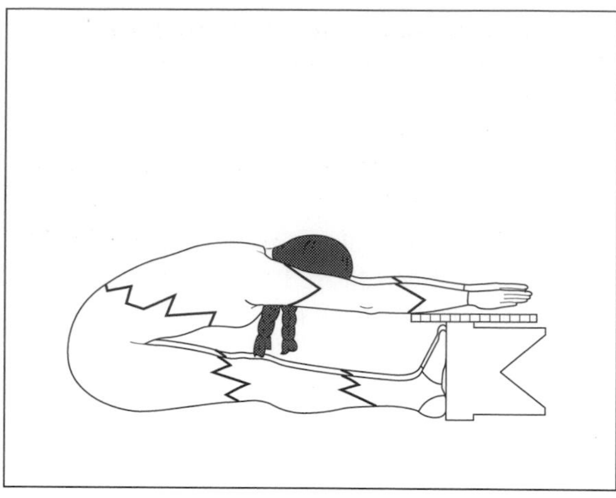

Figure 4.9 Sit and reach.

Table 31 : Sit and reach rating

Flexibility (cm) males	Flexibility (cm) females	Rating
> 14	> 15	excellent
11-13	12-14	good
7-10	7-11	average
4-6	4-6	fair
< 3	< 3	poor

Task Six—self-evaluation of body composition

Skinfold measurements: to test skinfold measurements taken at three sites on the body.

Materials: skinfold calipers.

Take three skinfold measurements at the three locations indicated in Figure 4.10. Add together these three skinfold measurements and evaluate your body fatness in relation to the skinfold rating chart.

Table 32 : Skinfold rating

Sum of skinfold thickness (mm) males	females	Rating
< 22	< 25	excellent
34-22	42-25	good
73-35	65-43	average
90-74	82-66	fair
> 90	> 82	poor

(The information for this rating chart has been taken from Pollock, Schmidt and Jackson, 1980.)

Figure 4.10 Skinfold measurements.

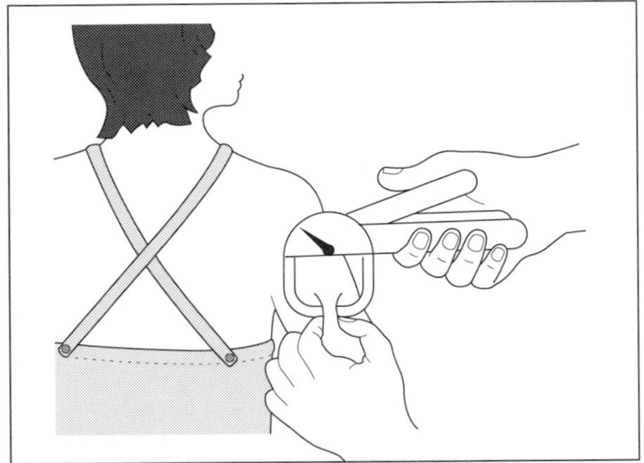

a. Triceps

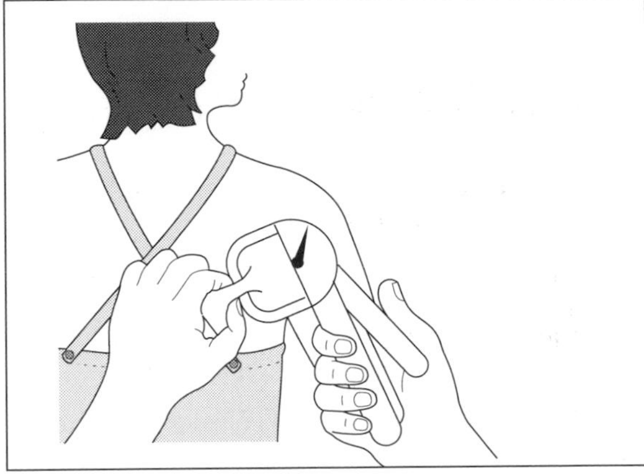

b. Scapula

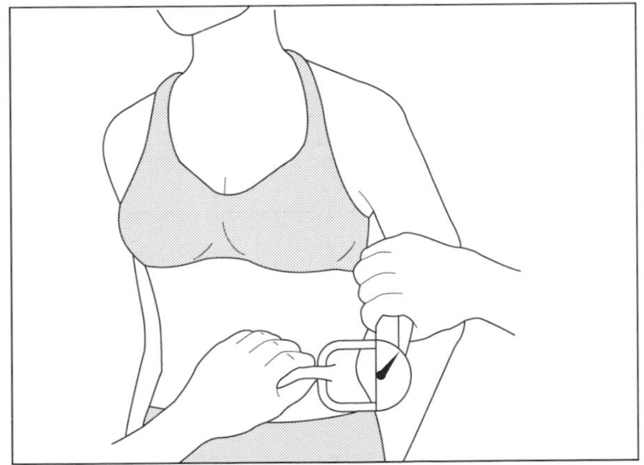

c. Abdomen

Task Seven—self-evaluation of agility

The Illinois Agility Run: to test speed and agility.

Materials: cones, tape-measure.

Mark out an area of 10 m in length and place four obstacles, 3.3 m apart as shown in Figure 4.11.

Lie prone, head to start line, hands beside your shoulders. On the command *'go'* run the course as fast as possible. Get a member of your group to issue the start command and time the run. Record your time and fitness rating.

Table 33 : Agility run rating

Time in seconds males	Time in seconds females	Rating
< 15.2	< 17.0	excellent
16.1-15.2	17.9-17.0	good
18.1-16.2	21.7-18.0	average
18.3-18.2	23.0-21.8	fair
> 18.3	> 23.0	poor

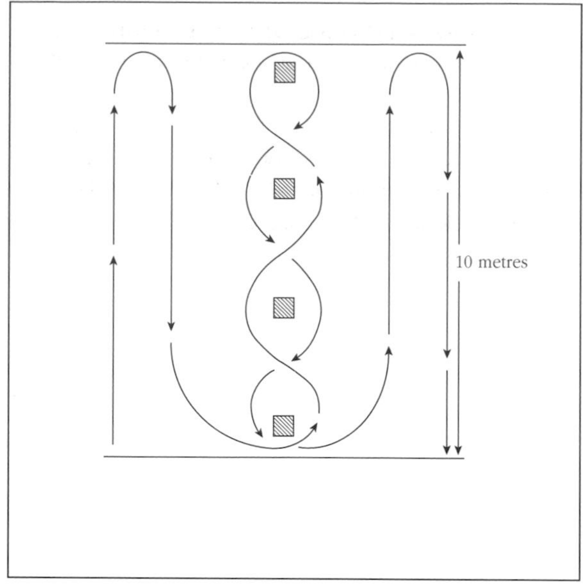

Figure 4.11 Agility run.

Task Eight—self-evaluation of static balance

Balancing on a beam: to test a timed static balance.

Materials: gymnastics bench.

Time how long balance can be maintained on one foot, with eyes closed, on a balance beam or inverted bench. Within your class use everyone's results to devise a rating scale.

Figure 4.12 Balancing on a beam.

Task Nine—self-evaluation of co-ordination

Juggling: to test how long it takes you to learn how to juggle.

Materials: tennis balls.

Time how long it takes you to learn to juggle three balls as illustrated in Figure 4.13. Within your class use everyone's results to devise a rating scale.

Figure 4.13 Juggling.

Task Ten—self-evaluation of reaction time

The stick drop test: to test the time it takes you to catch a ruler.

Materials: metre ruler.

Place a metre ruler against the wall. The partner holds the ruler against the wall at the zero end of the metre ruler. You place your preferred hand level with the 50 cm mark on the ruler, but not touching it. Without warning the partner lets go of the stick and you must catch it with thumb and index finger. Your score is the number just above your index finger. Assess your rating with results shown in Table 34.

Figure 4.14 Stick drop test.

Table 34 : Stick drop test rating

Reaction time (score in cm)	Rating
> 42.5	excellent
37.1-42.5	good
29.6-37	average
22-29.5	fair
< 22	poor

Task Eleven

1. Record all your results in Table 35 and, using these results, put together an assessment of your own personal physical and motor fitness profile.
2. How do your rating values compare with the given norms?
3. Describe the physiological value to the body of each of the tests you have done.
4. How could you use your results to best effect?

Table 35 : Results table — physical fitness and motor fitness tests

Exercise	Score	Rating
grip strength		
vertical jump		
chins		
sit-ups		
step test		
30 metre sprint		
flexibility		
skinfold measurements		
agility run		
static balance		
co-ordination		
reaction time		

VALIDITY OF FITNESS TESTING

Validity in any kind of testing is always a key issue for discussion. The major problem is whether the actual test measures precisely what it aims to measure. Nearly all tests measure other aspects of physical and motor fitness which are not defined in the test criteria. For example, a sit-up test measures dynamic strength. It could also be used to measure endurance and flexibility. A person may achieve a high score on the motor fitness components of the test and as a result inflate his/her overall test score, inspite of his/her possible weak physical fitness abilities.

To overcome this problem, pioneers of battery testing devised the theory of **construct validation**. This theory accounts for any measure of an aspect of physical or motor fitness which is not defined in the objectivity of the test (refer to *The Structure and Measurement of Physical Fitness,* by E.A. Fleishman, for a detailed discussion of this idea).

Simple tests, such as the 30 metre sprint, are also affected by motivation and previous experience. It is therefore important to recognize the limitations of such tests if they are to be used as assessment tools of physical fitness.

REVIEW QUESTIONS

1. How could a knowledge of physical and motor tests assist you in assessing the general training needs of the individual sportsperson?

2. Identify the specific physical fitness components in the following activities: gymnastics, sprint running, tennis, long-distance running. (AEB exam question.)

Summary

1. You should be able to identify physical and motor fitness components.

2. You should be able to devise tests for these components.

3. You should be able to appreciate that major dilemmas have been identified in the validity of fitness testing.

FURTHER READING

Biddle S. *Foundations of Health Related Fitness*, Ling Pub., 1987.

Bosco J.S. and Gustafson W.F. *Measurement and Evaluation in Physical Education, Fitness and Sports*, Prentice Hall, 1983.

Corbin B.C. and Lindsey R. *Concepts of Physical Fitness with Laboratories*, Wm. C. Brown, 1991.

Fleishman E.A. *The Structure and Measurement of Physical Fitness*, Prentice Hall, 1964.

Hockey R.V. *Physical Fitness, The Pathway to Healthy Living* 7e, Mosby–Year Book, 1993.

Pollock, Schmidt and Jackson. Measurement of cardiorespiratory fitness and body composition in the clinical setting, *Comprehensive Therapy*, 6 September 1980.

Prentice W. *Fitness for College and Life* 4e, Mosby–Year Book, 1994.

Safrit M.J. *Introduction to Measurement in Physical Education and Exercise Science* 2e, Mosby–Year Book, 1990.

Sharkey B.J. *Coaches Guide to Sport Physiology*, Human Kinetics, 1986.

Sharkey B.J. *Physiology of Fitness* 3e, Human Kinetics, 1990.

4.2 Training

KEY WORDS AND CONCEPTS

adaptation	**bradycardia**	**warm-up**
duration	**regression**	**cool-down**
progression	**inhibition**	**alveolar oxygen tension**
intensity	**specificity**	**acclimatization**
hypertrophy	**agonist/antagonist response**	**partial pressure of oxygen**
frequency	**variance**	**barometric pressure**
capillarization	**transfer**	**haemoglobin — oxygen saturated & unsaturated**
overload		

This is where the largely theoretical ideas involved in the discussion on the systems which provide the energy necessary for human exercise become directly related to day-to-day sporting activities.

The idea is that we should use our knowledge of the scientific basis of exercise to help us improve performance at our sport, and do this in a systematic and predictable way.

Unfortunately, nothing a human being does is ever thoroughly predictable, and psychological, cultural and emotive factors tend to upset the true progress of science. However, the aims of physical training can be enhanced only by using what we know of physiology to help us.

The aims and objectives of training are to improve performance, skill, game ability, and motor and physical fitness. Some individuals will use training purely as a recreational activity in itself, in which case the outcome will hopefully be to enhance fitness and personal health without relation to any other skill or game. This latter case will not make the activity any less worthwhile, but in the section below we aim to relate the needs of a sporting activity to the **extra** activities needed to enhance the quality of the sportsperson's performance.

THE PRINCIPLES OF TRAINING

Time—duration

The priority of training is that its aims must be long-term. Biological, physiological, psychomotor, neuromuscular and cardiovascular changes all take time to develop and become consolidated within human structures.

This idea is **not** about how often or how intense the training is, since it is true that light exercise/training done infrequently but regularly over a period of time has a beneficial effect on health and fitness. This is because the efficiency of the cardiovascular system and capability of the musculature to cope with day-to-day activities outside the sporting context are improved.

We have already discussed, and will discuss again below, how the human system responds to exercise—such **adaptation** response does not take place instantly.

Training intensity—overload

Overload is the term used to describe training activities which are harder/more intense/lengthier than the normal physical activity undertaken by an individual.

Overload places the human system under **stress**, and the human/biological system responds by becoming more capable of coping with this stress.

How does this happen? The following investigation gives a simple insight into one aspect of this effect.

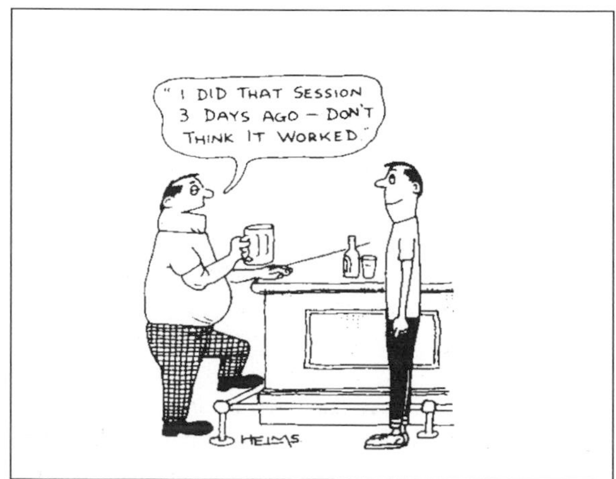

Figure 4. 15

Investigation 4.2 : Response to overload in weight training

As mentioned above, it will not be possible to obtain any measurable effect of any training or exercise regime which takes place within the teaching context, i.e. within only a short period of time. It is therefore suggested that the activity described below takes place over at least two weeks and preferably longer.

At least two students should undertake this investigation together, so that safety procedures and monitoring of the activity of one by the other can be ensured.

Task One—initial assessment

1. The aim of this session is to assess the maximal strength of the student on four different exercises. These are shown in Figure 4.16.

Figure 4. 16

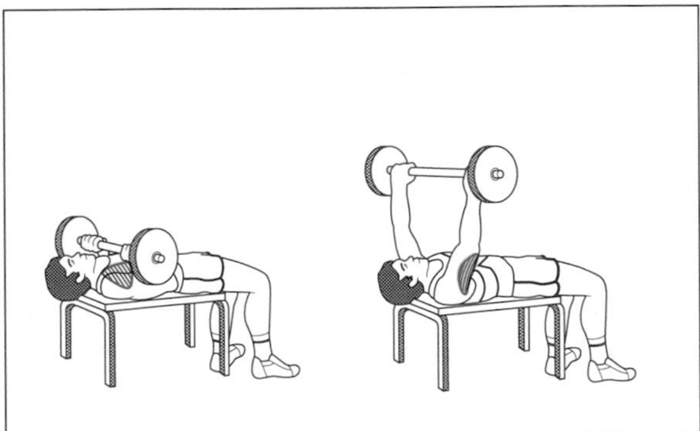

a. Bench press.

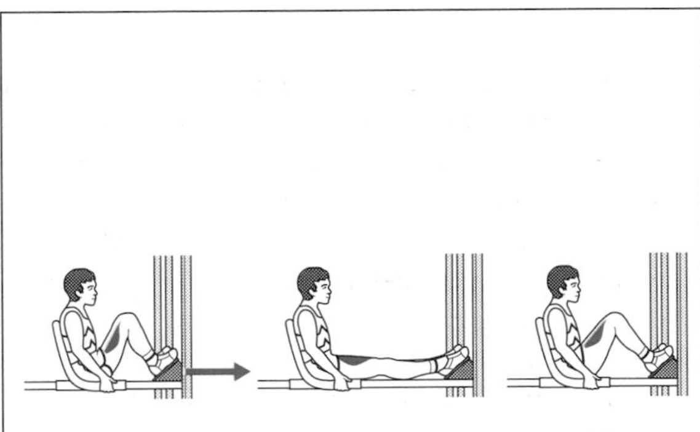

b. Leg press.

c. Pull down.

d. Sit-up or inclined sit-up.

2. The exercises have been chosen to be suitable for a multigym exercise machine. If one is not available, suitable free weight exercises should be used. If this is the case, take care over the safety of the lifter.
3. Students should perform a warm-up consisting of 5 minutes, jogging, 5 minutes, general muscle stretching, and 5 press-ups, 5 free squats, and 5 sit-ups.
4. The exercises should be done in turn starting at an easily achievable low level of weight or incline (sit-up), and then progressing by the smallest increases for each exercise until the student fails a lift. The highest successful lift is then recorded in Table 36.

For example, suppose the student starts at 20 kg for the bench press—he/she does this once, then progresses to 25 kg, does this once, and progresses to 30 kg—does this once, and so on, until no further weight can be lifted.

In the case of the sit-ups, the student could begin on the flat and gradually increase the angle of the inclined sit-up board until he/she fails—the highest rung/angle achieved being recorded. Alternatively, a disc weight may be used in the same way as the other exercises and the biggest disc lifted recorded.

Task Two—programme of exercise

1. The student then calculates 60 per cent of the maximum and notes this in the table below. This will be the load to be lifted for the first week of the programme.
2. The student will perform five **sets** of six **repetitions** of each exercise at the 60 per cent (or nearest possible below) level, with a 60 second interval between sets.
3. The schedule involves two sessions per week separated by at least two days—this must be continued for the period of the investigation.

Task Three—progression

1. It will make things more interesting if the student increases the load as the weeks go by—this is called **progressive overload.**
2. This can be done by increasing the load by one weight on the multigym per week (or, say, 5 kg for a free weight exercise).
3. Weights lifted should be recorded in Table 36.

Table 36 : Results table

Session	Bench press	Leg press	Pull down	Sit-up
assessment				
60 per cent				
session 1				
session 2				
session 3				
final session				
final assessment				
% improvement				

Task Four—final assessment

1. The student should have at least three days' rest between the last session of the main programme and this element.
2. The procedure of Task One above is now repeated and the results recorded in the final assessment row of Table 36.

Task Five—analysis of results

1. Now compute the percentage improvement for each exercise—results in the bottom row of Table 36.
2. Is the observed increase in measured strength a **real** increase in strength, or could there be other factors enhancing the results?
3. What other noticeable effects can you observe on your body?

Task Six—recovery after exercise

1. Comment on how your body has adapted to recovery between sets (of an exercise).
2. Make notes on breathing rates, pulse rates and whether or not you had recovered fully before the next set.
3. Did you have muscle soreness the next day?

Figure 4. 17

RESULTS OF LABORATORY TESTS ON STRENGTH TRAINING

Figure 4.18 shows the results of a strength training programme based on a single maximal contraction of a muscle group.

Note that the measured strength gain is most rapid at the beginning of the programme, but lessens towards the sixth week—this is called 'plateauing out', and is an inevitable outcome of regular training of the same muscle groups with the same exercise.

The question is, how much of this observed strength gain is **real**, and due to physiological adaptation (discussed below), and how much is a **learned response** due to **use** of the muscles and neuromuscular adaptation (of the brain and other parts of the nervous system)? Furthermore, would strength gain continue to increase if more stimulating and motivating exercise were substituted?

From this you will see that physiology is not the only consideration in producing training overload. Psychological and other motivational factors can contribute to making overload effective, in that the sportsperson needs to apply effort, without which overload is only apparent.

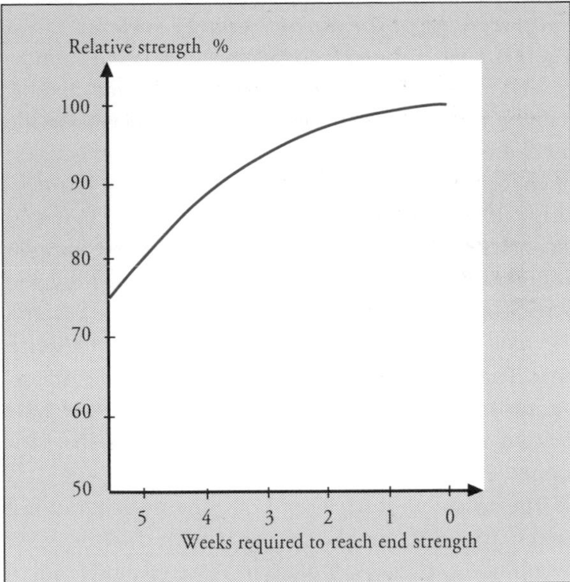

Figure 4. 18 Results of a strength training programme. (Following de Vries, 1986.)

EFFECTS OF OVERLOAD—ADAPTATION

The simple investigation above aims to show the effects of stressing the body a certain way. There are many ways of doing so, with different results. The effects of long term training on the body are that physiological adaptations occur in almost every tissue or system and these changes allow the body to perform more effectively. The simple investigation above aims to show the effects of stressing the body in a certain way. Overload training significantly improves a variety of aerobic and anaerobic functional capacities, the most notable including the following:

1. Effects on energy systems within cells

Enhancement of the ATP–PC energy system (see Figure 4.19)

If exercises requiring large amounts of instant energy lasting less than ten seconds are repeated, with full recovery between repetitions, then the stores of ATP and PC within muscle cell sarcoplasm are increased, thereby enabling more energy to be available.

If the other energy systems are **not stressed,** then it is found that these **diminish** in comparison with the ATP–PC system.

Enhancement of the lactic anaerobic energy system

Again, if overloads are experienced for periods of time up to 60 seconds (with only partial recovery between efforts), it is found that glycogen stores in muscle are enhanced (possibly by virtue of an increase in size and number of fast twitch muscle fibres/cells which preferentially and more rapidly store glycogen) and are more effectively utilized (through increases in the amount of glycogen-converting enzymes found in fast twitch muscle fibres that control the anaerobic phase of glucose breakdown—the cells themselves being increased in size and number). This is in addition to larger amounts of ATP. The buffering capacity of the muscle is increased because the muscle can work longer before the hydrogen ion concentration gets sufficiently high enough to inhibit enzyme action and therefore muscle contraction.

Enhancement of the aerobic energy system

There are several major adaptations that occur in muscle as a result of aerobic training. Prolonged aerobic training improves the aerobic system by increasing the number and size of mitochondria and also the levels of mitochondrial enzymes in skeletal muscle, particularly within slow twitch muscle fibres. This adaptation increases the ability of skeletal muscle to use oxygen at higher rates over longer periods of time. Prolonged aerobic exercise increases muscle glycogen stores and the trained muscles' capacity to mobilize and oxidize fats. This is beneficial to endurance-based athletes because it conserves carbohydrate stores (otherwise known as glycogen sparing) so important to prolonged exercise regimes.

The oxidative capacity of both slow twitch and fast twitch fibres is improved (particularly for the slow twitch fibres) as a result of an increase of muscle myoglobin content (which facilitates oxygen diffusion to the mitochondria) in addition to increasing the numbers and size of mitochondria and mitochondrial oxidative enzymes mentioned above.

Arteriovenous oxygen difference ($a\text{-}\bar{v}O_2$ *diff*) increases due to increased capillary density resulting in a shorter diffusion distance between the blood and the muscle cell and increased myoglobin and mitochondrial density. The net effect is for venal blood returning from working muscles to the heart is to be almost completely depleted of oxygen. However, this blood then mixes with venous blood from less active parts of the body and so overall the arteriovenous oxygen difference shows little change in the mixed venous return.

If aerobic exercise **only** is done (i.e. a training regime with **no** fast dynamic exercises), it is found that ATP and PC stores within muscle are depleted, thereby reducing the muscular capacity for strong rapid movements.

Threshold

This is the term used to describe the point at which use of one energy system is exhausted.

The moment exercise begins for a particular muscle or group of muscles, **all** mechanisms for remanufacture of ATP begin. However, high intensity exercise would deplete ATP so rapidly that the ATP–PC mechanism would be exhausted after a short period (ten seconds). At this point, the lactic anaerobic mechanism would provide the bulk of the ATP regeneration with a consequent reduction in power output as it takes longer for energy to become directly available to the muscle cell sarcoplasm.

Under full effort, eventually (after about 45 seconds in the trained athlete) the lactic system can no longer provide enough energy for demands made, so that the musculature will either cease functioning (collapse or tetanize) or require adjustment of effort to levels compatible with aerobic functioning, so that the oxygen debt can be purged.

These change-over times (thresholds) will vary between individuals, and depend very much on the **effort** put into the exercise, or the **rate** of energy use.

It is found that thresholds are delayed by training, so that the trained individual has greater capacity for ATP–PC and ATP regeneration, which means that high power exercise can continue longer. This is a direct consequence of the adaptation which provides more ATP in muscle sarcoplasm.

Figure 4.19 shows changes in ATP–PC to **lactic** thresholds between trained and untrained people.

The unbroken line shows how power output at maximum effort changes with time for the untrained person. The point at which power rapidly falls is the point at which ATP–PC stores are used up, and is therefore the ATP–PC to **lactic** threshold (at seven seconds in this example).

On the other hand, the trained athlete (dashed line) has a higher maximum power output and a delay in threshold (to about ten seconds) due to larger ATP–PC stores.

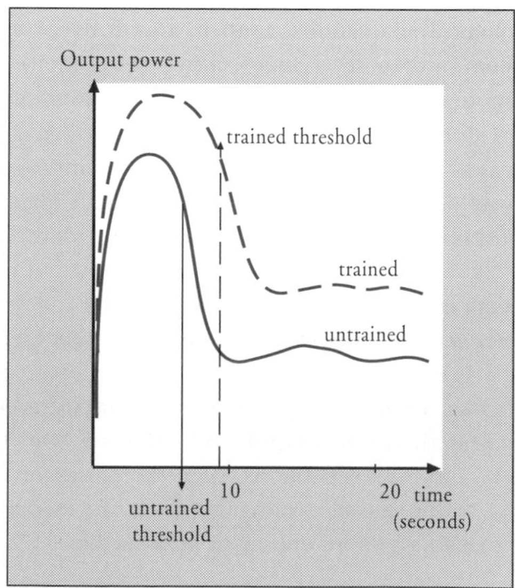

Figure 4.19 Difference in ATP—PC to lactic thresholds between trained and untrained people.

2. Muscle and soft tissue effects

Muscle adaptation

It is found that the most noticeable effect in muscle fibres of anaerobic training (particularly fast twitch, which respond when large forces are applied to a given muscle) is **muscle hypertrophy**. This is due to an increase in muscle width because more actin and myosin are assimilated: this will increase the strength of each fibre because more contractile protein allows for more cross-bridges to be formed (see p 41) and therefore the net effect will be an increase in the strength of contraction. In addition, there is evidence that more fibres are generated, possibly by longitudinal splitting of existing fast twitch fibres. The effect, therefore, is to make muscle bigger and stronger.

In highly trained anaerobic athletes fast twitch muscle fibres occupy a greater cross sectional area when compared with the slow twitch fibre content of a given muscle, whereas in highly trained aerobic athletes the reverse situation is found.

In trained sportspersons there is a noticeable increase in the recruitment of motor units (see p 44) and improved co-ordination of the firing of motor units to allow increases in strength (see p 45).

Capillarization

It is found that the blood supply to muscles undertaking aerobic exercise is enhanced by new capillaries being generated within the muscle bulk. An increase in capillary density results in a shorter diffusion distance between blood and muscle cells. This is in addition to the dilation, and therefore more effective use, of existing blood capillaries. The net effect is the evolvement of a more efficient oxygen transport system.

Bradycardia

One of the most obvious adaptations that occurs with endurance based training is a decrease in resting heart rate. Endurance athletes often have resting heart rates in the low 40's. **Bradycardia** is a term that describes a reduction in heart rate that is below 60 beats per minute caused by the enlargement of the heart muscle in response to its increased rate of activity, in the same way that skeletal muscle hypertrophy occurs. An increase in the thickness and strength of the left ventricular wall causes an increase in the stroke volume and a lowering of resting pulse for a given cardiac output (see Figure 2.8, p 57). This is the means by which greater blood volumes, and hence oxygen carrying capacity, are available to remaining musculature. Blood flow to the myocardium is slightly less during submaximal work rates since the heart is more efficient. Maximal cardiac output is increased to about the same extent as maximum stroke volume (see Figure 2.8, p 57).

Effects on tendons and other connective tissue

Tendon thickness and ligament strength and thickness are enhanced by stress. This appears to be a process of gradual protein assimilation. Articular cartilage also becomes thicker and more compressible when large forces are repeatedly applied. This has the effect of providing more cushioning to the ends of long bones under impact.

3. Respiratory effects

In response to the demand for oxygen, more lung alveoli become utilized, hence the lungs have a greater surface area for gaseous exchange. Also, the respiratory muscles become stronger, enabling larger gas volumes to be breathed per intake and exhaled more rapidly.

4. Recovery enhancement

This is not a separate effect, but more the combination of heart and lung adaptations which enable more oxygen to be available more rapidly during and immediately after exercise. Also, an enhanced capillary system supplies nutrients and glucose more efficiently to the muscular sites where they are needed.

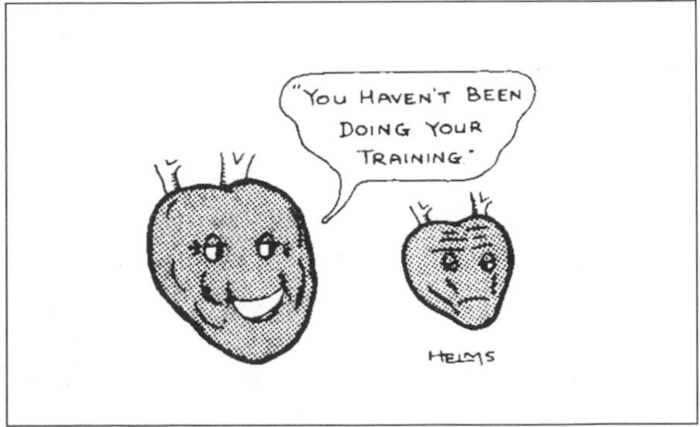

Figure 4.20

Sweating

Homeostasis is the maintenance of a constant internal bodily environment despite possible changes in external conditions. During exercise, the amount of heat energy produced is proportional to the intensity and duration of the exercise. The **thermoregulation centre**, which is situated in the **hypothalamus**, is sensitive to the temperature of the blood and sends out impulses to the skin, where appropriate action (for example, **sweating)** is taken. Another action is diversion of blood to the skin so that heat energy can be carried via blood from the musculature to the skin, where it is radiated away.

Sweating is therefore an evolutionary development which enables the human body to maintain approximately constant temperature, in spite of the inefficient energy transformation from chemical energy to useful work energy in the musculature.

Sweating provides moisture which evaporates from the skin surface. The energy required for this process is extracted from the skin which therefore loses heat energy and cools down. This response is again subject to adaptation when the body generates more heat as more exercise is done. Therefore, the capability of sweat production is enhanced by training. Similarly, if the individual moves to a warmer or more humid climate, bodily heat loss to the surroundings is reduced by external physical factors and the need to lose heat from the body surface is increased.

Figure 4.21

REGRESSION

It has been found that all the effects of training mentioned above **regress** to their normal untrained state if training ceases. Interestingly, it is found that effects established by **longer** periods of training remain for **longer** after training stops. Figure 4.22 shows an example of this.

Time is measured from the point at which training stops, which is when peak performance is observed. What is found is that exercise regimes which begin a long time before this point (*A* on the graph) enable the body to **retain** the increased fitness for a long time after training stops. On the other hand, training begun a short while beforehand (*B* on the graph), even though it may achieve high levels of fitness, will not promote much biological adaptation. In this case, fitness levels fall quickly after training stops.

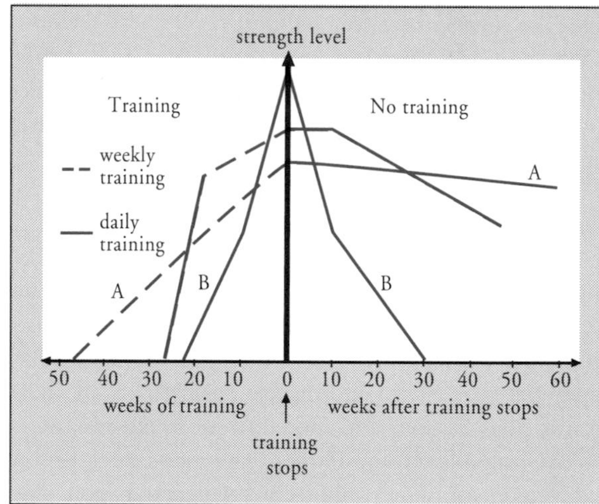

Figure 4.22 (After Harre *et al.*)

Figure 4.23

SPECIFICITY

This principle refers to the **relevance** of the **choice** of exercise to the activity to be improved. Choices to be made are:

1. Energy systems

Which energy system is to be stressed and therefore developed? (See Table 37.)

2. Strength/power or endurance

Which type of muscle fibre is to be stressed, and therefore made more efficient: fast twitch for stronger, faster more dynamic movements; or slow twitch for steady low force aerobic work?

3. Skill to be practised

Skills relevant to the sporting activity will need to be learnt. Perhaps some of the strength/endurance training can be done while skills are being practised?

The inference here is that the actual parts of the body to be used in the sport are to be stressed preferentially, leading to a direct improvement in the sport. This implies not only that their biology will be changed, but that **skill learning** will occur. Such learning is a product of the development of a **link** between the use of muscles and a **stimulus**; and also the development of more efficient use of the muscles in a sequence required by the stimulus. These changes occur in the brain and other parts of the nervous system.

Table 37

	% Emphasis according to energy system		
Sport/activity	**ATP–PC and LA**	**LA–O_2**	**O_2**
Basketball	60	205	20
Fencing	90	10	–
Field events	90	10	–
Golf swing	95	5	–
Gymnastics	80	15	5
Hockey	50	20	30
Long-distance running	10	20	70
Rowing	20	30	50
Skiing	33	33	33
Soccer	50	20	30
Sprints	90	10	–
Swimming 1500m	10	20	70
Tennis	70	20	10
Volleyball	80	5	15

(Adapted from Fox, Bower and Foss.)

The major problem here concerns the accuracy of the percentage contributions of the energy systems. The values in Table 37 are only estimates mainly because it is very difficult to accurately collect appropriate data. The important point to stress when using this table is that specific training programmes can be constructed. However, in activities lasting longer than three minutes and in all game situations, quick bursts of high intense activity are often interspersed with much longer periods of low activity. Therefore there is a need to develop aerobic conditioning with the ability to use the anaerobic mechanisms of energy supply when called on.

Investigation 4.3 : Training to learn a skill

Choose one of the following activities:

1. **soccer** (or field hockey): dribbling with the non-preferred foot (or reverse sticks for hockey).
2. **tennis** (or other racket game): striking a ball with the non-preferred hand.

Note: non-preferred means the limb not normally used for the game. We assume ambidextrous people don't exist.

Soccer or hockey: complete a course dribbling the ball **entirely** with the non-preferred foot (or reverse sticks). The course could be set up using cones and lines as in Figure 4.24. The course would be completed twice, and timed.

Figure 4.24

Tennis: hit a ball (completely free supply of balls) into a one-metre square marked on the gymnasium wall positioned one metre from the floor, as in Figure 4.25. This should be done if possible by hit and return. If the hit ball goes astray, the player should be fed another ball to continue the exercise.

This should be done for 30 seconds at each of 3 m, 6 m, and 9 m from the wall, the total number of accurate hits being recorded.

Figure 4.25

Task One—initial assessment

1. The chosen activity should be completed and the score recorded in Table 38.
2. This should be done in pairs, with the non-active student recording time/score, and, in the case of tennis, feeding balls when necessary. He/she should also check that the non-preferred limb is used.

Task Two—skill practice

The activity is repeated at least five times in two weeks (a total of six), and the times/scores recorded in Table 38.

Task Three—discussion of results

1. Have the scores improved over the period of the test?
2. If so, what factors have led to the improvement?
3. What other drills could you invent to enhance the skill chosen?

Table 38 : Results table

Session	Time / score
1	
2	
3	
4	
5	
6	

OTHER CHANGES OCCURRING WHEN MUSCLES ARE USED

1. Transfer

This is the idea that learning one skill will enhance the learning capability of another skill. For example, the practice of the skill of catching and throwing a ball rapidly and accurately may improve the sportsperson's ability to hit a ball with a racket firmly and accurately. This is discussed in more detail in Part Two, page 276.

2. The agonist/antagonist response

There is evidence that when a muscle is used, its **inhibition** to use is lessened. This enables more fibres to be activated and more force to be exerted. The antagonist is able to stretch without inhibition as the stretch reflex is repressed. This means that movements will become more fluent and less jerky as they are practised. The normal awkwardness of the first attempt at a skill is in part due to contraction of antagonists where they should be relaxing.

3. Body awareness

With repeated use of the musculature, even without a skill-related learning element (as in weight training), it becomes possible to learn complex skills more easily. The sportsperson becomes aware of how to operate certain muscle groups efficiently and can relate this to certain skill demands.

REPETITION

This principle underlies both overload and specificity. It seems essential to **repeat** an activity both to apply stress in suitable amounts, and to learn skills to a suitable degree of expertise. Generally speaking, it seems that the **more often** a system is stressed the **more rapidly** it will adapt to the stress. The **frequency** with which the exercise is repeated is therefore an important element of training.

MODERATION—INJURY

Unfortunately, the biggest cause of injury in the fit sportsperson is overtraining. Initially, most people find that training produces very noticeable effects on health and fitness, and it is tempting to increase overloads rapidly. If this process continues indefinitely, eventually the musculature and more probably other soft tissue (tendons, ligaments or cartilage, which take longer to adapt to increased stress) break down and injury occurs.

There is obviously a limit to what the body can cope with. The aim of training is to increase this limit **without exceeding** it. It therefore makes sense to apply the overload principle gradually and with moderation.

VARIANCE

The idea of variance is that training loads and skill demands should be varied with time. There are two sets of reasons for this:

1. Physiological reasons—the effects of repeated and prolonged stress on biological systems are:

- fatigue
- depletion of energy reserves
- raising of response threshold to stimulus (muscles do not respond as they ought)
- muscle soreness
- injury

Figure 4.26

It would therefore seem sensible to vary loads so that none of these factors causes regression.

2. Psychological reasons—varying training patterns and loads tends to:

- remove the emotive stress of coping with large amounts of exhausting and painful work
- enable learning and activity targets to be reassessed
- improve motivation

Figure 4.27

Investigation 4.4 : Variation of training loads

To research periodization

1. Write about two A4 sides on the training method known as **periodization.**
2. In your essay explain the meanings of **mesocycle**, **microcycle** and **period**, with suitable graphs or charts.
3. What advantage is there in choosing shorter mesocycles?

(*References*: Dick, 1984; Harre *et al.*, 1982.)

INDIVIDUAL RESPONSE

This training principle reflects the fact that no two individuals have the same training needs. The following factors need to be taken into account when designing a training programme:

1. Fitness needs

Differing fitness (endurance/strength/power) levels mean that different emphases will need to be placed on fitness factors in a training programme aimed at the same sport.

Fitness levels can be determined by a fitness testing assessment (see Section 4.1), which should also measure body composition.

2. Psychological needs

These include motivation, self-image, self-esteem and so on. The personal importance of these needs varies greatly between individuals.

Training should be organized so that clear goals are set and realistic targets for attainment agreed and understood.

Figure 4.28

3. Maturation

The individual's stage of development should be taken into account. It can be dangerous to subject people who have not reached maturity to high training loads. On the other hand, certain activities seem best learnt when young, and there is evidence that physical skill learning is a much slower process for older individuals.

4. Male/Female

Size and strength are usually less in the female, and therefore loads need to be adjusted accordingly. Menstruation can affect training loads, since there are body weight fluctuations as a result of monthly hormonal variations. There is also evidence that hormonal changes can affect joint stability. Generally, however, these effects are less important than size differences.

5. Cultural differences

Different attitudes to exercise and its place in one's lifestyle can play an important part in the effectiveness of training.

This applies particularly to female participation. Partner role, career prospects and self-image about size and muscularity still seem to be different between male and female sportspersons. The difference varies widely between societies and cultures. Roll on equal opportunities!

Figure 4.29

WARM-UP AND COOL-DOWN

The final principles of training to be discussed here are preparation of the body for exercise, and what to do immediately after exercise to minimize the risk of injury and muscle soreness.

1. Warm-up

Although anaerobic work can be done without using the oxygen carrying and delivery capacity of the cardiovascular system, replenishment of ATP and muscle glycogen depends on an efficient blood capillary system. Therefore, recovery from the oxygen debt is improved if light aerobic exercise is undertaken before training. This dilates capillaries and raises the pulse rate, pumping blood around the body more quickly.

A further effect of warm-up is to raise the body temperature. It has been shown that ATP conversion, glycolytic enzyme action and muscle reaction response times are speeded up at a slightly higher temperature.

Also, blood viscosity is slightly reduced at higher temperatures, so that the flow of blood (and its ability to pass through the capillary system) is improved. It is also found that light muscle stretching prepares the musculature for operation over its full range.

2. Cool-down

It seems important to do a small amount of aerobic work immediately after completion of a training session. This has the purpose of flushing the capillary system with oxygenated blood, thereby enabling oxygen debt in muscles to be fully purged, and lactic products of lactic anaerobic work to be converted and removed. This will hopefully limit muscle soreness and enhance recovery.

ALTITUDE TRAINING

Since the beginning of this century the effects of altitude on physical performance have been catalogued by mountaineers. The decision to hold the 1968 Olympic Games in Mexico City at an altitude of 2,242 metres (7,450 feet) resulted in intense physiological research into human acclimatization.

Human difficulties experienced at altitude

Sportspeople training or competing at high altitude suffer from acute drops in performance in sports relying on aerobic capacity. This is due to lack of oxygen. Figure 4.30 illustrates the oxygen transport system at sea-level and at altitude before and after acclimatization (Pugh, 1967).

The degree to which haemoglobin is saturated with oxygen depends on the partial pressure of the alveolar air. (See Chapter 2, p. 77, to review the concept of the oxygen–haemoglobin dissociation curve.) At sea-level, the partial pressure of oxygen in inspired air is sufficient to ensure that the haemoglobin is fully saturated. At altitude, the partial pressure of oxygen in the atmosphere and the pulmonary air is reduced. The result is that the haemoglobin is not fully saturated, therefore less oxygen is carried to muscle tissues and the aerobic working capacity of these tissues is reduced.

Physiological changes during acclimatization

Three major physiological changes occur in the body as a result of acclimatization:

1. Increase in blood haemoglobin concentrations

During acclimatization there is an increase in red blood cell count and therefore an increase in haemo-

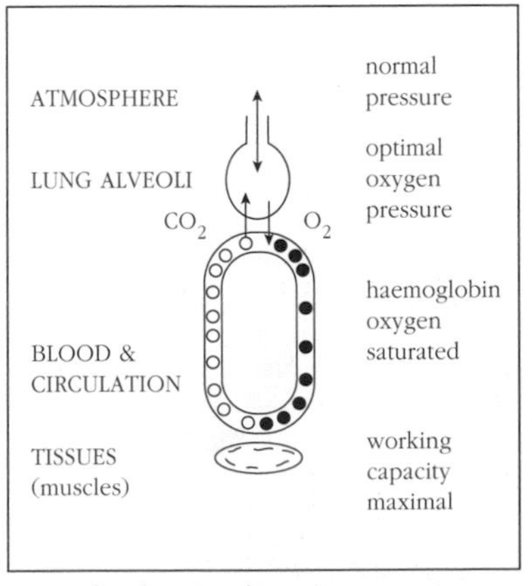

a. sea-level, normal

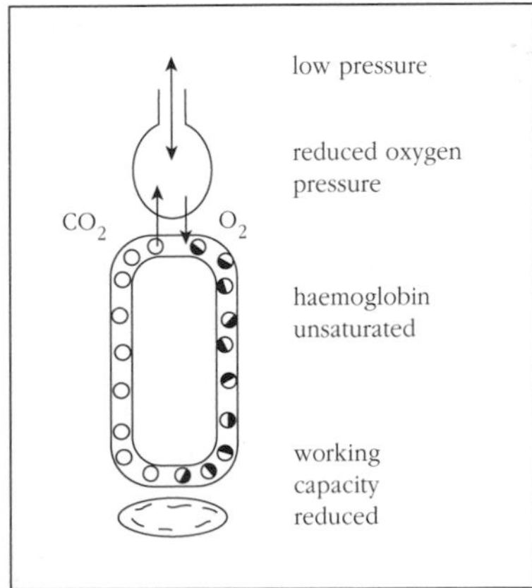

b. altitude, unacclimatized

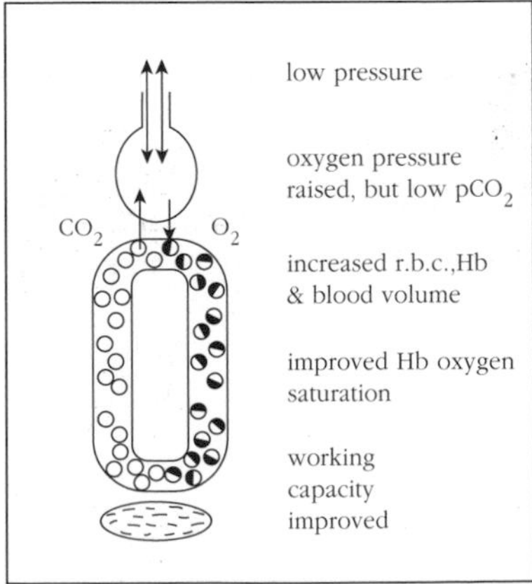

c. altitude, acclimatized

Figure 4.30 The oxygen transport system at sea-level and at altitudes, before and after acclimatization. (From Pugh, 1967.)
r.b.c. = red blood cells Hb = haemoglobin pCO_2 = partial pressure of carbon dioxide.

globin concentration, but the haemoglobin remains unsaturated with oxygen. The increase in red blood cell count is brought about by an increase in the manufacture of red blood cells, which is a rapid response made by the body to altitude; and a reduction in the plasma volume, which is a slow long-term response, as a result of acclimatization. It is found that haemoglobin concentrations of residents (who are presumably acclimatized) at altitude is inversely proportional to the prevailing barometric pressure (Pugh, 1964).

2. Increased rate of breathing

To compensate for a decrease in the partial pressure of oxygen in the alveoli, breathing rate increases. This response develops over several days (Pugh, 1967). Increased ventilation reduces the partial pressure of carbon dioxide which makes the blood too alkaline. This problem is corrected by the kidneys, and the urine secretion is more alkaline than normal.

3. Cellular changes

There is an increase in the myoglobin content of the muscles, and changes in characteristics and amounts of mitochondria (Tappen and Reynafarje, 1957).

The net effect of human acclimatization to altitude is to improve the aerobic working capacity of muscles to compensate for the reduced partial pressure of atmospheric oxygen, and to improve the capacity of the oxygen transport system to purge the oxygen debt. Pugh (1967) showed that at least four weeks of acclimatization are required if sea-level athletes are to stabilize their performances at altitude.

Investigation 4.5 : To consider the results of running events in the Mexico Olympic Games, 1968, and the benefits of altitude training camps on sea-level performances

Task One

Consider the information in Figure 4.31. Suggest reasons why world records were broken at 100, 200 and 400 metres.

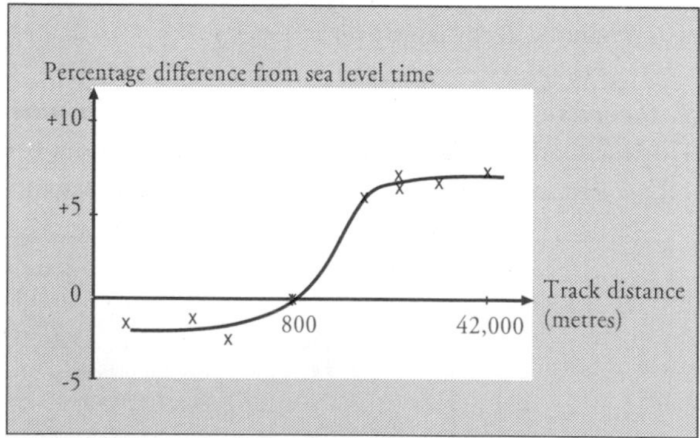

Figure 4.31 Results of running events in the 1968 Olympic Games.

Task Two

In the endurance events above 1500 metres, there was a uniform reduction in performance of about six per cent. Suggest reasons for this observation.

Task Three

The data in Table 39 refers to Olympic Games held at the sites stated. Carefully explain why acclimatized athletes were relatively successful during the 10,000 metres race at the Mexico Olympic Games.

Table 39 : Results of the 10,000 m race

TOKYO 1964 (200 m above sea-level)	MEXICO 1968 (2,242 m above sea-level)
1. M. Mills, USA	1. N. Temu, Kenya**
2. M. Gammoudi, Tunisia**	2. M. Wolds, Ethiopia**
3. R. Clarke, Australia	3. M. Gammoudi, Tunisia**
4. M. Wolde, Ethiopia**	4. J. Martinez, Mexico**
5. L. Ivanov, Russia	5. N. Sviridov, Russia*
6. K. Tsuduroya, Japan	6. R. Clarke, Australia*
7. M. Halberg, New Zealand	7. R. Hill, UK*
8. A. Cook, Australia	8. W. Masresha, Ethiopia**

** had lived at high altitude for most of their life
* trained at high altitude for an extended period prior to the Games

Task Four

Haemoglobin reversal occurs between three and eight days after return to sea-level. Any respiratory changes are reversed immediately and cellular changes reverse within one to two weeks.

Since the Mexico Olympic Games it has been common for endurance athletes to spend a period of several weeks at high altitude training camps and then return to sea-level to compete within about three days. How useful is the rationale of altitude camps to sea-level performances?

Task Five—aids to performance

Acclimatization is one way in which performance in sporting activities may be enhanced. What other methods are used by current sportsmen and women to aid performance?

Task Six—the ethics of aids to performance

Doping is defined as the administration or use of substances in any form alien to the body or of physiological substances in abnormal amounts and with abnormal methods by healthy persons with the exclusive aim of attaining an artificial and unfair increase in performance in competition. Furthermore, various psychological measures to increase performance in sports must be regarded as doping. (Statement by the International Olympic Committee.)

Using this definition of doping, and your answers to Task Five, decide whether you think there are any ethical objections to the use of such aids to enhance performance.

Summary

1. You should be aware of the aims and objectives of training with respect to enhancement of performance at sport or improvement of health.
2. You should be familiar with the concepts of the principles of training:
   - duration
   - overload
   - regression
   - specificity
   - repetition
   - variance
   - warm-up and cool-down
3. You should be aware of the physiological adaptations produced by training.
4. You should be aware of the neuromuscular adaptations produced by training.
5. You should understand that ceasing training allows the body to regress to fitness levels required by ongoing activities.
6. You should understand the effects on the body of a reduction in the partial pressure of oxygen in atmospheric air.
7. You should understand the changes brought about by acclimatization to altitude, and the beneficial effects to the athlete competing at altitude.
8. You should understand the benefits of altitude training camps on sea-level performances.
9. You should be able to discuss the issue of aids to performance.

FURTHER READING

Astrand P.O. and Rodahl K. *Textbook of Work Physiology – Physiological Basis of Exercise,* McGraw Hill, 1986.

Brotherhood J.R. Human acclimatization to altitude, *British Journal of Sports Medicine,* Vol. 8, No. 1, April 1974.

de Vries H.A. *Physiology of Exercise,* Wm. C. Brown, 1986.

Dick F.W. *Training Theory,* BAAB/AAA, 1984.

Fox E.L., Bowers R.W.and Foss M.L. *The Physiological Basis for Exercise and Sport* 5e, Wm. C. Brown, 1993.

Harre *et al. Principles of Training,* Sportverlag, Berlin, 1982.

McArdle W.D., Katch F.I. and Katch V.L. *Essentials of Exercise Physiology,* Lea & Febiger, 1994.

Pugh L.G.C.E. Man at high altitude, *The Scientific Basis of Medicine Annual Reviews,* British Postgraduate Medical Federation, Athlone Press, 1964, pp. 32–54.

Pugh L.G.C.E. Athletes at altitude, *J. Physio.,* **192** (1967), 619–646.

Tappen D.V. and Reynafarje B. Tissue pigment manifestations of adaptation to high altitudes *American Journal of Physiology,* **190** (1957), 99–103.

Voy R. and Deeter K.D. *Drugs, Sport and Politics,* Human Kinetics, 1991.

Types of training

KEY WORDS AND CONCEPTS

continuous training
interval training
set
cycle
repetition
interval
mesocycle
microcycle
period
circuit training
stage training
concentric
eccentric
active mobility
passive mobility
kinetic/ballistic mobility
isometric
isotonic
isokinetic
plyometric

The following two investigations attempt to bring out the essential differences between types of training.

Investigation 4.6 : Continuous training — jogging or swimming

Task One—initial assesment

1. Students should work in groups of at least two people, so that a conversation can be held during the exercise. For the purposes of this investigation, the jogging should be done as quickly as is allowed by the holding of a conversation—hard breathing without breathlessness should be aimed at. A similar breathing regime should be adopted for swimming. This will stress your body's aerobic energy systems, and we expect some adaptations to occur which will enhance aerobic capacity.
2. Pulse rate (beats per minute) and respiration rate (breaths per minute) are recorded before starting. Pulse rate is then recorded for the first 15 seconds after finishing, and then for 15 seconds after a rest of 60 seconds. Results are recorded in Table 40.
3. The initial jog is one mile (1600 m) in 10 minutes (the distance is a guide, the time is what is required), or a swim (any stroke) of 10 minutes. This forms an initial assessment of pulse rates and recovery rate.

Task Two—the exercise

The same measures are taken for three further sessions spread over a minimum of two weeks, results recorded in Table 40.

Table 40 : Results table

Pulse rate before activity	Respiration rate before activity	Approx. length of swim	Time to be taken	Approx. length of run	Pulse rate first 15 sec after activity	Pulse rate after 60sec rest
		metres	min	metres		
		250	10	1,600		
		375	15	2,400		
		500	20	3,200		
		250	10	1,600		

Task Three—conclusions

1. What effects are observed after the last session?
2. Make a direct comparison between the first and last session. Are any improvements found in either recovery or ability of the cardiovascular system to cope with the exercise?

Recovery rate can be expressed as:

recovery rate = pulse rate (per min) at end of run - pulse rate after 60 sec rest

CONTINUOUS EXERCISE

Exercise regimes lasting longer than 60 seconds, involving low forces and where breathing is comfortable, are essentially aerobic.

The following types of exercise fall into this category:

- jogging, variation by changing distance and speed
- swimming, variation by changing stroke, distance and speed
- aerobics (a means of total body exercise, aerobically)
- rowing
- game/skill simulations without full effort
- fartlek—speed play without full effort.

Investigation 4.7 : Interval training

Task One—sprint/swim interval training

1. The following session is attempted four times in two weeks. At least two students are needed to monitor timing of each other.
2. The session is:

   Running/sprints

   a) Five **repetitions** of 40 m sprint with a 30 second **interval** between repetitions. (This is written as 5 × 40 m sprint at 30 seconds, and is called a **set**.)

   b) Followed by five minutes' rest.

   c) Followed by a further **set** of 5 × 60 m sprints with 60 second interval.

   Swimming

   a) Five **repetitions** of 50 m (flat out, choice of stroke), with 30 second interval between repetitions.

   b) Followed by five minutes' rest.

   c) Followed by a further **set** of 5 repetitions at 75 m, with 60 second interval.

These sessions will stress the lactic anaerobic energy system for the muscle groups involved, and we will look for adaptations to thresholds and oxygen debt recovery.

3. Pulse rates are taken (for 15 seconds, and then multiplied by four to obtain pulse count per minute) before the session and immediately after completion of the exercise. A further count is taken after 60 seconds' rest, and counts entered in Table 41.

Table 41 : Results table

Session	Pulse rate before exercise	Pulse rate at finish	Pulse rate 60 sec after finish
1			
2			
3			
4			

Task Two—results analysis

1. Have recovery rates been enhanced by this training regime?
2. Has the alactic (ATP-PC) lactic threshold been changed?
3. Are there any advantages of this training system over the continuous exercise method?

INTERVAL TRAINING

As can be seen from Investigation 4.7, **interval training** is characterized by **repetitions** with an **interval** of time between, organized in **sets**, with a longer period of time between the sets. Figure 4.32 shows typical variations of a number of physiological indicators during interval training.

Figure 4.32 shows that this method can be more effective in establishing levels of fitness, and therefore biological changes, than the continuous exercise method. This is because of the repeated high level stressing of anaerobic systems for energy production, and the forcing of repetitions before full recovery is achieved (i.e. applying stress upon stress).

The idea can be used for acquiring fitness utilizing both anaerobic and aerobic energy mechanisms. The sorts of training incorporating the interval concept include:

- weight training
- circuit training
- stage training
- sprint training
- endurance training,
- training for a game utilizing game skills but composed of sets and repetitions.

Examples of endurance training for 5000 m runners could be:

4 × 1500 m at 80% 5000 m pace with 5 min intervals
20 × 40 m in 65 sec with 20 sec interval.

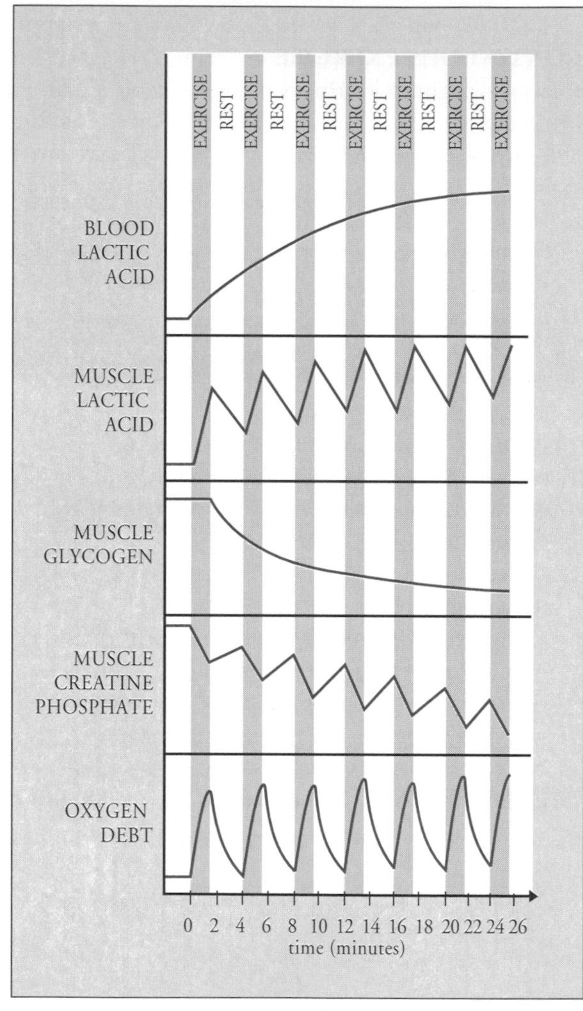

Figure 4.32 After Lamb, 1983 (Chapter 14).

Measurement of intervals

We have already mentioned the idea of using time for measuring the interval between repetitions and sets. Another way is to assess the pulse rate of the sportsperson immediately after a repetition. The next repetition is then begun when the pulse rate falls to a predetermined percentage of its value at the end of the effort, or to a value set beforehand (say 120 bpm).

For example, if the sportsperson has a pulse rate of 180 bpm at the end of an effort, then the next repetition would begin when his/her pulse rate falls to 70 per cent of this value, i.e. 126 bpm.

This means that pulse rate needs to be continually monitored by the sportsperson after each exercise effort. This has the advantage that the interval is individualized, and related to the person's recovery rate. As training progresses and the sportsperson becomes fitter, recovery rates become faster and the intervals smaller. This obviously enhances fitness even further, since now the individual is doing the same amount of work in a shorter time.

Training activities—weight training

There are a range of activities under this heading, the basic features of which are:

- intervalized exercises arranged in repetitions and sets
- **progressive resistance** exercises, in which the load can be increased by increasing either the forces applied or the number of repetitions.

Equipment which can be used includes:

- free weights with barbell, dumbbells and discs
- exercise machines of the multigym/Nautilus type in which slotted weights are moved by levers
- hydraulic exercise machines in which a system of levers operates a hydraulic dash pot which can be set for different forces
- exercises using body weight as the load.

Figure 4.33

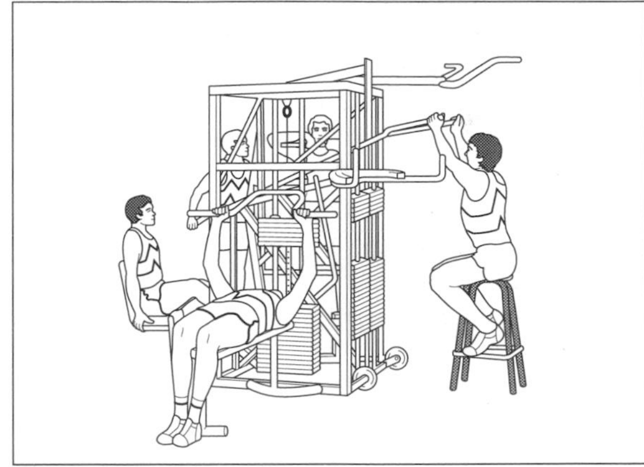

Figure 4.34

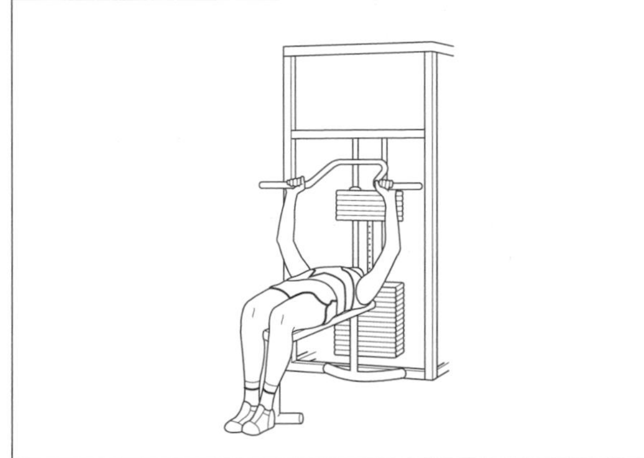

Figure 4.35

The exercises

Exercises are usually classified into four groups, from which a few examples are given in Figures 4.36–39.

If you need to know about more exercises than are shown here, refer to a specialist text on weight training.

(i) Shoulders and arms

Figure 4.36

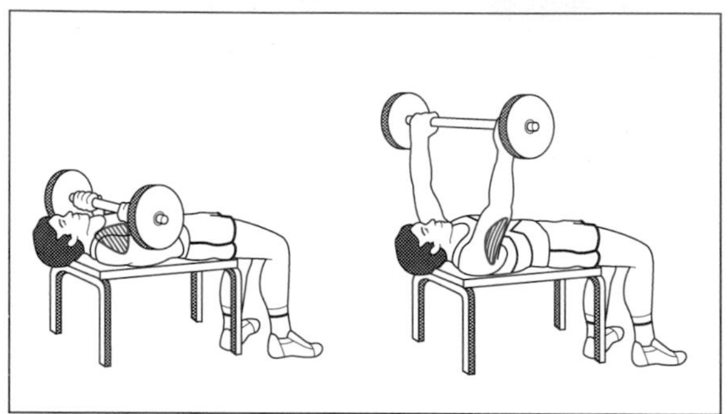

a. bench press.

b. curls.

c. Pull downs.

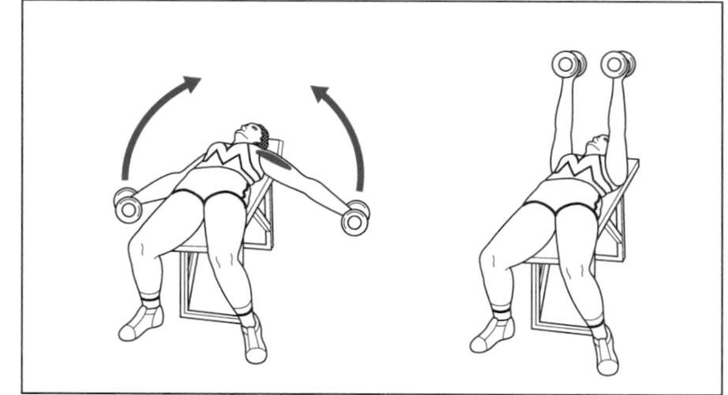

d. Flying exercise.

e. Bent over row.

f. Military press.

(ii) Trunk and back

Figure 4.37

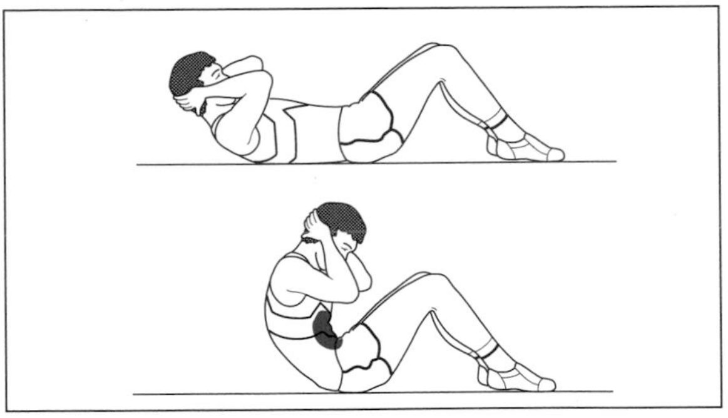

a. Sit-ups.

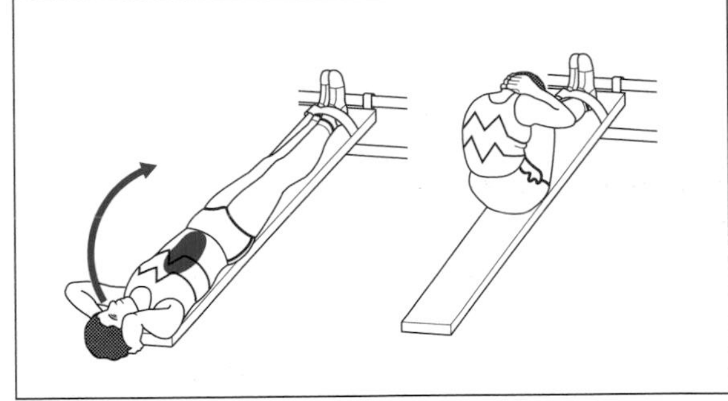

b. Inclined sit-up with twist.

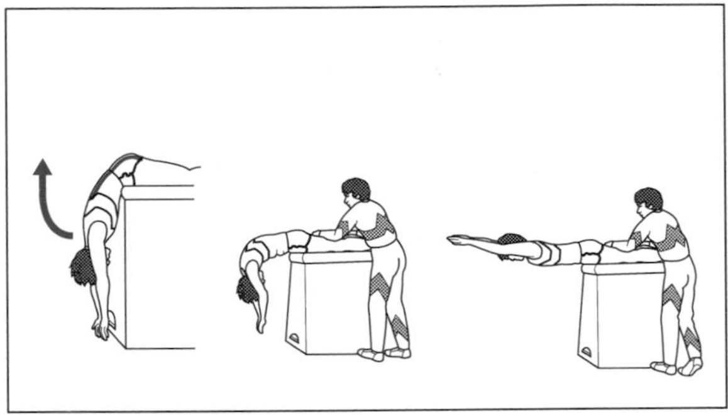

c. Back hyperextensions.

(iii) Legs

Figure 4.38

a. Squat.

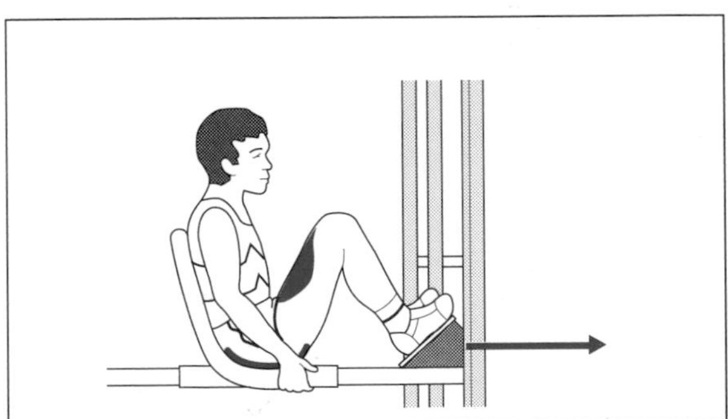

b. Leg press.

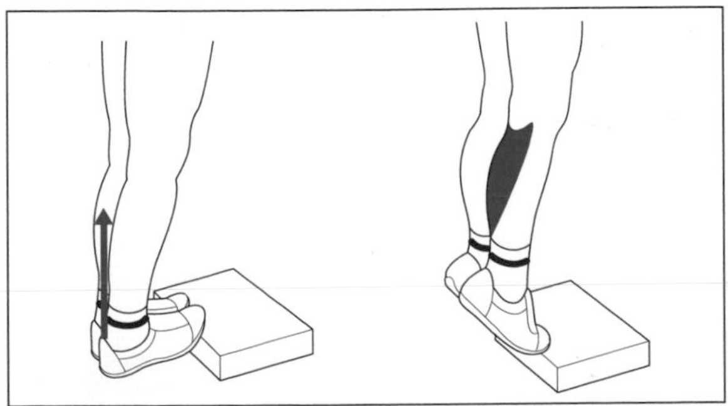

C. Calf raise.

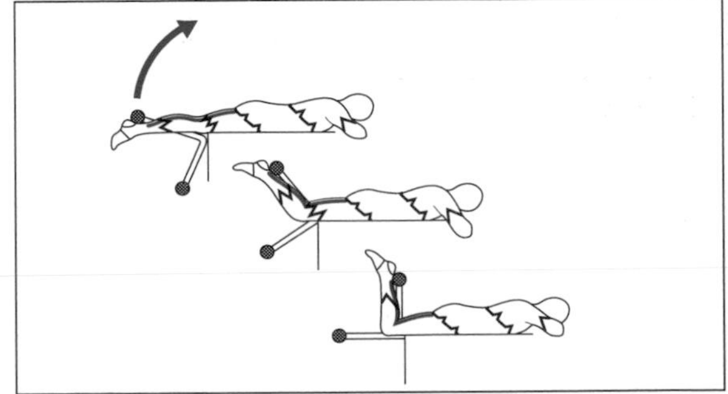

d. Hamstring curl.

(iv) 'All body' Exercises

a) **Power Clean** (see Figure 4.39).

b) **Snatch:** the snatch is a variation of the same technique as the clean, except that the bar is lifted overhead to arms length in a single movement.

c) **Dead Lift:** the bar is again picked up in the same manner as the clean, but the bar is lifted to thigh level only, with arms straight at all times.

Figure 4.39 Power Clean.

a.

b.

c.

Safety

First, it should be said that certain exercises can be dangerous if not performed correctly, particularly those in which the back is used (Power Clean, Snatch, Squat and Dead Lift). It is important for students to be aware that loadings at these exercises should be low until the skill of the activities is learnt.

Further injury can result from the dropping of bars and discs on the weight trainer. It therefore is essential for weight trainers to train in groups, and evolve a safety 'catching' protocol, wherever this danger is a possibility (exercises where this is particularly important are Bench Press, Snatch, Squat and Military Press).

Some exercises can involve very large loadings, and can be dangerous if too large a weight is attempted (squat and bench press, for example).

Frequency and intensity

The beauty of weight training is that almost any combination of exercises can be chosen (specifically related to the sporting activity for which the training is being done), with any combination of load and repetitions.

If 100% represents the maximal force which can be exerted (see Investigation 4.2) for any given exercise, then the following loadings and repetitions relevant to different requirements are suggested:

1. Alactic (ATP–PC) anaerobic energy system: fast twitch muscle fibres

a.
- 3 to 5 sets of up to 6 repetitions per set—between 80% and 100% load
- with full (one minute) recovery intervals between sets
- 2 to 3 times per week.

b.
- 3 sets of very fast dynamic work at 10 to 15 repetitions per set
- 60% load
- full recovery intervals
- 3 to 4 times per week.

2. Lactic anaerobic energy system: fast twitch muscle fibres

a.
- 5 sets of 6 to 10 repetitions per set
- 60–80% load
- restricted intervals (60 seconds)
- 2 to 3 times per week.

b.
- 5 sets of 4 to 6 repetitions per set
- 80% load
- 60 seconds' recovery
- 3 times per week.

c.
- 3 sets of 20 repetitions per set
- 50% load
- full recovery intervals
- 3 to 5 times per week.

3. Aerobic energy system: slow twitch muscle fibres

Any exercise done slowly at less than 50% load; most training programmes would have between 10 and 20 repetitions per set.

The above suggestions are examples of how an exercise regime can be organized to develop a particular energy system; there are many other possibilities.

Choice of exercise

It is usual to choose exercises which:

- relate to the muscle groups used in the sport
- exercise the antagonists to these muscle groups
- give all-round body fitness

Investigation 4.8 : The effects of circuit training

This investigation attempts to introduce the concept of **circuit training**, and its offshoot **stage training,** within a mini fitness programme.

Task One—the exercises

1. As its name implies, circuit training involves a **circuit** of exercises (which could be the same ones mentioned in the section on weight training). The circuit is organized so that the different exercises are done one after the other, instead of in multiple sets of the same exercise (see Figure 4.41a).
2. So, for our example we choose the bodyweight exercises in Figure 4.40 for our circuit.
3. Sessions consist of a warm-up followed by one set each of press-ups, sit-ups, free squats, squat thrusts, pulls to bar, and back hyper-extensions—this would be one **circuit** of exercises.
4. Three circuits would then be completed without rest between circuits.

Figure 4.40 Circuit training.

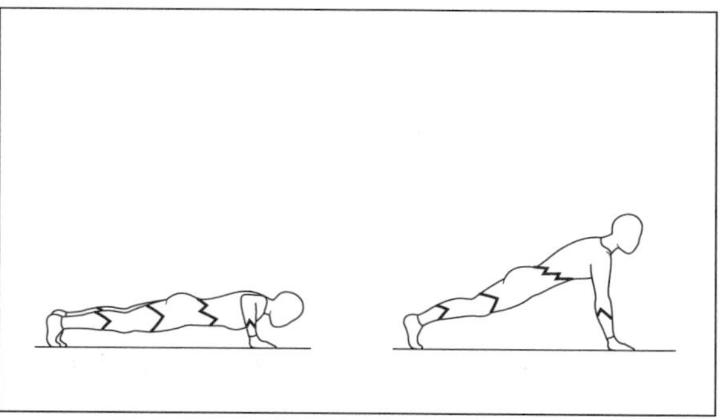

a. Press-up.

b. Sit-up.

c. Free squats.

d. Squat thrusts.

e. Pulls to bar.

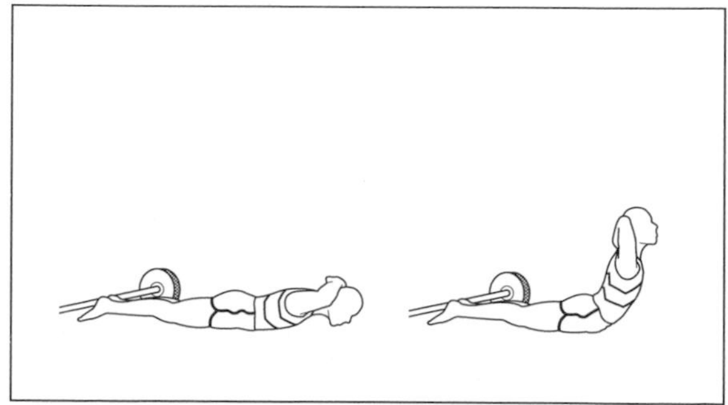

f. Back hyperextensions.

Task Two—determination of repetitions

1. Students should work in pairs, one scoring and timing the exercises while the other does the training.
2. The first session is used to assess the number of repetitions possible in 30 seconds for each exercise. So, the exercises are done in turn for 30 seconds, with 3 minutes' rest between each exercise. The count is recorded in Table 42.

Task Three—the training

1. Two further sessions are now done, with three circuits per session (as explained above). Each session is done continuously at **half** the 30-second loading per exercise.
2. For example, if the student achieves 30 press-ups in his 30-second assessment, he will perform 15 press-ups on each circuit (and so on for the other exercises).
3. Times for the second and third sessions are recorded. The aim is to improve on times.

Table 42 : Results table

Session	Press-up	Sit-up	Free squat	Squat thrust	Pulls to bar	Back hyper.
1						
2						
3						
4						

Time for session 2 = min sec Time for session 3 = min sec

Task Four—final assessment

1. Repeat Task 2, record reassessed 30-second counts for each exercise in the 'session 4' row of Table 42.
2. This should be done at least three days after the previous session.

Task Five conclusion

1. What improvement has been made over the short period of this investigation?
2. What other measures could be taken to assess improved fitness'?
3. Which energy system does this type of training develop?
4. What has been the effect on your body of this type of training?

Stage Training

This investigation could be modified by organizing the exercises in sets with the same exercise (at one-third of the number of repetitions found in the initial 30-second test) done three times at 15-second intervals before moving to the next exercise. This is more lactic than straight circuit training. It should be possible to detect differences between two groups of students, one performing circuits, the other stages.

Figure 4.41

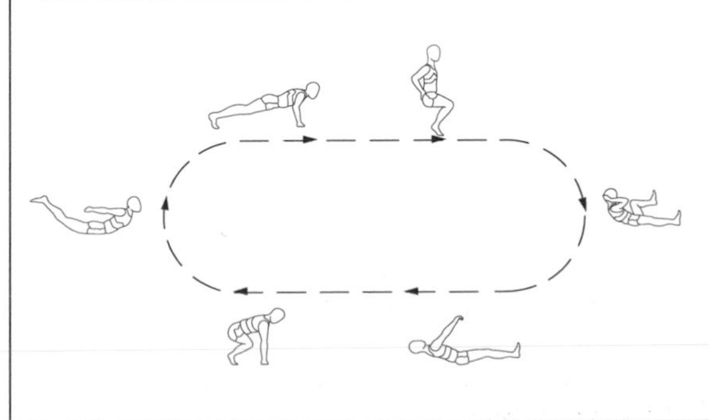

a. Circuit training.

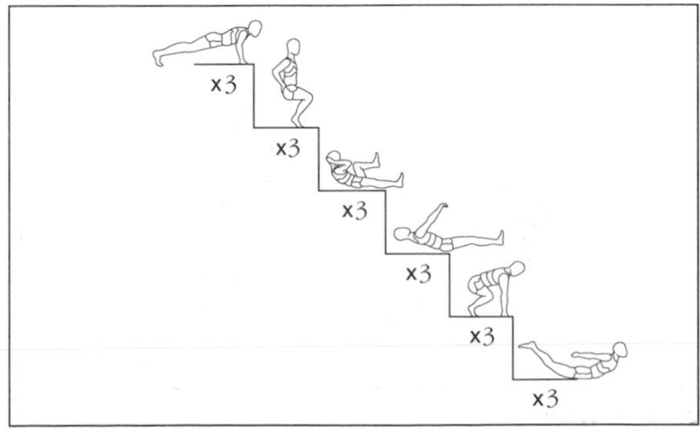

b. Stage training.

Other circuit training exercises

Circuits can be organized using any combination of exercises which give all body fitness; other exercises not already mentioned include:

- star jumps, bar jumping, straddle jumps to bench, full star jumps, bunny hops, shuttle runs, step-ups, box jumps, sergeant jumps.
- bench dips, burpees, alternate dumbbell press, chins, rope climbs, V sit-ups, hip thrusts, chinnies, alternate leg squat thrusts.

Categories of muscle use

The bulk of the discussion above has involved muscle **contractions**, in which the exercise is achieved by contracting the agonist (muscle which produces the desired body movement) more or less rapidly, depending on how vigorously the exercise is done and what the loading is.

It is, however, possible to exercise a muscle in several different ways, with different effects on strength gain. These aspects were discussed in detail in Chapter 1, p. 33 and Investigation 4.2, p. 127.

1. **Static contractions—isometric exercise**
2. **Concentric contractions—isotonic and isokinetic exercise**
3. **Eccentric contractions—plyometric exercises.**

During **static** contractions, the type of effort predominantly affects the ATP–PC anaerobic system. The main advantage of this **isometric** work is that it causes muscles to enlarge (**hypertrophy**). However, despite the physiological benefits of increase in size and strength of muscles, **isometric training** does little for cardiovascular fitness. Whereas in **concentric** and **eccentric contractions**, the physiological benefits include increased capillarization of skeletal and cardiac muscle tissues, improved **pulmonary** functioning and many other cardiovascular **adaptations** mentioned in the book.

Track intervals

As mentioned in the section on interval training above, any exercise organized in repetitions and sets with time intervals between them comes under the general heading of **interval training.**

The proportions of interval training which develop the different energy systems are set out in Table 43 below, and linked to the athletic event most suitable.

Table 43 : Percentage aerobic/anaerobic work within different interval training regime

Activity	% Aerobic	% Anaerobic
Continuous running	90	10
Fartlek running	75	25
Long slow running	60	40
Short fast intervals	40	60
Repetition intervals	25	75
Sprint running	10	90

(After *Athletics Weekly*, 29 October 1988.)

MOBILITY TRAINING

The purpose of mobility training is not to enhance energy production muscles, but to improve (or maintain) the range of movement over which muscle can act and joints can operate.

This works on the stress/overload principle in the same way as other types of training, only now the biological response is to make a muscle capable of operating more efficiently over a bigger range of joint movement. This happens by inhibiting the stretch reflex, and by forcing the contraction processes to operate in conditions of full stretch, thereby bringing into play more contractile fibres.

Investigation 4.9 : Mobility training

Task One—initial assessment

1. The four mobility tests shown in Figure 4.42 are completed.
2. Results are recorded in Table 44.

Figure 4.42

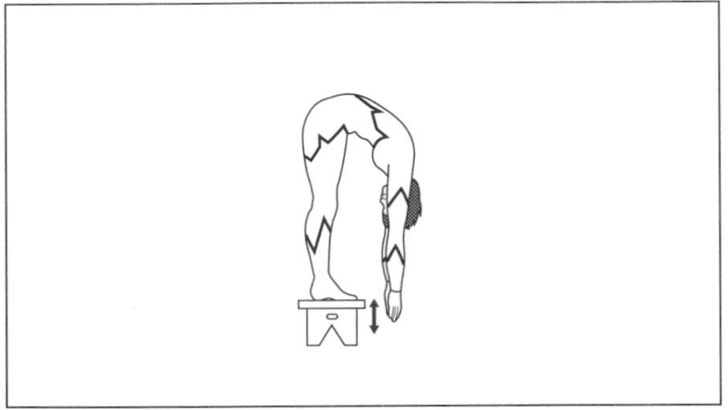

a. Hamstring stretch: distance of fingertips below soles of feet is measured.

b. Spinal hyperextension: feet are held, and height of nose above floor is measured.

c. Hip mobility: height of pubic bone above floor is measured.

d. Shoulder mobility: nose in contact with ground, height of fingers above ground is measured.

Task Two—the exercises

1. About 15 minutes of exercises are completed per day for two weeks.
2. The mobility exercises can be put into three categories:

   Active mobility (Figure 4.43): exercises in which joints are moved in as full a range as possible by the action of agonists and relaxation of antagonists. The exercise is done slowly without jerking or using bodyweight or a partner to extend the range of movement. Each exercise is performed five times by pulling, using muscle action only (hands must not grip another part of the body in the end position). The end position is held for five seconds each time.

   Passive mobility (Figure 4.44): again slow careful movements, but now by relaxation of all muscles, and increase of joint movement by a partner assisting or the sportsperson pulling him/herself into extended positions. Again the end position is held for five seconds for each of five repetitions per exercise.

Figure 4.43 Active mobility.

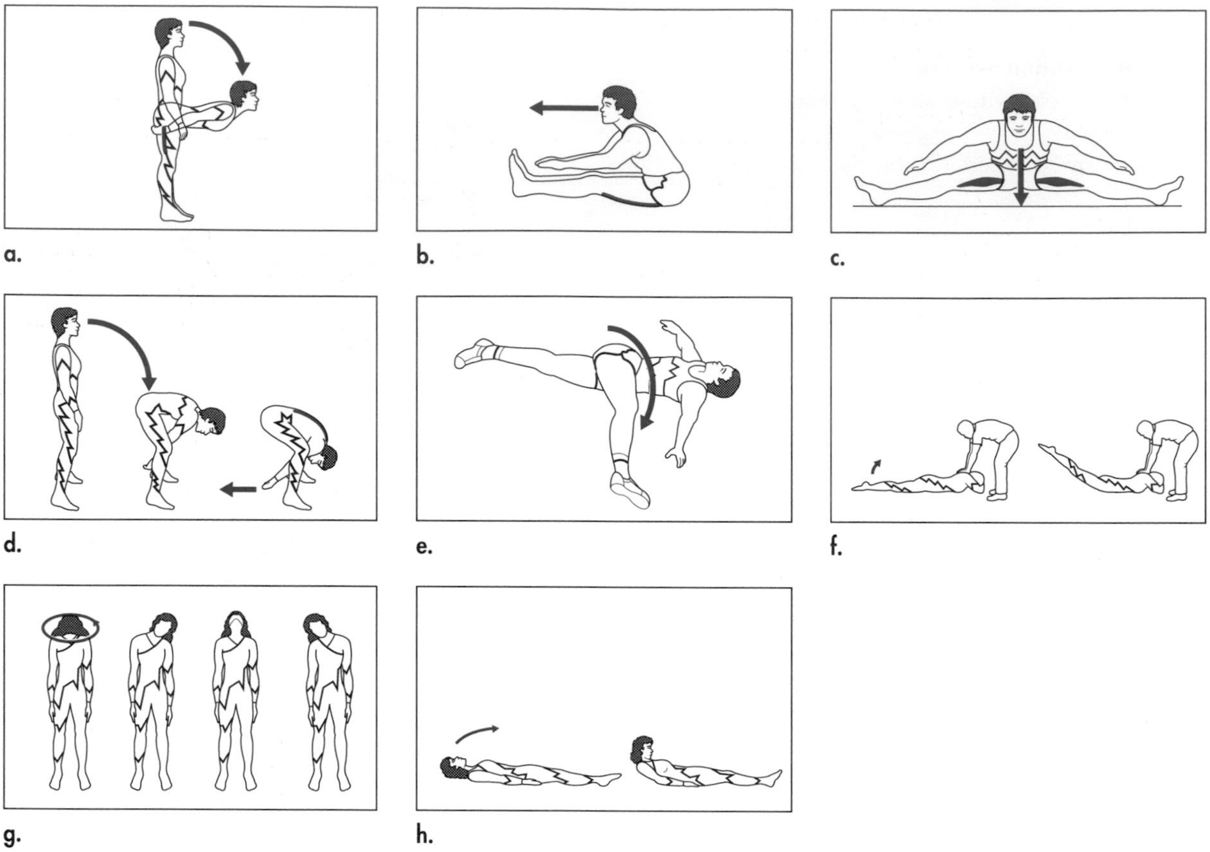

a. b. c.

d. e. f.

g. h.

Figure 4.44 Passive mobility.

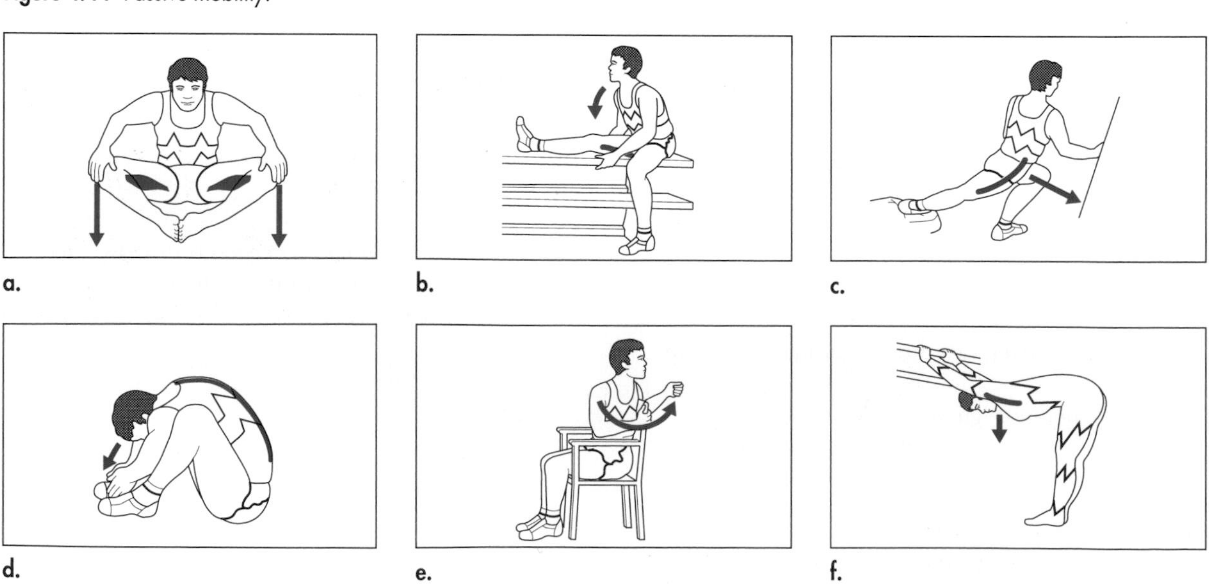

Kinetic or ballistic mobility (Figure 4.45): this style of exercise uses body movement to extend joint range. Each movement is done five times per exercise.

3. The exercises are done in sets of five without rest—a total of about 15 minutes per day.

Figure 4.45 Kinetic or ballistic mobility.

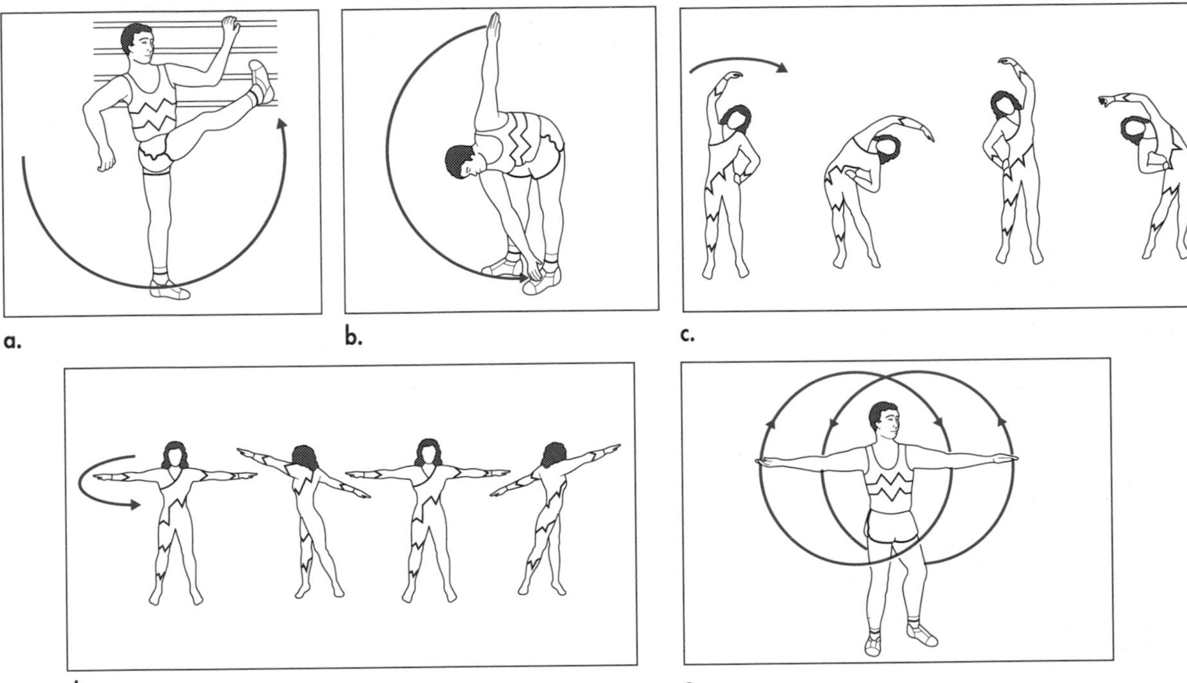

Task Three—final assessment

The mobility assessment test set out in Task One above is repeated and results recorded in Table 44.

Table : 44 Results table

	Hamstring stretch	Spinal mobility	Hip mobility	Shoulder mobility
initial assessment				
final assessment				

Task Four—conclusions

1. Has there been an improvement in joint mobility?
2. Which type of mobility exercise would you think is most effective?

Skill training and game simulation

This heading refers to the repeated practising of the skills involved in a sport or game. The aim is to improve **specific motor fitness**, that is to improve effectiveness or capability at the sport by isolating skills and rehearsing game situations.

Although some skills can be practised in situations which do not need a substantial degree of fitness, it is more usual to incorporate the skills involved in a game into the anaerobic and aerobic training elements of a programme.

Investigation 4.10 : Training programmes

This investigation puts into a practical situation the preparation of a training programme relevant to the student's own sporting interest.

Task One—selection of activities

1. Select *two* activities/games from:
   - athletics (choose an event)
   - basketball
   - tennis
   - gymnastics
   - swimming (select a stroke)

You will be setting out a training programme for your chosen activities.

2. Time allocation will be five hours' total per week. The age of the sportsperson will be 16 or 17.
3. Analyse the energy system demands appropriate to the chosen sport by using Table 37. Enter the percentage contribution for each system in the first row of Table 45.
4. Decide the **general** training elements and activities for each energy system. Make a list of these in the second row of the table.
5. Decide the **specific** training elements and activities relevant to the sport and the energy system demands. Make a list of these in the third row of the table.
6. Allocate time to warm up and cool down for each daily session.
7. Allocate time to each chosen activity over the weekly **microcycle**, according to the proportions required by the energy system demands of the sport (see first row of Table 45, as calculated at **3**, above). List activities and times in the fourth row of the table.

Task Two—choose details of activities

1. Decide on a battery of tests which will determine what the loadings will be for each chosen activity.
2. Carry out the tests on yourself so that the actual loadings produced for the training programme will be relevant to you.
3. Decide details of exercises, loadings, repetitions, distances run, rest, recovery times and so on.
4. Write down a programme of weekly activities to satisfy this—include warm-up and cool-down in each daily session.
5. Table 45 is a suitable *pro forma* in which the details of this investigation can be recorded.

Task Three—variations

1. Suggest *mesocycle* variations of loads for the schedule (**a mesocycle** is a training period of 3-8 weeks whose aim is to increase specific aspects of fitness and for which overload increases continuously).
2. Suggest variations in activities based on the mesocycle.
3. How would you modify the programme for progression to 17–18 and eventually 18–19 year olds?

Table 45 : Results table

	ATP–PC energy system		**LACTIC energy system**		**AEROBIC energy system**	
% demand of sport						
Appropriate general activities						
Appropriate specific activities						
Time allocation to activities	activity	time	activity	time	activity	time
Weekly schedule of activities	activity	time reps load	activity	time reps load	activity	time reps load
Sun						
Mon						
Tue						
Wed						
Thur						
Fri						
Sat						

Task Four—self evaluation of programme

1. Having carried out the pre-programme tests on yourself, now carry out the programme itself for a period of at least two weeks.
2. Carry out a post-programme test on yourself. Evaluate its effectiveness in terms of:

    fitness benefit
    skill learning
    mobility/agility.

3. Explain your feeling of well-being and fatigue as the programme progresses in terms of:

    energy system demands
    matching with food intake.

Summary

1. You should be aware that continuous training methods mainly utilize and enhance aerobic energy systems.
2. You should be aware of the applicability of interval training to the development of all types of energy system, its organization in terms of repetitions, sets and intervals, and how intervals are measured.
3. You should be familiar with the concepts of weight training as an intervalized progressive resistance form of training, some of the exercises used, how they can be used to enhance the different energy systems, and the safety problems associated with this type of training.
4. You should be aware of the organization and principles of circuit, stage, mobility and skill related training.
5. You should be able to construct a training programme for your personal fitness needs or those of a chosen sport.

FURTHER READING

Alter M.J. *Sport Stretch*, Human Kinetics, 1991.

Bowers R.W. and Fox E.L. *Sports Physiology* 3e, Wm C. Brown, 1992.

Dick F. *Training Theory,* BAAB/AAA, 1984.

Dintiman G.B. and Ward R.D. *Sport Speed,* Human Kinetics, 1988.

Hartmann J. and Tünnemann H. *Fitness and Strength Training,* Sportverlag, Berlin, 1989.

Fisher G.A. and Jensen C.R. *Scientific Basis of Athletic Conditioning,* Lea & Febiger, 1990.

Lamb D.R. *Physiology of Exercise,* MacMillan, 1983.

McArdle W.D., Katch F.I. and Katch V.L. *Essentials of Exercise Physiology,* Lea & Febiger, 1994.

Pauletto B. *Strength Training for Coaches,* Human Kinetics, 1991.

Prentice W. *Fitness for College and Life* 4e, Mosby–Year Book , 1994.

Sharkey B.J. *Coaches' Guide to Sport Physiology,* Human Kinetics, 1986.

Sharkey B. *Physiology of Fitness,* Human Kinetics, 1990.

Shephard R.J. *Exercise Physiology,* B.C. Decker, 1987.

Westcott W. *'Strength Fitness'—Physiological Principles and Training Techniques* 3e, Wm C. Brown, 1991.

Wirhed R. *Athletic Ability and the Anatomy of Motion,* Wolfe, 1984.

Chapter 5
Fitness for Life

People who exercise regularly, whether walking, jogging, swimming, cycling or playing team sports, are more likely to be able to carry on exhausting work for longer periods of time than sedentary people. This is due to the **adaptive** responses made by the body as a result of regular exercise (see Chapter 4, p. 130 onwards, for details of the long-term effects of exercise on the body).

Today's mass participation in jogging and distance running is a strong indicator that people generally value good health and work hard to keep their bodies in 'good working order'.On the other hand, modern day living with its sedentary life styles and increased leisure time has brought modern day illnesses such as **obesity, heart disease** and **cancers.**

This chapter will help you to understand the causes and consequences of **obesity** and **heart disease** and the role that regular exercise can take in the pursuit of **fitness for life.**

Figure 5.1

5.1 Obesity

KEY WORDS AND CONCEPTS

obesity	**negative energy balance**	**nutritional balance**
glandular malfunction	**energy input**	**basal metabolic rate**
neutral energy balance	**energy output**	**total metabolic rate**
positive energy balance	**overeating**	**underwater weighing**
		skinfold measurements

Obesity is a severe overweight condition of the body, defined as when a person has an excessive accumulation of body fat which is more than 20 per cent above the norm for his/her height and build. It is a serious form of **malnutrition** of the body (*mal,* of course, meaning bad).

THE PHYSICAL EFFECTS OF OBESITY ON THE BODY

Because of the increase in body size, the cardio-respiratory system has to work much harder since more energy is used in just moving the body mass.

In addition, an increase in adipose tissue (fat under the skin) and a decrease in sweat gland density make it much harder for the vascular system to remove waste heat energy, produced as part of the process of conversion of food fuel into useful work or energy in the body's muscles and organs. This heat energy has to leave the body from the skin surface, and therefore a thick insulating layer under the skin will tend to restrict flow of heat outwards. This means that the heart has to work harder to pump blood faster round the circulatory system, so that heat energy, carried by the blood, can be released more rapidly near the skin surface.

Also, a relatively poor circulatory system within adipose tissue, means that the blood (and therefore heat energy) cannot reach the skin surface in large enough quantities to release its heat as effectively as it would in a thin person.

All these factors result in **heart overload** and increased respiratory functioning, to keep pace with the increases in total metabolic functioning.

OBESITY AND DISEASE

Obesity has been strongly associated with a number of modern day cardiovascular diseases, such as atherosclerosis, hypertension, and coronary and cerebral thrombosis.

An obese person has an increased risk of suffering from mature diabetes, hernia, and gall bladder diseases, cirrhosis of the liver, and mechanical injuries to the body—such as backache and damage to joint structures. In addition, there are greater surgical risks and complications during pregnancy.

THE CAUSES OF OBESITY

Positive energy balance

Carbohydrates and fats are the fuels needed for energy production. The major cause of obesity is that energy intake (eating carbohydrate and fat) is far greater than energy output. In other words there is a lack of energy expenditure, so the obese person will continue to gain weight. This concept is known as a **positive energy balance** and can be expressed as:

ENERGY INPUT > ENERGY OUTPUT

Excess carbohydrate is stored as glycogen. When all the glycogen stores are filled, carbohydrate is converted to fatty acids and glycerol together with the excess fat content in the diet. Excess fatty acids and glycerol are stored as triglycerides (fat) in adipose tissue around major organs such as the heart and stomach, underneath the skin and in skeletal muscle.

Glandular malfunction

A small percentage of obese people suffer from a **glandular malfunction** which results in a hormonal imbalance in the body. This tends to create adipose tissue abnormally.

OVEREATING AND OVERWEIGHT

There is a strong relationship between a positive energy balance and being overweight. The latter is often associated with poor eating habits and **imbalanced** diets containing a high proportion of fat. This results in an individual becoming exhausted through work (exercise) more quickly than someone with a higher proportion of carbohydrate in his/her diet.

Figure 5.2

Over-indulgence in food is also associated with psychological, social and cultural factors. For example, the overeater may eat in an attempt to relieve anxieties. It has been shown that childhood obesity is strongly linked to adult obesity, i.e. the fat child grows into a fat adult!

Figure 5.3

The development of fat cells begins during the first two years of life. The fat cells in young children who are overfed may proliferate to five times the normal number of cells. So as the child grows she/he has thousands of extra fat cells just waiting to fill with fat. In the adult the number of fat cells remains constant, but the cells increase in size as weight is gained. Once this weight is gained it will be maintained unless a **negative energy balance** (described in detail below) is achieved.

Figure 5.4

Obesity and lack of exercise

There is strong evidence to suggest that overweight children and adults are far less active than their thinner counterparts. Obesity has the long-term effect of limiting the mobility of joints, thus restricting the person's ability to co-ordinate movements. It also places an additional strain on the cardio-respiratory system, as described earlier. Bodily strength, endurance and speed are impaired as a result of weight gain. So a combination of physical and psychological factors (such as self-image) often inhibit the person from participating in sport and leisure activities.

Figure 5.5

HOW TO LOSE WEIGHT

The only method of controlling obesity is to shift the energy relationship so that energy output exceeds energy intake. This concept is known as a **negative energy balance** and can be expressed as:

ENERGY OUTPUT > ENERGY INPUT

The result is that the body will mobilize the potential energy reserves stored in the fat deposits.

A combination of **balanced diet** and **regular aerobic exercise** is known to be the most effective means of weight control.

A balanced diet

Whilst dieting may be one effective way of losing weight, drastic dieting often leads to lethargy and illness as energy levels drop and resistance to infection decreases, as a result of vitamin and mineral deficiencies. The key to dieting is that a diet must be **well balanced,** i.e. containing all the nutrients for good health. Weight reduction will be achieved only when the normal proportions of fats, carbohydrates and proteins are maintained, but amounts are reduced.

Figure 5.6 A balanced diet.

Regular aerobic exercise

The long-term effects of aerobic exercise in alleviating obesity are well established. Long-term systematic exercise increases energy output, as **fat mobilization** takes place in the liver. Exercise causes lipids (fat-like molecules, insoluble in water, which form large parts of fat cells) to decrease and metabolic rate to increase. For example, an energy increase of approximately 5,000 kJ per day through exercise will burn off one kilogram of body fat in one week. The result of such an excess of energy output through exercise, against input via food, is a steady progressive long-term weight loss.

As weight decreases, physiological functioning and physical fitness improve, and so the obese person is able to increase the intensity, duration and frequency of exercise. In addition, there is a small reduction in the risk of heart disease.

Figure 5.7

ENERGY BALANCE

When energy input is equal to energy output a **neutral energy balance** is achieved, as a result of which a person's weight remains constant. This concept can be expressed as:

ENERGY INPUT = ENERGY OUTPUT

BODY FAT AND ITS MEASUREMENT

Body composition has two basic components:

1. **Body fat** or accumulated adipose tissue.
2. **Lean body mass** or the fat-free mass, including the mass of other tissues such as muscle, bone and skin.

Measurement of the proportion of body fat is one of the measures of physical fitness discussed in Chapter 4 (p. 121). It is possible to estimate the proportions of body fat and lean body mass by underwater weighing. The subject is weighed in air and reweighed under water whilst breathing out (see McArdle's *Essentials of Exercise Physiology,* 1994, p. 461 for details of this method).

PREPARING A WEIGHT CONTROL PROGRAMME

The principles of preparing a weight control programme involve a knowledge of the relationships between:

a. The quantity and types of nutrients required by the individual for perfect health.
b. Energy expenditure needed for **basal** and **total metabolic rates**.
c. The concept of **energy balance** and **body weight**.

Investigation 5.1 : The preparation of a weight control programme

Task One—calculation of energy intake over 24 hours

Record all details of food and drink taken in 24 hours in Table 46. Quantities of each item will need to be estimated so that energy values can be calculated using food energy tables from a standard table or chart such as that found in McArdle's *Exercise Physiology,* 1991, Appendix B.

Table 46 : Kilojoule intake

Meal	Food	Quantity	Kilojoules
Breakfast			
Snack			
Lunch			
Snack			
Evening meal			
		Energy Total	**kJ**

Task Two—calculating energy expenditure over 24 hours

1. Using Table 47, and the information that the Basal Metabolic Rate for a male is 100 kJ/kg/day and for a female is 90 kJ/kg/day, calculate your total metabolic requirements and insert value in Table 48 .
2. Specific Dynamic Action (SDA) accounts for the extra energy needed for digestion, absorption and transport of the nutrients to body cells. To calculate the SDA, refer to the food intake Table 46 and work out 10% of the kJ in food consumed. Now add this value to Table 48. You will observe that the total energy output is the result of the BMR + ***ALL*** energy requirements above BMR + SDA.
3. Discuss the relationship between your energy intake and energy expenditure. What type of energy balance is there?
4. Using the information from Tables 46 and 48, describe the different ways in which positive and negative energy balances could be achieved.

Table 47 : Energy expenditure for various activities

Subject's weight (kg): ____________

Activity	kJ/kg/min over BMR requirements
Sitting at rest	0.14
Walking	0.2
Jogging and swimming (moderate)	0.6
Cycling (moderate)	0.46
Vigorous exercise	0.8

Table 48 : Energy expenditure table

Activity	Duration of activity	kJ/kg above BMR needs	Total kJ for body mass
			+SDA =
			+BMR =
			TOTAL MR ____________

Task Three

Write an equation reflecting energy relationships for:

a. maintaining body weight

b. losing weight

c. gaining weight.

REVIEW QUESTIONS

1. What are the effects on health of obesity, and what are its causes and its cure, based on energy considerations. Describe the most effective ways of reducing weight.
2. What do you understand by 'Healthy Eating'? How can this concept be applied to dieting?
3. How could an evaluation of body composition assist in:
   a. The control of body weight
   b. As an aid to sportsmen and women preparing for competitions?
4. How can exercise be used as a means of weight control?

FURTHER READING

Allsen P.E., Harrison J.M. and Vance B. *Fitness for Life* 5e, Brown & Benchmark, 1993.

Ashton D. and Davies B. *Why Exercise?* Basil Blackwell, 1986.

Hockey S. *Physical Fitness—the Pathway to Healthy Living* 7e, Mosby–Year Book, 1993.

Katch F.I. and McArdle W.D. *Introduction to Nutrition, Exercise and Health* 4e, Lea & Febiger, 1993.

Lamb D.R. *Physiology of Exercise,* MacMillan, 1983.

McArdle W.D., Katch F.I. and Katch V.L. *Exercise Physiology* 3e, Lea & Febiger, 1991.

McArdle W.D., Katch F.I. and Katch V.L. *Essentials of Exercise Physiology,* Lea & Febiger, 1994.

Prentice, W. *Fitness for College and Life* 4e, Mosby–Year Book, 1994.

Sharkey B.J. *Physiology of Fitness* 3e, Human Kinetics, 1990.

Wootton S. *Nutrition for Sport,* Simon and Schuster, 1988.

5.2 Cardiovascular Diseases

KEY WORDS AND CONCEPTS

cardiovascular disease
atherosclerosis
coronary thrombosis
angina
hypertension
cardiac arrest
atheroma

Cardiovascular diseases include diseases of the heart and blood vessels. The majority of patients suffering from cardiovascular diseases have **hypertension** or high blood pressure (this is diagnosed when the diastolic pressure consistently reads over 95 mmHg or 11.9 kPa). Hypertension is a major contributing factor in **atherosclerosis, coronary heart disease** and **strokes.**

Atherosclerosis, commonly described as **furring up of the arteries**, is caused by lipid deposits accumulating in the inner lining of arteries, resulting in a narrowing of the arterial lumen, thereby impeding blood flow. When the deposits silt up one of the coronary arteries, a coronary heart attack results—illustrated in Figure 5.8b and c.

Coronary heart disease (CHD) is one of Britain's greatest killers and encompasses diseases such as **angina** and **heart attacks** or **coronary thrombosis**. The first symptoms of coronary heart disease are often manifested as a result of an increased heart rate caused by physical exertion or excitement. Heavy, cramp-like pains are experienced across the chest. This kind of pain is known as **angina** and is normally treated and controlled with drugs and relaxation. A person suffering from angina has a higher risk of suffering from a **coronary thrombosis**.

A **coronary thrombosis** or heart attack is a sudden severe blockage in one of the coronary arteries, cutting off the blood supply to the cardiac tissue. This blockage is often caused by a blood clot forming in an already damaged furred up coronary artery, as illustrated in Figure 5.8c. Heart attacks can be severe or mild, depending on the positioning of the blockage.

In Figure 5.9 a severe blockage has occurred in a

Figure 5.8

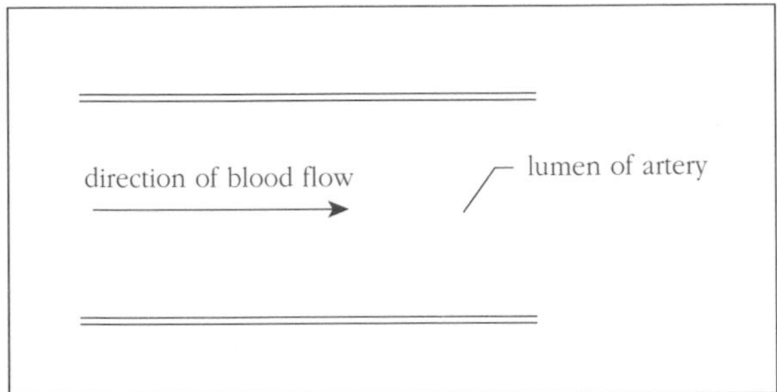

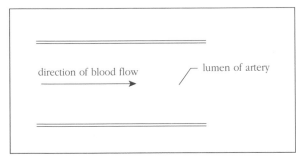

a. Normal artery.

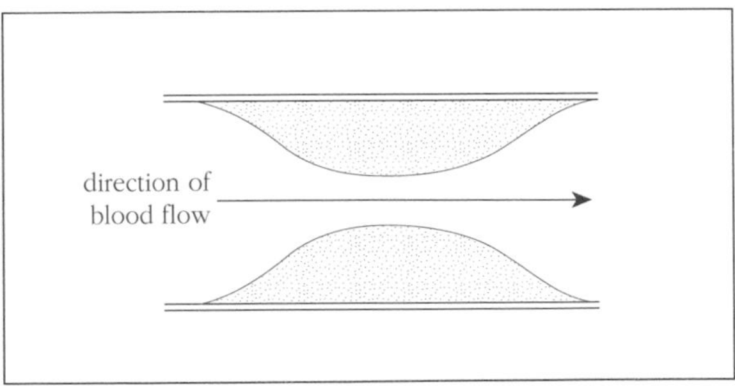

b. Narrowing.

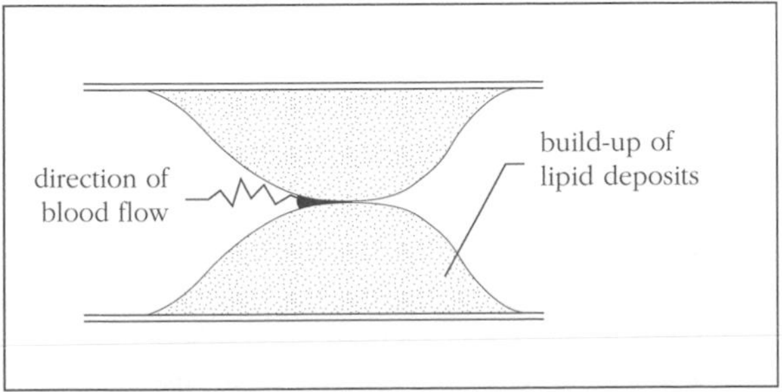

c. Blocked.

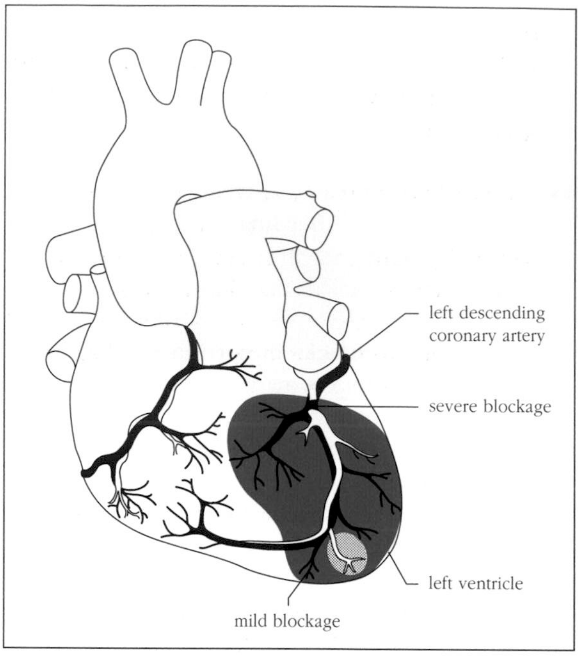

descending coronary artery. The amount of heart tissue involved is great, causing a major heart attack. The mild blockage is towards the end of the coronary artery and therefore the amount of heart tissue involved is minimal. In this instance the patient would have a better chance of full recovery.

In a severe blockage the heart may stop beating. This is called a **cardiac arrest.** About half of all cardiac arrest cases die.

Figure 5.9 Blockage leading to a heart attack.

Investigation 5.2 : To examine death rates from coronary heart disease

Task One

Coronary heart disease accounts for 30 per cent of all deaths in the UK to people aged under 75. Suggest possible reasons and causes for this.

Task Two

Figure 5.10 shows different death rates from heart disease for 55–64-year-olds in different countries of the world.

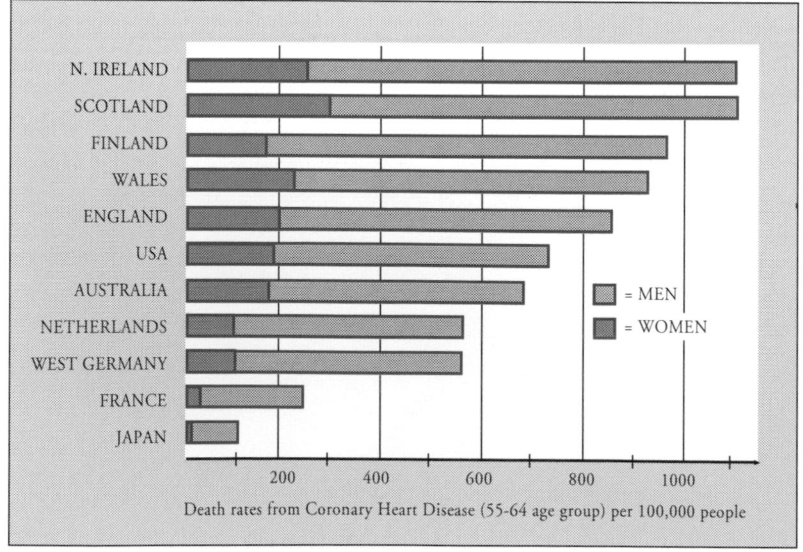

Figure 5.10 Comparative death rates from coronary heart disease. (*Source:* WHO, 1982–84.)

1. Using examples from this chart, suggest reasons why the death rate from coronary heart disease varies so much from one country to another.
2. Suggest reasons why men are more likely than women to suffer from coronary heart disease.

PROTECTION AGAINST CORONARY HEART DISEASE

The advice usually given is to watch your weight, do not smoke, do not drink too much alcohol, reduce your salt intake, relax, but take regular exercise. This is because, although some individuals who smoke, eat too much and drink too much, live to old age without heart trouble, a higher proportion contract heart disease than the average for the population as a whole. There is therefore a higher statistical risk of heart disease among people who drink, smoke, eat too much and take salt in their food.

EXERCISE AND CORONARY HEART DISEASE

There is good evidence that regular exercise can have a protective effect on the heart. Stamina building activities such as jogging, cycling and swimming will improve the efficiency of cardiac tissue and circulation.

Regular exercise reduces resting heart rate and increases heart stroke volume because of a stronger, more efficient, heart. Resting blood pressure is lowered and the balance of cholesterol (a constituent of animal fat in the diet) and triglycerides (fat) is improved. Amounts of cholesterol and triglycerides which reach the fuel transport system of the body are statistically associated with a high incidence of atherosclerosis, and therefore there is an increased probability of heart disease and coronary thrombosis. Diets should therefore include less animal fat (saturated fats) to reduce this risk.

In addition to the positive physiological effects of exercise on the body, a person will feel and look better.

The type of exercise undertaken to protect your body from coronary heart disease will depend on your present physical condition. The major questions to be asked in devising an exercise programme are: how often, **frequency**; how much, **intensity**; and how long, **duration**.

1. **Frequency:** at least two to three times a week.

2. **Intensity:** hard enough to make you breathless. This should mean that your heart rate should be at least sixty per cent of your maximal heart rate and increase in proportion to your maximal heart rate as your fitness improves.

3. **Duration:** the length of each session will depend on the intensity of the exercise, but should last between twenty and sixty minutes for it to be beneficial to the body.

4. Finally, **what activity?** Something that you enjoy doing! It is important that the selected mode of exercise is aerobic and uses large muscle groups so that stamina is improved.

Figure 5.11

Investigation 5.3 : To devise an activity programme

Task One
Consider the information in the stamina rating chart (Table 49) and devise two exercise programmes—one for a male and one for a female aged 42. Give reasons for your selection of activities, frequency, intensity and duration of the schedule.

Task Two
Why would a medical examination be advised for anyone who decides to start regular exercise at this age?

Task Three
Why should an exercise session be preceded with a warm-up and finished with a cool-down?

Table 49 : Stamina rating

	Stamina rating
Badminton	• •
Canoeing	• • •
Golf	•
Jogging	• • • •
House work (moderate)	•
Mowing the lawn by hand	• •
Swimming	• • • •
Tennis	• •
Walking (briskly)	• •
Yoga	•
KEY	
not much effect	•
beneficial effect	• •
very good effect	• • •
excellent effect	• • • •

Investigation 5.4 : The application of energy concepts

Task One
Select a team game and individual sport and briefly describe the ways in which energy is supplied to working muscles. How can an understanding of the ways in which energy is produced help you in devising a training programme for your selected activities?

Task Two
How can an understanding of energy production enable us to find out about the causes of fatigue and how it can be delayed or even avoided during competitive performance?

Task Three
How does information regarding nutrition and its potential energy supply assist performance?

Task Four
What principles of body weight need to be applied to energy requirements of the body?

Task Five
Why is it important for the athlete to keep a stable body temperature?

Investigation 5.5 : A training programme for health-related fitness

The aim of this investigation is to build an exercise/training programme based on improving fitness for health, as opposed to a particular sporting activity.

The student should choose a single subject for the investigation from among parents, brothers/sisters or friends.

Task One—initial assessment

Decide on a battery of tests from Section 4.1 on fitness testing and energy balance which would determine the fitness levels of the chosen subject. Take into account:

- age and sex
- general build of individual
- physical fitness assessment (any step test duration must not be so long as to initiate heart failure!)
- body composition tests
- dietary intake
- energy demands of occupation.

Task Two—the programme

1. Decide on a **gradual, progressive** exercise regime which would help the health needs of your subject **without overstrain**.
2. Research one of the many available texts to help in sorting this out.
3. Set out in detail the day-to-day activity programme for the subject for a period of four weeks.

   Make this **realistic** for the subject to contemplate. There is no doubt that he/she would definitely not co-operate with an exercise regime which is thought to be too difficult or time-consuming.

DO NOT TRY TO IMPLEMENT THE PROGRAMME BEFORE CONSULTATION WITH YOUR TEACHER—WE DON'T WANT FATALITIES AS A RESULT OF YOUR EFFORTS!

4. Explain in your programme how warm-up and cool-down are incorporated.

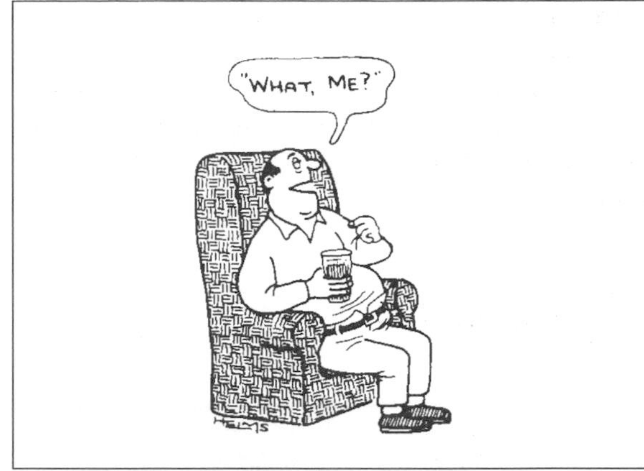

Figure 5.12

Task Three—evaluation

1. If it is possible to implement the suggested regime with your subject, then do so after consultation with her/his doctor if necessary!
2. How would you assess the effectiveness of your programme?
3. Devise a **before and after** questionnaire which would assess the impact of the programme on:

- physiological factors:
  - pulse rate
  - breathlessness
  - circulation
- body composition
- feeling of well-being
- feeling of coping with the physical demands of life:
  - work
  - hobbies
  - sex
- feeling of coping with emotive stress-related demands:
  - coping with work loads
  - interpersonal relationships
- states of exhaustion
- sleep patterns
- eating habits
- personal cleanliness habits and so on.

REVIEW QUESTIONS

1. Describe the ways in which exercise can reduce the risk of getting coronary heart disease.
2. How might changes in life style go some way to preventing coronary heart disease? (AEB exam question.)

Summary

1. You should understand the causes, cures and effects of obesity on health; and appreciate the long-term effects of exercise on weight control.
2. You should understand the concepts of neutral, positive and negative energy balance; be able to compare energy intake with energy output using investigational procedures; and relate this information to the concepts of the role of exercise and nutrition in body weight control.
3. You should be able to understand what is meant by a 'balanced diet'.
4. You should appreciate the two components of body weight through investigational procedures.
5. You should appreciate the effects of changes in modern life styles on the general state of health of populations.
6. You should understand what is meant by coronary heart disease; appreciate its risks and causes; and the long-term effects of different types of exercise in protection from coronary heart disease.
7. You should be able to devise an activity programme based on the three criteria of duration, intensity and frequency, to improve the health profile of a subject of your choice.

FURTHER READING

Allsen P.E., Harrison J.M. and Vance B. *Fitness for Life* 5e, Brown & Benchmark, 1993.

Ashton D. and Davies B. *Why Exercise?* Basil Blackwell, 1986.

Corbin B.C. *Fitness for Life,* Gage, 1980.

Corbin B.C. and Lindsey R. *Concepts of Physical Fitness with Laboratories,* Wm. C. Brown, 1986.

Cundiff D.E. (ed.) *Implementation of Health Fitness Exercise Programs,* American Alliance for Health, Physical Education, Recreation and Dance, 1985.

Fox E.L., Bowers R.W., Foss M.L. *The Physiological Basis for Exercise and Sport* 5e, Wm. C. Brown, 1993.

Franks B.D. and Howley E.T. *Fitness Leaders Handbook,* Human Kinetics, 1989.

Franks B.D. and Howley E.T. *Fitness Facts,* Human Kinetics, 1989.

Gavin J. *The Exercise Habit K,* Human Kinetics, 1992.

Hartmann J. and Tünnemann H. *Fitness and Strength Training,* Sportverlag, Berlin, 1989.

Hockey *Physical Fitness—The Pathway to Healthy Living* 7e, Mosby–Year Book, 1993.

Prentice W. *Fitness for College and Life* 4e, Mosby–Year Book, 1994.

Sharkey B.J. *Coaches' Guide to Sport Physiology,* Human Kinetics, 1986.

Sharkey B.J. *Physiology of Fitness,* Human Kinetics 3e, 1990.

Shephard R.J. *Exercise Physiology,* B.C. Decker, 1987.

Sorrell L.S. and Schmied M.A. *Feeling Fit—Instructors Guide,* Human Kinetics, 1988.

Sorrell L.S. and Schmied M.A. *Feeling Fit—Participants Guide,* Human Kinetics, 1988.

BIBLIOGRAPHY

Anatomy and Physiology

Ashton D. and Davies B. *Why Exercise?* Basil Blackwell, 1986.

Astrand P.O. and Rodahl K. *Textbook of Work Physiology,* McGraw Hill, 1986.

Biddle S. *Foundations of Health Related Fitness,* Ling, 1987.

Bowers R.W. and Fox E.L. *Sports Physiology,* Wm. C. Brown, 1992.

Corbin B.C. *Fitness for Life,* Gage, 1980.

Corbin B.C. and Lindsey R. *Concepts of Physical Fitness with Laboratories,* Wm. C. Brown, 1986.

Cundiff D.E. (ed.) *Implementation of Health Fitness Exercise Programs,* American Alliance for Health, Physical Education, Recreation and Dance, 1985.

Davis D., Kimmet T. and Auty M. *Physical Education Theory and Practice,* Macmillan, 1988.

de Vries H.A. *Physiology of Exercise,* Wm. C. Brown, 1986.

Diagram Group. *Life Sciences on File: Human Biology,* Facts on File, 1986.

Dick F.W. *Training Theory,* BAAB, 1984.

Edington D.W. and Edgerton V.R. *The Biology of Physical Activity,* Houghton Mifflin, 1976.

Fox E.L. and Bowers R.W. *The Physiological Basis for Exercise and Sport* 3e, Wm. C. Brown, 1993.

Harre D. *Principles of Training,* Sportverlag, Berlin, 1982.

Hartmann J. and Tünnemann H. *Fitness and Strength Training,* Sportverlag, Berlin, 1989.

Katch F.I. and McArdle W.D. *Introduction to Nutrition, Exercise and Health* 4e, Lea & Febiger, 1993.

Lamb D.R. *Physiology of Exercise,* Macmillan, 1983.

McArdle W.D., Katch F.I. and Katch V.L. *Essentials of Exercise Physiology,* Lea & Febiger, 1994.

National Coaching Foundation. *Physiology and Performance,* NCF, 1987.

Ross J.S. and Wilson K.J.W. *Foundations of Anatomy and Physiology,* Churchill Livingstone, 1981.

Sharkey B.J. *Physiology of Fitness* 3e, Human Kinetics, 1990.

Sharkey B.J. *Coaches' Guide to Sport Physiology,* Human Kinetics, 1986.

Shephard R.J. *Exercise Physiology,* B.C. Decker, 1987.

Simpkins J. and Williams J.I. *Advanced Human Biology,* Unwin Hyman, 1987.

Solomon E.P. and Davis W.P. *Human Anatomy and Physiology,* The Dryden Press, 1987.

Wirhed R. *Athletic Ability and the Anatomy of Motion,* Wolfe, 1984.

Wootton S. *Nutrition for Sport,* Simon and Schuster, 1988.

Exercise Physiology

Allsen P.E., Harrison J.M. and Vance B. *Fitness for Life* 5e, Brown & Benchmark, 1993.

Ackermann U. *Essentials of Human Physiology,* Mosby, 1992.

Alter M.J. *Sport Stretch,* Human Kinetics, 1991.

Barrow M.B. *Man and Movement—Principles of Physical Education,* Lea & Febiger 1988.

Chu D.A. *Jumping Into Plyometrics,* Human Kinetics, 1992.

Fisher G.A. and Jensen C.R. *Scientific Basis of Athletic Conditioning,* Lea & Febiger, 1990.

Franks B.D. and Howley E.T. *Fitness Leaders Handbook,* Human Kinetics, 1989.

Franks B.D. and Howley E.T. *Fitness Facts,* Human Kinetics, 1989.

Gavin J. *The Exercise Habit K,* Human Kinetics, 1992.

Hockey *Physical Fitness—The Pathway to Healthy Living* 7e, Mosby Year Book, 1992.

McArdle W.D., Katch F.I. and Katch V.L. *Energy, Nutrition and Human Performance,* Lea & Febiger, 1991.

Pauletto B. *Strength Training for Coaches,* Human Kinetics, 1991.

Prentice W. *Fitness for College and Life* 4e, Mosby–Year Book, 1994.

Safrit M.J. *Introduction to Measurement in Physical Education and Exercise Science,* Mosby, 1990.

Seeley R.R., Stephens T.D. and Tate P. *Anatomy and Physiology* 2e, Mosby 1992.

Sharkey B.J. *New Dimensions in Aerobic Fitness,* Human Kinetics, 1991.

Sorrell L.S. and Schmied, M.A. *Feeling Fit—Instructors Guide,* Human Kinetics, 1988.

Sorrell L.S. and Schmied, M.A. *Feeling Fit—Participants Guide,* Human Kinetics, 1988.

Thibodeau G.A. and Patton K.T. *Anatomy and Physiology* 2e, Mosby–Year Book, 1993.

Thompson C.W. *Manual of Structural Kinesiology,* Mosby, 1989.

Voy R., Deeter K.D. *Drugs, Sport and Politics,* Human Kinetics, 1991.

Wuest D.a. and Bucher C.A. *Foundations of Physical Education and Sport* 11e, Mosby–Year Book 1993.

Journals

Brotherhood J.R. Human acclimatization to altitude, *British Journal of Sports Medicine,* Vol. 8, No. 1, April 1974.

Karlsson J. Lactate and phosphagen concentrations in working muscle of man, *Acta Physiologica Scandinavia,* supplement 358, 1971.

Newsholme E. and Leech T. Fatigue stops play, *New Scientist,* 22 September 1988.

Pugh L.G.C.E. Man at high altitude, *The Scientific Basis of Medicine Annual Reviews,* British Postgraduate Medical Federation, Athlone Press, 1964.

Pugh L.G.C.E. Athletes at altitude, *Journal of Physiology,* **192**, 1967, 619–646.

Tappen D.V. and Reynafarje B. Tissue pigment manifestations of adaptation to high altitudes, *American Journal of Physiology,* **190**, 1957, 99–103.

Chapter 6
Biomechanics: Linear Motion

Chapters 6 to 8 deal with the study of **biomechanics**.

This area of study applies the concepts of physics and mechanics to the way in which the human body moves, and how it applies forces to itself and other bodies with which it comes into contact.

Figure 6.1 All motion and no speed!

6.1 Linear Motion

KEY WORDS AND CONCEPTS

speed	**force**	**air resistance**
acceleration	**weight**	**fluid friction**
velocity	**friction forces**	**work**
deceleration	**reaction forces**	**kinetic energy**
	streamlining	

Linear means *in a straight line*. This chapter attempts to put into place concepts involving movement in a single direction such as speed, velocity, acceleration and force (through Newton's second law of motion), as directly applied to a practical situation.

Investigation 6.1 : Motion of a sprinter during a 100 m run

This investigation comprises the bulk of the work in this chapter and requires the use of a video camera (with on-screen timing facility), a tape measure (50 m), 10 traffic cones or markers, bathroom scales, and a video playback machine with slow and stop facility.

Task One—production of video film

Work in groups of at least four.

1. Mark out a 100 m (or 50 m) stretch of straight track with cones (or other easily visible objects) at 10 m intervals down the track.
2. Set up your video camera viewing at right angles to the screen, at about 50 m from the track.
3. Student A will then perform the run from a standing start (flat out from the start—otherwise important features of the exercise will be lost);
   Student B will call the start commands;
   Student C will operate the video camera (which will need to follow the runner as he/she runs down the track);
   Student D will have the very important task of operating the timer start on the on-screen timer display of the camera.
4. The latter facility is essential for all practical uses of a video camera in measuring the motion of a sportsperson.
5. Trial runs of the investigation showed that only a couple of 'takes' were needed to obtain very usable film.
6. An alternative method of obtaining the data is to station a student armed with a stop-watch at each cone , who then measures the time from the start to the moment the runner passes.

Figure 6.2

a The start.

b The finish.

Task Two—production of primary data from the film

1. Locate the beginning of a suitable run on the film.
2. Using the pause and frame advance facility on the video machine, move the film forward until the runner is level with the first 10 m marker (i.e. at 10m from the start line) and record the time in the second column of Table 50.
3. Continue this process, moving the runner to successive 10 m points down the track and record the times on the chart. Note that it will be important to allow for the fact that the camera is not alongside the runner. Therefore you will have to estimate when he/she passes each marker, and not line up the marker with her/ him in the field of view.
4. Now complete the third column of Table 50: time for the previous 10 m (by subtraction of times).

Table 50 : Times at 10 m intervals during the run

Distance moved (m)	Time at this point (sec)	Time interval for previous 10 m (sec)
0	0.0	
10		
20		
30		
40		
50		
60		
70		
80		
90		
100		

Task Three—graph of distance against time

1. Plot a graph of distance (y-axis) against time from the second column of Table 50 (x-axis). *Note: For the purpose of this text the y-axis is the vertical axis and the x-axis the horizontal axis of a graph.*
2. Mark on your graph any straight (or almost straight) portions—note that when drawing a line through your graph points, **do not** connect up the points but draw a smooth curve or line which best fits the motion that is represented.
3. Mark on your graph any obviously curved portions.
4. Write a brief description of what you understand may be happening during the straight and curved bits of the graph.
5. Using the equation below, work out the slope (gradient) of the graph at 1.0 and 5.0 seconds after the start. What do these values tell you about the motion of the runner?

$$\text{gradient} = \frac{\text{change in } y \text{ value of graph}}{\text{corresponding change in } x \text{ value}}$$

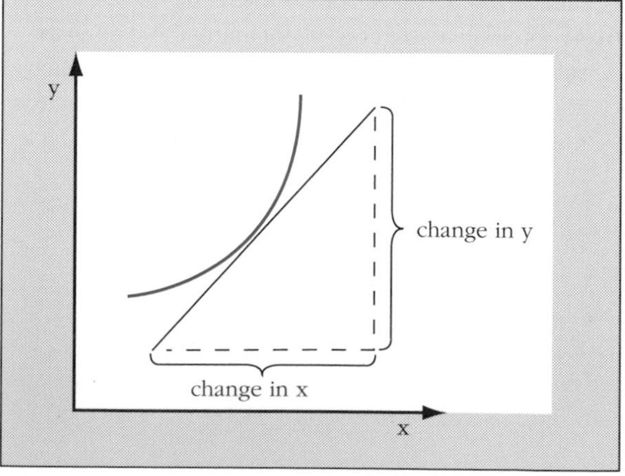

Figure 6.3 Sketch graph of a gradient.

Task Four—computation of the speed of the runner

1. Using a calculator and the information that:

$$\text{speed} = \frac{\text{distance moved}}{\text{time taken}}$$

(units—metres per second or ms^{-1})
calculate the speeds of the runner for successive 10 m intervals. Record these values in the second column of Table 51.

Note: remember that the distance moved is always 10 m and the time taken is the time recorded in the third column of Table 50.

Table 51 : Speed against time for the runner

Section of race (m)	Speed for the section (ms^{-1})	Time at the middle (sec)
0–10		
10–20		
20–30		
30–40		
40–50		
50–60		
60–70		
70–80		
80–90		
90–100		

2. Now work out the average time at which each speed was reached. For example, for the 10–20 m section of the table, calculate the time half way between the 10 m and the 20 m times. This should be done for all sections of the run, and entered in column 3 of Table 51.

This can also be done approximately by taking the times at 5 m, 15 m, 25 m, 35 m and so on from the **distance–time** graph produced in Task Three above.

3. This may seem complicated, but is necessary so that the average speed over each 10 m distance is linked to the average time at which this speed occurred.

Task Five—speed–time graph

1. Now plot a graph of the speed of the runner (*y*-axis) against the time at the middle of the section (*x*-axis), using the data from columns 2 and 3 of Table 51.

2. Try to make the graph as big as possible within your paper—include the origin of the graph (0,0).

Also you should draw a smooth curving line of best fit to your points on the graph; **don't** connect up the points (as this will result in a graph showing rapid and sharp changes in speed, which cannot be the case). Such a smooth curve will average out the errors made in taking measurements.

Task Six—analysis of motion

Now put into writing what you understand from your graph actually happens to the athlete during the run. This should be between half and one side of A4 paper in length and include comments on:

a. What happens between 0 and 2 seconds after the start?

b. When does the athlete reach maximum speed?

c. What happens to the athlete in the last three-quarters of the run?

d. Does the athlete slow down at any time during the run in spite of maximum effort?

e. When is the biggest **net** force being applied to the runner (to enable him/her to accelerate)?

Task Seven—calculation of initial acceleration

1. From your speed–time graph, write down the speeds at time = 0.0 seconds, and time = 1.0 seconds.
2. These two values give you the change of speed in one second, which is the acceleration of the athlete at the start of the run. Write down the value of this acceleration:

acceleration = change of speed per second
unit of answer = metres per second per second or ms^{-2}.

Task Eight—calculation of final deceleration

1. During the last part of the run the runner will be slowing down. Why do you think this is?
2. Deceleration is very similar in definition to acceleration, only slowing down instead of speeding up. Complete the following sequence to calculate the final deceleration of the runner. Use values from your speed–time graph.
3. Calculate the speed at 2.0 seconds from the end of the run and the speed at the end of the run. Calculate the deceleration using:

deceleration = change of speed per second.

Task Nine—forward force at start of run

1. Use Newton's Second Law of Motion to compute the accelerating force on the athlete at the start of the run. Newton's Second Law of Motion says:
Force (in newtons) = mass (kg) × acceleration ($m\ s^{-2}$) (provided the mass which is accelerating remains constant, which in this case it does).
2. Find the mass of the runner **in kilograms** (using bathroom scales).
3. Compute the force at the start of the run using:
Force = mass × acceleration
(unit of answer—newtons or N)
4. What is the nature of this forward force acting on the athlete?
Note: it must be a forward force since the athlete is accelerating forwards, but the athlete pushes **backwards** on the ground.
5. Does friction play a part in this force?
Note: the runner probably would not be able to accelerate as quickly if he/she wore flat shoes instead of spiked ones. How could we test if friction is the cause of this forward force, and in any case how does this friction force manage to push the runner forwards when he/she obviously pushes backwards?

Task Ten—forces acting on the runner

1. Consider Figure 6.4 of our runner one second into the run. Copy this diagram and sketch on him the forces which might be acting.

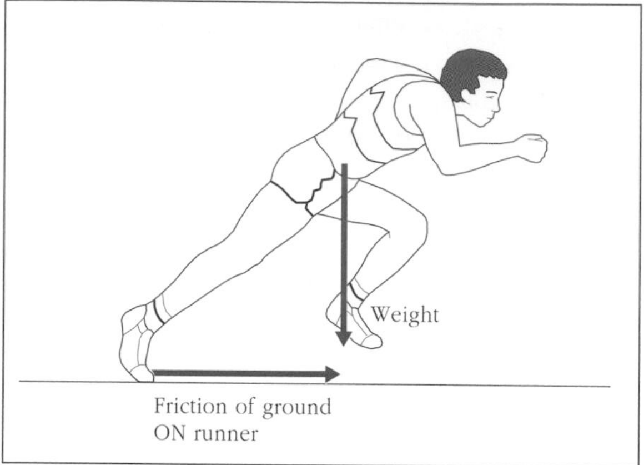

Figure 6.4

2. To extend the list a little, remember that gravity acts downwards (towards the centre of the earth) on all objects on the surface of the earth and the **force** due to gravity is called **weight.**
3. Newton's First Law of Motion says that an object which is not accelerating has **no net force** acting on it. Our runner is **not** accelerating vertically, therefore there can be **no net** vertical force acting on him.
4. Using the bathroom scales again, stand still on them and read the force (or, better still, get a partner to read the force) you are exerting on them.
5. Bend your knees very slowly until they are at about 90°, then jump violently upwards (making sure you don't land on the scales, thereby breaking them or your ankle!).
What do the scales read during the act of jumping? (It will be important here to get a partner to read the scales.) More or less than your weight?
Why should the scales read more, since your weight obviously remains the same?
Perhaps the fact that you push hard down on the scales means that the scales push hard up on you and enable you to accelerate upwards off the ground?
This is Newton's Third Law of Motion—that for every action there is an equal and opposite reaction.

6. This means that when the athlete pushes hard against the ground during the start, the ground pushes back **on the runner** with an exactly equal force, **but in the opposite direction**.

   Now extend your force drawing to include **all** forces which might be acting on the runner.

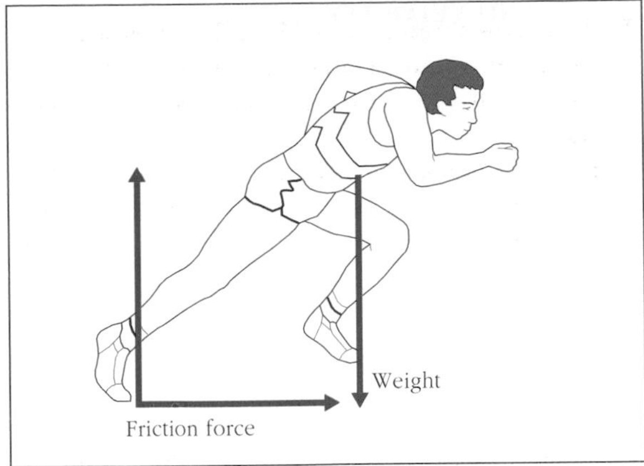

Figure 6.5

Task Eleven—does air resistance affect the runner?

1. Near the end of the race (when the runner is moving at considerable speed) another force may come into play; what could this force be, and how does it depend on the speed of the runner?
2. Air resistance (or fluid friction) crops up in various forms in other sports and sporting situations. Write about one side of A4 paper describing this, mentioning as many examples as you can. (Hint—water has a much bigger fluid friction than air, and very fast-moving objects, like golf balls or motor cars, generate much more fluid friction.)
3. What about the shape of the moving object?

   Streamlining occurs naturally in fish, birds and some animals, and less naturally in cars and planes; boats also are streamlined to reduce water fluid friction.
4. Look at the drawing of our runner (Figure 6.6) which includes the forces acting on the runner **near the end of the run**. Will the friction force now be as large as it was at the start?

Note: since the runner is running at almost constant speed, Newton's First Law of Motion can be used to answer this.

At the end of the run, the fact that the runner is going at almost constant speed means that the forces (although each is large) cancel out to produce almost zero **net** (or resultant) force.

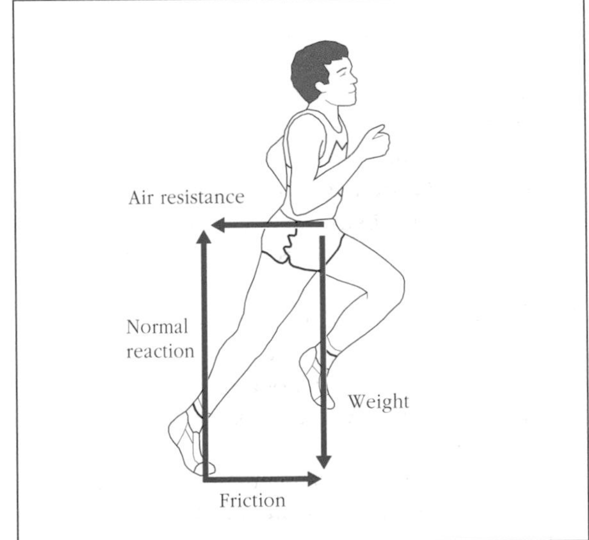

Figure 6.6

SPEED AND VELOCITY

At this point it would be worthwhile to explain the difference between these two apparently similar concepts.

Although both are expressed as metres per second and are defined by the same formula (v = distance/time), **velocity** is a **vector** and has value **and** direction, whereas **speed** is a **scalar** and has value only.

There is a discussion on vectors in Chapter 7 (p. 179 onwards), when we look at the concept of **force,** which is also a vector.

In Investigation 6.1, it doesn't actually make any difference whether we use speed or velocity to describe the motion of our sprinter, because he/she always moves in the same direction. But once the direction changes, then it is important to use **velocity** to describe the motion. This is because the definition of acceleration is:

change of VELOCITY per second

and if the **direction** changes, so will the velocity and there will be an acceleration and a **force** (by Newton's Second Law).

Note: remember Newton's First Law which says that an object on which no net forces are acting has no change in velocity; and Newton's Second Law which gives a value for the force needed to provide an acceleration: $\boldsymbol{F} = \boldsymbol{m} \times \boldsymbol{a}$.

For example, imagine a football, soccer, tennis or rugby player swerving (see Figure 6.7). The friction force of the ground on his feet causes a change of direction but **no change of speed**. The fact that there has been a change of direction means that there has been an acceleration in the **direction of the force**.

Another sporting example of this idea being important is in the hammer throw (Figure 6.8). As the hammer head moves in a circle, its direction is continually changing, so there is a force causing this change **along the hammer wire towards the thrower**, and the hammer head is continuously accelerating towards the thrower, as the hammer head continuously changes **direction** towards the thrower.

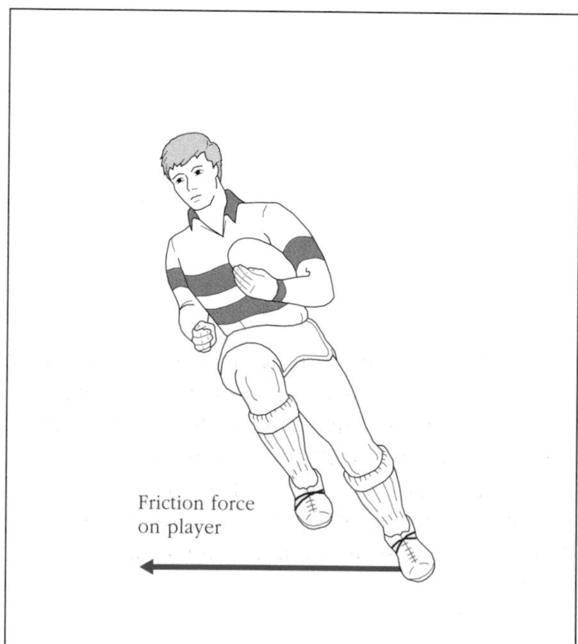

Figure 6.7

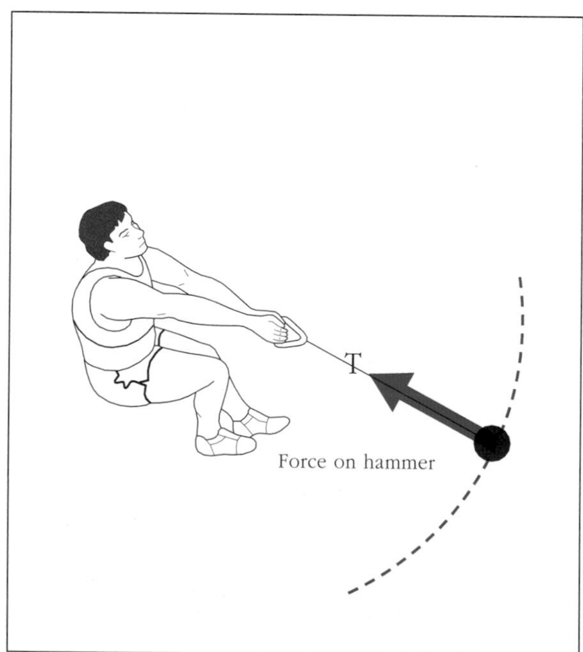

Figure 6.8

Further optional reading on linear motion

Linear motion can be described by a set of equations called **equations of motion**, some of which we have come across already:

$$\text{speed/velocity} = \frac{\text{distance travelled}}{\text{time taken}} = v = \frac{s}{t}$$

$$\text{acceleration} = \frac{\text{change of velocity}}{\text{time taken}} = a = \frac{v - u}{t}$$

where s = distance travelled
t = time taken
u = starting velocity
v = finishing velocity
a = acceleration

Further equations can be derived from these, and are:

$$v = u + at$$

$$s = ut + \tfrac{1}{2} at^2$$

$$\text{average speed} = \frac{u + v}{2}$$

$$v^2 = u^2 + 2as$$

all of which apply to uniformly accelerating motion of acceleration a.

The student who wishes to use these formulae to describe the motion of people or objects should obtain advice from a Physics text book (see bibliography at the end of Chapter 8)—since this is more a physics matter than a biomechanics matter.

ENERGY AND MOTION

The discussion in Chapter 3 (p. 93) on human energy systems outlines the ways in which the human body as a machine can transfer energy from food as fuel (from chemical energy) into movement of the skeleton. The implication is that energy can be neither created nor destroyed, but only transferred from one form to another (this is the Law of Conservation of Energy). One of the forms into which energy can be transferred is **motion energy** or **kinetic energy.**

Kinetic energy (KE) is mechanical energy possessed by any moving object or body **by virtue of its motion.** This motion can be **linear** (in a straight line) or **rotational** (spinning or turning). A formula for KE can be derived from the **work** definition:

work = force × distance moved in the direction of the force

$$\text{KE} = \tfrac{1}{2} \times \text{mass} \times (\text{velocity})^2 = \tfrac{1}{2} \times m \times v^2$$

(Answer in joules)

Note that this concept includes dependence on the mass as well as the speed of the moving body.

An application of this idea to a sporting context is in the throwing of an implement (such as a shot or javelin or ball).

Mechanical work is done by the thrower who applies a force over a distance in order to accelerate the thrown object:

$$\text{work} = \text{force} \times \text{distance} = F \times s$$

At the point of release, this energy has been transferred into kinetic energy:

$$\text{KE} = \tfrac{1}{2} \times m \times v^2$$

So it can be seen that in order to make the release velocity (v) of the thrown object as big as possible, it will be necessary to **increase** the **force** (F) *or* **distance** (s) over which the force is applied. This is the reason throwers do so much weight training (to increase strength and hence F) and mobility and skill training (to improve the distance over which force is applied).

Looking at Figure 6.9, it can be seen that the skilful shotputter starts applying force on the shot from a position where the shot lies on a vertical line passing outside the back of the circle, to a point on a vertical line passing outside the front of the circle, and therefore applies force over the maximum distance possible.

Figure 6.9

Summary

1. You should be able to calculate speed, acceleration and deceleration from primary data

$$\text{speed} = \frac{\text{distance moved}}{\text{time taken}}$$

$$v = \frac{s}{t}$$

$$\text{acceleration} = \text{change of speed per second}$$

$$a = \frac{v - u}{t}$$

2. You should be able to plot distance-time and speed-time graphs. and understand the meaning of the slope (gradient) of each.
3. You should be able to apply Newton's Second Law to accelerating sportspeople and objects:

$$\text{force} = \text{mass} \times \text{acceleration}$$

$$F = m \times a$$

4. You should be able to apply Newton's First Law to stationary or constant velocity systems.
5. You should begin to understand Newton's Third Law and how this leads to the idea of reaction forces.
6. You should begin to be able to appreciate the place of air resistance and streamlining.
7. You should be able to distinguish between the concepts of speed and velocity.
8. You should be familiar with the concept of the conservation of energy as applied to thrown objects, and be aware that:

$$\text{Kinetic energy} = \tfrac{1}{2} \times \text{mass} \times (\text{velocity})^2$$

$$\text{KE} = \tfrac{1}{2} \times m \times v^2$$

Chapter 7
The Nature and Application of Force

Figure 7.1 'Grunt'

Very broadly speaking, **force** involves the idea of 'pushing' or 'pulling', the idea that one object exerts a force on another object, and the idea that a force will cause motion (that is, **accelerated** motion).

7.1 Force as a Vector

KEY WORDS AND CONCEPTS

force	**air resistance**	**gravitational field strength**
vector	**Bernoulli effect**	**reaction force**
resultant force	**Magnus effect**	**drag**
component	**momentum**	**fluid friction**
weight	**gravity field**	**streamlining**
mass	**scalar**	**laminar flow**
friction	**net force**	**impulse**

Force is also a **vector**, and therefore has a **direction** as well as a size or value. This point is very important to anyone thinking about what happens when forces are applied, because it enables a force in one direction to cancel out completely an equal force in the opposite direction, so that—in spite of very large forces being involved in a given situation—they can cancel out to give a zero (or very small) **net** or **resultant** force.

For example, consider the weight lifter in Figure 7.2. As he pulls upward on the bar. he exerts a force of 1000 newtons **upwards** on the bar and gravity exerts a force of 980 newtons **downwards** on the bar.

(See section below on measurement of force for a definition of the newton as the unit of force.)

The **resultant** or **net** force acting on the actual bar is therefore only about 20 newtons **upward**—just enough to accelerate the bar off the floor.

The idea that **net** force causes **acceleration** is linked with Newton's First and Second Laws of Motion, and is a fundamental property of force.

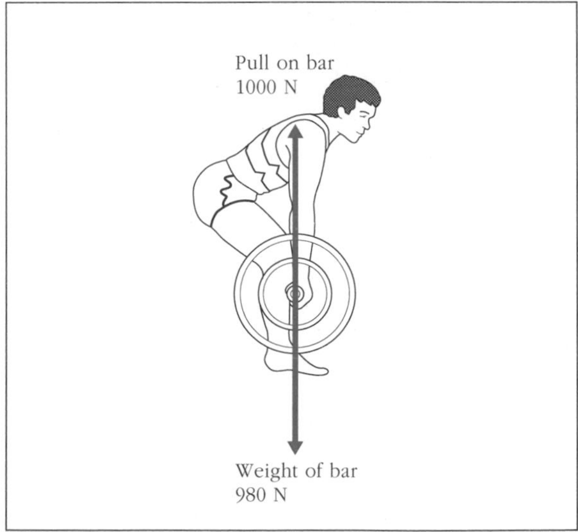

Figure 7.2

Also, it is possible for many forces acting in all sorts of different directions to cancel one another out. When this happens, from Newton's First Law we know that the object (or sportsperson) on which the forces act will either be stationary or moving at constant velocity (in a straight line). This situation is called **equilibrium**—where the object is stationary, **static equilibrium** and moving at constant velocity, **dynamic equilibrium**.

FURTHER NOTES ON VECTORS

There are specific mathematical rules which enable you to add together vectors which are **not in the same direction**. You may notice from Figure 7.3a and b that the resultant of two forces at an angle has been drawn by completing a parallelogram (in Figure 7.3a) or a rectangle (in Figure 7.3b, where the forces are at right angles). The **resultant** then lies along the **diagonal** of the parallelogram.

Figure 7.3

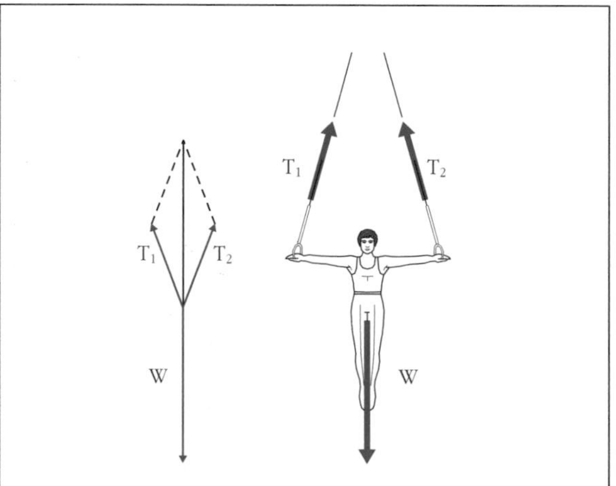

a. The resultant of the forces in the wires (T_1 and T_2) supporting the gymnast **upwards** cancels out exactly his weight (W) **downwards** (static equilibrium).

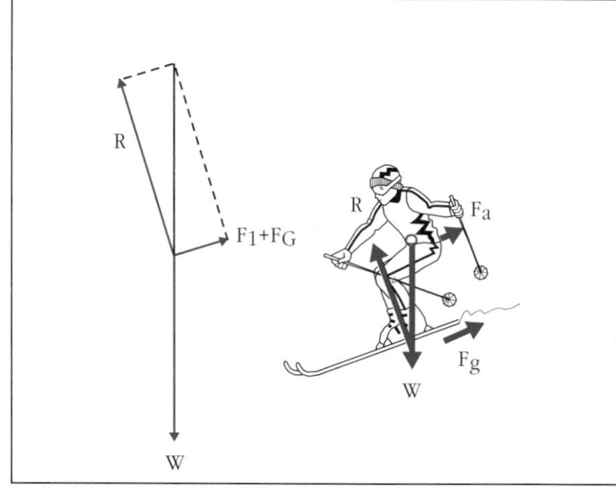

b. Again, the resultant of the normal reaction force (R) and the combined friction forces (air resistance and friction with the ground) exactly cancels out the weight of the skier—note the geometric vector diagram (dynamic equilibrium).

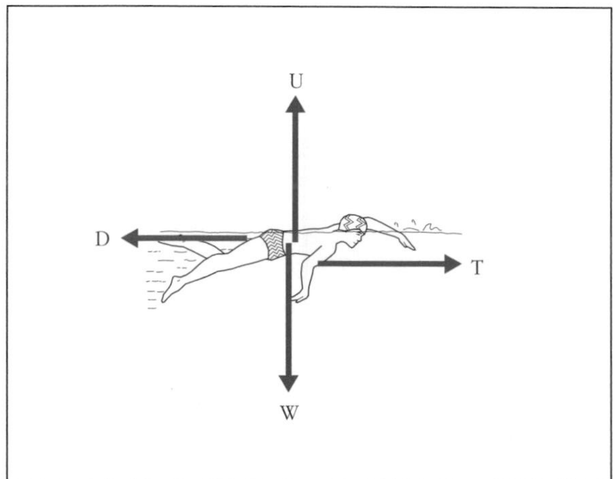

c. For the swimmer, his **weight** (W) is balanced by the **upthrust** of the water (U) and the forward **thrust** (T) cancels out the backward **drag** (D) of the water (again dynamic equilibrium).

It turns out that it is possible to do the opposite of this process, and split a **single** force into two parts at right angles to one another—this is called **taking components**. This is particularly useful when looking at vertical and horizontal components of a force—it might enable you to see how a complicated set of forces could add up or cancel out in relation to the **weight** of an object, which is always vertical.

The components together with the original force form a right angled triangle (see Figure 7.4)

Then we see that $\frac{F_V}{F} = \sin\alpha$ and $F_v = F.\sin\alpha$

and $\frac{F_h}{F} = \cos\alpha$ and $F_h = F.\cos\alpha$

where F_v = vertical component of F; F_h = horizontal component of F (the original force); and α = angle the original force makes with the horizontal.

Note that **either** the original force **or** the components can be used, but **not both together**.

It is beyond the scope of this book to progress these ideas further—physics text books will provide many examples of the use and practice of the formulae—and the Teachers Guide to this text (2nd edition) gives examples related specifically to sporting situations.

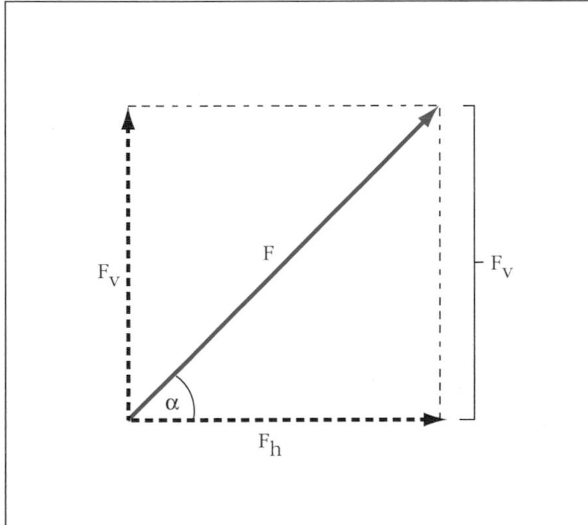

Figure 7.4

MEASUREMENT OF FORCE

Force is measured in **newtons**, one newton being defined as that force which produces an acceleration of one metre per second squared in a mass of one kilogram. (This is linked with Newton's Second Law of Motion, mentioned in Task Nine of Investigation 6.1.)

A more convenient measure is that one newton is approximately one tenth of the **weight** of a one kilogram mass, as in Figure 7.5.

The following paragraphs deal with the nature of force, and **how** forces are applied.

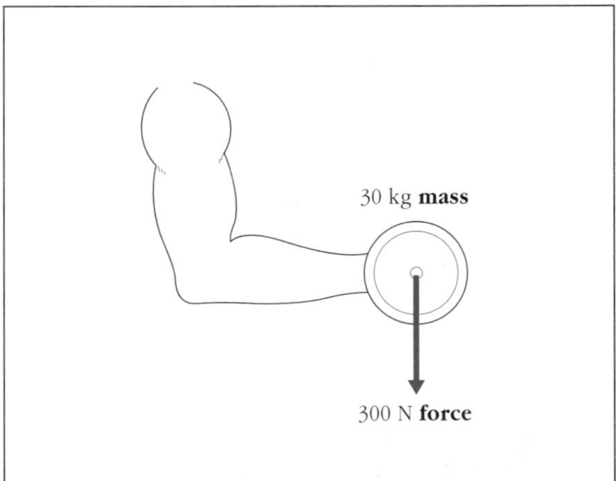

Figure 7.5 The lifter lifts a **mass** of 30 kg and exerts a **force** of 300 N.

WEIGHT

Gravity is an example of a **force field** (others occurring in nature are electromagnetic and nuclear and are not relevant to this text).

A force field is a means by which a force can be exerted **without touching**. So, for example, a ball in flight is accelerated towards the earth's centre continuously, and therefore has a **net** force acting on it without being in contact with the earth.

When thinking about this, you may be confused by the fact that the air *surrounds* the ball (since the ball is in contact with the air, which in turn is in contact with the earth). However, experiments on falling objects have been done in a vacuum which confirm the concept of the 'non-touching' force.

For our purposes, what is relevant is the gravity field at the earth's surface. This field exerts a force of 10 N for every kilogram of mass; this figure is known as the **gravitational field strength** (g) (the actual figure is 9.81 N kg^{-1} but it is usual to approximate this to 10 N kg^{-1} to simplify calculations). In other words, every kilogram mass has a force of 10 N acting on it towards the earth's centre, regardless of whether the mass is in contact with the ground or other surface, or whether it is moving through the air without contact.

Figure 7.6

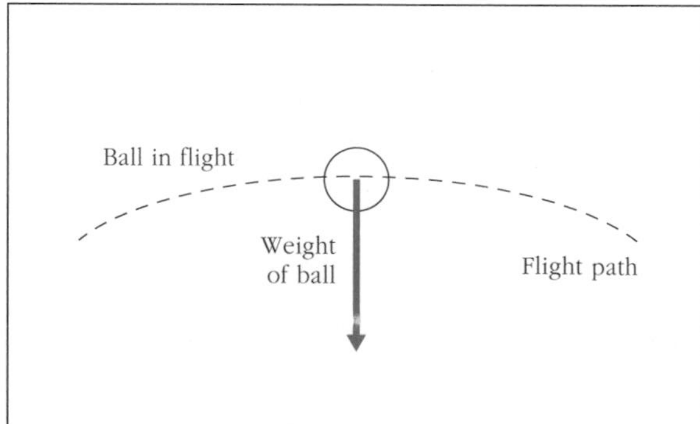

a. A ball in flight experiences a force (its weight) which causes acceleration towards the earth.

THE DIFFERENCE BETWEEN WEIGHT AND MASS

At this point it is worth mentioning that in scientific terms **weight** and **mass** are **not** the same.

Mass of a body is the same everywhere for a given object and does not change with, for example, the gravity field. So someone on the moon, where gravity is one-sixth of the earth's value, would have the same mass as on earth. **Mass** also depends on the quantity of matter present in the body and is related to the **inertia**.

b. The gymnast hangs high from the high bar; he is stationary and experiences his weight and an upward reaction force of the bar on his hands, which cancel to give a net zero force on his body (he is in static equilibrium).

Inertia is explained as resistance to acceleration. The more inertia an object has, the harder it is to accelerate when a given force is applied. This is why it is a good idea for any sportsperson who has to change speed or direction rapidly, or accelerate from rest, to have the least body mass possible consistent with necessary strength.

The **concept of inertia** is derived from **Newton's First and Second Laws**; the quantity m in the formula $F = m \times a$ relates exactly to this, and **inertia** is therefore a property of **mass**, and a property of all objects. **Inertia** also applies to decelerating objects or people, so that, once moving, an object requires a force to slow it down or stop it. For example, at the end of an indoor 60m sprint, runners have difficulty in stopping—this is because of their inertia/mass.

Weight, in comparison, is the **force** due to the gravity field and changes with the gravity field (for example, on the moon). It is therefore always present as a vertical downward force acting on either a sportsperson or an object in flight. In most situations, it is **very large** relative to other forces such as air resistance, friction, the Bernoulli effect and so on. Weight can be calculated using the formula:

$$\text{weight} = \text{mass} \times \text{gravity field strength}$$

$$w = m \times g$$

$$\text{where } g = 10 \text{ N kg}^{-1}$$

Figure 7.7

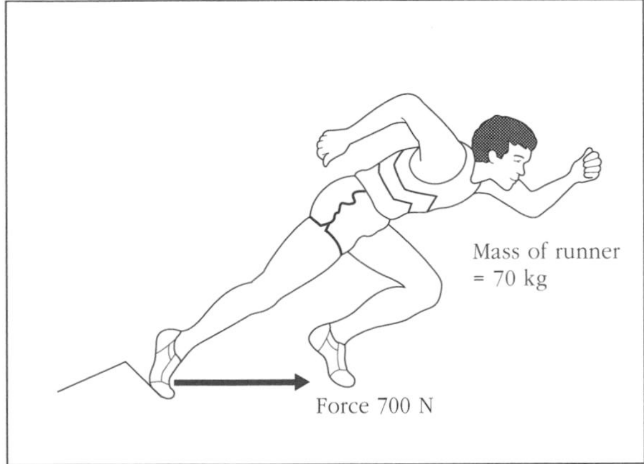

a. Mass of runner = 70 kg
Driving (Friction) force = 700 N
Therefore using Newton's Second Law:

$$\text{acceleration} = \frac{\text{force}}{\text{mass}} = \frac{700}{70} = 10 \text{ m s}^{-2}$$

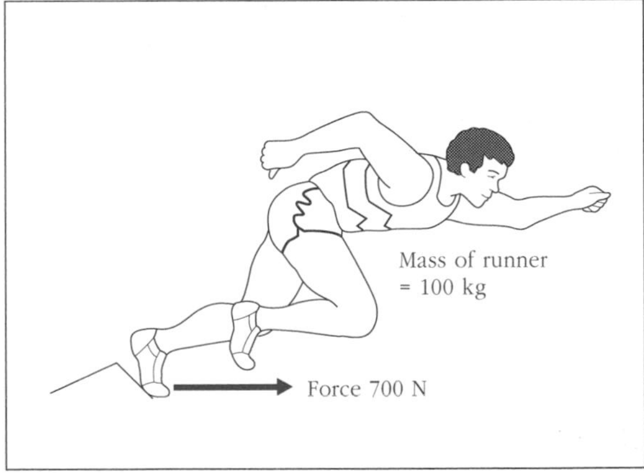

b. Mass of runner = 100 kg
Driving (Friction) force = 700 N
Therefore using Newton's Second Law:

$$\text{acceleration} = \frac{\text{force}}{\text{mass}} = \frac{700}{100} = 7 \text{ m s}^{-2}$$

Figure 7.8

As weight is proportional to mass, the acceleration produced by weight alone is always the same (i.e. the acceleration due to gravity is always 9.81 m s^{-2} or approximately 10 m s^{-2}). This means that sportspeople or objects in flight have **weight** as the predominant force.

The examples in Figure 7.9 assume air resistance to be small compared with the effect of the weight. Note that in each case the flight is a parabolic arc—this is discussed in more detail in Investigation 7.2 below.

Figure 7.9

a. After take-off, the flight of the jumper is governed by his weight only.

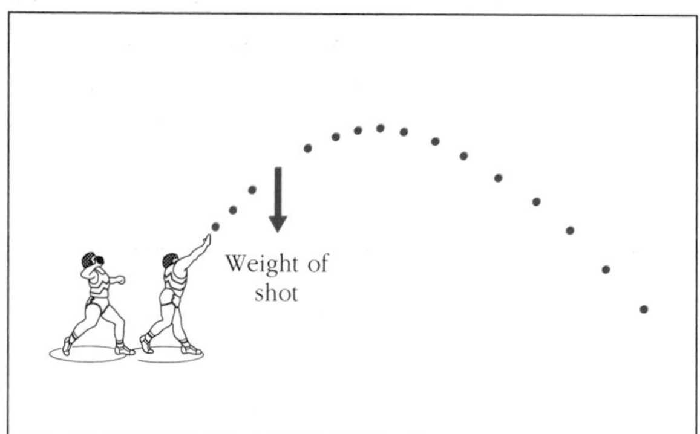

b. After release, the flight of the shot is governed by gravity only, i.e. its weight.

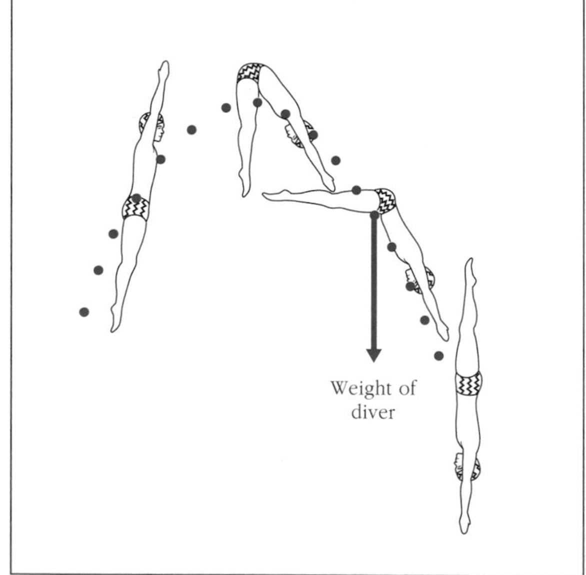

c. After leaving the board, the flight of the diver is governed by his weight.

REACTION FORCES

Reaction forces are those produced as a result of Newton's Third Law of Motion and were discussed in Investigation 6.1. This law states that when **any** object exerts a force on another, then **it** experiences an equal, but opposite in direction, force exerted by the other (Figure 7.10).

Figure 7.10

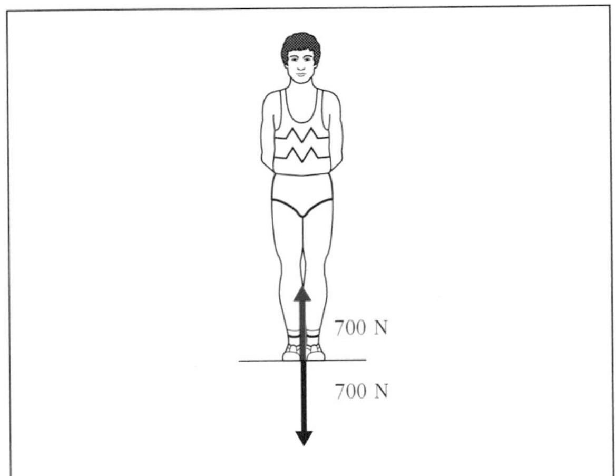

a. The athlete pushes **down** on the ground with a force of 700 N—the ground therefore pushes **up** on the athlete with a force of equal value.

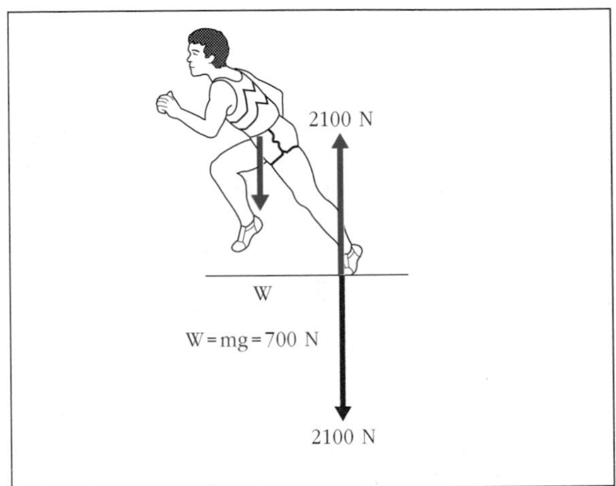

b. The athlete drives hard **into** the ground with a force of 2100 N—the ground therefore pushes up on him with a force of 2100 N. Here the **net upward** force on the athlete is 1400 N. which would cause an **upward** acceleration of 20 m s^{-2}. (Using $F = m \times a$, with $F = 1400$ N and m = mass of athlete = 70 kg.)

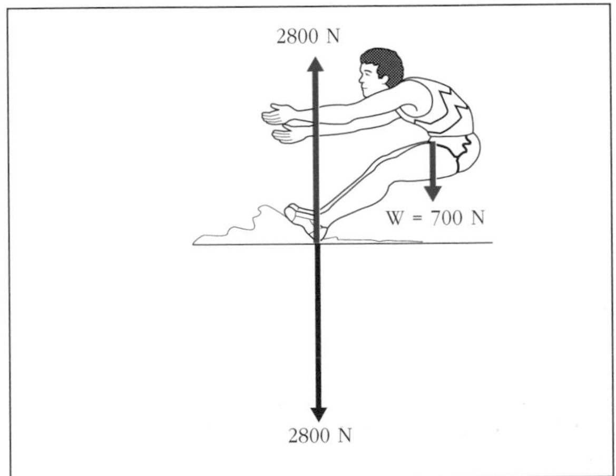

c. As the jumper lands, he pushes **into** the sand at 2800 N. which in turn pushes up on him at 2800 N. The **net upward** force is now 2100 N—producing a deceleration of 30 m s^{-2}. (Again using $F = m \times a$, with $m = 70$ kg.)

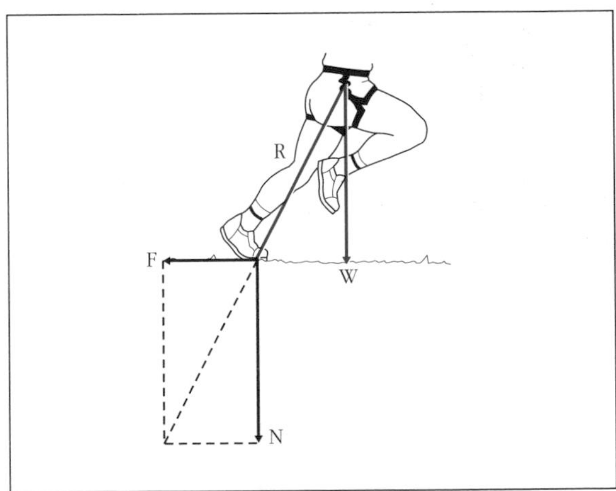

d. The total reaction force is the resultant of the **normal** reaction (i.e. at right angles to the ground) and **friction** forces (parallel to the ground). In this example, the **reaction resultant** (R) **on the athlete**, is a reaction to his pushing both **backward** (F) **and downward** (N) on the ground.

Reaction forces with the **ground** (or by the ground **on the athlete**) are caused as the athlete pushes hard down on the ground. These forces enable the **ground** to **push upwards** on the athlete and hence cause acceleration upwards of the athlete. The skilful person can vary this force by swinging or moving any body segment such as the trunk, arms or legs as demonstrated in Figure 7.11.

A detailed discussion of reaction forces is to be found in Wirhed, pages 95–96.

Figure 7.11

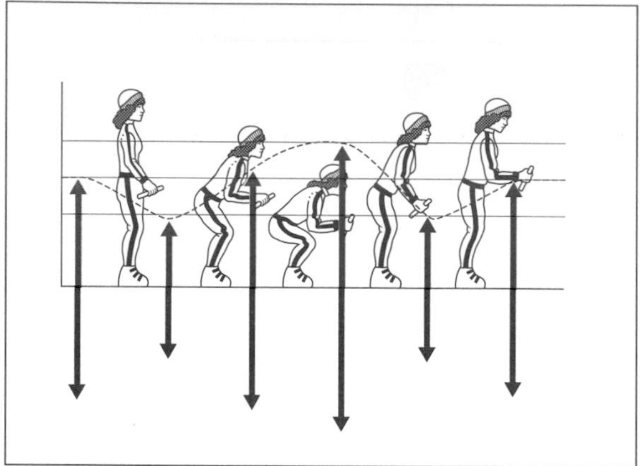

a. As the skier in this example moves her body down and then up, as shown in the sequence, the downward force she exerts on the ground (black arrows) changes, and hence the reaction force of the ground **upward on** her (red arrows) varies.

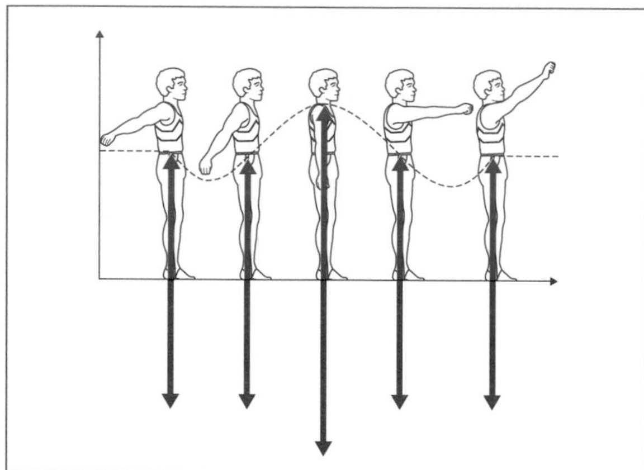

b. A similar example to **a.** is of a person swinging his arms. As the arms accelerate downwards or decelerate upwards (!), the force exerted on the ground is less, and as the arms swing violently at waist level, the effect is to pull down on the shoulders and hence increase the force on the ground. The reaction force **upward** on the body exactly mirrors this.

Reaction forces during the strike of a ball

Reaction forces can also be applied to the impact between sportsperson and ball, as in striking a ball with the foot, golf club, tennis racket etc. The force forward on the ball is equal and opposite in direction-backward on the foot and so on. In Figure 7.12, the force forward on the ball is marked in red and the reaction in black.

Figure 7.12 Reaction forces during strike of a ball.

a.

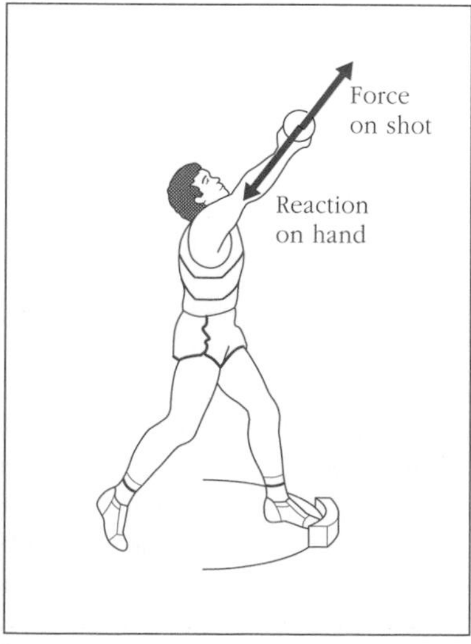

b.

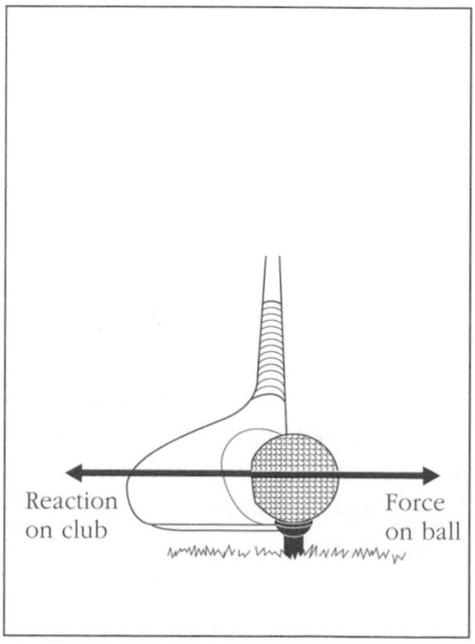

c.

Reaction forces within the body

Action and reaction forces within the body are caused when any muscle contracts. The two ends of the muscle pull equally on one another. In Figure 7.13 the **insertion** of the muscle is pulled to the **left**, and the origin to the **right**. The effect this has on the body shape or relative position of the different limbs and attachments depends on which of these are able to move.

Examples of muscle contraction causing changes in body shape, as origins and insertions are pulled towards one another are shown in Figure 7.14.

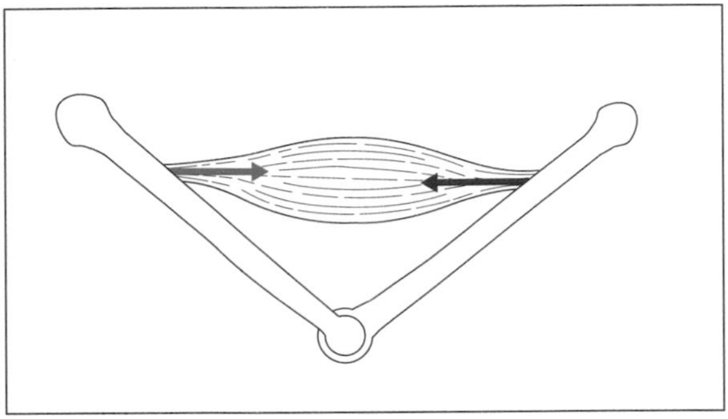

Figure 7.13 Reaction forces within the body.

Figure 7.14 Muscle contractions causing changes in body shape.

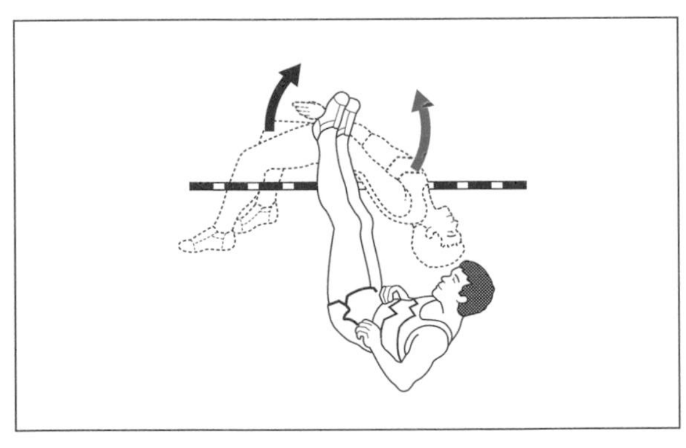

a.

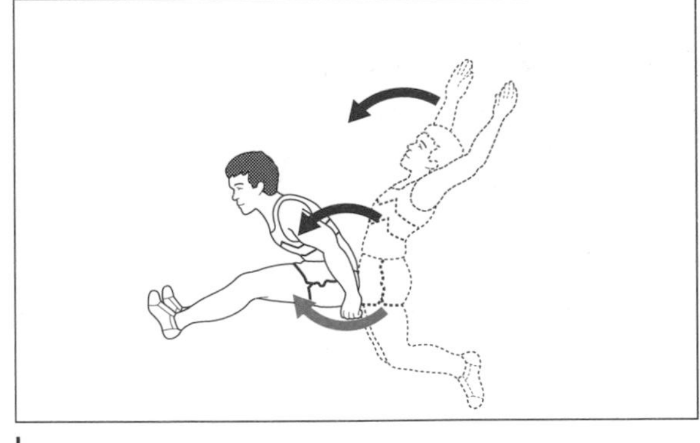

b.

c.

d.

FRICTION FORCES

Friction forces act sideways to any two surfaces which are sliding or trying to slide or slip past each other.

Friction forces are extremely important to the athlete or sportsperson since even walking would be impossible without them. Forces which enable a person to accelerate, slow down, or swerve and change direction are due to friction between the footwear and the ground. Therefore, anything which changes the friction (mud, flat shoes, ice, etc.) will drastically affect the ability of the person to do these things.

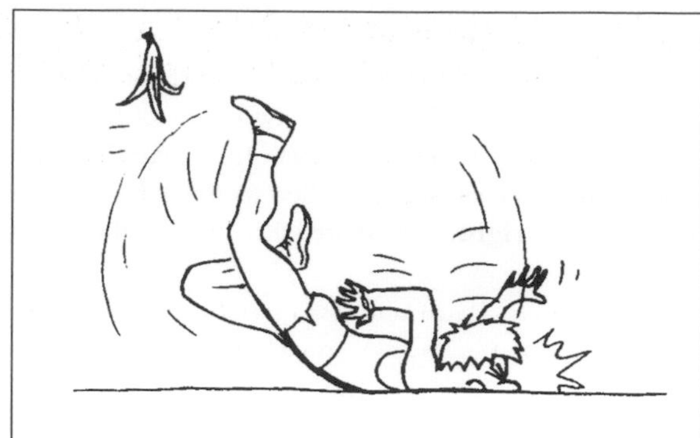

Figure 7.15 'Ouch! No friction.'

Figure 7.16 The **forces** acting on the sportsperson are marked in **red**. Note that in each case the jnormal reaction force (at right angles to the ground) is marked R, and the **friction** force *F*. *T* is the **thrust** of the athlete **on the ground** (marked in **black**), i.e. the force the athlete applies to the ground in order to achieve the swerve or acceleration required.

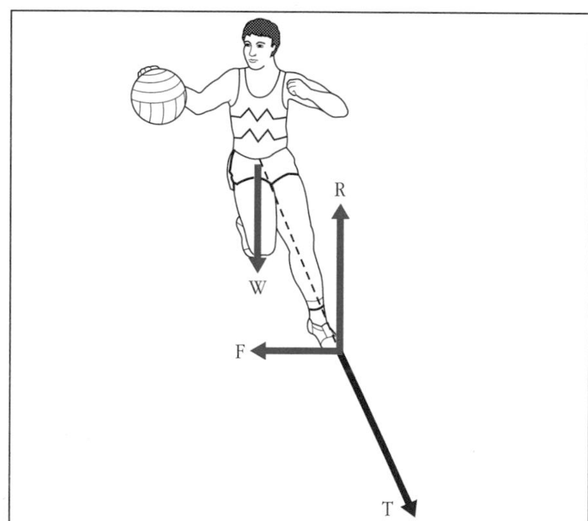

a.

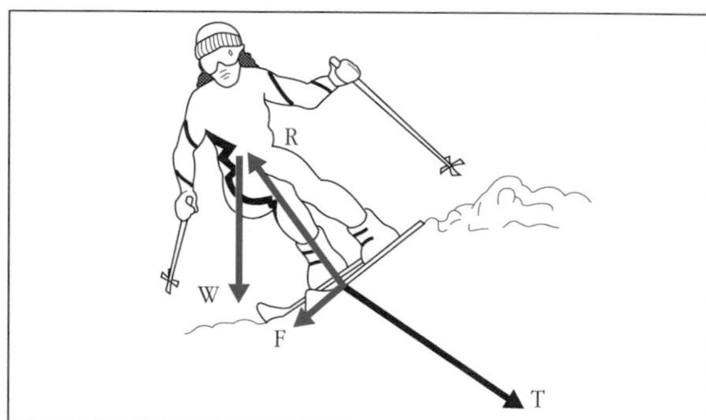

b.

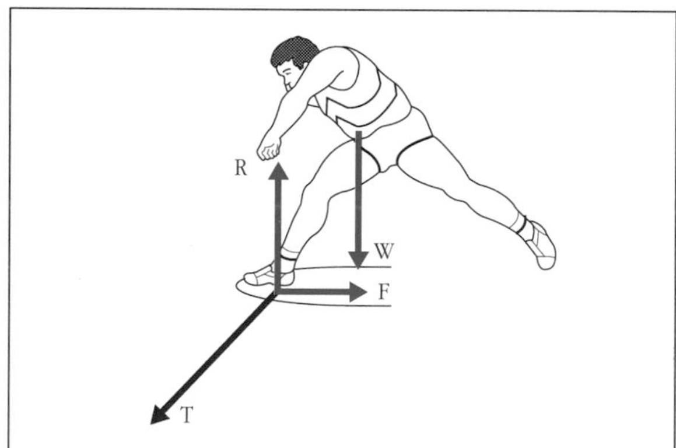

c.

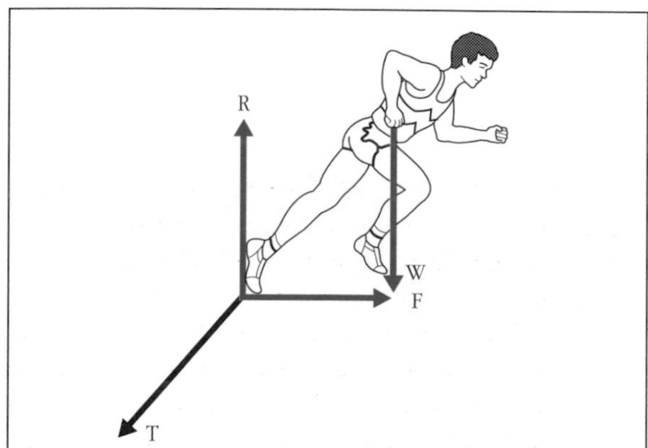

d.

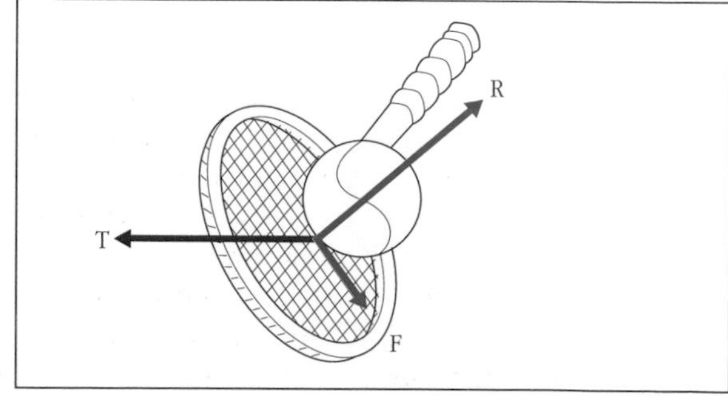

Figure 7.17 Forces acting **on** the ball are marked in **red** and the thrust of the ball **on** the racket in black.

Investigation 7.1 : The effect of different footwear and surfaces on friction forces

Aim: to demonstrate how friction forces change as footwear and surface change.

Task One

1. There is an almost unlimited number of combinations of the two factors; in fact, any combination from:

spikes	rubber track surface
flat trainers	shale track surface
studs	grass
ridged trainers	sand
walking boots	mud
climbing boots	ice
discus shoes	concrete
etc.	etc.

2. Some measure of comparability can be gained from a timed run over 20 m.
3. Each student can perform the 20 m run with a range of footwear and surfaces.

Table 52 : Results table

Time for 20 m	Footwear	Surface

Task Two—tabulation of results

Complete Table 52 by putting the fastest time at the top of the chart and the slowest at the bottom.

Task Three—analysis of results

1. Obviously, it will be difficult to prove anything scientifically from this investigation, but it should be possible to place the footwear–surface combinations in some sort of grouped order—the most friction to the least.
2. What factors increase friction?

   It would be simple to say clean dry fixed surfaces (with no loose material), but is it always the case that ridged/spiked/studded shoes have the most friction?

   What about smooth soled shoes on concrete?
   What effect does surface water have?
   Why are rock-climbing boots completely smooth-soled?
   Does the area of contact between shoe and surface play a part?
   Do spikes completely eliminate the effect of surface?

In conclusion, the amount of friction which can be exerted depends on the nature of the footwear and the surface, and on the normal reaction forces between the footwear and the surface. This is particularly significant in the case of the racing car with inverted wings which force the car **down** onto the road, thereby **increasing** the reaction force on the car **and** therefore **increasing** cornering friction between tyres and road.

For an athlete, running spikes are an attempt to remove completely the differences between various footwear and surfaces, and considerable research has been undertaken by shoe companies to find variations (bobbles, nylon barbs, spike plates, brush spikes, etc.) which would be more effective in this aim. Studs do the same job for games players, and shoe companies lay great store by the efficiency of their shoe stud patterns for different conditions of playing surface.

AIR RESISTANCE AND FLUID FRICTION

Investigation 7.2 : Flight of a ball or thrown or struck object

Aim: to consider the flight paths of different objects. The word object is meant to include badminton shuttles, discuses, javelins, as well as light and heavy balls.

Task One

Work in threes—one acting as thrower, one as catcher and the other as viewer/sketcher.

1. Throw or strike the following objects outdoors—remember that you are watching the flight path **not** playing a game:

   a. Shot
   b. Discus
   c. Football
   d. Tennis ball
   e. Golf ball
   f. Cricket/Hockey ball
   g. Javelin
   h. Frisbee

   To obtain the most simple shapes, try to make the release height as near as possible to the landing or caught height.
2. In each case sketch the flight path as you see it **from a position some distance from the flight and observed at right angles to it**. The stress is laid on this because we want a view of the flight undistorted by the perspective of the thrower (or striker) or receiver of the ball or object.
3. It may be helpful to take a video film of these flights, so that the shape of the fight path can be assessed more carefully. This would then be viewed indoors later and corrected versions of the flight paths drawn up.

Task Two

1. The same sequence is repeated indoors, this time with a gently thrown or struck:

   a. Badminton shuttle
   b. Tennis ball
   c. Indoor shot
   d. Squash ball
2. This lends itself more to observation by video film.
3. Drawings of flight paths should be sketched.

Task Three—analysis of flight paths

1. Collect together drawings (from the whole group) into groups:
   a. flight paths almost exactly symmetrical, circular (?) or parabolic in shape;
   b. flight paths nearly symmetrical but obviously not so;
   c. flight paths definitely asymmetric.
2. What characterizes groups a, b and c?

   Make a list of factors which might affect the shape of flight for each group.

   Consider effects like: weight of the object, speed of the object, spin of the object and so on.
3. Create a chart of possible factors in the three categories above.

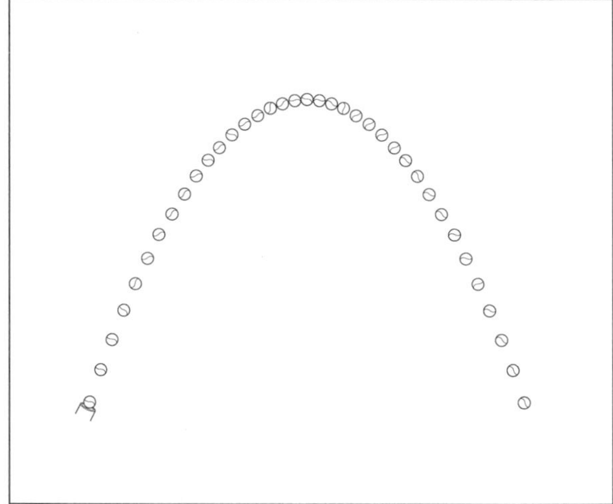

Figure 7.18 A typical shape of a symmetrical flight path. Note that the shape is parabolic and not circular—and is that mentioned in the section on the effect of weight on objects.

Task Four—what forces affect the flight path?

1. Sketch a diagram of the flight path of:
   a. a shot
   b. a badminton shuttle
   c. a football (outdoors).
2. Indicate the forces acting on each object. Assume that the object is well clear of the ground and moving upwards (at an angle of about 45° to the vertical) with considerable speed.
3. Remember that once the object is in flight and moving with whatever velocity it started with (at whatever angle to the horizontal), the only things that can affect the flight are the earth's pull of gravity (force = its weight) and the effects of the atmosphere.

   In which direction will the **gravity force** (its **weight**) always act?

   In which direction will the **air resistance force** act (relative to the direction of motion at any given point in the flight path)?

Task Five—how do the forces affect the flight path?

1. If gravity always acts in the same direction (downwards, towards the centre of the earth), what shape would this give the flight path if there were no air resistance? (Sketch your answer.)

   Would the shape of the flight path always be the same (regardless of shape or mass of object) if there were no air resistance?
2. What factors does the air resistance force depend on?

   Fluid friction (scientific term for air resistance) depends on the speed of the object (the faster it goes the more the force) and on the shape of the object. How do these factors fit in with what happened to our real objects in flight?
3. What effect will air resistance have on the motion of our flying objects?

   This depends on the property of inertia (mass) of the object. The argument goes like this:

a. For any two objects of the same **size** and **shape** moving at the same speed, the air resistance will be the same and in the same direction.

b. If the two objects have different **masses**, then the effect of the same air resistance force on each would be different, the heavier (more massive) object would be decelerated less than the lighter (less massive) object.

   (This follows from **Newton's Second Law of Motion** i.e. $F = m \times a$. For a given force, $m \times a$ remains the same, so if m is bigger, a must be smaller and vice versa.)

4. Write about one side explaining how these ideas explain what you have observed in the first parts of this investigation.

Task Six—the effects of spin during flight

You will now perform a series of experiments indoors with a table tennis ball.

1. Attempt to observe and draw diagrams of the flight paths for:
   a. Sidespin—left- and right-handed
   b. Topspin
   c. Underspin (backspin).
2. In each case mark on your diagram the direction (or sense) of spin—clockwise or anticlockwise to the direction of view; also show the direction of swerve or dip of the ball.

   The Bernoulli effect, which enables winged objects heavier than air to fly, is thought to be responsible for these effects. This is discussed in more detail later in this section.
3. Go and practise (and then write an explanation of how you did it) the spinning and swerving of one or more of:
   a. a tennis ball b. a cricket ball
   c. a soccer ball d. a golf ball.

Further reading —stability in flight by spin

This brief section is to draw your attention to the fact that an american football/rugby, javelin or discus has much more stability in flight when spun. The reasons for this are beyond the scope of this book, but form the same basis as the reason that a spinning gyroscope always attempts to point in the same direction.

AIR RESISTANCE AND FLUID FRICTION

As discussed in Investigation 7.2, **fluid friction** is the scientific term used to describe resistance to motion of any object or body moving through a fluid—gas or liquid. This force (marked A in Figures 7.19–21) depends on the shape of the object moving, and on its speed, and acts in the opposite direction to that of its forward motion. In each of the diagrams, the weight of the moving object or person is marked W.

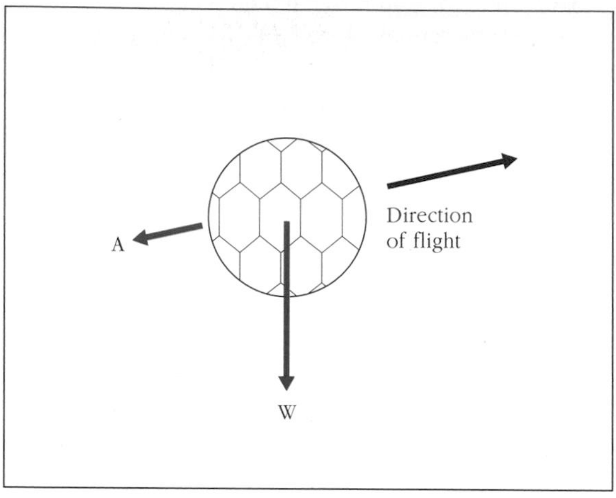

Figure 7.19 Forces acting on a ball in flight. The most simple object has the shape of a sphere, and in this case the fluid friction force is proportional to the radius of the sphere and to its forward velocity. So it can be guessed that the size of swimmer or boat or free fall diver as seen from the forward direction affects the size of the fluid friction force.

Figure 7.20

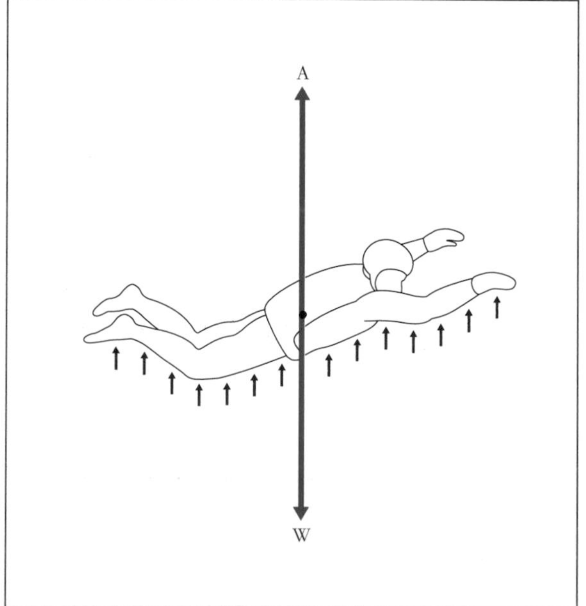

a. The free faller moves at terminal (constant) velocity with air resistance force exactly balancing the weight.

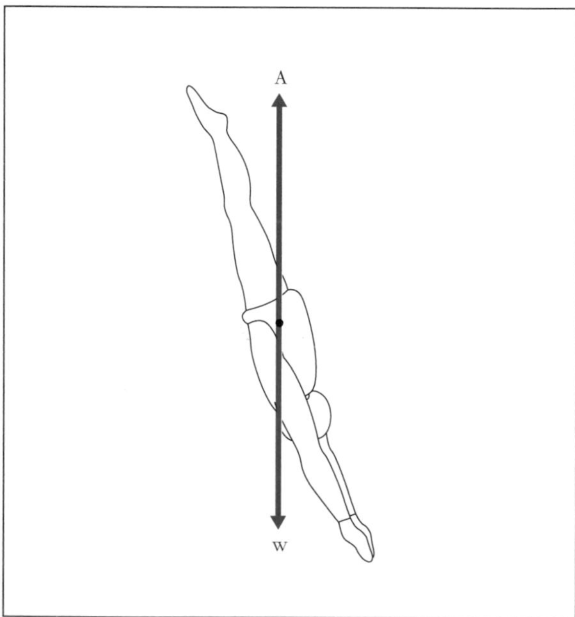

b. In a diving position, he would move faster because the air resistance force would be too small to balance the weight at the slower speed. He would therefore speed up and increase the fluid friction force until the two forces balance again.

Figure 7.21 The swimmer in **a** has a bigger shape, when viewed from the forward direction, than the swimmer in **b**; therefore **a** would have a bigger fluid friction force A than **b**.

As the object moves through the fluid. it has to move fluid out of its way, and obviously the more fluid moved the greater the fluid friction force.

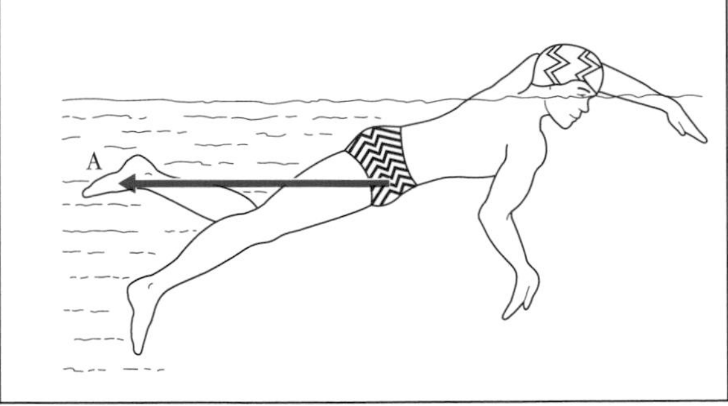

a.

b.

STREAMLINING

If we can make the fluid flow smoothly past the object, as opposed to being flung into vortices, then the fluid friction drag will be less. Smooth flow means that the fluid flows in layers (scientifically termed **laminar flow**). It is the design of wings, car bodies, racing cyclists' helmets, ski and speed skating outfits and swimming gear which tries to reduce the tendency for fluid to be flung sideways into vortex patterns. The rough texture of certain types of cloth can also create vortices when moving through air. The two profiles of racing cyclists' helmets shown in Figure 7.22 are moving at the same speed, and have the same profile if looked at from the forward direction, but helmet **b** has less fluid friction because the air flows smoothly past.

Figure 7.22 Streamlining of racing helmets.

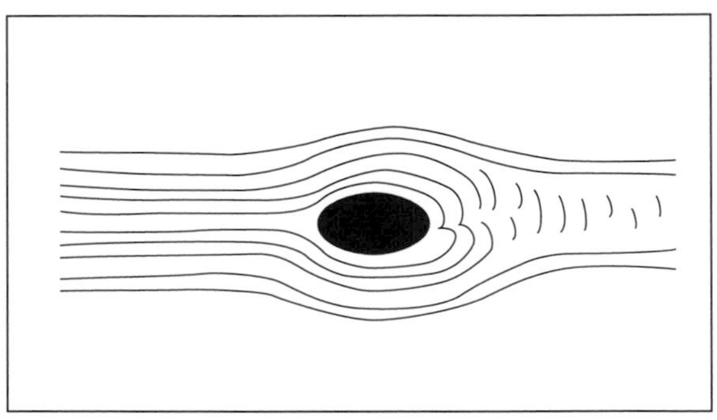

a.

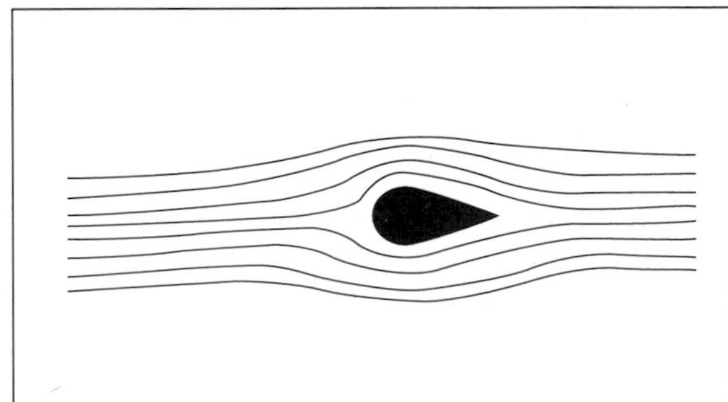

b.

Investigation 7.3 : Drag on swimmer in pool

Aim: to look at how the shape and speed of the body (or boat) moving through water affects the fluid friction drag of the water. You will need a force meter measuring up to 500 N.

Task One—towing the swimmer

1. Students should work in pairs one towing, and one in the water. The person doing the towing will need to practise two speeds of moving (walking and trotting) and try to maintain these when actually towing.
2. Student A will then tow the swimmer using rope and either fastening it to the swimmer's wrist or a body harness. The rope will be attached to a force meter.
3. Four different tows are suggested (see Figure 7.23).
4. Tow at the two speeds practised and tabulate the results.

Task Two—discussion of observations

1. What effect does speed have on drag force?
2. What effect does shape or area of body, when viewed from the forward direction, have on the drag force?
3. Look for water turbulence in the four situations, which has most and which least?
4. What conclusion would you draw for the best body shape and position when swimming?

Figure 7.23

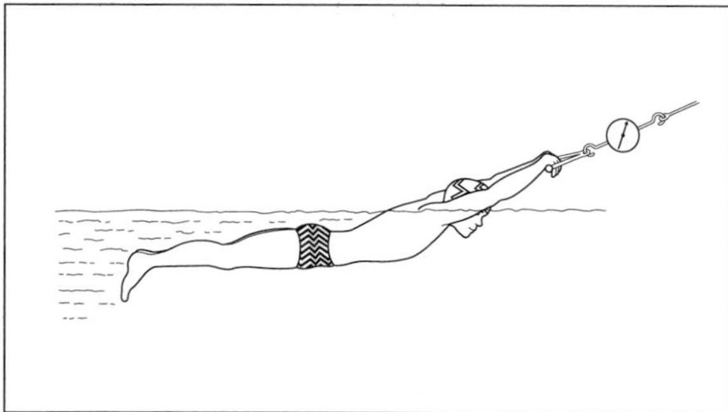

a. Swimmer streamlined.

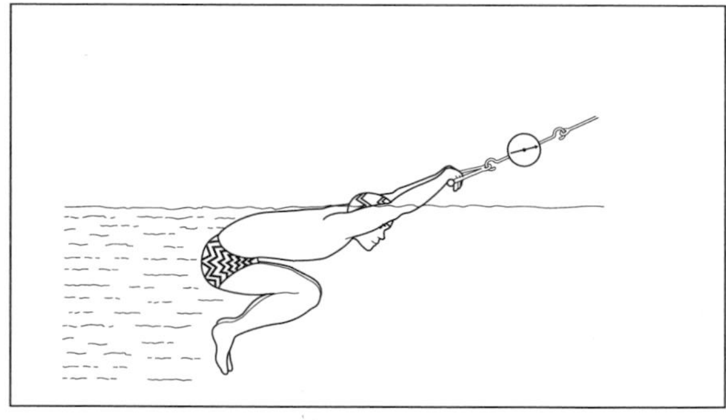

b. Swimmer in tight ball.

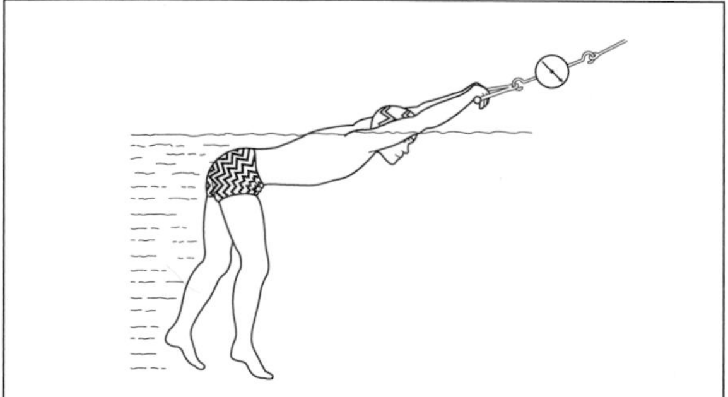

c. Swimmer making as big a shape as possible.

d. 'Swimmer' in a canoe (or on an air bed).

THE BERNOULLI EFFECT

As mentioned briefly above, this is the effect which enables wings to fly and which can be applied to spinning and swerving balls in flight. Essentially, the pressure on a surface is reduced when a fluid flows past, and the faster the flow the greater the reduction in pressure. On a very simple level, this is because there is less chance of a fluid molecule striking the surface if the fluid is flowing rapidly—hence an effective reduction in pressure.

Application of this idea to a spinning ball is called the **Magnus effect**, and concerns the way the air flows past the ball (see figure 7.24).

Figure 7.24

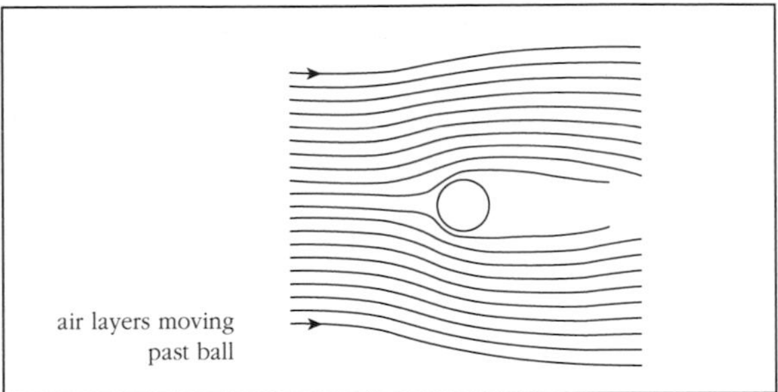

a. For a non-spinning ball, the air moves past symmetrically—there is no sideways force.

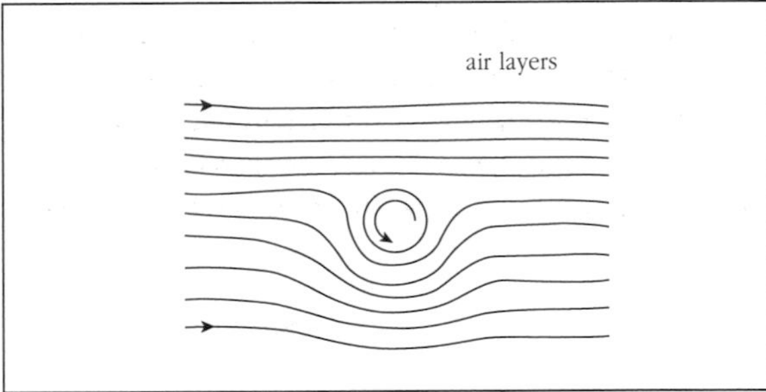

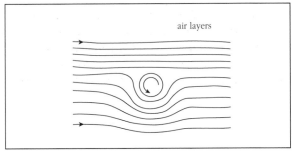

b. For a spinning ball, air flows further past the lower edge. and therefore travels faster on this edge—hence pressure is reduced on the bottom of the ball and the ball swerves downwards.

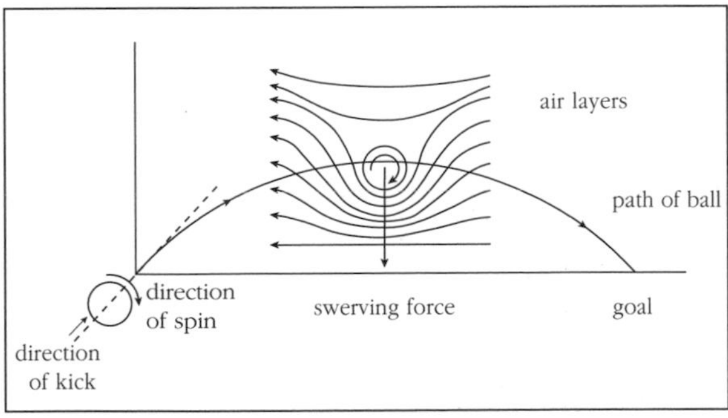

c. This diagram shows how a soccer corner kick can be made to swerve into the goal.

IMPULSE AND IMPACT

When a foot, bat or club strikes a ball, there are often very large forces acting on the ball during the period of contact. These cause correspondingly large accelerations of the ball as it moves from rest to its speed at the start of its flight. Since such forces act over very short times, it is convenient to use a different approach from that of the straightforward definition of acceleration and Newton's Second Law of Motion when dealing with such cases.

The same idea is applicable to tennis, squash, cricket and baseball where the ball is already moving rapidly on contact with the racket or bat.
This new approach is as follows.

Strictly, Newton's Second Law should read:

Force applied to a body = rate of change of momentum of the body

Force = change of momentum per second

$$\text{Force} = \frac{\text{change of momentum}}{\text{time taken to change}}$$

or Force × time = change of momentum

This brings in two new constructs as below:

Momentum: defined by **mass × velocity**

or **momentum** = $m \times v$

Impulse: defined by **force × time**

or **impulse** = $F \times t$

Therefore Newton's Second Law becomes:

impulse = change of momentum

$F \times t$ = change of $(m \times v)$

Note: this formula is compatible with our original Newton's Second Law formula since:

change of $(m \times v)$ = $m \times$ (change of v)

therefore $F \times t$ = $m \times$ (change of v)

$$\text{or } F = m \times \frac{(\text{change of } v)}{t}$$

and $F = m \times$ acceleration

Use of impulse in impacts

In Figure 7.25 we see the force of impact on the ball (F), and its reaction on the foot of the kicker (R). This force of impact lasts for a short time (t in the formula). Figure 7.26 is a graph of force of impact against time. It shows a force of 250 N lasting for $^1/_{50}$ s. It can be seen that the product $F \times t$ has the value $250 \times {^1/_{50}} = 5$ N s.

This can be equated to the area under the graph (shaded red). The area under a force–time graph is a convenient measure of impulse.

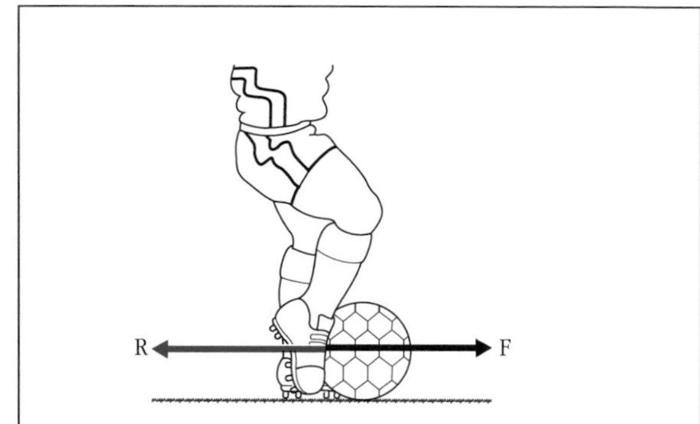

Figure 7.25

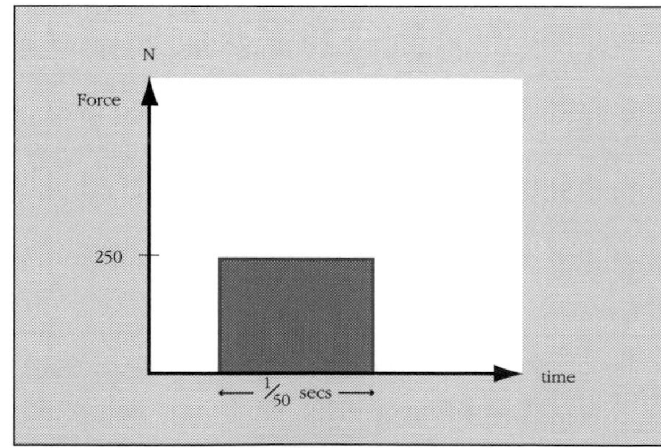

Figure 7.26

In practice the force of impact is not constant, but varies with time. It is possible to measure how F changes with time using a force sensor mounted on the ball or foot. Figure 7.27a shows how a graph of force (F) against time would look.

Impulse is defined as the area under the graph (shaded red), which represents the total force × time added up over the time of contact. Note that the maximum force is large, 500 N, and the time of contact short, $^1/_{50}$ s.

impulse = area under graph

= $^1/_2 \times {}^1/_{50} \times 500$ approximately

(this assumes that the shape in Figure 7.26a is a triangle, and its area = $^1/_2$ × base × height).

= 5 N s

If the mass of the ball, m = 0.5 kg

then the change of momentum

= m × change of velocity of the ball

= 0.5 × final velocity

Therefore

impulse = change of momentum

5 N s = 0.5 × final velocity

therefore

final velocity = 10 m s^{-1}

Figure 7.27b shows the graph of the reaction force (R) on the foot of the kicker with time. Note that the graph exactly mirrors that of the force on the ball—this fits in with Newton's Third Law—since at all times the reaction force must be exactly equal and opposite (and therefore negative) to the force on the ball.

Figure 7.27

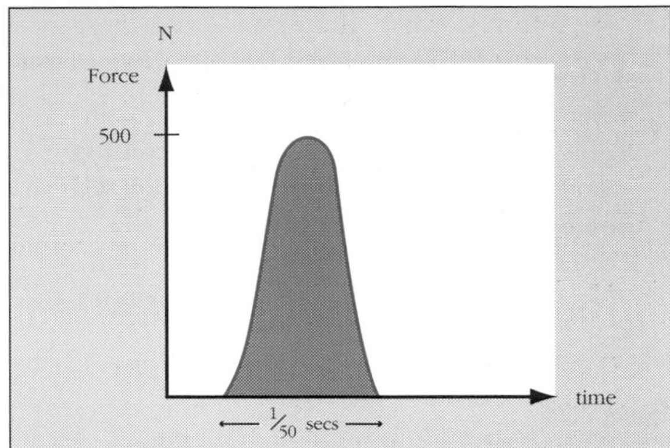

a.

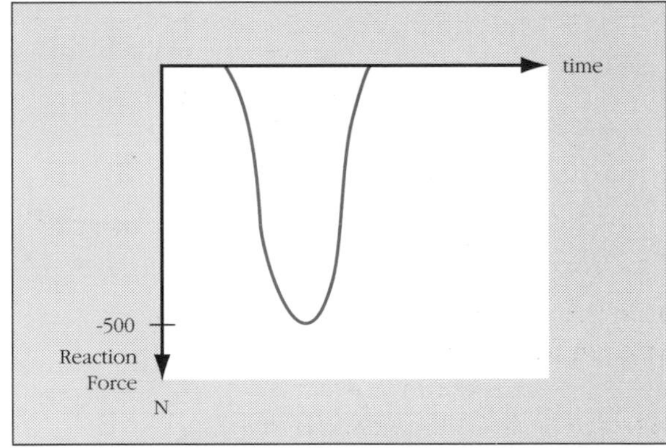

b.

Investigation 7.4 : Impulse and impacts

Task One

1. When a tennis ball is struck by a racket, as in Figure 7.28, the ball arrives with an **incoming** velocity of 15 m s^{-1}, and leaves the racket with an **outgoing** velocity of 25 m s^{-1}.
   The mass of the ball is 200 g = 0.2 kg.
   Time of contact between ball and racket is 0.1 seconds.
2. Calculate the **incoming momentum** of the ball (*remember:* momentum = $m \times v$).
3. Calculate the **outgoing momentum** of the ball.
4. Calculate the **change of momentum** of the ball.
5. Using the formula:
   $F \times t$ = change of momentum
   calculate the average **force of impact** between ball and racket.

Figure 7.28

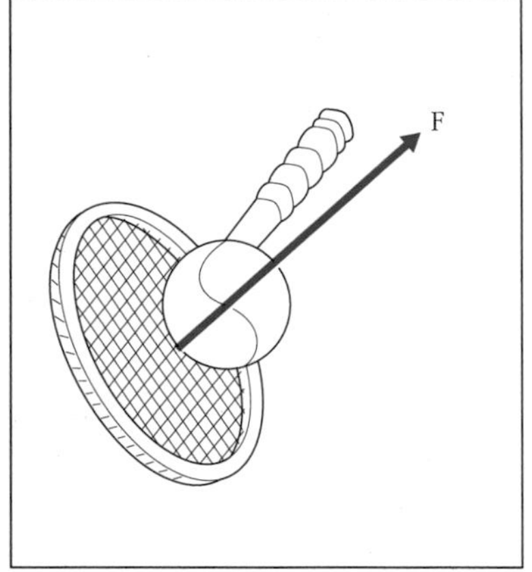

a.

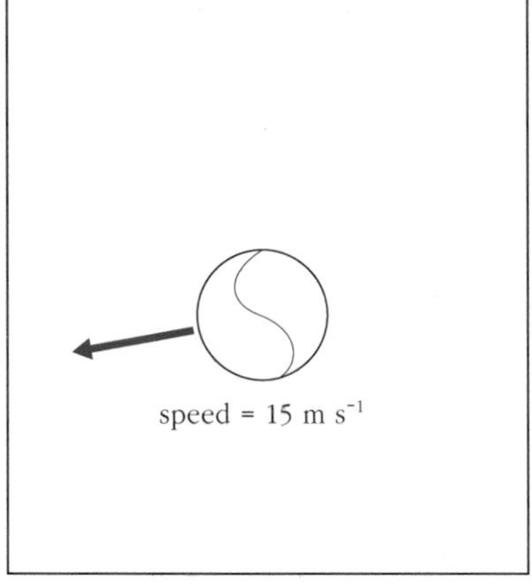

b.

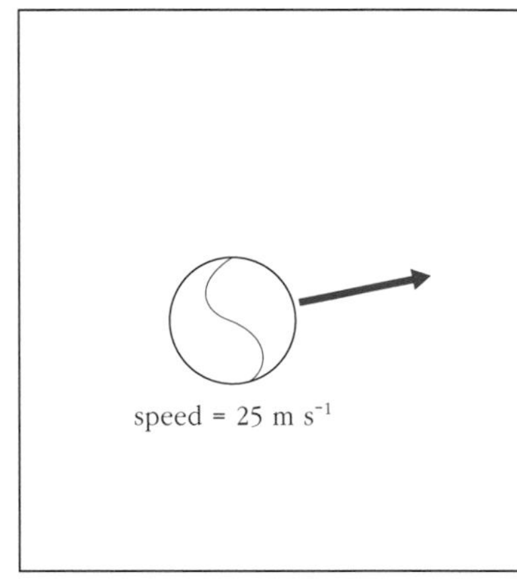

c.

Task Two

1. Look at the two graphs in Figure 7.29 of force of impact against time for a baseball bat striking a ball.
2. Explain why follow-through increases the outgoing velocity of the ball.

Figure 7.29

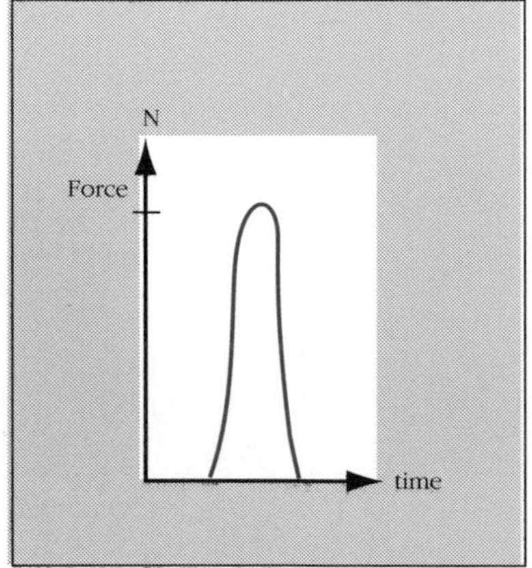

a. Shows the force *without* follow-through.

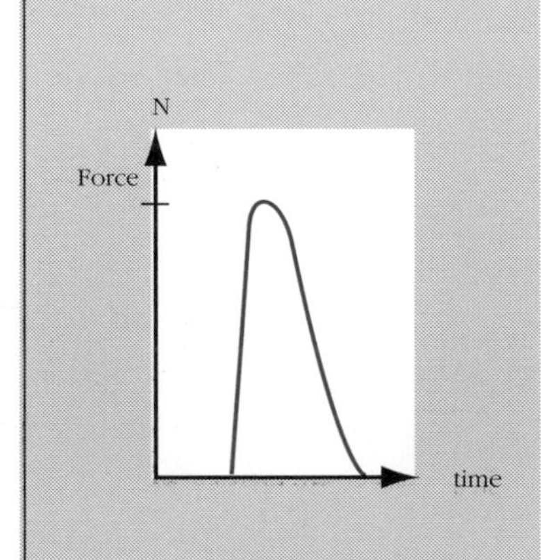

b. Shows the force *with* follow-through.

Task Three
Explain why the catcher of a hard ball finds it more comfortable to let his hands ride with the ball on catching.

Figure 7.30

a. Short time of impact – large force. **b.** larger time of impact – moderate force. **c.** long time of impact – . . . .

Task Four
Research other areas of possible application of the impulse concept, particularly in connection with forces of impact of the human foot with the ground, and impacts of a moving body with other objects.

Force platforms linked to a computer have been developed to analyse scientifically impacts between take-off foot and ground, at the point of take-off for a high or long jumper. These allow comparison of the way in which force is applied for jumpers of different standards, and so point the way towards improvements in technique of the less competent performer.

Figure 7.31

a. Sprinter stops quickly!

b. Sprinter doesn't stop quite as quickly.

Task Five
1. Look at the properties of ball and surface which may affect the outgoing velocity of the ball from an impact.
2. Where does the energy come from in ball/bat impacts?
3. What effect does spin of the incoming ball have on the outgoing spin, direction and velocity of the ball?

Summary

1. You should have an understanding of the concept of force, and you should be aware of the unit of measurement of force—the **newton**.
2. You should be familiar with the concept of force as a vector, and the idea of a vector as a quantity with **direction** as well as size. Also, you should understand the way in which several forces in different directions can combine to form a **net** force or **resultant** force.
3. You should be able to distinguish between **weight** and **mass**, and use the formula:

   weight = mass × gravitational field strength
   = mass × g
   = mass × 10 (newtons)
4. You should understand the nature of **reaction forces**:

   a. applied on the sportsperson by his/her surroundings
   b. applied by one part of the body to another.
5. You should have an understanding of the nature of **friction** forces and the factors affecting them.
6. You should be aware of **air resistance** and **fluid friction** acting on objects and the human body moving through fluid, and the factors affecting them.
7. You should be aware of the **Bernoulli effect** (and Magnus effect) as it affects spinning balls in flight.
8. You should be able to use the concepts of **momentum** and **impulse** in respect of the analysis of forces of impact between bat and ball, and foot and ground.

   momentum = mass × velocity
   = $m \times v$
   impulse = force × time
   = $F \times t$
   impulse = change of momentum
   $F \times t = mv - mu$

7.2 Internal Forces

KEY WORDS AND CONCEPTS

internal forces	**lever**	**fulcrum**
moment of a force	**couple**	**stability**
principle of moments	**effort**	**stable equilibrium**
clockwise	**centre of mass**	**base of support**
anticlockwise	**load**	**unstable equilibrium**
torque	**equilibrium**	**neutral equilibrium**

Wirhed (p. 98) uses this term to describe those forces exerted by one part of the body on another, via the musculature and internal system of ligaments and tendons of the body.

Simply, a muscle contracts when a suitable string of nerve impulses arrives and causes muscle fibres to shorten via a complex series of biochemical reactions, involving the consumption of glycogen and the release of energy. When this happens, both ends of the muscle, i.e. origin and insertion, are pulled towards each other—in the manner described in the section on reaction forces and in Figure 7.32. The effect that this has on body shape, limb orientation and motion of the body or parts of it depends on the relationship of the muscle insertion to the joint complex which enables movement in any particular case, and whether or not the body is in contact with the ground. For example, consider the gymnast in Figure 7.33a who is performing a pike action while in flight. Here, both upper and lower body move towards each other as the abdominal muscles contract.

In Figure 7.33b the feet are fixed in position so that the upper body **only** moves when the stomach muscles contract.

Figure 7.32

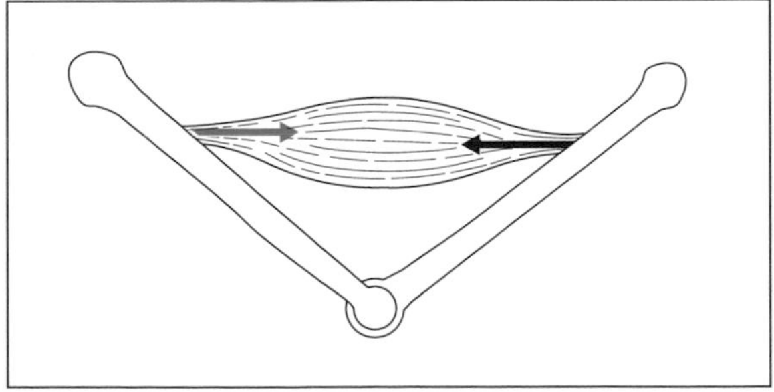

Figure 7.33

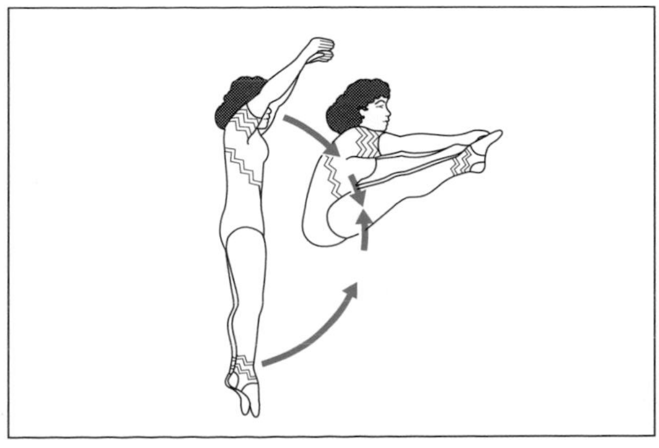

a.

b.

Investigation 7.5 : Force developed in a muscle

This investigation uses the concepts involved in levers and the principle of moments applied to specific muscles in certain joint complexes. Since it is very difficult to isolate one muscle (or closely located group of muscles) in a body movement, two examples have been chosen—others may be developed by students, but they must take care when using these ideas that several muscle groups and joint complexes are not used. The simple technique here applies only to the simplest situations.

Materials: a range of force meters (or weight training equipment) to measure forces up to 500N, and rulers or soft tape measures.

Task One—levers

1. Most of you will be familiar with the concepts behind levers and what is meant by **pivot** or **fulcrum**. This is the balance point for the lever: the point about which the 'lever arm' turns, or the **axis of rotation** of the lever system.
2. '**Effort**' is the force applied by the user of the lever to some point on the lever arm.
3. The '**load**' is the force applied by the lever system; this can be more than **or** less than the effort depending on the type of lever used.
4. Draw sketches of the following lever systems, identifying clearly the positions and directions of the **fulcrum**, **effort**, and **load** in each case:
   a. a wheelbarrow
   b. nutcrackers
   c. a spade
   d. a screwdriver
   e. scissors or pliers
   f. a crowbar.

Task Two—the principle of moments

1. The **moment of a force** about a fulcrum is defined by:
   moment of force = force × distance to the fulcrum
   (Distance is measured at right angles to the force.)
   Moment of force is also known as **torque**. **Couple** is defined as the moment of a pair of equal forces applied in opposite directions to a lever arm, as shown in Fig. 7.34.
   The **couple** $= F \times d$
2. Looking at Figure 7.35:
   Moment of force = Force × distance to the fulcrum
   (distance measured at right angles to the force)
   = 200 (newtons) × 0.3 (metres)
   = 60 N m
3. This **moment** tends to turn the lever clockwise (the opposite direction of turn being anticlockwise).
   The **principle of moments** says that:
   For a system of balanced forces about a fulcrum or pivot:
   total anticlockwise moment = total clockwise moment about the fulcrum.
   A system in balance in this way is said to be **in equilibrium**.

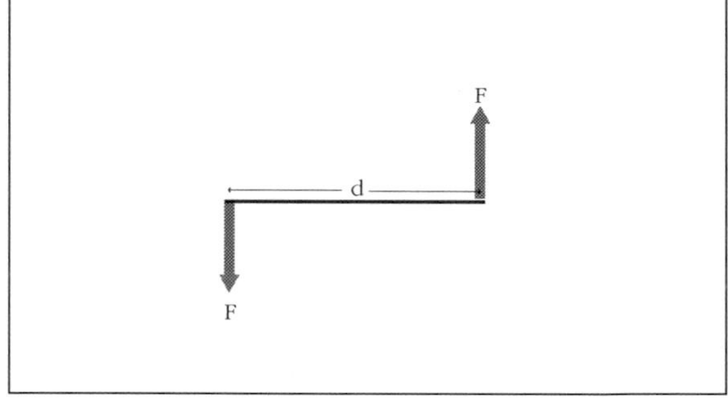

Figure 7.34

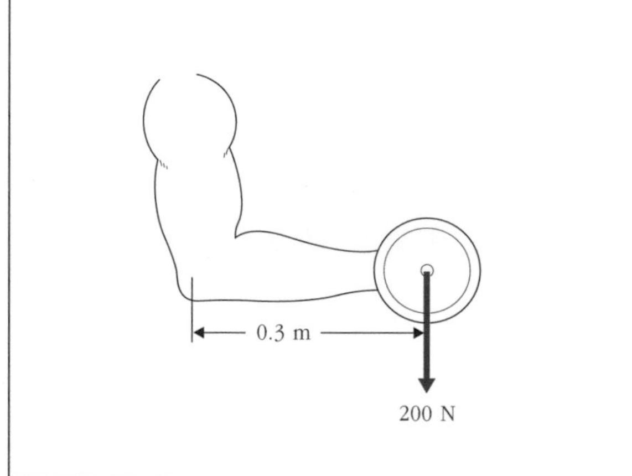

Figure 7.35

4. Consider the elbow joint complex in Figure 7.36. Calculate the moment of the weight held in the hand about the elbow joint as a fulcrum (this force, the weight, is the **load** on the lever) using:

   Moment of force = Force × Distance from fulcrum (fulcrum is at elbow)

   This moment would be the **clockwise** moment, i.e. tending to turn the forearm in a clockwise direction.

5. The **anticlockwise** moment is provided by the force in the biceps muscle group (this is the **effort** on the lever) as it pulls upwards to balance the force in the hand. Now calculate this force using the principle of moments:

   Anticlockwise moment = Force × Distance of biceps insertion from elbow joint

   This must be equal to the final answer obtained in **4** above; therefore, we arrive at the equation:

   Anticlockwise moment = Clockwise moment

   Thus you can now calculate the force in the biceps muscle.

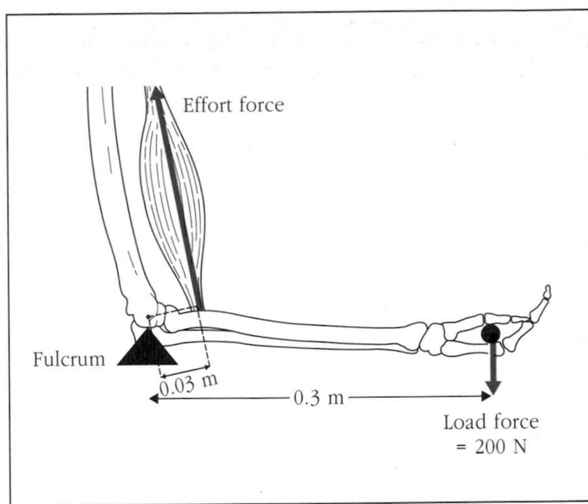

Figure 7.36

Task Three—calculation of the force in your own biceps muscle

1. You are now going to measure this force using the same method as above.
2. Make measurements with a ruler of the two distances marked in Figure 7.37, i.e. distance of hand from elbow (x) and distance of insertion of biceps tendon to elbow (d).
3. Measure the load force you can apply with your hand in the position shown in the diagram—the position is chosen so that the angles between the effort and the forearm and the load and the forearm are both right angles.

   The force can be measured by using weights, a multigym, or a force meter.

   Remember: the weight of 1 kg is 10 newtons force.

4. Following exactly the procedure in **Task Two** above, calculate the force developed in your biceps muscle.

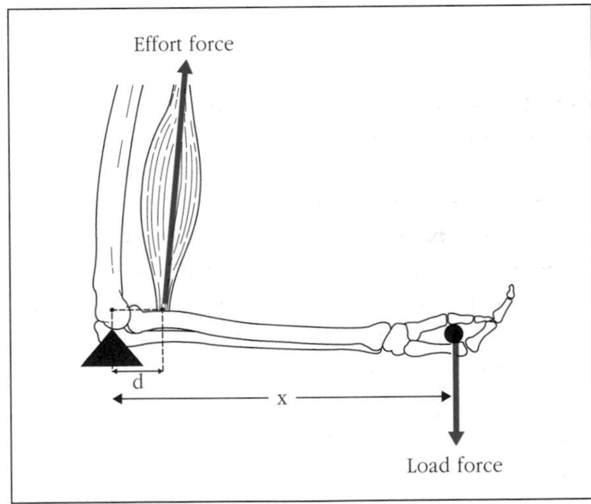

Figure 7.37

Task Four—force in achilles tendon and calf muscles

1. The aim now is to repeat this procedure for a further joint complex, i.e. the ankle.
2. From Figure 7.38, measure carefully the distances shown **on yourself** (it may be easier if a partner takes the measurements). Note that the fulcrum is under the ball of your foot.
   i.e. Distance from tibia/ankle joint to fulcrum (x) and distance from achilles tendon to fulcrum (d)
   Note: distances must be measured at right angles to the forces.
3. Calculate the force lifted by this system through your leg by adding together your weight (in newtons) to any weight or force exerted by your body (for example, a weight on your shoulders).
   Remember: 1kg mass weighs 10 N force
4. Now calculate the force in the achilles tendon using the same process developed in **Task Three**.

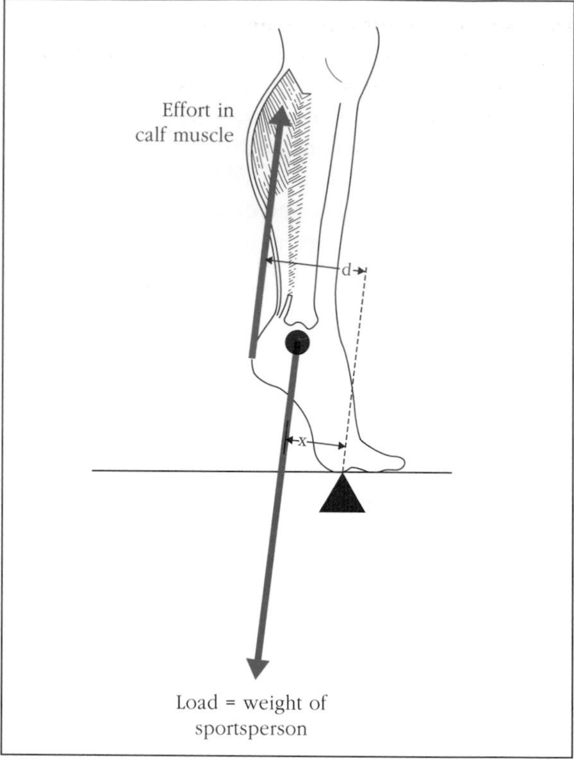

Figure 7.38

Task Five—another force in muscle calculation

Try to find another joint complex and range of muscles and an appropriate exercise, which will enable you to calculate the force in the muscles in the same manner as in Tasks Three and Four.

Task Six—extension study

1. This further study examines the relationship between force developed in a muscle and the muscle girth or cross section. It involves measurement of:
   a. muscle girth (using tape measure) OR
   b. cross-sectional area.
   Estimate maximum width of the muscle, w.
   Assuming a circular cross section
   and using the formula: $A = \frac{\pi \times w^2}{4}$
   find an approximate value for the area (A).
2. Create a table of force developed in a muscle from Tasks Three, Four and Five and girth or muscle cross-sectional area.
3. Next plot a graph of force developed in the muscle (y-axis) against muscle girth or cross section (x-axis).
4. What can you conclude from the graph?

Task Seven—changing the angles

1. Taking the biceps group as an example, explore what happens when the angle between the effort and the lever arm (in this case the forearm) changes, as in Figure 7.39.
2. You will need to measure the angle between the 'pull' of the biceps and the forearm and note whether the force at the hand changes.
3. This task is left open for the student to explore the method of displaying his/her results, and deciding on a conclusion from these.

Figure 7.39

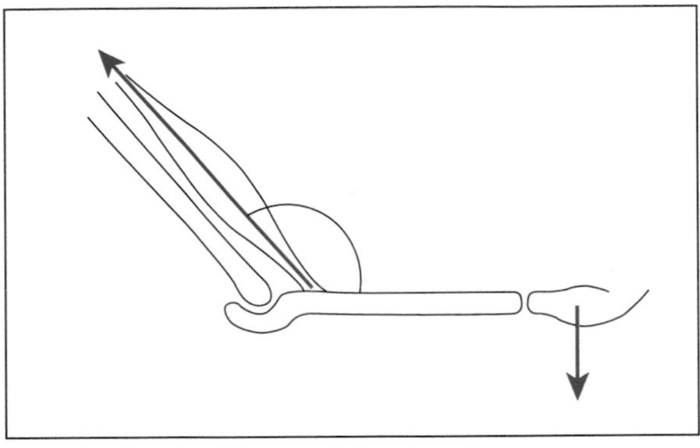

a.

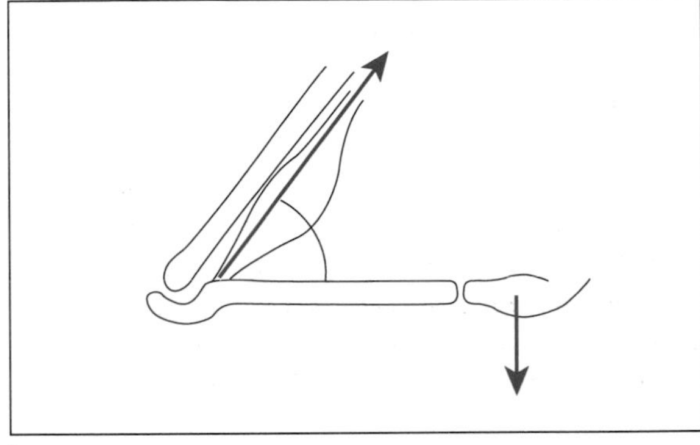

b.

CLASSIFICATION OF LEVERS

Another way of looking at lever systems is to classify them in the following way:

Class 1 lever

The fulcrum lies **between** the effort and the load, as in Figure 7.40a. Note that if the system is in balance the principle of moments applies.

An example from a human joint complex is the action of the **triceps** muscle on the elbow joint—the **effort** lies in the muscle, the **fulcrum** at the elbow joint, and the **load** at the hand which would be exerting a force as shown in Figure 7.40b. This particular arrangement has the load smaller than the effort (effort is closest to the fulcrum).

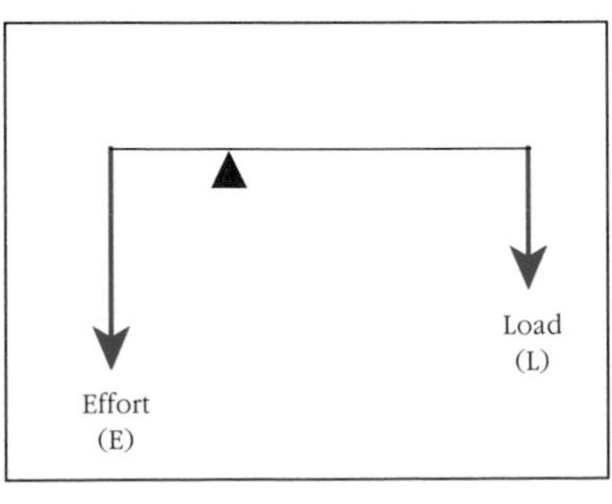

a.

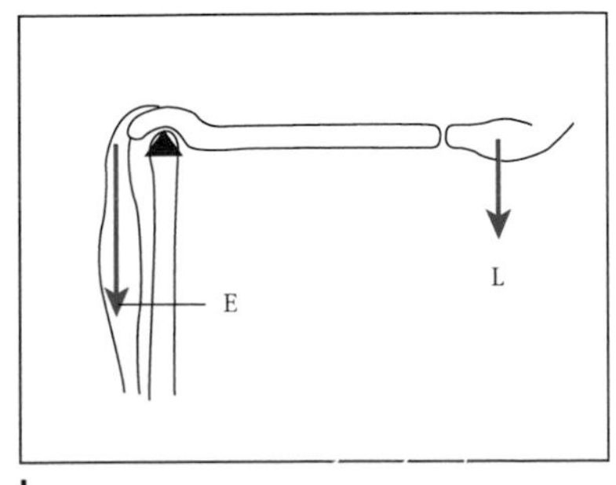

b.

Figure 7.40

Class 2 lever

In this type of lever the fulcrum is at one end of the lever arm, the effort at the **other end**, and the load between fulcrum and effort (Figure 7.41).

The example of this in the human body is the ankle joint as discussed in Task Four of Investigation 7.5. Here the load is bigger than the effort (effort is further from the fulcrum).

Class 3 lever

The fulcrum and **load** are at opposite ends of the lever arm, with the effort somewhere in the middle. In this case the effort is **always** bigger than the load, since the effort is nearer the fulcrum. This is the most common class of lever to be found in human joint complexes (Figure 7.42a).

The easy example from the human system is the biceps/elbow complex used frequently above (Figure 7.42b).

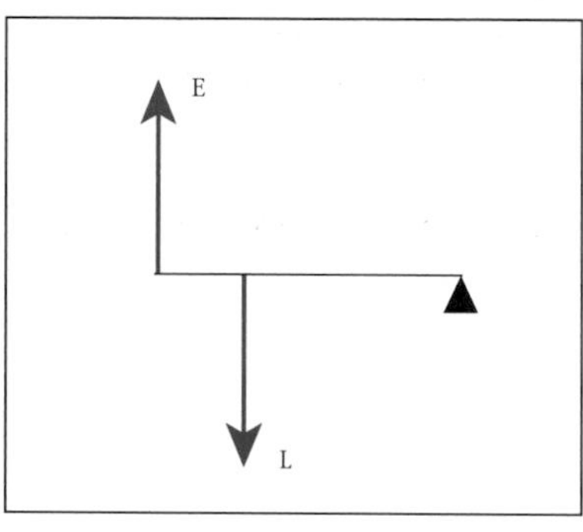

a.

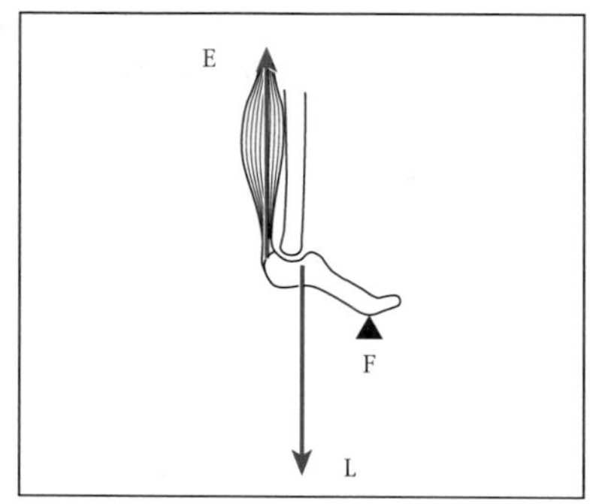

b.

Figure 7.41

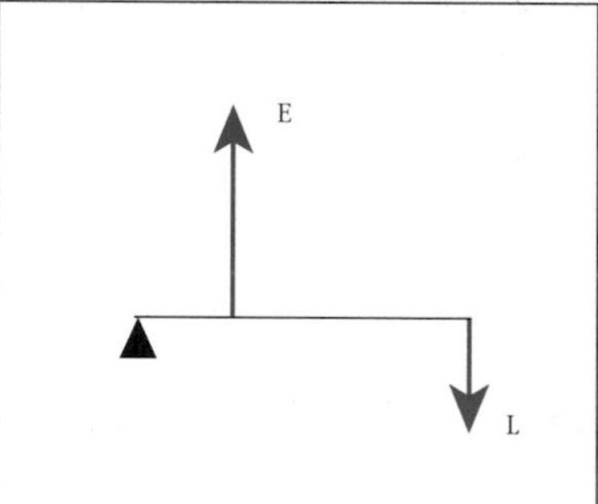

a.

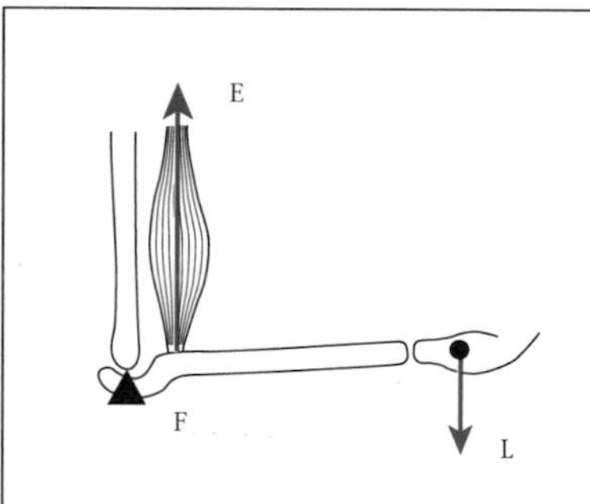

b.

Figure 7.42

REVIEW QUESTIONS

1. Classify the lever systems mentioned in Task One of Investigation 7.5.
2. Research the human joint complexes and classify the lever class of as many muscle groups on the joints as you can.

A MORE ADVANCED LEVER REPRESENTATION

In the interests of simplicity, the discussion above has been restricted to those cases where the muscle (effort) action and the load direction are at right angles to the lever arm. This is because the definition of a moment includes the idea that all distances from the fulcrum are to be measured at right angles to the force involved.

In practice, of course, it rarely if ever happens that these angles are 90°, so it is necessary to be able to represent diagrammatically in a simple way real muscles and joints as they would naturally operate. From such diagrams it will be possible to calculate the forces acting in muscles in the same way as in Investigation 7.5. Figures 7.43–46 show how this can be done.

In each case:

a. shows the location and directions of forces (Load and Effort) and Fulcrum

b. shows the simplified lever representation.

The load is in each case the weight of object, limb or head.

In Figure 7.46, we have two antagonistic muscle groups working on opposite ends of the lever arm; the forces exerted by these muscles are marked M_1 and M_2, respectively, and perpendicular distances from the fulcrum x_1 and x_2 (After Hochmuth *et al.*)

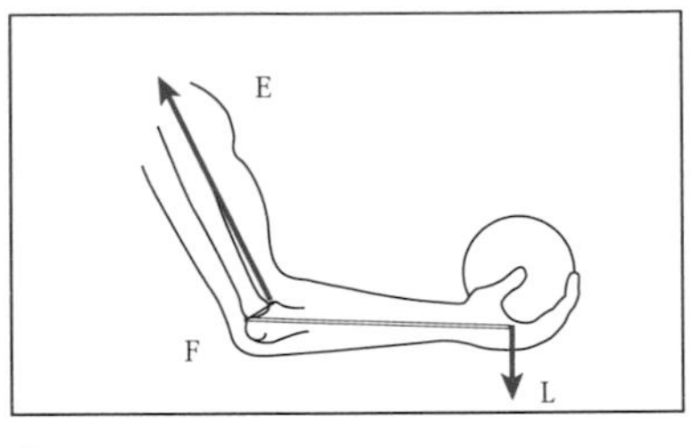

a.

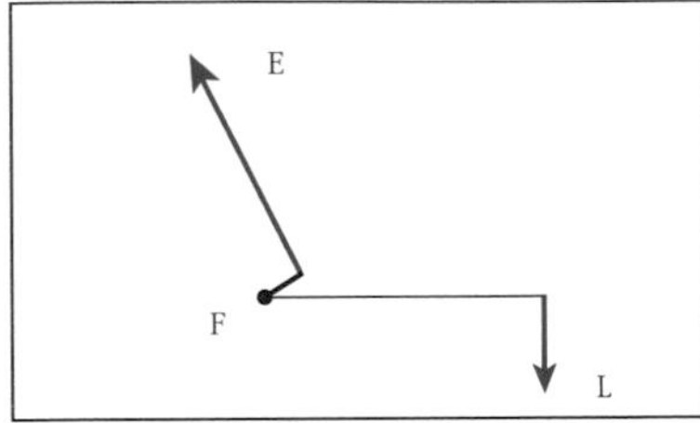

b.

Figure 7.43 The biceps/elbow system.

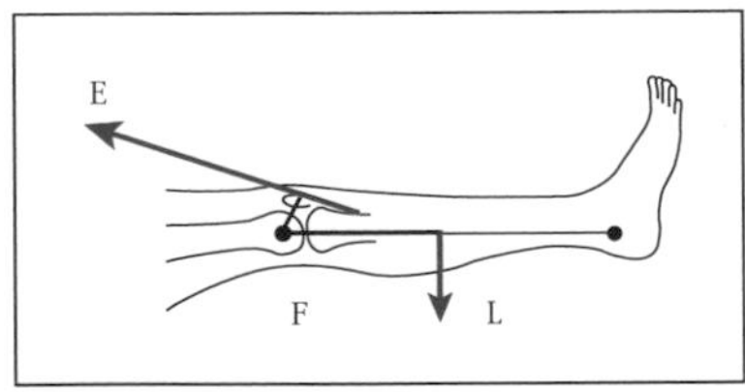

a.

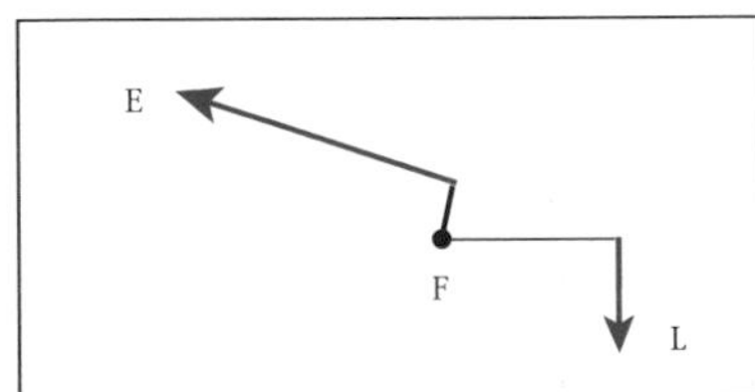

b.

Figure 7.44 The patella tendon/lower leg system.

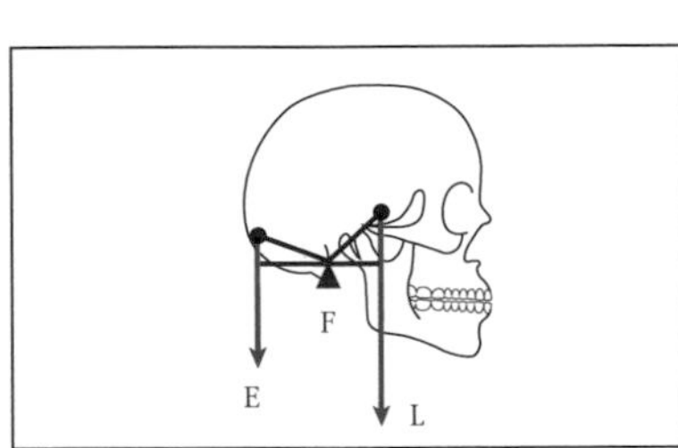

a.

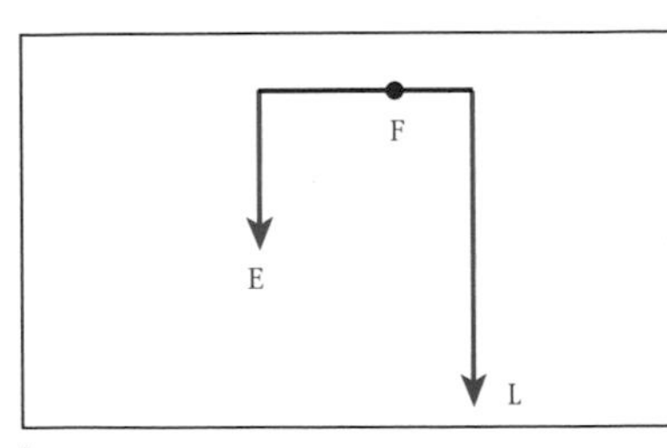

b.

Figure 7.45 The neck muscles/head system.

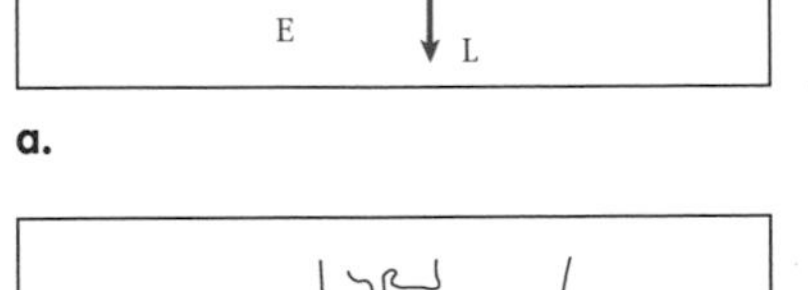

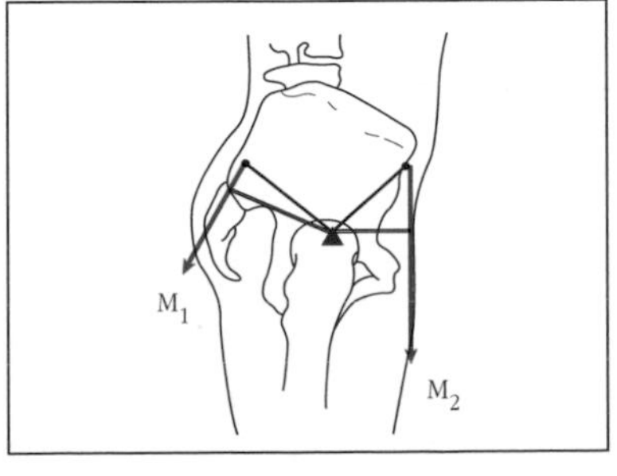

a.

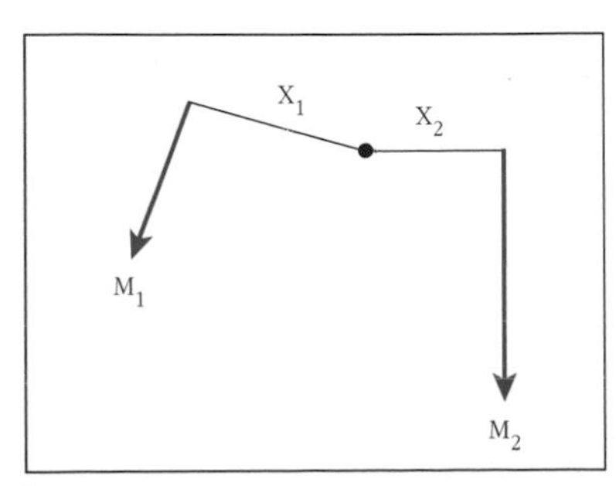

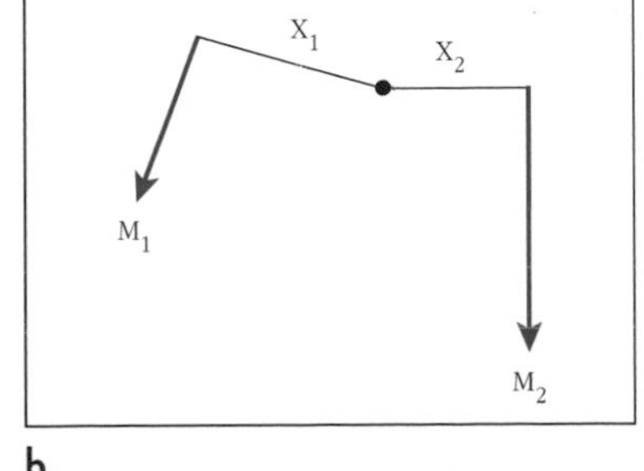

b.

Figure 7.46 The pelvic system.

CENTRE OF GRAVITY—CENTRE OF MASS

This is the idea that the mass of a body behaves as if it is all at one point in the body instead of spread out into arms, legs, torso, head, etc.

Strictly speaking, the concept is **not** dependent on gravity, and would be relevant in weightless situations as well as on the surface of our planet. We will therefore use the term **centre of mass** from now on.

Consider the simplified object in Figure 7.47 in balance (equilibrium) at the fulcrum marked. That is where the moment of the left-hand weight (anticlockwise) balances the moment of the right-hand weight (clockwise). If we were now to apply a force to the system as a whole it would behave as if the mass was entirely at the balance point instead of in two parts.

Therefore, you can see that the definition of the position of the centre of mass is that at which the body would balance at any angle, if suspended at that position.

Also, if the body were suspended or hung from a point, the centre of mass would lie vertically below the point, since if it were not there would be a **moment** of the weight tending to turn it towards this position—as shown in Figure 7.48.

The idea of **centre of mass** can be extended to any body (or object) spread out in space—like the human body. This is obviously much more complicated than the simple example above, but the same principle applies—only now with variable masses and distances from the fulcrum.

In Figure 7.49a the dots mark the approximate positions of the centre of mass of the body segment, with the numbers representing the percentage of the total length of the segment on each side of the centre of mass. Figure 7.49b shows the percentage of total body mass of each body segment (after Wirhed).

The application of the concept to the human body

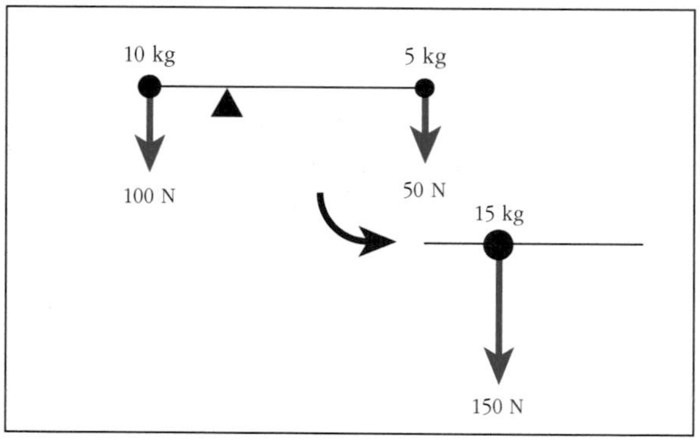

Figure 7.47

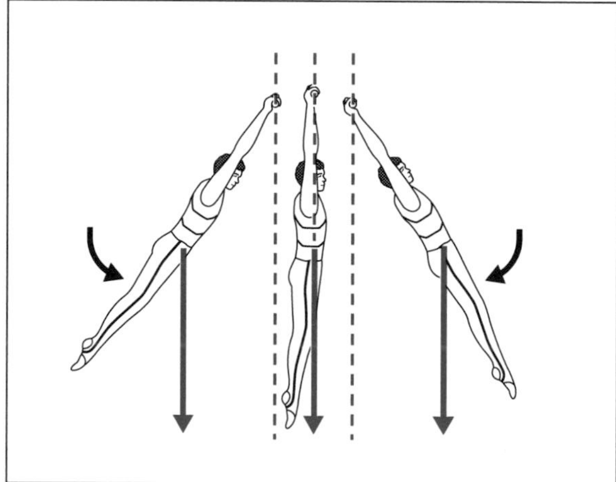

Figure 7.48

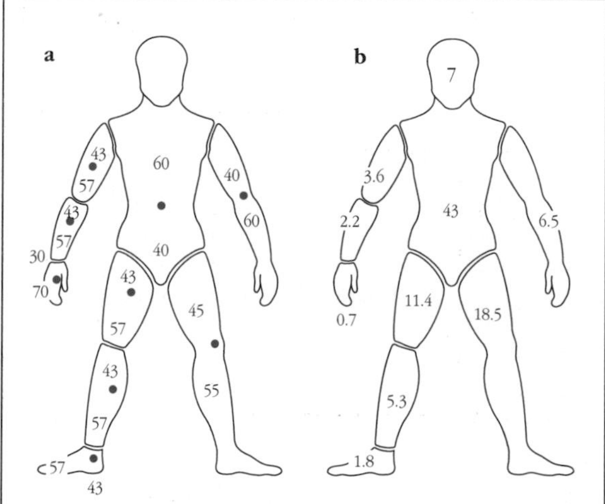

Figure 7.49

revolves around the fact that the position of the centre of mass will change as the shape of the body changes (Figure 7.50). The red dot marks the position of the centre of mass.

The detailed position of the centre of mass can be calculated (and computerized) using the method of Wirhed (p. 102), or Hochmuth (p. 96).

It is also possible to use a mannikin (cardboard model, with jointed movable limbs weighted in proportion to actual body parts—see Hay and Reid (p. 397) to simulate body shapes and discover the position of the centre of mass. This is done by hanging the mannikin from at least two points, determining a line vertically below the point of suspension, and finding the intersection of the lines from each suspension.

It is now possible to simplify the mechanics of any given sporting situation to a single mass and a single **net** force (and a **couple**, which is a turning moment, as explained in Task Two of the previous investigation).

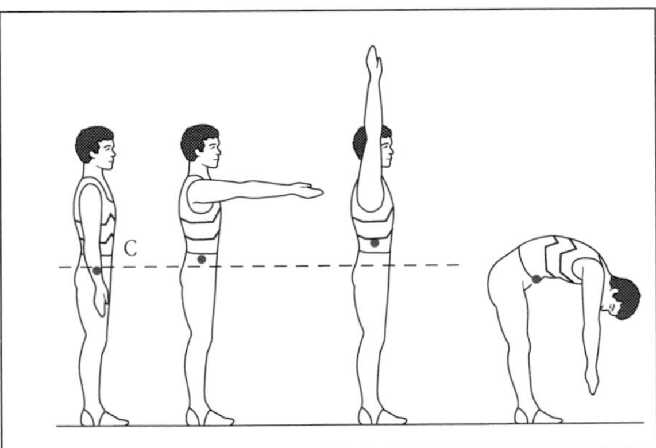

Figure 7.50

MOTION OF A JUMPER

We will take this example to illustrate how the mechanics of a situation involving the human body in a sporting situation can be simplified. Whether a high jumper, long jumper or basketball dunker, gymnast or trampoline tumbler, the mechanics can be split into two sections:

1. Before take-off

While in contact with the ground (or trampoline) the combination of **reaction force**, **friction force** and **weight** will produce a **net** force on the jumper, as shown in Figure 7.51.

This **net** upward force will produce an upward acceleration on the body, which can be increased by the skilful swinging or moving of trunk, arms and legs—as discussed in the section on reaction forces (p. 186). We can therefore represent the vertical motion of the athlete on a velocity–time graph, as in Figure 7.52.

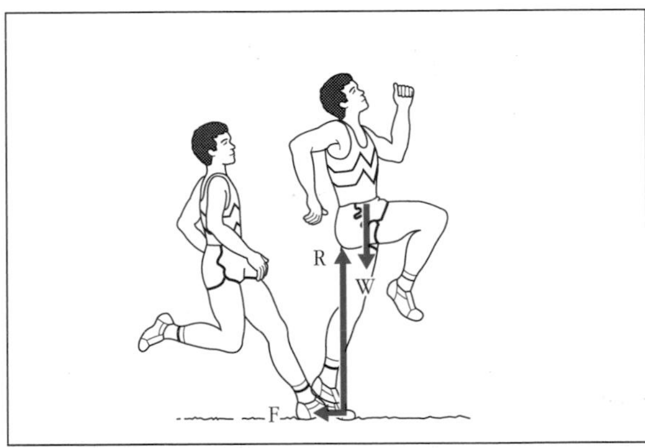

Figure 7.51 The resultant of R, W and F will be upwards and slightly backwards.

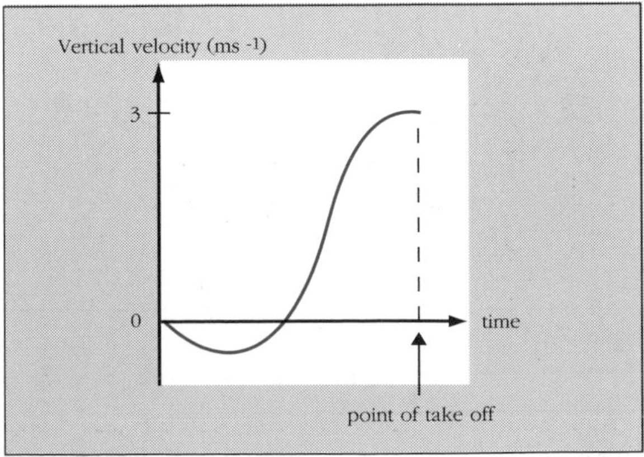

Figure 7.52

So at the instant of the foot leaving the ground the jumper has a velocity of 3 m s^{-1} (in this example). In fact, the **centre of mass** of the jumper has an upward vertical velocity of 3 m s^{-1}, and following this the **centre of mass** will follow a flight path similar to (and following the same rules as) that of the objects in flight discussed in Investigation 7.2 above.

2. Flight of the jumper after take-off

Now the force diagram (Figure 7.53) consists of just two forces: **weight** and **air resistance**. Since the jumper will be moving relatively slowly (so that air resistance will be relatively small) the force will be almost entirely the weight acting vertically downwards; hence the centre of mass of the jumper's body will accelerate vertically downwards at 10 m s^{-2}, and will describe a parabolic path of the sort discussed in Investigation 7.2.

This is where the **flexibility** of the human body affects the pattern of the activity in the air. As you can see from Figure 7.53, the body changes shape considerably during flight, but the path of the centre of mass remains parabolic.

In the case of the high jumper, a skillful performer can actually have the centre of mass pass underneath the bar whilst clearing the bar with his body —in Figure 7.54 this is not quite achieved.

Similarily, the basketball dunker can gain extra height for his dunking hand by lowering the arm and free leg rapidly near the top of the jump (Figure 7.55).

Note that the centre of mass still follows a parabolic path.

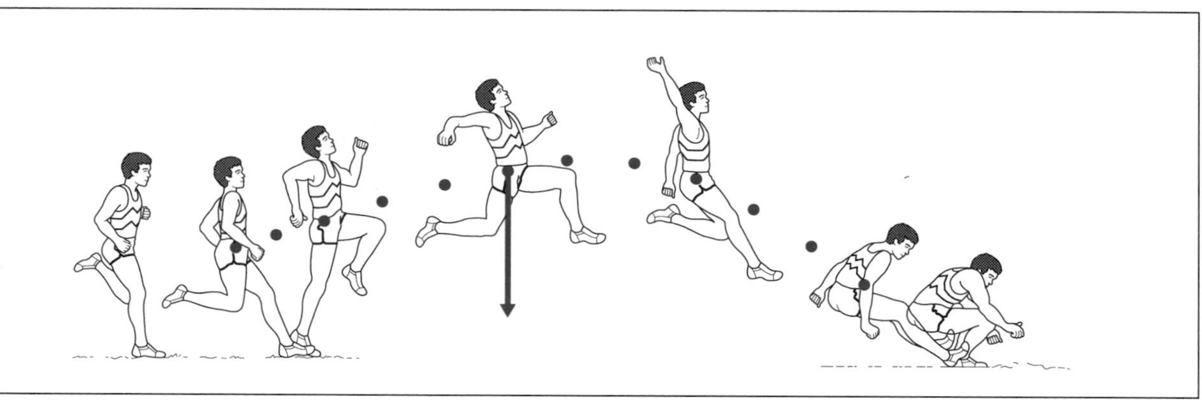

Figure 7.53

Figure 7.54

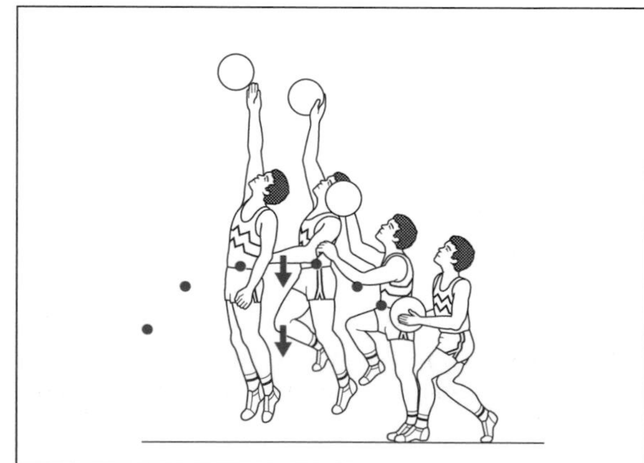

Figure 7.55

EFFECT OF DIRECTION OF NET FORCE ON MOTION OF JUMPER

In Figure 7.56, of the jumper before take-off, the basketball player has the **resultant** (of reaction and friction) force of the ground on the jumper acting in a direction **through** the centre of mass, whereas the high jumper has this force acting in a direction to the **left** of the centre of mass.

The effect of this is for the basketball player to keep the same body orientation throughout the jump, whereas the high jumper's body rotates in a clockwise direction.

In the case of the high jumper this is because the **net** force has a **moment** about the jumper's centre of mass, which will cause rotation about this point as a fulcrum or axis of rotation.

This process is more or less violently initiated by a tumbling gymnast or vaulter, and it is the skill of being able to apply forces to the body **before take-off** in this way which makes one athlete more successful than another.

Once the athlete (jumper) has taken off, then the **path** of the centre of mass, *and* the **rotational momentum** of the body has been determined and **cannot be changed** (assuming the effect of air resistance can be ignored).

Figure 7.56

a.

b.

STABILITY

Another issue related to the concept of centre of mass is that of **stability**.

As mentioned above, a body suspended from a point will tend to hang so that the centre of mass will be vertically below that point. This is called **stable equilibrium** since whichever way the gymnast is pushed he will tend to return to the same position (Figure 7.57a).

On the other hand, a gymnast doing a handstand would fall over if pushed, although in balance (equilibrium) while he holds the handstand: this is called **unstable equilibrium.**

Neutral equilibrium is where on pushing the system, it immediately adopts a new equilibrium position—as for the gymnast lying on the floor.

a. Stable.

b. Unstable.

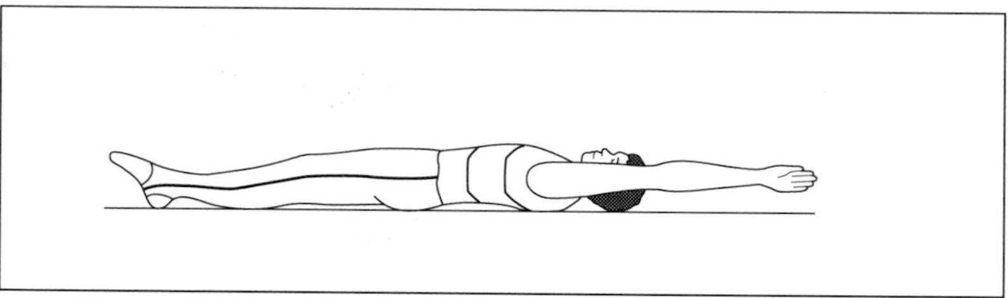

c. Neutral.

Figure 7.57 Stability.

In practice, all sportspeople need to perform movements in balance and this is done by ensuring that the line of action of his/her weight lies between his/her **base of support**. In other words, the centre of mass lies **above** the base of support. If on the other hand the centre of mass lies above a point **outside** the base of support, then the sportsperson will lose balance and be unstable.

For example, in Figure 7.58 the martial arts player adopts a stance with his feet as wide apart as possible, so that his opponent has to apply a large force in order to move his centre of mass to a position in which it lies over one of his feet—this is then unstable equilibrium, and he can be thrown.

In order to increase stability the martial arts player can bend his legs, thereby lowering his centre of mass and increasing the moment needed to tip him off balance.

Similarly, the rugby/football player making a standing tackle will adopt the stance in which the centre of mass must be moved further in order to be above a point outside the base of support (Figure 7.59).

A slightly more sophisticated example is that of the beam gymnast who needs careful control of the position of her centre of mass if she is not to fall off (Figure 7.60).

Figure 7.58

a.

b.

Figure 7.59

a.

b.

Figure 7.60

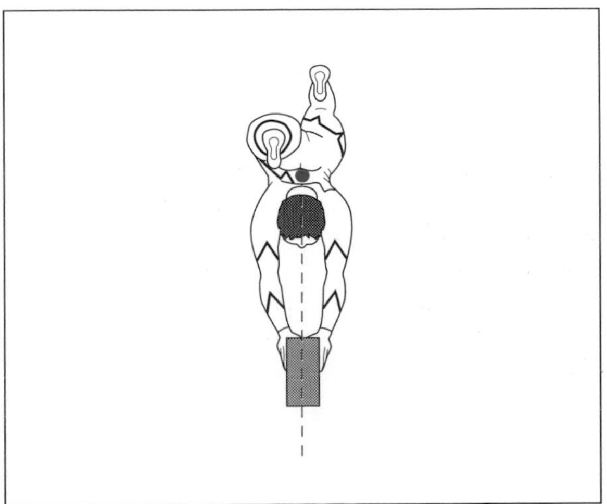

a.

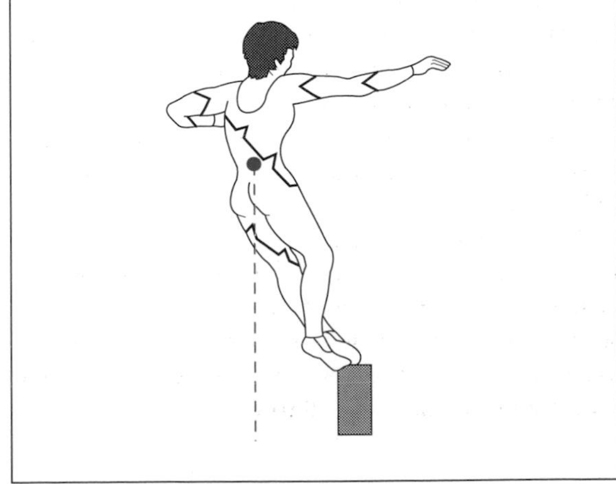

b.

Summary

1. You will be aware of the concept of **moment** of a force:
   moment of a force = force × perpendicular distance from fulcrum to line of action of force.
2. You will be able to apply the **principle of moments** to lever systems, and to classify such lever systems:
   clockwise moment = anticlockwise moment.
3. You will be able to describe some of the lever systems within joint complexes of the human body.
4. You will understand how **internal forces** are applied within the body and some of the effects produced by them.
5. You will be aware of the concept of **centre of mass**, and how its position in the body can be changed by changing the shape of the body.
6. You will understand that the weight and mass both appear to act at the centre of mass, and that the centre of mass of the body follows a parabolic path when in flight.
7. You will be aware that the **stability** of your body position depends on the position of your centre of mass relative to your base of support.

Chapter 8
Rotating Systems

This final chapter on biomechanics deals with some examples of rotating systems in sport, and the physical concepts involved.

Figure 8.1

Investigation 8.1 : Rate of turn of a tumbling gymnast

Aim: to examine the concepts of angle, angular velocity and the law of conservation of angular momentum in the context of a gymnast (or trampolinist) performing a somersault. Further study will enable the student to extend application of the concepts to other sporting situations.

Materials: a video camera with timer, together with a 360° protractor and a video playback machine with stop and slow controls.

Task One—production of video film

1. The video camera is set up so that the field of view is at right angles to the tumble to be performed and far enough away for the student performing the action to fit within the field of view.
2. The student performs a variety of straight, piked and tucked forward or backward somersaults. If you have an expert student who can perform double somersaults, even better.
3. The student doing the filming will need to follow the action with the camera—**with the on-screen timer running**.

Task Two—information on angle

1. Although we are used to measuring angles in degrees, this will not do for scientific measurements.
2. Without adding to the complications of this investigation, we shall use a simple conversion factor from degrees into **radians**. The radian is the scientific unit of angle.
   1 radian = 57.2958 degrees
   1 degree = 0.017453 radians
3. Convert 30°, 60°, 105°, 360°, 47° into radians (use a calculator—some have automatic conversion).

Task Three—analysis of video of motion

1. Locate the beginning of a suitable piece of film.

2. Using the pause and slow forward facility on the video machine, position the gymnast at the point at which his/her feet are just about to leave the floor (or trampoline bed). Note the time on the auto on-screen timer when this occurs.

3. Measure the angle **of the gymnast's upper body** to the vertical at this time.

4. Record in Table 53: angle (in degrees) against time (actually recorded on the film), and elapsed time

Figure 8.2

(the difference between the film time and the answer to **2** above).

Make your measurements with a protractor on the screen every 30° of turn of the **upper** body of the gymnast. This is so that measurements are made at regular intervals of angle, and the time is just sufficient to register a difference on the tenth of a second timer on the video film.

Note: the first angle recorded, i.e. answer to **3**, needs to be in the first row of the angle column. This will not necessarily be 0°, since at the instant the gymnast's feet leave the ground he/she will be leaning into the action of the tumble.

(We are aware that the measurement of the upper body angle does not reflect the true averaged whole body angle of the gymnast. However, this is an attempt to simplify the process without losing sight of the basic idea behind the investigation.)

You will need a bigger chart if the gymnast does a double somersault!

5. Complete the fifth column of the table by subtraction of successive times.

Table 53 : Angles against time

Angle (degrees)	Time (film) (sec)	Elapsed time (sec)	Angle (radians)	Time for previous 30° or 0.523 radians
		0.00		
30			0.5236	
60			1.0472	
90			1.5708	
120			2.0944	
150			2.6180	
180			3.1416	
210			3.6652	
240			4.1888	
270			4.7124	
300			5.2360	
330			5.7596	
360			6.2832	

Task Four—calculation of angular velocities

1. Now comes the hard bit. Angular velocity is defined as 'angle moved through per second' and is measured in radians per second. A formula would be:

   $$\text{angular velocity} = \frac{\text{angle turned through in radians}}{\text{time taken}}$$

2. Using your calculator and the data from Table 53, complete Table 54 of angular velocity against time for each segment of the somersault.

   Note: each segment of 30° is approximately 0.52 radians. Apart from the first calculation, this figure will appear on the top of the formula.

3. Finally, compute an elapsed time half-way between the elapsed times for the beginning and end of each segment for column 3 of the table.

   For example, if at 30° the time is 0.2 seconds, and at 60° 0.3 s, the average time for that segment will be 0.25 s.

Table 54 : Angular velocity against time

Segment of tumble	Angular velocity (rad s^{-1})	Average time for segment
–30		
30–60		
60–90		
90–120		
120–150		
150–180		
180–210		
210–240		
240–270		
270–300		
300–330		
330–360		

Task Five—graph of angular velocity against time

1. Plot a graph of angular velocity, from the second column of Table 54 (y-axis) against time, from the third column of Table 54 (x-axis). Use as big a scale as possible so that the graph occupies as much of the paper as possible.
2. Draw a smooth curve through the points on the graph.

Task Six—interpretation of results

1. What does this graph show?

   Angular velocity means rate of spin—can you relate the rate of spin to body shape?

   Examine again the video film from which the data were taken—the tucked or piked position adopted by the gymnast during the middle part of the somersault somehow made him/her spin faster. Why?
2. Examine a few text books (Wirhed, Watkins) on spinning sporting systems. See if you can come up with a general rule which governs changes in rates of spin during a movement.
3. Sketch pin men diagrams of body positions which lead to high rates of spin and compare them with similar diagrams for body positions within the **same** activity leading to low rates of spin.
4. For example, with our tumbler the tightly tucked position seems to lead to a higher rate of spin than the open or straight position—what happens with the spinning skater?

Figure 8.3

a. Tucked

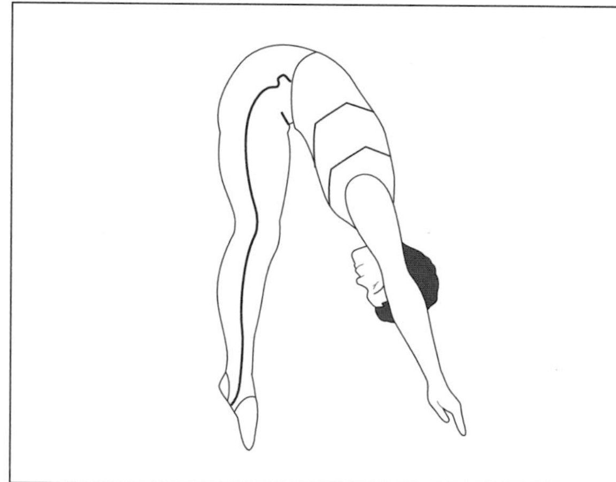

b. Piked.

Task Seven—the spinning skater

1. Take a small turntable and stand on it with arms outstretched. Another student should now spin you as quickly as possible.
2. The spinning student should now bring his/her arms to the side—what happens?
3. The experiment can continue with various positions being adopted: hands overhead; one leg held out at right angles; body adopting a sideways 'V' shape (>) and so on (see Figure 8.4).
4. Each position should be drawn with a pin man diagram, and relative rates of spin mentioned.
5. What factor induces change of spin?

Figure 8.4

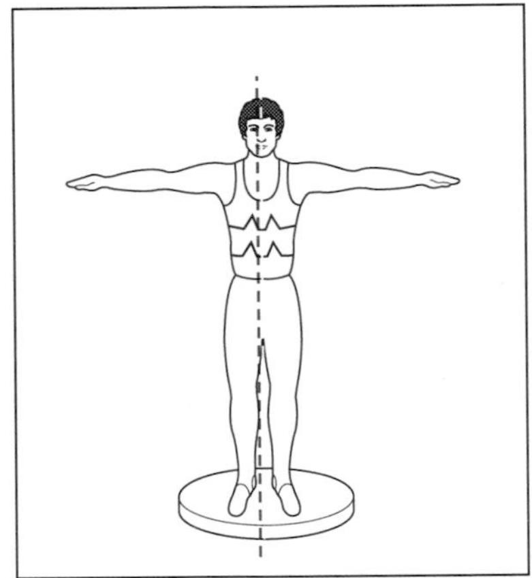

a.

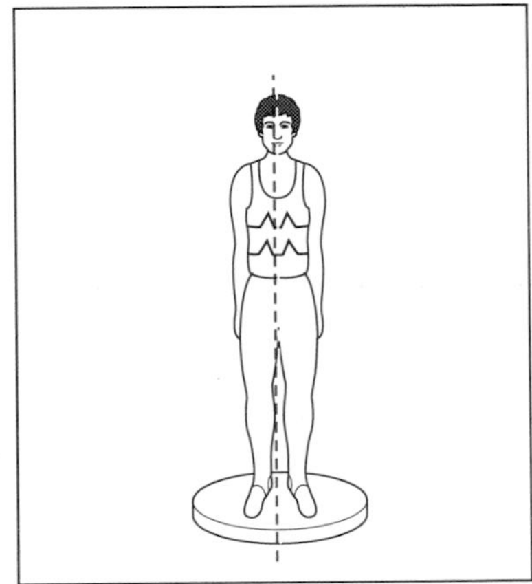

b.

c.

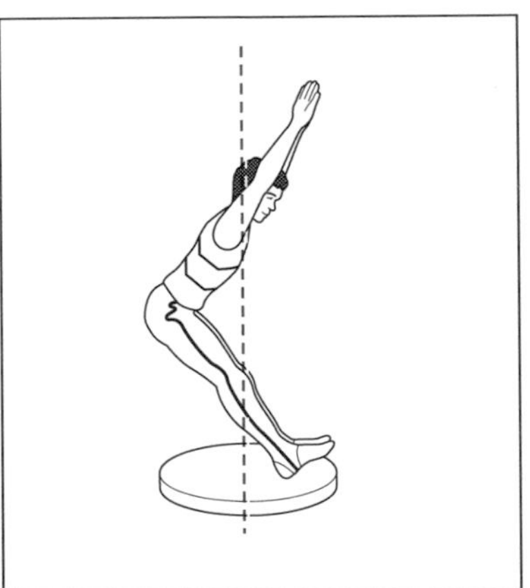

d.

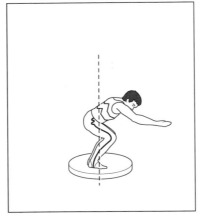

e.

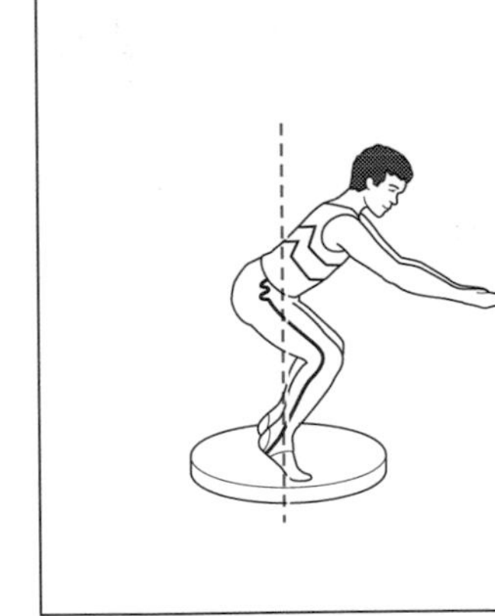

f.

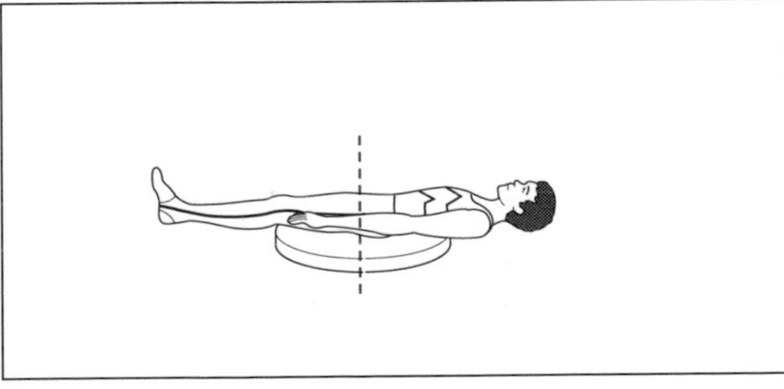

g.

8.1 Moment of Inertia

KEY WORDS AND CONCEPTS

radian	**axis of rotation**	**angular acceleration**
angular velocity	**moment of inertia**	**angular momentum**
	rotational energy	

Various texts have a lot of detail about this concept. See intermediate level physics and maths books, and Watkins pages 118–122, Wirhed pages 107–110, Page pages 45–56 for application of the idea to the sporting situation.

Basically, moment of inertia is the resistance to rotational motion of a body (directly comparable with mass/inertia for objects moving in straight lines—see p. 182–183 for explanation of this).

The bigger the **moment of inertia,** the bigger the **moment of force** (or **couple** or **torque**) needed to provide the same **angular acceleration** in the body, and vice versa.

This is the same as the linear situation only now, instead of going in a straight line, the object is spinning about an **axis**; instead of acceleration (in m s^{-2}) we have **angular acceleration** (in radians s^{-2}); and instead of force we have **turning moment**.

Angular acceleration is the change of (increase of) angular velocity per second of the spinning body.

The concept of **moment of inertia** (MI) depends on the distribution of mass about the axis of rotation of a spinning system, i.e. the further away from the axis a mass is the greater the moment of inertia, and the harder it is to make it spin, or stop spinning if it is already doing so.

A simple example of this idea applied to sport is the leg action during running. As the leg drives through at the moment of leaving contact with the ground, it is (or should be) as straight as possible in order to maximize the range of movement in the stride (see position 2 of Figure 8.5).

The next action that needs to be performed is to bring that leg through as rapidly as possible to the fully forward position (as in position 9 of Figure 8.5). It takes the least possible **moment of force** applied by the abdominal muscles to the leg, if that leg is as bent as possible and therefore has the **least possible moment of inertia** about the hip joint as an axis of rotation. This is why the more efficient sprinter will have his/her heel as close to his/her backside as possible (as in position 7 of Figure 8.5).

To relate to the tumbling gymnast in Investigation 8.1, the act of spinning in a straight position (as opposed to a tucked position) means that some of the gymnast's mass is further away from the axis of spin and therefore the **moment of inertia** is bigger.

Similarly, for the skater, if the body is straight with no 'bits' sticking out, the moment of inertia is low—but as soon as a leg or arm is put out at right angles to the body, the moment of inertia increases since more of the person's mass is further from the axis of spin.

Figure 8.5

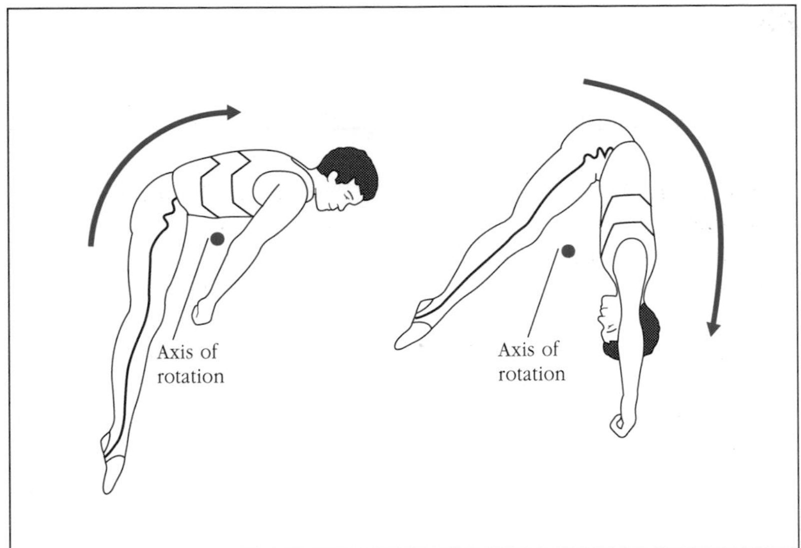

Figure 8.6
Piked position = small moment of inertia
Straight position = large moment of inertia

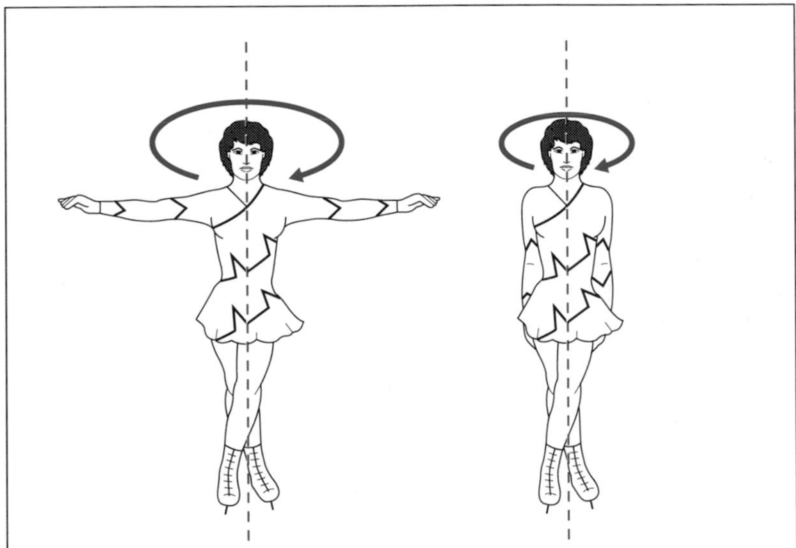

Figure 8.7
Arms held in = small moment of inertia
Wide arms = large moment of inertia

EVALUATION OF MOMENT OF INERTIA

The definition of MI is:

moment of inertia

= the sum of [(mass of body part)
× (distance from the axis of rotation)^2]
for all parts of the body

or MI = $\Sigma\ (m \times r^2)$ (UNIT of MI - kg m^2)

It can be seen that the computation of MI is not simple for the complex shape and variations of the shape the human body can adopt in the sporting situation.

In Figure 8.8, a range of spinning body shapes is shown, the axis of spin is marked with a red dotted or continuous line, and the corresponding moment of inertia relative to the first example is shown (this first example has a nominal value I). I has the value 1.0–1.5 kg m^2 for a person of 60 kg mass.

Therefore, it can be seen that it is possible to double the moment of inertia by holding arms out, or one or more legs! The practicalities of the use of this idea are that the skilful sportsperson is able to vary his/her moment of inertia by changing body shape and hence the properties of the body in so far as spinning, tumbling, turning or twisting are concerned. This is done in a similar way to the variation of centre of mass of the body, but in different situations.

Figure 8.8 Axis of spin and moment of inertia in spinning bodies.

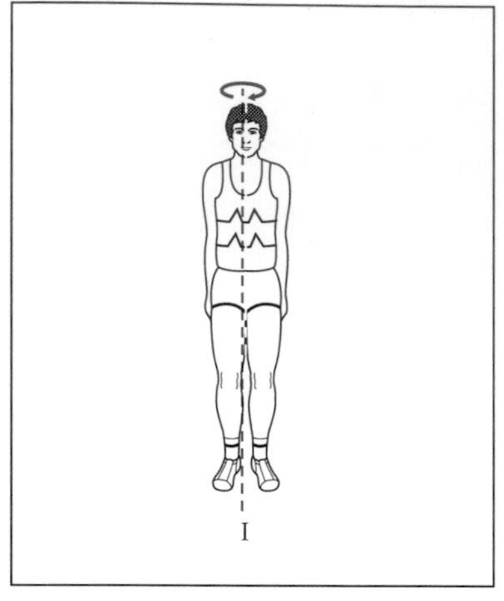

a.

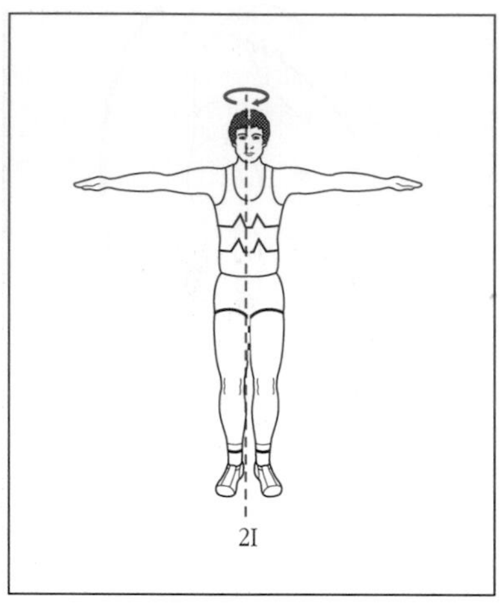

b.

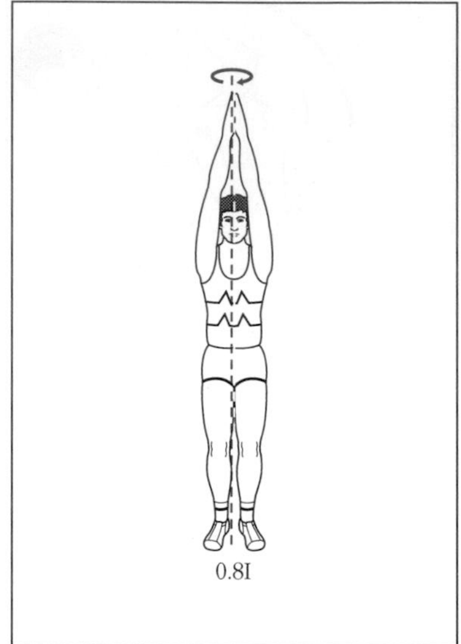

c.

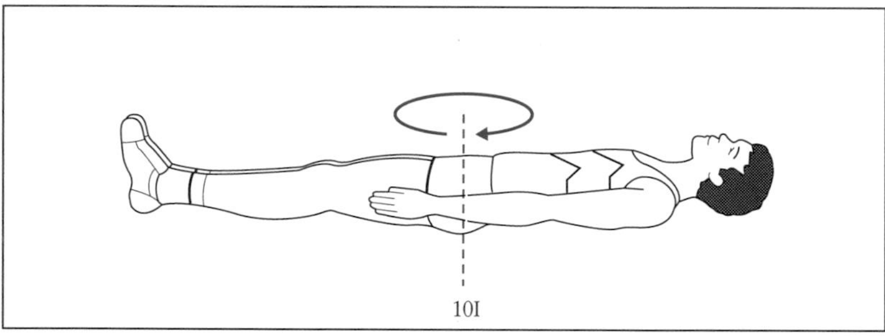

d.

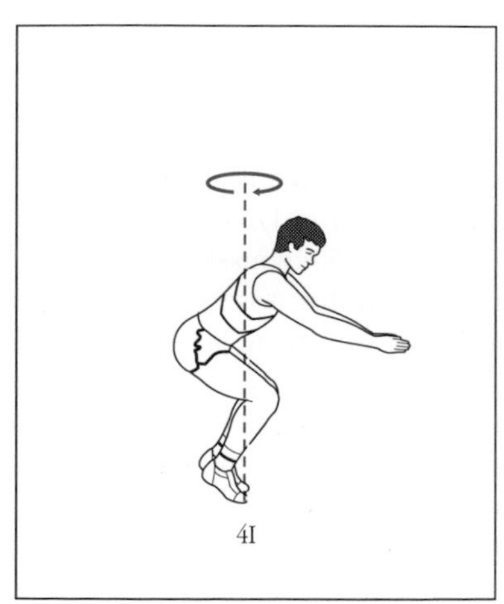

e.

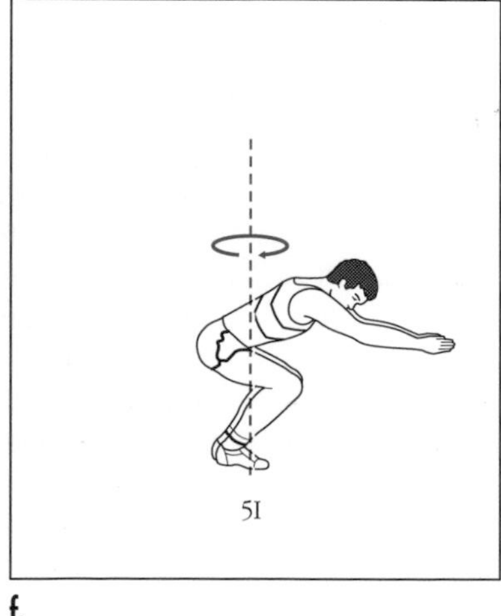

f.

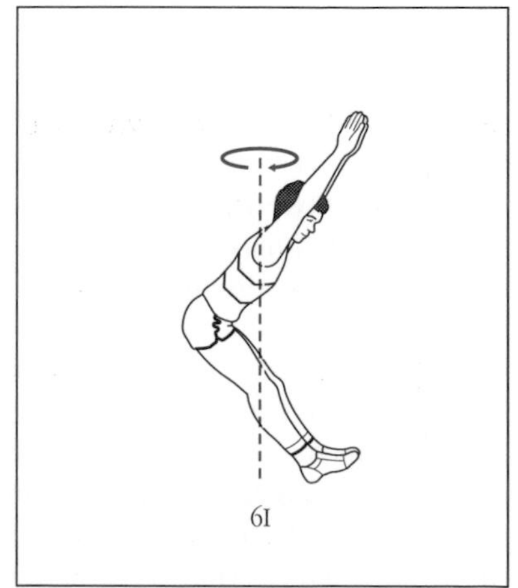

g.

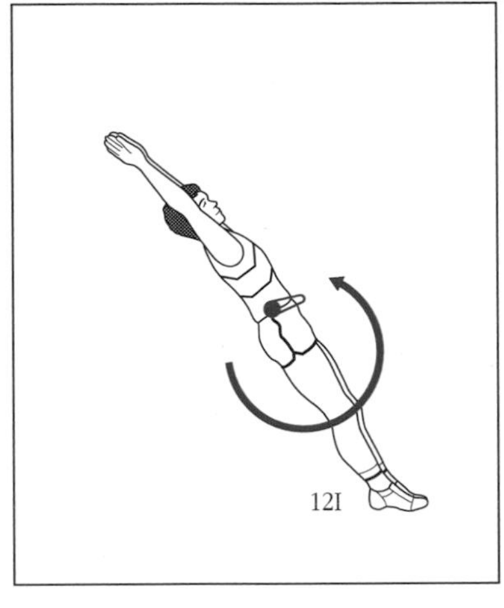

h.

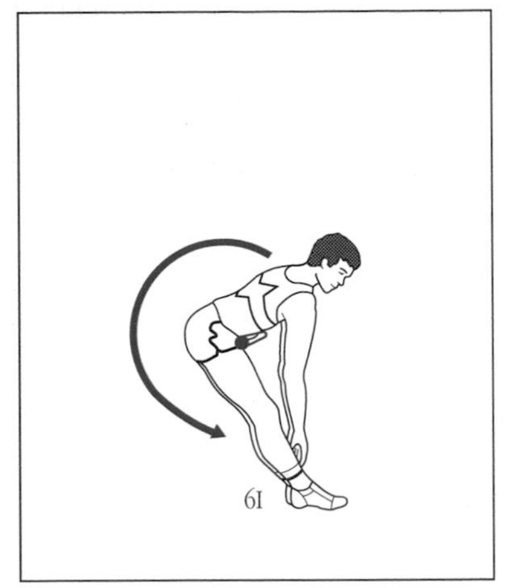

i.

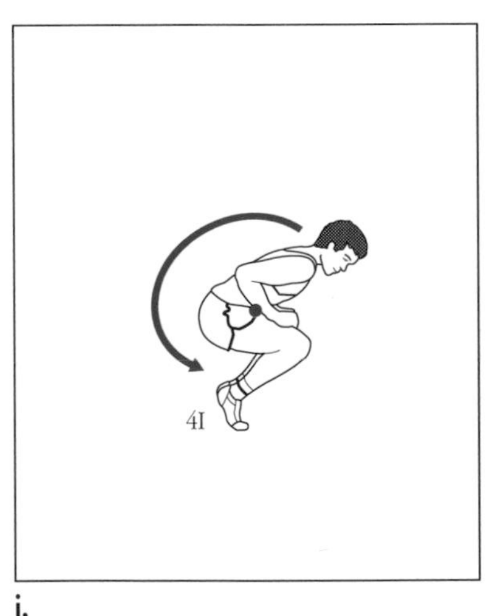

j.

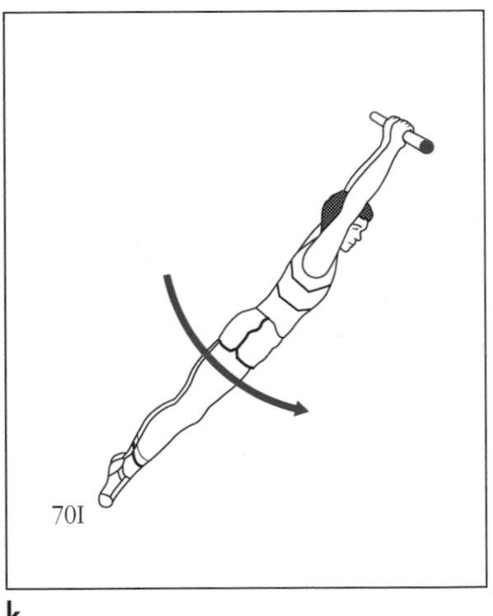

k.

ROTATIONAL KINETIC ENERGY

This is defined by:

rotational energy = $^1/_2$ × moment of inertia × (angular velocity)^2

It can therefore be seen that the spinning energy stored in a system depends on both the **moment of inertia** and the **angular velocity** (Figure 8.9).

Figure 8.9

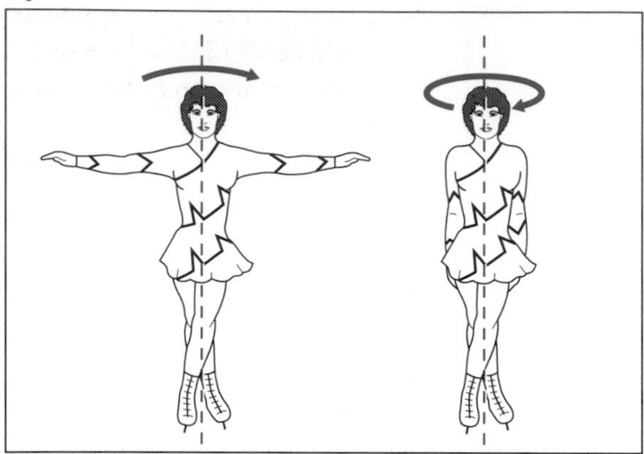

a. Large moment of inertia, slow rate of spin.
Small moment of inertia, large rate of spin.

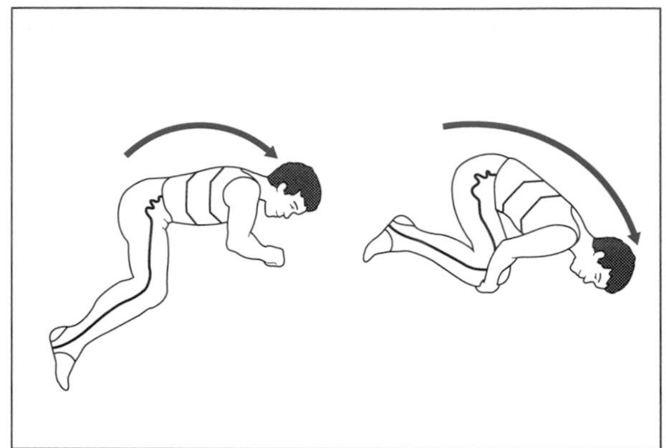

b. Large moment of inertia, slow rate of spin.
Small moment of inertia, large rate of spin.

ANGULAR MOMENTUM

Angular momentum is defined as:

angular velocity × moment of inertia.

This very difficult construct combines our two most difficult concepts together in a slightly different way to the rotational energy concept discussed above. However, it enables us to explain why the rate of spin changes when the moment of inertia changes because:

Angular momentum of a system remains constant throughout a movement provided nothing outside the system acts with a turning moment on it.

This is known as the **Law of Conservation of Angular Momentum** and as far as is known it is obeyed by all rotating systems. (There is a similar universal law in linear dynamics—this is **not** the same law.)

In simple terms, this 'conservation law' means that if our gymnast or skater, **when already spinning,** changes his/her moment of inertia (by changing body shape), then the rate of spin will also change.

So, if the skater spins rapidly with arms and legs held near the body then the moment of inertia is **increased** by sticking out an arm and the rate of spin **decreases** (and in fact the angular momentum remains the same).

Similarly the tumbler goes from an open shape with large moment of inertia, into a tucked position with small moment of inertia—and in doing so speeds up the rate of spin.

Other examples of this law applied to sporting systems are illustrated in Figures 8.10–8.13.

Figure 8.10 The dancer begins her movement with arms wide. and therefore large moment of inertia. and as she jumps and turns. brings her arms to her side reducing her moment of inertia and increasing the number of turns possible in the air before landing again.

Figure 8.11 The discus thrower kicks his right leg wide at the start of the turn, thereby giving his lower body rotational momentum with a large moment of inertia. As he moves to the centre of the circle he brings his leg closer to the body, reducing his MI and increasing the rate of spin of the lower body so that it moves ahead of the upper body in the movement.

Figure 8.12 The slalom skier begins his turn in a low squat position with high moment of inertia and, as he passes the gate, straightens his body into a shape with half the moment of inertia, doubling the rate of turn past the gate. After passing the gate, he reverts to the high moment of inertia position in order to slow down the rate of turn again.

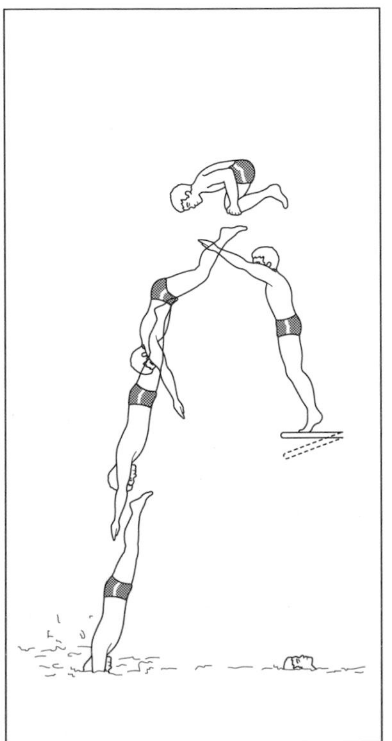

Figure 8.13 Like the gymnast, the springboard diver varies his shape from straight (large moment of inertia, low rate of turn) to tucked (small moment of inertia, high rate of spin) and back to straight again before entering the water.

Investigation 8.2 : Spinning systems

1. Write in your own words a detailed explanation of why the rate of spin changes in the examples in the diagrams above or researched in Investigation 8.1.
2. Using the graph produced in Task Five of Investigation 8.1, how would you expect the graph of moment of inertia against time to look?

Sketch a graph of the moment of inertia of our gymnast against time. Estimate the values from the chart of MI in Figure 8.8 (don't worry about precise values—they aren't important at this stage).

The graphs should have the properties shown in Figure 8.14.

Figure 8.14

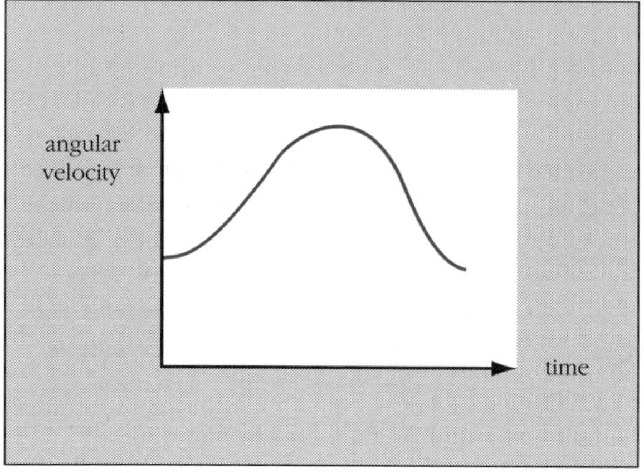

a. Graph of angular velocity against time. Note that the rate of spin increases in the middle of the movement to about double that at the start and finish of the movement.

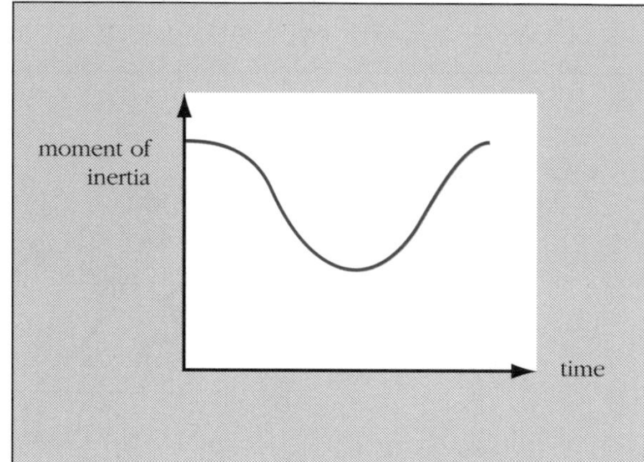

b. Graph of moment of inertia against time. Here the moment of inertia falls in the middle of the movement to about half that at the start and finish of the movement, so that the product of moment of inertia and angular velocity remains the same throughout the movement.

Summary

1. You should be familiar with the measurement of angles in **radians**.
2. You should be aware of the use of a video system for analysis of rotating human systems.
3. You should understand the concept of **angular velocity** as:
   angular velocity = angle turned per second.
4. You should have an understanding of the concept of **moment of inertia** as applied to the human body when rotating about various axes.
5. You should be aware of the concepts of angular acceleration and rotational energy.
6. You should understand the concept of **angular momentum** as applied to human body rotations, where:
   angular momentum = angular velocity × moment of inertia
7. You should be familiar with the Law of Conservation of Angular Momentum as applied to rotating human bodies, and how this enables the sportsperson to vary his/her rate of spin.

BIBLIOGRAPHY: BIOMECHANICS

Dyson G. *The Mechanics of Athletics* 6e, London, ULP, 1973.

Ecker T. *Basic Track and Field Biomechanics,* Los Altos, USA, Tafnews Press, 1985.

Hay J.G. and Reid J.G. *Anatomy Mechanics and Human Motion* 2e, New Jersey, USA, Prentice Hall, 1988.

Harre D. *et al. Principles of Sports Training,* Berlin, Sportverlag, 1982.

Hochmuth. *Biomechanics of Athletic Movement* 4e, Berlin, Sportverlag, 1984.

Jardine J. *Mass in Motion,* London, Longman, 1970.

Page R.L. *The Physics of Human Movement,* Exeter, UK, Wheaton/Pergamon, 1978.

Walder P. *Mechanics and Sport Performance,* Hampshire, UK, Feltham Press, 1995.

Watkins J. *An Introduction to Mechanics of Human Movement,* Lancaster, UK, MTP Press Ltd, 1983.

Wirhed R. *Athletic Ability and the Anatomy of Motion,* London, Wolfe, 1984.

FURTHER READING IN ADVANCED PHYSICS

Akrill T.B. and Osmond S.J. *Work Out Physics – A Level,* Basingstoke, UK, Macmillan, 1986.

Breithaupt J. *Understanding Physics for A Level* 2e, Cheltenham, UK, Stanley Thornes, 1990.

Duncan T. *Physics: A Text Book For Advanced Level Students,* London, John Murray, 1982.

Hutchings R. *Physics,* University of Bath, Macmillan Science 16–19 Project, Basingstoke, UK, Macmillan, 1991.

Muncaster R. *A Level Physics* 2e, Cheltenham, UK, Stanley Thornes, 1985.

ADVANCED READING

Adrian M.J. and Cooper J.M. *Biomechanics of Human Movement,* Dubuque, USA, Brown and Benchmark, 1989.

Hall S. *Basic Biomechanics* 2e, St. Louis, USA, Mosby–Year Book, 1995.

Hay J.G. *The Biomechanics of Sports Techniques* 4e, Prentice Hall International Edition, New Jersey, USA, Prentice Hall, 1993.

Luttgens K., Deutsch H. and Hamilton N. *Kinesiology–Scientific Basis of Human Motion* 8e, Dubuque, USA, Brown & Benchmark, 1992.

Part Two:

The Performer as a Person

So far in this book we have been considering the way in which the body works when we are performing physical tasks. In physical education the body is central to what we do; if it is not trained and functioning properly we cannot achieve our intentions. But we must not ignore the mind in our studies, for in complex skills and movements, such as we employ in physical education and sport, body and mind work together. Next time you hear a sportsperson interviewed on television or radio, note how he or she talks about the mental aspects of preparation and performance as well as the physical aspect.

The science which studies how people's minds work and how they behave is called psychology. Behaviour is a result of how people think and feel in a situation, and may or may not be an 'automatic reaction'. So when we are interested in what sportspeople do to prepare for competition and how they react in the competition itself, or when we study dancers as they perform and choreograph, or when we observe and analyse what motivates the water sportsperson or mountaineer, then we use psychological theories and methods. You will be introduced to some of these aspects as you work through this section. This is Sport Psychology.

People have a number of different motives for participating in sport: to stay fit, to meet the challenge of competition and prove themselves, to share an enthusiasm with friends. But research has shown that what people tend to put high on their list of reasons for involvement in sports is the desire to improve skill and achieve excellence. So it is important for students of sport to understand how we become skilful in physical activities; in other words how we learn, or acquire, skill, and the factors which makes this process easy or difficult. Chapters 9 to 12 deal with this topic. Chapters 13 and 14 consider how sportspeople prepare themselves for performance or competition; we look at some of the things that could go wrong and what coaches, teachers and the performers themselves can do to optimize their performance. We look at the performance itself, how people behave, how they achieve success (or failure) and what factors influence their performance in physical activities. Although we will tend to focus our attention on sport, and most of the additional reading you do will be about sport, you should remember that the ideas apply equally to any form of physical activity—dance or outdoor pursuits, for example. They apply when anyone is learning and trying to do something to the best of her or his ability.

As you read you will find that associated with each section of work are suggestions for practical activities, which either illustrate the theory presented or else which form the basis for investigations. These can be carried out during class work. Additional reading is suggested, and the ideas contained therein might prove useful when you come to discuss your practical work, its results and your observations. It will also extend your knowledge and understanding of the key concepts and issues.

Chapter 9
The Nature and Classification of Skill

Chapters 9–12 consider how we acquire skill. You will be introduced to the nature of skill, to some ways in which skills may be classified, and to a consideration of the way in which people learn to become skilful in an activity. A theoretical model is presented which sets out to analyse performance and learning in terms of the way in which information is processed, and we also look at learning from the teacher's or coach's point of view.

KEY WORDS AND CONCEPTS:

ability	**discrete skills**	**self-paced skills**
balance	**externally-paced skills**	**serial skills**
closed skills	**general motor ability**	**skill**
continuous skills	**open skills**	**strength**
co-ordination	**perceptual-motor skill**	

9.1 Skill Defined

At the end of this section of work you should be able to:

a. define skill and say what makes a performance skilful;
b. describe the bases of three different classifications of skill and analyse physical tasks in terms of their characteristics
c. distinguish between 'skill' and 'ability'.

The concept of 'skill' is used in several different ways.

- We use the word to mean an element of a game or sport, a technique—for example, passing, volleying or somersaulting.
- Later in this section we shall be referring to sports themselves as 'skills', for example, diving, archery or tennis.
- Also, we use the word 'skill' to imply a quality which a sportsperson possesses. We use the word 'skilful' in the same way. In using the concept of skill in this way we must ensure also that we are differentiating between 'skill' and 'ability', for in the literature on motor learning and skill acquisition these mean different things.

Let us first identify three different types of skill:

1. When you do arithmetic in your head (for example, when you are computing a darts score) you are employing **intellectual** or **cognitive** skill.
2. If you look at Figure 9.1 you can probably see two different images. With practice you will be able to switch between these two images at will. You are employing **perceptual** skill.

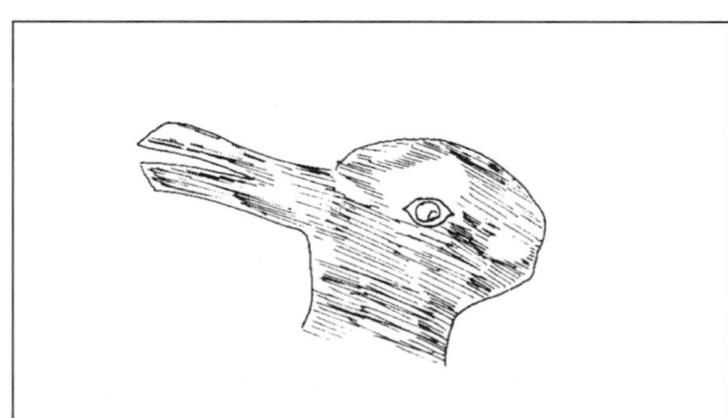

Figure 9.1

3. As you write your name, your hand is moving across the page and you are thus using essentially **motor** skill.

Imagine you and a team-mate are throwing and catching a ball between you. Which of the above types of skill would you be using? You will come across the term **perceptual–motor** skills in your reading. You will find that often it is shortened to 'motor skill'; the perceptual element is usually implied, however.

Investigation 9.1 : To identify the characteristics of skill

Method: Work in pairs. One demonstrates a perceptual–motor skill which can be performed very well; for example, a badminton serve. If you are short of space or equipment, throw and catch one or two tennis balls.

Observations: Note down all the things about the performance which enable you to describe it as 'skilful'. In other words, what is it about the performance which suggests that 'skill' is being demonstrated? You may find it helpful to contrast this performance with one where lack of skill is evident; for example you might ask your partner to try to juggle two or three tennis balls with one or two hands.

Discussion: From your observations, outline the characteristics of skilled performance and suggest a definition of skill.

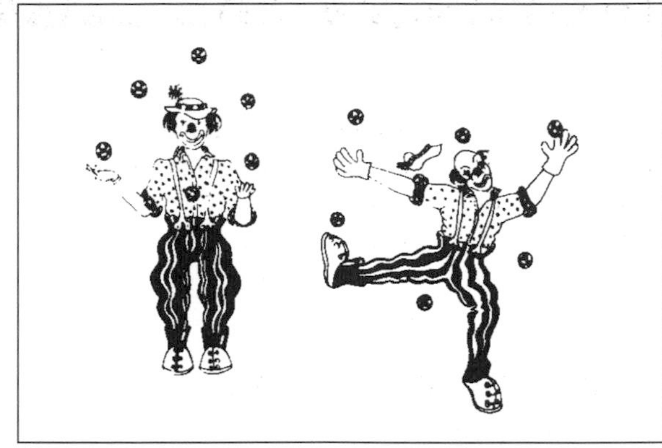

Figure 9.2

Knapp's definition

Knapp has defined skill as:

'the learned ability to bring about pre-determined results with maximum certainty, often with the minimum outlay of time or energy or both.'

(Knapp, 1963, p. 4)

To what extent does your definition match hers?

- Skill is learned. It requires practice and results from experience. Learning is usually defined as a relatively permanent change in behaviour/performance which persists over time. We recognize this idea when we refer to an early success as a 'fluke' (accidental, or not the usual performance) and when we acknowledge a skilful gymnast as one who can reproduce a vault successfully time after time.
- Skill has an end result. We refer to it as 'goal-directed'. It is obviously important that the learner is aware, before the skill is attempted, of what this goal is and the reasons for aiming to achieve it. These are the 'predetermined results'.
- A skilled performer achieves his/her goals consistently. There is much more likelihood than not that a skilful racket sports player will place shots exactly as intended; there is 'maximum certainty'.
- Skill results in economic and efficient movement, which is well co-ordinated and precise. A skilled performer can vary the timing of the movement, performing it quickly or slowly according to the demands of the moment. A beginner may use a lot of energy and still not succeed, but an experienced performer will be able to fit the energy required to the demands of the task. The movement will be efficient.
- A skilled performer makes accurate analyses of the demands of a sports situation and appropriate decisions about how to deal with these. Skill is not just about being a good technician, but about being able to use techniques at the right moment.

You will notice that two terms keep occurring in this description: 'learning' and 'performance'. You will come to a clearer understanding of these concepts as you progress through this section (in particular, Chapter 12), but we need to be able to distinguish these terms at this stage.

Learning is a process, a life-long process. Even top class sportspeople will claim that they are still learning about their sport and aiming to improve. But a sport has definable elements or stages of learning associated with it, so that a gymnast, for example, could claim to have learned to perform a back somersault. What we mean is that her early performances were unsuccessful (or that she was reliant on her coach for support) but that with practice she became able to produce a well-formed somersault that would achieve good marks in a competition and was able to produce this performance consistently. A good coach or teacher will define stages of learning (i.e. intermediate goals) within a learning process so that the gymnast knows which elements of the skill have been mastered and which need further refinement. Learning is thus shown by improvements in peformance and we have learned a skill when we can show a relatively permanent improvement. Of course, what we mean by 'relatively permanent improvement' depends to some extent on the accuracy requirements of the task. We would not say that a professional golfer had not learned to putt just because she/he occasionally misses! We return to this subject in Chapter 12.

9.2 Skill Classified

Let us now return to the idea of skills being activities, such as climbing, dancing or playing a shot in badminton. Clearly, these are very different and may well have to be learned in different ways. Teachers, coaches and performers themselves, therefore, find it useful to be able to classify skills so that they can be analysed and their differing characteristics taken account of.

As you complete your further reading, see how many different classifications you can find. For example, Singer (1982) suggests that the following factors can each form the basis of a classification:

bodily involvement
duration of movement
pacing conditions
cognitive involvement
feedback availability.

Stallings (1982) has a similar list:

continuity
coherence
pacing
environmental conditions
intrinsic feedback.

Let us see how **three** of these classifications work and you can then investigate the others for yourself. Most classifications are represented as a continuum (Figure 9.3, for example).

CONTINUOUS/DISCRETE CONTINUUM

Continuous skills are those which have no obvious beginning or end; in theory they could be continued for as long as the performer wished. The end of one cycle of the skill becomes the beginning of the next.

Discrete skills, on the other hand, have a clear beginning and end; the skill can be repeated, but the performer 'starts again'.

Serial skills are composed of several discrete elements, strung together to produce an integrated movement. The order in which the elements are performed is important; for example, in a high jump or a triple jump, the run up, take-off and the components of the jumping phase happen in a particular order. Note that whereas we refer to these as serial skills, they are also clearly discrete, so the two terms are not mutually exclusive.

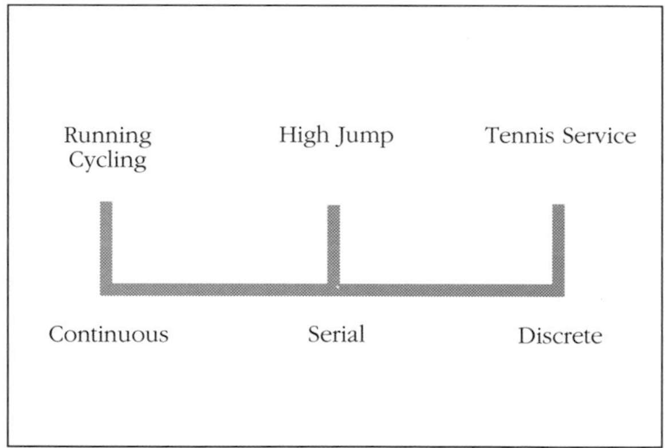

Figure 9.3 The continuous/discrete continuum.

PACING CONTINUUM

The 'pacing' continuum (Figure 9.4) is concerned with the extent to which the performer has control over the timing of the action. Actions are said to be 'self-paced' or 'externally-paced' (or somewhere between these two extremes) according to the extent to which the performer can decide when to start the action.

Some skills are self-paced—that is the performer has control over the rate at which the action takes place. For example: a tennis player determines the timing of the action of the serve; some floor-work moves in men's gymnastics may be done slowly or quickly, depending on the effect required; a climber may move up a pitch slowly and carefully, savouring the technical problems posed, or may decide that the weather is closing in and it would be better to hurry. In others the start of the action can be controlled but thereafter the movement takes place at a given rate; for example a diver decides when to start his dive, but once he has left the board he cannot slow down his rate of progress to the water! At the other end of the continuum are externally paced skills, those in which timing and form are determined by what is happening elsewhere in the environment; for example, a sailor adjusts the trim of the sails and the direction to be taken according to the wind.

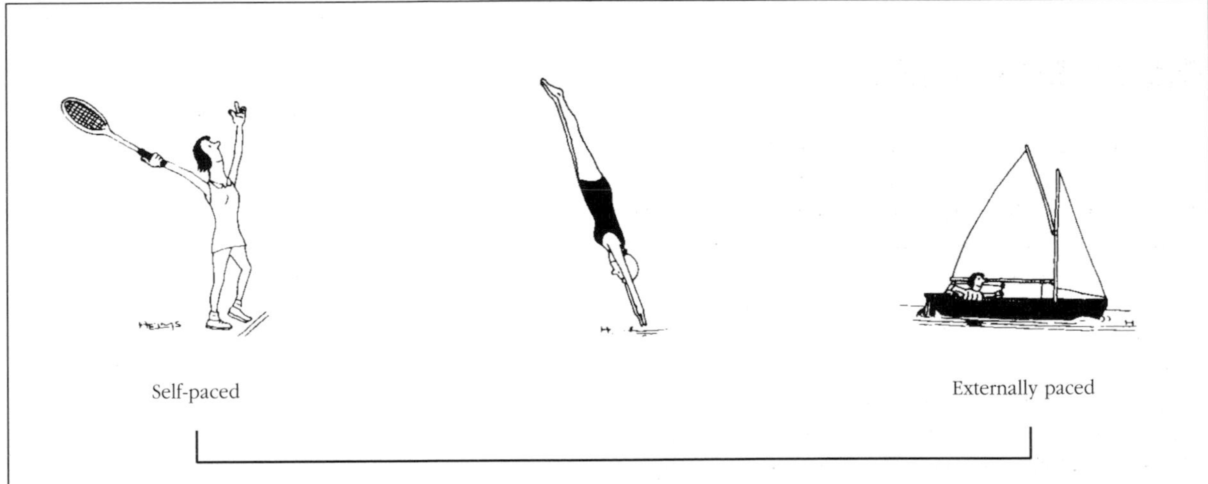

Figure 9.4 The pacing continuum.

OPEN/CLOSED CONTINUUM

The 'pacing' continuum leads us to an important classification proposed by Poulton (1957) and developed in relation to sport skills by Knapp (1977). The continuum is based on the extent to which environmental conditions affect the performance.

You can see that **open skills** are those in which the form of the action is constantly being varied according to what is happening around the performer whereas a **closed skill** is a pre-learned pattern of movements which can be followed without (or with little) reference to the environment.

At first sight this seems to be a fairly straight forward idea, but as one tries to identify skills as more or less open or closed, complexities arise. For example, one might identify soccer as essentially an open skill because players are constantly reacting to other players, but within the game there are skills which are clearly closed, for example taking a penalty. We call these 'closed skills in open situations'. It is very important that performers, teachers and coaches recognize where a skill lies on the continuum, because open skills need to be practised differently from closed skills.

When learning and practising a closed skill, such as in trampolining or athletics, the performer and coach have a model of the required movement pattern in mind and the task of the performer is to make the performance conform as closely as possible to that model. Practice therefore entails gradually refining performance and, once the movement pattern has been established, repeating it until it becomes habitual and the performer can reproduce the movement consistently without having to give too much attention to it.

Open skills, on the other hand, require practice which takes into account the many different ways in which the techniques are to be used. For example, a fielder in cricket, rounders or baseball must be able to throw an infinite variety of diatances to ensure the ball reaches the receiver at just the right height.

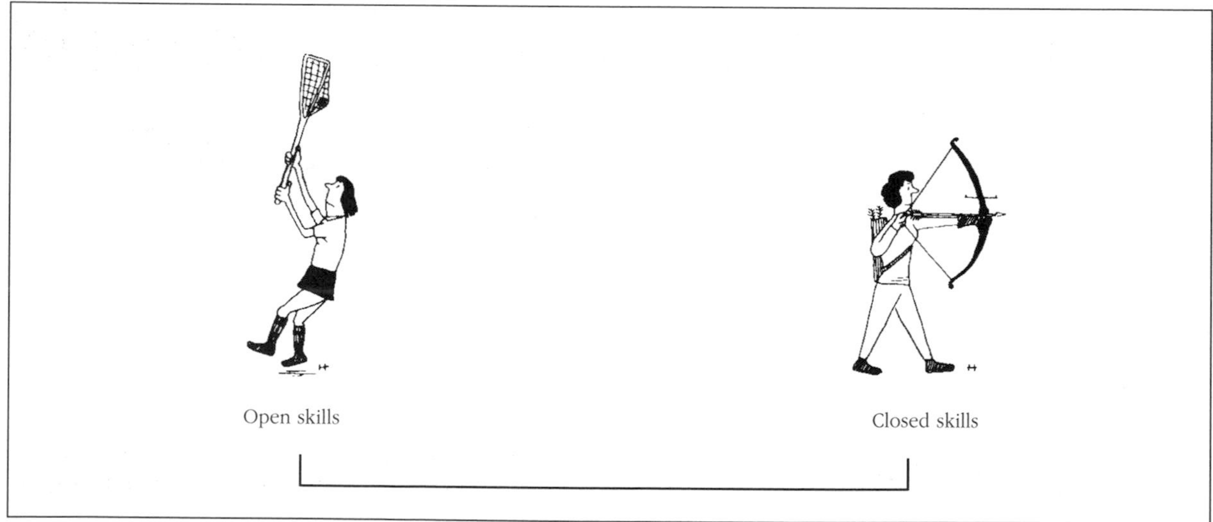

Figure 9.5 The open/closed continuum.

Investigation 9.2 : To explore the classification systems

Method: Work in pairs. Each makes a list of physical education skills. Exchange lists and place the activities you have been given into the three classifications we have studied so far.

Observations: As you think about these classifications, you will realize that to assign a particular activity a place on a continuum can be a complex task. Much will depend on the circumstances. For example, skiing could be open or closed depending on the state and gradient of the piste. And one could argue that whereas a game such as tennis clearly demands open skills, once a player has decided what sort of shot to make, has positioned him/herself correctly and has read the pace and spin of the ball, then the resulting stroke is closed, hence the idea of 'closed skills in open situations'.

Discussion: Try to come to some agreement with your partner about the placing of the various activities. Suggest what some of the implications of this classification for sportspeople might be.

In spite of the difficulties you may have identified, the idea of classifying skill is an interesting one and gives us food for thought when deciding how a skill should be practised. We will return to it later, in Section 12.2.

Investigation 9.3 : To identify motor abilities

Method: Perform a handstand, or other balance, using a partner for support if necessary, but try, if only for a short time, to balance alone.

Observations: Analyse the requirements of this skill. What does the performer need to be able to do, or have, in order to be successful?

Discussion: Note that the balance itself is 'a skill'. The performer brings a certain amount of 'skill', as we have defined it above, to its execution.

9.3 Skill and Ability

We need at this stage to differentiate between two more terms which are often used, in everyday language, to mean the same thing; but to sport psychologists they are technical terms. Skill is learned, but an ability (for example, to react quickly) is a general characteristic of the performer and can be used in a variety of skills.

- **Affective characteristics**, such as courage or confidence. An affective characteristic is one which is associated with the emotions.
- **Motor abilities**, such as balance, strength, co-ordination. An ability is a personal characteristic, or trait, which contributes to proficiency in a number of skills (Stallings, 1982, page 10). It is an enduring quality and is both inherited and affected by experience.
- **Perceptual abilities** concern the way in which we notice important things that are happening around us, and thus determine how quickly and effectively we make decisions about how to deal with these.

Abilities contribute to skill; for example, someone with good natural balance, shoulder flexibility, upper body and wrist strength, has the prerequisites to perform a handstand. Of course, they have to learn to use these abilities effectively.

We will be considering motor abilities in more detail in Chapter 11, when we study individual differences in learning and performance.

Summary

1. The terms 'ability', 'skill' and 'technique' mean different things. Skill is learned; it the efficient attainment of a pre-specified goal; it involves speed, accuracy, and the adaptation of movements to the requirements of the task. Ability is a function of both inheritance and experience; though it may be developed and extended with use, it is not learned. Abilities underpin skill. A technique is a movement pattern. It may be performed more or less skilfully.
2. Skills may be classified in a variety of ways. Three of the most useful classifications in terms of an understanding of how skills are acquired, relate to (i) continuity, (ii) pacing and (iii) environmental requirements.

REFERENCES

Knapp B. *Skill in Sport,* Routledge and Kegan Paul, Chapter 1, 1977.

Poulton E.C. On prediction in skilled movements, *Psychological Bulletin,* 54, 6, 467-78, 1957.

Singer R.N. *The Learning of Motor Skills,* Macmillan, Chapter 5, 1982.

Stallings L.M. *Motor Learning From Theory to Practice,* Mosby, 1982.

FURTHER READING

Schmidt, R.A. *Motor Learning and Performance: from Principles to Practice,* Human Kinetics, Chapters 1 and 11, 1991.

Scottish Sports Council. *Acquiring Skills, Coach Education Module 1,* Scottish Sports Council, 1987.

Sharp, B. *Acquiring Skill in Sport,* Sports Dynamics, Chapter 2, 1992.

Chapter 10
Information Processing in Perceptual–motor Performance

So far we have defined skill by describing it. Knapp's is thus a **'descriptive definition'**. Let us now consider a different form of definition—one which analyses how the skill is performed. This is known as an '**operational definition**'.

At the end of this section you should be able to:

a. differentiate between learning and performance;
b. use an information processing model to analyse a skill;
c. understand the relationship between sensory input, perception, decision making, memory and motor output in the performance of skilled actions and in the learning process;
d. measure reaction time and test hypotheses using reaction time data;
e. understand the difference between open and closed modes of motor control;
f. define, and apply to physical education activities, the key words listed at the end of the section.

At this stage we need to review the important distinction between learning and performance.

Investigation 10.1 : To differentiate between learning and performance

Method: Work with a partner. One is the learner, one the instructor. The instructor, out of sight of the learner, composes a sequence of movements, chosen at random. Keep the movements simple and 'nonsense'. About ten separate movements will be sufficient. Practise this sequence so that you can demonstrate it fluently to your partner. Teach your partner the sequence by demonstrating it in full **once only** and asking him/her to perform it as best (s)he can. This performance will probably contain some errors, so, without any explanation or correction, show them the sequence again and request another demonstration. Repeat this procedure until a completely correct sequence is produced by your partner.

Results: Note how many mistakes of movement pattern or sequencing are made at each performance. Draw a graph as in Figure 10.1.

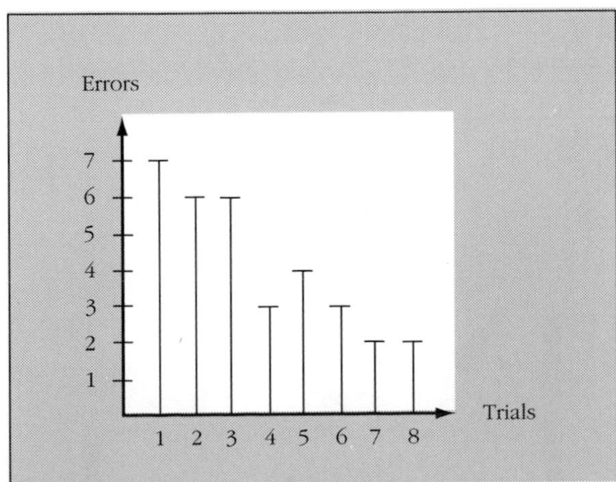

Figure 10.1 A graph of decreasing errors to demonstrate learning.

The graph you drew in Investigation 10.1 is one of decreasing errors—one way of measuring learning. Another way would be to note **increases** in performance; for example, the number of successful consecutive catches in a juggling task. The graph would then look like Figure 10.2.

Each attempt at the task is a performance, a demonstration of the learner's ability in that task at that time. While a person is learning, each performance is likely to be different from (and hopefully better than) the last. As the skill is learned, the performance becomes more consistent. So learning is the process by which performance is refined and it represents a relatively permanent change of behaviour.

Both the process of learning and the result of that learning, the performance, can be described using a model, a representation of what we think may be happening inside our central nervous system. Several such models exist and you will come across them during your further reading, but they all have the same basic components. They are called **human information processing models**, because they describe the performer or learner as a system for processing information from the environment in order to produce a response to a situation. The information is carried from the sense organs to the brain by the nerves, and commands are sent similarly from the brain to the muscles. You will have dealt with this process as part of your work in physiology, and you should refer back to Section 1.4 to ensure that you understand this. The simplest model looks like Figure 10.3.

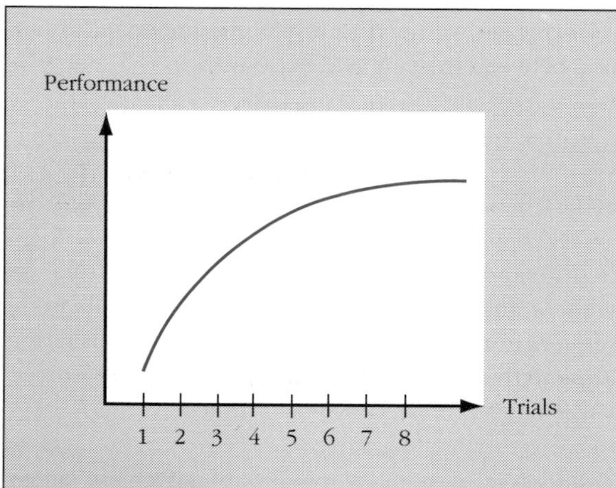

Figure 10.2 A learning curve.

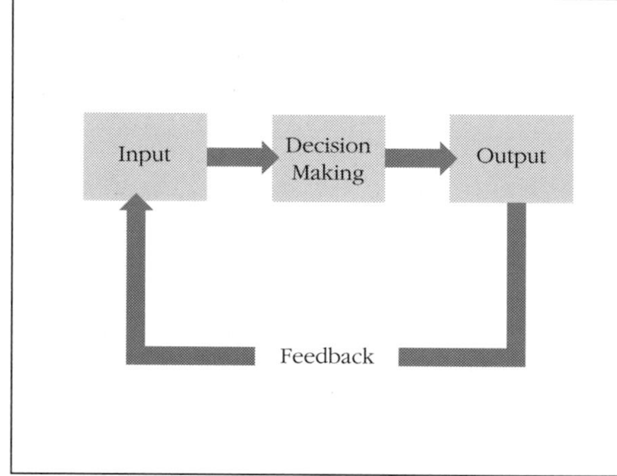

Figure 10.3 A simple information processing model.

Investigation 10.2 : To use an information processing model to analyse a skill

Method: Work in pairs. Select a striking skill (tennis, badminton, hockey, etc.). The 'feeder' sends to the striker' who aims at a target.

Observations: Using the three 'boxes' in Figure 10.3, describe what is happening as the striker performs the skill. What is the significance of the 'feedback' loop?

You will probably have found that in your description you started to analyse aspects of your performance which were not in the model; so let us expand it (Figure 10.4).

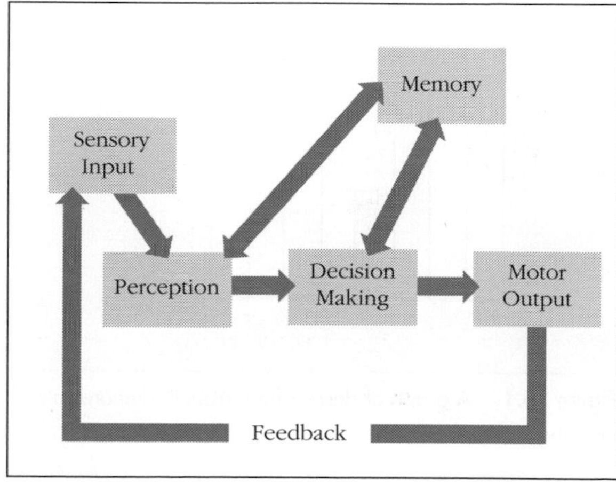

Figure 10.4 An expanded information processing model.

10.1 Sensory Input

KEY WORDS AND CONCEPTS

proprioception **touch** **kinaesthesis**
equilibrium

When we are doing any physical activity we are aware of our surroundings. We use all our senses to locate ourselves in space and to decide on the requirements of the task, whether it is to pass a ball or perform a gymnastic/dance movement. Taste and smell are not used to any great extent in physical activity, but vision, hearing and proprioception are. **Proprioception** is the means by which we orientate our body in space or know by how much a muscle is contracted. If the amount of sensory input normally present is not available for some reason, problems occur.

Vision and hearing deal with information from the external environment. We also receive information from the internal environment—that is, from within our own bodies.

Proprioception is the means by which we know how our body is oriented in space, the extent to which muscles are contracted or joints extended, and allows us to feel the racket or ball. The three components of proprioception are **touch, equilibrium** and **kinaesthesis.**

Touch (or the tactile sense) enables us to feel pain, pressure and temperature. In sports and dance we are mostly concerned with the pressure sense to tell us how firmly we are gripping a racket, for example, or whether our climbing partner is on a tight rope, or whether we struck the ball hard or 'stroked' it. If we are sensible we take heed of any pain warnings we are being sent.

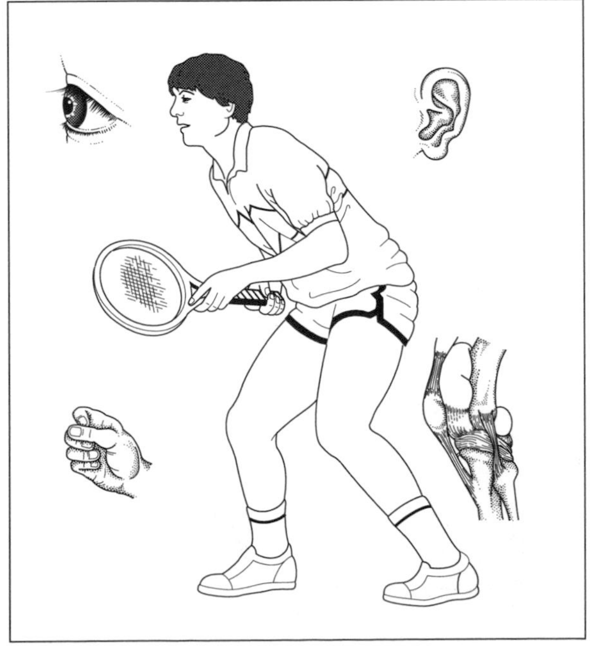

Figure 10.5 Major sensory input systems in games.

Investigation 10.3 : To investigate the effects of sensory deprivation on performance

(a) VISION

Task One

Method: Play a game of five-a-side soccer or basketball (or any passing/striking game). One team plays as normal. Players in the other team have one eye covered with a medical eye patch. **Do not continue this activity for too long.**

Observations: What are the effects on the visually deprived players? What does it feel like to play like this?

Task Two

Method: Reverse team roles so that the other team is visually deprived. This time restrict peripheral vision (your ability to see 'out of the corner of your eye' things which you are not looking at directly). You can do this by cutting a strip of card 8 × 60 cm, stapling the narrow ends to form goggles and attaching it round your eyes with elastic or string (Figure 10.6).

Observations: What is the effect of the goggles? What does it feel like to play like this?

Figure 10.6 Goggles to restrict peripheral vision.

Task Three

Method: Try a gymnastic or dance sequence with which you are familiar, using the same vision restrictors.

Observations: What are the problems? What does it feel like?

We use vision a great deal in physical activities. Imagine the difficulties for a blind or partially sighted person. Discuss with a partner any knowledge you have of visually handicapped people participating in sport or physical activity. How do they compensate?

(b) AUDITION

Task Four

Method: Select an activity in which sound is an integral part (for example, the sound of the ball against the racket in tennis or the bed in trampolining). Try this activity wearing headphones or ear-plugs to block out the sound.

Observations: How does this affect your performance? To what extent do we use sound in these activities?

(c) PROPRIOCEPTION

Task Five

Method: Play a ball-handling game such as basketball, netball or softball in thick gloves. Perform a gymnastic or dance sequence, with which you are familiar, in stiff trainers.

Observations: It will obviously feel strange, but what are the particular problems?

Discussion: Explain the difficulties in terms of your loss of some tactile sense.

Equilibrium is the sense which tells you when your body is balanced and when it is tipping, turning or inverting. It is obviously important for divers, gymnasts and trampolinists as well as dancers to be able to orientate themselves in space. This is done by means of the sense organs in the vestibular apparatus of the middle ear.

Kinaesthesis is the sense which informs the brain of the movement or state of contraction of the muscles, tendons and joints. A skilled performer will know whether a movement has been performed correctly or not, not only from seeing its effect, but also from sensing how the movement felt to perform. You may have experienced a foot or a limb 'going to sleep' and you will know how difficult it is not only to move the limb, but to know what is happening to it. The messages to and from the muscles have been interrupted and kinaesthetic sense impaired. Investigation 10.4 illustrates how we use our kinaesthetic sense.

Investigation 10.4 : To illustrate kinaesthesis

Method: Make a loop of fairly strong elastic and loop it round your fingers as in Figure 10.7.

Your partner holds a ruler horizontally and you stretch the elastic to a length specified by your partner. You relax the elastic, your partner removes the ruler and you try to repeat the exact stretch again but this time with your eyes closed.

Repeat this several times, each time with a different length to reproduce.

Observations: How accurate were you? Calculate your percentage error each time.

Discussion: Discuss with your partner how kinaesthesis is being used.

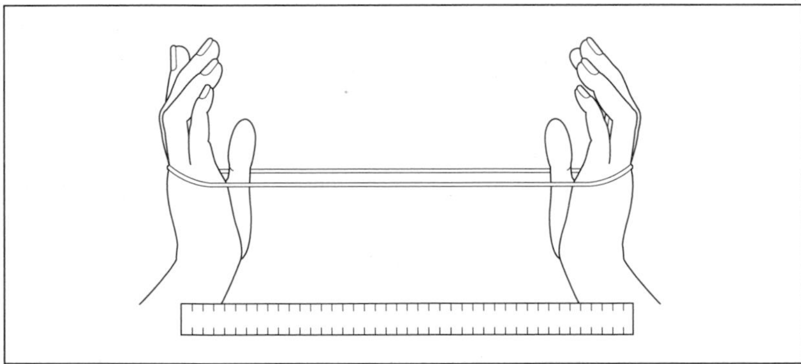

Figure 10.7 Equipment to illustrate kinaesthesis.

We take our sense organs very much for granted in sport and recreation and do not always appreciate that our ability to make appropriate decisions is based on receiving the right information. Whether or not we get the right information depends on:

a. the efficiency of our sense organs
b. the intensity of the stimulus
c. our ability to interpret the stimulus correctly.

10.2 Perception

KEY WORDS AND CONCEPTS

open skill	**stimulus identification**	**short-term memory**
noise	**DTR**	**long-term memory**
stimulus	**detection**	**selective attention**

This is the process by which the brain interprets and makes sense of the information which it is receiving from the sensory organs.

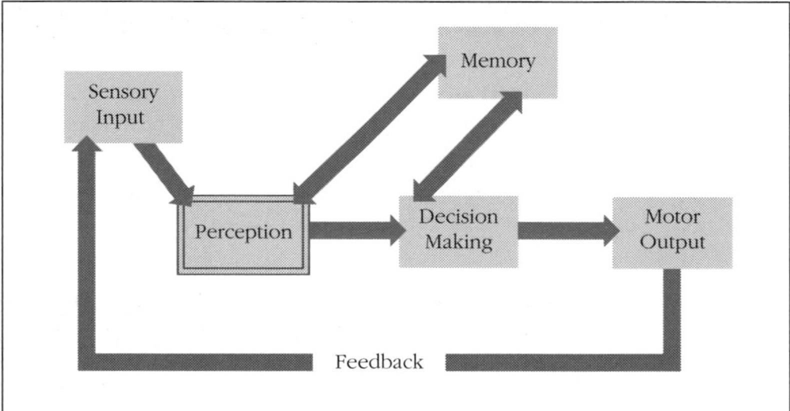

Figure 10.8 Perception in the information processing model.

Investigation 10.5 : To investigate perception in physical activities

Method: Participate in any **open skill**. Remember that an open skill is one in which the important aspects of the environment are constantly changing. As you participate, be aware of all the aspects of your surroundings to which you are paying particular attention.

Observations: List all the things that you take notice of in order to perform well. In a ball game you will need to note the flight of the ball as it comes towards you; as you climb you will be attending to the changes in the rock or the wall; as you canoe you will be watching for waves, rocks and currents.

Discussion: Talk these over in detail with a partner.

Each of the factors you noted in Investigation 10.5 is a **stimulus:** the spin of a ball, the flight path of a shuttle, the size of a hold on a climb. The word 'stimulus' is being used here to mean any item of information which is standing out from the background. Psychologists refer to the background information (for example the crowd) as 'noise'. **Noise** used in this sense is information which is present and which we might be aware of, but which is not directly relevant to the task in hand. We will see later that the ability to differentiate background from stimuli is partly learned, but partly a personality trait. We will also see that noise can be a problem for decision making.

We are more likely to sense and identify something if it is intense, i.e. loud, bright, large, contrasting, fast-moving, unusual.

With the person sitting next to you, discuss each of the concepts above (for example brightness, size, etc.) in relation to games, giving examples of how performers, coaches and organizers take account of each in their particular sport.

Investigation 10.6 : To investigate the effect of background and ball colour in tennis

Method: Play two games of short tennis, one with balls that contrast with the surroundings and one with balls which blend with the court and wall colour. (Experiment with dyeing a few tennis balls to get a colour which blends with your particular sports hall.)

Observations: How did the colour of the balls affect your game?

The process by which we can pick out a particular stimulus from all those bombarding our brain is known as **stimulus identification**.

Investigation 10.7 : To investigate the effect of early and late stimulus identification in the catching/returning of a ball

Method: a) Work in threes, a 'feeder', a 'catcher' and a 'scorer'. A cross is marked in chalk or tape on the ground about one meter from the catcher's feet.

First, the feeder bounces the ball on the cross for the catcher to receive. You will need to adjust your position and that of the cross so that the ball can be received comfortably by the catcher. Have 10 trials. The feeder should try and make the bounces consistent. The scorer notes successful catches out of ten.

The catcher then has a further 20 trials, but this time the catcher has eyes closed until the feeder shouts 'now!'. This should be done at varying points on the trajectory of the bounce, ten times early (i.e. shortly after it has left the feeder's hand) and ten times late.

Results: What are the effects on catching of early and late opportunity for stimulus identification?

Discussion: How do you explain the results you obtained?

b) Repeat the experiment playing badminton or volleyball, with a server, two or more receivers and a scorer as before.

Discuss examples from a variety of sports by which a player can inflict late signal opportunity on an opponent.

There are three elements to stimulus identification:

detection
comparison
recognition.

We shall call this the **DCR** process and will be returning to it throughout this section.

Detection is the process of registering the stimulus by the sense organ. Some things that happen in games we simply do not see, because we are not looking in that direction. But it is also possible for our senses to receive information which we do not notice. This is because of a process known as **selective attention**. Let us look at this in more detail, by expanding our model further to include memory processes.

SELECTIVE ATTENTION AND MEMORY

All the senses are feeding a vast amount of information into the central nervous system. Think for a moment of all the aspects of your surroundings and your body on which you can focus your attention if you choose. We are able to concentrate only on a very small proportion of these at any given moment. However, all this information is stored briefly in a 'memory box' which is called the **short-term memory**.

If we are looking out for some particular stimulus, or if a particular happening catches our interest, then we focus on that by the process of **selective attention**. This focusing of attention lengthens the period during which the stimulus is stored in the short-term memory. If we do not attend to it, we quickly forget it.

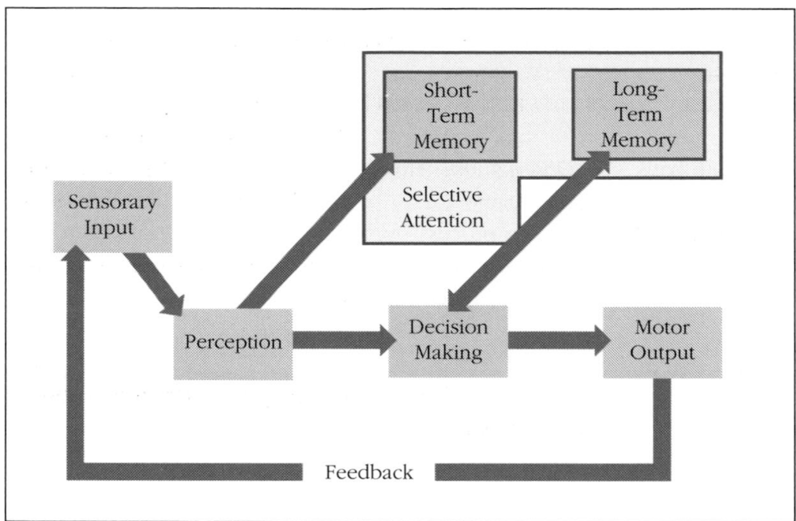

Figure 10.9 Memory and selective attention in the information processing model.

Investigation 10.8 : To investigate selective attention

Task One
Method: Listen through stereo headphones to an audio tape, which has been recorded with two separate passages of prose on the two tracks of the tape.

Observations: Can you listen to them both simultaneously? What strategies did you adopt to make as much sense as you could of both passages? What aspects of the passages made you switch your attention?

Task Two—To investigate the effect of selective attention on the performance of a motor skill
Method: You will need five yellow tennis balls and one of a contrasting colour. A catcher stands two metres from a line of six throwers, each of whom has a tennis ball held so that it cannot be seen.

a) On the command 'throw', given either by one of the throwers or by the scorer, the throwers throw simultaneously and gently to the catcher who attempts to catch the contrasting ball. Score successful catches out of ten trials.
b) The instructor gives the command 'throw'—and the name of one of the throwers. All throw; the catcher is to catch the ball thrown by the nominee. Score successful catches out of ten.
c) The instructor gives the command as in b) above, but only the nominee throws. Score successful catches out of ten.

Results: Draw a **bar chart** to illustrate the mean scores for the whole class on each of the three tests. An example is given in Figure 10.10. Note that a bar chart, with spaces between the bars, is used because the horizontal axis shows three separate trials: it does not represent a scale, as it would if a histogram was drawn

Discussion: In which of the three tests is selective attention easiest? Suggest reasons.

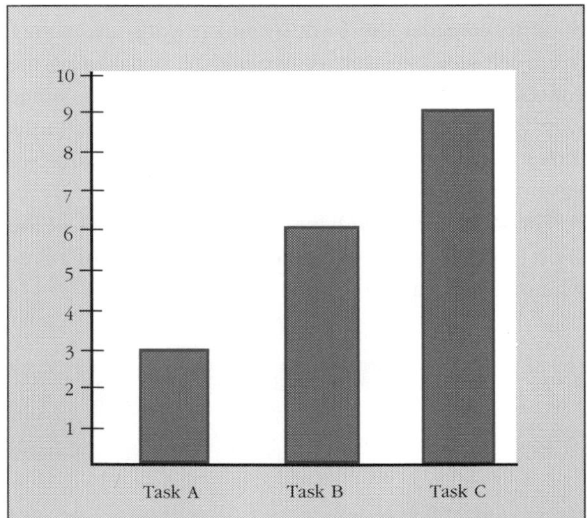

Figure 10.10 Hypothetical group mean scores on three tests to illustrate selective attention.

As we learned earlier, intensity of the stimulus may attract our attention—for example, loudness, brightness, colour contrast, speed of movement; but we are also attracted to unusual stimuli (we try to make sense of them) or stimuli in which we are particularly interested, as in Task Two of Investigation 10.8.

Task One indicates that our capacity to attend to several stimuli at once is severely limited. The process of selective attention ensures that only a small amount of information can be processed at a time. We shall see later that this is not necessarily a disadvantage, for it means that the decision making system is not overloaded. Imagine what it would be like to decide when and who to pass to in a team game if we had to analyse all the available information coming in through our senses before making a move!

Investigation 10.9 : To investigate the capacity of the short-term memory

Method: Play 'Kim's Game'. About 15 everyday items are placed on a tray and all the subjects are given about 15 seconds to study them. The tray is removed and the subjects attempt to write down as many of the items as possible.

Results: Record the total number of correct items recalled.

Discussion: People's short-term memory capacity varies, but the norm is between five and nine items. If you have a longer period to study the contents of the tray, or if you have mastered memory skills, you will be able to remember more than this because you are able to extend retention in the short-term memory by a process of rehearsal or practice.

Long-term memory is also used in this process because, as you first perceive the objects on the tray, you recognize them; that is, you compare the object that you see with a memory of it from earlier experiences stored in the long-term memory, and this allows you to identify it, name it, recall its characteristics and how to use it. Remember the DCR process?

It has been suggested that this process of comparison and recognition takes place in the short-term memory, often referred to as the 'workspace' of the system. Incoming signals are held there and the long-term memory is scanned for an identical image, or something like it. When this is found it is transferred to the short-term memory and compared with the incoming image, so that the image can be recognized.

For example, you might have learned from past experience that when your opponent in tennis or badminton 'shapes up' to serve in a particular way, then he/she is going to produce a particular type of serve. You see this happening; you detect, compare and recognize. We will discuss what you do about it in Chapter 11. We monitor our surroundings in this way all the time; our brain is constantly operating the DCR process, even when we are not consciously aware of it.

Long-term memory is also the store for information which we constantly need to refer to or which has been so well learned or practised that it remains in permanent store. It has an almost limitless capacity, as long as information is stored effectively and the memory not interfered with. It is beyond the scope of this book to consider the form in which skills are memorized, but in a later section we will be considering the concept of motor programmes, which takes us some way to an understanding of this. Some continuous motor skills seem to be stored particularly well; we never forget how to ride a bicycle.

The knowledge we have about the capacities of the short- and long-term memories is important to us when we are learning or practising skills.

Investigation 10.10 : To investigate the implications of the characteristics of short-term memory

Task One

Method: Work in pairs. One composes two lists of five three-letter sequences. Five are meaningful words, e.g. cup, dog; five are nonsense, e.g. frz, xvu.

Present one list to your partner, for a period of ten seconds, then ask him/her to repeat the list. If a mistake is made, return the list for another 10-second viewing and repeat until your partner can repeat the list accurately to you. Repeat the exercise with the other list.

Results: Score the number of attempts before a correct list is reproduced. Which list took fewer attempts to remember?

Discussion: What strategies did you adopt to try and memorize the 'nonsense' list?

Assuming you found that the meaningful list was easier to remember, there are two reasons for your answer. Can you suggest what they are?

Included in your suggestions should have been:

(i) the short-term memory is better at storing information which is meaningful;

(ii) since its capacity would seem to be about seven items, it is more efficient to 'chunk' items together if this can be done. So the letters C-A-T instead of being three items become one, CAT, which also has a meaning (a visual image) attached to it.

Task Two

Method: Change roles and repeat the task, but as the memorizer is studying the list, the partner asks questions for which answers are demanded; anything to distract.

Discussion: What are the effects on the memory task? What are the implications of your findings for learning in physical education? If you were helping a friend to master a particular skill in your favourite activity, how would you present the information?

Task Three—to try out coaching strategies based on an understanding of memory processes

Method: Think up a discrete sports hall skill which you can coach, but with which your partner is not very familiar. It could be a game or gymnastic skill, a particular set of moves on a climbing wall, a dance step to a complex rhythm. Work out how you are going to introduce and coach the skill, bearing in mind the principles we have just identified.

Teach your partner the skill you have devised. As you coach, be aware of your own teaching points and also analyse your partner's performance. If possible, video the session.

Observations: Afterwards, analyse the recording and/or discuss with the learner (i) when your comments were helpful and (ii) when your comments were not helpful and why. Remember we are focusing on the extent to which you helped your partner to **remember** what you wanted them to do.

Attention, relevance, meaning, 'chunking', brevity are the key words. Did you use **demonstration?**

Figure 10.11 (Adapted from Singer, 1982.)

10.3 Decision Making

KEY WORDS AND CONCEPTS

reaction time	**simple reaction time**	**psychological refractory period**
response time	**choice reaction time**	**attend**
movement time	**initiations**	**anticipate**

Our perceptual ability allows us the information with which to make decisions about what to do next in a physical task. This might be intrinsic to the skill itself ('I can feel my body is vertical—now is the moment to push against the box-top to complete the vault'); or it might be extrinsic ('my opponent has pushed the ball a little too far ahead—now is the moment to tackle'). The speed at which we make decisions, or **reaction time**, is of great interest in this area of study. This is partly because, in many sports and activities, being able to react quickly allows the performer to be in greater control; the quicker you respond to the gun and are away from your blocks in a 100 metre track event, the more you can dominate the race; the more quickly you can respond to an unexpected eddy in white water, the less likely you are to capsize. The study of reaction time is also important because it tells us a lot about the process of making decisions.

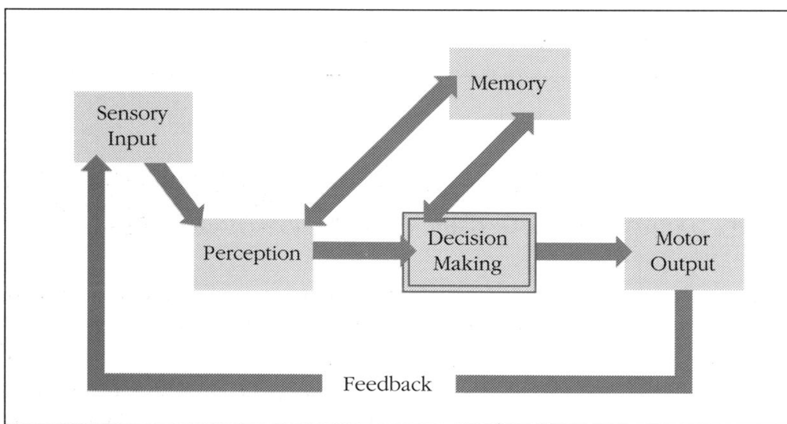

Figure 10.12 Decision making in the information processing model.

As you can see from Figure 10.13, responding to a stimulus is a complex business. You will recognize the DCR process at work. You will also notice that:

Response time = reaction time + movement time

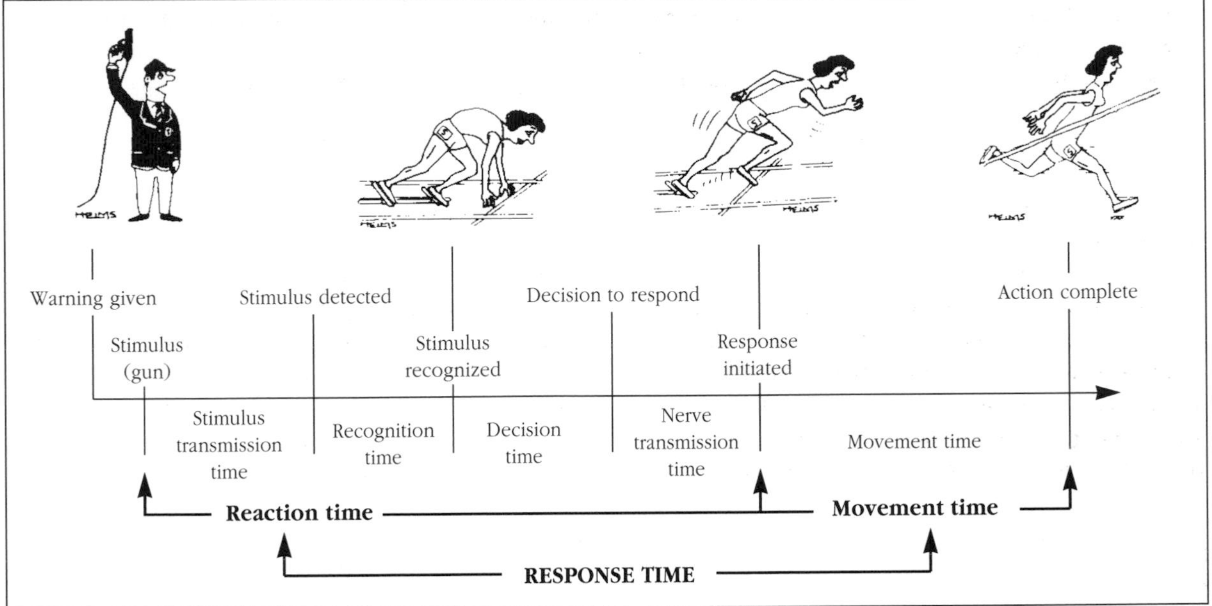

Figure 10.13 The components of reponse time.

Investigation 10.11 : To calculate the timing of a baseball swing

Study Figure 10.14. The pitcher delivers the ball at a velocity of 32 metres per second. The reaction time of the batter is 0.18 seconds and the time to swing from back to contact is 0.2 seconds. How far out of the pitcher's hand can the batsman afford to let the ball travel before he starts to swing?

Did you get an answer of 5.8 metres?

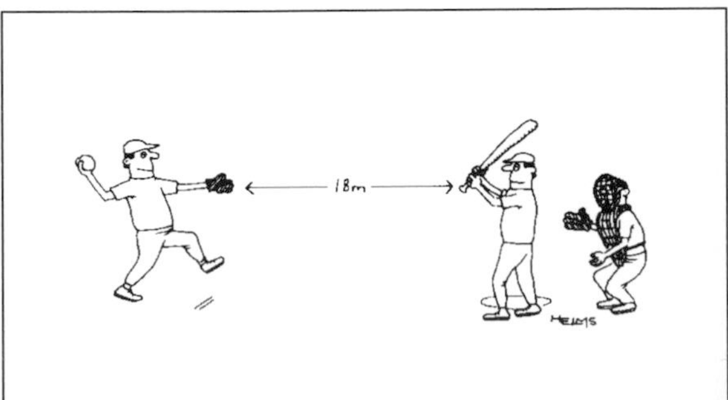

Figure 10.14 (Adapted from Davis *et al.*, 1986.)

Obviously, when we are playing striking games we do not consciously make this kind of calculation each time we play the ball, but the faster we react the more time we have to make a decision about the kind of shot to play. A fast reaction or response time is more important in some skills than in others. Refer back to the section on classification of skill in Chapter 9, p. 232.

DISCUSSION

Discuss the extent to which fast reaction times contribute to performance in (i) self/externally paced skills; (ii) open/closed skills.

Method: Work in pairs. Make a list of skills which you can identify as lying at various points on the two continua. Decide, for each skill, the advantage of a fast reaction time or the disadvantage of a slow reaction time for effective performance.

Reaction time is an ability. It varies between individuals and is also influenced by the demands of the task and the nature of the stimulus. Some of these influences are:

- the intensity of the stimulus
- the probability of the stimulus occurring
- the existence of warning signals/the extent to which the stimulus is expected
- the sense being used for detection.

So far we have considered reaction time as if it were to one stimulus only. At the start of a track event, this is so—there is one gun and the athlete is expecting it; but in other events there may be several stimuli and the performer has to choose which one to respond to, or which of several possible responses, for example shots in a racket game, to make for a given stimulus. These two forms of reaction time are known as **simple** and **choice reaction time** (SRT and CRT).

Investigation 10.12 : To measure reaction time

There are a variety of ways in which reaction time can be measured in the laboratory or classroom. Choose the one(s) for which you have the appropriate equipment. Most are more accurately measures of response time, because it is not possible to identify the point at which reaction is complete and movement starts (refer to Figure 10.13).

Methods:

a. Use a microcomputer programme to measure eye–hand or possibly ear–hand SRT and CRT (for example, 'Reaction Timing', Jordanhill College of Education).

Compare SRTs and CRTs.

Explain why CRTs are longer.

Devise an experimental hypothesis which compares RTs with another variable, for example dominant/non-dominant eye or preferred/non-preferred hand. Collect appropriate data and test out this hypothesis.

b. Use reaction time apparatus (described in many motor learning text books) to investigate:

SRT, CRT and movement time; preferred and non preferred-hand reaction to auditory and visual stimuli; foot reaction as above (if the apparatus includes foot-pads).

Devise a hypothesis which predicts association between two of the variables you have measured, and test this.

c. Use the 'ruler drop' test, full details of which appear in Arnot and Gaines (1984), to measure SRT and CRT. The only apparatus you will need for this test are two metre rulers.

a.

b.

Figure 10.15 Ruler drop test.

Convert the distance the ruler drops into a response time using the formula:

$$d = ut + {}^1/_2\, at^2$$

where d is the distance the ruler falls (cm)
u is the initial velocity of the ruler which in this instance is 0 cm s^{-1}
t is the response time (s)
a is the acceleration of the ruler due to gravity. This is constant at 981 cm s^{-2}

You will need to use some simple algebra to arrive at an expression for t.

Compare your score on this test with your score on a comparable version of one of the other tests, if possible.

Explain any differences in the scores in terms of:

a. reaction and movement time
b. experimental procedure.

d. Work in pairs. You will need a stop-watch and a set of playing cards. The task is to sort the shuffled pack. Your partner will give a start signal, time you to completion of the sort and note the time.

a. Separate red cards from black (two groups).
b. Separate the four suits (four groups).
c. Separate four suits of court cards and four suits of non-court cards (eight groups).

Calculate the mean time for the whole class on each of the three tasks.

Plot a graph of time against the number of choices which have to be made for each card (two, four or eight).

What does this graph tell you about the relationship between response time and the number of choices available? Explain this relationship in information processing terms. Is it likely to be reaction which takes longer, or movement?

Your answer to method (d) in Investigation 10.12 should lead you to an important principle for the learning of motor skills. The more choices are available to us, the longer we take to react. So when we are in the early stages of skill learning, when we need to concentrate on the production of effective movement as well as choose an appropriate response, it is best if we are not presented with too many choices. This allows the learner more time to operate the DCR process and relate recognition of the stimulus to the production of the appropriate movement. Hence not only should instructions be simple and brief (as you learned earlier) but the task should not involve too much decision making. Two against two or three against three games induces better learning than a premature introduction to the full 7- or ll- or 15-a-side game.

When we are involved in physical education activities we have to respond to a constant stream of stimuli. If these are well spaced and we have time to respond to each in turn, reaction time seems not to be affected. But often a second stimulus will arrive before we have had a chance to complete, or even initiate, our response to the first.

Opponents often do this to us on purpose; for example, by disguising a shot or 'selling a dummy' in slalom canoeing a wave may hit just as the canoeist is negotiating a gate. This is illustrated in Figure 10.16.

S_1 and S_2 are two stimuli and R_1 and R_2 are the **initiations** of the responses to these stimuli; thus the distances S_1/R_1 and S_2/R_2 represent **reaction** time. This is not easy to demonstrate with simple equipment but Investigation 10.13 illustrates what happens.

You can see from Figure 10.17 that the reaction to the second stimulus is longer. The time between S_2 and R_1 is known as the **psychological refractory period** (PRP).

Figure 10.16 'Selling a dummy'.

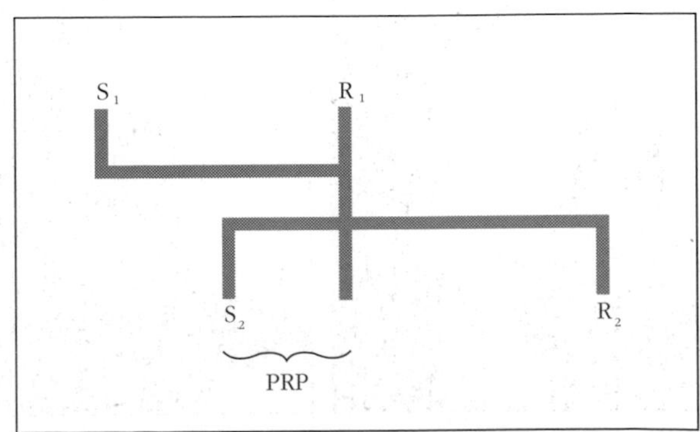

Figure 10.17 The psychological refractory period.

It would appear that when a performer detects a stimulus and starts to select a plan of action/response, he must devote his attention to the process. Research summarized in Figure 10.17 suggests that whilst he is doing this he is unable to deal with any other decision requiring attention. This is where 'faking' or 'selling a dummy' comes in. The attacker makes a fake move and then uses the defender's PRP to move the other way or play a different shot. Martenuik (1976, p. 24) suggests that this strategy 'is effective even if the player does not usually begin to move in response to the fake. All that is necessary is to have him begin the search for an action, since he cannot amend this process until the search is completed'.

Investigation 10.13 : To illustrate the psychological refractory period

Task One

Work in pairs. One acts as 'catcher', the other as 'feeder'. The feeder needs to be able to throw underarm consistently with both hands. Stand approximately five metres apart.

The feeder holds a tennis ball in each hand. There are twenty trials. Each trial consists of the thrower saying a warning 'ready!' and then throwing gently to the catcher who attempts to catch with two hands. The throws should be consistent and accurately placed into the catcher's hands. In ten of the trials one ball only is thrown, sometimes from the feeder's left and sometimes from the right hand. In the other ten trials (which should be mixed in with the former trials at random), one ball is thrown immediately followed by the other—not both together (this takes some practice by the feeder!). One point is scored by the catcher a) if he catches the ONLY ball thrown or b) if he catches the SECOND thrown (no points for catching the first). Note the score out of ten when one ball is thrown, and the score when two balls are thrown.

Which score do you think will be the highest and why?

Task Two

Play a game in which faking or dummying is a realistic strategy. When attacking make the most of opportunities to do this. Practise the timing necessary. Remember that if your second move comes more than one normal reaction time (200 ms) after the first, then your opponent will be able to read it, unless you have actually 'wrong-footed' him or her in which case the opponent must recover and you have gained even more time.

Task Three

If you have the appropriate equipment (a film camera and frame analysis equipment, or a video camera and playback machine with a freeze-frame facility) experiment with analysing reaction time and the PRP by film. Select a variety of activities in which reaction time is an important aspect of the skill and film them, making sure that the initial stimulus as well as the response can be identified.

CHANNEL CAPACITY

It can be seen from our study so far, summarized in Figure 10.18, that the amount of information we can process and deal with is dependent on our ability to **attend** and this seems to be limited. Theorists have argued for there being a channel of limited capacity or 'bottleneck' through which coded information must travel as we process it, and this seems to operate at at least two points in the system.

Bearing in mind the fact that information is stored in the short-term memory for only a very short time, it is important that a learner should focus attention on important instructions, or on significant cues in the activity, and practise the skill as soon as possible following instruction.

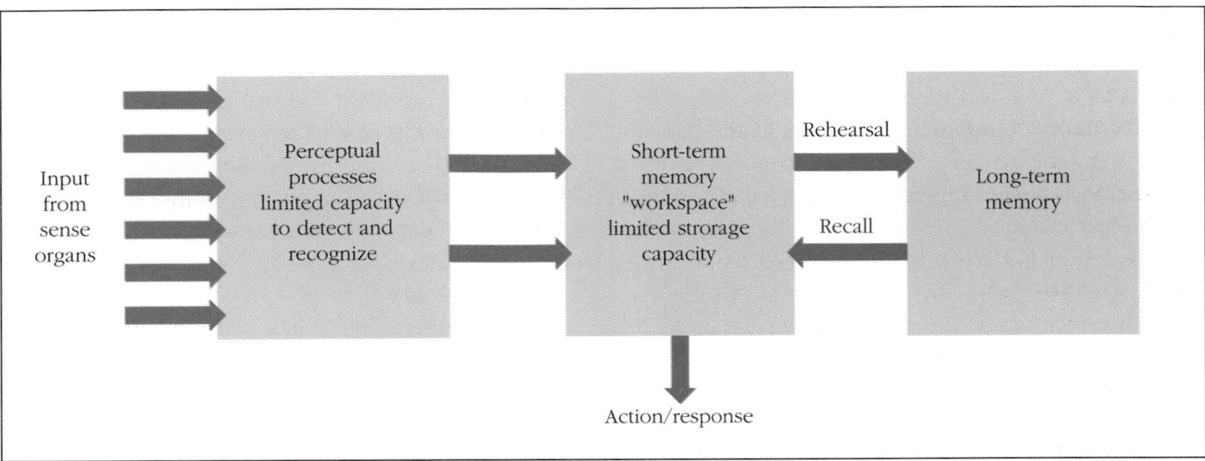

Figure 10.18 Channel capacity.

ANTICIPATION

One of the problems which beginners face in any physical education activity is that of information overload. There is just too much to think about and do and their information processing channels cannot cope with it as fast as they would like. One of the things they learn as they become more experienced is to interpret events in relation to similar things that have happened before. They learn to detect cues early in the sequence of events which help them to **anticipate** the outcome, and thus overcome the problems of delay due to reaction time. Figure 10.19 shows three types of anticipation

Perceptual anticipation is interesting in that we take it so much for granted, but it is the essence of skilful performance. It allows the performer to anticipate proprioceptive feedback and thus correct errors, perhaps even before the result of the movement is known. Errors are corrected in this way by comparing anticipated feedback with feedback from the proprioceptors.

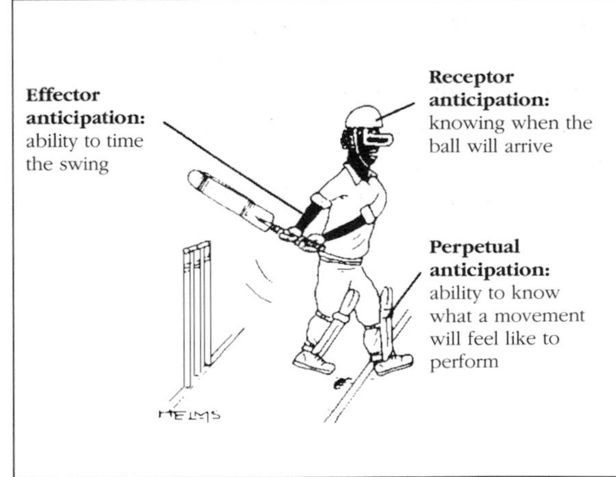

Figure 10.19 Receptor and effector anticipation.

10.4 Motor Output and Feedback

KEY WORDS AND CONCEPTS

effector mechanism	**subroutines**	**hierarchical**
plan of action	**new skills**	**open loop control**
motor programmes	**executive programme**	**closed loop control**

This section is concerned with how the performer learns to produce the movements required for a skilled action. This part of the process is controlled by the **effector mechanism**. This consists of the nerves and muscles which serve the limbs involved in the movement. As a learner practises a skill, images of the movements required are built up in the long-term memory. Gradually, less effective aspects of the movement are eliminated and successful actions are reinforced. With repetition this becomes stored as a **plan of action** associated with the set of stimuli which normally precedes it. So the hockey goalkeeper knows that as the ball arrives at her feet from a shot, the plan required is a long, low kick to the side.

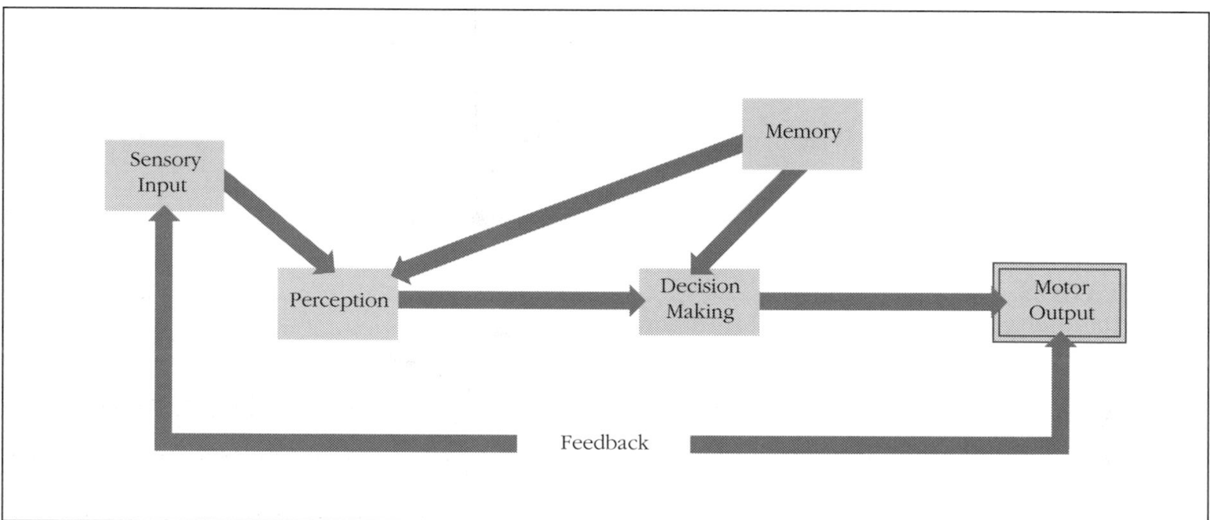

Figure 10.20 Motor output in the information processing model.

MOTOR PROGRAMMES

Before we consider how this process works, let us look in more detail at these plans of action or **motor programmes**. You should note that different writers give different definitions of the term 'motor programme'. In this text we define a motor programme as a set of movements stored in memory, regardless of whether or not feedback is used in its execution.

The motor programme specifies what movements the skill is composed of and in what order these occur. It can be seen from Figure 10.21 that a skill such as a tennis serve (which is known as the **executive programme**) is made up of shorter movements known as **subroutines**, which in turn operate at several levels. In open skills the executive programme has to be adaptable and flexible in order to cope with the variety of environmental requirements. Each pass or shot that you make will have a different trajectory, pace and distance programmed in. The subroutines are short fixed sequences which, when fully learned, can be run off automatically, without conscious control.

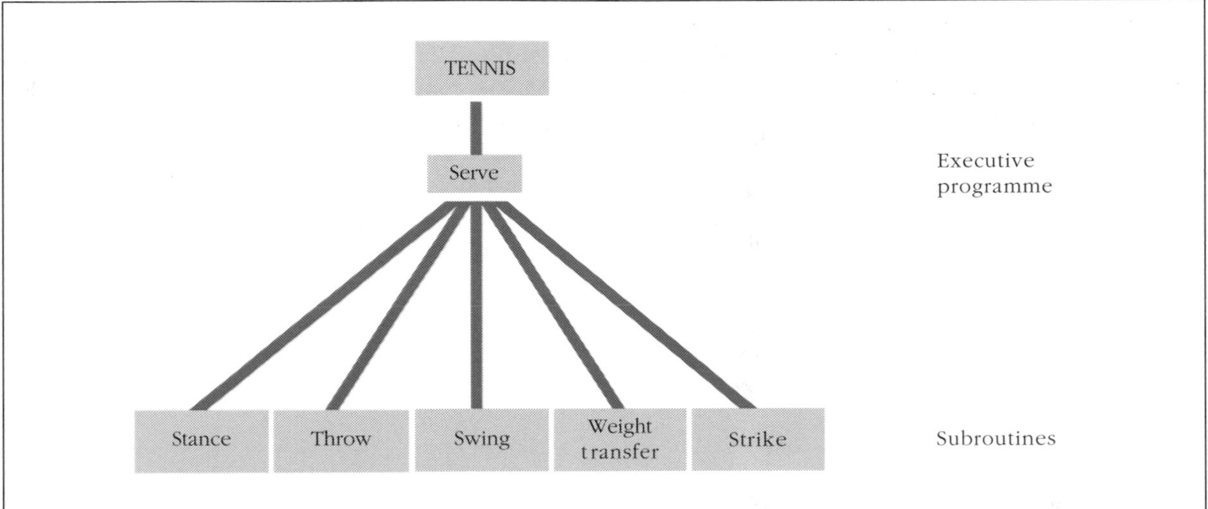

Figure 10.21 The hierarchical structure of a skill.

Investigation 10.14 : To identify executive programmes and subroutines

Method: Work in pairs. Each selects a skill which can be well demonstrated repeatedly. Partner observes and analyses the skill to produce a model similar to Figure 10.21.

Analysis: If you compare your analysis with others in the class you will find that some subroutines are common to several skills.

Motor learning in early childhood is about the establishment of these subroutines; the youngster learns to run, jump, turn, grip, strike, etc. To him these are executive programmes—but as he develops more complex activities, these become the subroutines for his **new skills**. As he becomes more versatile, the learner becomes adept at transferring subroutines already learned into new executive programmes.

The importance of this **hierarchical** organization of motor programmes is that it allows parts of the skill, or indeed the whole skill, to be stored in the long-term memory as a complete programme and recalled for use automatically, leaving the performer to concentrate on the perceptual or interpretive aspects. Speaking of Torvill and Dean's strategy of always running through their whole ice dance at final rehearsals (rather than isolating sections for practice) Christopher Dean commented:

> *Every time you do the programme in full you're adding to your store of experience and self-confidence. The more you can drill yourself into automatic mastery on the ice, the more you can give yourself to presentation when the big moment comes.*
>
> (Hennessy, 1984)

MOTOR CONTROL

Let us look in more detail at how this 'automatic mastery' works. As you practise, so the skill becomes programmed into the long-term memory. When you recall the programme and ask the muscles to put it into operation, research (Martenuik 1976, p. 139) suggests that there are three levels at which this happens.

Some movements seem to be produced without reference to any feedback, because they happen too quickly for feedback to have any effect. Fast typing would be an example of this kind of skill. This is known as **open loop control**. It happens at a subconscious level and does not make any attention demands on the system.

At Level 2, feedback does operate but the loop is a short one. As you will know from your work in exercise physiology, the muscle spindles have sensory receptors which can act as error detectors. If a muscle contraction during a movement is not what was prescribed by the motor programme (for example, if a skier hits a patch of ice when expecting soft snow), then a message is sent directly to the muscle to correct the error (with a copy to the brain to tell it about the ice!). This allows the correction to take place quickly (within 50 ms), because the important part of the mes-

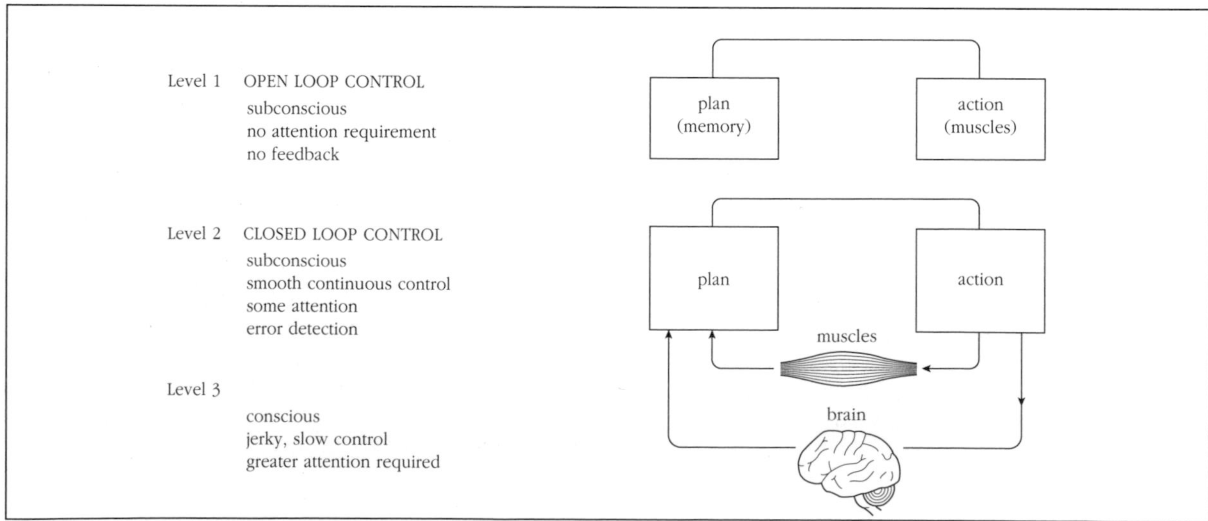

Figure 10.22 Levels of motor control.

sage did not have to be brought to the level of consciousness. You can experience this kind of control yourself if you set yourself the task of balance-walking along a narrow beam. This is known as **closed loop control**. It is essentially subconscious, but because feedback is operating it demands some of the attention channel. Its function is to provide smooth continuous movement whilst allowing for error detection. Because it relies on comparing what is actually happening with the demands of the motor programme, it develops as expertise develops, when the programme is well established.

Level 3 is also an example of closed loop control in that it, too, relies on feedback. In this case visual and kinesthetic feedback is used and thus the control is conscious and voluntary. The performer checks on the outcome of the first part of the skill before moving on to the next and thus there may be delays between successive movements; the whole appears jerky and unco-ordinated. As we learned earlier, perceptual anticipation can speed things up, but even then a considerable amount of the attention channel is being used up, and the performer does not have much capacity left to focus on the environmental demands of the task. This type of control is characteristic of beginners and experts who suddenly experience a problem, for example a skater whose triple jump has gone wrong and who finds himself having to concentrate very hard on regaining balance and getting back into the routine.

We will be returning to a consideration of the application of these theories to the learning of skills in Chapter 12, and you might like to turn to Section 12.1 now.

Summary

1. Learning is the process by which discrete performances of skilled behaviour are refined. It represents a relatively permanent change of behaviour.
2. Human information processing models offer an operational definition of performance and learning in motor skills.
3. All such models identify receptor, translator and effector mechanisms and at least one feedback loop.
4. Sense organs allow the input of information into the central nervous system. They initiate the process of stimulus detection.
5. Selective attention is the means by which information overload in the system is prevented. Attention is determined by stimulus intensity, relevance and pertinence.
6. Memory serves as a 'workspace' for information processing and as a store for information and skills.
7. Motor skills are stored as motor programmes, organized hierarchically.
8. Decision making in response to stimuli takes time. This is because the system contains 'bottlenecks'; the channels between the perceptual, decision making and output processes have a limited capacity.
9. Three different methods of motor control allow problems associated with this time delay to be overcome to some extent by skilled performers, but it is a limiting factor in early learning and must be accounted for in teaching strategies.

REFERENCES

Arnot R. and Gaines C. *Sports Talent,* Part l, New York, Penguin, 1984.

Hennessy J. *Torvill and Dean,* London, David and Charles, 1984.

Martenuik R.G. *Information Processing in Motor Skills,* New York, Holt, Rinehart and Winston, 1976.

Singer R.N. *The Learning of Motor Skills,* London, Collier Macmillan, Chapters 2, 4, 5, 7 & 9, 1982.

Stallings L.M. *Motor Learning From Theory to Practice,* St. Louis, C.V. Mosby,Chapters 4 and 5, 1982.

FURTHER READING

Davis D. *et al. Physical Education: Theory and Practice,* Part 4, Melbourne, Macmillan, 1986.

Hawkey R. *Sport Science,* London, Hodder and Stoughton, Chapter 7, 1981. (A basic text, but a useful starting point.)

Rothstein A. *et al. Motor Learning: Basic Stuff Series 1,* Number 3, Reston, Va, AAHPERD, Chapters 1, 2, 6 & 8, 1981.

Schmidt, R.A. *Motor Learning and Performance: from Principles to Practice,* Human Kinetics, Chapters 2–5, 1991.

Sharp, B. *Acquiring Skill in Sport,* Sports Dynamics, Chapter 1, 1992.

Whiting H.T.A. *Acquiring Ball Skill,* London, Bell and Sons, 1969.

Chapter 11
Individual Differences

In Chapters 9 and 10 we considered the nature of skill and some theoretical models which define and explain what might be happening as we learn to become skilful. This chapter makes the important point that individuals differ in their physical and psychological make-up. This means that they will learn at different rates and vary in the activities in which they choose to become successful.

On completion of this chapter you will be able to:

a. appreciate that people grow and mature at different rates and within different genetic parameters;
b. understand that early childhood experiences affect the development of basic motor skills;
c. analyse the main features of several fundamental movement patterns in terms of immature and mature motor behaviour;
d. explain the extent to which psychomotor abilities contribute to rate of learning and to performance;
e. measure certain motor abilities.

11.1 Fundamental Movement Patterns

KEY WORDS AND CONCEPTS

agility	**development**	**psychomotor abilities**
autonomic nervous system	**dynamic flexibility**	**physical proficiency**
co-ordination	**perceptual ability**	**physique**

As we grow and develop, so our motor behaviour changes. **Growth** means a change in size. **Development** implies changes in the way in which the systems of the body work. People achieve their potential in physical activity by means of a combination of growth, development and experience. **Experience** is enhanced by the help and intervention of others; older siblings, friends, parents and teachers.

GROWTH

Growth potential is largely inherited from our parents. Environmental factors such as diet or disease can affect this potential but in modern, developed societies this effect is minimal. Physique is the combination of bone structure, muscle size and fat content. It results from growth but lifestyle also affects it. You will have a basic genetic blueprint for your physique but what you eat and the amount of exercise you take can affect this, as you have seen in earlier chapters.

Whereas growth and development follow general patterns, considerable individual variation occurs, particularly during the **'growth spurt'** at adolescence.

As the skeleton grows, so do the muscles, but muscle growth is also related to exercise and hormone levels in the body.

Investigation 11.1 : To analyse growth during pre-adult years

Method: Study the graphs shown in Figure 11.1.

Observations: Which characteristic of the graphs illustrates the adolescent growth spurt? According to these graphs, when does this spurt start and finish in males and females?

Discussion: How do growth and physique influence learning in physical education?

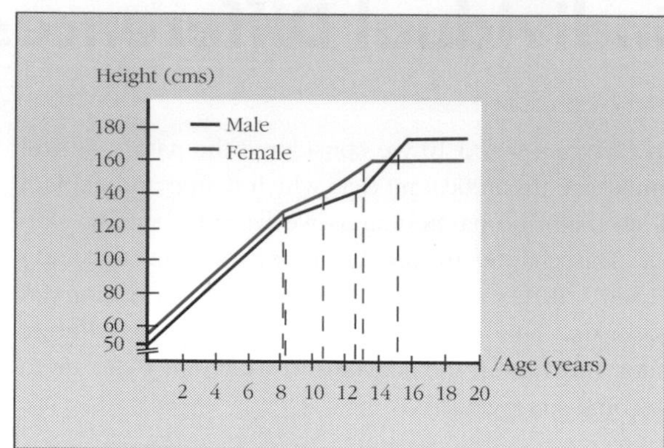

Figure 11.1 Increase in height for males and females (Adapted from Malina, 1975, p. 19.)

In general, increased growth improves physical performance, hence youngsters who start their growth spurt early often appear more advanced in skill than their contemporaries. Two factors may work against this, however: first, perceptual and sensory development may lag behind growth, making co-ordination less effective; and secondly, changes in length of limbs often affect motor mechanics. Thus skills which were well developed in the pre-adolescent child may need to be partly relearned by the youth because of the difference in body shape.

Our physique will to some extent determine those skills which we find easy to learn and those which we find more difficult. For example, if you have a high percentage of lean body tissue and a corresponding low percentage of fat, you will find floating in water and hence learning to swim quite difficult at first. This is not to say you are incapable of becoming a good swimmer, just that in comparison with your 'chubbier' friends the early stages of skill learning may be more difficult. The danger is that you tell yourself 'I won't ever be any good at swimming'.

FUNDAMENTAL MOVEMENT PATTERNS

As we learned in Chapter 10, physical education activities are composed of complex skills (executive programmes) which are underpinned by basic/fundamental movements (subroutines) (Figure 11.2). These fundamental movement patterns can be seen to fall into three categories and are underpinned by a range of perceptual abilities (Figure 11.3).

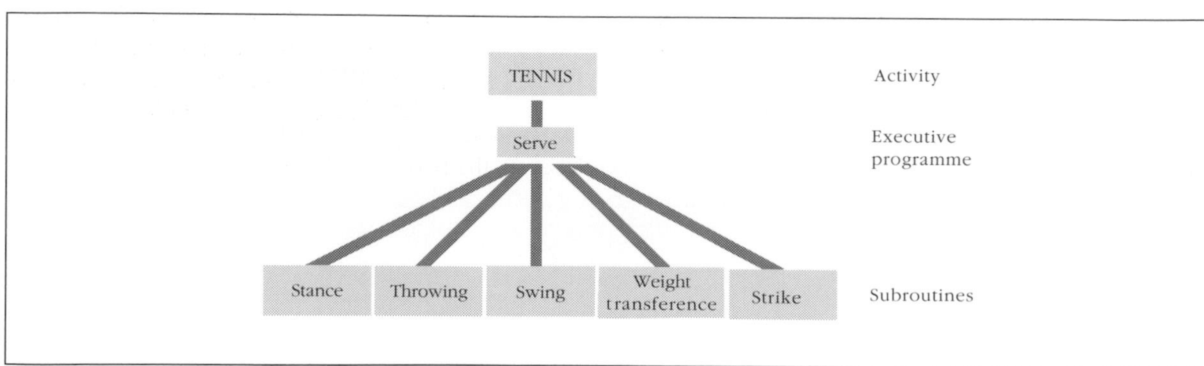

Figure 11.2 Executive programmes and subroutines.

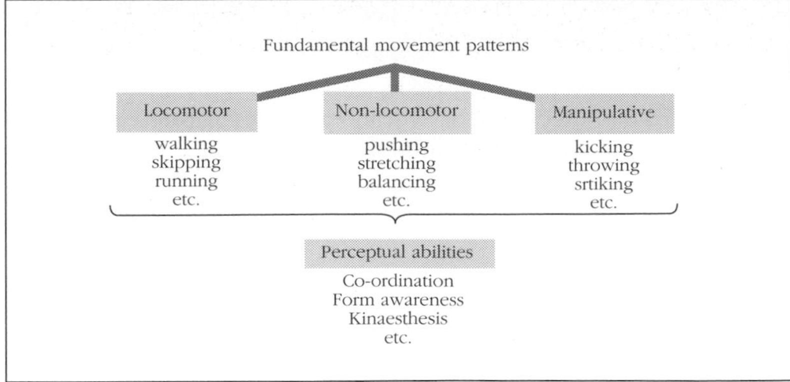

Figure 11.3 Fundamental movement patterns.

Investigation 11.2 : To analyse a skill in terms of its fundamental movement patterns

Method: Video a performance of a motor skill. Choose an unusual skill if possible.

Observations: Use Figure 11.3 to analyse the skill in terms of the fundamental movement patterns.

Development of these patterns is a complex mixture of growth, development and experience. Maturational processes will ensure that they develop to a certain extent in all children, but varied movement experiences, together with sound instruction, will ensure maximum development.

In normal circumstances, simple non-locomotor movements develop in the first few months of life, some even before birth; basic locomotor movements such as crawling and walking may be mastered by the age of two, but more complex activities such as skipping or hopping take longer. Manipulation of stationary objects with the hands is possible very early, but manipulatory skills involving other body parts or of moving objects need advanced perceptual abilities which may not be evident until late childhood. Thus there is little point in trying to teach young children particular skills before the basic abilities are laid down. However, broad and varied movement opportunities will encourage development. If such opportunities are not available, development will not occur at the same rate.

You can now see that the combination of genetic differences and variation in opportunity and experience means that children come to physical education lessons at very different levels of readiness.

Investigation 11.3 : To study differences in skill level in pre-adolescent children

Method: Ask your teacher to arrange a visit to a primary school which has an infant and a junior department. Work with your teacher and the class teachers in the school to plan a PE lesson for each of three classes, one in the infant department, a first year junior class and a top junior class. The class teacher should take the lesson but you should ask her/him to include a range of fundamental skills—running, jumping, balancing, skipping, striking, throwing, etc. You will be able to help with the lesson, perhaps by working with a small group of children, with the class teacher directing the activities. Two of you should act as director and cameraman to video particular children.

Results: Back at school/college compare each activity across the three age groups. Note differences in physique, growth, skill level.

Video yourselves doing the same activities.

Discussion: How do the movement patterns change as the performer gets older? To answer this question, analyse the lower level subroutines, e.g. limb, trunk and head movements, hand and foot positioning, etc.; consider rhythm and timing.

Some excellent checklists for this analysis, together with action photographs, can be found in Haywood (1988).

11.2 Psychomotor Abilities

KEY WORDS AND CONCEPTS

dynamic precision	**static strength**	**speed**
dynamic strength	**extent flexibility**	**stamina**
explosive strength	**trunk strength**	**static precision**

Maturation, the result of growth and development, will vary with individuals and will cause differences in the rate at which individuals learn. A second factor which leads to individual differences in rate of learning is motor ability; this may also set limits on the level of performance in any one skill which an individual is capable of achieving. For example, if you have not inherited enough fast-twitch muscle you will never make a top class sprinter, no matter how hard you train.

In Chapter 9 we identified motor abilities as being innate and stable (though some writers disagree with this) and as underpinning skilled behaviour. Here we are concerned with how abilities (and hence differences) affect performance.

It is important to remember that there is as yet no definitive list of psychomotor abilities. Different researchers categorize ability in different ways and even the terms used to describe the abilities vary slightly. Stallings (1982), for example, selects her list on the following grounds: that each ability has been identified in a number of studies; that they can be developed and assessed; and that they are relevant to physical educators (Figure 11.4).

Fleishman (1972) identified the characteristics of performance in a major research programme involving over 200 tasks and many thousands of subjects. In addition to a series of psychomotor abilities derived from limb co-ordination tasks, he suggested nine **'physical proficiency abilities'**, referred to later as **'gross motor abilities'** (Figure 11.5)

Guilford (1958) had earlier produced a similar list: **impulsion**, **speed**, **static precision**, **dynamic precision**, **co-ordination and flexibility**. There are some interesting differences between the two theories.

Figure 11.4 Stallings' (1982) motor abilities.

a. Muscular power and endurance

The contraction capacity of muscles

Short-term, high intensity, anaerobic

Long-term, low intensity, aerobic

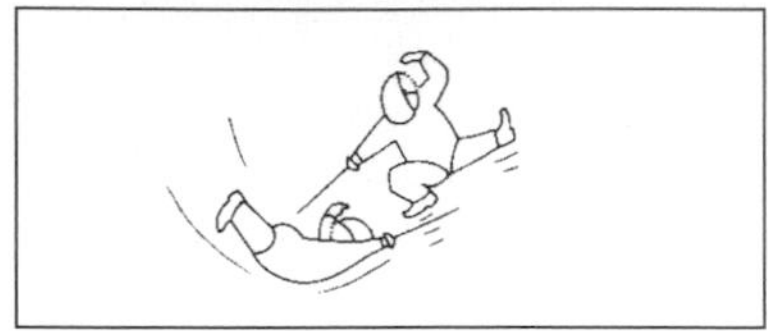

b. Flexibility

The range of movement in a joint or group of joints

Static —range of motion

Dynamic use of range of motion within a movement task

c. Balance

The maintenance of position and equilibrium

Static—fixed position

Dynamic —whilst in motion

Rotational—whilst turning

d. Co-ordination

The integration of all aspects of an action

Timing

Agility

e. Differential Relaxation

The selective adjustment of muscle tension

Investigation 11.4 : To consider the abilities required for particular skills

1. Discuss with a friend the similarities and differences between Fleishman's and Guilford's inventories of abilities. Check up on the meanings of the terms if you are not sure.

2. Look at the photographs of PE skills in Figure 11.6. List the abilities which you think are very important for good performance in each skill.

EXTENT FLEXIBILITY:	flexing or stretching the trunk and back muscles as far as possible in any direction.
DYNAMIC FLEXIBILITY:	making repeated rapid movements in which the ability of the muscles to recover is critical.
EXPLOSIVE STRENGTH:	expending a maximum amount of energy in one or a series of strong, sudden movements.
STATIC STRENGTH:	the maximum force which can be exerted for a brief period.
DYNAMIC STRENGTH:	exerting muscular force repeatedly or over a period of time.
TRUNK STRENGTH:	dynamic strength specific to the abdominal muscles.
GROSS BODY CO-ORDINATION:	co-ordinating the simultaneous movements of different body parts whilst involved in whole body action.
GROSS BODY EQUILIBRIUM:	maintaining balance whilst blindfolded.
STAMINA:	continuing to exert maximum effort over time.

Figure 11.5 Fleishman's gross motor abilities.

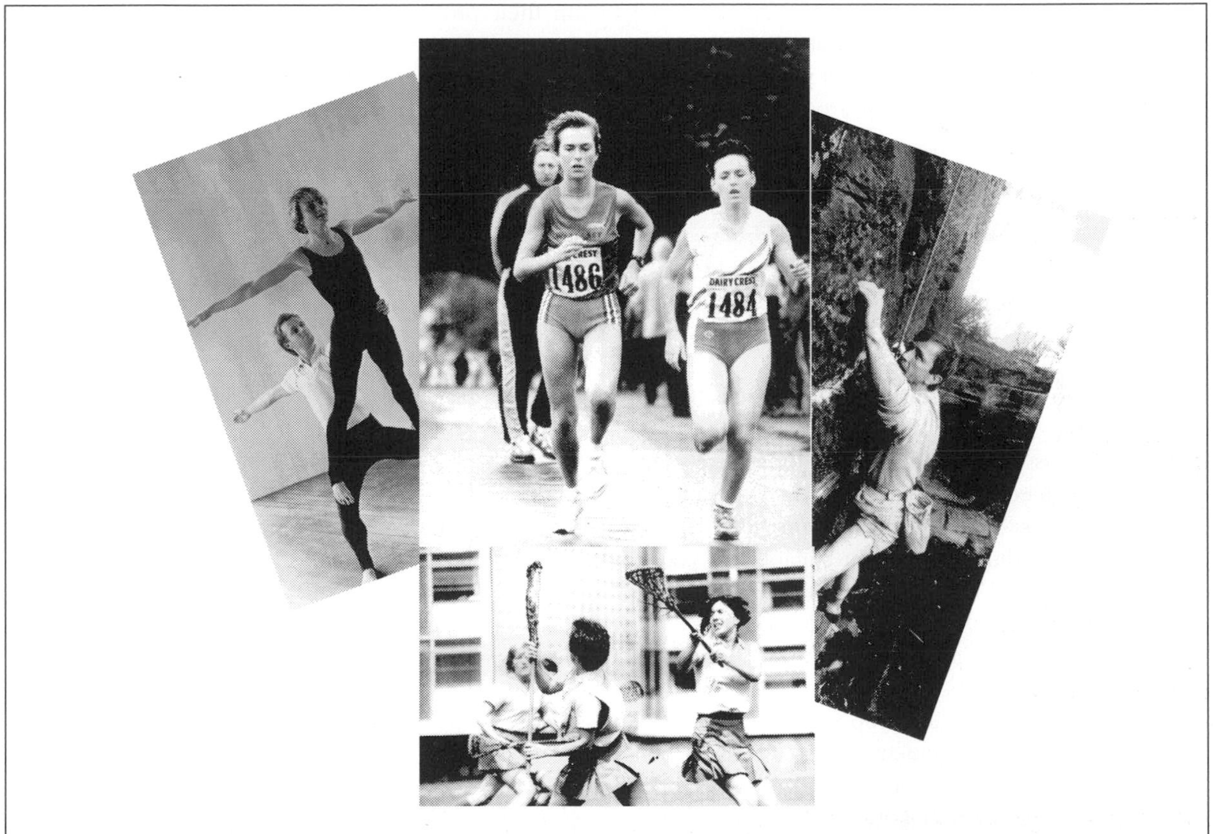

Figure 11.6 Physical education activities.

You have probably found that several abilities keep being mentioned over and over again. Strength, speed and co-ordination seem to be requirements for most motor skills. This has lead some writers to argue for the idea of a general motor ability. We hint at this when we say that someone is a 'natural' games player, meaning that they are good at most sports. But research tends to show that this is **not** the case and that **specific skills require specific abilities**. The co-ordination required to kick a ball is not the same as that required to execute a complex dance step. There are more than one hundred motor abilities; so when we talk about a 'natural' sportsperson we mean someone who has inherited and developed a large number of the abilities which underpin skill in sport, including the ability to learn motor skills efficiently. This implies that in addition to motor abilities, we could also argue that there are perceptual abilities that are important in sport, concerning the way in which we notice significant things that are happening around us and how quickly and effectively we make decisions about how to deal with them. These abilities, which Stallings (1982) identifies as visual, auditory, tactile and kinaesthetic, were discussed in Chapter 10.

The measurement of psychomotor abilities

If psychomotor abilities are fundamental to the learning and performance of skills then it is useful for us to be able to measure ability in sportspeople, either for research purposes, to add to our knowledge of how skill works, or to find out our own personal ability make-up. Arnot and Gaines (1984), in their book *Sports Talent*, show how a knowledge of the specific tasks of an activity such as windsurfing or tennis can lead to participants being able, with simple 'home-made' tests, to measure the strengths and weaknesses in their profile of relevant abilities. They can then choose activities they have the potential to be good at, or compensate for, say, lack of strength with good co-ordination.

Investigation 11.5

In the three tasks below, work in pairs. The scorer has a stop-watch.

Task One—to measure static balance (gross body equilibrium)

Method: This test measures the ability to balance using the inner ear mechanism only; that is, not using the considerable positional information provided by the eyes. It is quite difficult and not suitable for young children; if you find difficulty in scoring, perform the test with eyes open.

The subject stands as in Figure 11.7. It is best to wear 'trainers' and to be standing on a hard surface. Stand on your preferred leg; keep your bent knee well out to the side. The experimenter starts timing as soon as you close your eyes (don't cheat!). The watch is stopped when you open your eyes or move your hands or take your foot off your knee or move your standing foot from the spot. Wobbling is permissible as long as you don't do any of the above. Take the test three times (with rests in between) and record your best time.

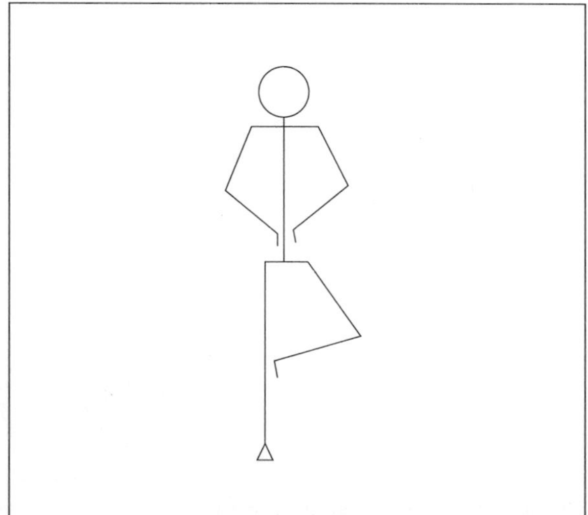

Figure 11.7 Stork balance.

Results: Use Table 55 to find your score in points. Record your points score.

Table 55 : Blind-Stork Balance

Men		Women	
Best time (secs)	Points	Best time (secs)	Points
60	20	35	20
55	18	30	17
50	16	25	14
45	14	20	11
40	12	15	8
35	10	10	4
30	8	5	2
25	6		
20	4		
15	3		
10	2		

(Arnot and Gaines, 1984, p. 175)

Task Two—to measure co-ordination (agility)

Method: Measure out a 66 cm-per-side hexagon on the floor as shown in Figure 11.8.

Cover the lines with masking or plastic tape so that the outside edge of the tape becomes the outside of the hexagon.

Stand in the middle of the hexagon, facing side A; face this way throughout the test. On the command 'go', when the watch is started, jump with both feet across line B and immediately back into the hexagon (remember to keep facing front). Then jump over side C and back and continue until you are back in the hexagon, having jumped over side A. This is one complete circuit; do three circuits altogether. The watch is stopped when you have completed the third circuit. Record your time. If you make a mistake, by treading on a line or jumping over the wrong line, start the trial again. Count the times for successful trials only. Have three 'goes' with rests in between and note your best time.

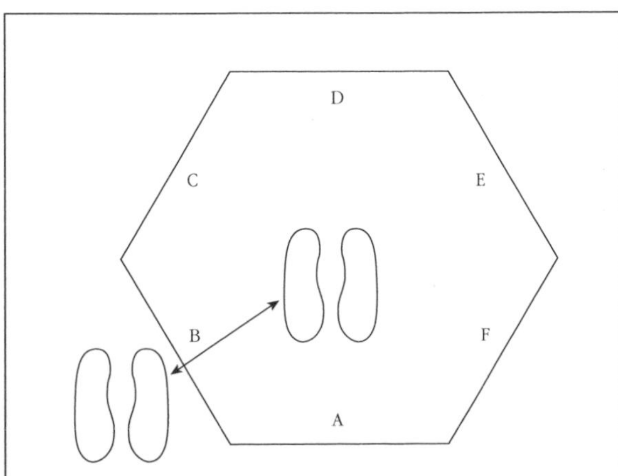

Figure 11.8 The hexagon

Results: Use Table 56 to record your points score.

Table 56 : Hexagonal Obstacle

Best time without sides (seconds)		Points
Men	Women	
9.0	9.0	10.0
10.1	10.6	9.0
11.2	12.2	8.0
12.3	13.8	7.0
13.4	15.4	6.0
14.5	17.0	5.0
15.6	18.6	4.0
16.7	20.2	3.0
17.8	21.8	2.0
18.9	23.4	1.0
20.0	25.0	0.0

(Arnot and Gaines, 1984, p. 145)

Task Three—to measure the endurance strength of the quadriceps

Method: The subject stands with his/her back against a smooth wall. Do the test barefoot or in trainers that will not slip, as your feet will tend to slide. When you are ready, gently slide your back down the wall until you are in the position shown in Figure 11.9. Your feet should be comfortably apart.

There should be ninety degree angles at the hip and knee.

Lift one foot about 5 cm off the ground. Your partner should start timing now. The watch is stopped when you put your foot back down on the floor. Stand up by putting your hands against the wall by your hips and pushing forwards slowly. Stand up gently. Record your time. Take a rest and then repeat the test with the other leg supporting. Again record your time.

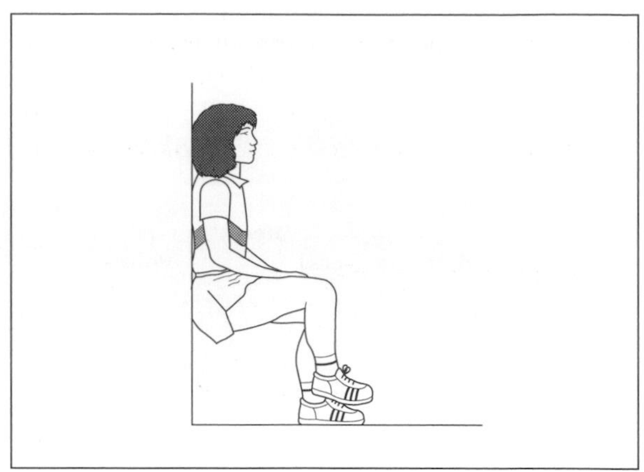

Figure 11.9 The wall squat

Results: Taking the lowest of the two times, record your points score using Table 57.

Table 57 : Wall Squat

Time (seconds) Men	Time (seconds) Women	Points
120	70	8.0
111	65	7.6
102	60	7.2
93	55	6.8
84	50	6.4
75	45	5.6
66	40	4.8
57	35	4.0
48	30	3.2
39	25	2.4
30	20	1.6
21	15	0.8

Discussion: Look at your profile of points for the three tests. Which is your highest points score? Is this what you would have expected?

As you read further you will find many other examples of psychomotor ability tests. Sometimes you will recognize that these measure more than one ability, for it is often difficult to isolate abilities in simple tests.

The above three tests measure the motor aspect of ability, i.e. the work that the muscles are doing. In your further reading you will find tests that measure the perceptual aspects of ability.

Summary

1. Individuals differ in both their physical and their psychological make-up. This means that they will learn at different rates and vary in the activities in which they can find success. People achieve their potential in physical activity by means of a combination of growth, development and experience. Underpinning all physical skills are fundamental movement patterns of, for example, running, striking and throwing, and the development of these is affected both by maturation and by the experience a child has of them.

2. The learning and performance of skills is also affected by the stage of development of motor abilities. It is possible to measure the extent to which any ability has developed at a given moment; however, we must remember that it is not always easy to isolate motor abilities and tests often measure several at once.

REFERENCES

Arnot R. and Gaines C. *Sports Talent,* Harmondsworth, Penguin, 1984.

Bunker L.K. *et al. Sport Psychology,* Ithaca, N.Y., Mouvement Publications, Section II, 1985.

Carron, A.V. *Social Psychology of Sport,* Ithaca, N.Y., Mouvement Publications, Chapter 2, 1980.

Cattell R.B. *The Scientific Analysis of Behaviour,* Harmondsworth, Penguin, 1965.

Eysenck H.J. *The Biological Basis of Behaviour,* Springfield, Ill., Charles C. Thomas, 1967.

Fleishman E.A. The structure and measurement of psychomotor abilities. In: Singer R.N. (ed.) *The Psychomotor Domain: Movement Behaviour,* Philadelphia, Lea & Febiger, 1972.

Guilford J.P. A system of psychomotor abilities, *American Journal of Applied Psychology,* 71, 164–174, 1958,

Haywood K.M. *Laboratory Activities for Lifespan Motor Development,* Human Kinetics, Champaign, Ill., 1988.

Stallings L.M. *Motor Learning: From Theory to Practice,* Part 4, St. Louis, Mosby, 1982.

FURTHER READING

Davis D. *et al. Physical Education: Theory and Practice,* Part 4, Melbourne, Macmillan, 1986.

Schmidt R.A. *Motor Learning and Performance: From Principles to Practice,* Champaign, Ill., Human Kinetics, Chapter 6, 1991.

Sharp B. *Acquiring Skill in Sport,* Eastbourne, Sports Dynamics, Chapter 6, 1992.

Chapter 12
Principles of Learning and Teaching

In this chapter you will:

a. become familiar with some theories about what learning is and how we learn;
b. use information processing models to analyse some aspects of motor learning;
c. examine the processes of transfer of learning and mental rehearsal;
d. realize the importance of feedback to learning;
e. examine the way in which styles of teaching, modes of presentation, forms of guidance and types of practice can affect learning.

In Chapter 9 we defined learning in general terms and contrasted it with performance. Let us look again at these definitions.

> *Learning may then be considered to be a more or less permanent change in performance associated with experiences but excluding changes which occur through maturation and degeneration, or through alterations in the receptor or effector organs.*
>
> (Knapp, 1973)

> *Performance may be thought of as a temporary occurence . . . fluctuating from time to time because of many potentially operating variables. We usually use performance to represent the amount of learning that has occurred, for the process of learning must be inferred on the basis of observations of change in performance.*
>
> (Singer, 1975)

Discussion
Work in groups of two or three. Discuss the meaning of the two definitions above to make sure you understand them. In particular, explain:

'permanent change of performance'
'associated with experiences'
'maturation and degeneration'
'alterations in receptor or effector organs'
'potentially operating variables'
'inferred on the basis of observations of change in performance'.

12.1 Learning

KEY WORDS AND CONCEPTS

command style	**mechanical guidance**	**spaced practice**
distributed practice	**mental rehearsal**	**task complexity**
fixed practice	**reciprocal style**	**teaching style**
manual guidance	**simplification**	**transfer**

ASSOCIATION AND REINFORCEMENT

In Chapter 9 we illustrated the relationship between learning and performance by drawing a learning curve; that is, we allowed practice of a skill to occur and tested performance at time intervals, charting changes in performance to indicate whether or not learning had occurred.

In Chapter 10 we considered learning to be the commitment of skills and knowledge to memory. We saw that this process requires that we view what is to be learned as relevant, that we are attentive to what we are doing and that we are prepared to practise so that the information or movement becomes 'grooved' in memory. In other words we must have the will, or the need, to learn; effective learning cannot take place without this. This will/need to learn can be called **motivation**. Motivation has been defined as 'the internal mechanisms and external stimuli which arouse and direct behaviour' (Sage, 1977, p. 457).

DRIVE REDUCTION THEORY

There are many theories of motivation. One, attributed to Hull (1952), views learning as the development of 'habits', i.e. in this case the most appropriate behavioural responses to movement problems which need to be solved. This is illustrated in Figure 12.1. This is a very complex theory in its totality, but stated simply and applied to physical activity it suggests that as a movement problem arises, for example in a dance choreography, or the performance of a particular skill in a game, this generates a need for competence, a need to solve that problem. This need in turn develops a drive and an incentive to learn to solve the problem and also a habit (the way of performing the skill). So we start to practise. At first the performance will not be effective, but as success comes it is perceived as a **reward** and thus acts as **reinforcement**. As a result a memory bond is forged between the **stimulus** (the problem) and the **response** (the effective performance). The two become **associated** in the memory and a 'habit' (a successful performance) is developed. As our performance gets better, so the habit is strengthened and the drive to go on learning reduced. At this point the teacher or coach will extend the problem to maintain interest and motivation.

CONDITIONING

Notice the connection here between the **stimulus** (the physical problem) and the **response** (the performance). Theories of learning which focus on this are known as 'stimulus–response' or S–R theories. There are many of these (sometimes called **'connectionist'**

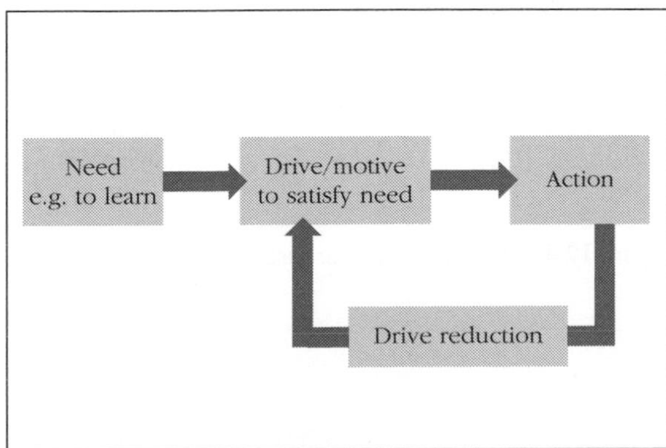

Figure 12.1 Drive reduction theory.

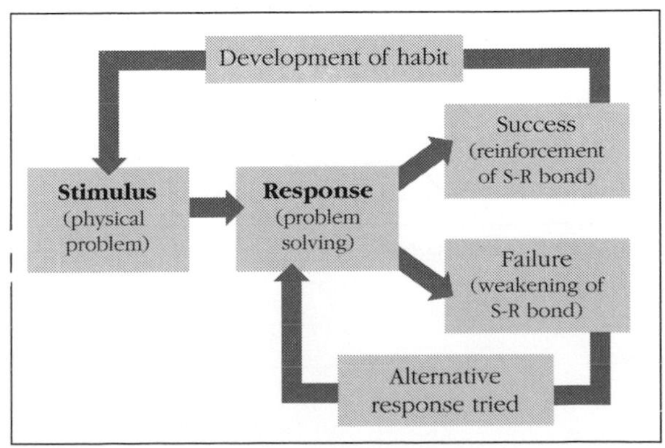

Figure 12.2 The stimulus–response bond.

theories) and you will find reference to them in Stallings (1982) and Neate (undated), and in other general psychology text books. Thorndike (1932) established the idea that when a response to a stimulus is associated with a feeling of satisfaction ('great, I won that point'), then the likelihood of the response occurring again when the same stimulus is presented is increased. If the response is not effective, the S–R bond is not confirmed (it may even be weakened) and the individual will try another approach.

This process has become known as 'trial and error' learning. It depends on the learner being able to recognize success and to feel satisfaction with the response or alternatively to admit that a response is not appropriate and try another. The problem for skill learning of this approach is that it can allow learners to establish 'bad habits', i.e. responses that are immediately successful at beginner stage but will not allow further development.

Thorndike's theories emphasized the importance of positive reinforcement in strengthening the bond between stimulus and response. Skinner (1974) stressed the relationship between an action and its results. He suggests that much behaviour is **'operant'** in that it does not necessarily happen in response to a specific stimulus, or that the relationship between a stimulus and a response may not be obvious to a learner. For example, in learning a game a young player may make exactly the right move, say, to cover a gap in defence, but not know either what he did or why it was sensible. Skinner suggests that a teacher may use a process of **'operant conditioning'** by praising, or in other ways rewarding, the desired response as soon as he/she sees it. In the early stages of learning the right action may not be there for the teacher to reinforce, so the teacher 'shapes' the action by encouraging successive approximations to it. Skinner emphasizes the importance of immediate reinforcement for effective learning. In recognizing that for teachers of normal sized classes this is not always possible, he developed the idea of programmed learning using 'teaching machines' or computers. In Section 12.2 we shall consider other ways for the teacher to organize immediate reinforcement for pupils' learning.

All S–R theorists stress the importance for effective learning of the close temporal relationship between the stimulus and/or the response and the reward which acts as reinforcement. Remember that the 'reward' may be praise, or the satisfaction gained from positive **knowledge of results** or **knowledge of performance**. We can learn from negative feedback (see Figure 12.3) but this information tells us only what **not** to do; it does not act to strengthen the S–R bond.

MOTOR LEARNING AND FEEDBACK

The awareness of the difference between knowledge of performance and knowledge of results leads us to a more detailed consideration of **feedback** and its role in the learning process. You should re-read Section 10.4 to remind yourself of the role of feedback in information processing.

Feedback could be considered to be the single most important factor in learning. It is the information which occurs after or during an activity and allows the

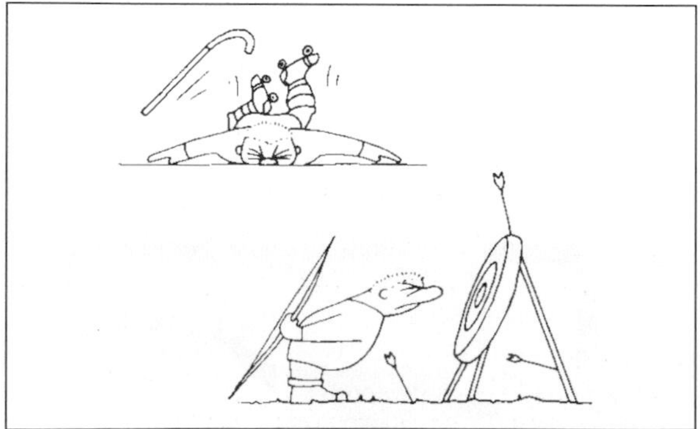

Figure 12.3 Knowledge of performance and ... knowledge of results.

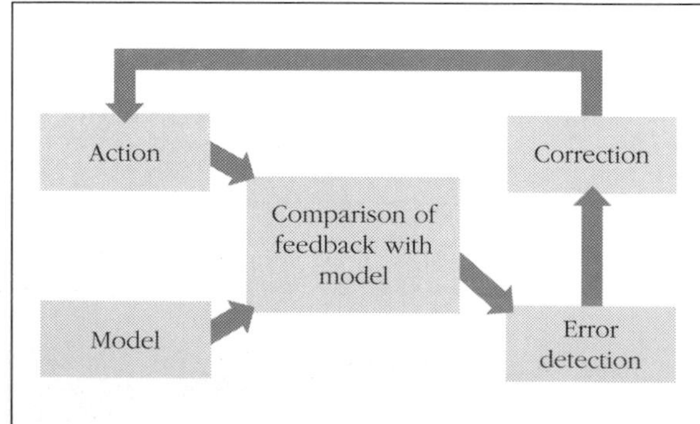

Figure 12.4 Feedback as error detection.

performer to determine how successful he/she has been. The learner may or may not be consciously focusing on the available feedback, or may be helped to be aware of it by a teacher or a coach; but in any case feedback affects learning. It does this in three distinct ways:

1. **motivation**—encouragement from friends or teacher acts as a form of reward and as an incentive to continue;
2. **reinforcement of learning**—we saw in Figure 12.2 how perception of success strengthens the S–R bond and enhances learning;
3. **change in performance**—feedback about performance allows the learner to compare his/her attempts with an established 'model' of the required skill and thus to detect and correct any errors.

If feedback is to be of value, there must be a '**model**', that is a reference, or a picture of the action, of which the learner is aware. Often these models are provided by a demonstration or by a specific description of the action. Such models are particularly important in closed skills and it is important that models are appropriate for the level of experience of the learner. The learner uses the model to compare the attempt that has just been made with what the action should be like. This is where feedback comes in. In the early stages of learning, visual and verbal feedback from a teacher or coach is useful since the learner does not have a clear mental image of the skill; as experience is gained, experts can use kinesthetic information to decide for themselves whether a movement 'feels right' or not.

Information processing theory views feedback as an **error detection** mechanism. One of the problems that a teacher has in applying this idea is that S–R theory suggests that positive feedback is more effective in enhancing learning than negative feedback (or error detection). However, it is also clear that people learn by their mistakes and that errors should not be ignored. A good coach or teacher will ensure that information about errors is balanced (and preferably preceded by information about what was correct).

There are many different forms of feedback and further reading will show you in more detail how these can be used. You should bear in mind that:

- different forms of feedback seem to be appropriate at different stages of learning;
- individuals differ in the form of feedback they prefer and respond to best;
- one form of feedback may be more appropriate for a particular sport or activity than another.

Figure 12.5 shows some of the categories of feedback that you may come across in your reading.

What does the research tell us about how these various forms of feedback may be used? The data to answer this question have usually been obtained from studies which aim to remove, control or distort feedback.

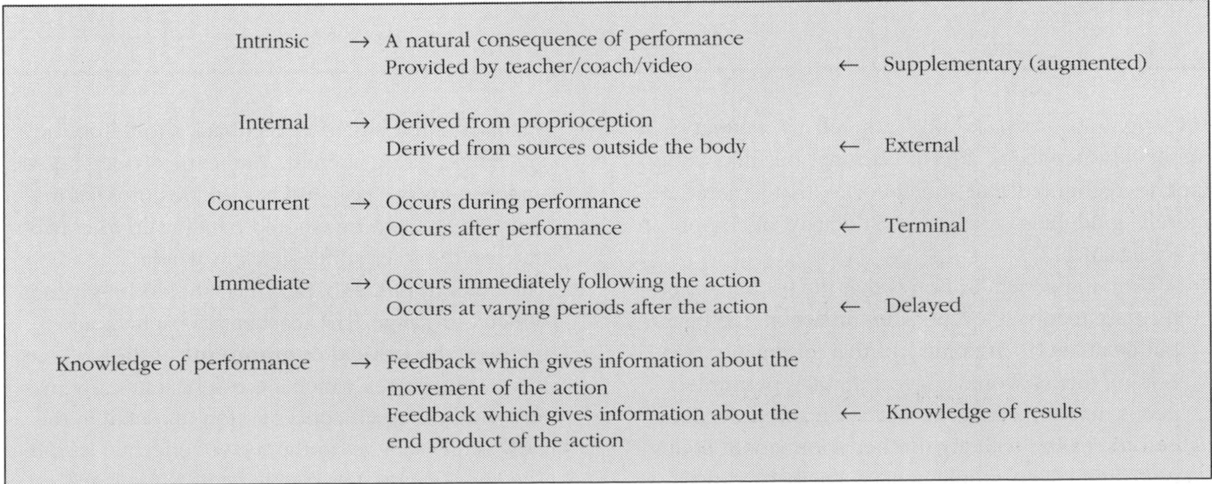

Intrinsic → A natural consequence of performance
Provided by teacher/coach/video ← Supplementary (augmented)
Internal → Derived from proprioception
Derived from sources outside the body ← External
Concurrent → Occurs during performance
Occurs after performance ← Terminal
Immediate → Occurs immediately following the action
Occurs at varying periods after the action ← Delayed
Knowledge of performance → Feedback which gives information about the movement of the action
Feedback which gives information about the end product of the action ← Knowledge of results

Figure 12.5 Categories of feedback.

Investigation 12.1 : To investigate the effects of knowledge of performance on learning

Method: Work in two groups of subjects with one person acting as the experimenter. Ideally, once the task has been decided upon, the subjects should not be aware of the details of the experiment. Devise a closed skill motor task which is unfamiliar to all members of both groups and which is likely to show some learning over a short period of time. Aiming at a target with the non-dominant hand might be an example, but you can probably think of a better one. Organize about ten blocks of practice which can be scored. At the end of this phase, give a five minute break and then about five 'performance' blocks. Group A is given both knowledge of results and knowledge of performance after each of the first ten blocks of practice; Group B is given knowledge of results and social reinforcement (encouragement without reference to either KP or KR) (Singer, 1982, p. 167).

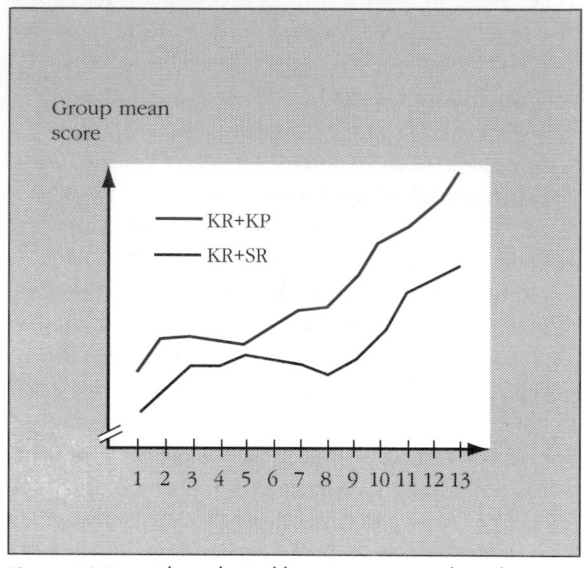

Figure 12.6 A hypothetical learning curve to show the effects of different forms of feedback on learning (Adapted from Wallace and Hagler, 1979.)

Results: Record your data for each member of the group and obtain a mean score for each group, for each block of practice. If your data are appropriate, plot a learning curve as in Figure 12.6.

Discussion: What do your results, or the hypothetical results in Figure 12.6, suggest about the importance of knowledge of performance to learning? How would you adapt the methodology to investigate other forms of feedback?

Investigations such as 12.1 can tell us a great deal about how feedback affects learning, but it is important to recognize that the theories that emerge are merely guidelines for action and may not apply in every instance.

1. A common generalization is that the sooner supplementary feedback occurs after an action, the better; but Gentile (1972) points out that information processing theory would suggest that the performer needs time to process intrinsic/concurrent feedback before dealing with any further information. In any case, immediate supplementary feedback is not always practical.
2. Supplementary feedback should not delay the next attempt at the skill too long, otherwise forgetting will occur.
3. Similarly, supplementary feedback should not be given after every attempt. The learner, once he/she understands the task and has an idea of what it feels like to perform, should be allowed to concentrate on the internal feedback available.
4. The amount of feedback which should be given is difficult to gauge. The teacher or coach should focus on the **critical components** of the skill, i.e. those subroutines which are essential to early mastery. But too much concentration on detail in the early stages can get in the way of effective learning.
5. The specificity of the supplementary feedback required depends on the age and stage of the learner and his/her capacity to process information.

MOTOR LEARNING AND MOTOR CONTROL

Feedback affects learning at every stage. Fitts and Posner (1967) and Adams (1971) describe three phases of learning (Figure 12.7). Progression through the phases/stages will be determined by practice, effectiveness of information processing, and the nature and extent of the guidance and feedback available. These are discussed in more detail later in this section.

Feedback is an important aspect of the concept of **motor control** which was introduced in Section 10.4. Re-read about **open- and closed-loop control** to remind yourself. From your increased knowledge of feedback you will now understand how the two theories give rise to different teaching/coaching philosophies. For example, if a skill is thought to be under closed-loop control, as in Figure 12.8, then the learner will be encouraged to focus on how the movement feels and, as he becomes more competent (the associative phase), will be operating an error detection system. For example, a gymnast on a balance beam will sense the beginning of 'over-balance' and will correct with an adjusting movement. At the autonomous phase of learning, this may happen subconsciously. Coaching will therefore emphasize the kinesthetic sense. Closed-loop theories are known as **peripheral theories**.

Central (open-loop) theories of motor control suggest that feedback is not essential to the control of the movement. This is achieved by the use of pre-learned motor programmes (see Section 10.4). Coaches/teachers using this theory would decide that a skill is best learned by breaking it down into parts, into its subroutines, and practising these until they are mastered and can be stored as motor programmes for use in the executive programme, i.e. the whole movement pattern.

Some sports psychologists are dissatisfied with this polarized view of motor control and believe that performance involves both open- and closed-loop processes. Schmidt (1980) suggests that both are used at different points in an action. Consider a serve in tennis. Which elements do you think are under closed-loop control and which are under open-loop control? Evidence from experiments involving continuous tracking movements (e.g. using a joy-stick to play a computer game) indicates that short bursts of activity may be programmed centrally and the outcome checked (peripherally) for error and correction before the next burst of activity is initiated (Schmidt, 1980, p. 127).

A second theoretical alternative to the 'open-loop versus closed-loop' perspective is **schema theory**. This claims that what is stored in memory is not a fixed pattern of movement (programme) but a set of relationships determining the performance of the skill. This 'set of relationships' could be thought of as a programme of sorts, but a generalized one, which can be run differently according to the demands of the situa-

Fitts and Posner (1967)		Adams (1971)
Cognitive (early) phase	Understanding of the nature of activity. Analysis of techniques. Establishment of 'models'.	
Associative (intermediate) phase	Focus on movement. Comparison of action with model. Error detection and correction. Movement is variable and inconsistent.	Verbal-motor phase
Autonomous (final) phase	Action has become automatic. Attention can be given to environmental aspects of game/activity. Strategy can be focussed on.	Motor stage

Figure 12.7 Phases of motor learning.

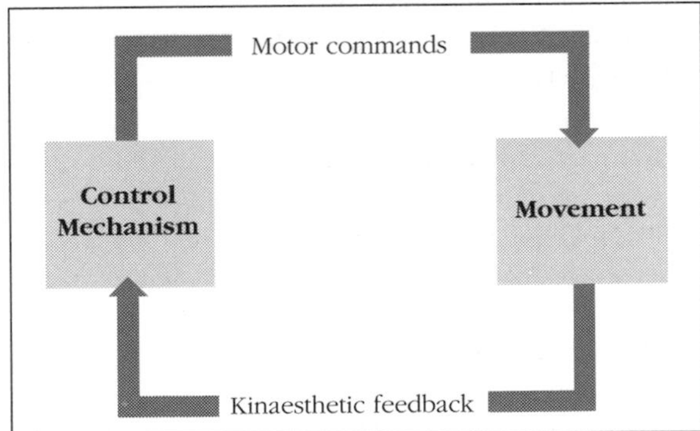

Figure 12.8 Closed-loop control.

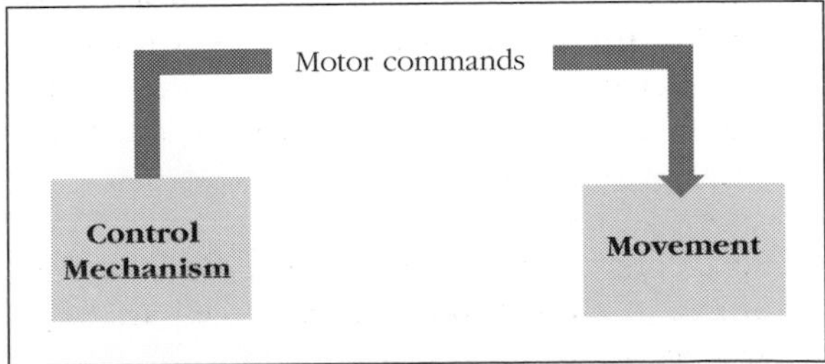

Figure 12.9 Open-loop control.

tion. So a player will practise and develop a schema for kicking or throwing a ball, which has established a relationship between the distance the ball is to be sent and such variables as muscular force, limb speed, angle/direction of release, etc. This schema will be adapted to his/her perception of the specific requirements of the task. Schema can apply at any part of the skill hierarchy (see Figure 11.2). Thus you will have developed a schema for throwing a ball as a youngster; this will have been refined for throwing, for example, a basketball; it can be generalized to help you learn a new throwing action, for example the javelin. Schema theory is essentially, though not exclusively, an open-loop theory and in it learning is seen as the generation of increasingly more comprehensive general programmes. You should be beginning to see that schema theory fits in with several ideas we have discussed earlier: fundamental motor patterns (Section 11.1) and open skills (p. 234) in particular.

Schmidt (1977) develops some important implications of his schema theory for the learning of motor skills:

- People learn from errors. Where appropriate, errors could even be included in practice to up-date and strengthen the schema. For example, how far can you 'lean' on your paddle before capsizing your kayak? There's only one way to find out!
- Terminal feedback is important in learning in order to strengthen the schema in memory.
- Practice must be varied. In open skills in particular, do not spend too long practising a specific move or stroke over the same distance and in the same direction.

Motor control is an aspect of skill acquisition which is still developing and it is important to view the various theories as hypotheses still to be adequately tested. Whereas they can be usefully applied to the practical problems of learning skill, equally we need to be aware of their limitations.

TRANSFER OF LEARNING

Schema theory seems to imply that certain aspects of a skill learned in one situation can determine performance in another similar situation. Singer (1982, p. 168) refers to this as 'relating the now with the then' and suggests that we rarely learn a totally new skill after our early years. This is named **'transfer'** in the skill acquisition literature.

Transfer is defined as the effect of the learning and performance of one skill on the learning and performance of another. It is important to note that not all transfer enhances learning:

- **Positive transfer** occurs when learning in one task is promoted by previous learning in another; for example, you may initially be better able to throw a ball with a lacrosse stick if you have a good basic throwing action with your hand.
- **No transfer** at all may occur, even between skills which appear on the surface to be similar.
- **Negative transfer** occurs when the learning of a new task is interfered with by knowledge of a similar activity; for example, the flexible use of the wrist in a squash or badminton shot may interfere with learning the firm wrist needed for a tennis drive, or vice versa.

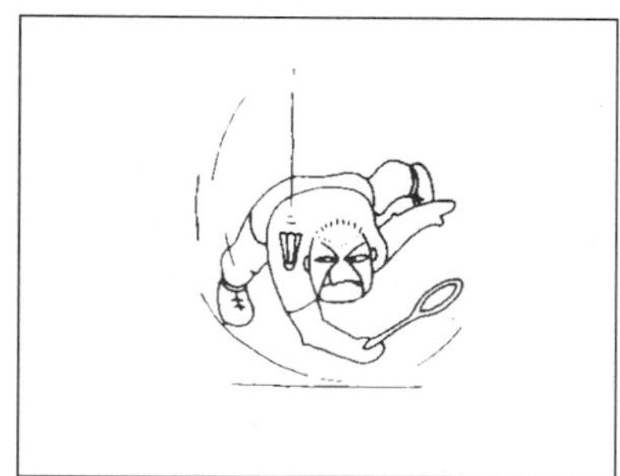

Figure 12.10 Negative transfer.

Teachers and coaches attempt to use positive transfer whenever possible.

Stallings (1982) identifies a variety of forms of transfer in addition to the general categories listed above.

1. **Skill-to-skill**	Between two skills. Evidence suggests little long-term positive transfer.
2. **Practice-to-performance**	Positive transfer likely only to occur if environmental conditions are similar in both situations. Practices should simulate the stimuli and cues which occur in performance.
3. **Abilities-to-skill**	Abilities do not transfer totally to the performance of skills which they underpin, but contribute significantly.
4. **Limb-to-limb (bi-lateral)**	Positive transfer of learning and training occurs between limbs (hand–hand; leg–leg). Effect most obvious in transfer from preferred to non-preferred limb.
5. **Principles-to-skill**	Under particular learning conditions (Stallings, 1982, p. 213) knowledge of a skill principle, e.g. body shape/speed of rotation, will enhance the learning and performance of the skill.
6. **Stage-to-stage**	Motor skill development depends on building each new skill upon those learned previously. See Sections 10.4 and 11.1 on fundamental motor patterns and hierarchy of motor control.

Figure 12.11 Categories of transfer (Adapted from Stallings, 1982.)

Investigation 12.2 (a) : To investigate positive transfer effects in skill learning

Method: Select one form of transfer from categories 1–5 in Figure 12.11. Select two groups of subjects, Group 1 and Group 2, matched for motor learning ability as far as possible.

Devise two novel tasks (A and B) by which you might expect learning in Task A to transfer positively to learning in Task B. Make your tasks relevant to the category of transfer you have chosen. Ensure that the tasks are 'learnable' in the time you have available, but they should present some degree of difficulty.

Decide on the criteria you will use to determine that learning has taken place; for example, you might decide that seven accurate shots out of ten in a novel aiming task constitutes learning.

Group 1 learns Task A and then Task B.
Group 2 learns only Task B.

Results: Determine which group learned Task B more quickly.

Discussion: Assuming all other variables have been controlled (a dangerous assumption under the circumstances of a class experiment), what do your results tell you about the possibility of transfer between Task A and Task B for Group 1?

How might you improve the experiment so that you could be more confident of your results?

Transfer is a complex concept and is not easy to apply in the learning/teaching situation. What can we learn from the research? Let us consider this question by taking the example of a good gymnast who goes to college and follows a beginners' dance course as part of his or her A level or undergraduate studies. To what extent will successful experience in gymnastics aid learning in dance?

- The student's attitude to the new activity will contribute considerably to early learning. Our gymnast will be confident about his/her body image in a movement task and will enjoy showing a competent individual performance. In this respect there is likely to be positive transfer. On the other hand, a gymnast is used to having performance choreographed by a coach or trainer and may approach the creative element of dance with trepidation. The rule- and technique-governed nature of competitive gymnastics may even cause negative transfer initially.

- In skill transfer terms, evidence suggests that the actions he/she has learned as a gymnast will not transfer readily to dance unless the choreography is particularly gymnastic in style. In this respect there will be no obvious transfer effects.
- In terms of ability–skill transfer, there is much more likely to be some positive effect. Balance, co-ordination, flexibility and many other abilities developed in gymnastics can be used very effectively in dance. The rhythmic ability so necessary for dance may or may not be present.
- Practice-to-performance transfer will depend on how well the gymnast has learned to use later practice sessions as rehearsal for the 'real thing'. If this strategy is also used in preparation for dance performances, then transfer could occur.
- Repetition and variation are two important dance choreography principles. One way of both repeating and varying the movement is to use both sides of the body in a dance phrase. If the gymnast has developed this skill, then positive transfer to dance will occur, but gymnasts tend to be 'one-sided', for example, by always using the same foot for take-off, and this may be a difficulty in dance work.
- Movement principles are universal, though they are analysed and expressed differently. The gymnast's knowledge of, for example, biomechanics, will transfer directly to the production of good technique in dance. Research does, however, show that we must have reservations about the extent to which knowledge of principles of action aids in the performance of that action.

For teachers and coaches to make transfer work positively they must make a careful analysis of the relevant tasks, and the teaching environment, to ensure that all the potential points of transfer are stressed. Positive transfer is most likely when:

1. the performer is well motivated and understands the principles of transfer;
2. the similarities between the tasks are stressed;
3. the learning conditions are similar;
4. the new task is easier than the first.

Investigation 12.2 (b) : To investigate stages of learning and feedback

To summarize our work on learning, use this investigation to study the relationship between stage of learning and appropriate feedback.

Before you start, re-read Section 12.1 carefully, noting in particular Figures 12.4–12.7. Schmidt (1991, pp. 172–174) gives an excellent expansion of the 'stages of learning' model and also a detailed analysis of feedback (Chapter 10).

Method: Work in threes, with roles of 'learner', 'teacher' and 'observer'. Before the start of the investigation, each member of the trio selects a simple, novel psychomotor skill to teach; a short sequence of hopping and stepping would be appropriate, or a mirror-tracing task if such a task has not been used before. Exchange roles for each of the following learning episodes. If videoing the episodes is possible, this will aid your analysis and discussion.

(i) Teacher demonstrates the skill to the learner, who practises it. No feedback is given but the skill is demonstrated by the teacher at intervals. The observer attempts to identify when learning changes from 'cognitive' to 'associative' to 'autonomous' (see Figure 12.7). If videoing the learning is possible, this would allow review.

(ii) Teacher demonstrates the skill to the learner, who practises it. Teacher focusses on giving instructions appropriate to the phase of learning, i.e. demonstration and general verbal guidance in the cognitive stage; error detection and specific guidance in the associative stage and a focus on style and or speed in the autonomous stage. Observer checks the appropriateness of the instruction given.

(ii) Teacher demonstrates the skill to the learner, who practises it. Teacher has identified beforehand examples of supplementary feedback which gives (a) knowledge of results (KR) and (b) knowledge of performance (KP) and gives these during the learning episode. Observer notes these and attempts to identify which are intended as KR and which as KP.

Discussion:

- Were the skills essentially open or closed?
- How does instruction in the different stages differ between open and closed skills?
- What evidence did the observer use to identify the different stages of learning?
- How effective was the teacher in giving appropriate instructions?
- Do teacher and observer agree about the examples of KR and KP?
- How helpful did the learner find the instruction and the feedback in terms of amount, timing, specificity?

12.2 Teaching

KEY WORDS AND CONCEPTS

modification of display
variable practice
negative transfer
verbal guidance
positive transfer
visual guidance
problem solving
whole method
progressive part presentation
whole-part-whole method
pure part presentation
organization

So far in this chapter we have considered some elements of the learning process. This section focuses on how learning may be structured so that it is achieved efficiently. You should bear these points in mind when planning your own practice or training, or when helping others with theirs.

STYLES OF TEACHING

Most of our learning is achieved by being taught in one way or another, although 'trial and error' learning or 'learning by experience' also occurs. Teaching others is a process we are all involved in, even though we may not consider ourselves to be teachers. Teaching is about giving experiences or advice which will aid learning. There are many different ways to teach. These are known as styles and have been analysed and classified in much the same way that we have previously classified skill, that is by observing action, noting the characteristics of that action and devising a theoretical framework to fit the observations.

Mosston and Ashworth (1986) have produced a classification (based on observations of physical education but applicable to all teaching) which they have labelled the 'Spectrum of Teaching Styles'. They suggest that teaching and learning are essentially about making decisions: what to teach/learn; when to teach/learn; how to present/acquire the ideas/skills, etc. Their model suggests that at one end of the spectrum the teacher makes all these decisions, and at the other end the learner makes them all. In between are a range of styles in which the teacher and learner are both involved in decision making. The styles are distinct and Mosston gives them letter labels and names (for example, Style A = Command Style).

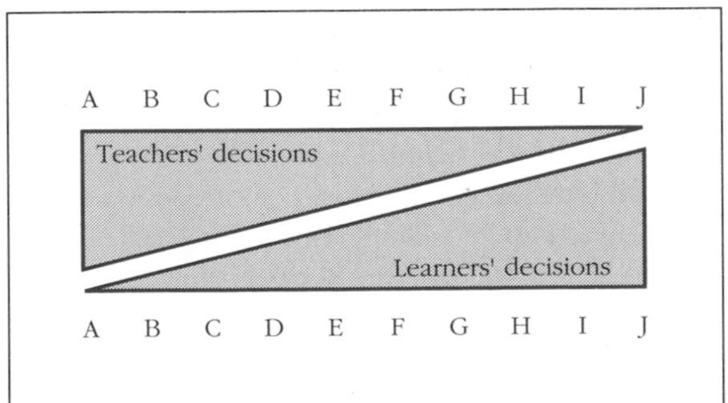

Figure 12.12 The Spectrum of Teaching Styles.

Investigation 12.3 : To investigate decision making in teaching and learning

Method: Work in pairs. One is the teacher and one the learner. The teacher devises a simple task to teach the learner. It may be something the learner can already do and wishes to improve. It can be classroom or sports hall based, but it should have a motor component. Spend some time teaching and practising the task. This period of time is known as an 'episode'.

Discussion: When the episode is over, discuss with each other and list all the decisions which were made by both the teacher and the learner:

a. before the episode
b. during the episode
c. when the episode was over.

Who made each decision?

What was the ratio of teacher decisions to learner decisions? Do you think the teacher was nearer to Style A or Style J?

The teacher in Investigation 12.3 was probably nearer to Style A. This style is one in which the teacher makes all the decisions. It is very difficult to teach for long in this style and it is not advisable to do so, because we usually want to hand some of the decisions to the learner, e.g. 'start when you're ready'. Style A is known as the **'command style'** and is used when a teacher wants tight control over what the learner is doing, or wants uniformity in a class. A lot of aerobics and keep fit teaching is done in Command Style.

Style C is an interesting style. Pupils work in pairs. One is the 'doer' and the other the observer'. In this style the teacher hands over all the contact with the learners (the 'doers') to fellow pupils (the 'observers'). The teacher makes sure, either by a work sheet or by very explicit instructions, that all the pupils understand the task and the criteria for successful completion of it. It is then up to the observer to help the doer; the teacher helps the observers with their teaching. This is known as **reciprocal** teaching; it is a useful style with large groups because it allows each learner a lot of immediate feedback. Look back to pp. 272–273 to remind yourself of the advantages of this. No doubt you can think of some disadvantages, however.

In both Styles A and C the teacher is concerned not only with what the learners learn, but with how they learn it; a specific product and process. At other times the teacher may focus on 'how-to learn' and may adopt a **problem solving** style. A task or problem is set which the pupils have to solve in their own ways. The problem may be defined by a single solution which the teacher wishes the pupils to **discover** (Style F); or there may be several possible solutions (not all of which the teacher may have thought of) and the pupils' task is to investigate these and select the one which most interests them (Style H). Teachers of creative dance and educational approaches to gymnastics use these styles a lot; so, in a different way, do teachers of outdoor pursuits.

There is not the space here to discuss the whole spectrum of styles, nor to go into much detail about each, but it is important that you begin to grasp that there are many ways of learning and therefore of teaching, and the skilful teacher will select appropriately from the range. So when you are next helping a friend or group of juniors with an activity, consider ways in which you can vary your approach.

MODES OF PRESENTATION

Teaching style is concerned with the way in which a teacher opts to deal with the range of decisions which the teaching process imposes. One of these decisions is, 'How do I present this new information/skill to my pupils?'. The answer to this question depends on the teacher's analysis of two important factors. These are illustrated in Figure 12.13.

Task analysis involves deciding what the important elements of the task are. Information processing theory will help here.

What are the perceptual requirements?
What are the decision making requirements?
What techniques does the performer need?
What feedback is available?

Answers to these questions indicate the **complexity** of the task. Note that complexity relates to the nature of the task; whether a task is simple or difficult depends upon the experience of the learner. Analysis should also indicate the extent to which the skill is **organized**. Skills which are not easily broken down into constituent parts are said to be highly organized. Swimming strokes are examples of low organization, because the leg, arm and breathing actions are all different and separate, though obviously they need to be well co-ordinated for effective performance (Singer, 1982). All this analysis should be compared with the state of readiness and the capabilities of the learner.

Ideally, a skill should be taught as a **whole**. The learner can then appreciate the end product and can develop a feeling for the flow of movement necessary for smooth, efficient production of the skill; he/she can see the relationship between the movements which constitute the whole action. However, for some skills it is not appropriate or sensible to teach the whole all at once, e.g.:

if the skill is too complex and/or difficult for the learner;
if there is an element of danger.

In these cases the skill is broken down into its constituent parts (sub-routines); these parts are taught as separate actions and then put together. This can be done in a variety of ways (see Figure 12.14).

Part methods of teaching are useful when the skill is complex and/or difficult, not highly organized, and when the mechanics of the movement are important. It lessens fear and risk in dangerous skills and allows the teacher to focus on key elements of the skill. It may help motivation, as the teacher can structure the teaching of the parts as 'mini wholes', thus giving the learner a feeling of success and progress. The main problem is one of transfer, for it is essential that the separately taught elements should be practised in the same way as they are performed within the whole skill and this is not easy to achieve. It is also important that the whole skill is demonstrated to the learner initially so that the end product can be appreciated in terms of its purpose, pace, flow and organization.

Many skills can be taught by the **whole-part-whole** method, whereby the learner first tries out the whole skill to get the feel of its performance requirements and to identify the easy and difficult elements. These may be different for each individual. By careful observation the teacher can isolate the difficult elements and teach them as parts, finally integrating them into the whole again.

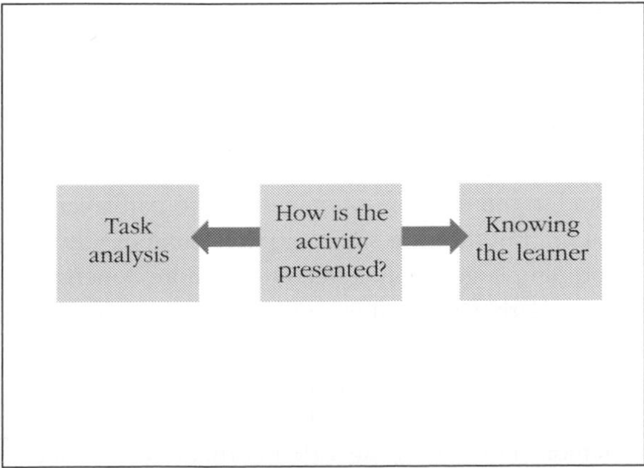

Figure 12.13 Deciding on presentation.

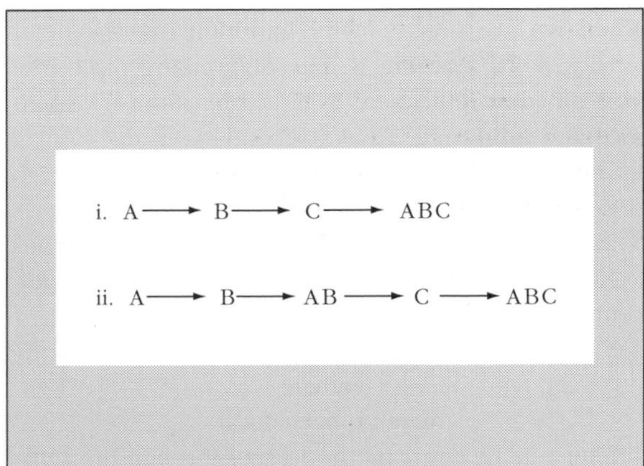

Figure 12.14 'Part' methods of presentation.

Investigation 12.4 : To investigate the effectiveness of whole and part methods of teaching a novel sequence of movement

Method: The class is divided into four groups. Four group leaders are appointed. The class teacher has previously devised and taught to the group leaders a sequence of movements which flow into one another and which contains some complex (but not impossible) moves. The constituent parts of the sequence are agreed.

Group A learns the sequence by the **'pure parts'** method (Figure 12.14(i)).

Group B learns the sequence by the **'progressive part'** method (Figure 12.14(ii)) .

Group C learns the sequence as a whole.

Group D learns by the whole-part-whole method.

Discussion: Which group takes the longest to learn? Which group performs the sequence best? What seems to be the best method of teaching for **this particular skill**?

You have been investigating teaching methods, but what are the 'confounding variables' in this experiment, i.e. factors other than teaching method which may have affected the result?

Whole and part methods assume that the parts of the skill are taught as if they were being performed within the whole. If, however, the whole is complex but not easily broken into parts that are meaningful, then the task itself may be **simplified**. A good example of this is the current focus on the 'mini-game' for youngsters. Short Tennis and Pop Lacrosse have many of the elements of the full adult game, but are played with modified rules and equipment.

If simplification of this kind is inappropriate, the idea of **shaping** the performance may be used. This is an aspect of operant conditioning as described in 12.1. The coach or teacher rewards aspects of the performance as the correct technique is approached and so the performer gradually acquires the skill. This is also known as **gradual metamorphosis** of the skill.

FORMS OF GUIDANCE

When we are practising or experiencing a skill or activity, some learning is inevitably taking place; but we learn most efficiently by a combination of experience and **guidance**. Thus a second set of decisions a teacher must make is about the type of guidance to give.

There are three basic forms of guidance or methods a teacher may use to transmit information about performance:

visual
verbal
manual/mechanical

Guidance is received by the learner through the senses and because we have several of these, information can be communicated to us in a variety of ways. Two points are important here:

a. the senses interact, so a combination of forms of guidance can be effective;
b. people differ in their preference for the type of guidance offered.

Visual Guidance

This is used at all stages of teaching and learning but is particularly valuable in the early (cognitive) phase to introduce the task and set the scene.

1. **Demonstration** relies on imitative learning and is a powerful tool. It is efficient, 'on-the-spot' and interesting to learners, but it must be accurate and relate to their age, experience and gender. It must show the activity as it occurs in real life. Teachers should avoid talking too much as a demonstration is taking place (remember channel capacity), but it is important to focus the pupils' attention on important performance cues.
2. **Visual aids** can be of value if constructed and presented thoughtfully. Photographs, charts and models are cheap and readily available; they can be tailored to the exact requirements of the particular situation; but they are static and thus limited. Video, and film, is generally agreed to be more beneficial, particularly since action can be slowed down, but it is expensive and the need for bulky play-back equipment currently curtails its usefulness, particularly outdoors. Video can be used either in place of demonstration or to provide information feedback on the learners' performances.

Investigation 12.5 : To produce a visual aid

Method: Select a skill or aspect of an activity with which you are especially familiar. Decide on a particular aspect which you might focus upon when helping a friend to learn the activity. Produce a visual aid to support your proposed coaching. Try making a video if you wish, but it is a time consuming task and you are probably better advised to avoid the technicalities of filming and concentrate on producing a good chart or model. Think about:

a. simplicity
b. clarity
c. use of colour
d. highlighting the important performance cues.

Try out your visual aid on a friend and invite constructive criticism of it.

3. **Modifying the display.** Sometimes it is appropriate to give assistance by enhancing perception of the important aspects of the surroundings. We discussed signal detection in Section 10.2 and the way, for example, the colour of tennis balls might affect play. Areas of space might be highlighted; for example, a coach might mark a target on a court for serving practice, or chalk the points on a gymnastic mat where the hands should be placed for a cartwheel. Coloured bibs or different strips not only help the referee, but they help player identification in a team game.

Verbal Guidance

A great deal of teaching and coaching is done using verbal guidance. A good coach will be able not only to set the task clearly and unambiguously and to describe the actions; he/she will be able to highlight the important performance cues and even be able to express these in ways which may not be entirely accurate, but which will convey the feel of the movement to the learner: 'Climb with your eyes!'; 'Stretch your toes to the ceiling!'. The advantages of using verbal guidance are that it is 'on-the-spot' and, when used by a knowledgeable and perceptive teacher, is directly relevant to the problems and capabilities of the individual learner.

There are some difficulties which a teacher must work to overcome:

- Does the learner understand the instructions?
- Can the learner remember what has been said (remember the capacity of the short-term memory)?
- Can the learner translate from the spoken word to movement?

Manual/mechanical guidance

This form of assistance involves physical contact, for example by the coach supporting and guiding the movement (as in the practice of a gymnastic vault) or by the support of a device such as a swimming armband, a trampoline belt or a 'tight rope' in climbing. It allows the learner to discover the timing and spacial aspects of the movement, but does not help with a knowledge of the forces acting on the body or the movement cues. The aim is to reduce error and fear—important when there are safety considerations. Such support is therefore generally used with youngsters and people with special needs. Two forms of manual guidance have been identified:

1. **physical restriction:** a person or an object confines the moving body of the performer to movements which are safe, e.g. a trampoline belt;
2. **forced response:** the learner is guided through the movement, e.g. a coach may physically guide a player through a forehand drive in tennis.

Both these forms are used primarily with open skills.

TYPES OF PRACTICE

The concept of open and closed skills also gives the teacher guidance in deciding how to structure the practice of a particular activity. We saw, in Section 10.4, how, as a general rule, open skills should be practised with as much variety as is feasible (**variable practice**), to allow a general schema to be developed. Whereas in closed skills (in which the replication of a specific movement pattern is the aim), **fixed practice**, with repetition to allow the movements to be over-learned, is appropriate.

A third decision about practice which the teacher needs to make concerns the length of the practice periods and the extent to which the learners need rest during practice. If they do need rest, how long should the rest periods be and what should the learners do in them? This is an important question for, as you probably know from your own experience, if fatigue or boredom sets in, learning decreases markedly.

If the performers are highly skilled, fit and well-motivated, **massed practice** may be the most appropriate form of organization. This means that they will work continuously at an activity without any breaks until the skill is mastered or time runs out. Massed practice is efficient and allows concentration and over-learning.

The alternative is **distributed** (or **spaced**) **practice**. In this form, the total practice session is split into several shorter periods with intervals between. These intervals may be rest periods or the teacher may set alternative tasks. From what you now know about negative transfer (see p. 276), what must the teacher be careful about in organizing alternative tasks in the intervals?

What is the best form of organization? There really is not a straightforward answer to this question. Motor learning proceeds best when the learner is trying hard, concentrating fully on the task and when feedback is available. People vary greatly in their capacity to maintain attention to and interest in a task, and thus what is a good practice session for one will be inappropriate for another. If success is being achieved, learners can continue longer than if the task is hard and progress is slow. In general, both researchers and teachers agree that distributed practice is the most effective in the majority of cases.

One of the advantages of distributed practice is that the rest intervals can be used for **mental rehearsal**. This is the process whereby the performer, without moving, runs through the performance in his/her mind. The learner can do this in several ways:

- by watching a demonstration or film;
- by reading or listening to instructions;
- by mental imagery, if the skill is established.

Obviously, this is a useful strategy for experienced performers, and many use it in preparation for competition, but interestingly it also appears to enhance the learning process. Research cited by Cratty (1975) suggests that, when mental rehearsal is occurring, the muscular neurons are firing as if the muscle is actually active. Because of this, it is suggested, mental rehearsal has a real learning effect. Though few sports psychologists would claim that a skill can be learned entirely by mental rehearsal, evidence would suggest that a combination of physical and mental practice is beneficial.

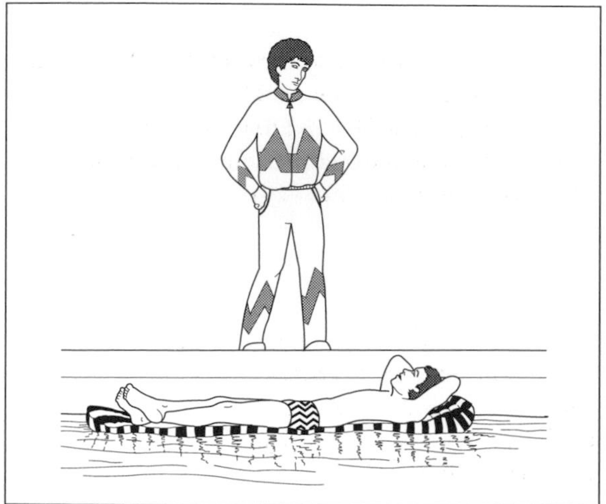

Figure 12.15 'But coach, you told me to include mental rehearsal in my training!'

Summary

1. In order to learn we must be motivated. Effective teaching relies upon this motivation. The relationship between motivation and learning has been highlighted in 'drive reduction theory'. There are many different theories of learning. One group, the S–R theories, see learning as a process of conditioning, i.e. the establishment of a connection between stimulus and response, with success seen as a reward or reinforcement. Feedback is an important part of S–R bonding and is therefore an integral part of the learning process. It provides motivation and reinforcement and thus effects changes in performance. But if feedback is to be effective, there must be a frame of reference, a model by which error detection can function. There are several forms of feedback and much research has been done into its effects on learning.
2. Feedback is central to the concept of motor control. Closed- and open-loop theories of control give rise to different coaching philosophies but modern thinking tends to integrate the two; an important outcome of this is schema theory which suggests that what is stored in memory is not a fixed pattern of movement but a set of relationships. An important practical implication of this is the need for the practice to be as varied as possible.
3. There are many factors which teachers need to consider in structuring learning for their pupils. Possible transfer from previously acquired to new skills is one, and teaching style is another. Decisions on what material to present and how to present it leads to a need for task analysis and a knowledge of the stage of motor development of the pupils. Skills which a learner will find relatively straightforward can be taught as a whole, but more complex skills may need to be broken down into, and taught as, parts. The interaction of task complexity and learner capability will also necessitate a consideration of the kind of guidance which is most appropriate, and the way in which practice of the activity may be structured.

REFERENCES

Adams J. A closed loop theory of motor learning, *Journal of Motor Behaviour,* 3, 111-150, 1971.

Butt D.S. *Psychology of Sport,* New York, Van Nostrand Reinhold, 1987.

Carron A.V. *Social Psychology of Sport,* Ithaca, N.Y., Movement Publications, 1980.

Fitts P.M. and Posner M.I. *Human Performance,* Belmont, Cal., Brooks Cole, 1967.

Fleishman E.A. The structure and measurement of psychomotor abilities. In Singer R.N.: *The Psychomotor Domain: Movement Behaviour,* Philadelphia, Lea & Febiger, 1972.

Gentile A.M. A working model of skill acquisition with application teaching, *Quest,* 17, 3-23, 1972.

Neate D. *Motor Skills and Sport Performance,* Cambridge, University of Cambridge Local Examination Syndicate.

Sage G.H. *Introduction to Motor Behaviour: a Neuropsychological Approach,* Reading, Ma., Addison Wesley, 1977.

Schmidt R.A. Schema theory: implications for movement education, *Motor Skills: Theory into Practice,* 2(1), 36-38, 1977.

Schmidt R.A. Past and future issues in motor programming, *Research Quarterly,* 51, 122-140, 1980.

Skinner B.F. *About Behaviourism,* New York, Vintage Books, 1974.

Thorndike E.L. *Fundamentals of Learning,* New York, Columbia University Press, 1932.

Wallace S.A. and Hagler R.W. Knowledge of performance and the learning of a closed motor skill, *Research Quarterly,* 50, 265-271, 1979.

FURTHER READING

Bunker L.K. *et al. Sport Psychology,* Ithaca, N.Y., Movement Publications, 1985.

Mosston M. and Ashworth S. *Teaching Physical Education* 3e, Columbus, Ohio, Merrill, 1986.

National Coaching Foundation. *Planning Your Programme,* Leeds, NCF, 1992.

National Coaching Foundation. *Improving Techniques/Planning and Practice: Introductory Study Packs 4 & 6,* Leeds, NCF, 1993.

Singer R.N. *The Learning of Motor Skills,* New York, Macmillan, 1975.

Stallings L.M. *Motor Learning,* St Louis, C.V. Mosby, 1982.

Chapter 13
Psychology of Sport

In Chapters 9–12 we considered the processes by which people become skilful and the factors which influence motor skill **learning**. We now turn our attention to the idea of **performance**, and study what is happening whilst people are taking part in physical activity for recreation and competition, once they have become proficient (though of course we never stop learning).

We call this study the **psychology of sport**. Psychology is the study of the behaviour of individuals. Most researchers in this area have dealt with behaviour in a sports context, though many of their findings apply to other physical activities such as dance and outdoor pursuits. Sport psychology (as it is alternatively called) has a great deal to offer sportsmen and sportswomen; indeed some claim that it will be the main factor in future improvement in performance.

> *Our biomechanical, physiological and sports medicine counterparts will all contribute—but ultimately it will be the athlete's ability to control his or her own body and mind in action and in all areas of life that will determine the level of ultimate athletic performance.*
>
> (Bunker and McGuire, 1985, p. 13)

The field of study of sport psychology covers a range of topics, some of which we deal with in this book. Sport personality is an important area; we study how psychologists have attempted to identify what makes up personality and whether the kind of person you are affects your performance in sport. We develop this further in Section 13.2. We also take our study of motivation further, and in Section 13.4 consider the effects of stress on sportspeople and how they can optimize their performances. In Section 13.3 you will study how being a part of a team or group affects behaviour.

The knowledge we have about the psychological aspects of physical activity derives from research by an 'army' of psychologists, teachers, coaches and sportspeople themselves. This research uses, for the most part, social science **methodology**, and it is important that you understand the basis of this in order both to carry out your own investigations and to appreciate how others have derived their theories. Your practical work in Chapters 9–12 and in other chapters of the book will have introduced you to this methodology, but as you work through this chapter you should further develop your awareness of the importance of:

- asking appropriate questions
- deriving hypotheses and identifying variables
- selecting a method of enquiry such as interview, questionnaire, test or measurement, observation and analysis
- choosing your subjects appropriately
- analysing, presenting and evaluating your data.

As an example, look back to an investigation in which you have been through the process outlined above (e.g. Investigation 12.2). Identify for that particular investigation, each of the stages. For example: what were the variables you were interested in; what data collection techniques were used; how were the subjects chosen; how were the data presented and analysed; and what were the issues for discussion which arose? These questions ask you to describe what you did; to 'tell the story' of your investigation. You must also evaluate and ask yourself: (i) how representative was my sample of the general group (population) I was interested in; (ii) were the data collection techniques I used valid, i.e. did they actually measure what was intended; (iii) were my methods reliable, i.e. likely to produce similar results in similar circumstances; (iv) were my observations objective, i.e. free of variation or bias due to the experimenter, or was there an inevitable element of subjectivity; and, finally, (v) did I respect my subjects' rights to refuse, to remain anonymous and to have their physical and emotional well-being protected.

There is not the scope in this book to deal with this methodology in detail. Suitable additional texts are Roberts, Spink and Pemberton (1986) and Harris (1986).

13.1 Personality

KEY WORDS AND CONCEPTS

trait
Sheldon's constitutional theory
psychometric methods
source traits
surface traits
self-report questionnaires
trait theories

What is personality? In Section 11.2 we became aware of the need to recognize that sportspeople are individuals. We all have different abilities and are most skilful in different activities. We also know that we differ in terms of how we behave and react in sporting contexts.

On completion of this section you will:

a. appreciate the importance of psychology as a variable for learning and performance;
b. understand the relationship between learning/performance and the development of the self concept.

Investigation 13.1 : To derive a common sense definition of personality

Method: Work in groups of three or four. Think of a televised sport with which you are all familiar. Select two 'personalities' within that sport who contrast in the way they behave as they play. An example from tennis a few years ago might have been Bjorn Borg and John McEnroe.

Discussion: What is it about them that differs? What characteristics do they show through their responses to things that happen in the game/competition?

You have been talking about a pattern of characteristics which makes each of these two people different. You have begun to define their personalities.

Guilford (1959) defines personality as 'a person's unique pattern of traits'. A **trait** is a general, underlying, enduring predisposition to behave in a particular way each time a given situation occurs. So if you always believe you have a good chance of winning the competitions you enter, you could be said to show the trait of 'optimism'. Eysenck (1969) suggests that personality is the more or less stable and enduring organization of a person's **character**, **temperament**, **intellect** and **physique** which determines the unique adjustment to the environment'. Since, in Investigation 13.1, we, with Eysenck, are defining personality in terms of how someone behaves in a particular situation, then it seems that situations and behaviour and personality are in some way related. Most theories about what personality is accept this interrelationship.

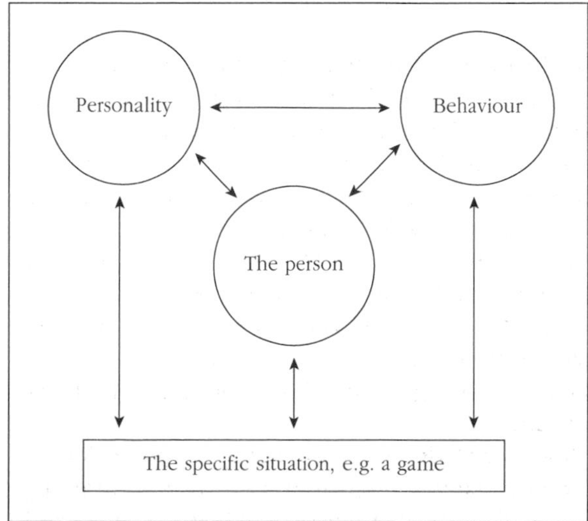

Figure 13.1 Personality, behaviour and the situation.

There are many different theories about what personality is and how it develops. A good review, which considers those theories most applicable to sport and physical activity, can be found in Carron (1980). There are two which have been most often used in trying to explain behaviour in sport:

1. **Sheldon's constitutional theory.** This theory has never been fully accepted, but maintains credibility partly because it has a certain 'folklore' validity. In Chapter 4, you will have measured body type by means of a process known as somatotyping. Sheldon (1942) associated each of the three somatotypes with a personality type.
2. **Trait theories.** These theories assume that a trait is a general, underlying, enduring predisposition to behave in a particular way each time a given situation occurs. For example, if we always feel nervous before a competition we could be said to possess the trait of 'competitive anxiety'. Trait theories suggest that our personality is made up of many traits. Two theorists in particular (Eysenck and Cattell) have suggested that these traits are organized in a hierarchical way. Their research has led to a model of personality in which those traits which seem to cluster together are given a label which summarizes a group of behaviours. For example, think of a sportsperson whom you would label as 'extrovert'. Now list some words which describe his/her behaviour and which define the term 'extrovert' in this case. Did you think of words like outgoing, confident, talkative, publicity seeking?

SOMATOTYPE	PERSONALITY TYPE
Ectomorphy Linearity	Cerebrotonia Tenseness, introversion
Endomorphy Plumpness	Viscerotonia Sociability, affection, comfort-loving
Mesomorphy Muscularity	Somatotonia Risk taking, adventure-seeking, extrovert

Figure 13.2 Sheldon's somato-personality typology. (Adapted from Carron, 1980.)

HOW IS PERSONALITY ASSESSED?

Just as there are many theories of personality, so there are several distinct ways in which personality can be assessed. The methods most usually used in sport research are known as **psychometric** methods; that is, they set out to quantify personality—to say, for example, just how extrovert someone is. This is normally done by means of **self-report questionnaires**.

Cattell's Sixteen Personality Factor Questionnaire (known as the 16PF) has been widely used in sport research. Cattell first identified 171 behaviours, which he believes we all exhibit to a greater or lesser extent. He grouped these into 16 clusters which he labelled **source traits** or **first order (primary) factors**. He then constructed a questionnaire which, after considerable preliminary work, he proved to be a valid and reliable measure of these 16 surface traits. The scoring system allows, if the researcher wishes, further grouping of

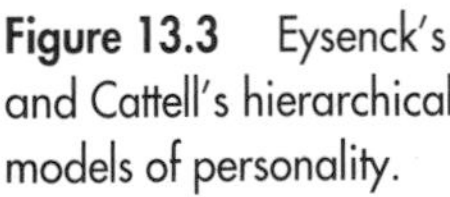
Figure 13.3 Eysenck's and Cattell's hierarchical models of personality.

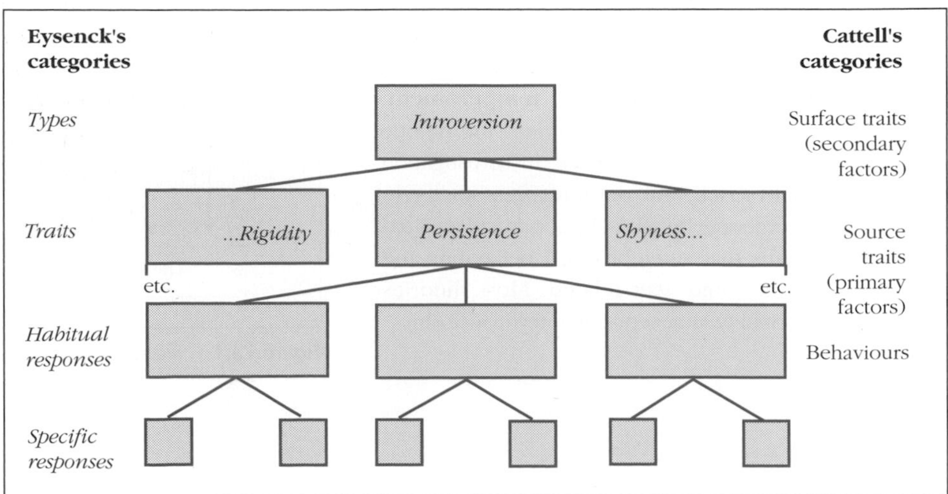

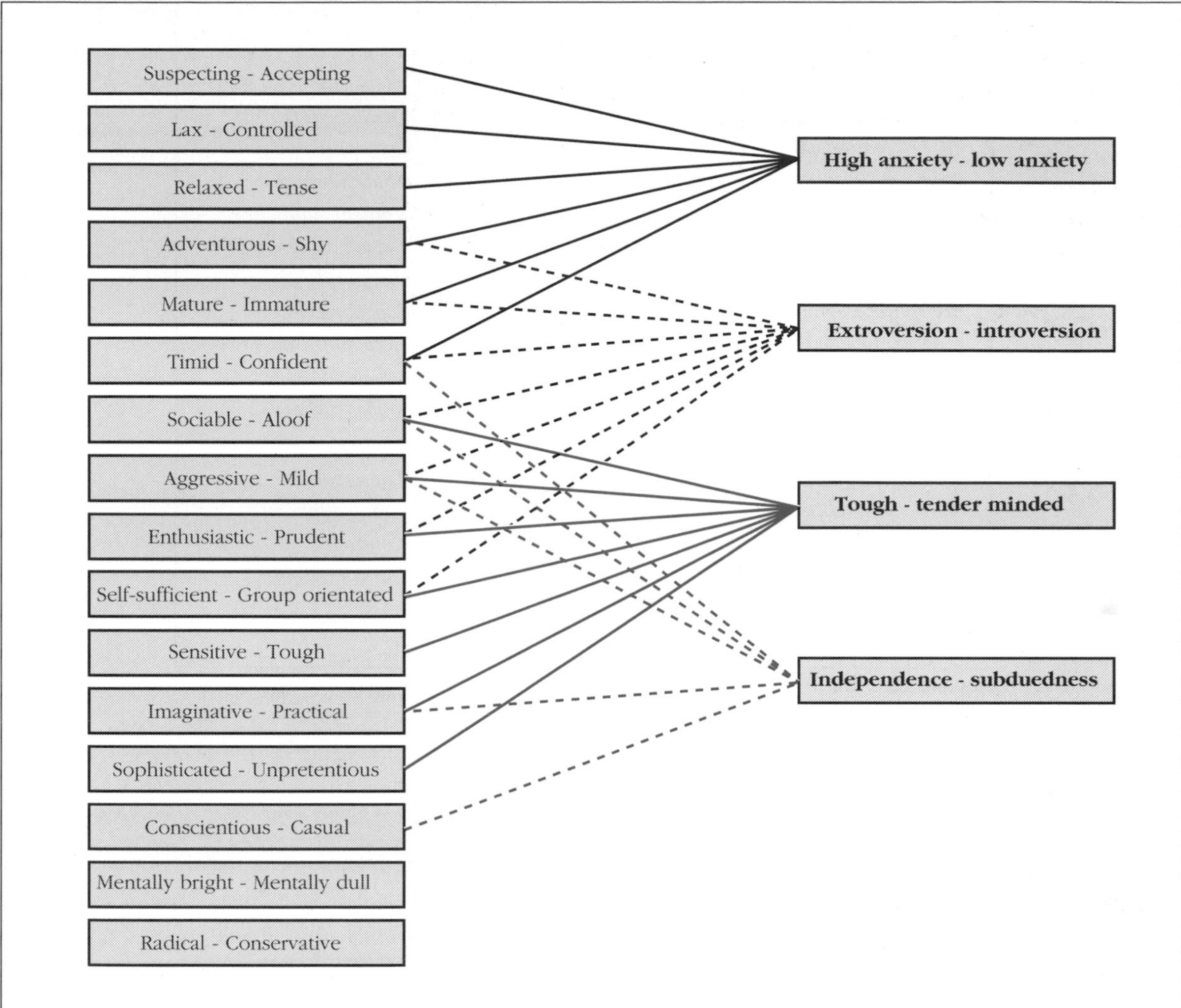

Figure 13.4 The structure of Cattell's 16 Personality Factors.

the source traits into four **surface traits or second order (secondary) factors**. The slight differences between Eysenck's and Cattell's terminology can be a little confusing but are illustrated in Figure 13.3.

There are 141 statements in the 16PF questionnaire, each assessing a particular trait. The statements are similar to the following example:

'I feel the need every now and then to engage in tough physical activity.

a) Yes

b) In between

c) No'

When the scoring of the questionnaire is completed, the subject has a standardized score out of ten (known as a **STEN** score) on each of the 16 factors and his/her profile might look like that in Figure 13.5

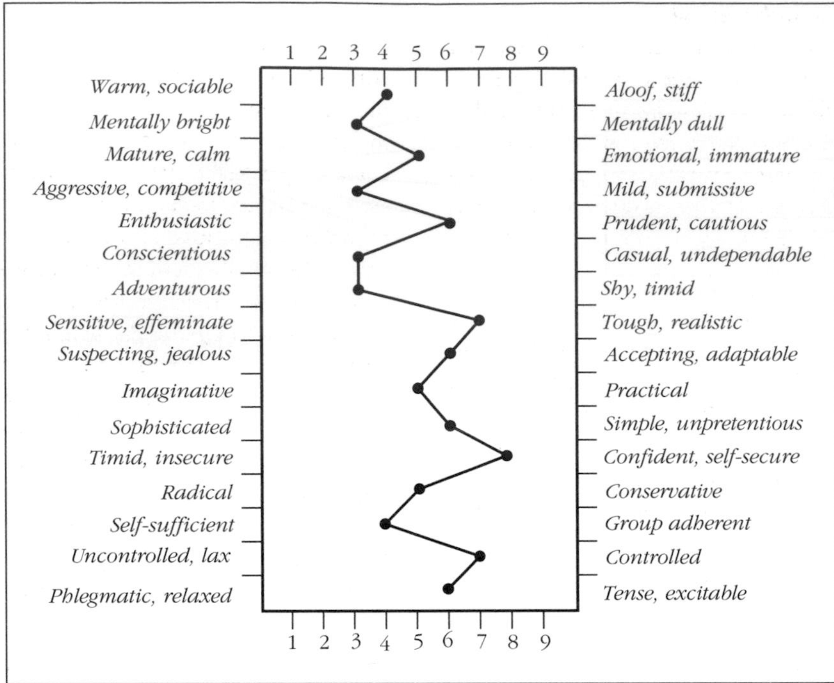

Figure 13.5 The 16PF profile of an athlete.

Investigation 13.2 : To analyse a 16PF profile

Method: Imagine you have collected data on an athlete's personality using the 16PF questionnaire and have constructed a profile as in Figure 13.5

Observations: Analyse the profile, noting particularly those traits in which the athlete's scores fall outside the range 3.5–6.5. We shall be considering the implications of scores such as these later in the section.

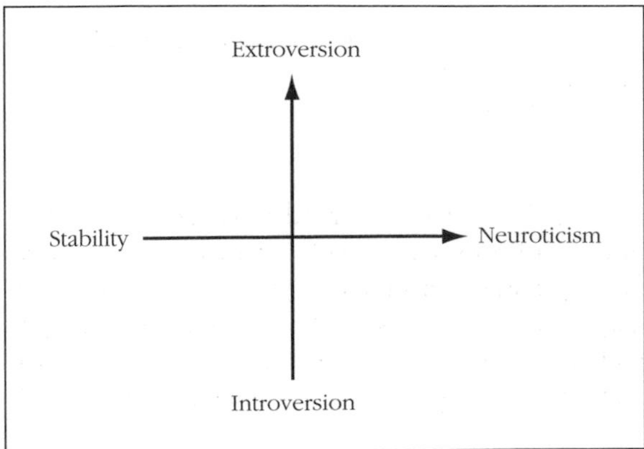

Figure 13.6 Personality dimensions: extroversion and neuroticism.

Eysenck developed a similar self report questionnaire, shorter and with a 'Yes/No' answering format in contrast to Cattell's three-point scale. This is known as the Eysenck Personality Inventory (or Questionnaire), the EPI or the EPQ. There is also a version for children. The major difference between this and Cattell's questionnaire is that Eysenck's directly identifies second order factors; the two most usually refered to are **extroversion** and **neuroticism**. Neuroticism is associated with **emotionality** and is extroversion and neuroticism. characterized by a tendency to worry, to exhibit physical symptoms associated with anxiety and to tend to experience unstable mood states. These are usually represented as **dimensions** and can be illustrated as in Figure 13.6.

What does the research tell us?

During the 1960s and 1970s a great deal of research was carried out, using mostly Cattell's and Eysenck's inventories, into the relationship between personality and sport. Sport scientists were interested in answers to three questions. Is there an athletic 'type'? Can success in sport be predicted from measures of personality? Does personality change as a result of participation in sport?

Is there an athletic type? Do certain groups of sportspeople, performers or recreationists differ from the norm in terms of their personalities (for example, do they have scores which fall outside the 3.5–6.5 range in the 16PF)? The results of research into these questions are very unclear, largely because of theoretical and methodological problems associated with the research itself. The most clear-cut evidence seems to emerge when second order factors are considered. A good review of the great wealth and variety of data is given in Butt (1987). We must remember that it is mean scores which are reported and within any group of athletes there is a wide variety of personalities. However, what does seem to emerge is that both male and female sportspeople show traits of extroversion, dominance, enthusiasm, confidence, aggression and high activity levels (Butt 1987). There is some evidence that people involved in team sports are more extrovert than those who prefer individual sports and also that extroversion for all groups increases as participation continues.

A physiological explanation has been offered for the relationship between sports chosen and extroversion/emotionality. The Reticular Activating System (RAS), located in the brainstem, is stimulated by sensory information from many sources, including hormonal (adrenalin). It has both an exciting and inhibiting effect on the cerebral cortex. You can think of it as a telephone bell if you like. In introverts the RAS is strong; a little stimulation triggers the mechanism, a lot may cause overload. So introverts prefer situations where the stimuli from the environment are limited. In extroverts, however, the RAS is weak. They need a lot of stimulation to get really going; they perform best in situations where there is a lot happening (a team game, for example); they are 'stimuli-seekers'. In a similar way, individual differences in the functioning of the Autonomic Nervous System (ANS), which you will have dealt with in Chapter 2, and which has been called the 'centre for emotions', will affect the extent to which an individual copes with anxiety-producing situations to be found in many sports.

One of the questions which has been asked about personality and sport is whether or not a particular personality profile is necessary for performance at the top level. In some countries psychological testing is used, in addition to measures of performance and body composition, to identify children who are suitable for intensive training in a sport. You will be aware of the increasing use of personality testing in the selection of people for executive positions in industry and commerce in this country.

REVIEW QUESTION

Discuss the use of personality testing in the selection of, for example, young people to attend a programme of training in a sports school or centre of excellence. What do you see to be the main problems associated with such testing?

Perhaps personality research in sport has been asking the wrong questions. This has led Martens (1979) and other sports psychologists to suggest that we still know very little about the relationship between personality and sport. Others view this as too sceptical a position and argue that the results summarized above do provide us with some useful information. Perhaps research has not taken enough account of the situational variables we considered earlier. Perhaps we need to turn our attention to those aspects of personality which seem to be particularly important in sport and performance: the 'Three As', aggression, anxiety and ambition. We will be considering these later in this chapter.

13.2 The Self Concept

KEY WORDS AND CONCEPTS

self concept
self-esteem
body image
models
roles
significant others

An interesting element of personality, and one which certainly affects the way in which we participate, learn and perform in physical activities, is the **self concept**. As you read you will find many different terms and definitions in this area. We will confine ourselves to two: **self concept** and **self-esteem**.

- The **self concept** is the descriptive picture we have of ourselves. It includes physical attributes, attitudes, abilities, roles and emotions. It is important to remember that it represents how we see ourselves and this may not reflect reality or the way others see us.
- **Self-esteem** is the extent to which we value ourselves. Again this may or may not match up to the expectations of others. For example, a player may take pride in an ability to tackle hard, whereas the referee and the coach see it as unnecessary aggression.

Several theories describing the structure of the self concept exist. These are summarized in Fox (1988). In this case we shall assume that the self concept is built in levels, as illustrated in Figure 13.7.

The development of the self concept

Developmental psychology tells us that the newly born child cannot distinguish between itself and its environment. Growth and maturation bring an increasing awareness of self, of other people and of control over the surroundings and events. At this point the self concept comes into existence. Some aspects of the self concept are enduring; others change as our experiences, our roles and our position in society change.

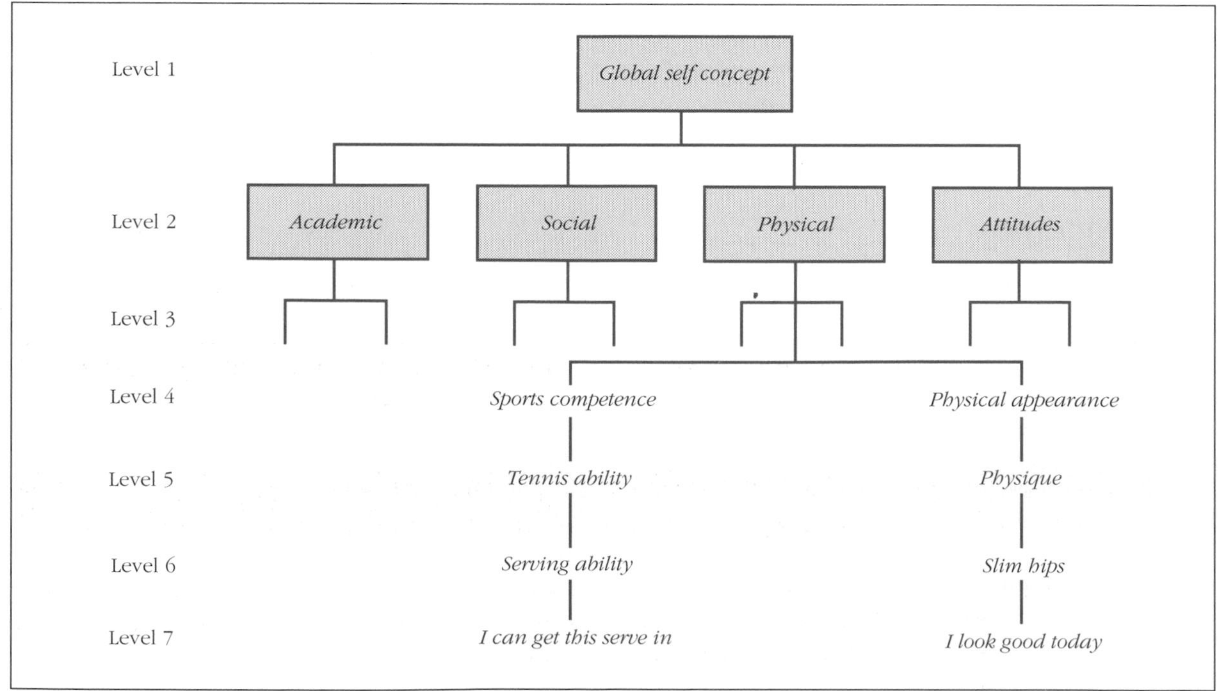

Figure 13.7 The structure of the Physical Self Concept (adapted from Fox, 1988).

Factors which influence the self concept

Figure 13.8 represents the internal and external factors which give rise to a particular self concept and self-esteem. Some are objective; they are aspects of yourself which can be measured or readily agreed upon. But others are socially developed and depend upon how you and other people view or value the objective characteristics. This is illustrated in Figure 13.9 in relation to **body image**, that is, the view a person has of his or her body and physical make-up.

Let us consider in a little more detail the social or interactional view of the development of the self concept, referred to in Figures 13.8 and 13.9. We are interested in how other people see us and we take note of their reactions to things we do and say. In this sense other people act as a mirror to reflect us and we internalize what we perceive. If you have received praise and encouragement as you learned to participate in physical activity, then you are likely to have begun to think of yourself as good at sport or dance or gymnastics. As this picture of self begins to clarify we ask ourselves, 'Well, how good am I?'. We start to compare ourselves with others to see how we 'measure up'. Interestingly, we appear to be sensible about this, and in order to get a reasonable evaluation we do not compare ourselves with others who are out of our league'. For example, if you are a good college tennis player you will, for the moment, compare yourself with your team-mates and those above you in the club ladder, not the Wimbledon champion!

Our **roles** in society determine very much how others see and react to us. A role is a set of behaviours associated with our position in a family or group or organization. The longer and more fully we play a particular role, the more we internalize it. You are interested in sport or dance or other forms of physical activity. Others begin to think of you as a sportsperson, or dancer or climber. You may like the idea of being seen in this role and reinforce it by, for example, wearing clothes which identify you with it and adopting the role behaviours.

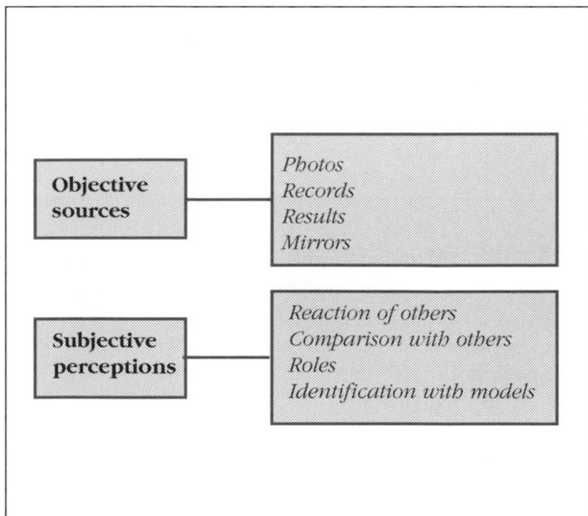

Figure 13.8 Factors affecting self concept and self-esteem.

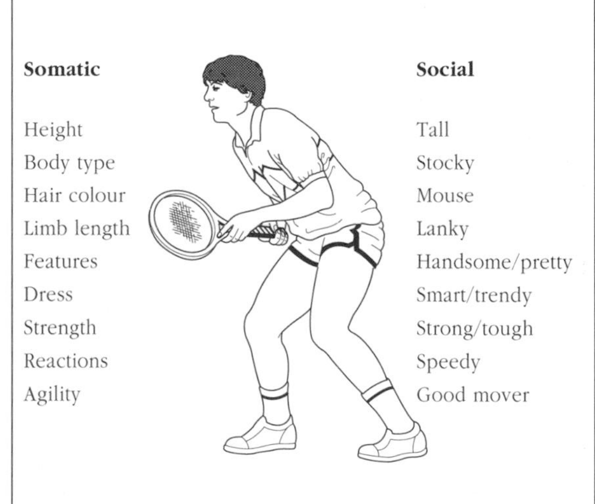

Figure 13.9 Objective/somatic and subjective/social aspects of body image.

Investigation 13.3 : To identify aspects of role

Method: Each member of the group makes a list of the roles they play. Examples might be sister, team captain, student. Select six or so which are common to all members of the group. Each person then writes down the behaviours which are inherent in that role. In groups of two or three devise a 'role play' which illustrates one of the roles but which does not directly name it. Other members of the group have to identify the role being acted out.

Discussion: What were the behaviours and attitudes that most obviously characterized each role?

Part of learning to play a particular role is the way in which we identify with others who we see to be playing the role successfully (this is assuming that we want to). Sports heroes act as **models** in this respect. which is partly why sports authorities believe it to be important that players at the top of a sport behave in a way which is going to 'set a good example' to youngsters.

The establishment of self-esteem

The process described above allows us to develop a particular view of ourselves and also to place a value on that view. If the majority of our experiences with people and of events are enjoyable and satisfying we will develop a positive self concept and high self-esteem. If we often feel 'put down' and incompetent we will have a correspondingly negative self concept/low self-esteem. But in fact it is not quite as simple as this for two reasons:

1. Self-esteem is a reflection of how **significant others** value us. We do not seem to be so interested in the evaluations of people who are not important to us. So if parents, teachers, coaches treat our efforts with respect and support, self-esteem will be raised independently of how competent we actually are or even perceive ourselves to be. People are significant at different periods of our life; early on it is parents; later the evaluations of our peers become much more important to us.
2. Self-esteem in relation to a particular activity or attribute is a reflection of how important we see it to be. So friends laughing at you for being 'hopeless' at soccer, when you are not very interested in it, will not have as much effect on your self-esteem as they would if you really wanted to be seen to be a good player. This is illustrated in Figure 13.10.

The effects of levels of self-esteem on learning

Research has shown that differing levels of self-esteem give rise to differing personality profiles. People with high self-esteem tend to be optimistic, resilient, adventurous and to enjoy challenge. People with low self-esteem tend to lack confidence, to be self-protective and to be critical of others. It must be remembered that self-esteem can be specific to one particular activity or area of life, or it can be global, but high or low global self-esteem colours all our ideas about ourselves. Once self-esteem is established, it predisposes us to view new experiences in particular ways. This is known as attribution and we will be considering it in more detail in Section 13.4, but we should note the contribution of the self concept to this process. This is shown in Figure 13.11

	Perceived competence	Perceived importance	Self-esteem
Basketball	L	L	O
Fitness	L	H	L
Gymnastics	H	L	O
Dance	H	H	H

Key: L = Low rating
H = High rating
O = Little effect

Figure 13.10 The effects of perceived competence and perceived importance on self-esteem. (Adapted from Fox, 1988.)

	Existing positive self concept	Existing negative self concept
Positive experience of PE	Self concept enhanced	Self concept may become positive
Negative experience of PE	Self concept may become negative	Self concept reinforced

Figure 13.11 The relationship between experiences and the self concept.

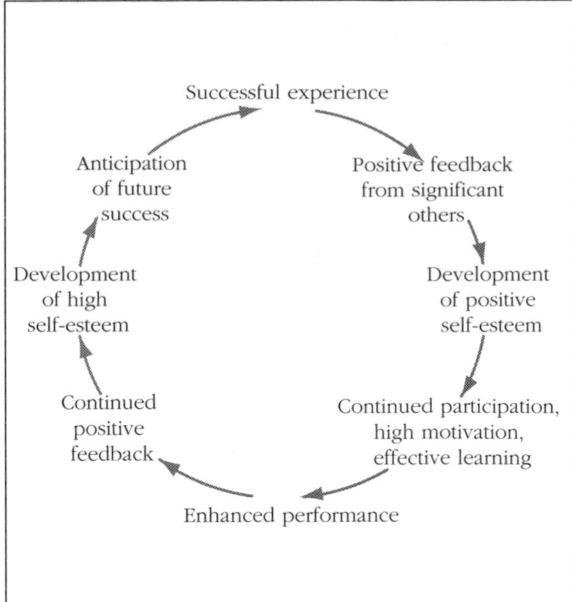

Figure 13.12 The self concept wheel.

This relationship, together with the personality factors we know to be associated with high and low self-esteem, suggest that self-esteem is an important variable in learning, and the self concept in the avoidance of or adherence to physical activity. It seems to be a cyclical relationship.

If this is the case and if we believe that physical activity is something which everyone should have the opportunity of enjoying and being successful in, then what are the implications for the way in which we present and teach and coach physical activity?

Discuss this question in terms of:

a. the range and type of activities offered to young people;
b. the teaching and coaching styles used;
c. the place of competition in physical education;
d. the place of fitness training in physical education;
e. the role of dance and adventure activities in physical education;
f. the use of award schemes, e.g. RLSS Aquapack.

Summary

A significant way in which individuals differ in how they learn and perform is in their personalities and the way they view themselves. Research into personality and sport has tended, in the past, to focus on finding an 'athletic type' but more recently sports psychologists are trying to find ways of using sportspeople's self-knowledge to help them get the best out of themselves (see also Section 13.3). The extent to which we value ourselves seems to play a large part in effective learning and satisfying performance.

13.3 Social Influences

KEY WORDS AND CONCEPTS

interaction	**cohesion**	**leadership**
influence	**sociometry**	**competitors**
awareness	**sociogram**	**supporters**
co-ordination problems	**social cohesion**	**aggression**
motivation problems	**task cohesion**	**attitudes**

This section deals with the fact that most recreative, artistic and competitive physical activity takes place within the context of a group, squad or team. It thus happens within a social context. The broad implications of this are considered in Part Three, but here we are concerned with the effects that team-mates, spectators and others have on individuals, their behaviour and performance.

We also consider the concept of motivation, and study the way in which an individual's perception of the costs and benefits of participation in an activity affect performance.

At the end of this section you should be able to:

a. define a sport/activity group;
b. describe the relationship between individual and group performance;
c. understand the nature of leadership and cohesiveness within a group context;
d. discuss the possible effects of spectators and team-mates on individual performance;
e. define and classify motivation;
f. explain how a sportsperson's perceptions of the reasons for success or failure affect subsequent participation.

GROUP PROCESSES

Most sports and activities take place within a social context. Whilst there certainly are people who derive satisfaction from training and competing alone, dependent upon their own psychological and physical resources, most are drawn to activity because of the opportunity to join people who share their enthusiasm. Personal experience and research tell us that we tend to react differently when we are in a group from when we are alone, and thus investigating these differences and considering their implications for teams and squads is an important, if somewhat neglected, branch of sport psychology.

What is a group? Shaw (1976, p. 11) defines it as *'two or more persons who are interacting with one another in such a manner that each person influences and is influenced by each other person'*. McGrath (1984, p. 7) states that *'groups are those social aggregates that involve mutual awareness and potential interaction'*.

Both definitions highlight the importance (whether actual or potential) of **interaction**.

Shaw sees **influence** as an important component; McGrath prefers **awareness**.

GROUP DISCUSSION

If you accept these definitions, would you consider a crowd at a football match, or a collection of people at a public swimming session, to be a group?

Select some other examples of groups and non-groups in sports and activity contexts.

Don't be concerned if you have some difficulty in deciding; the borderline between group and non-group is not clear-cut.

Of interest to sport psychologists and coaches is the question of how people interact in sports groups and how that interaction can be made most productive. Gill (1986) has used Steiner's model of group productivity to suggest that:
team success = potential for success – co-ordination and motivation problems

- **Potential for success:** in general, the most skilful individuals make the best team. Jones (1974) correlated the individual success of members of a team against the overall success of the team and found high positive correlations in all his cases. The lowest correlation (0.6) was in basketball, a sport in which there is a great deal of interaction.
- High interaction presents **co-ordination problems** for players: if one player is being selfish or aggressive, or if a defence is not working together, overall team performance suffers.
- **Motivation problems:** people seem to work less hard in a group than they do on their own. For example, in the 1972 Olympics, the time of the winning double sculls was only four per cent faster than the single sculls, and the eights only six per cent faster than the fours. Obviously, there might be a technical explanation for this in terms of the sizes and weights of the boats, but the effect seems to be general and is known as the Ringelmann Effect (Gill, 1986) or **'social loafing'**.

Social loafing is the tendency for individuals to lessen their effort when they are part of a group. Work by Williams *et al.* (1981) suggests that this is eliminated if players think that their contribution within the team is identifiable. Thus team coaches who are aware of this will develop strategies for recognizing individual performance in a game. The use of player statistics in American football is an example of this.

Figure 13.13 Co-ordination and co-operation may be a problem!

Figure 13.14 'Social loafing'.

Interaction

In some teams, the need for interaction between players is high; basketball has already been suggested as a game requiring a lot of co-operation. In other teams, such interaction is not as important.

Investigation 13.4 : To discuss interaction within sports teams

Method: Make a list of sports included in the Olympic Games. Construct a continuum, based on the extent to which the members of a particular team in each sport **need** to interact with one another during competition.

Results: You might have, for example, volleyball near one end (as a highly interactive sport) and archery near the other.

Discussion. Compare your list with others in your group and discuss any discrepancies.

Cohesion

In sports where the need for co-operation between team members is high, coaches will take the interactional skills of players into account and hence may sometimes select a slightly less able player who 'fits in' better than a more skilful, but selfish, colleague. The nature of these interactional skills in sport has not been extensively researched. Cratty and Hanin (1980) suggest that players like and value each other more when the team is doing well. Strong competition for places on a team can lead to personal rivalry and even hostility. Friendships within a team can aid team spirit and **cohesion**. Cohesion is the extent to which members of a group exhibit a desire to achieve common goals and group identity. But friendship groups can have negative effects; some research (Klein and Christiansen, 1969) shows that passing patterns in team ball games reflect friendship groups, though observation suggests that this does not happen at the top level or in professional sport.

Friendship patterns in a team can be measured by a technique known as **sociometry**. You will find more details of this in a text such as Saunders and White (1977), but essentially it involves asking members of a group to nominate, in confidence, two or three other members who they would choose in the situation being investigated. The situation might be a friendship choice or it might be a task; the ways in which the technique can be used are very varied. These choices are then represented on a diagram, known as a **sociogram**.

Several researchers (Carron and Ball, 1977; Williams and Hacker, 1982) have studied the relationship between success and cohesion in sports teams. The results of this research are equivocal. Some studies show that high group cohesion leads to better performances; others suggest that good performance leads to increased cohesion. There would seem to be a 'cause and effect' problem in interpreting the data. This may be resolved if we consider cohesion to have two facets, i.e. 'social' and 'task' elements. **Social cohesion** refers to interpersonal attraction within the group; **task cohesion** is determined by how well the group works together.

Investigation 13.5 : To interpret a sociogram

Method: Look at the sociogram in Figure 13.15. The arrows represent choices, for example 'N' has nominated 'K' as a friend.

Can you identify the following individuals and subgroups:

a. a 'star'—someone who is chosen by many others
b. an isolate—someone who is not chosen by anyone else
c. a mutual pair—two people who choose each other?

Discussion: What effect might friendship patterns such as this have on the way the players interact as a team? How would you rate the cohesion of this group?

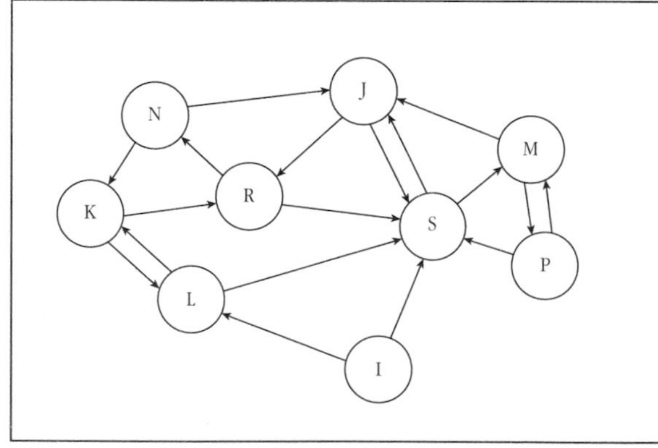

Figure 13.15 A friendship sociogram within a sports team.

Investigation 13.6 : To investigate the relationships between social cohesion, task cohesion and team success

Methods:

(i) Use one of the learning experiences described in Carron (1981) or Roberts *et al.* (1986), or

(ii) organize a tournament in your class or college in a small-team sport, such as basketball or volleyball, such that the teams can be ranked at the end. Select the teams so that intra-team friendship groups are avoided as far as possible. Ask the individual members of the teams who were ranked highest and lowest to complete the following simple questionnaire to assess task cohesion (Q1) and social cohesion (Q2).

Q1 Did the members of your team play well together?

9	8	7	6	5	4	3	2	1
very much							not at all	

Q2 Do the members of your team like one another?

9	8	7	6	5	4	3	2	1
very much							not at all	

Results: Calculate a mean score on each question for each team. From your results, draw a bar chart similar to that given in Figure 13.16.

Discussion: What do your results tell you about the relationship between task cohesion, social cohesion and team success?

Most coaches would accept that members of a team interact more effectively in task-oriented situations if they like, or at least respect, one another. This does not apply in just sport. Consider the implications for a climbing team or a dance company if excessive rivalry develops between its members.

Leadership

The development of team cohesion often depends on the **leadership** of the coach or team captain. Leadership has been defined in a variety of ways, but most definitions view it as the process by which a particular individual is instrumental in fulfilling the expectations of a group or team, and develops an environment in which the group is motivated, rewarded and helped to achieve its goals. Martens points out that it should not be confused with management, which deals with routine organization; leadership is about vision.

Analysis of the concept of leadership reveals two kinds of leader (Carron, 1981). **Emergent** leaders are those who come from the group itself, either informally because of their skills and abilities, or formally through nomination/selection. **Prescribed** leaders are those appointed by the organizing body. What do you see to be some of the advantages and difficulties for leaders themselves of being in each of these two categories?

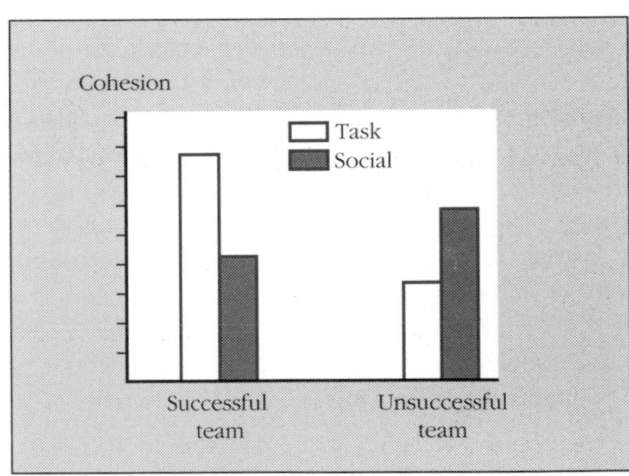

Figure 13.16 Task cohesion, social cohesion and team success.

Characteristics of Leaders

The characteristics of effective leadership are difficult to pin down, but it is generally recognized that there are three main factors which interact to affect a person's capacity to lead. These are represented in Figure 13.17.

Chelladurai's theory is that the more the leader's actual behaviour matches the expectations and preferences of the group, and the specific demands of the situation, the greater the group's satisfaction, enjoyment and performance will be. The problem is, however, that each group, and each activity context, is different, so defining just what these behaviours are is very difficult.

The results of research and your own experience of leading and being lead will help us to clarify these factors.

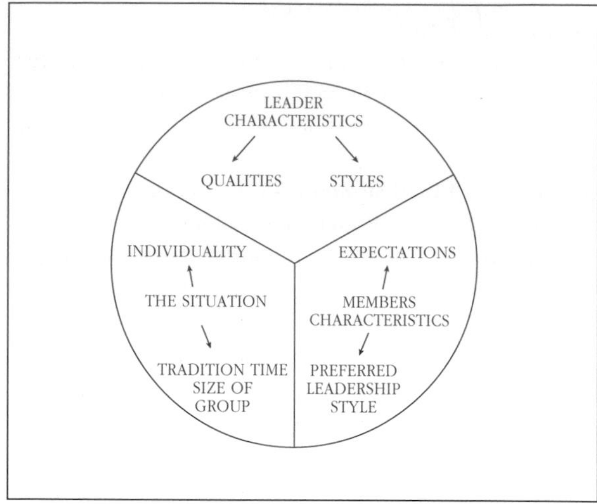

Figure 13.17 Components of leadership. (Adapted from Chelladurai, 1984.)

Investigation 13.7 : To identify the qualities of an effective leader

Method: From your own experience, make a list of the qualities you would associate with a good team captain. Compare your list with others and derive a definitive list of about twelve qualities which you all agree on. Think of opposites for these. For example, if you chose 'self-confident', the opposite might be 'diffident'. Construct a questionnaire by separating your opposites by a five-point scale, for example:

self-confident	5	4	3	2	1	diffident
unfriendly	1	2	3	4	5	friendly

Try out your scale on yourself. To get an overall score you will need to reverse the scoring on some items, e.g. unfriendly–friendly.

Discussion: How did you rate as a leader? Of course, you may have all these qualities and not be your team's captain; there are many other factors.

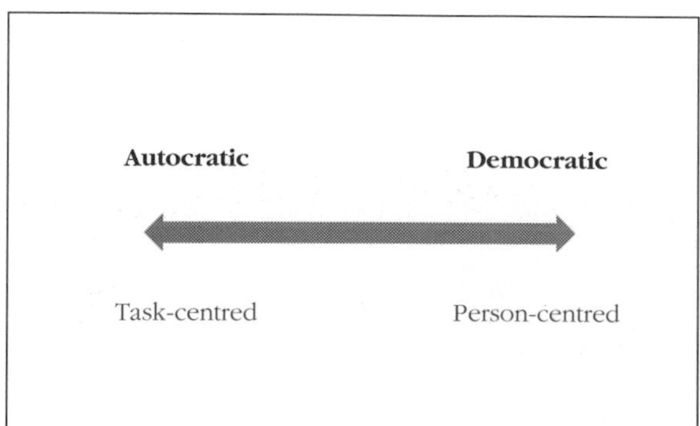

Figure 13.18 Leadership style.

One of these factors is leadership style. Two styles have been identified at opposite ends of a continuum (Fielder, 1967).

Of course, it is possible for a leader to adopt both styles, according to the situation, and a good coach or captain does this.

Situational Factors

There are a range of situational factors which a leader needs to be aware of in selecting an appropriate style. Research has shown that players in team sports look for a captain or coach who is directive and uses his/her authority to organize and structure the group. Individuals, for example skaters or athletes, prefer a more person-oriented approach. This seems to relate to the size of the group; the more team members there are, the less easy it is to take each person's individual needs and preferences into account. Similarly, if decisions have to be made quickly an autocratic style is usually adopted. Another interesting research finding, probably backed up by your own experience, is that groups tend to be traditional: once they have got used to a particular style they resent change.

Members' Characteristics

This leads us to the third section of the model (Figure 13.17). We tend to think of captains and coaches and leaders influencing the behaviour of the group members, but of course it works the other way too. If, for example, a team captain senses that the team is hostile, he/she will tend to develop a more autocratic style than if the team is friendly and co-operative. A team/group which is working towards a particular goal, an important competition, expedition or performance, will look towards the leader to help it succeed, and will have ideas about how this should be done—particularly if its members are experienced. Problems can arise if the strategies for training and preparation adopted by the leader do not match their expectations. Good leaders are sensitive to the expectations, knowledge and experience of group members.

You will find some interesting investigations on leadership in sport in Carron (1980) and Saunders and White (1977).

SOCIAL FACILITATION

Most of us involved in sport or dance recognize the effect that the presence of spectators has on the way we play or perform. This is known as **social facilitation**. People watching us **may** tend to make us nervous, but their presence often means that we try a little bit harder. Investigating these effects experimentally has interested sports psychologists for a long time, but there is still some difficulty in isolating the different variables operating. Early research, which contrasted performance **with** an audience with performance **without** one, proved unexpectedly inconclusive, until Zajonc (1965) clarified the terms which were being used. He first defined different kinds of audience. These are shown in Figure 13.19.

It is important for you to note that in this model, the **audience** and **co-actors** are completely passive; i.e. not communicating in any way with the performer. **Competitors** and **supporters** interact with him/her in a variety of ways. Co-actors are involved in the same activity at the same time as the performer, but are not competing directly.

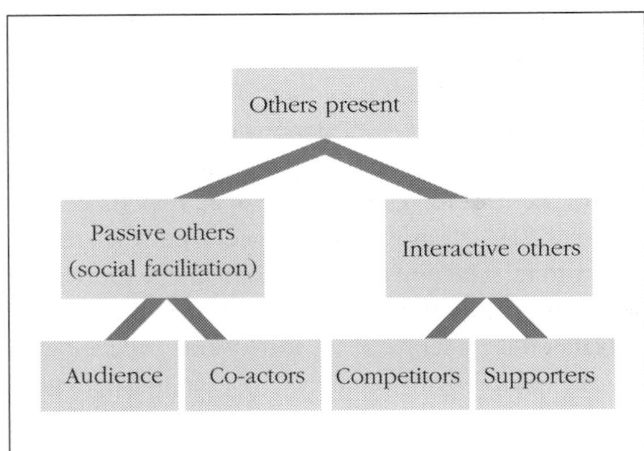

Figure 13.19 Different types of audience (adapted from Zajonc, 1965).

Investigation 13.8 : To interpret Figure 13.18

Method: Study Figure 13.18. Take each of the four categories of audience, co-actors, competitors and supporters, and give sport-related examples for each category. Remember that 'audience' and co-actors' are not interacting or communicating in any way with the performer. You may have to select particular periods in a game or event to illustrate these categories.

Discussion: Compare and discuss your ideas with others in the group.

Investigation 13.9 : To investigate whether performance on a simple endurance task is improved by the presence of (i) an audience and (ii) co-actors

Method: For the task, use a wall squat as illustrated at Figure 11.9. Divide the subjects available into three groups, A, B and C. Arrange your data collection so that all the subjects are timed on their ability to hold a wall squat under three different experimental conditions: (i) alone; (ii) in the presence of co-actors; (iii) in the presence of an audience. Measurements are taken in the following order:

Group A: audience, alone, co-actors;
Group B: co-actors, audience, alone;
Group C: alone, audience, co-actors.

Once you have got results from the three groups for three conditions, treat all three groups as one.

Results: Obtain a mean score for the three conditions and plot these on a bar chart, as in Figure 13.20.

Discussion: To what extent do your results match those in Figure 13.20? Explain any discrepancies.

What is the reason for collecting the data in groups? Does the presence of an experimenter pose a problem of validity?

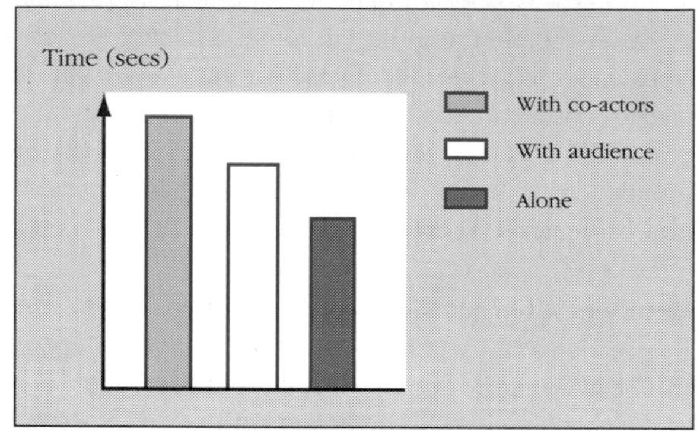

Figure 13.20 The hypothetical relationship between scores on an endurance task, under three different experimental conditions.

On the basis of this, Zajonc suggests that an audience affects a performer differentially, according to the part of the learning curve he/she is in. Experiments by Martens (1970) show that learners perform better alone than with an audience, but that experienced performers do better with an audience. Zajonc explains this in terms of an increase in psychological arousal caused by the audience. For the inexperienced performer, still in the associative phase of learning, this increase causes interference with the production of the skill, but for the expert the increased level of arousal is motivating. We will be considering this idea further in Section 13.5.

Thus, according to Zajonc, the mere presence of others creates arousal which then affects performance. Cottrell (1968) disputes this model and suggests that it is not 'mere presence' which creates arousal, but the fact that the audience may be perceived as evaluating the performance, thus creating what Cottrell calls **evaluation apprehension**.

There would seem to be still a lot of work for sport psychologists to do in this area. We do not fully understand audience effects, particularly aspects such as the 'home advantage', which is very obvious in professional football.

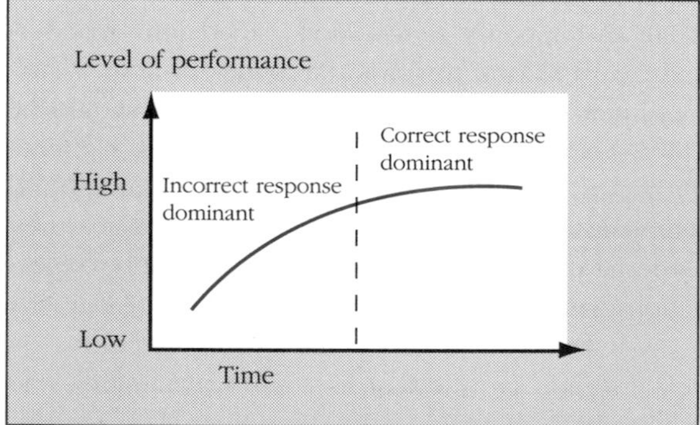

Figure 13.21 A learning curve to show the development of a correct dominant response.

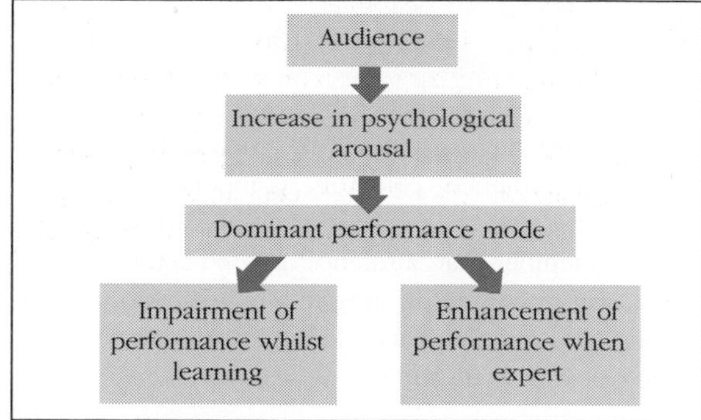

Figure 13.22 The relationship between audience, arousal level and performance.

AGGRESSION IN SPORT

The aggressive behaviour of players or spectators is one aspect of group interaction in sport which is currently attracting particular attention. As the rewards of winning become increasingly more substantial, at both professional and amateur levels, so emotions tend to run high and some players (and coaches) believe that almost any means can justify the end—that of winning. That is not to say that this is a modern phenomenon (look at some of the photographs of mob games in the 'history' section of this book!) but the organization and codification of games during the nineteenth century was designed to bring a spirit of control and 'fair play' to potentially violent activities.

Definitions of Aggression

One of the main difficulties in studying this area from a psychological point of view is that there can be confusion in defining the term, since we use the word extensively in everyday life. A good starting point for your study of aggression would be to video a game and then identify, and discuss as a group, all the incidents of aggressive behaviour you find. This will raise some interesting questions: Is a strong but fair tackle aggressive? Is it aggressive to shout at the referee? What about throwing your racket to the ground after a bad line call? Are some soccer fans' chants aggressive? The answers you arrive at will depend on how you define 'aggression'. In this section we will differentiate between aggression (as defined below) and **assertion** (which is forceful, decisive play): Sport psychologists generally agree that aggression is behaviour in which a deliberate intent to harm or injure others is evident (Gill 1986, page 196). Gill goes on to identify several issues which arise from this definition:

- aggression is behavioural, so willing or wishing harm to someone is not aggression and neither is anger, unless it is expressed as intention to harm
- aggression must be intentional, so accidentally causing injury or harm is not included in the definition
- the inclusion of the idea of 'harm' in the definition implies that aggression can be verbal if the words are such that they are intended to embarrass or hurt, but it seems to rule out 'eyeballing' an opponent
- the definition refers to other people, so smashing your racket into the ground would not be aggressive.

Taking this view of aggression as **hostile**, with the notion of intent to injure as central, we can see that the frequency of aggressive acts in sport is less than we might have at first thought. There may well be players who set out with the intent to injure, because their coach has told them to, or because they have a score to settle, or because taking out a skilful opponent will make victory more likely, or perhaps because they enjoy hurting others. But it is likely that these are very much a minority. What is probably more worrying to governing bodies of sport, and to those who value the socialising potential of sport, is the apparent increase in **instrumental aggression**, i.e. acts which whilst not having the intention to injure as the primary purpose, are carried out without due care for others, so that injury is a possible, or even likely, outcome. Invasion games and contact sports offer plenty of scope for this kind of behaviour. The difficulty is that in many games/sports the boundary between hostile aggression (which is nearly always illegal), instrumental aggression (which is sometimes condoned as merely hard play) and assertiveness is not easy to distinguish. This is a task for referees and officials, however. As sport psychologists we are concerned with how aggressive behaviour arises and its effects on the individuals concerned and on sport performance.

Theories of Aggression

There are three main groups of theories about aggression and each warrants further reading to fully appreciate what they have to say.

- **Instinct theories** (Lorenz, 1966). These theorists believe that aggression is innate and instinctive, developed through evolution to help us survive as a species. According to this theory, we all experience a build-up of aggression which must be released in some way. Sport is seen as an appropriate way of dissipating pent-up aggression; it acts as a catharsis. This is an interesting theory, but from your own experience, can you see any flaws in it?
- **Drive theories** (Dollard, 1939). The best known of these is the frustration–aggression hypothesis which suggests that frustration (being blocked in the achievement of a goal) causes a drive to be aggressive towards the source of the frustration. If this is a

person, then aggression automatically follows. This idea was amended (can you suggest why?) by Berkowitz (1974), who suggested that frustration causes anger, which in turn creates a 'readiness' aggression. The important point here is that anger is not a drive (which has to be resolved), but an emotion which people can learn to deal with.

- **Social learning theories** (Bandura, 1973). These theories claim that aggression is learned, in the same way that much other behaviour is learned. Bandura's experiments suggest that aggression is learnt by observation and by social reinforcement. This would suggest that if players are frequently exposed to the aggressive behaviour of others and particularly if they are praised/rewarded (either directly or indirectly) for their own aggression, then they are likely to develop aggressive responses to some situations in sport. However, an individual can also learn non-aggressive ways of dealing with the same situations; hence the importance of teachers and coaches establishing clear, unambiguous behavioural codes for themselves and their players and helping players deal positively with sources of frustration.

A number of questions arise from these theories and from observing examples of aggressive play or spectator violence. Whereas sport psychology is addressing these questions there is some way to go before definitive statements can be made. The answers given below are therefore speculative but are suggested by the research.

Does competition cause aggression? Probably not directly, but it can lead to frustration, and to provocative behaviour by opponents, both of which may prompt aggressive responses. There is also some evidence that sport increases arousal levels and that this causes people to over-react or make wrong judgements.

Does participation in sport reduce aggression or prevent people being aggressive in non-sport settings? Probably not, though there are many 'common-sense' claims that this is the case.

Does watching a 'bad-tempered' game cause spectators to be more violent towards each other? Research does tend to show that watching aggressive sport does increase feelings of hostility and therefore the likelihood of aggressive acts.

Does aggressive behaviour aid or inhibit sport performance? If we relate assertive behaviour with arousal levels, theory suggests that up to a certain point, we need to be assertive to be playing/performing at our best, but that normally aggression is associated with over-arousal, which in turn will interfere with decision making and concentration.

ATTITUDES IN SPORT

Whether or not you are a player who tends towards aggressive behaviour will, to some extent, depend upon your attitude to sport and its purposes and in particular to winning and losing.

Attitudes are a combination of beliefs and feelings about objects or people or situations which predispose us to behave in a certain way towards them. Thus if I feel angry about being constantly fouled by my opponent I may well behave aggressively towards her; more positively, if you believe it to be important to keep fit and enjoy exercise, then you are likely to participate in sport, or an exercise programme, regularly.

This relationship between attitude and behaviour is not quite as simple as this, however. Can you think of any examples from your experience when having a particular attitude about something does not necessarily mean you do anything about it? However, if your attitude includes an intention to behave in a particular way, then research shows that you are likely to follow your intention. Thus:

Attitude - - - Behavioural Intention - - - Behaviour

So although I might believe in the value of exercise, I am much more likely to actually exercise regularly if I also plan to do so.

Research into attitudes to and in sport tends to focus on establishing the views of particular groups about issues or situations. Some examples are:

- children's attitudes to their school PE programmes
- women's views on the availability of sport opportunities in their area
- athletes' attitudes to training
- teachers' attitudes to the physical and intellectual abilities of black children
- general attitudes to women in sport.

The results of this research show no general patterns of attitude to sport, which is to be expected, since attitude is by definition an individual variable.

Research into the value of Physical Education in schools has shown generally positive attitudes of teachers, parents and pupils, though pupils are somewhat more critical of the content of the programme. Society seems to becoming more egalitarian in its view of women in sport, though evidence of gender stereotyping still exists, as does racial stereotyping.

This research is based on measurement of attitudes. This may be done in a variety of ways. Since attitude is closely linked with behaviour, we can observe, record and analyse people's behaviour in situations which are likely to reflect their attitudes and then infer their attitudes from that behaviour.

Can you think of some sport and non-sport examples of how you might do this? For example, how might you collect information about students' attitudes to the meals provided in your school/college canteen?

There are problems of validity with such methods, however, and the most usual form of attitude measurement is a scale. A scale is a questionnaire which has been carefully constructed to be valid and reliable and to give a score for an individual on a particular attitude. There are three major types of scales, named after their authors: **Thurstone scales**, **Likert scales** and **Osgood Semantic Differential scales**. They differ slightly in their construction, but all consist of asking respondents to indicate the extent to which they agree or disagree with a particular statement. Investigation 13.11 contains an informal example of such a scale. Gill (1986, page 98) gives a useful comparison of the different types.

There are two important things to remember about attitude scales.

(i) They appear simple to construct, but in fact it is very difficult to ensure that you have composed a valid and reliable measure. If you wish to use an attitude scale in an investigation it is sensible to use one that has already been constructed and validated for the attitude which you are interested in.

(ii) Although scales are composed of a number of questions, each scale represents the same attitude (though you may have more than one scale in a questionnaire). Ensuring that you are only dealing with one attitude with the questions you have constructed is one of the problems affecting validity.

13.4 Motivation

KEY WORDS AND CONCEPTS

performance	**achievement motivation**	**attribution**
intrinsic motivation	**personality**	
extrinsic motivation	**situational factors**	

In Section 12.1, we briefly considered motivation as a factor in the learning process. In this section we study it as a factor in **performance,** particularly in terms of the role it plays in people's continuing participation in physical activity.

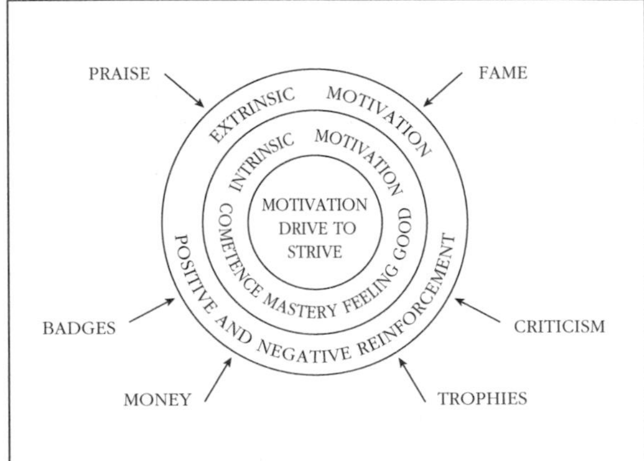

Figure 13.23 Intrinsic and extrinsic motivation.

Intrinsic and extrinsic motivation

Figure 13.23 identifies two forms of motivation, **intrinsic** and **extrinsic**. People who are intrinsically motivated pursue an activity for its own sake, for the pride and satisfaction they achieve, regardless of what anyone else thinks of their efforts. Extrinsic motivation stems from other people, through **positive** and **negative reinforcement**, (see Section 12.1), and from **tangible rewards** such as trophies, badges and payment (for professionals).

Behavioural psychologists have, for many years, recognized the power of extrinsic rewards to develop and modify behaviour. A very basic principle of human behaviour is the Law of Effect, which states that rewarding a particular behaviour increases the probability that that behaviour will be repeated. Coaches and teachers recognize this and many of the governing bodies of sport have produced **award schemes**, which encourage youngsters to work at skills in order to increase their proficiency and thus be awarded a badge or certificate.

Extrinsic rewards			**Intrinsic sources**
Tangible	**Intangible**		
Badges	**negative**	**positive**	Satisfaction
Trophies	criticism	praise	Achievement
Certificates	defeat	fame	Feeling good
Money		winning	

Figure 13.24 Extrinsic rewards and intrinsic sources.

Investigation 13.10 : To identify a range of governing body award schemes

Method: Go to your local/school/college library and look up the magazines and journals produced by the governing bodies of sport, e.g. *The Swimming Times*. Note details of any award schemes which are described. As a class group write to several governing bodies, asking for details of their award schemes.

Analyse these schemes in terms of the age range for which the award is designed; the level of difficulty of each stage of the award; the nature of the award (certificate, badge, etc.); the general attractiveness of the presentation; and the potential interest which the award might generate in its target population.

Until recently, few would have questioned the appropriateness or effectiveness of such schemes. It was assumed that extrinsic rewards would encourage initial participation, and that adding an extrinsic reward to a situation in which youngsters were already intrinsically motivated at best increased motivation, and at worst did no harm.

Recent research has led us to question this, however.

intrinsic motivation + extrinsic reward = ?

Deci (1971) and Lepper, Greene and Nisbett (1973) show that, in certain circumstances, adding external reward to a situation that is already intrinsically motivating actually **decreases that intrinsic motivation** and may eventually replace it, so that when the reward is no longer available interest in the activity wanes.

Can you suggest some explanations for these findings? Can you think any occasions when you have found the receipt of an extrinsic reward irrelevant or even de-motivating?

Explanations which have been suggested:

- the reward acts as a distraction to the sportsperson's intrinsic desire to work at his/her own pace;
- individuals may feel that being given a reward turns what they thought of as play into work and thus changes the nature of
  - (i) the relationship between themselves and the person giving the reward and
  - (ii) the activity itself;
- people like to determine their own behaviour; participating for the sake of a reward makes them feel that someone or something else is in charge.

Does this mean that we should scrap all award schemes, leagues, certificates etc.? Certainly not. Rewards do not automatically undermine intrinsic motivation. They may be used to attract youngsters to an activity they might not otherwise try, or to revive flagging motivation, or to get an athlete over a bad period in his/her training. The psychological borderline between intangible extrinsic rewards such as praise and fame and the intrinsic rewards of satisfaction and sense of achievement is by no means clear. Thus, if extrinsic rewards provide information about levels of achievement and competence, they will enhance motivation. However, current thinking does suggest that as intrinsic motivation and participation for its own sake develops, so tangible rewards become redundant and should be withdrawn or used very sparingly.

Achievement Motivation

So far we have considered motivation in terms of the sportsperson's interest in participating in physical activity. In taking this stance, we have recognized that an important part of intrinsic motivation stems from perceived success in achieving competence and mastery. An individual's drive to achieve success for its own sake is known as **achievement motivation**. In sportspeople this is closely related to competitiveness; in other aspects of physical activity, we would refer to the persistence of a climber in the face of difficulties, for example, or the striving for perfection of a dancer. Achievement motivation is about what happens when we are faced with a choice to seek out or to avoid situations where we might or might not be successful. For example, you might have a choice of routes to climb on a rock face, or of opponents to make up your school–college fixture list. Which or who do you choose? Research shows that two factors contribute to the decision: personality and situation.

Personality

Atkinson (1974) suggests that there are two personality factors contributing to achievement motivation:

a. the need to achieve (Nach); and
b. the need to avoid failure (Naf).

These are shown in Figure 13.25.

We all have both characteristics, but those with a high need to achieve usually tend to have a low need to avoid failure (subject 'A'), and those who have a high need to avoid failure generally have a low need to achieve (subject 'B'). What is not so clear to sport psychologists are the characteristics of people who might appear in the other two quadrants (Gill, 1986).

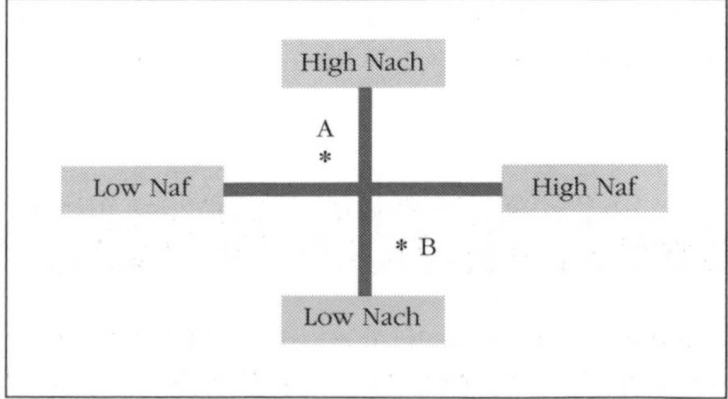

Figure 13.25 The personality components of achievement motivation.

This aspect of personality explains why some people seek out success while others avoid situations where they might be seen to fail, but it does not give the full picture or account for behaviour in those **situations** where someone is committed to participate, but the level of task difficulty can be chosen; for example, deciding on an easy or difficult rock route once you have arrived at the base of the cliff.

Situational factors

We judge the situation in terms of:

a. the probability of success; and

b. the incentive value of that success.

This is shown in Figure 13.26 and is derived from the work of Atkinson (1974). The model shows that if the probability of success is low (for example, if you were playing squash against a world class player), the incentive value of success is high (you would be very excited if you won). Similarly, if you are playing against weak opposition, winning doesn't mean so much to you.

Research (e.g. Roberts, 1974) shows that people with a low achievement orientation (high failure avoidance) tend to choose tasks which are either very easy or very difficult. Can you suggest why this is? High achievers, however, tend to select tasks where there is a fifty–fifty chance of success. Thus, high achievers tend to be risk takers.

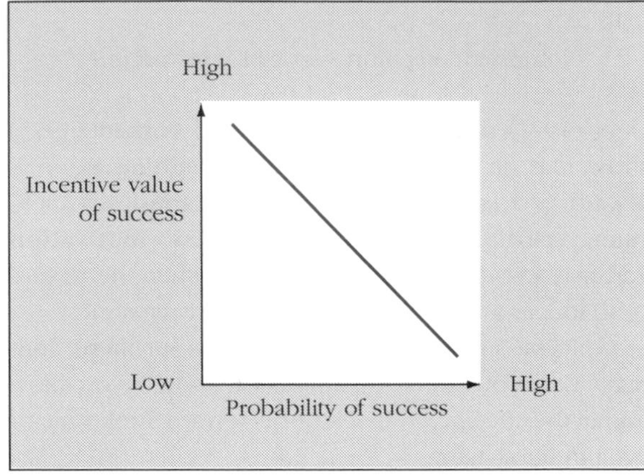

Figure 13.26

Investigation 13.11 : To investigate the hypothesis that high achievers are high risk takers

Method: Select a group of subjects who are not aware of the nature of the experiment.

1. Measure the achievement motivation of your subjects either by using the Lynn Survey of Achievement Motivation (Carron, 1981) or by means of the following scale (circle the score which most represents your feelings about each of the paired statements):

1. Success in sport is very important to me.	5	4	3	2	1	Winning doesn't matter; it's the game that counts.
2. I prefer to play opponents I know I can beat.	1	2	3	4	5	I like playing opponents who are about my level.
3. I enjoy a challenge.	5	4	3	2	1	I like doing things I know I will succeed in.
4. I don't enjoy close games.	5	4	3	2	1	I enjoy a close game.
5. I don't worry about the result of a game.	1	2	3	4	5	I don't like having to tell people I lost a game.
6. I tend to make errors when I'm under pressure.	5	4	3	2	1	I play best when I'm under pressure.

Scoring: Statements 1–3 are achievement orientation scores, and statements 4–6 are failure avoidance scores.

3–6: Low achiever/avoider

7–10: Average achiever/avoider

11–15: High achiever/avoider

(Note that this is an informal scale and has not been tested for validity and reliability.)

2. Set up a basketball/netball shooting task (Figure 13.27). Each subject has ten shots from a point of her/his choice on a line drawn at a radius of four metres from the base of the post. Scores are noted.

The next ten shots can be taken from anywhere. Subjects are told that successful shots will be added to their score, but they will be penalized for unsuccessful shots by the deduction of one point from their overall score. Record scores for feedback purposes, but for the **purposes of the research**, note whether each of the second ten shots was taken from nearer the post than the first ten (1 point), from the same place (2 points), or from further away (3 points). Total the **points** (not the scores) for the ten shots.

10–15: Low risk taker
16–24: Average risk taker
25–30: High risk taker

Results: Draw two scattergrams which correlate:
(i) achievement and
(ii) failure avoidance with risk taking.

Figure 13.27

Atkinson's theory suggests that your achievement graph will look something like Figure 13.28. Does it?

Discussion: Analyse your findings and discuss any discrepancies you note between your results and the hypothetical ones in Figure 13.28.

De-brief your subjects on what the experiment was about and what their shots scores were. Why is it important to do this? Bear in mind what you know about the **ethics** of psychological investigation.

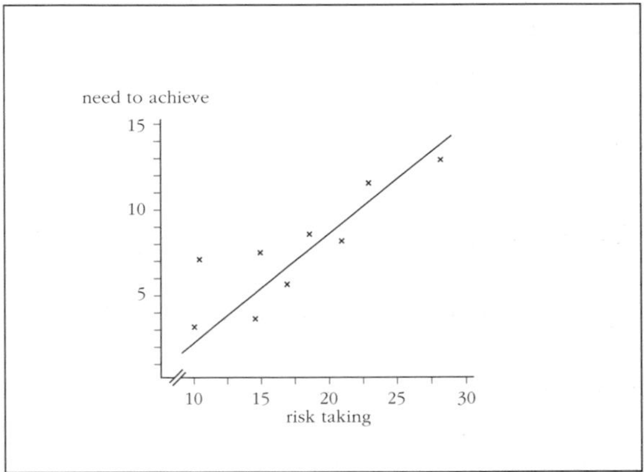

Figure 13.28 The relationship between need to achieve and risk taking.

Investigation 13.12 : To introduce the concept of attribution

Method: Play a small-sided game such as basketball, netball or five-a-side soccer. Play to a result, i.e. avoid a draw. After the game, each player individually writes down four reasons why they think **their own** team won or lost. In addition, each states whether or not they would like to play against the same team again, with the same team-mates, in the near future.

Discussion: As a class group, pool these statements. Categorize them into groups of similar reasons, e.g. 'we played well as a team' with we had some good players'. These reasons are known as **attributions.** How many categories did you construct? Consider the relationship between wanting/not wanting to play again and winning/losing? Does any pattern emerge?

THE ATTRIBUTION PROCESS

The process of ascribing reasons for, or causes to, events and behaviours is known as **attribution**. When something significant happens to us, such as winning or losing an important game, we ask ourselves 'why?'. Sport psychologists have asked two important questions about this:

a. What sorts of reasons do sportspersons give?
b. How does this affect their future participation and chances of success?

Weiner's (1974) attributional theory of achievement behaviour has been widely applied to sport contexts. He suggests that one of the differences between high and low achievers (see p. 307) is the way in which each group develops attributions about success and failure. He proposes a model of four types of attribution. This is shown in Figure 13.29.

Weiner's four types of attribution are:

a. **Ability:** the extent of the performer's capacity to cope with the task.
b. **Effort:** the amount of mental and physical effort the performer gave to the task.
c. **Task difficulty:** the extent of the problems posed by the task, including the strength of the opposition.
d. **Luck:** factors attributable to chance, such as the weather or the state of the pitch.

To what extent did your categories derived in Investigation 13.12 correspond to these?

Weiner also organized his categories into two dimensions (see Figure 13.29) which he termed **locus of causality** and **stability**. The word 'locus' is derived from the Latin 'place'; thus the 'locus of causality' indicates where the individual perceives the cause of success or failure to lie. In this case, the two categories are internal (ability and effort) or external to the individual (task difficulty and luck). The stability dimension implies that two of the factors (ability and task difficulty) are relatively stable, i.e. not subject to change, in the short term at least, whereas the other two (effort and luck) can vary from competition to competition or even within an activity.

Weiner did not claim that these dimensions were exclusive and further research (Weiner, 1979) has identified a third, that of **controllability**. This is the extent to which the outcome of a situation is under control (by the individual or others) or is uncontrollable.

How do these attributions affect a sportsperson's view of his/her sport?

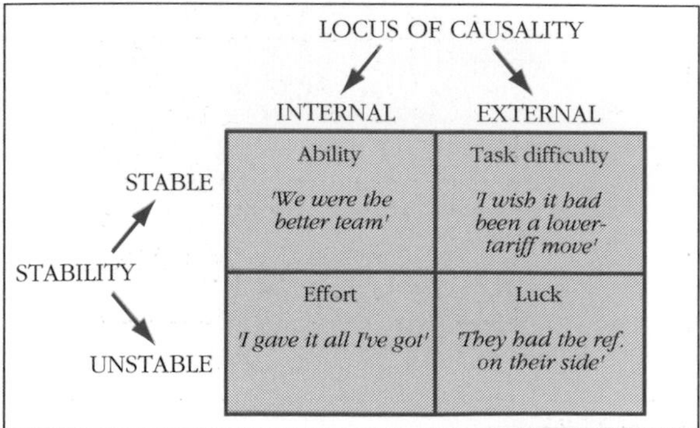

Figure 13.29 Weiner's model of causal attribution.

Figure 13.30 The Control Dimension!

1. Feelings of pride and dissatisfaction (affective responses)

Figure 13.31 shows the results that were obtained when two teams of basketball players were asked to state the extent to which they felt satisfied with their performance after a game, in terms of the four categories of attribution. These results would appear to be fairly typical (Weiner, 1974) and suggest that if we attribute our success in an activity to internal factors, such as ability and effort, we are more likely to feel satisfaction with our performance than if we put our winning down to luck or the ease of the task. In the same way, we experience greater feelings of disappointment if we perceive our losing to be due to internal rather than external factors.

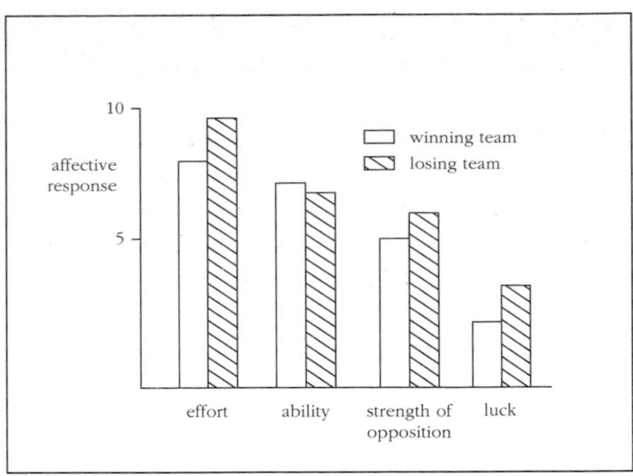

Figure 13.31 Affective responses and attributions.

2. Expectancy

In addition to predicting the probability of a performer feeling satisfaction or disappointment with the outcome of an activity, the attribution theory attempts to explain the way in which we come to **expect** certain things to happen.

Investigation 13.13 : To investigate the effect of attribution on the expectation of subsequent success or failure

Method: Select a group of students who do not know the purpose of the task. Divide this group into four.

1. Devise four motor tasks, one for each group. The tasks should have a clear goal to be attained and should be as follows:
   a. **luck** plays a major part in success or failure; e.g. throwing a dice for a specified number (code letter U);
   b. **effort** plays a major part; e.g. improving previous performance on a simple strength task (code letter U);
   c. **ability** is of importance—any novel motor task (code letter S);
   d. **task difficulty** is central—this can be simulated by selecting a relatively simple task, but distracting the performer during it (code letter S).

   The code letters refer to whether the task is likely to produce stable or unstable reasons for the result.
2. Measure the subjects' performance in their particular task by noting whether they succeed or fail.
3. Suggest to them that they are going to do the task again (in fact they are not). Ask each subject whether they think they are going to succeed or fail at the second attempt.
4. Mark each subject in one of the boxes in Figure 13.32: for example, if they succeeded in their task but couldn't predict the outcome of the proposed second attempt, they would be marked in box 'C'. Mark the subject with a letter to correspond with the attribution task they did, as in Figure 13.32.

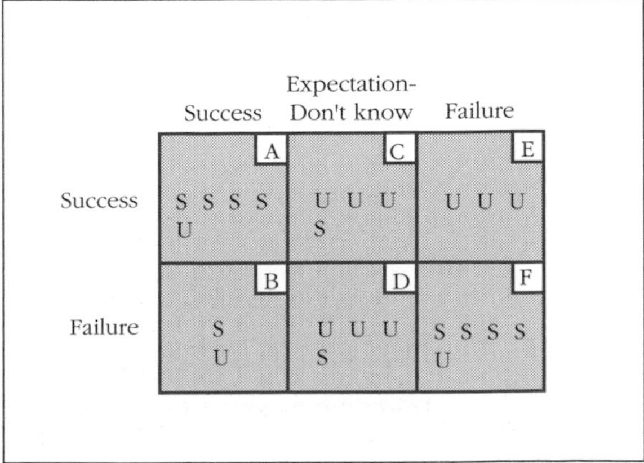

Figure 13.32

Discussion: Theory suggests that you might obtain results as in Figure 13.32. If you did not, can you offer an explanation? Do you think the hypothesis is faulty, or was there something different or special about your sample or your method. For example, do you think it is legitimate to assume that the subjects would attribute success/failure in the way suggested by the tasks?

Figure 13.32 suggests that people who attribute success or failure in an activity to stable factors are more likely to expect the same outcome next time they perform than if unstable attributions are made.

3. Learned helplessness

Why is it that some people seem to give up very easily if a task is difficult? If you ask some of your non-sporting friends why they don't join, for example, the badminton club, the initial response will probably be 'I don't like sport' but if you persist you may get answers such as 'I'm no good at badminton', 'I never was any good and I never will be' or 'I'm useless at all sport'. Dweck (1980) calls this **learned helplessness** and sees the cause as the individual attributing early difficulties to internal, stable and global factors. The **global/specific** dimension relates to whether failure is seen to be specific to the particular activity or generalized to other areas of sport ('I'm useless at sport' is a global attribution). The attribution process can be summarized by Figure 13.33.

Clearly, the attribution theory carries implications for coaches and trainers. Performers are more likely to do well if they think they are going to do so, and this in turn depends on how they attributed their success and failure in the past. It is part of the coach's job to help the performer achieve initial success and then attribute this to stable, internal and controllable factors.

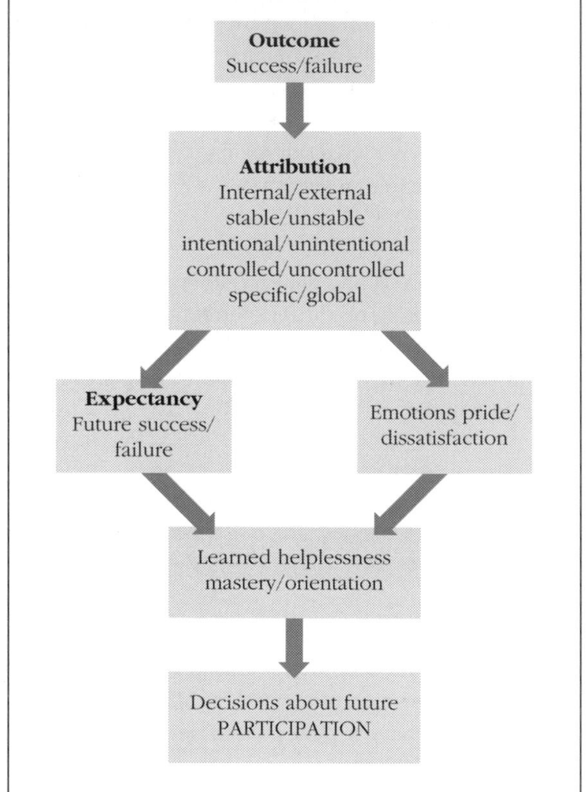

Figure 13.33 The attribution process.

Summary

1. Most sports and activities take place within a social context, in groups. A group is defined as two or more people who are interacting with each other. In general, the most skilful individuals make the best sports team, but co-ordination and motivation are controlling factors. In sports where the need for co-operation between team members is high coaches will take the interactional skills of the players into account, and will try to develop social cohesion since it would appear that members of a team interact more effectively during the game if they like/respect one another.

   Leadership is an important element in the effectiveness of a team or squad. It is the process by which an individual is instrumental in fulfilling the expectations of the group.
2. Social facilitation is the effect that certain types of audience have on performance. Four types of audience have been identified: passive audiences, co-actors, competitors and supporters. Audiences appear to have both positive and negative effects on performers: learners perform better alone than with an audience and experienced performers do better with an audience. One theory suggests that the mere presence of others has an effect, another that it is the perceived evaluation ability of the audience that inhibits or enhances performance.
3. Motivation can be categorized into intrinsic and extrinsic forms. Extrinsic rewards have a powerful effect in developing and modifying behaviour. In certain circumstances, adding an external reward to a situation that is already intrinsically motivating decreases that motivation. Rewards do not automatically undermine intrinsic motivation, but current thinking suggests that as intrinsic motivation and participation for their own sake develop, so tangible rewards become redundant and should be withdrawn or used very sparingly.
4. An individual's drive to achieve success for its own sake is known as achievement motivation. Four factors contribute to this: two personality factors—the need to achieve and the need to avoid failure; and two situational factors—the probability of success and the incentive value of that success. Research shows that people with a low achievement orientation tend to choose tasks which are either very easy or very difficult, whereas high achievers tend to select tasks where there is a 50–50 chance of success.
5. The process of ascribing reasons for, or causes to, events is known as attribution. Weiner (1974) suggested that one of the differences between high and low achievers is the way in which each group develops attributions about success and failure. He developed two dimensions of attribution: locus of causality, and stability. Later, other dimensions were added. If success in an activity is attributed to internal factors, such as ability and effort, satisfaction with performance is more likely to be felt than if external attributions, e.g. task difficulty or luck, are involved. In addition to the emotions of pride in, or dissatisfaction with, performance, certain expectations of outcome (future success or failure) accrue. Sportspeople who attribute success or failure in a task to stable factors are more likely to expect the same outcome next time than if unstable factors are involved. Attribution theory contains many implications for coaches.

REFERENCES

Alkinson J.W. The mainsprings of achievement—oriented activity. In: Alkinson J.W. and Raynor J.O. (eds), *Motivation and Achievement,* New York, Halstead, 1974.

Bandura A. *Aggression: A Social Learning Analysis,* Englewood Cliffs, N.J., Prentice Hall, 1973.

Berkovitz L. *Roots of Aggression,* New York, Atherton Press, 1969.

Bult D.S. *Psychology of Sport,* New York, Van Nostrand Reinhold, 1987.

Bunker L.K. and McGuire R.T. Give sport psychology to sport. In: Bunker L.K. *et al. Sport Psychology,* Ithaca, N.Y., Mouvement Publications, 1985.

Carron A.V. *Social Psychology of Sport: an Experimental Approach,* Ithaca, N.Y., Mouvement Publications, 1981.

Carron A.V. and Ball J. An analysis of the cause–effect characteristics of cohesiveness and participation motivation in inter-collegiate hockey, *International Review of Sport Sociology,* 2, 49–60, 1977.

Chelladurai P. Leadership in sports. In: Silva J.M. and Weinberg R.S. *Psychological Foundations of Sport,* Champaign, Ill., Human Kinetics, 1984.

Cottrell N.B. Performance in the presence of other human beings: mere presence, audience and affiliation effects. In: Simmell E.C. *et al.* (eds.) *Social Facilitation and Imitative Behaviour,* Boston, Allyn and Bacon, 1968.

Cratty B.J. and Hannin Y.L. *The Athlete in the Sports Team,* Denver, Love Publications, 1980.

Deci E. Effects of externally mediated rewards on intrinsic motivation *Journal of Personality and Social Psychology,* 18, 105–115, 1971.

Dollard J. *et al. Frustration and Aggression,* New Haven, Yale UP, 1939.

Dweck C. Learned helplessness in sport. In: Nedeau C. *et al.* (eds.) *Psychology of Motor Behaviour and Sport,* Champaign, Ill., Human Kinetics, 1980.

Eysenck H.J. *The Biological Basis of Behaviour,* Springfield, Ill., Thomas, 1969.

Fiedler F.E. *A Theory of Leadership Effectiveness,* New York, McGraw-Hill, 1967.

Fox K. The child's perspective in physical education: Part 5, the self-esteem complex, *British Journal of Physical Education,* 19, 6, 247–252, 1988.

Gill D.L. Individual and group performance in sport, In: Silva J.M. and Weinberg R.S., *Psychological Foundations of Sport,* Champaign, Ill., Human Kinetics, 1984.

Harris P. *Designing and Reporting Experiments,* Milton Keynes, OUP, 1986.

Jones M.B. Regressing group on individual effectiveness, *Organisational Behaviour and Human Performance,* 11, 426–451, 1974.

Klein M. and Christiansen G. Group composition, group structure and group effectiveness of a basketball team. In: Loy J.W. and Kenyon G.S. (eds.), *Sport, Culture and Society,* New York, Macmillan, 1969.

Lepper M., Greene D. and Nisbett R. Undermining children's intrinsic interest with extrinsic rewards, *Journal of Personality and Social Psychology,* 28, 129–137, 1973.

Lorenz K. *On Aggression,* Harcourt Brace and World, 1966.

Martens R. Social reinforcement effects on pre-school children's motor performance, *Perceptual and Motor Skills,* 81, 787–792, 1970.

McGrath J.E. *Groups: Interaction and Performance,* Englewood-Cliffs, N.J., Prentice-Hall, 1984.

Roberts G.C. Effect of achievement motivation and social environment on performance of a motor task, *Journal of Motor Behaviour,* 4, 37–46, 1974.

Roberts G.C. et al. *Learning Experiences in Sport Psychology,* Champaign, Ill., Human Kinetics, 1986.

Saunders E. and White G.B. *Social Investigation in Physical Education and Sport,* London, Lepus Books, 1977.

Sheldon W.H. and Stevens S.S. *The Varieties of Temperament: A Psychology of Constitutional Differences,* New York, Harper and Row, 1942.

Weiner B. *Achievement Motivation and Attribution Theory,* Morristown, N.J., General Learning Press, 1974.

Weiner B. A theory of motivation for some classroom experiences, *Journal of Educational Psychology,* 71, 3–25, 1979.

Williams K. *et al.* Identifiability and social loafing: two cheering experiments, *Journal of Personality and Social Psychology,* 40, 303–311, 1981.

Zajonc R.B. Social facilitation, *Science,* 149, 269–274, 1965.

FURTHER READING

Biddle S. and Fox F. The child's perspective in physical education, Parts 2 & 4, *British Journal of Physical Education,* 19, 2 & 4/5, 1988.

Gill D.L. *Psychological Dynamics of Sport,* Champaign, Ill., Human Kinetics, 1986.

Silva J.M. and Weinberg R.S. *Psychological Foundations of Sport,* Champaign, Ill., Human Kinetics, 1984.

13.5 Optimizing Performance

KEY WORDS AND CONCEPTS

arousal	**stress**	**biofeedback**
trait anxiety	**GAS**	**self-confidence**
state anxiety	**PRT**	**goal-setting**

AROUSAL AND PERFORMANCE

Most of us have at some time or another felt keyed up before an important sport performance. Perhaps it was the first time your parents watched you play, or at a selection trial, or before a college dance performance.

The term we use for this state of alertness and anticipation is **arousal.** You will recognize the physical symptoms: your heart beats faster, your breathing quickens, you sweat more. As you get more nervous, these symptoms increase and you may feel sick or shaky, or your mouth may feel dry.

Arousal then has both physiological and cognitive components; the mind interacts with the body. The purpose of arousal is to prepare the body for action. When we are just waking from sleep, arousal level is very low. As more demands are made on the body, so arousal level is raised to cope with these demands. Arousal is a function of the autonomic nervous system and is a response that was built in to our central nervous system as we evolved. When danger threatened our primitive ancestors, they had to be immediately ready to fight or run.

Coaches and sport psychologists are very aware of arousal in sport and the effect it has on performers; they try to manipulate it, for example by 'psyching up' a team for an important event in the hope that a good performance will result, or by calming down a nervous athlete. We need to be aware of it ourselves so that we can control our own level of arousal. So what do the theories tell us?

Drive Theory

One influential approach is Drive Theory. You have already met it as the basis for Zajonc's theory of social facilitation (see Section 13.3).

Drive theory proposes that as arousal increases to meet the perceived demands of the task, so the performance is more likely to reflect the most usual behaviour (dominant habit). If you have not learned a skill very well, the dominant performance habit is full of mistakes and, as arousal increases, so will the number of mistakes you make. If you are an expert, the dominant habit is correct, effective technique and judgement and you may well play even better as your arousal level increases.

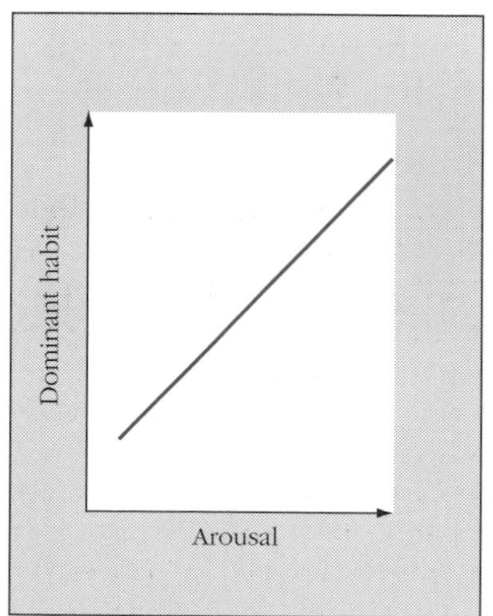

Figure 13.34 Drive Theory.

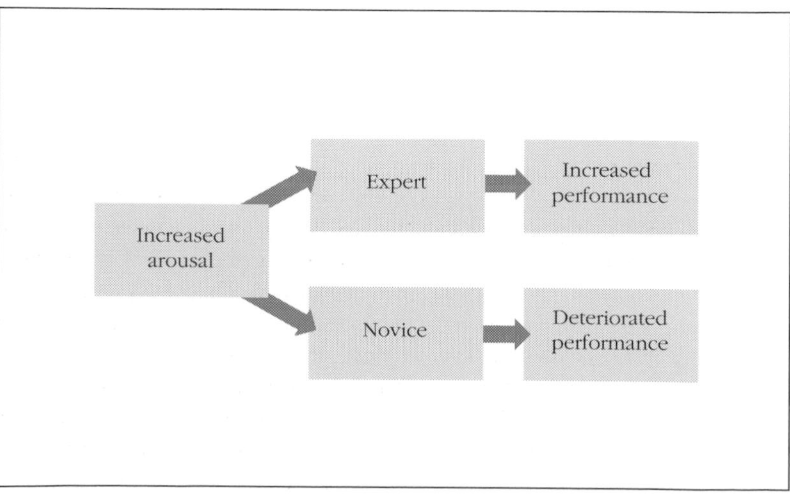

Figure 13.35 The effect of arousal on experts and novices according to Drive Theory.

Inverted U Theory

The problem with Drive Theory is that it does not easily explain the 'choking' effect at an important event that can occur with even the most experienced sportsperson. A more currently acceptable theory is the Inverted U Theory (hypothesis).

This suggests that, up to a certain point (A in Figure 13.36), arousal levels are too low for best performances. The sportsperson is just not 'psyched up' enough. But there comes a point (B in Figure 13.36) when arousal turns to anxiety and performance seems to deteriorate; the sportsperson is 'psyched out'. Between these two points is an optimal arousal zone, at which performers are able to give of their best. This has not been an easy theory to verify for reasons discussed below, but Sonstroem and Bernardo (1982) have obtained some confirmatory results using female university basketball players during competition.

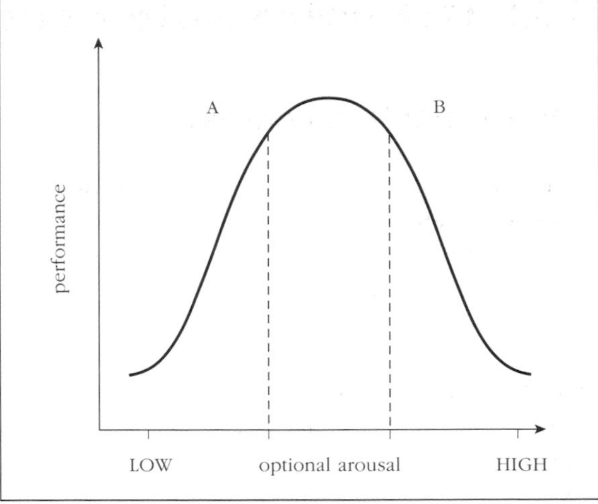

Figure 13.36 The Inverted U Theory.

Individual differences

REVIEW QUESTIONS

What does the graph in Figure 13.37 tell you about the three athletes whose arousal curves are depicted?

1. Who is capable of the best performance?
2. Who needs to be really psyched up before he performs at his best?
3. Whose level of arousal needs to be very carefully controlled for good performance?

Your answers should be 1. Sam, 2. Jon and 3. Ted.

You should note, however, that these are stylized graphs. Actual arousal-performance curves are much more variable than these.

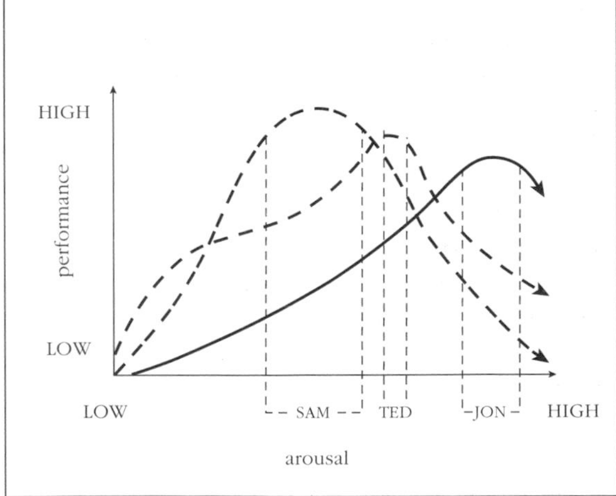

Figure 13.37 Individual differences in the optimal arousal zone. (Adapted from Martens, 1989.)

Task Differences

It is not possible to predict exactly what level of arousal is best for any one sport activity; so much will depend on circumstance and the personalities of the competitors, but there are some general rules which help competitors and coaches.

1. **Simple and complex tasks**—we consider it to be easier to kick a penalty in rugby from in front of the posts than from the side-line. What we usually mean in saying that a task is easier is that there is a greater margin for deviation from the movement plan, whilst still staying within the boundaries of successful execution. Note that we are referring here to **inherently** simple and complex tasks. Obviously, a task becomes easier for an individual to perform as he/she becomes more practiced at it. Thus, simple tasks have a broader optimal arousal zone than complex tasks; that is, they can tolerate greater arousal levels before successful turns into unsuccessful performance.

2. **Fine and gross tasks**—as with complex tasks, fine motor tasks have less margin for error than gross motor tasks; they require precision of movement. Compare putting in golf with weightlifting. If you watch these two sports on television you will notice

that a golfer tries to relax and calm down before putting, whilst the weightlifter really tries to 'psych himself up'. Gross motor tasks can tolerate greater levels of arousal before errors start than can fine motor tasks.

3. **Strength/endurance and information processing tasks**—another difference between golf putting and weightlifting is that the former has information processing as a key component. High arousal levels seem to interfere with information processing; thus skills in which this is important are more likely to be adversely affected than skills such as weightlifting in which the performer's concern is to summon as much of his/her strength and/or endurance as possible.

Figure 13.38 illustrates the optimal arousal levels for the six types of task we have been discussing, but again you should note that these are largely hypothetical and that obtaining research data which confirms the relationships indicated is not easy. What seems to be clear from experience, however, is that:

a. optimal arousal levels can be identified;
b. these vary across individuals and activities;
c. ability to control arousal is the key to successful performance. (Gill, 1986).

Martens (1989) has put forward an interesting critique of arousal theory, suggesting that it is more useful to think in terms of positive and negative psychic energy. This discussion is outside the scope of this book, but interested students might like to follow up his ideas by reading further.

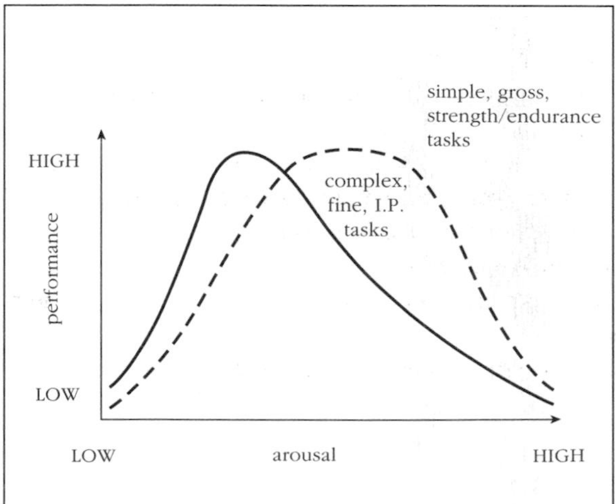

Figure 13.38 Arousal–performance curve for gross/fine, simple/complex and strength/IP motor tasks.

ANXIETY

You will now be aware that a certain level of arousal is necessary for your best possible performance in sport. Arousal responses are generated by a variety of means; some are automatic, some are associated with emotion (you will recognize the physical symptoms of, for example, anger). Those associated with physical performance are generated by our perceptions of the demands of the situation. We know that in a practice or recreational game it is less important that we do not fail. In a championship game, however, it is very important that we live up to the demands of the situation, of our team-mates, and of our supporters; even the most confident of us has occasional doubts. These doubts can, if we dwell on them, generate **anxiety,** 'a vague form of fear which involves bodily responses or stress reactions' (Pargman, 1986). It is this additional arousal which, if allowed to build up, can tip us from the 'psyched up' side of the inverted U curve to the 'psyched out' side.

Because of the negative effects on performers of too much anxiety, coaches and sport psychologists are very interested in measuring anxiety levels. Attempts to decide what exactly we are measuring have lead to a more specific definition of anxiety. Spielberger (1970) proposes that we should differentiate between **trait anxiety** and **state anxiety.**

Trait Anxiety is a personality variable which predisposes us to perceive certain situations as threatening. If a person has high trait anxiety, he/she will tend to be fearful of unfamiliar situations and to respond with obvious anxiety symptoms.

State anxiety is an emotional response, often temporary, which exists in relation to particular situations. For example, if you get nervous before a dance production but not a team game, you are showing state anxiety in relation to dance.

Spielberger developed a self-report inventory to measure levels of state and trait anxiety in general situations. It is known as the **State Trait Anxiety Inventory (STAI).** It is not easily obtained, but an excerpt from it can be found in Carron (1980). Research using STAI has not generated any conclusive results in sports contexts, but Martens (1977) developed a sport specific competitive trait anxiety measure, the **Sport Competition Anxiety Test (SCAT)**. This has proved more helpful in investigating anxiety in sportspeople because it deals specifically with sport. You should note, however, that it is a test of competitive **trait** anxiety; that is the tendency to be anxious in sport contexts in general.

Investigation 13.14 : To investigate the relationship between competitive trait anxiety as measured by SCAT, and state anxiety prior to an important sport event

Method: Select a group of people who are involved in competitive sport at a high level, for example your school/college first team or a local club team. Obtain their permission to administer two simple questionnaires, at a mutually convenient time.

Use the SCAT (Roberts *et al.*, 1986, p. 68) to obtain a trait anxiety score, and the following question to obtain a crude state anxiety score for each player:

Imagine that it is a few minutes before a very important league or championship game/event. You have been beaten only once this season, by today's opponent(s). How do you feel with a few minutes to go before the start of the game/event?

Very anxious 9 8 7 6 5 4 3 2 1 Not at all anxious
(adapted from Roberts *et al.*, 1986, p. 66)

Results: Follow the scoring system for SCAT in Roberts (1986).

Using each respondent's SCAT and state anxiety (SA) scores, compute the Spearman's Rank Correlation Coefficient.

Discussion: What does the correlation coefficient tell you about the relationship between SCAT and SA scores? Discuss the implications of this for the team's coach or the sportspeople themselves.

Research along the lines of that which you have just carried out (Scanlan and Passer, 1979) suggests that:

- competitive trait anxiety and pre-game state anxiety are correlated;
- high trait anxiety tends to cause high pre-game state anxiety;
- winners tend to experience less post-game anxiety than losers. The SCAT and the STAI are self-report, psychometric approaches to anxiety measurement. In this sense they are equivalent to the personality tests (Eysenck and Cattell) which you studied in the section on individual differences (p. 272).

REVIEW QUESTIONS

List:

1. the assumptions researchers make in using these tests;
2. the advantages of 'pencil and paper' tests such as these over, for example, psychoanalytical interviewing or physiological measures;
3. disadvantages or drawbacks.

Use your experience of Investigation 13.14 to help you with this.

Discuss your findings with others in your class.

STRESS

So far we have been using the term 'anxiety' to refer to the negative aspects of arousal. Another term which you will come across in your reading and with which you are familiar is '**stress**'. Often the two terms are used interchangeably. Arriving at a generally agreed definition of stress is difficult because of the differing theoretical perspectives adopted by researchers. For example, is stress what **causes** us to feel sick before an exam, or is stress the **result**? Current usage, led by the work of Selye (1976), tends to favour the latter. Thus, stress is defined by Selye as 'the non-specific response of the body to any demand made on it'. The sources of stress are referred to as **stressors.**

Some stressors are universal; everyone would be worried by a loud, unexplained noise in the night. But others, for example performing in front of an audience, may be stressful to one person but not to someone who is used to the experience and enjoys the challenge.

Stressors come in many forms. Pargman (1986) lists the following:

social
chemical/biochemical
bacterial
physical
climatic
psychological

Those involved in physical activity will be very aware of the last three. The physical pain resulting from a sports injury, a dancer's shoes, or the final stages of a long distance race or walk, causes the participant considerable stress, as perhaps you know.

The weather can be a stressor. Heat stress is something that marathon runners have to be able to deal with, and very cold, wet weather brings the danger of hypothermia for those involved in outdoor pursuits.

Psychological stress results from a mismatch between a person's perception of the demands of a situation and a self-assessment of his/her ability to cope, given that the outcome is important. This is illustrated in Figure 13.39.

Selye's (1976) theory of stress proposes that the body reacts to all these stressors in the same way. He suggests that there is a **General Adaptation Syndrome (GAS)** which has three stages. The GAS is illustrated in Figure 13.40.

In the alarm reaction stage, the body is alerted to deal with the stressor. This is when breathing and heart rate quicken and adrenalin is released.

During the resistance stage, a series of hormonal and chemical changes attempt to maintain **homeostasis**; that is, the delicate biochemical and fluid balance which allows our body to function effectively. Selye defines a stressor as anything which disturbs this balance.

The final stage is that of exhaustion, when the product of the strength of the stressor and the length of time during which it acts is such that the body can no longer put up any resistance. Exhaustion is the body's last defence. If this stops the stressor (if, for example, you have been pushing yourself too hard in a 13 km run and you drop out) then the body recovers homeostasis. But if you drop exhausted in a blizzard on Ben Nevis without having gained shelter, then the stressor (the cold) persists in spite of your body having stopped, and you may well not recover.

Psychological stressors do not have such a powerful effect on the body as the others, but over a long period of time will take their toll on general health.

You should note at this stage that several writers (e.g. Harris and Harris, 1984) discuss **eustress**, or 'good' stress, associated with thrill and excitement.

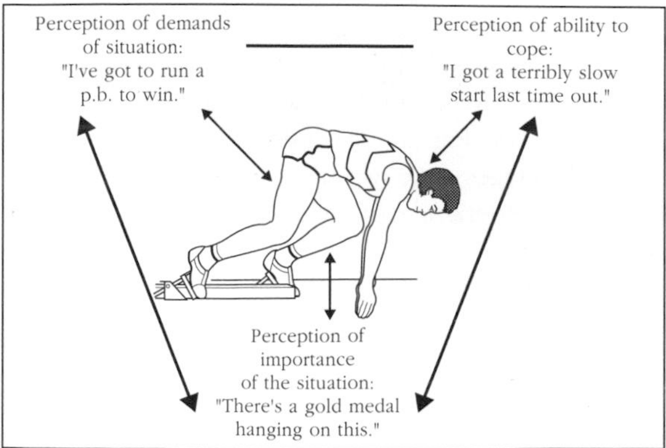

Figure 13.39 Psychological stress.

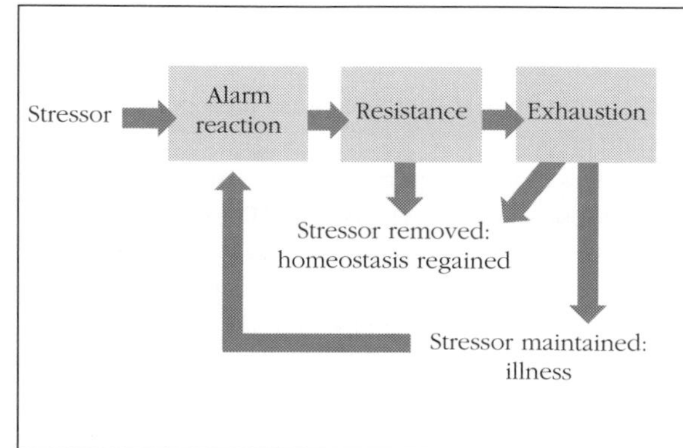

Figure 13.40 The General Adaptation Syndrome (Selye, 1976).

This should not be confused with optimal levels of arousal. The stressor is there and the body is resisting but the individual enjoys, and may even seek out, the sensation. Mo Anthoine, a climber and mountaineer, said:

> *'The truth is, I like an unforgiving climate where if you make mistakes you suffer for it. That's what turns me on. I think it's because there is always a question mark about how you will perform.*
>
> (Alvarez, 1988, p. 151)

In general, however, stress is something to be avoided in sport, for its effects, as with anxiety, are to inhibit performance.

- It may act directly on the information processing and motor elements of skill. Muscles tense, muscular control is reduced, concentration is difficult, our span of attention is narrowed and we don't attend to the things we should.
- Our awareness of being under stress may itself act as a stressor (see Figure 13.43).

Martens (1989) suggests that there are three forms of stress symptoms, physiological, psychological and behavioural.

Physiological symptoms: increased heart rate; increased blood pressure; increased sweating; increased respiration; decreased blood flow to the skin; increased oxygen uptake; dry mouth.

Psychological symptoms: worry; feeling overwhelmed; inability to make decisions; inability to concentrate; inability to direct attention appropriately; narrowing of attention; feeling out-of-control.

Behavioural symptoms: rapid talking; nail biting; pacing; scowling; yawning; trembling; raised voice pitch; frequent urination.

Figure 13.41 Climbers as stress-seekers?

Figure 13.42 Attentional narrowing.

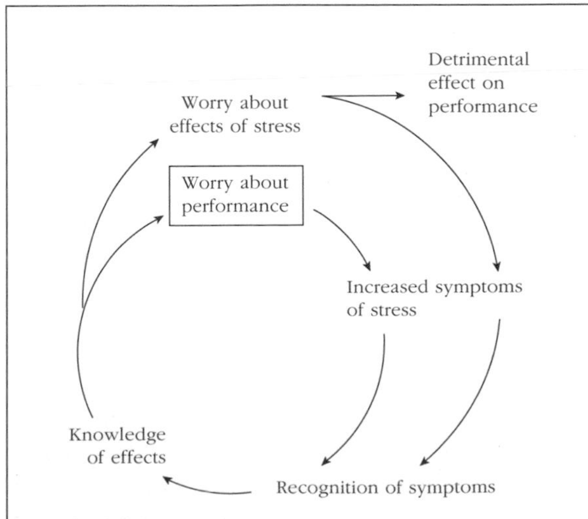

Figure 13.43 The stress spiral.

Measurement of stress

These symptoms are used to identify and measure stress. There are essentially three types of stress measurement:

1. **Self-report questionnaires:** two examples of these have been dealt with on p. 319; there are many other similar inventories.
2. **Observation techniques:** these are used extensively by coaches and consist of observing and monitoring the behavioural aspects of stress listed above in relation to particular aspects of competition and training; thus over a period of time the coach learns what the athlete finds stressful and can work to avoid or overcome this.
3. **Physiological responses:** many of the physiological responses listed above can be measured directly; for example, heart rate, temperature, oxygen uptake, sweating by a galvanic skin response apparatus. Under appropriate supervision, blood analysis can be carried out to measure hormonal responses. All these are useful to establish pre-game levels of stress, but it must be remembered that exercise itself produces similar responses and therefore to measure stress **during** or immediately after performance is very difficult.

STRESS MANAGEMENT TECHNIQUES

It should now be clear to you that in, sport and other physical activities, the most damaging form of stress is that which is self-induced through worrying about the performance to come. Physical activity is inherently arousing so that in most cases getting adequately 'psyched up' is no problem; the difficulty is in limiting anxiety to manageable levels. This means breaking the 'stress spiral' (see Figure 13.43). Since you know that the mind and the body work in very close harmony in the production of skilled movement, it will be no surprise to you that there are two places we can break the spiral; we can deal with the mind by replacing negative thoughts with positive ones and we can eliminate many of the harmful physiological responses to stress by persuading the body that the stressor does not exist. For this we use **relaxation.** Martens (1989) calls this somatic stress management and cites four forms of relaxation:

a. imagery
b. self-directed
c. Progressive Relaxation Training
d. biofeedback.

Imagery relaxation involves picturing yourself in a place where you feel very comfortable and safe. You should try to see yourself there as vividly as you can, relaxed, warm, at ease; evoke the sounds, the smells, the whole 'feel' of the place. It will help if you are in a quiet and comfortable setting in reality, but eventually you will learn to use the technique whenever you feel stressed. To make imagery relaxation work well for you, you need to:

a. think of a place which has clear associations of warmth and relaxation;
b. possess good imagery skills;
c. practise the technique initially in non-stressful situations before using it to control competitive stress. (Martens, 1989)

Self-directed relaxation is a simplified form of **Progressive Relaxation Training (PRT)**, developed in the 1930s. PRT involves learning to tense and then deeply relax separate muscle groups. Tensing a muscle is not difficult but thoroughly relaxing it is, and takes several weeks of practice. Self-directed relaxation involves focusing on each of the major muscle groups in turn, simultaneously allowing the breathing to become slow and easy. As you focus on each muscle, visualize the tension flowing out of it until it is completely relaxed. Work through all the muscle groups in this way. Whereas initially you will need to relax muscles separately to get the required relaxation effect, as you become more proficient you will be able to combine groups and achieve total body relaxation very quickly. Martens (1989, p.123) gives a useful script which you could get someone to read to you, or which you could tape, in order to get you started. Alternatively, there are several relaxation audio tapes on the market.

A similar technique is suggested by Benson (1976), but his focus is just on breathing and hence is closer to meditation than relaxation. You should find a quiet setting and concentrate totally on your breathing. As you breathe out, silently repeat a single syllable word which has no particular meaning for you. If you find your attention wandering, just bring your mind back to your breathing.

You may find that it is difficult to feel the difference between tension and relaxation in your muscles. In this case, **biofeedback** may be helpful, for it is a technique which gives you direct information about what is happening in your body. We have suggested that physiological responses to stress can be measured. Biofeedback does this and teaches you how to use your mind to change the reading. There are three main types of biofeedback:

1. Skin temperature: when muscles are relaxed, more blood flows to the skin and skin temperature rises; this can be detected by sensitive electrothermometers taped to the skin. If you are stressed, blood will be diverted from the skin to the tense muscles and the skin will be cold. As you relax, using imagery relaxation techniques, you will see the reading change and this provides feedback and reinforces the relaxation.

2. The galvanic skin response (GSR) is a means of measuring the electrical conductivity of the skin, which increases when the skin is moist. When the muscles are tense sweating occurs to get rid of the heat generated, thereby increasing the skin conductivity which can be measured using a simple battery-operated device. This device provides immediate feedback on how successful you are at relaxing.

3. Electromyography (EMG): electrodes are taped to the skin over specific muscles whose state of tension or relaxation can then be monitored. This is very helpful if you have a problem with tension in a specific muscle group during performance.

Relaxation techniques can be invaluable for reducing stress prior to an important sport event. They sound easy, but in fact it takes some time to learn to do them really effectively. The drawback is that whereas you do wish to remove stress, you do not want to remove all muscle tension before your game or event. Your aim, therefore, is to prepare the body, to remove unhelpful tension, so that you can then effectively direct your thoughts and attention to the task in hand.

MENTAL PREPARATION FOR PERFORMANCE

Cognitive stress management involves controlling emotions and thought processes prior to, during and after competition or performance, and is closely linked to the achievement and attribution processes discussed in Section 13.4. It is about eliminating negative feelings about oneself and the sports situation, and developing confidence. Coaches and performers use a great variety of methods and there is not scope here to go into these in any depth, but many recent Sports Psychology texts, written for sportspeople and coaches (e.g. Bull, 1991, and Nideffer, 1992), deal with these issues in detail.

Self-confidence is an important aspect of our personality in everyday life. As with any aspect of character, if taken to extremes it can be annoying to others; but there is no doubt that, if you believe in yourself and your ability, you are more likely to succeed in reaching your goals than if you do not. Research indicates that this is particularly true in sport (Gill, 1986). Discuss with your colleagues the extent to which specific, well-known, successful sportspeople could be said to be self-confident. How do they show this?

Bandura (1982) presents a useful theoretical model for how coaches can set about developing self-confidence in their performers. He refers to **self-efficacy**, which is self-confidence in a specific situation; you will be aware of feeling confident in one sports context, but not in another. He suggests that there are four ways in which self-efficacy can be developed:

- Performance accomplishments: helping a performer to succeed in a task is the most effective way of developing confidence.
- Vicarious experiences: watching someone else successfully performing the same activity and imagining being as successful oneself.
- Verbal persuasion: less effective than other methods, but often a coach will successfully persuade a performer or team that they *are* capable of succeeding.
- Emotional arousal: which must be controlled for optimum performance.

Mental rehearsal, (sometimes referred to as mental imagery or mental practice) is increasingly being recognized as an important skill and many top class sportspeople use it in some form, although it takes some time to learn how to rehearse effectively. In essence, it involves consciously imagining the performance, either by re-running a past experience as if in 'action replay', or by previewing a hoped-for success. Sharp (1992) gives a fuller explanation of the concept.

Evidence shows that mental rehearsal can help a sportsperson concentrate before an event, can create self confidence, help he or she focus on strengths and weaknesses, and also assist in the learning and improving of skills. However, Nideffer warns that 'no amount of mental rehearsal will help you perform well if you lack technical skill. There is no substitute for actual practice' (Nideffer, 1992, p.4).

Research (e.g. Hird *et al*, 1991) suggests that mental rehearsal is not as effective in skill acquisition as well-structured physical practice, but can still have a positive effect on learning.

Goal-setting is an important aspect of any sportspeoples' preparation, whether for competition or performance. If performer and teacher/coach are aware of what is being aimed for, then success is more likely.

This is because:
learning is focused;
uncertainty is reduced;
confidence is increased;
practice is planned and structured;
evaluation/feedback is specific.

Goals should be identified and training planned, first by specifying a long-term goal, something that can be worked towards over the next 9–12 months. You might, for example, be aiming for a place in an Olympic team or for a particular competition score. This is then broken down into intermediate and short- term goals which lead to the long-term goal. For example, a skater might have the long-term goal of becoming the national junior champion in 12 months' time. One of the intermediate goals might then be to learn a routine which would catch the judges' eye and be awarded a high score, and the short-term goal would thus be practising particular sections of this routine.

Goals should be:

stated positively;
specific to the situation and the performer;
challenging;
achievable;
measurable;
negotiated between the sportsperson and coach.

Goal setting is increasingly used not only as a means of ensuring that training targets are met, but also so that a sportsperson feels prepared for, and therefore confident about an event. There is a wealth of literature now on optimizing performance and managing stress in sport; the National Coaching Foundation material is a useful and interesting starting point, particularly in terms of goal-setting.

As we have already indicated, being a good performer involves training the mind as well as the body, so that both work together in harmony. Understanding and helping sportspeople achieve this are the important contributions that sport psychology can make to physical endeavour.

Summary

1. Arousal is the state of alertness and anticipation that exists before, during and after a sports performance—and indeed throughout our lives. It has physiological and cognitive components.

   Drive theory suggests that as arousal increases to meet the demands of a task, so the dominant motor habit is increasingly likely to be reflected in performance.

   The Inverted U Theory suggests that as arousal increases, so up to an optimal level- does potential performance, after which that performance deteriorates. Coaches and sportspeople accept that optimal arousal levels can be identified, but that these vary between individuals and with the type of task. Ability to control arousal would seem to be avital aspect of successful performance.
2. Anxiety is an emotional response which causes physiological reactions similar to, but less specific than, fear. Two forms have been identified: state and trait anxiety. Competitive trait anxiety has been shown to correlate with state anxiety in competitive situations, as measured by self-report questionnaires.
3. Stress is the non-specific response of the body to the demands made on it by stressors. Stressors have many forms, but the three most applicable to sportspeople are physical, climatic and psychological. Selye's General Adaptation Syndrome outlines three stages in the body's response to stressors. Symptoms of stress may be behavioural, psychological or physiological and are used to monitor stress in athletes by means of self-report questionnaires, observational techniques and physiological measurements.
4. In controlling stress, coaches and athletes use two types of technique: somatic, and cognitive stress management. Somatic techniques deal with the physiological effects of stress. The two examples given were self-directed relaxation and biofeedback.
5. Cognitive stress management techniques deal with emotions and thought processes prior to, during and after competition/performance. The development of self-confidence, mental rehearsal and goal-setting was used as an example of this. It was emphasized that whereas the development of these skills is often initiated by the coach or trainer, the long-term aim is for the athletes themselves to understand amd learn the principles of stress management and sport preparation, and thus to use them to manage their own performances.

REFERENCES

Alvarez A. *Feeding The Rat*, London, Bloomsbury, 1988.

Bandura A. Self efficacy: toward a unifying theory of behavioural change, *Psychological Review,* 84, 191-215, 1977.

Benson H. *The Relaxation Response*, New York, William Morrow, 1976.

Carron A.V. *Social Psychology of Sport: an Experiential Approach,* Ithaca, N.Y., Mouvement Publications, 1980.

Hird, J.S. *et al.* Physical practice is superior to mental practice in enhancing cognitive and motor task performance, *Journal of Sport and Exercise Psychology,* 8, 281–293, 1991.

Martens R. *Sport Competition Anxiety Test,* Champaign, Ill., Human Kinetics, 1977.

Scanlan T.K. and Passer M.W. Sources of competitive stress in young female athletes, *Journal of Sport Psychology,* 1, 151-159, 1979.

Selye H. *The Stress of Life* (rev. ed.), New York, McGraw-Hill, 1976.

Sharp B. *Acquiring Skill in Sport,* Eastbourne, Sports Dynamics, 1992.

Sonstroem R.J. and Bernardo P.B. Individual pre-game state anxiety and basketball performance: a re-examination of the inverted U curve, *Journal of Sport Psychology,* 4, 235-245, 1982.

Spielberger C. *et al. State Trait Anxiety Inventory Manual,* Palo Alto, Ca., Consulting Psychologists Press, 1970.

FURTHER READING

Bull, S.J. *Sport Psychology: A Self-Help Guide,* Crowood, 1991.

Gill D.L. *Psychological Dynamics of Sport,* Champaign, Ill., Human Kinetics, 1986.

Hardy L. and Fazey J. *Mental Training Package,* Leeds, NCF, 1990.

Harris D.V. and Harris B.L. *The Athlete's Guide to Sports Psychology,* Champaign, Ill., Leisure Press, 1984.

Martens R. *Coaches Guide to Sport Psychology,* Champaign, Ill., Human Kinetics, 1989.

National Coaching Foundation. *Mind over Matter: Introductory Study Pack No. 5,* Leeds, NCF, 1990.

Nideffer R.M. *Psyched to Win,* Champaign, Ill., Human Kinetics, 1992.

Pargman D. *Stress and Motor Performance: Understanding and Coping,* Ithaca, N.Y., Mouvement Publications, 1986.

Roberts G.C., Spink K.S. and Pemberton C.L. *Learning Experiences in Sport Psychology,* Champaign, Ill., Human Kinetics, 1986.

Roberts, G.C. (Ed.) *Motivation in Sport and Exercise,* Champaign, Ill., Human Kinetics, 1992.

Silva J.M. and Weinberg R.S. *Psychological Foundations of Sport,* Champaign, Ill., Human Kinetics, 1984.

Willis J.D. and Campbell L.F. *Exercise Psychology,* Human Kinetics, 1992.

Part Three:

The Performer in a Social Setting

It is very easy for us to turn to the sports pages and consider that information about players' performances is all there is to know. If we are to gain a useful knowledge and understanding of physical education and sport we must recognize that any group activity involves relationships between people, and that any group activity is influenced by the society to which it belongs.

There are three main dimensions to be examined under the title of the **Performer in a Social Setting.** These consist of **contemporary socio-cultural aspects, historical perspectives** and **comparative studies** of physical education and sport.

The **contemporary socio-cultural** and **comparative studies** have been deliberately integrated because of the international nature of much of physical education and sport. The section starts with a critical analysis of concepts, ranging from play to professional sport, and involves the reader in the process of understanding words and notions. Having established what we mean by certain concepts, it is useful to review the administration of these in a number of countries. The third phase involves an examination of physical education and sport using a number of sociological techniques at both intra- and inter-group level. Finally, these components are integrated to examine a number of contemporary issues in physical education and sport.

The **historical perspective** consists almost entirely of British sports history, on the ground that this represents the nucleus from which most international developments have stemmed. It is presented in four phases: popular recreation, public school athleticism, rational recreation and elementary school physical training, and can be readily linked with the contemporary scene.

Bibliographies are presented at regular intervals to encourage additional reading, and a large number of models and illustrative material are offered to involve the student in decision-making activities.

Inevitably, a text is dated almost as soon as it is written and so this 2nd revised edition includes changes which have occurred in our field of study since 1991 as well as elements which have emerged as a result of reflective study by teachers and young people.

The main additional input concerns the political changes which have recently occurred in what was once the Soviet Union, and, in Eastern Europe; and while it will take some years for socio-economic and political systems to stabilize, there is a need to review trends and speculate on eventualities. Similarly, there is an increased interest in the impact of developing countries on sport, and in their sometimes disproportionate allocation of funding to specific activities.

Chapter 14
Important Concepts in Physical Education and Sport

Introduction

You have read about the structure and function of our subject through the eyes of the scientist and the social scientist. It is now time to look at physical education and sport in a social setting. If we put that in the form of a model, it should look something like Figure 14.1.

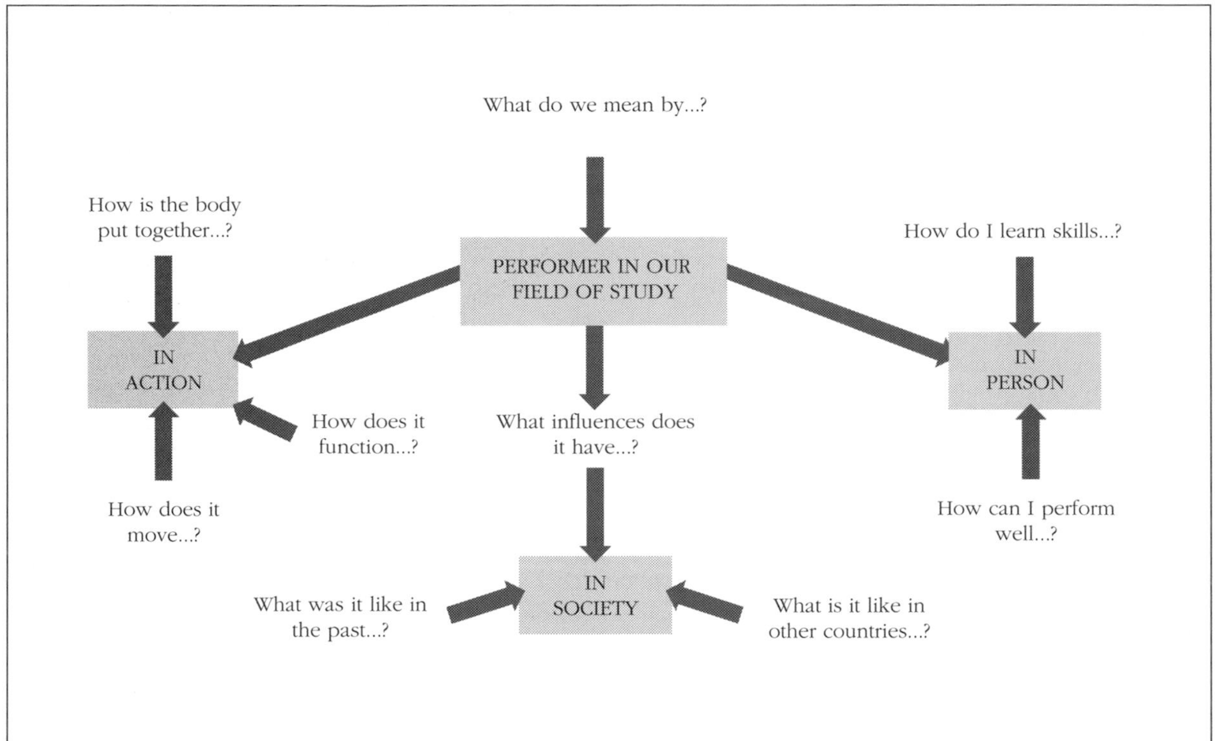

Figure 14.1

Do you understand what each of the nine questions is getting at? Have you been able to give a brief answer to each of them? You need to know the meanings of words and notions and be able to express them accurately. Get into the habit of asking two basic questions whenever you meet new words or situations:

What do we mean by?
If you can answer this, you will get your definitions sorted out and that will allow you to discuss things rationally.

How do we know?
If you go on to this second level of questioning and establish authoritative back-up to what you have said, you have changed a point of view into a worthwhile, public statement which will stand up to a certain amount of scrutiny.

So, what does this model tell us?
It would seem that most of what you have been reading has been centred on the **performer** and his or her involvement in a family of activities which we variously call **physical education, sport** or **physical recreation.**

You have looked at the **performer in action** through the eyes of the physiologist; at the **person involved in the activity** using the techniques of the psychologist; and you are about to examine the nature, structure and function of **physical performance in a social setting.** This implies that you should know about physical education and sport in your own country; that it helps to know what it is like in other countries; and that it is important to know what influence the past has had.

Let's try to establish some **terms of reference:**

- We are concerned with a particular **field of study** which we have called **physical performance.**
- Our initial task, therefore, is to establish the boundaries of *this* term in *this* book.
- Our definition of **physical performance** is limited to activities which fall within the categories of **play, physical recreation, sport** and **physical education.**
- Other forms of physical performance exist and may have common features with those categories we have identified, but they are outside our present **field of study**.

All four categories can also be experienced in the natural environment, where alternative motives arise and different types of challenge have to be met, producing recreative and educative sub-categories.

Having identified four categories we now apply our questioning technique by asking, **what do we mean by them**?

Figure 14.2 shows what they *might* mean.

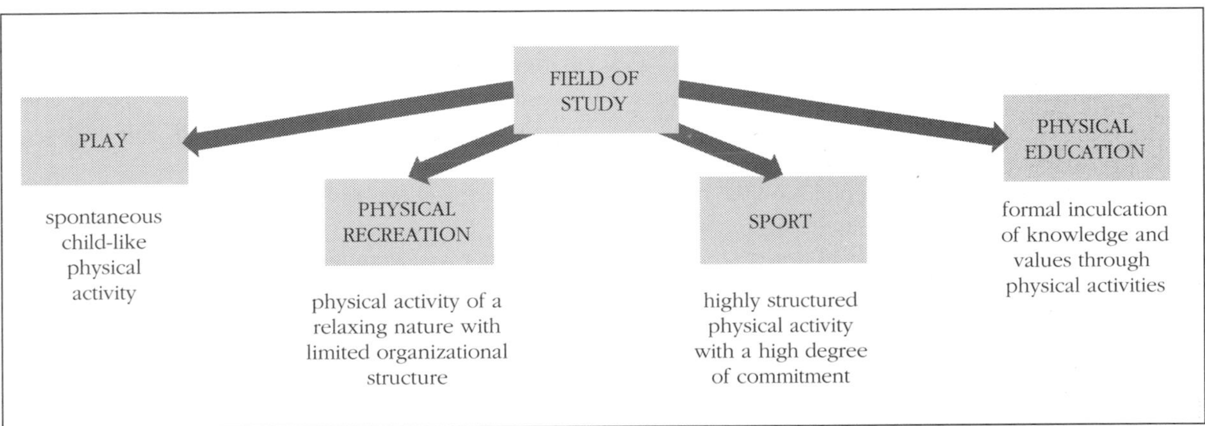

Figure 14.2

REVIEW QUESTIONS

To test the definitions

1. See if you can think of an experience you have had in each of the categories in Figure 14.2.
2. Put the following activities into these categories:
   a. two children playing hopscotch in the street;
   b. Miami Dolphins playing the Redskins in the Superbowl;
   c. a school gymnastic lesson;
   d. a group of backpackers rambling in the English Lake District.
3. Make sure that you understand the words in each definition, and try to find some exceptions.

If you have gone about this in the right way, you will be starting to come up with some **characteristics** which all four categories **share**, but you will also be aware that each has certain characteristics which make it **different** from the others.

Do you agree with the **shared characteristics** in Figure 14.3?

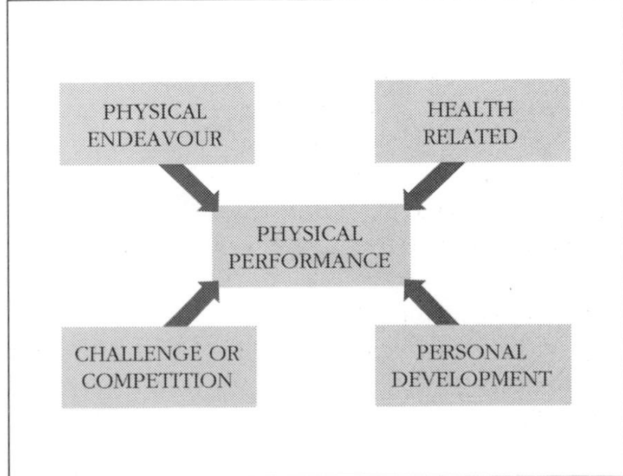

Figure 14.3

Now let's look at a few other **physical performances** which we suggest are outside our terms of reference: acting in a play; playing chess; pulling a tooth out; and gardening.

It is suggested that none of these fits into our notion of play, physical recreation, sport or physical education because they don't have a **sufficient** number of the **shared characteristics** we expect to find in our **field of study.**

See if you can establish why these four activities are outside our terms of reference. What you will find is that there is a core of activities which can be applied to **all four categories**, and others which may fit into only one. Motor racing, for example, is certainly a sport, but it is hard to see it as play, physical recreation or physical education. Football, on the other hand, can consist of some children kicking a tin can down the road; being taught it at school; playing a game in the park with coats for goals; or fulfilling a league fixture. It is all football, but each of these examples fits into a different category of physical performance.

Most of the examples we are going to use will be like football; in other words, it depends on the players and the way they play as to whether they are involved in play, a formal educational experience, a sport or a recreation. Figure 14.4 identifies some of these **core** activities and 'dares' to **classify** them into five major groups.

We are suggesting that all these activities belong to the same **family** or **field of study,** but they have a number of **unique features** which makes them rather like the fingers of one hand.

Try to identify some of these **unique features.** You will probably come up with words like **game, combat** and **conquest;** you might decide that some are **objective** while others have **subjective** elements; you might conclude that the key lies in the number of players and their relationship. It is always easier if you relate your definition to a specific activity and test it.

A **combat,** for example, involves you in beating an opponent in a stylized war game. Do you agree, or is there more to it than that? Test your definition by looking at judo or fencing. What do you think about archery being in this category?

Can you define a **conquest** activity? Does it involve competition or challenge? Is it against man or nature? Does it have to be the first time? What are its physical and psychological components? Is it basically an objective or a romantic experience? If you ask these questions and link them with an acknowledged conquest activity like mountaineering, you should come up with certain characteristics, which will give you a clearer understanding of the term.

You are still left with the difficult notion of what a **game** is. For example, would you agree that basically it is a contrived competitive experience existing in its own time and space? That is quite a difficult statement. Can you simplify it and then pick a game to test it?

However, Figure 14.4 divides the games into **partner** and **team.** We also know that there are **invasion** games, like hockey and football; **court** games, like

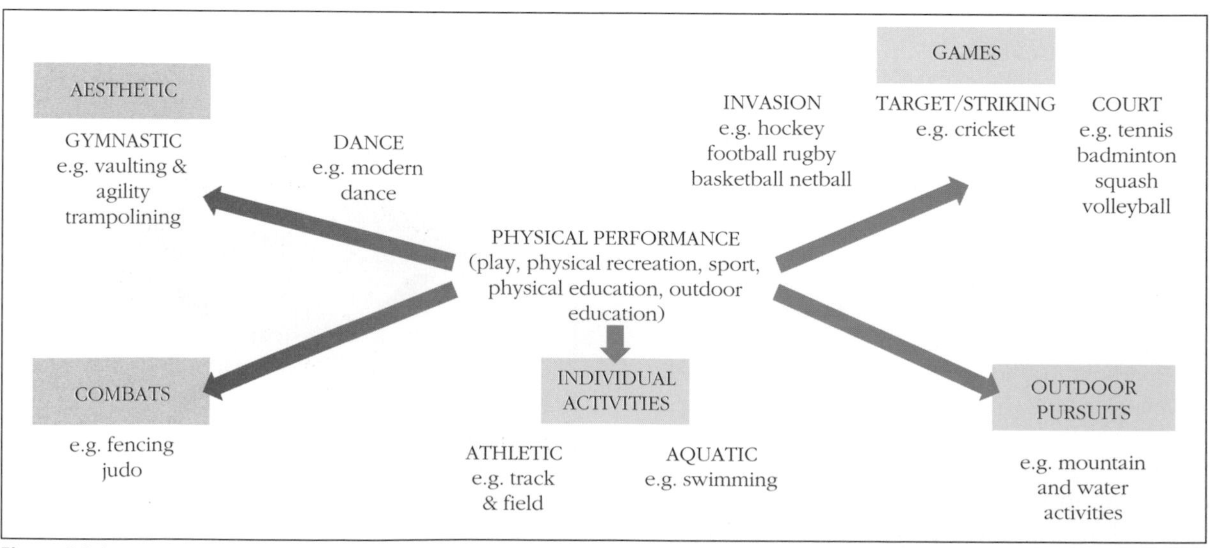

Figure 14.4

tennis and squash; and **target** games, like cricket, baseball and golf. Can you set up some sets of characteristics to differentiate these *types* of game?

Unfortunately, this degree of analysis simply takes us into another round of **what do you mean by** and **how do you know?** For example, can you differentiate between a **contest** and a **game?** Or what is the notion of combat? Is it a description of certain activities or a potential feature of all contests? Can you establish the difference between a **competition** and a **challenge?** We are probably getting more questions than answers by this point. Don't worry too much; the debate itself is valuable, and the more we question, the more you will realize that there are very few absolutes.

Let's make a decisive statement and if it holds we are ready to make a start.

> *Our field of study includes a number of specific activities which share a number of characteristics. There would seem to be four main categories within this field of study: play, physical recreation, sport and physical education. Most of the core activities can exist in each category, dependent on the attitude of the performer and the level of performance and organization.*

Test this statement by using different examples and different situations.

We now have one more basic step to take. Having just used the word **situation,** we need to recognize that we are concerned with a **dynamic experience** which is **complete in itself,** an intrinsic whole. Like a watch, once it is put together successfully, it works independently.

In model form, the **components** of this working dynamic can be arranged as in Figure 14.5. Can you make this model more meaningful by putting it into a real situation? For example, if you are performing, what are you performing? Where are you performing? Why are you performing? These are the most important components. Now, what about the influence of the coach, the spectators and the administrators? They all have a direct bearing on you as a performer and the direct function of the activity.

However, this activity does not exist in a vacuum. All the time, outside forces are acting on it. In the case of the watch, someone winds it up, wears it, looks after it, uses it, looks at it and values it. These outside influences are what we have called the **social setting,** or they could be called extrinsic factors.

Terms like 'spheres of influence' and 'affective horizons' can help to explain the way in which society changes the **performer and the performance.** You probably belong to a sports club. What factors outside the club influence it? Are they human, financial, geographical or perhaps political? Or all four?

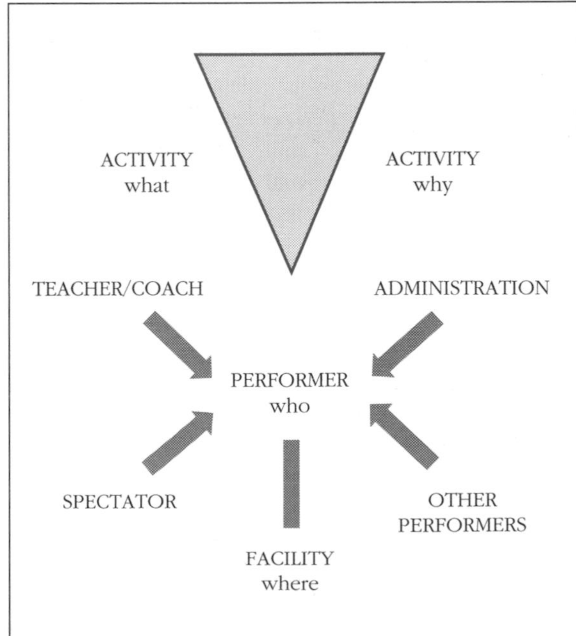

Figure 14.5

Figure 14.6 identifies the main extrinsic factors which influence the performance situation. It is often said that performance situations reflect the society and culture they exist in, but there are occasions where such is the impact of sport on society or physical education on education that the opposite occurs and our field of study changes aspects of society as well as some of its cultural patterns.

The extent to which this interaction takes place varies from a local influence to an international one, in waves of reaction which have been variously called 'spheres of influence' and 'affective horizons'. At a local level, you probably belong to a sports club and would be aware of the influence of the local community on it. Conversely, you would be able to recognize the influence your club has on the town. Similarly, but on a wider scale, you could assess the wave-like impact of the 1992 Olympic Games on Barcelona itself, but also on Spain, Europe and ultimately the whole world. These examples of interaction remind us that to understand the performance situation we must be aware of its social setting. These relationships do not always reflect intrinsic values—for example, the selection of Atlanta instead of Athens for the Centenary Olympic Games may well have hinged on the influence of the Coca Cola Company.

If these are the dimensions in which our field of study operates, we can appreciate the Contemporary Scene; but we then need to unravel traditional behaviour, through the time perspective of historical knowledge, and environmental influences, through the spacial perspective of comparative study, to understand parallel developments in other countries.

Clearly, **play** is likely to have a predominance of local influences, whereas the impact of high-level **sport** can result in world wide determining factors. England being allowed to re-enter European football is one example, but the exclusion of South Africa from the Olympic Games had even wider implications.

In addition to **dimensions,** we need to be aware of **perspectives** if we are to get a coherent picture of the social setting. We will understand **our own contemporary society** more fully if we use **historical perspective** to establish what has caused the present; and a **comparative perspective** to understand parallel developments in other countries.

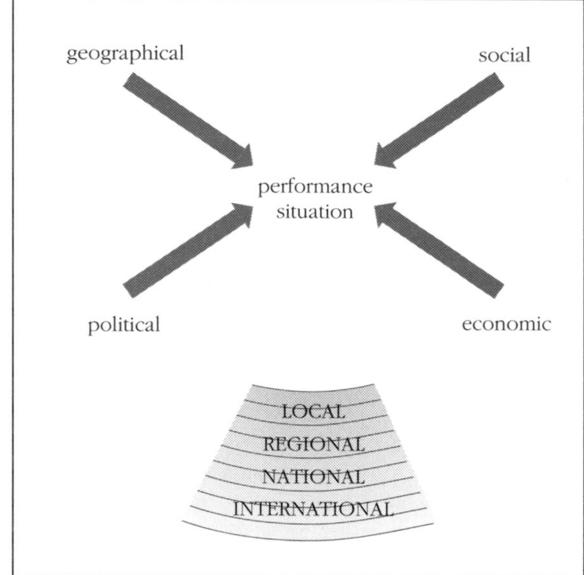

Figure 14.6

14.1 Towards a Concept of Leisure

The ordinary citizen has to **work** for a living. He or she then has certain **obligatory activities** which have to be performed, such as sleeping and eating. What is left is **leisure time.**

All the activities in our **field of study** either take place in leisure time, are themselves leisure activities or prepare us for active leisure, and it is therefore essential that we understand what is meant by the term **leisure.**

Let's start by making a list: (Figure 14.7).

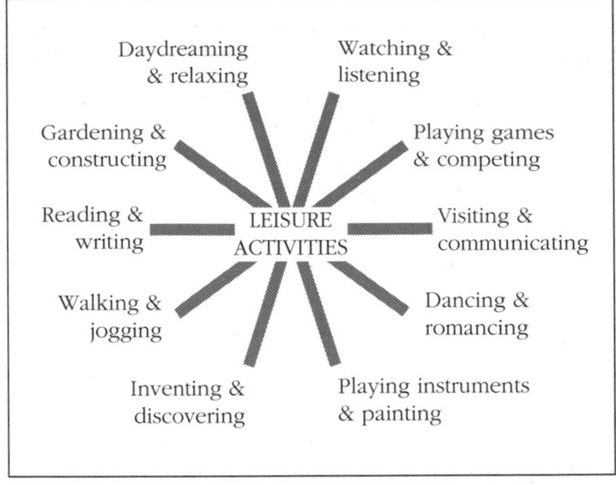

Figure 14.7

How clever are you at recognizing differences between these activities? Well, there would seem to be two major variables.

a. Not all **leisure** involves **physical performance**; for example, watching TV sport.
b. **Physical performance** is not always a **leisure time experience**; for example, professional sport has work connotations.

It looks as if it might not be as simple as we thought! Let's play safe and look at what other people think it is.

> *Leisure is time in which there is an opportunity for choice.*
>
> (ARNOLD, 1978)

> *Leisure has three functions: relaxation of energies consumed by daily life; free development—compensation for the specialization of movement and knowledge imposed by modern industrial life; and recreation—relief from the boredom and restrictions of daily life.*
>
> (McDONALD, 1965)

> *Leisure helps people to learn how to play their part in society; it helps them to achieve societal or collective aims; and it helps the society to keep together.*
>
> (PARKER, 1971)

> *Leisure is a mental and spiritual attitude—a condition of the soul, not the inevitable result of spare time.*
>
> (PIEPER, 1965)

> *A necessary prerequisite for practising the more civilized virtues—the adoption of a critical attitude to life and developing a taste for excellence.*
>
> (BELL, 1947)

> *Leisure is the complex of self-fulfilling and self-enriching values achieved by the individual as he uses leisure time in self-chosen activities that recreate him.*
>
> (MILLER & ROBINSON, 1963)

> *Leisure is an activity—apart from the obligations of work, family and society—to which the individual turns at will.*
>
> (DUMAZEDIER, 1967)

> *Leisure consists of relatively self-determining activity-experiences that fall into one's economically free-time roles.*
>
> (KAPLAN, 1975)

REVIEW QUESTIONS

1. Remember, anyone can select quotations to make a biased case. Look for quotations by other authors and make an attempt at your own definition of leisure.
2. Before reading on, pick out the key words in each quotation and assemble them in a model. These key words should represent characteristics of leisure and you should try to fit them into a number of categories if you can.

Compare your presentation of the **concept of leisure** with the analysis that follows. Don't worry too much if your format differs from ours, as there are many ways of presenting characteristics of a complex experience like leisure. However, we tend to use the same order of presentation with all models: **structure** (what); **function** (how); **interpretation** (why); **conclusion** (key).

Figure 14.8 Leisure!

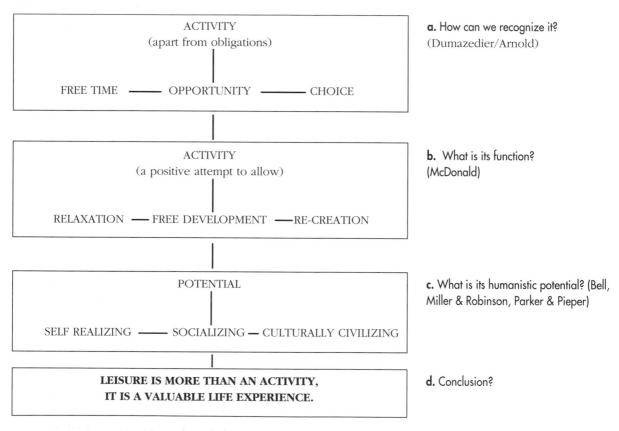

ACTIVITY
(apart from obligations)

FREE TIME —— OPPORTUNITY —— CHOICE

a. How can we recognize it? (Dumazedier/Arnold)

ACTIVITY
(a positive attempt to allow)

RELAXATION — FREE DEVELOPMENT — RE-CREATION

b. What is its function? (McDonald)

POTENTIAL

SELF REALIZING —— SOCIALIZING — CULTURALLY CIVILIZING

c. What is its humanistic potential? (Bell, Miller & Robinson, Parker & Pieper)

LEISURE IS MORE THAN AN ACTIVITY, IT IS A VALUABLE LIFE EXPERIENCE.

d. Conclusion?

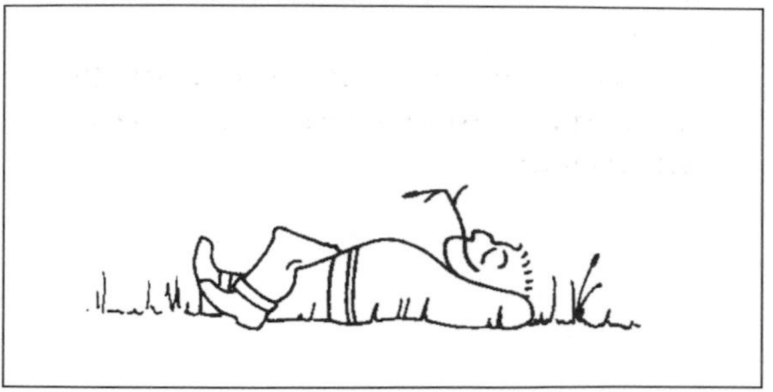

Figure 14.9 Don't be a 'jock' all your life! Remember the reflective and the sportive should complement each other.

Well, we have produced a list of words here, characteristics of leisure, maybe, but now you need to establish what each word means and explain it in a **physical performance** situation that you have experienced.

Investigation 14.1

Read this short case study:

I'm John and I spend much of my leisure time gardening, but my wife, Jane, prefers the theatre and my two children love swimming.

We all pursue our favoured activities when we have the free time to do so, but once in a while we share each other's hobbies. Both my wife and I work, but on summer evenings I am able to visit my allotment, while she settles down to a good play on the TV. We don't have to do either of these things, but we enjoy them and respect each other's right to choose. Similarly, the children swim whenever they have the chance, which amounts to two or three times a week. Mary is a little more serious than Bill and so she tends to train quite hard while he just plays around. Either way, they come home tired, but happy.

Our hobbies certainly take us away from the boredom, conformity and stress of the working day and we find that we can relax within a few moments of tasting the atmosphere of our chosen activities. Funnily enough, although we often feel quite jaded when we start our various activities, the tiredness falls away as we accept the responsibilities of our chosen activity. There are always new situations which are totally unpredictable and my wife tells me that her greatest joy is to experience a play unfolding for the first time. Nor is she limited to watching plays on the TV, as she belongs to a small amateur company, which puts on plays twice a year and she also visits the West End occasionally as a special treat.

It is as if we are genuinely part of the experience. I sometimes feel that I am actually growing with the plants and Jane says that she often loses herself in the story she's watching.

The children, of course, with their practical activity, are able to express themselves physically, as well as test their temperament in the hurly-burly of the swimming baths, and they invariably come away from the pool exhausted but glowing inside.

Unfortunately, we find that our work is not very fulfilling. I work on a conveyor belt in a car factory and my wife is a typist in an office. We seem to spend each day doing the same thing, surrounded by the same noises and petty anxieties. Only our leisure activities seem to give us a chance to achieve something as individuals. I've learnt so much more about myself as a result of my leisure activity, sometimes reflecting on life's many foibles as I dig the ground each Autumn; at other times realizing, as I pick my own strawberries, that I am totally responsible for their existence; and, honestly, is there anything to equal the peace and quiet of a garden on a balmy summer evening?

Not that any of my family particularly want solitude, gosh, on the contrary, we seem to spend most of the time chatting to friends, sharing and caring, as they say, with a kind of sincerity that doesn't seem to occur very often at work.

I know I'm a better person as a result of the time I spend on the garden and the allotment, it's as if nature is slowing me down and actually giving me roots.

No one can tell me that gardening is just an activity. It is a diversion which is at once relaxing and invigorating; it broadens my experiences and has given me lasting friendships; it really is the free exercise of my creative capacity; and it's the only time in my life when I feel I actually taste excellence.

OK, so my family is involved in a pretty purposeful approach to leisure, but if I can paraphrase John Ruskin,

> *'True creative fulfilment comes from the exertion of body or mind to please ourselves.'*

1 Pick out the key words which reflect the potential value of leisure. It is only a question of looking at Figure 14.8!
2 Establish your own role-play groups so that you can 'score points' in illustrating characteristics of leisure.

Always remember, however, that an **activity** is only the **vehicle** which allows a person to **experience leisure**.

LEISURE IN A CULTURAL SETTING

At first sight, it would seem that **leisure** is a **universal concept.** However, all activity-experiences are influenced by their cultural setting, and so where there are societal differences between countries there will also be variables in the structure and function of leisure. Kaplan (1975) produced a six-model analysis, but we will use the less sophisticated approach suggested by Jelfs (1970).

Leisure is spare time

The most common concept of leisure is the negative view that **leisure is non-work.** It presents **work** as the valued ethic in society and tends to devalue **leisure,** presenting it as a means of restoring individuals for work. This leaves leisure with little or no independent identity and minimal cultural status.

This view still exists in the United Kingdom as a result of the **industrial revolution** and the **protestant work ethic.** To paraphrase Huizinga (1956), '**Work was first of all the IDEAL and then the IDOL of the age**.'

This sums up 19th-century English industrial society and the ethic can still be seen today. Less evident in France and what was once the Soviet Union, it does have links with **capitalist economics** and so has found some favour in the United States.

Try to explain Figure 14.10, establishing what each term means and illustrating it wherever possible.

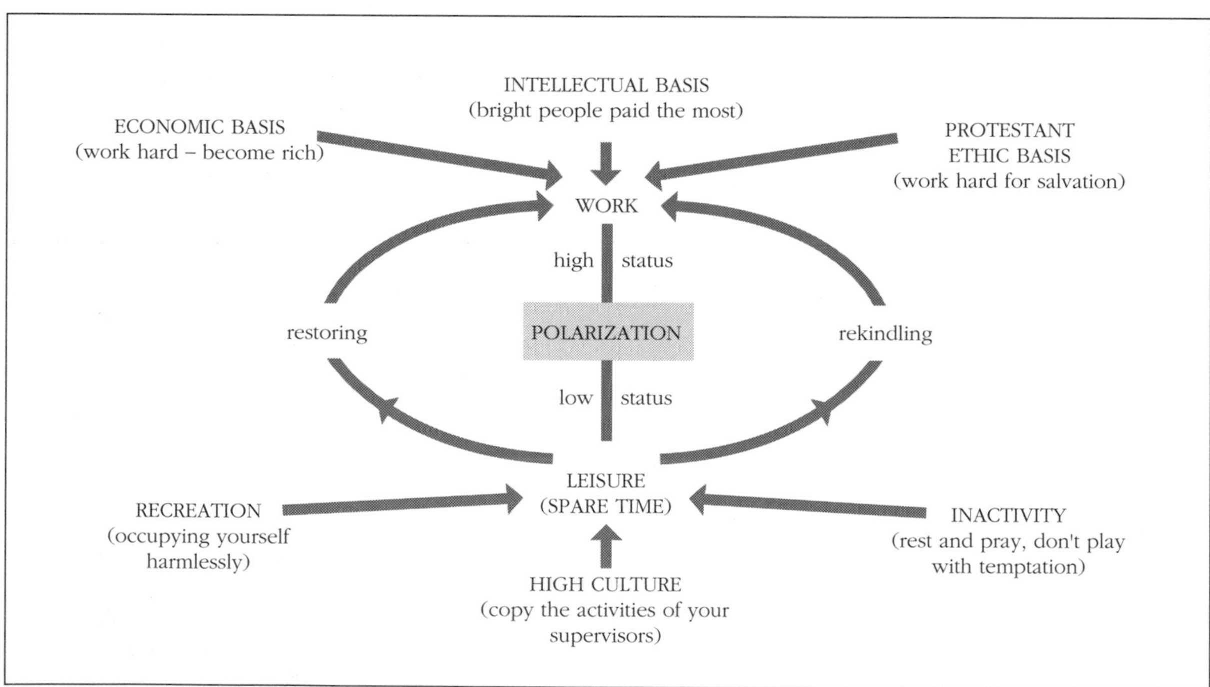

Figure 14.10

Leisure as an economic condition

This second concept of leisure is very closely identified with the first. An expression which describes it is: **leisure as a reflection of cultural life style**; the point being that any inherent form of social inequality will be evident in a society's pattern of leisure.

See if you can explain Figure 14.11 using illustrations from your experience.

If we look at the British and American leisure scene we find a high and a low culture which is partly determined by status in society. This may reflect social class variables, racial discrimination or gender inequalities. In England it is evident in the group who play polo, as against those who play soccer. In the States a comparison might be made between golf and baseball. Even in activities which involve a mixture of social groups, cultural demarcation is often evident, even if this is only a vestige of the past. The English Derby, for example, has the Grandstand and Enclosure for 'Society', and the Downs, where popular culture continues to thrive.

As egalitarian trends reduce these traditional boundaries, fewer leisure activities are completely exclusive, but the traditional conservatism of many leisure activities gives them a permanence which resists change.

Leisure as a form of social control

This is identifiable in a society where social equality is very important, but also where deviance from a culturally acceptable pattern of behaviour is not tolerated. The key phrase here is **purposeful leisure**.

So far, we have seen leisure as an optional extra and as a feature of privileged groups in society. In both cases the values have tended to be **intrinsic,** and that means the activities are seen to have little value outside themselves. This view is common to most of the Western World, and most strongly evident in Britain.

However, the former Soviet Union and other 'socialist' societies reflected this third concept much more strongly than America or Common Market countries, because the former Soviet Union tended, and still does, to be more authoritarian, even though committed to an egalitarian political system. Such statements as 'good socialist principles' and 'for the good of the State' were commonplace until the break-up of the

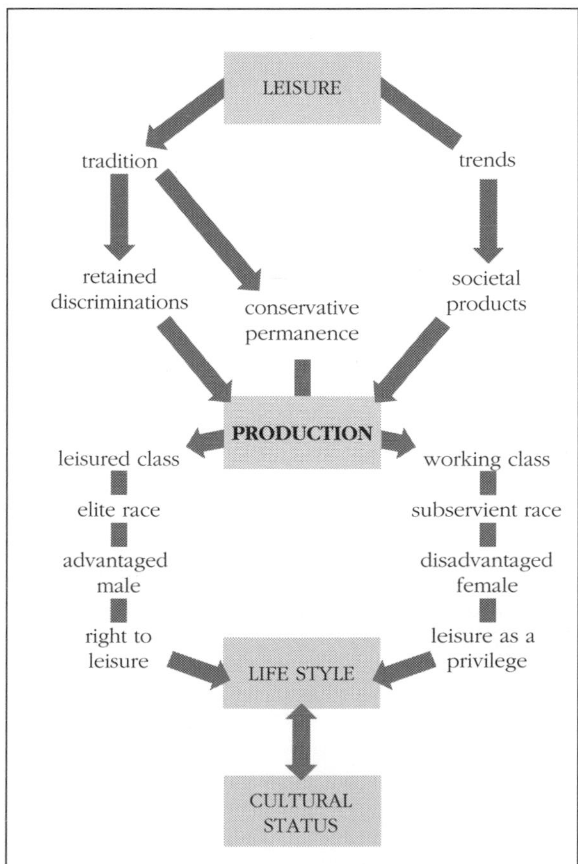

Figure 14.11

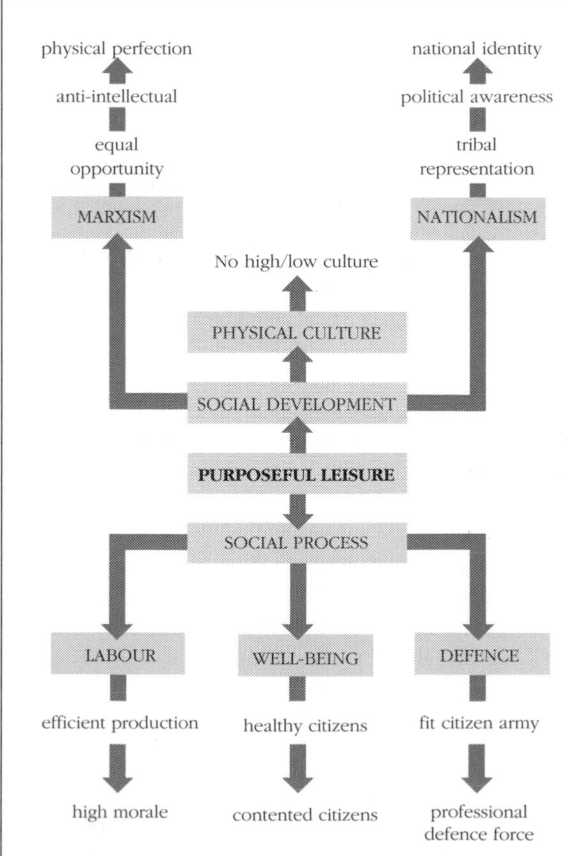

Figure 14.12

Union. Leisure was given considerable social status, designed to reinforce socio-political values and based on the belief that leisure had **extrinsic** value—which meant that it could influence the **social development** of a society and also exist as a **social process** in its own right.

See if you can work your way through Figure 14.12 and try to grasp why leisure had such prominence in societies like the former Soviet Union.

Leisure as a basis of self-realization

Finally, we have the most difficult concept to look at. We need to pick up the comments made by several of the authors we quoted earlier, where they wrote about humanistic values like self-realization and socialization.

The potential of leisure as a medium for creative fulfilment is being increasingly recognized. It takes the social conditioning of the last model an extra step, where, in addition to the extrinsic usefulness of leisure, it is felt that in the modern world of sedentary jobs, packaged goods and repetitious work, the only creative moments may arise in our leisure experiences; that only leisure can give us all a **taste of excellence.** Though you might think that all this is pretty revolutionary, the notion goes back to Aristotle, who argued that leisure is the most serious human occupation or activity. If you combine this with Ruskin's comment in the 19th century that leisure is the exertion of body or mind to please ourselves, we have an enlightened view of leisure as the key to personal development in a democratic society and as an art form in the context of cultural advancement. Select a leisure experience you have had and trace it through 14.13.

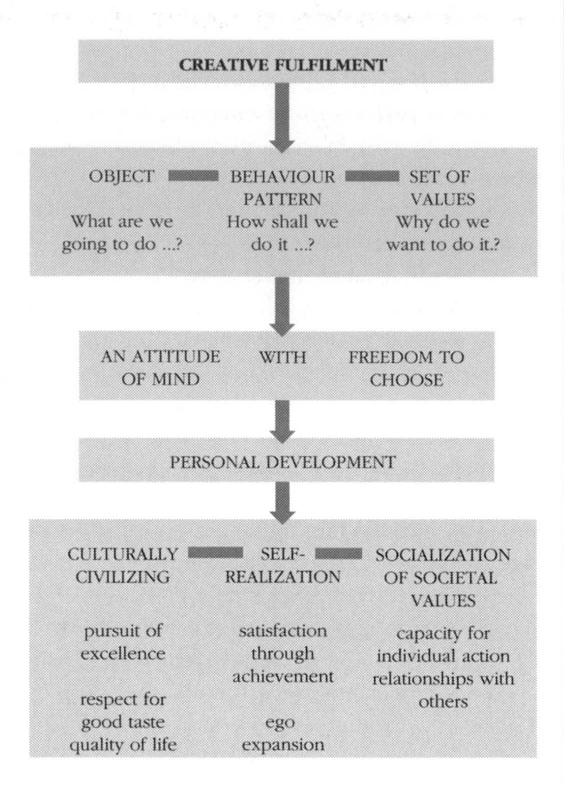

Figure 14.13

Summary

Leisure:

1. **Freedom**; **relaxation**; **choice**; **opportunity**; **recreation**.
2. Leisure time is **time** without **obligation**; an activity which is also an **experience**; a **performance** depending on **attitude**.
3. It is a **non-work** experience; **an economic condition**; **a social process**; and a **basis for self-fulfilment**.

14.2 Towards a Concept of Play

It is very important for us to understand what we mean by the term **play.** We use the word all the time and yet when we go to psychology books we find we are getting into a highly complex area. Let's take it gradually.

Play is something we do. It involves ourselves and others in action. It tends to make us feel good, but it has little or nothing to do with the real world; in fact, we often play to get away from the real world. Children play much more than adults, and if it was not for the use of the word in the theatre and in sport we would probably feel that it concerned only children. Play is not necessarily a physical experience, but because it normally involves the whole person there is often a physical component.

When we are playing, we are behaving in such a way as to retain attitudes which have their origin in **play**; and when we are **playful** we are having fun.

Let's compare **war** and a **football match** for a moment. War is real. You fight and the consequence may be death. The intention is to kill. Jokingly, you might suggest that you have seen football matches like that! Well, first of all, football is kicking a ball about, it is fun. A match is contrived to test the temperament and skill of one group against another, through football. It is played according to fixed rules with playing area and timing strictly controlled. When the whistle goes it is over.

Figure 14.14 Go on! Enjoy yourself!

These are all characteristics of play, but occasionally rules are broken, violence breaks out, and aggression goes on after the whistle. When this happens the game has left the world of play and become real; it can even become war!

Similarly, playing the game means you have made an undertaking to 'play the game'. If you cheat or commit fouls, you have stepped outside the play concept. We would argue that you have also stepped outside the moral concept of the game. The result of such behaviour will lead to the destruction of the **play element** immediately, and of the **game situation** eventually.

Can you identify any characteristics of play in these two photographs?

Figure 14.15

Figure 14.16

If you have an opportunity, do a critical review of the film *Rollerball* to explain what has happened to the twin concepts of **play** and **game**.

Finally, you will find that theorists invariably look at a pure form of **play**, largely because it is much easier to categorize. However, when you see play operating, it is clear that you are looking not at a pure form of it but at elements of play mixed in with moments of reality. This is almost always the case in our **field of study.**

Try to pick out the key words which help to identify this thing called **play** from what has been written above.

We have come up with the model in Figure 14.17. Compare it with your own.

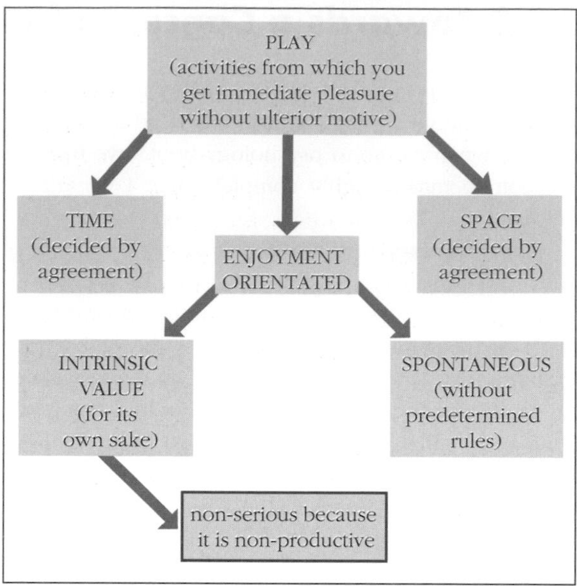

Figure 14.17

REVIEW QUESTIONS

There has been a lot of theory written about **play**. What we need to do is to test some of these views against our own experiences.

1. Divide the following notions between members of the group, establishing the meaning of the different phrases and giving examples: civilization preparation; role rehearsal; surplus energy; recreation; instinctive practice; recapitulation; transmission of culture; personality development; cathartic function; ego expansion.

   Alternatively, take a simple play activity like hide and seek and see how many of these interpretations can be linked with it.

   What we are discovering is that **play** has many sides to it and, therefore, can have a wide range of interpretations and uses.
2. Now explain Figure 14.18.

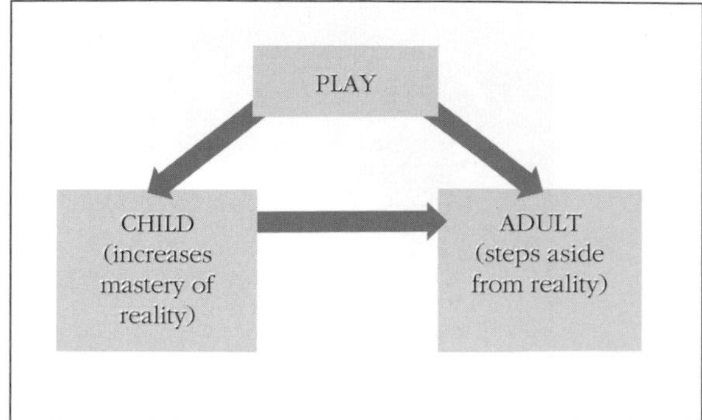

Figure 14.18

3. The final test as to whether we understand the term **play** in the context of **physical performance** is to turn to Huizinga (1949).

   Select a physical performance activity that you have **played.** Test the extent to which you were really **playing** from the following criteria:

   a. Play is a voluntary activity, never a physical necessity or a moral duty. It is not a matter of leisure and free time, it is freedom.

   b. Play is not ordinary or real life, but this is not to say that play may not be intense or serious . . . an interlude in our daily lives, an end in itself.

   c. Play is a temporary world within and marked off from the ordinary world. It begins and is over in a specific moment and functions within limitations of time and space.

   d. Play creates order; in fact it is order. Slight deviation from the rules spoils the game.

   e. The play community tends to become permanent, because in the course of playing you become part of an 'in-group', sharing a common existence.

   If you have managed to understand these principles in the context of your chosen activity, you will realize that many of the components of play are immediately identifiable in physical recreation and sport. The more structured and commercially orientated sport is, the less play is evident, and one might argue that the sheer joy of participation is often lost because of the work-orientated values which exist in high-level sport, resulting in an obsession with a 'win at all cost' ethic.

And so we end with the Huizinga definition:

> *Play is an activity which proceeds within certain limits of time and space, in a visible order according to rules freely accepted, and outside the sphere of necessity or material utility. The play mood is one of rapture and enthusiasm and is sacred or festive in accordance with the occasion. A feeling of exaltation and tension accompanies the action, mirth and relaxation follow.*

You will no doubt recognize these characteristics from your own experiences of games, individual activities and outdoor pursuits, and so there is every justification for us to continue to use the word **play** freely in our field of study and to expect **sport for all** to live up to the qualities which are an inherent part of the play concept.

It may not be obvious, but the application of play theory to playing games takes us away from the original emphasis by Huizinga and Caillois in that they stressed the temporary nature and spontaneity of play, largely discounting its developmental potential. The concept of play which we are adopting presumes that, given a retention of play attitudes, rules can facilitate rather than destroy a play situation. Secondly, that whether the game is won or lost, the experience can yet increase a person's ability to know themselves and others with greater emotional and social skill.

This explanation is very much part of the education in physical education and the test of temperament which exists in most sporting situations. It is also a counter to the 'win-at-all-costs' ethic, which presumes that only winners gain from a sporting competition.

Summary

Play:

1. **Free time; free space; spontaneity; intrinsic; enjoyable; unreal.**
2. Play is something we do: it is an activity-experience.
3. It is associated with children, but vestiges are retained into adulthood.
4. Play is **non-serious** because it is **non-productive,** and yet it may be a major factor in self-development.

14.3 Towards a Concept of Recreation

Recreation is a positive aspect of **leisure** and is widely used in the Western World to describe **active leisure.**

Two major problems with its universal acceptance concern its traditional association with the privileged classes, and the built-in presumption that it has only intrinsic value. 'Socialist' societies have tended not to use the term on these grounds. Let's see how others define it.

> *Activity voluntarily engaged in during leisure and motivated by the personal satisfactions which result from it . . . a tool for mental and physical therapy.*
>
> (Kaplan, 1975)

> *Recreation embodies those experiences or activities that people take part in during their leisure for purposes of pleasure, satisfaction or education.*
>
> *Recreation is a human experience or activity, it is not necessarily instinctive, it may be considered purposeful.*
>
> (Zeigler, 1964)

> *Recreation carries away the individual from his usual concerns and problems. The attitudes derived from this are those involving feelings of relaxation. Contentment not complacency might best describe an attitude which is a product of a recreative experience.*
>
> (Vanderswaag, 1972)

> *Recreation is a concept closely related to play. . . It means literally to re-create or to refresh oneself in body and/or engagement. Recreational activity is also limited in time and space by the actor and requires no preparation or training. Recreation is also non-utilitarian in product.*
>
> (Edwards, 1973)

If you go through the same exercise of selecting key words, you will notice strong links with the analysis we have already done on leisure, but also be aware of the conflict between those who label recreation **non-utilitarian** and others who acknowledge that it can be **purposeful**. Significantly, all the authors quoted are American, and yet they cannot agree. Little wonder writers in the now disbanded Soviet Union find it an outmoded concept!

You will find that the four basic conceptual models we used to analyse leisure apply also to the slightly narrower field of recreation. We have taken characteristics mentioned in the quotations and built a model (Figure 14.19). Take a particular recreation and identify it in the context of each stage.

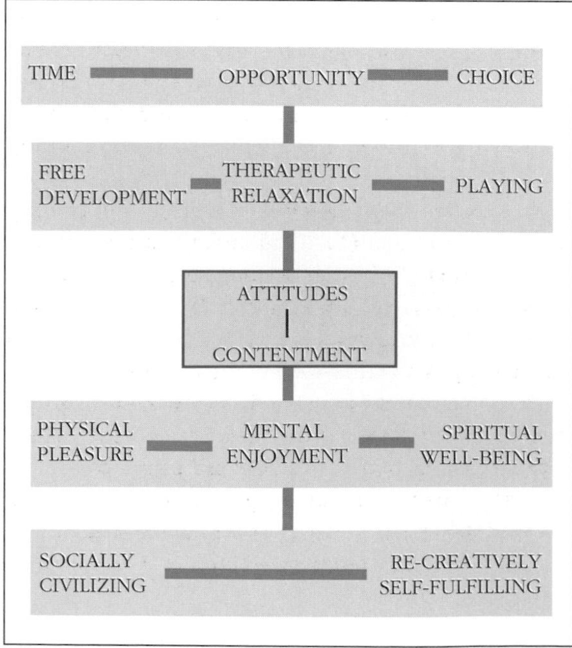

Figure 14.19 Towards a concept of recreation.

14.4 What do we mean by Physical Recreation?

To date, you have been asked to identify the characteristics of leisure and recreation from a series of models and the occasional photograph. It is important that you should now get some practice in recognizing the characteristics yourself, from a series of statements which we will call **notional propositions**. It is for you to think them through and decide whether you accept them or wish to question them. At the end of the exercise, however, you should have a list of the central characteristics of **physical recreation**.

Having made the progression from the general concept of **leisure** to the narrower experience of **recreation**, it should be a relatively straightforward step to reduce the field that much more to include only **physical recreation**. This notion of narrowing is an important one, because the conceptual elements identified in the **leisure analysis** still hold true, but also because some of the cultural bias evident in **recreation** continues to operate in **physical recreation**.

The former Soviet Union, for example, tended to suspect that discrimination and non-functional values were still applied to the term **physical recreation** in the West. They chose to use the term **massovost,** which avoided these limitations. In Britain and France, the slogan **sport for all** is extremely popular and tends to be replacing the term **physical recreation** to describe physical performance opportunities for all members of the community, where emphasis is on **participation** rather than **performance standards.** Loy, Jun. (1970) in the United States has coined the phrase **game occurrence** to describe physical activity which is playful, competitive and strategic, with physical skill and prowess, but is played at a relatively unsophisticated level.

Probably the main reason why the term **physical recreation** is still used is simply tradition, but it would also seem that none of the other expressions are able to replace it completely. It is a wider concept than **game**; and the recreative can be at odds with the sportive. Similarly, how can we still incorporate the concept of **outdoor recreation**, which is very much in vogue, when we are suggesting that the concept of **physical recreation** is outmoded?

Outdoor recreation

This term survives not only because of the traditional romanticism associated with the countryside, but also because it invariably involves challenge of self in the natural environment, which is more obviously **recreative** than the contrived **competition** of a game.

Outdoor recreation and the **frontier spirit** remain symbolic features of American ideology, and the late Soviet Union gave considerable political and national recognition to its outdoor policy, under the heading of **tourism**.

Participation for its own sake

This is the key to the identity of **physical recreation** and is also the reason why academics and politicians have claimed that it is **non-serious.** The assumption here is that if there is no intellectual or commercial value, it is not functionally important in a society.

The fact that, in the 19th century, recreative opportunity was to some extent limited to wealthy people who had the 'right', the money and the time to participate is no more than an accident of history, but may yet remain as a vestige of those times.

The privilege of a few has now become the right of the majority and so the social impact of **physical recreation** is that much broader. Now that almost everyone has the opportunity to recreate physically, we are increasingly motivated to gain from it: as a therapeutic experience; as a frontier experience, where we learn more about ourselves; and as a social experience, where we can make lasting friendships.

The key democratic factors are the right to choose; the opportunity to participate; and the provision to facilitate that freedom.

Little wonder that the Soviet Union was prepared to take these intrinsic elements and give them cultural status, on the ground that here was an experience which would influence productivity and social well-being by improving health and increasing group morale.

American writers like Slusher (1967), Vanderswaag (1972) and Hellison (1975) all argue that the self-realizing potential of physical performance makes it a vital element in personal development. This would seem to be particularly true in a country where individual decision-making is a cornerstone of the culture.

There may even be a case for using the term **physical recreation** in a more general context, where **sport** is identified as one specialized aspect of it.

In societies where **taking part** is more highly valued than **winning**, the **recreative** component may be stronger than the **competitive** one. After all, there is

Figure 14.20 This is my idea of heaven!

not so much a conceptual difference between **physical recreation** and **sport**, as a gradually increasing intensity of efficiency at the professionalized end of the continuum.

Hold on a minute: it would seem that **professional sport,** as a means of livelihood, can hardly be identified as a **physical recreation!**

We have already made the point that physical activities can be recreational, sporting or educational, depending on the level of commitment. Furthermore, certain words specifically identify activities at a recreative level. For example, **rambling, pony trekking, hill-walking, paddling, cycle touring** and **boating** reflect outdoor activities as pastimes rather than as sports; **jogging, bathing** and **aerobics** are recreative forms of individual activity; in addition, there are phrases like **kick about** at football, **knock about** at tennis, or a **friendly** game of golf, which imply that a game is being played at a low competitive key.

These words and phrases tell us that the physical activity is recreative and being enjoyed with minimal organization. We have now gathered enough characteristics of physical recreation to produce our own conceptual model as a framework to test our understanding.

It is most important that you should be able to operationalize this framework and so take a physical activity which you have experienced at a recreative level and use it to illustrate the key words in Figure 14.21.

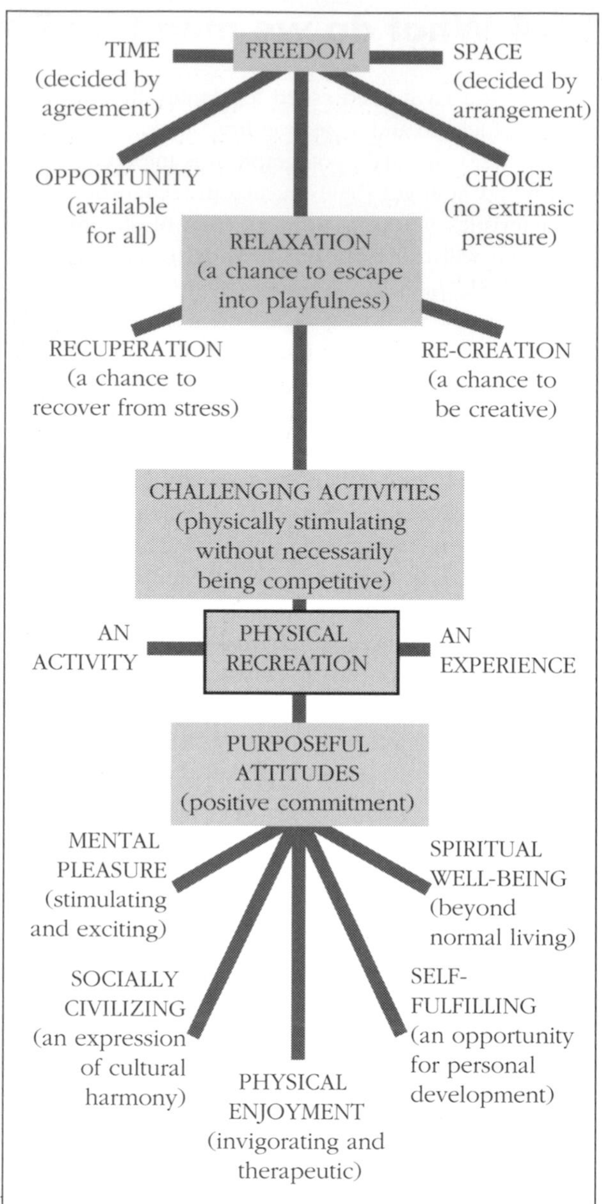

Figure 14.21

REVIEW QUESTIONS

You have your experience of recreating; you have made a systematic analysis of leisure characteristics earlier in this chapter; and you now have a range of notions outlining the qualities one would expect in **physical recreations**.

1. Using this knowledge, select one outdoor activity, one individual activity and one game from the following photographs, and describe the characteristics you would expect to find if you were playing these at a **physical recreation** level.

a. Outdoor activities Study Figure 14.22. What have these outdoor pursuits got in common?

Figure 14.22

b. Individual activities Why are the individual activities in Figure 14.23 'recreative' rather than 'sporting'?

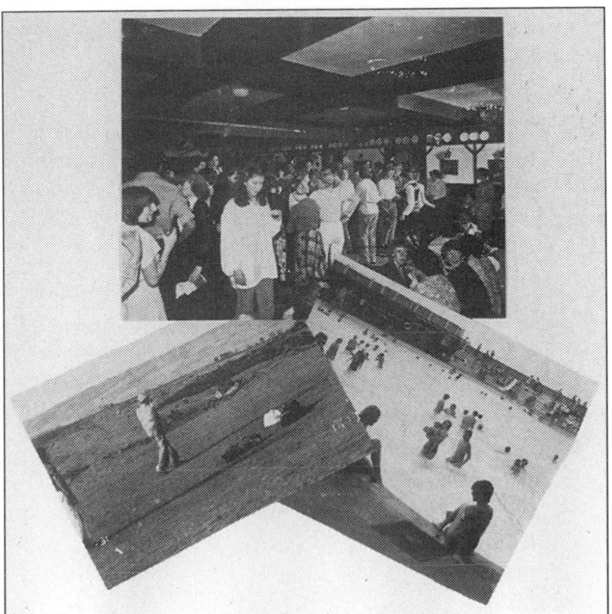

Figure 14.23

c. Games

What clues are there in the pictures in Figure 14.24 to suggest that the players have a recreative attitude? Could we be wrong?

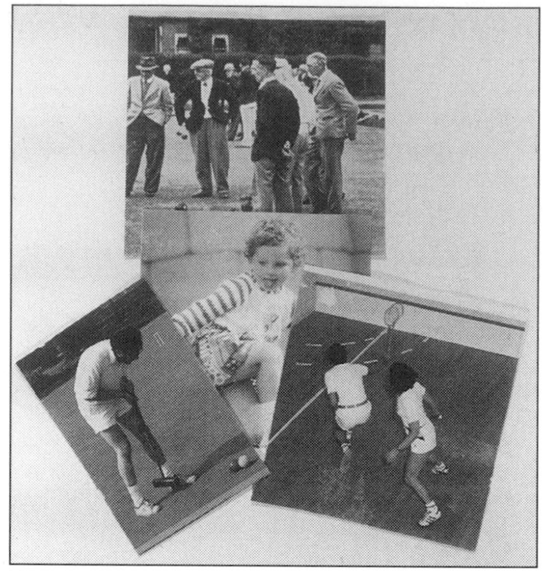

Figure 14.24

2. As an alternative, you may find it more beneficial to attempt some structured questions.
   a. **Outdoor recreation** allows man and woman to re-create in ideal surroundings.
      i) What qualities are you likely to find in the natural environment which could lead to the use of the term 'romanticism'?
      ii) Use any one photograph to explain the association of freedom and adventure.
      iii) Explain how therapy appears to result from considerable effort in the outdoors.
      iv) Why do you think bonds of friendship are so strong after expeditions similar to those shown in the photographs?
   b. **Individual activities** do not have to be based on competition.
      i) Explain the idea of being 'free to move'.
      ii) Select any one picture and discuss the 'health related' qualities depicted.
      iii) What can you learn about yourself if you become involved in an individual activity at a recreative level?
   c. The most important element in a **game** is the enjoyment which arises from taking part.
      i) Why do you think a game should always be 'friendly'?
      ii) Why is participation in a game so rewarding even when the standard of play is low?
      iii) We say that we 'play' a game. Explain the elements of play which can exist in any one of the games in the photographs.

Summary

Physical recreation:

1. **Free time; free space; enjoyment orientated; recuperative; spiritual well-being.**
2. **Physical recreation** is a part of **recreation**. It can include most sporting activities, but also includes physical activities which are not competitive.
3. **Participation** is invariably more important than **results** where the recreative component is dominant.

14.5. Towards a Concept of Sport

Sport is commonplace and yet always controversial. It is universal in the sense that every country practises it, and yet it does not always take the same form in each country. Everyone seems to know what it means, but it doesn't always mean the same to everyone.

There are three levels at which we can attempt to explain these apparent contradictions:

1. **Sports and pastimes** are as old as civilization and many features and values of modern **sport** are vestiges of the past.
2. **Sport** reflects the **culture** to which it belongs and, therefore, it also reflects cultural variables.
3. **Sport** is a sophisticated concept and, while it is relatively easy to identify its universal characteristics, the more we refine our definition the more varied the cultural interpretation.

Let's first of all clarify the historical connotations. You must be well aware that **sports and pastimes** are as old as civilization itself. There is ample archaeological evidence that ancient societies indulged in physical activities ranging from bull-leaping in the Minoan Culture of Crete to the football game of Tsu Chu played in China over 3,000 years ago. You will be aware of the Ancient Greek Olympic Games but you may not realize that Olympian Games also took place in Medieval England, as witnessed by the Dover Games; and re-emerged in Victorian England with the Much Wenlock Olympian Games, well before the 1896 modern revival.

REVIEW QUESTIONS

1. Do you know a sport when you see one?

- Under the heading of **games**, football, hockey, baseball and tennis, for example, all seem to be acceptable—but what about poker, chess or table skittles?
- **Individual activities,** like track and field, swimming and gymnastics, are unquestionably sports, but what about sunbathing, skipping or body building?
- We have no doubts about **outdoor pursuits** like canoeing and rock climbing, but what about cycling, motor racing, hunting, angling and horseracing?

Take some of these activities and discuss your reservations about them being part of **sport.**

2. Look at Figures 14.25 and 14.26. What characteristics determine whether these are sports or not?

In answering these questions, you have been determining what is **necessary for an activity to be a sport.** This is the first level of definition.

Figure 14.25

Figure 14.26

If, on the other hand, we look briefly at the **cultural** factors, there is ample evidence that different primitive cultures have evolved **sports and pastimes** which reflect their needs. The sports of the Canadian Eskimo have little in common with those of the Australian aborigine. Even where cultures are geographically related, there are major differences. In Melanesia, for example, the war-like contests in Fiji are very different from the land-diving festival in the New Hebrides.

Controversially, a case has been made by Elias (1970) that these ancient and primitive **sports** are not **sport** in the modern definition of the term. He suggests that the **Genesis of Sport** is the product of the European industrial revolution in the 19th century, and is consequently a highly sophisticated institution matching the technology of such advanced societies as the United States and Western Europe.

After making our own attempt to classify sport, let's find an authoritative view.

The International Council for Sport and Physical Education (ICSPE) (1964) has suggested that:

Any physical activity which has the character of play and which takes the form of a struggle with oneself or involves competition with others is a sport.

Did you pick out elements like **physical, play, struggle with self, competition**, when you were identifying those activities earlier?

Michener (1976) has a similar definition:

An athletic activity requiring physical prowess or skill and usually of a competitive nature.

Should we take the Kaplan (1975) notion on board again and suggest that they are more than **activities** in that they are also **experiences**? Certainly, we could argue that participation in a sport can be a most worthwhile experience.

The notion of **sport** as an **experience** is supported by Inglis (1977) when he suggests that:

Sport is a scrapbook of memories which defines life. It involves a peculiar and intense awareness of yourself, a self-consciousness, in which the point of awareness is to get something right which is quite outside yourself.

Let's not forget our definition of **physical recreation** and the associated term, **game occurrence**. We have not defined anything which is exclusively **sport** as yet, have we? However, it is worth making the point that we are reinforcing the notion that **sport** is at one end of a **physical recreation continuum** (Calhoun, 1986).

Don't worry if you are still unsure whether some activities are **sports** or not. Many others have also tried with only limited success.

Caillois (1961), in his analysis of *paida* to *ludus* (play to games), classified sports into four main categories:

- Agon (competition)
- Mimicry (pretence)
- Alea (chance)
- Ilinx (vertigo)

Huizinga (1964) extended these to eight:

- Pursuit (chase)
- Enigma (mental)
- Chance (gamble)
- Vertigo (heady)
- Strategy (planning)
- Imitation (pretence)
- Dexterity (skill)
- Exultation (excitement)

McIntosh (1987) suggested

- Competition
- Aesthetic
- Combat
- Chance
- Conquest

There is considerable overlap between these three attempted classifications. It should also be clear that, whereas some activities/experiences are within one criterion, other sports include a combination.

If you use the Huizinga classification, it also seems reasonable to suggest that the more criteria operating in any particular activity, the more secure its status as a sport.

Test these propositions by describing the sport criteria evident in:

a. horseracing
b. rowing

We are now ready for a second level of analysis. Are there any set conditions as to **how an activity should be performed** before it can be accepted as a **sport?**

The ICSPE (1964) claimed that:

If this activity involves competition, then it should always be performed with a spirit of sportsmanship. There can be no true sport without the idea of fair play.

The assumption is that **sport** and **sportsmanship** are inseparable, definitive components of the **sporting experience.**

Noel-Baker (1965) suggested that:

Fair play is the essence, the sine qua non, of any game or sport that is worthy of the name.

Similarly, the following words of Baron de Coubertin are displayed at all the modern Olympic Games:

The most important thing in the Olympic Games is not to win but to take part, just as the most important thing in life is not the triumph but the struggle.

This **moral intention** is further reinforced in the Olympic oath, where reference is made to

. . . respecting and abiding by the rules that bind them, in the true spirit of sportsmanship, for the glory of sport and the honour of our teams.

Before you point to the cheating and corruption, the drug abuse and the political intrigue, which are commonplace in the modern Olympics, remember we are trying to establish what sport ought to be. Time enough later to recognize all the shortcomings.

An explanation of this moral requirement is best achieved at the three levels used earlier: historical, cultural and ideological.

Ancient and primitive societies have consistently used sport festivals as a ritual expression of their cultures. The Ancient Olympic Games reflected the **Man of Action** concept held by citizen Greeks: the Tournament reinforced the **Chivalric Code** in 12th-century Europe; the **Courtly Mould** was a cornerstone of Tudor England and Renaissance Europe; and the emergence of the **Gentleman Amateur** in 18th- and 19th-century England reflected the lifestyle of a leisured class.

In each case, the elite members of a civilization used sport to reflect the ideals they held most dear.

It is important to recognize that sport was the arena in which physical prowess and temperament were tested.

There were various times when these ethics were closely tied to religious beliefs: Greek gods were idealized humans; the chivalric code fueled the Crusades; and Muscular Christianity was inspired by Gentlemen Amateurs who were also social Christians. Nor must we forget that 19th-century **Athleticism** in the English Public Schools was a duality of **physical endeavour** and **moral integrity,** not one or the other.

The bonding through tradition, therefore, is very clearly defined. However, we need to recognize that cultures differ and this means that, in addition to sport differing, the values associated with it vary from one country to another.

Gardner (1974) examined the American 'Win' ethic, linking it with the 'Lombardian' commitment of American professional sport and the pressures of capitalism and commercialism in American society.

See if you can discover who Vince Lombardi was and why he is quoted so much by American sports commentators.

Little wonder that the European ethic of 'doing your best' has been regarded as an excuse for weakness. Mind you, professional British sport is equally sceptical of this amateur ethic.

Lombardism, on the other hand, defends the view that only winners matter in sport and society, turning the Olympic model on its head and emphasising the triumph rather than the struggle.

If you want to continue this dialogue, it is probable that the humanist would reply that the struggle to do one's best is socially desirable and open to all, but that triumph is a reward for a few and a mark of failure for the rest.

There is a very interesting relationship here with rewards. The Greeks had a laurel wreath and 19th-century amateurs had medals—token reminders of the struggle. Today, an elite group of athletes receives great wealth, because commercialism idealizes the champion in order to sell products to the envious. We find emergent cultures promoting their champions for such reasons as giving their citizens a sense of national pride or, more questionably, as an opium to forget hardship or revolution.

The Soviet culture, interestingly, needed winners to reinforce its political identity and yet could not justify the promotion of individualism in a so-called socialist society. Consequently, 'to do your best' was a very real Soviet concept, but it had to be for society rather than for self.

Fair play, therefore, is under attack from professional and commercial forces. Sport and sportsmanship have become political instruments and expedients. In both instances they represent a dominance of extrinsic factors, undermining intrinsic values.

We must defend sport from these external excesses, if we believe that the essence of sport is sportsmanship.

As early as 1967 Lüschen pointed out that sport had the potential to be **functional** or **dysfunctional**. It is an arena where 'man' is tested and may fail to cope with the situation. How many of you have fouled in a game in the heat of the moment, hopefully to regret it later?

If you want to achieve the highest moral experience from sport, you should be able to play to the rules regardless of having a referee present. Jimmy White, the professional snooker player, repeatedly acknowledges when he has committed a foul stroke, regardless of whether the referee has seen it. Here is the principle of 'walking at cricket'.

In life, there are those of us who would not steal on principle, while others do not steal because they are afraid of being caught. Similarly, some of us need the referee to be there to make decisions for us. Hopefully, we accept his decision even if we don't agree with it, but there are times when we argue with the referee or even retaliate against an offending player. When we do this the experience is detrimental to us as a person and detrimental to the game.

Nash developed this concept in the context of Recreation and Leisure and Figure 14.27 is an adjustment of his model to match the sporting situation.

The third level of analysis is the one which allows us to distinguish between **physical recreation** (a **game occurrence**) and **sport**.

You will recall that Inglis (1977) identified an 'intense awareness... to get something right'. Similarly, McIntosh (1987) wrote about 'striving for superiority against man and/or nature'. Weiss (1967), Loy (1970) and Howell (1986) all define sport as a **highly organized game requiring physical prowess**.

This is the identification of **sport as an institution**. To understand this we need to take it through three stages:

1. As an administrational feature. To paraphrase Dunning (1969)—sport has a stringent organization; fully standardized codification; a high level of permanence and regularity; and technological sophistication.
2. It requires a performer to embark on a high level of physical preparation, involving fitness and skill ability.
3. It invariably demands an attitude of commitment, a struggle to focus the mind and body on attaining the goals of the competition or challenge situation.

HIGH 3 (functional)	personal decision in the true spirit of the game	creative participation	inventive player/coach
2	personal decisions regarding the rules of play	active participation	playing the part: role-play
1	acceptance of the referee	emotional participation	observational appreciation
0	reluctant acceptance of the referee	entertainment amusement escape from monotony of killing time	antidote for boredom
–1	arguing with the referee	injury or detriment to self	excesses
–2 (dysfunctional)	retaliation	violence against other players	crime

Figure 14.27. Application of Nash's model.

We need look only at great athletes like Daley Thompson (UK), Mark Spitz (USA), Jean-Claude Killy (Fr), and Ludmilla Turishcheva (former USSR) to identify the time and attitude commitment; the outstanding quality of performance; and the administrative support system necessary for them to have achieved their optimum level of performance.

What we have, therefore, is a three tier analysis: certain activities/experiences involving a spirit of fair play at the highest level of personal excellence.

What will have become obvious is that the more professionalized the sport, the less affinity there is with Huizinga's play criteria. Edwards (1973) goes so far as to say that sport has nothing in common with play, but this seems too categorical. Howell (1986) seems nearer the mark when he writes that:

> *an individual has to have satisfaction from playing the sport, otherwise it ceases to be a sport. A professional athlete whose only concern is money and who does not care for the activity itself would no longer be engaged in sport, but work.*

It might seem that this combination necessarily excludes the **Sport for All** concept. However, though attention is automatically drawn to a professionalized elite, the term **personal excellence** has been deliberately chosen because it describes any person with the commitment to strive for his or her own optimum level of achievement. The Sport for All campaign is designed to give everyone this opportunity, and if they choose to retain a recreative attitude, so be it, but the provision, opportunity and esteem are all there to be grasped in the fullness and freedom of a leisure-time decision.

It is important that you should be able to illustrate Figure 14.28 from your own experience of a sport. You could trace a sport at which you have competed and then take the likely path of a successful professional performer. Comparing these two pathways is worthwhile, but it is also important that you refer back to Figure 14.21 and compare it with Figure 14.28, explaining the extent to which the concepts of physical recreation and sport can differ.

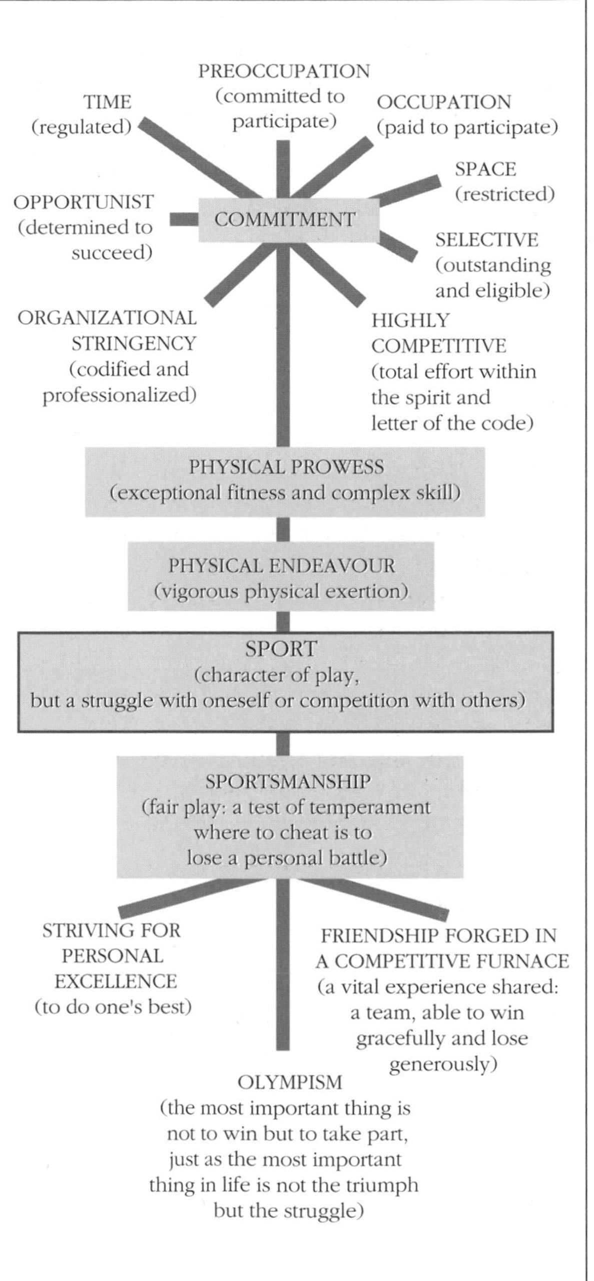

Figure 14.28.

TEST YOUR UNDERSTANDING OF THE CONCEPT OF SPORT.

Select a specific sport with which you are acquianted and use it to explain the following definition of sport:

> *Sport is an institutionalized competitive activity that involves vigorous physical exertion or the use of relatively complex physical skills by individuals whose participation is motivated by a combination of the intrinsic satisfaction associated with the activity itself and the external rewards earned through participation.*
>
> (Coakley, 1978)

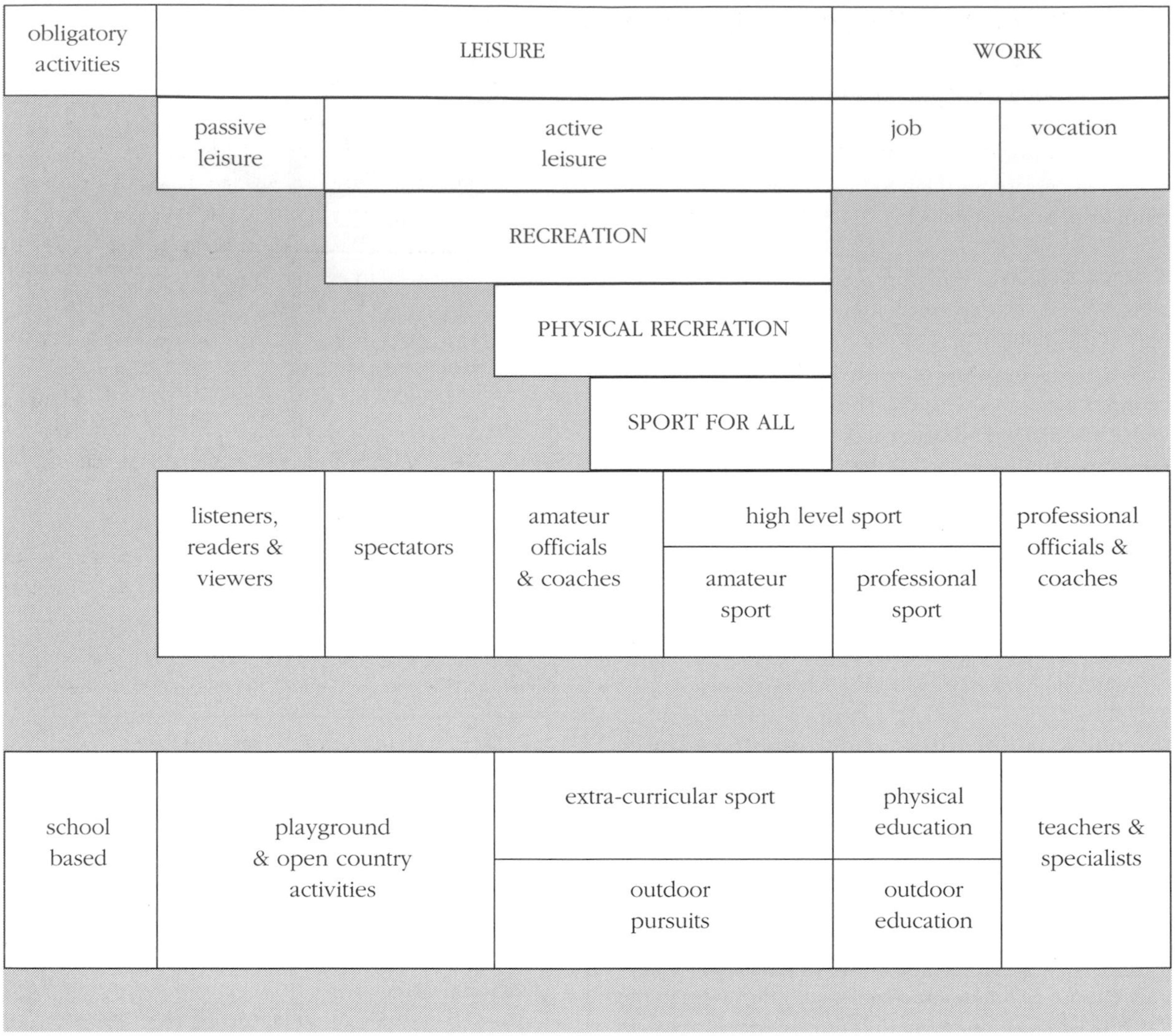

obligatory activities
LEISURE
WORK
passive leisure
active leisure
job
vocation
RECREATION
PHYSICAL RECREATION
SPORT FOR ALL
listeners, readers & viewers
spectators
amateur officials & coaches
high level sport
amateur sport
professional sport
professional officials & coaches
school based
playground & open country activities
extra-curricular sport
physical education
teachers & specialists
outdoor pursuits
outdoor education

REVIEW QUESTION

Test your understanding by identifying one of your own experiences in each of the labelled boxes, briefly explaining what is happening as you move from top left to bottom right.

This is a good time to reaffirm that no classification in our field of study is going to be perfect and so have fun trying to point out the errors in this one. Then, if you are brave enough, produce your own format and defend it.

Summary

Sport:

1. **Sport for all** or **sporting excellence; amateurism** and **professionalism; commercialism** and **spectatorism; sport** and **sportsmanship.**
2. **Sport** consists of **contests, conquests, games** and **chance.**
3. Sport is an **activity-experience,** reflecting **dynamic attitudes.**
4. Sport and society are **intertwined.**
5. Sport is an **institution** and a **social process.**

14.6 What is Physical Education?

It might help to get us started to establish where the term is used:

- numerous Universities award degrees in physical education;
- it is a subject taught in all schools and is part of the core curriculum;
- the main administrative body is the Physical Education Association (PEA);
- the term is used to describe several GCSE syllabuses and an Advanced level GCE syllabus.

However, authors tend to write about physical education *and* sport, and so presumably they are not one and the same thing. And although the term appears to have a similar currency in the United States, France and Britain, this is less the case in the diverse group of countries, federation of republics etc., that once comprised the Soviet Union.

Let's look first at the situation in the former USSR. Though the term physical education is used, **physical culture** is a more common expression. Riordan (1975) suggested that this more general concept could be defined as:

The sum total of social achievements connected with man's physical development and education.

If this is to be accepted, what was once the Soviet Union has a collective term for the whole of our field of study.

We intend to work from a very narrow definition of **physical education**, where it is limited to:

The formal inculcation of knowledge and values through physical activity/experiences.

As a direct result, physical education is most likely to be practised in educational institutions. The Leeds Study Group (1970) defined physical education as:

A term used to describe an area of educational activity in which the main concern is with bodily movement.

(Where the words 'educational activity' are presumed to mean the formal inculcation of socially desirable knowledge and values.)

The actual activities are often common to those already identified in play, physical recreation and sport, and are those found in the school curriculum.

REVIEW QUESTIONS

1. a. Using your own school as an example, explain Figure 14.29 in terms of curriculum PE, extra-curricular programmes and recreational activities.
b. Why is a pyramid such a useful analogy?

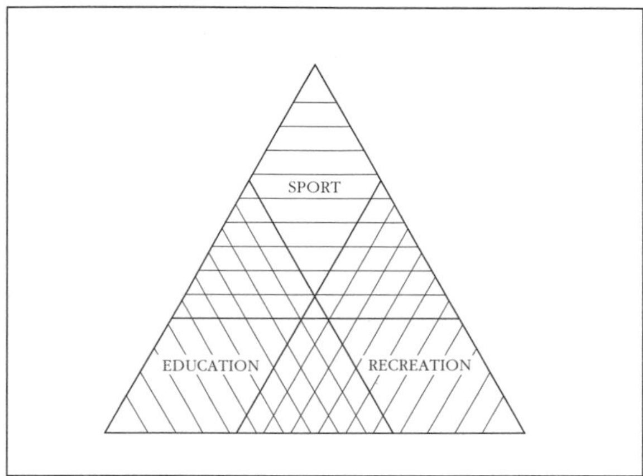

Figure 14.29

2. a. Again using your own school as an example, explain Figure 14.30 in terms of relationships.
b. Why are circles such a useful analogy in this context?

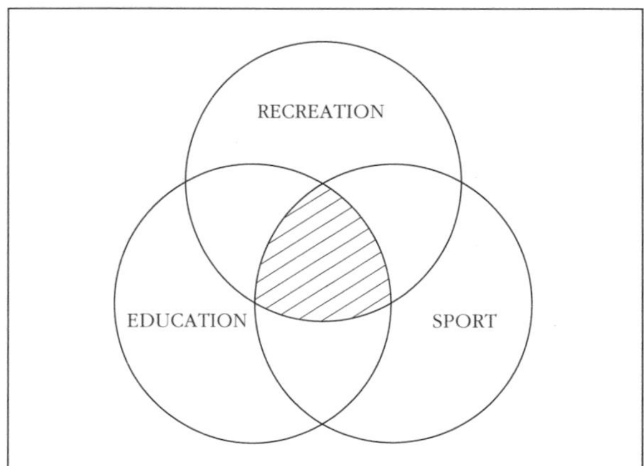

Figure 14.30

3. List the activities on your curriculum under two headings, **core subjects** and **options**.

4. Select one of your favourite physical education activities and use it to explain these three ways of knowing and understanding physical performance.

The core subjects will probably be common to most schools and include major games, gymnastics, track and field, and swimming. These are normally compulsory activities, but may vary according to gender and age group.

It is very important at this point to recognize that curriculum physical education is only one of a number of physical performance opportunities in the average school. Groves (1972) produced two diagrams to illustrate this relationship between physical education, physical recreation and sport in schools (Figures 14.29 and 14.30).

The optional subjects will probably be less common because they have not been a traditional part of the curriculum; because they are less physical; or because they are too expensive in terms of time, space or cost. Some of the activities we have recognized as sports may not be included in the school curriculum for these reasons, but some sports may not be suitable for children, for example, they may be too dangerous to be pursued at school.

There are a number of traditional reasons why certain activities are included in the PE curriculum. For example, gymnastics has military and therapeutic roots; games owe much to the character building ethic of the English public schools in the nineteenth century; and swimming has had links with cleanliness and safety.

There is also a very strong cultural association. Examples of high prestige activities dominating the curriculum for economic and popularity reasons include American football and basketball in the United States; gymnastics and skiing in the one-time Soviet Union; and cricket and football in England.

However, the overriding reason for teaching a particular activity should be its potential as a **medium for education**. Lüshchen (1967), for example, subdivided sports into functional and dysfunctional, meaning that the latter had a detrimental influence on society. In England today, the behaviour associated with professional soccer might lead educationists to the conclusion that the game should not be taught in schools. Conversely, it can be argued that there is an even greater need to teach it, to reform its popular image.

It would seem that certain activities have more potential as a vehicle for the inculcation of desirable values. Currently, in England, gymnastics is regarded as an ideal medium by educationists, whereas table tennis is generally presumed to have only recreative value. These are dangerous presumptions as most sporting activities can become educational vehicles in the right hands.

A great deal also depends on the knowledge and values being promoted; for example, the choice of gymnastics in England is linked with heuristic, therapeutic and individualistic values, currently in vogue in educational circles. Alternatively, the importance of football in the American high school is tied to the significance of the sports ethic in the community and the socio-economic importance of competition and manliness.

We certainly need to tease out these societal variables before we can suggest what **physical education** ought to be in any one particular country. What we need to do, therefore, is to produce a series of models which you can easily adjust to meet the needs of different societies.

First of all, we will look at **knowledge**.

We teach **physical education** because we think it has a useful body of knowledge, the implication being that having this knowledge will make us better people and enhance our lifestyle.

We can assess its usefulness at three levels:

1. **Knowing about physical activities** should help us to understand them and enable us to talk about them.
2. **Knowing how to perform** allows us to express ourselves through physical skills and competitive performance.
3. **Knowing how it feels to perform** gives us an enriching experience which is possible only in a performance situation.

We teach **physical education** because we can promote desirable values both as an intrinsic experience and to achieve extrinsic ends. Let's look at these values under four main headings. Where you can, illustrate each one from your experience of a game, an individual activity, a contest and an outdoor pursuit.

1. **Instrumental values:** those directly linked with physical performance (see Figure 14.31).
2. **Economic values:** those which are useful in everyday life and valuable to the community (see Figure 14.32).
3. **Humanistic values:** those which help in the development of a wholesome personality (see Figure 14.33).
4. **Quality of Life:** those which carry experience beyond the ordinary in terms of awareness and commitment (see Figure 14.34).

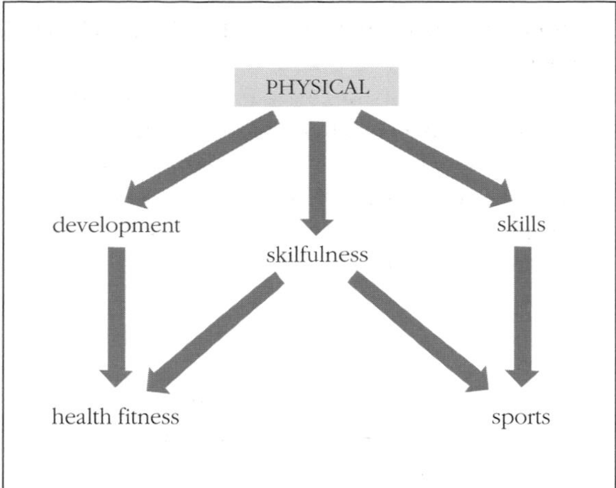

Figure 14.31 Instrumental values.

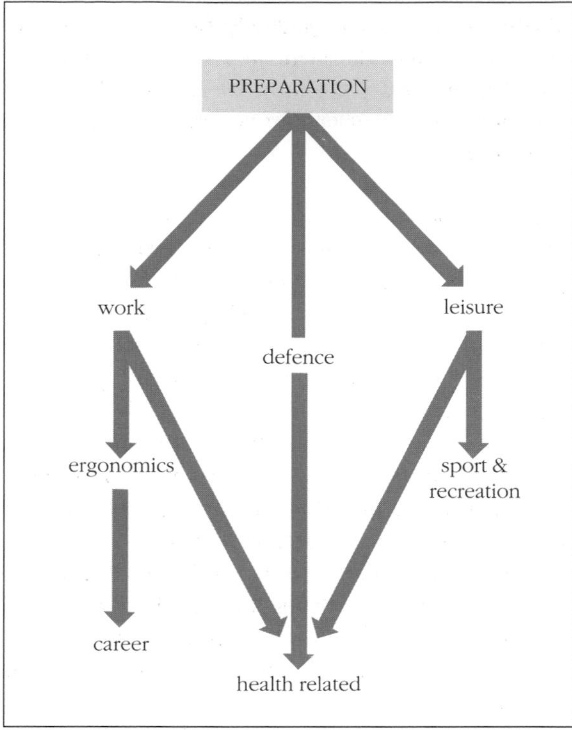

Figure 14.32 Economic values.

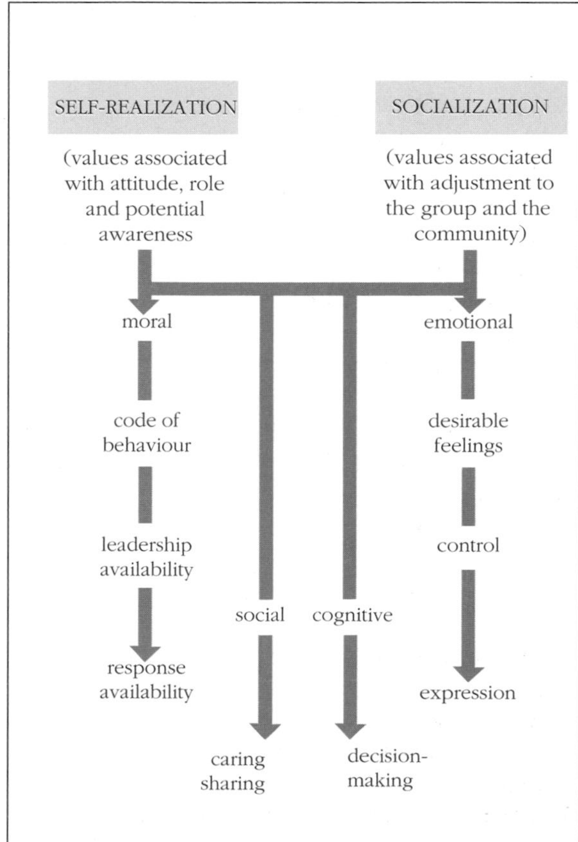

Figure 14.33 Humanistic values.

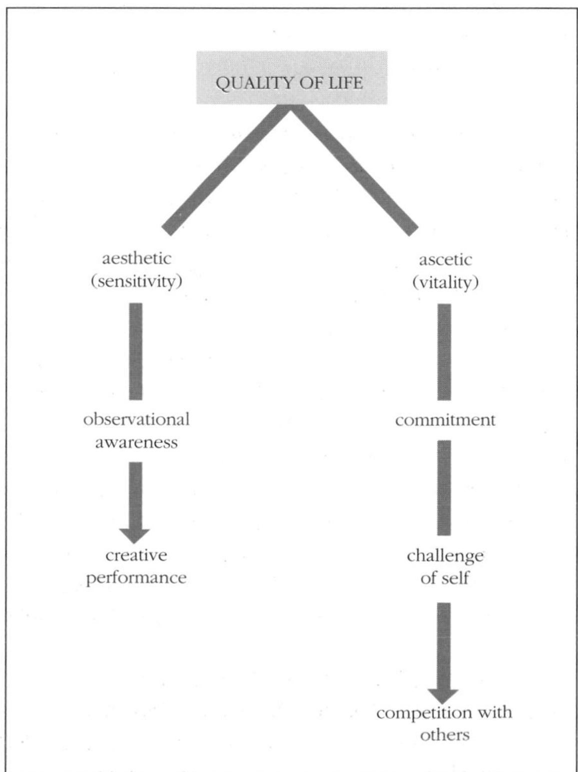

Figure 14.34 Quality of Life.

If you have explained each of these models in the context of a particular physical education activity, you should be aware of the potential range of intensions in the mind of a teacher. It is not enough to claim that this experience is physical education because the children are learning skills. Performance skills have obvious values in active leisure terms, but a good teacher looks for an opportunity to educate the performer at each of the four levels identified.

Remember, the first concern of a sports coach is performance, but for the physical educationist it is the person. The all-important factor is that if a comprehensive knowledge and a wide range of values are inculcated through physical education during the formative years of childhood, it is more likely that physical recreation and sport will have a functional rather than a dysfunctional influence on adult lifestyle.

When looking at the concept of physical recreation, a special case was made for outdoor recreation. A similar situation arises between physical education and outdoor education. Conceptually, outdoor education is a part of physical education in that outdoor pursuits are sports which are included in the physical education curriculum, and the use of the term education implies that both involve the formal inculcation of knowledge and values.

However, we make special mention of outdoor education because, whereas games, contests, and individual activities function in controlled surroundings, outdoor pursuits tend to be undertaken in a natural environment which is not entirely predictable. Also, in most physical activities, the environment simply **regulates** the activity, but in outdoor education the natural environment **stimulates** the activity.

A series of definitions may be useful at this point:

> *Outdoor education is not a separate discipline, but part of a method of teaching which utilizes the natural environment.*
>
> (Jagger, 1971)

> *Outdoor education is learning in and for the outdoors.*
>
> (Passmore, 1973)

> *Outdoor education contains within it a combination of outdoor pursuits and studies in the rural environment, but it is not necessary for them to be practised simultaneously or even in proportion to one another.*
>
> (Parker & Meldrum, 1973)

> *Outdoor education is a means of approaching educational objectives through guided direct experiences in the environment using its resources as learning materials.*
>
> (NAOE, 1974)

Mortlock (1984) advanced the understanding of outdoor education in his analysis of the *Adventure Alternative*. His analysis of natural examination, the instinct for adventure, and an awareness of risk, suggests that outdoor education has an advantage over games and individual activities because it places the individual at the decision-making frontier.

Bonnington (1981) examines this powerful element of adventure, an experience which is not always evident in other physical activities; and Mortlock (1984) suggests that it requires an individual to differentiate between real and perceived risk, and it helps a person to become a part of nature rather than a conquerer of it.

The word 'escape' is often used in sports history, where people have tried to find an alternative experience. In our urbanized society, the need for an escape to the simplicity of the natural environment has never been greater.

REVIEW QUESTIONS

1. Select an outdoor activity and use it to examine one of Mortlock's propositions.
2. We have now analysed the concepts of **leisure, play, physical recreation, sport** and **physical education.**

As we have progressed from one to the other, relationships between them have been discussed. Test your understanding of these conceptual relationships by writing a critical evaluation of the model in Figure 14.36.

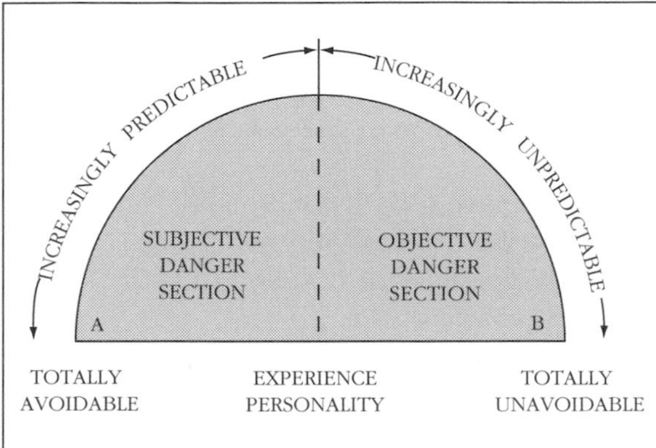

Figure 14.35 Danger diagram.

Subjective danger: that potentially under the control of the human being, e.g. correct choice and use of equipment.
Objective danger: that over which the human being has no control, e.g. avalanches, blizzards, floods, storms.

Beginners will be working at the left end of base line (A). Committed experts will be taking on challenges at the right end of base line (B). (Mortlock, 1984.)

Figure 14.36 Physical activity/experiences.

Summary

Physical education:

1. Formal inculcation of knowledge and values; an educational instrument.
2. May include outdoor education.
3. Fundamentally a physical experience, it is also concerned with cognitive and moral development.

FURTHER READING

Armstrong N. (Ed) *New Directions in Physical Education, Vol. 1*, PEA, Human Kinetics, 1990.

Arnold P.J. *Education, P.E. & Personality Development*, Heinemann, 1968.

Bonnington C. *Quest for Adventure*, Hodder & Stoughton, 1981.

Caillois R. *Man, Play and Games*, N.Y., Free Press, 1961.

Calhoun D.W. *Sport, Culture and Personality*, Champaign, Illinois, Human Kinetics, 1987.

Coakley J.J. *Sport and Society: Issues and Controversies*, St. Louis, Mosby, 1982.

Edwards H. *Sociology of Sport*, Homewood, Illinois, Dorsey, 1973.

Elias N. & Dunning E. *Sociology of Sport*, Frank Cass, 1970.

Fine G.A. (Ed) *Meaningful Play, Playful Meaning*, TAASP, Vol. 11, Human Kinetics, 1987.

Gardener P. *Nice Guys Finish Last*, N.Y., Allen Lane, 1974.

Groves R. PE, recreation & competitive sport, *PE Bulletin*, Vol. IX, 3, July 1972.

Hellison D. *Humanistic PE*, Prentice Hall, 1975.

Hellison D.R. *Goals and Strategies for Teaching Physical Education*, Human Kinetics, 1985.

Howell R. & Howell M. *Physical Education Foundations*, Queensland, Brooks Waterloo Pub., 1986.

Huizinga J. *Homo Ludens: A Study of the Play Element in Culture*, Boston, Beacon, 1964.

Jelfs B. *Towards a Concept of Leisure*, ATCDE (PE) Conference Papers, 1970.

Kaplan M. *Leisure, Theory and Policy*, N.Y., Wiley, 1975.

Kenyon G.S. & Loy J.W., Jnr. *Sociology of Sport*, Chicago, Athletic Institute, 1969.

McIntosh P.C. *Fair Play. Ethics in Sport and Education*, Heinemann, 1979.

McIntosh P.C. *Sport in Society*, West London Press, 1987.

Michener J.A. *Sports in America*, N.Y., Fawcett, 1977.

Morgan R.E. *Concerns and Values in PE*, Bell, 1974.

Mortlock C. *The Adventure Alternative*, Milnthorpe, Cicerone Press, 1984.

Riordan J. *Sport in Soviet Society*, Cambridge U.P., 1977.

Weiss P. *Sport: A Philosophic Inquiry*, Carbondale, S. Illinois U.P., 1969.

Winnifrith T. and Barrett C. (Eds) *Leisure in Art and Literature*, Macmillan A & P Ltd, 1992.

Chapter 15

The Social Setting of Physical Education and Sport in Four Countries

We need to have a knowledge of the **cultural background** before we can hope to understand how organized physical activity functions in different societies. We will call these influences **cultural determinants** and look at them under **three** main headings: **geographical, historical** and **socio-economic.**

15.1 Geographical Influences on Physical Education and Sport

Geography is a very broad field of study, but is limited in this analysis to comments on population, land area, topography, climate, urbanization and communications in the context of sport and physical education.

UNITED KINGDOM

Population (to the nearest million):

1851	1881	1921	1951	1961	1981	1991
20	29	42	49	51	54,147,000	53,917,000

Ethnic minority (Afro-Caribbean and Asian) approx. 2% in 1981.

Over the last decade the anticipated population increase did not occur, but there were shifts in population from old industrial areas into rural districts, suburbs and new towns. There are also urban centres where there is a disproportionately high concentration of ethnic minorities.

Size: 94,247 sq. miles.

Topography: Britain has mainly rolling country with the Pennines and the Cotswolds as its major hill features. The hills and meadows are ideal for rambling and field sports. The East Anglian Fens are very flat and popular for boating, angling and ice skating. The mountains are limited to the Lake District, the Scottish Highlands and the Welsh Mountains, and are attractive for climbing, game fishing and shooting, with skiing in Scotland. There are extensive coastal waters which are ideal for sailing and other water sports and, traditionally, the British have an annual holiday by the sea. Numerous rivers make angling the most popular sport in the country, but there are also a large number of canoe and inland sailing clubs.

Climate: The weather is temperate—western maritime, with a moderating influence from the Gulf Stream Drift. Generally, there is less rainfall on the east coast, which also has colder winters as a result of the Continental influence.

The four clearly identifiable seasons have shaped the pattern of sport, but the weather is so changeable and unpredictable that it may account for the durable British temperament, particularly in the context of sport. Though the area is small, the climate and terrain is so variable that the diversity of sporting opportunity is considerable, with the possible exception of winter sports.

Urbanization: The population density is very high, 596 per sq. mile, with many urban-industrial conurbations, surrounded by green belts.

Communications: There are six international ports. The railways were reduced after 1945, but there is a fast inter-city service. Roads include four major motorways, with A-roads radiating from London. There are airports serving each of the major cities. All areas in Britain can be reached in the same day for sporting fixtures and tourism.

FRANCE

Population (to the nearest million):

1931	1954	1962	1982	1989
42	43	47	54	56,184,000

Ethnic minority (so-called foreign residents) approx. 2% in 1982, mainly North African Arabs and Portuguese.

Size: 210,000 sq. miles.
In comparative terms, France and the U.K. have approximately the same sized populations, but France is twice as large, resulting in Provincial France retaining its rural nature.

Topography: A wide plain covers half the country, with the Massif Central, a mountainous plateau, in the centre. The Alps are famous for winter sports and climbing and there are numerous canoeing rivers in the Massif Central. An extensive coastline makes sailing and other water sports as popular in France as in Britain.

Climate: This is much more varied than in Britain, with western maritime in Normandy and Britanny; Continental inland from Paris; Alpine in the mountainous areas; and Mediterranean along the south coast. Clear pattern of winter skiing holidays in the Alps and seaside summer holidays on the Landes (Atlantic) and Mediterranean coasts.

Urbanization: The population density is 260 per sq. mile (less than half that of Britain). Dominated by Paris, but there is an industrialized north east, where soccer is popular, and extensive vineyards in the south west, where the main game is rugby football. Ethnic activities include Breton wrestling; kick boxing or 'savate'; boule or petanque, a form of street bowls; and pelote and bull fighting.

Communications: These are totally dominated by Paris, with roads and railways radiating from it. Marseilles, Le Havre, Nantes, Bordeaux and Rouen are the main ports, with numerous ferry ports along the English Channel. The country is geared for tourism, but the French themselves tend to have fixed holidays at Eastertide and in July/August.

UNITED STATES OF AMERICA

Population (to the nearest million):

1930	1950	1960	1980	1988
106	151	179	227	245.8

In 1980: 188 m. Caucasian; 26.5 m. Afro-American; 12.5 m. others.

Size: 3,539,289 sq. miles
In terms of different individual States in 1980:

Texas, a population of 14 million with an area of 262,000 sq. miles; California, 23.6 million with an area of 156,000 sq. miles; New England, 12.3 million with an area of 63,000 sq. miles.

In comparative terms, the UK is about two-thirds the size of California, but has well over twice the population; France is four-fifths the size of Texas, but with over four times the population. Geographically, therefore, each State is equivalent to a European country.

Topography: Every type of terrain from wide plain and deserts to the high mountains of the Rockies. Wide expanses of 'frontier country', with back packing, and winter sport provision. Extensive coastal waters, with New England the centre of ocean sailing.

Climate: Ten climatic zones:
Pacific Coast, ranging from polar to warm temperate to desert in the south. Mountain States, with relief and latitude factors. High Plains, with a cold continental, ranging from blizzards to dust bowls. Central Plains, with temperate continental and high rainfall. Mid-West, continental with hot summers and cold winters. Great Lakes, similar to the Plains, but very cold winters. Appalachian Mountains, with cool temperate moving south to warm temperate, but very high rainfall. Gulf Coast, subtropical. Atlantic Coast, temperate maritime (similar to UK). New England, cool temperate with severe winters and warm summers.

All sports and recreational pastimes are possible in such a complex pattern, but distance can be a problem.

Urbanization: Population density 65.3 per sq. mile. Massive areas are virtually unpopulated, while some areas, such as parts of California, have huge urban sprawls and air pollution problems.

Communications: Sophisticated inter-state air travel and trans-continental railways. Complex freeways, with Greyhound coach services. Extensive car use, with custom of travelling long distances compared to Europeans.

SOVIET UNION

Population (to the nearest million):

1970	1979	1983	1989
242	262	273	286.7

The most important 'ethnic' comment is the Soviet policy of encouraging Russians to settle in all the other Republics.

Size: 8,649,490 sq. miles.

Before its dramatic disintegration, the Soviet Union consisted of 15 republics, where each might be compared with an American state or European country. West of the Ural Mountains is much more technically developed and with a more rapidly expanding population than on the East or Oriental side of the Urals, which remains rural and under–developed.

With the break up of the Union in 1991, it is important to provide data for at least some of the individual republics:

Russia, a population of 147.4 million with an area of 7,625,000 sq. miles;

Ukraine, 51.7 million with an area of 174,412 sq. miles;

Georgia, 5.5 million with an area of 26,611 sq. miles;

Lithuania, 3.7 million with an area of approx. 26,000 sq. miles.

In comparative terms, Russia covers seven-eighths of the old Soviet Union, but has about only half its population. It is over twice the size of the United States with around two-thirds the population. The Ukraine is about the same size as California, but has similar population figures to France and the United Kingdom.

Topography: Covering one-sixth of the earth's land surface. Full range of land features, similar to the US, but with a limited seaboard, mainly in the Arctic Circle.

Climate: Full range of climates, but without any tropical conditions. Very much Continental, giving cold winters and hot summers, but with large areas in the colder latitudes making winter sports a central feature. The Steppes have a traditional reputation for equestrianism; and wrestling is very popular in certain southern republics (Georgia, etc.). The extreme cold of the Siberian winter has delayed development until the advent of the 'Sunshine Cities' over the last 20 years.

Urbanization: Population density 31 per sq. mile (half that of the US, but with more uninhabitable areas). Major cities in the West with Leningrad and Moscow, and a high population on the Black Sea, where many of the tourist resorts are situated.

Communications: Complex road and rail networks in the European republics, but only two trans-continental rail links. Air travel the only hope for speedy communication. Many of the Asian republics isolated by distance and primitive roads.

It is important that these statistics be updated regularly. There are numerous year-books available in most libraries. The two used for this material were Paxton, 1991, and Lane, 1986.

Summary

Geographical:

1. **Population; size; topography; climate; urbanization; communications.**
2. **United Kingdom:** small, densely populated; western maritime.
3. **France:** larger, same population as UK; diverse climate and topography.
4. **United States:** isolated from the world; large, with diverse climate, topography and ethnic groups.
5. **Soviet Union:** double the size of US with similar population; massive diversity, but limited coastline.

FURTHER READING

Bale J. *Sport and Place,* Hurst, 1982.

Paxton J. (ed.) *The Statesman's Year Book, 1988-89,* 127e, Macmillan, 1991.

Lane Hana Vinlauf (ed.) *The World Almanac,* N.Y., Newspaper Enterprise Association, 1986.

OPCS. 1991 Census. Preliminary Report for England and Wales. London, HMSO 1991.

15.2 Historical Influences on Sport and Physical Education

UNITED KINGDOM

Chapters 19–22 examine the development of sport and physical education in the United Kingdom as a major area of study.

FRANCE

The first comment about sport in France must belong to the high culture of Louis XIV, and with it the extension of the 'courtly mould' and the art of fencing, associated with the sophistication of real tennis in the 17th century.

This elite culture finally collapsed as a result of the French Revolution, which in turn led to the Napoleonic period. From this time, militarism and nationalism have dominated French physical activity, reflecting the phrase 'every Frenchman is born a soldier'.

As early as 1817, Amoros was invited to Paris to open a gymnasium matching the German and Scandinavian developments. It was built at Joinville and destined to be the centre of French military and sporting endeavour for well over a century.

By 1845 Clias was at Joinville, training school PT instructors as well as military personnel. Drill was central, particularly after France had lost a war with Prussia, but in 1887 Demeny identified therapeutic exercises, and in 1906 Hebert introduced his 'Natural Method', a lasting influence, partly because it so closely reflected the philosophy of Rousseau.

Teacher training, as we know it today, began at Joinville in 1920, and in 1934, despite Hebert's condemnation of sport, attempts were made to quantify PE with a series of Brevets Sportives (tests). Throughout these years sport had been excluded from PE and even today PE is known as 'la Gym'. Sports development consisted of popular recreations, as in England, but very clearly provincially orientated.

Conversely, rational recreations radiated from Paris and, stimulated by such aristocrats as Baron de Coubertin, amateur sport spread among the middle classes in the last quarter of the 19th century, based very much on the Olympic ideals.

Although professionalism did not occur in games, there were semi-professional cycling races between Rouen and Paris as early as 1869, and eventually these developed into the Tour de France.

Sporting links with schools were established with the formation of OSU (later ASSU) in 1934, where university sports clubs helped in the coaching of school children.

The collapse of France in the Second World War, followed by failure in the 1952 Olympics, led to an upsurge of nationalism, which was encouraged by President de Gaulle.

M. Herzog, alpinist, led a High Commission for Youth and Sport in 1958 to improve the organization and finance of sport, and this was followed in 1961 by a four-year plan and £46.5 million to improve sports facilities nationwide.

Figure 15.1 Breton wrestling. (*125 Sports in France*, 1985.)

UNITED STATES

In the 18th century, only the eastern seaboard had been settled—by Europeans—but a primitive version of lacrosse was already being played by a number of Indian tribes. European culture steadily took over and, according to Baker (1988), the geography of colonial sports reflected the varied origins of the settlers. In the English colonies, courtly activities like hunting and horse racing were evident, as well as popular recreations; international cricket matches were being played by 1751.

As in Europe, many of the popular recreations suffered at the hands of Puritanism. Following the War of Independence, field sports continued in the east, but the phrase 'frontier sport' reflected the spirit of survival and individualism through such festivals as 'barn-raisings'.

The Civil War took American society yet another step away from the 'courtly mould' of the English gentry, and sport became a key element in the emergence of an American identity. Both codes of English football were played at American universities in the 1870s, but it was the rugby style at McGill and Harvard which became more popular. At Princeton in 1879, 'guarding the runner' marked the first step towards the Grid Iron game. Amateur rowing and athletics were also part of a collegiate input which established the tradition of Collegiate Sport.

Alternatively, the 'American National Game of Baseball' was well established by the 1860s, with the National Association of Professional Baseball Players coming into being in 1871, marking the popular replacement of cricket.

The great John L. Sullivan and Jack Johnson made America the centre of world professional boxing, a status it still retains.

Although American sport was extremely masculine, the traditional role of the female was less entrenched than in Europe, and so lawn tennis, croquet and cycling were popular among middle-class women, with bloomers and rational dress accepted much earlier than in England.

The influence of the YMCA was also considerable and the combination of James B. Naismith and the Springfield YMCA University led to the birth of basketball in 1891, followed by volleyball in 1895. Significantly, women were encouraged to play both games from the beginning.

Gymnastics and physical training were very popular among German and Scandinavian ethnic communities, to the extent that both activities were well established in Massachusetts by the 1820s, with fully qualified civilian instructors. However, such was the significance of sport in the universities and high schools that there it was gymnastics which emerged triumphant, epitomized by the American cry of 'Health and Sport' as against 'health through physical education!'.

The frontier was a reality until 1918, personified by the dynamic lifestyle of President Theodore Roosevelt. When it finally disappeared, the rugged scenery became the vehicle whereby national pride was sustained through backpacking in wilderness environments, with well-administered National and State Parks.

Figure 15.2 The American National Game of Baseball. A print by Currier and Ives dating from 1866 (Baker, 1989.)

SOVIET UNION

Whereas the UK had an industrial revolution in the 19th century, Russia was very much a feudal society until the October Revolution in 1917. This meant that there were nobles who pursued the 'courtly' activities of field sports and horse racing, and peasants who retained their occasional festivals. These folk activities were tribal, with horse riding on the Steppes, troika in the north and wrestling in the south.

The emergence of rational recreation was restricted to a wealthy elite except in a few industrial towns like St. Petersburg (Riordan, 1977). Gymnastics and drill did develop as a part of the European Movement, with Swedish influences from 1835 and the Czech Sokol Movement from 1870. It was soon after this that Lesgaft introduced a system of drill gymnastics and this was adopted in most grammar schools by the 1880s.

The second phase of development followed the 1917 Bolshevik Revolution, but sporting developments were limited because of the poverty of the people; the political focus on education; industrialization and militarism; and the ravages of a civil war which continued until 1921.

Lesgaft became a cult figure and the Sokol Movement was encouraged because of its social basis. Lenin recognized the need for 'improved health for the young' and in 1920 the Supreme Soviet of Physical Culture was established. This led to the formation of the Pioneer Movement in 1927 and the GTO in 1931. Meanwhile, the trade union movement had started to encourage sport for the workers and sports clubs were formed by such societies as Dynamo and Spartak.

The first Moscow Spartakiad was held in 1928, and school spartakiads were established from 1935. It was around this time that Sportsmen's Awards were introduced.

Alongside the GTO and sport, there was a strong military component and the encouragement of ethnic sports.

All this was internal and designed to be politically conforming as well as bringing the republics together in friendly competition. After the Second World War, Moscow Dynamo Football Club toured Britain, and in 1956 the Soviet Union felt ready to compete in the Olympic Games for the first time since 1908.

This process of Nation Building and the formal political and economic integration of the 15 republics continued until the appointment of Mikhail Gorbachev in 1985. Though apparently a confirmed communist, he was unhappy with the old-style authoritarian form of government and concerned about the Soviet economy. By 1989, two words symbolized the reforms he started to enact. **Glasnost**, reflected a policy of public frankness and accountability, and **perestroika** was a policy whereby Soviet institutions and the economy were modernized and westernized.

The political consequences were that after nearly 70 years of authoritarianism, free speech was encouraged among groups of people, the newspapers and the media. At republican level, this released all the old nationalist and racist hates held in check by the communist regime, resulting in calls for independence by different republics. The Baltic States of Latvia, Lithuania and Estonia led this fight for political freedom, and though there was pressure for Gorbachev to subdue this nationalism by force he allowed them to achieve independence.

It was only a very short time before all the remaining republics called for levels of independence and so the Supreme Soviet ceased to be the centralized controlling body. Gorbachev tried to keep this revolutionary trend in check by establishing an elected Soviet President to hold the various republics together, whilst

Figure 15.3 Traditional archery is still seen (Yearbook USSR, 1987.)

allowing the individual republics to make their own decisions on how far down the democratic path they wished to go. However, the emergence of nationalist leaders, like Boris Yeltsin of Russia, led to the removal of Gorbachev and the emergence of individual Presidents for each republic. By 1993 no single, stable political pattern had emerged as the liberals competed with the old-style communists in the battle for power.

There is little doubt that democratic policies would have the support of the majority in the old Soviet Union in the name of glasnost, but perestroika is meeting opposition because of the linking of liberal politics and racial emnity with a market economy which is causing extreme hardship. (This pattern can be seen at its worst in the former Yugoslavia with its combination of racial hatred, territorial bitterness and religious bigotry.) The same thing could easily happen in a number of the old-style Soviet republics, resulting in civil war and the abhorrent 'policy' of ethnic cleansing.

Summary

Historical:

1. Ancient traditions and popular recreation.
2. Industrialization and the rise of rational recreation.
3. Influence of colonialization on sporting tradition.
4. Changes in physical education and sport, caused by war, civil war and revolution.
5. Continuing political and economic reform in the name of glasnost and perestroika.

FURTHER READING

Baker W.J. *Sports in the Western World,* new edn, University of Illinois, Urbana, 1988.

Holt R. *Sport and Society in Modern France,* Macmillan, 1981.

Lucas J.A. & Smith R.A. *Saga of American Sport,* Lea & Febiger, 1978.

Riordan J. *Sport in Soviet Society,* CUP, 1977.

15.3. Socio-Economic Factors Influencing Sport and Physical Education

NATIONALISM

United Kingdom: Decentralized Civil Administration

The UK consists of four major racial groups, the English, Scots, Welsh and Irish. A number of nationalists in Scotland and Wales would prefer more independence in a Union dominated by London.

Sports fixtures between the four countries have been held annually for over a century and remain highly emotive, but the sporting ethic normally prevails and so they may be seen to act as a safety valve in the long term. In these traditional international confrontations, England is invariably the 'old enemy' and constantly finds itself involved in the defence of ancient transgressions, well in excess of normal rivalry. Rugby against Wales, soccer against Scotland, and cricket against Australia are all ritual battlefields.

In the Irish context, we have the divisive rivalry in soccer where Northern Ireland and Eire have separate administrations, but there is also the bridge-building situation of players from both sides of the border playing for the Irish Rugby Union.

Large numbers of Afro-Caribbean and Asian immigrants have settled in Britain since the Second World War, and although they are British citizens they retain links with their mother countries. This is never more evident than during cricket tours by the West Indies, India and Pakistan. This can be seen to be separatist, but at the same time it allows cultural identity to be expressed.

Despite some initial discrimination, the Afro-Caribbean contribution to British athletics and both codes of football is considerable, as is the Pakistani influence on hockey and squash. Significantly, Afro-Caribbean women have successfully broken in to British sport, but cultural barriers still prevent Muslim girls from widespread participation.

There is also a tradition of regional loyalty being expressed through sport. The county championships in cricket and rugby are highly competitive and charged with territorial pride. Similarly. the sense of belonging to an urban community is achieved through loyalty to a professional soccer club, although the football fan may also be attracted for a variety of other reasons.

France: Centralized Civil Administration

France has a very strong sense of national identity, largely because of the constant threat from outside. In sporting terms this is more closely associated with amateur representation like rugby union, than with professional soccer and cycling, which is seen to be commercially based. Even in the case of rugby, however, appearances are deceptive. The French cockerel is displayed with great pride against England, but a closer scrutiny shows that the players are largely drawn from provincial clubs in the south of the country, suggesting that the game has national appeal only when representing the 'tricolor'. There are similarities here with rugby league in the north of England.

In France, as in Britain, there are powerful ethnic minorities like the Basques and the Bretons who are trying to keep a cultural and a political identity and, in addition to retaining their own language, there is a major attempt to revive many of the old ethnic sports.

A second comparative point is that sport and nationalism have never had political ties in England, but President de Gaulle made French sport a rallying point for the revival of national pride.

Unlike the British, the French have always regarded their colonies as part of France. Consequently, there is a substantial North African minority resident in the country with little evidence of discrimination in terms of sport participation. Significantly, middle-distance runner Said Aouita, the Moroccan Olympic gold medallist, received a great deal of his coaching in France.

United States: Decentralized Civil Administration

The United States has a 'pluralist' policy, unlike Britain and France, whose policies are 'assimilative'. This means that every cultural group living in America is encouraged to keep its ethnic identity, on the ground that this is one of the basic freedoms in the **'Land of the Free'.** The various racial groups retain a cultural identity; they seem to dominate certain geographical areas and vary considerably in terms of economic wealth and social status.

Generally speaking, the last group to enter the country has the lowest status. Consequently, Caucasians tend to have a higher status than members of the black community, but they in turn are higher up the social ladder than the Puerto Ricans, Mexicans and Vietnamese. Each of these racial groups has been identified with particular sports—for example, there have always been strong links between the Italian community and baseball, and there are a disproportionate number of black professional basketballers. To some extent this may reflect the social exclusivity of certain sports; for example, track and field has a very broad racial input, but the majority of top golfers and tennis players are white.

The autonomy of the 50 states is another obstacle to a national identity. Federal control is resented and the diversity of lifestyles is such that a state identity is far more identifiable than a generalized national character, which tends to be meaningless except in international affairs. It can be seen, therefore, that national pride is not easily established in a young country, particularly one which has a decentralized administration and is practising pluralism.

Yet another problem has been the country's history of isolationist policies. However, the post-war role of America as the champion of the Western World has brought them into the international arena.

Sport most certainly plays its part in all these facets of nationalism. In addition to being a vehicle for ethnic and racial identity, activities like professional boxing have allowed individuals to climb out of the social gutter. American football, baseball and basketball are uniquely 'American', culturally fashioned to meet the needs of a confident, get-up-and-go society, and endowed with a status which makes sport one of the unifying features in a country where competitiveness is an esteemed quality, and where the mass media are the main conforming agency.

The extent to which the honour of citizenship is respected and the ritual associated with the **Oath of Allegiance** and the **Star-spangled Banner** reflect a country which is striving to achieve the **American Dream.**

It is important to recognize that loyalty functions on a continuum from support for the local community to concern for the starving world. For example, New Yorkers can choose to support either the Jets or the Giants, but when one of them plays any other football team the whole city rallies behind them. Probably, if this happens to be a game against a Californian team, they will gain not only the support of the State of New York, but of the whole East Coast. Should they reach the Rose Bowl, they are now representing a Conference, in other words half the American football public. As for the rest of the world, the game is a spectacle of excitement and athleticism; a mixture of showbiz and gladiatorial combat. Like Hollywood, it is a dream rather than a reality: symbolizing American competitiveness and commercial enterprise, but not necessarily reflecting the conscience of the American people.

Soviet Union: Centralized Civil Administration

The Soviet Union was faced with even greater problems of national identity. Many of the 15 republics which constitute the Union had been independent countries in the past. It was acknowledged that within these republics there were at least a hundred distinct nationalities and 180 spoken languages. In literacy terms, 60 of these were taught in schools; there were 65 newspaper languages, and books were published in 76.

The political uniformity and authoritarianism of the Soviet Union did tend to cement relations between the constitutionally autonomous republics, but attempts had also been made to establish a cultural unity through the policy of making the Russian language compulsory in schools. Inevitably, this 'Russianization' programme met with a great deal of opposition from the various republics.

Most of Eastern Europe has in recent years moved dramatically from single-party communist authoritarianism to multi-party democracies and this has been followed by the break-up of the Soviet Union. With the three Baltic States leaving the 'Union', the remaining 12 republics are tied only temporarily by trade agreements and specific treaties. As a result, the centralized civil administration between the republics no longer exists in a formal sense, but arrangements, such as the C.I.S. grouping for the 1992 Olympic Games, acts as interim arrangements. It is probable that each republic will enter future international competitions as an individual state, (in fact, this is already starting to happen) however, there is little likelihood that the administration of sport and physical education within each republic will become decentralized in the short-term. On the one hand they have more pressing issues to occupy them and, on the other, the centralization of Soviet Sport is likely to change to the nationally based centralization of Russian or Ukrainian Sport.

Howell (1975) used the phrase 'sport and politics intertwined', and this expressed the dual role of sport to reinforce a Soviet identity on the one hand, and to allow continued ethnic expression on the other. The significance of ethnic minorities remains in the independent republics, but politics is being take out of sport as liberalism overtakes communism. The association between sporting excellence and communism may yet cause a backlash, where the replacement of authoritarianism by 'people power' may lead to an emphasis on popular and ethnic sport.

It remains to be seen whether the nationalistic significance of excellence in sport, evident in France and Germany, is adopted by Russia and the other republics. The infrastructure already exists and so it depends on the strength of nation building and integration intentions.

INTERNATIONALISM

United Kingdom

Ireland retains special links with the United Kingdom, particularly at a sporting level: Cheltenham Races is probably the best example.

The United Kingdom contribution to world sport is extended by the influence of Commonwealth countries. They have perpetuated and even developed many of the British games and activities, resulting in international competitions like the Commonwealth Games and Test matches.

France

Undoubtedly, the Common Market has drawn Western Europe together in sporting and tourist links. More recently, commercial interests have broadened with several European soccer competitions and the European Athletics Grand Prix.

France also has the Tour de France cycle race, which is probably the biggest annual international event in Europe and which in 1994 will include a UK stage—emphasising, with the Channel Tunnel, the ever-growing European unity (what with English soccer players playing for French teams and French players for English).

As a Continental country, France has close sporting and recreative ties with various European countries—for example, the special relationship with Britain and Ireland in rugby union and horse racing; the shared winter sports and tourist amenity of the Alps; and the business of attracting tourists to its Mediterranean resorts and casinos.

United States

As the major power in the North American subcontinent, the United States has attempted to keep an economic and political hold on the other countries. This is particularly true of Mexico and Central America, but their policy suffered a considerable setback when Fidel Castro gained control of Cuba.

Several games have been limited in expression to the subcontinent, such as American football and baseball, and until recent years the same was true of ice hockey, basketball and volleyball.

The international political status of the United States has meant that it has had to defend its reputation on the sports field.

In terms of games, the greatest threat in ice hockey and basketball until the recent past came from the Soviet Union. And for Americans, to be beaten in games which *they* originated has always been the bitterest of pills to swallow. The same attitude has applied to Cuban and Soviet successes in track and field athletics, boxing, and volleyball.

Soviet Union

The Soviet Union supported international communism and used sport as a vehicle to promote accord, but also to allow nationalistic rivalries to be released in the relatively harmless sporting arena. This was achieved through contests against Eastern Bloc countries.

The Soviets also poured money and coaching expertise into Cuba to beat the Americans on their own doorstep. Cuba remains a communist power at the moment, but from 1992 has of course had to retain its political stance as well as its sporting excellence without money from 'Mother Russia'. It may well be that several of the old-style 'Soviet' republics will remain communist and continue to use sport as a shop window, or perhaps, like China, try to embrace a market economy without relaxing communist control.

When the United States and the Soviet Union boycotted each other's Olympic Games they were using sport as a pawn in international politics. That the boycotts should have been in the context of the Olympic Games, a festival which supposedly involves individuals rather than nations, was a sad reflection on both the USA and the USSR and its satellites. In Britain and France athletes were allowed to choose in each case.

The principle of political boycott in international sport is nowhere more evident than in links with South Africa. All communist and non-white countries exercised a total boycott, but, though the majority of white countries would not send national teams, individuals could still play in South Africa from choice in certain sports.

The political reforms by the South African government, symbolised by the release of Nelson Mandella, and steps taken by governing bodies of sport in the country to make their activities multi-racial, have resulted in the international boycott being called off and South Africa being re-admitted to the Olympics.

POLITICAL

United Kingdom

The monarchy, with wealth and romantic influence but little political power, has a strong impact at Commonwealth level. Sporting members of the Royal Family include Prince Philip, Prince Charles and the Princess Royal, who have a considerable impact on national and world sport. The Queen Mother and the Queen have maintained a lifelong love of horse racing.

With two Houses of Parliament, Lords and Commons, in a Western Democracy, with an elected lower House, opposition parties function at local and national level. There is a Minister of Sport with limited executive powers and a Sports Council which remains politically autonomous.

Conservative governments for the last decade have dramatically changed many features of this 'Welfare State', but it continues to have a Mixed Economy.

United States

A republic with an elected president and two elected Houses, Senate and Representatives, there is a two-party system with the Democrats and Republicans, both on the political right. Socialism remains a political taboo in a strongly capitalist economy.

State legislation is highly significant, with the State Governor having as much power as most national leaders in Europe.

As a relatively young society, it is still striving for an identity. It continues to admire the 'macho' image and has romantic associations with the 'frontier spirit of the Wild West', much as the English warm to the notion of 'Merrie England' at the time of Shakespeare. This promotes an energy in America to forge a modern, unified nation from a melting-pot of exiles and immigrants.

Figure 15.4 Who is really running the show?

Figure 15.5 Playing the American Way.

France

A republic with an elected president, it tends to be identified as a bureaucracy. A western democracy, but with a larger number of minority parties than the UK and a much wider political spectrum. There is a disturbinlgy influential right-wing Nationalist Party and an equally large Communist Party. This results in moderate parties having to establish coalitions with extremists to gain a majority. Very much a Mixed Economy.

Soviet Union

Politics was intertwined with sport in the Soviet Union, and was responsible for the USSR not sending a team to the Los Angeles Olympic Games.

Tsarist elements ended with the 1917 Revolution. Until the recent break-up of the Soviet Union, the Marxist ideology, implemented by Lenin on the basis of socialism working towards communism ruled. Being an egalitarian society, mass participation in sport was central and part of a 'collective' system. It is still to early to say whether communism is finished in the independent states which were the Soviet Union. It is likely that the old style authoritarianism is outmoded, but various forms of 'socialism' might well emerge in some states while others might revert to a form of democratic socialism having found the market economy and capitalism unpalatable.

If it is unlikely that single party politics will reappear, some of the Marxist precepts may survive, including man as a social animal; working for the state; living in a changing world; and the spread of international 'socialism'. The old protectionist consumer-based society is being replaced by a market economy in Russia and the Ukraine, which idealizes the entrepreneur and a supply-based society. Whether this can be maintained in the face of efforts to slow down the change or even initiate a counter reform has yet to be settled.

What has now to be decided is whether the image of the manual worker or the bourgeois intellectual is going to dominate Russian thinking and whether sport will continue to be the shop window. Much depends on whether sporting excellence is linked with the old order.

Figure 15.6 Traditional Dancing. (Yearbook USSR, 1987.)

FINANCE AND RESOURCES

United Kingdom

The UK owes its status to industrialization, the raw products of coal and iron ore, but most of all to its skilled workforce and business expertise. The 1980s saw a decline in heavy industry, and now it is technological advance which holds the key to the future.

Depression and resultant unemployment are major social problems which might promote a more enlightened view of leisure in the future. The increasing importance of tourism is also highly relevant.

The Sports Council publication *Into the 90s* (1988) gives detailed figures of grant aid from central government and local government, as shown in Table 58.

It is anticipated that there will be a rise in revenue from tourism and from the commercial and voluntary sections.

Feeling exists that the revenue from the football pools should go directly to sports aid rather than to the general exchequer.

The British government has introduced a Bill to establish a national lottery. It will be under the control of the National Heritage Secretary of State and will be shared by sport, the arts and national charities. The government will also take revenue from it, but, despite all these dividends, it is expected to make much more money available for sport, particularly as the Government have promised not to reduce existing grants to the Sports Council.

Table 58

	£m
Sports Council	7.1
Local Authorities	4.0
Governing Bodies (net of Sports Council grants)	16.0
Sponsorship	109.5
Sports Aid Foundation	0.5
British Olympic Appeal	2.0
TOTAL	£139.1

France

Much less urban than the UK, France depends a great deal more on agriculture and the tourist industry.

The significance of sport in France can be measured in the increases in the size of the sports budget since 1958.

1982 French Sports Budget.

> *It is expected that the Ministry of Youth and Sport will receive 1,626 million francs as compared with 1,300 last year.*
>
> *In addition, the Ministry of Leisure is to receive 587 million francs as compared with 423 last year.*
>
> *Sport itself will get some 168 million instead of 148 but this is less than inflation. Top level sport will get approx 28 million with Sport for All receiving 134 million francs.*
>
> *Sports grants for clubs (FNDS) up to 102 million francs from 76 last year. This money is outside the sports budget.*
>
> (Extract from, *L'Equipe* Nov. 16th 1981.)

A Sports Lottery began in 1985 involving soccer, tennis, rugby and cycling with an expected three billion francs available for sports federations and clubs each year.

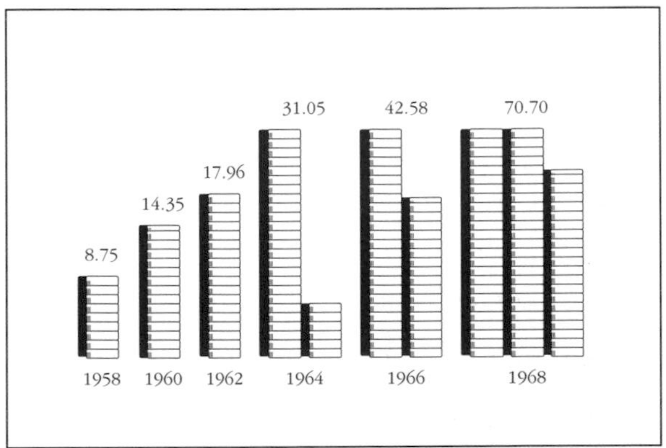

Figure 15.7 Evolution of the Sports Budget—1958 to 1968.

United States

The capitalist economy is based on the self-made man who has risen 'from rags to riches'. This is a key factor in American competitiveness, tying in closely with the 'win-at-all-costs' philosophy.

> *'Winning isn't the most important thing—it's the only thing.'*
>
> Vince Lombardi, professional football coach.

> *'How can you be proud of a losing team?'*
>
> Jim Tatum, college football coach.

> *'If it's under W for Won, nobody asks you how.'*
>
> Leo Durocher, professional baseball manager.

> *'A team that won't be beaten can't be beaten.'*
>
> Bill Roper, college football coach.

(Some American sports slogans taken from Paul Gardner's *Nice Guys Finish Last.)*

Advanced technology and material wealth give the United States the confidence to accept its role as the major world power, with the demise of the Soviet Union. It also takes its responsibility as a benevolent society seriously through aid to the Third World and American support for the Voluntary Overseas Service.

The affluence is also evident in the extent to which Americans travel abroad on business and tourist visits. Europe is a major attraction for many Americans as they attempt to find their roots.

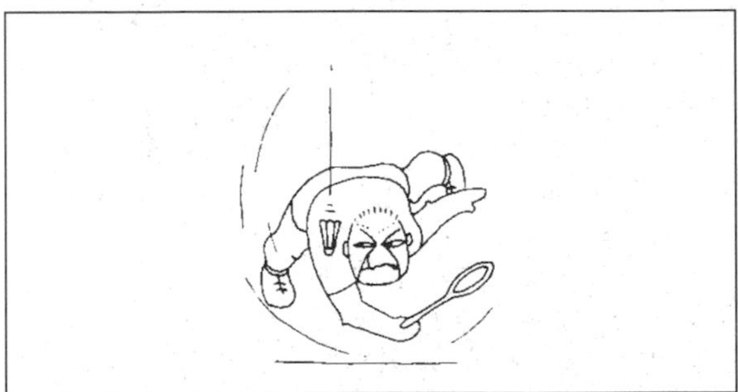

Figure 15.8 'A winner never quits, a quitter never wins.' (Anon.)

Soviet Union

A socialist economy where the source of money was from the State with the bulk of its distribution through work and trade unions. Wealth did not lie in the hands of the individual or private enterprise, but not all workers had the same wages. The industrialization of European USSR led to population growth in towns and increased wealth and hopefully this trend will not only continue but will to spread to the Eastern republics.

Raw materials are abundant in the Urals and elsewhere. The amazing speed at which industrialization has taken place has been the result of authoritarian, directed labour policy emanating from the Stalin era. Sputnik and the success of the USSR in space demonstrated a technological advance which at the time shocked the USA.

Considerable sporting and tourist developments have been sponsored by the trade unions through the factories and collective farms. Each union had its own holiday camps and sports facilities, where workers were rewarded with holidays which reflected their level of productivity. The economic reforms will probably mean that the factory owners or management panels will take over organization and sponsorship, given that state and union money is no longer available. The principle of rewards for working hard, however, could still apply as an incentive.

In the past, every Soviet citizen who wanted to take up a sport had to pay a token 30 kopek admission fee to use the local facility. Any representative expenses were paid by the sports society or the USSR Sports Committee. This is standard procedure in all advanced countries, but there will certainly be some difficult times still to come as the transition continues and before adequate commercial money can be negotiated, given the beleagured state of the economy that still persists despite the disunification of the Union.

Some commercial money has already been available within Soviet sport, such as gate money, the sale of sports goods and publications, and the promotion of various lotteries. It is likely that these lotteries will continue, given that the rest of the Western World has now followed the Soviet example.

One can also expect an extension of the American win-at-all-costs philosophy as Russia and the Ukraine change to adopt professionalism and the commercialism attached to television advertising. Not only are Soviet sports stars and coaches being lured abroad by high wages, but performers like Sergei Bubka have considerable international advertising credibility.

Figure 15.9 The most practised sports (number of people involved, in millions).

DISCRIMINATION

Cultural variables have inevitably led to certain groups being discriminated against in a specific community and in a society. Normally, whatever form this takes, it is reflected in a country's sport.

In order to compare one community or society with another it is useful to have a structural framework which helps us to tease out the variables. Three basic questions need to be asked:

What **opportunities** do you have to participate in sport and physical recreation?

CHOICE OF ACTIVITY — TIME TO PLAY — MONEY TO PAY

SUITABLE STANDARD — ACCEPTABLE COMPANY

What **provision** is there for you to participate in sport and physical recreation?

VARIED TYPES — ACCESSIBLE — REASONABLE COST — SUFFICIENT SPACE

EQUIPMENT FOR USE — SOCIAL AMENITIES — DEGREES OF PRIVACY

Do you have sufficient **esteem** to play a full part in sport and physical recreation?

SELF (how do you see yourself?) — OTHERS (how do others see you?)

STATUS — EXPECTATIONS — RESPECT

SELF FULFILLING — SOCIALLY STRATIFIED

Western Europe

Regional: Regional differences have always existed between England, Scotland, Wales and Ireland; and between the industrial Midlands and the North, the rural South West and South and the suburbanized London and the Home Counties.

This has influenced the pattern of sport, largely on a class/occupation basis, but with the decline in the industrial economy, there is now a North–South divide in wealth terms and this directly influences the pattern of leisure. France has a similar division between north and south and between Paris and provincial France.

Class: Clearly identifiable cultural patterns, particularly in tourism, becoming a major problem when associated with racial and gender discrimination.

Traditional: Upper-class: exclusivity, land ownership and schooling: dominance of rural sports.

Middle-class: salaried, urban influence; dominates many sports with strong club control.

Working-class: wage earning, traditional sports; soccer spectator dominance.

There is a gradual breakdown of elitist divisions, evident in such sports as rowing and sailing.

Gender: The pattern is linked with the class variable. Upper-class women are fully emancipated, but Victorian values have delayed equal opportunity for other women. Some problem areas remain in sport, e.g. girls and soccer; femininity and aggressive sports; and payment of professionals.

Religion: Divisions still exist in Northern Ireland and Scotland with the separatism between Catholics and Protestants. This influences community recreation and determines sporting loyalty. However, sport does have a bridge-building potential, e.g. the Irish Olympic Boxing Team (1988) is drawn from Northern Ireland

Investigation 15.1

One of the most necessary questions for you to answer is to establish the extent to which our society handicaps the disabled.

The second question involves all problems of discrimination. You must attempt to assess the suitability of separation, pluralism and/or assimilation in any discriminatory situation.

and Eire and includes boxers from both religious groups. The rivalry between Glasgow Rangers and Celtic is a classic example of religious allegiance being expressed on the terraces.

There is still some conflict over sport on Sundays (Sabbatarianism) in Britain, but the 'Continental Sunday' is very much a day for sport. The limited sporting opportunities for Muslim females is an area for concern.

Race: Until 1948, there was only a very small non-white community in the UK and sports like professional boxing helped Jewish and black boxers to improve their social status.

This picture has changed dramatically since 1948, with the influx of Afro-Caribbean and Asian immigrants into Britain, Algerians into France, and Turkish workers into what was then West Germany. Legally, there is no discrimination, but colour, language and cultural variables result in social discrimination still being practised. The baiting of professional black soccer players and cricketers still occurs in England (even though it is the country of their birth). But generally it is not simply colour, rather the combination of race and lower class in traditional activities which has prevented black performers from having access to certain sports.

Age: As welfare states in the Common Market, all age groups should be catered for equally. Schools are of a high standard nationally, but the British have failed to make the strong links between youth and sport which, in the past France and West Germany did. In sporting terms, the post-school 'gap' reported by the Wolfendon Report (1960) is still evident in the UK.

Disabled: There is an increasing awareness that physical education, sport and physical recreation concerns the whole of society, not just the able-bodied. If we start from our own interest and ability, it should be possible for all of us to express ourselves through a physical experience. To exclude those with special needs is unfair and fails to recognize the potential of our field of study to make life more worthwhile. Most of us are disabled in some way or other and it is for society to help us through these problems. Regrettably, in Western Europe, societies seek to separate, forget, and even deny, the disabled.

The Sports Council publications, *The Next Ten Years* (1982), *Which Way Forward* (1987) and *Into the 90s* (1988), identify 'target groups' which do not make full use of Britain's sports provision. These groups are invariably the ones which are still discriminated against socially.

United States

Regional: The historical division of America is North–South and the racial variable remains much more evident in the South. However, there is also a major differential East–West, where the eastern seaboard has a much greater affinity with Europe.

The most important regional comment is that there is no such thing as an American view, only a Californian or a New Yorker view, suggesting that it is always dangerous to generalize whenever you comment on American attitudes and traditions.

The underprivileged group varies according to the region, in that it is the Mexican in California, but the Puerto Rican in New York. The general principle is that the latest immigrant group finds itself at the bottom of the social ladder.

Class: There is no clearly defined class element in the USA, but early English settlers took it to the eastern seaboard; there is a clear meritocracy based on wealth; and this is also linked with old families such as the Dutch families of New Amsterdam (New York) and the Irish families around Boston.

Figure 15.10 If only I'd been given a chance to participate in an organized sport!'

Gender: Feminism is strong in the USA. The Frontier Spirit gave the American woman a more dynamic role, but it also produced a society with chauvinistic tendencies, epitomized in the masculine sports scene. Women's rights have been fought at a political and an educational level, but it is the extent to which women have inherited wealth which has made some commentators suggest that America is a matriarchal society. There is less traditional separation of the sexes in terms of occupations and community games. Methany (1965) and others, have analysed the feminine image in America, where, in the major games, girls appear to accept the limited role of cheerleaders.

Title IX of the Education Amendment Act of 1972 stated:

> *No person in the United States shall, on the basis of sex, be excluded from participation in, be denied the benefits of; or be subjected to discrimination under any education programme or activity receiving federal financial assistance.*

Where competitive sport existed in the early 1970s, it was often financed with a budget of less than one per cent of the men's athletic programmes. Title IX required equality of opportunity, facilities, practice time, coaching and travel—though it is important to recognize that private organizations can opt out.

Religion: In a pluralist society, with so many religious minorities, decisions are left to the communities themselves, sometimes resulting in individuals losing various freedoms for religious reasons.

Race: The subjugation of the Red Indian and the slavery of black Americans have resulted in a form of racial inequality, which continues to exist despite legislation. Wealth, education and sport have helped to break this down, but there are very few black quarterbacks at top level; only one leading black golf professional; and one black female tennis professional. On the other hand, there is a black dominance in basketball, athletics and positions in American football other than quarter-back. This suggests that freedom of opportunity is still being denied in certain privileged sporting situations.

A considerable amount of research is being carried out in this area. There are two basic hypotheses being tested. One is concerned with **centrality**: that the dominant male WASP society (white anglo-saxon protestant) tends to control all the central/decision-making playing positions in professional football and baseball. This research is also being undertaken in England in the context of rugby, soccer and cricket. The second research area is concerned with **stacking**: that certain playing positions are directly linked with promotional prospects, on the ground that, as decision-making positions, the successful player has a capacity for management. This would appear to hold for American football, baseball and basketball at a professional level. The vast majority of players in these privileged positions are white and so this limits the prospects of ethnic minorities reaching coaching or management status.

Finally, the views of Professor Harry Edwards is worth noting. He suggests that, in any discriminatory situation, there are three groups of people: a small group of conservatives who do not want change and, therefore, seek to retain the dominance of one minority group; the reformists at the other end of the scale who actively seek equal opposrtunity; and the mass of people in the middle who, apathetically, go along with the existing system as a self-prophesying admission of their own inadequacies.

Age: Though undoubtedly the wealthiest country, with the highest level of recreational provision, the highest standard of performance, and the largest Olympic team in 1988, television news coverage has shown a New York scene of young black boys tumbling on old mattresses on a derelict building site. Without wishing to make too much of a spontaneous street activity, it would seem that a self-help policy inevitably means that the most talented and the wealthiest gain most. The plight of the loser in the competitive society, identified by Arthur Miller in *Death of a Salesman*, could also be referring to a social administration which pays little attention in recreative terms to the underprivileged, except as a law and order issue or as a source of potential commercial profit. A similar criticism could be levelled at Britain.

Disabled: America has a very active physical activity policy for disabled people, particularly in education. They call it an adaptive programme on the ground that they are helping those with special needs to adapt and to cope with their particular disability, but also to alert able-bodied people to the needs of others. There is an active programme of assimilation, but also an awareness that special needs sometimes need special attention.

Soviet Union

Regional: The standard of living in European republics was higher than in the East, but this is more a case of emergence than discrimination.

Class: The presumption is that, with the Bolshevic Revolution in 1917, the class system was destroyed. Such is the nature of man that the ambition to get on and do the best for his children inevitably leads to an undercurrent of meritocracy. This was called the 'white collar cult' in the Soviet Union. Party policy has been directed against this in the past, but the new era of glasnost may change this. Sport has been one of the few areas where individualism has been encouraged and even here the rewards of success tend to be wrapped up in social benefits.

Physical aptitude has been the key factor in sporting achievement. Societal status has come as a result of this, not as a prerequisite.

In a political system based on economics, the value of an individual lay in his/her contribution as a worker. Unions had a range of holiday camps and choice was linked with effort.

> *Soviet trade unions show particular concern for the organization of holiday activities for working people and their children. In the summer of 1983, for example, nearly 14 million children spent their holidays in 68,000 Young Pioneer camps. The cost of maintaining a child at a camp for one shift (26 days) is 100 roubles. But half the accommodations at Young Pioneer camps is free, for the other half parents pay only 20 per cent of the actual cost. The last few years have seen an expansion of facilities for the summer holidays and recreation of parents with their children. In 1985, trade union-sponsored holiday homes and hotels have three times more accommodation for families than ten years ago.*
>
> (*Novosti Press*, 1985.)

It is probable that, if Russia and the Ukraine continue to introduce a market economy, the old infrastructure of full employment and a narrow differential between rich and poor will be eroded. The Soviet Union had already built up a wealthy class of high ranking party officials, but the reforms are producing a new class of rich entrepreneurs. However, long term, the old 'white collar tradition' will probably re-emerge. The consequence of these trends may be a widening of the wealth continuum, resulting in a large deprived sub-class, and, if jobs become scarce, there may also be a backlash associated with ethnic minorities, similar to happenings in Britain and France.

Gender: The Soviet Union attempted to adopt universal female equality. In a society based on both parents working there was no differential and, therefore, no discrimination. To some extent this accounted for the success of Soviet and East European female athletes. They were not handicapped by traditional myths and roles as is the case in Western democracies.

However, having quoted Articles 34 and 35 of the Soviet Constitution on sexual equality, the text *Women in the USSR* went on to explain that:

> *unlike several Western countries, such popular men's sports as football, judo and boxing are not cultivated.*

This was supposedly on health grounds, but the suggestion was made that women had many other alternatives. To some extent, this was cultural pressure to deter women from taking part in these activities and it may well be that there was more freedom for women to play soccer in Britain than in the Soviet Union. There is certainly more freedom for girls to play soccer in the United States than anywhere else in the world.

Religion: There has been a political policy of atheism, but it has been based on education rather than a destruction of churches. It was hoped that religion would die with the old generation, but a strong Christian and Muslim minority still exists and glasnost has allowed more religious freedom in Russia and the Ukraine.

Race: There has been a level of discrimination against the Jewish community. This was partly because they were accused of putting their race and religion before 'socialism', but also because the Soviets feared a 'brain-drain' to Israel. Perestroika has allowed Jews to go to Israel, but the future may yet bring a re-emergence of anti-Semitism in Russia and the Ukraine.

Even in the case of the Jewish problem, there was no question of discrimination influencing sporting opportunity. The desire to maintain the economy and to produce champions was far too strong to allow racial discrimination to exist in sport.

It might be argued that individuals who were not party members lost some of the advantages associated with pioneer palaces and workers camps, but even in this context appeasement was a vital factor in an authoritarian society, and recreation was regarded as a conforming instrument.

Age:

> *Every Soviet child, regardless of the financial state of its family, enjoys equal opportunities for physical and intellectual development. Apart from free medical care and universal free education, the state fully finances the development of the interests and abilities of every child at art studios, music and sport schools, young technicians' and young naturalists' centres, etc.*
>
> (*Novosti Press*, 1985.)

The Soviet Union was politically aware that the future of its community ideology lay in the hands of its children. From a very early age, therefore, the State was presented as a benefactor. Children's groups from the Octobrists (young children) to the Pioneers (adolescents) were given the best possible facilities, complete with a high level of political education. The Komsomol, which represented the politically active youth of the country, had considerable influence on impressionable young people.

With both parents employed, the State recognized the need to keep children occupied in a positive way, and sports' palaces and outdoor camps were very popular inducements to keep young people 'off the streets', complete with a reward system of competitive 'pins' and prestige camps available for those who tried hardest.

Finally, the 'Olympic Reserve' policy encouraged the identification and promotion of young talent in sport, with a view to selection and special treatment—an attraction to children and parents alike.

It is important to recognize that this appealed to the politically committed citizen, and also to ambitious parents who saw a chance of using the system for their own ends.

Perestroika has removed the political indoctrination motives and this, together with the end of funding, has led to a breakdown in organizations for young people. In time, there may be a re-emergence of scouts and guides, but in the meantime children are increasingly being left on the streets, encouraging deviance and lawlessness. It will be a tradegy if the superb pioneer palaces for young people fall into disrepair before an alternative programme can be implemented.

Disabled: In the dark days of the Cold War, the Soviet authorities would not have admitted to the existence of a handicapped group in their society. However, glasnost has shown that it is just as big a problem in Russia and the Ukraine as it is in the rest of Europe. The problem is that if these 'new' republics continue to descend into economic depression, the less able are likely to suffer most.

Summary

Socio-cultural:

1. **Ideology** reflected in sport; **pluralism** and the survival of ethnic sports.
2. **Centralized administration** in France and the Soviet Union; **decentralized administration** in the UK and the US.
3. **Political** influence in all countries, but was strongest in the Soviet Union.
4. **Financial aid** determined by ideology: ranging from **subscriptions** and **commercial sponsorship** to **state aid.**
5. Elements of **discrimination** reflected in the sporting inequalities which exist in different cultures.
6. As a result of the reforms republics like Russia and the Ukraine are going through a transition which is largely unpredictable, but in 1993 they showed signs of becoming increasingly democratic and market led.

FURTHER READING

Calhoun D.W. (ed.) *Sport, Culture and Personality,* Human Kinetics, 1987.

Gardner P. *Nice Guys Finish Last,* Allen Lane, 1974.

Howell R. The USSR: Sport and politics intertwined, *Comparative Education,* Vol. 11, No. 2, June 1975.

Lucas J.A. & Smith R.A. *Saga of American Sport,* Lea & Febiger, 1978.

McPherson B.D. *et al. The Social Significance of Sport,* Human Kinetics, 1989.

Rigby F. The place of PE and sport in a centralized system—France. *PE Review,* Vol. 1, No. 1, 1978.

Riordan J. *Sport in Soviet Society,* Cambridge U.P., 1977.

Sage G.H. (ed.) *Power and Ideology in American Sport,* Human Kinetics, 1990.

Sports Council. *The Next Ten Years,* 1982.
Which Ways Forward, 1987.
Into the 90s, 1988.

A/72//2/70 *et al. Sport in France,* France Information, 125, 1985.

Chapter 16
The Administration of Physical Education and Sport in Four Countries

16.1 The Administration of Physical Education

UNITED KINGDOM

Traditionally, the British educational system has been divided into a private sector for a social elite and a State sector for other children. At the end of the Second World War, a major building programme was necessary following widespread destruction by bombing. The victory resulted in a general feeling of well-being and a need for an extension of recreational opportunity, and a tripartite system of education allowed able children to get a free grammar or technical education. In the 1960s, the tripartite system was largely replaced by comprehensive schools, but the old style grammar schools persisted in some authorities and the private schools continued as a separate system, functioning as private institutions or as charitable trusts. Then, in the 1980s, central government encouraged schools to consider becoming independent from local authority control.

Throughout these changes, the British educational system has remained **decentralized**. This means that the basis of decision-making is in the hands of the teacher responsible for physical education in the individual school. That person can select from a variety of objectives, activities and teaching styles. There are a number of common features operating, however. Teachers appear to retain habits and interests from their own school experiences; they often select colleges which reflect these interests, but they are also influenced by innovations experienced at college; they are very much at the mercy of local attitudes and provision in the school; and although they are 'responsible', the Head of the school always has the final word.

The considerable increase in the quality of physical and human resources in physical education has had a marked effect on the PE curriculum. On the physical resources side, the new sports halls and swimming pools have broadened PE beyond gymnastics and field games, and the introduction of an all-graduate profession has increased the general quality of input and the status of the subject.

Another major area of change arises from the cluster of ethnic minorities. In certain schools, the proportional dominance of Asian and Afro-Caribbean children is such that the traditional PE programme is being questioned. The overall trend of increased coeducational PE is being criticized by Asian parents; they also prefer their boys to play hockey rather than traditional soccer and rubgy; and swimming for Muslim girls is a particular problem.

The local authorities, representing shire counties and urban conurbations, are the pivot on which decentralized administration functions. They have the communicative role of relaying government policy and maintaining local standards. The personnel involved are professionally qualified and highly experienced and, despite the recent move to give them inspectorate status, their traditional role has always been as advisers, helping teachers with their problems; initiating in-service programmes; recommending and supplying equipment; and stimulating innovation.

Finally, the central government is responsible for general educational legislation and they have maintained this decentralized policy. However, the 1988 Educational Reform Act has resulted in a number of major changes being directed by the government, apparently, reducing the level of decentralized autonomy. The 1988 Act introduced a National Curriculum; increased the extent to which schools are open to public scrutiny, through the increased powers of school governors; increased influence by parents; and increased the extent to which market forces can determine the success of schools. While on the one hand this would appear to increase governmental control, it significantly reduces the powers of local government, particularly where schools decide to 'opt-out' of local government control.

There was an initial adverse affect on physical education as local management of schools (LMS) took policy decisions often resulting in a reduction in the priority of swimming because of costs, a policy of basing programmes on costs rather than benefits; school facilities being closed to the public; and many schools selling off part of their playing fields.

This policy has now been checked as a result of

pressure from the Sports Council, PE associations and parents. It has become obvious that sports facilities can generate a steady income for a school; that a successful record by sports teams and PE examinations can increase status and improve admissions; and that as a subject on the core curriculum, PE remains a vital part of education.

The latter has become increasingly apparent as attainment targets and programmes of study have been written for PE (The Education Order, 1992), where the purpose of the attainment target for PE is to 'demonstrate the knowledge, skills and understanding involved in areas of activity encompassing athletic activities, dance, games, gymnastic activities, outdoor and adventurous activities and swimming'. There are four Key Stage Tests; Stages 1–3 came into effect in August 1992 and Stage 4 is scheduled for August 1995. Stages will take place in years 1, 3, 7 and 10 of schooling, respectively, and be followed by the national examinations of GCSE and Advanced GCE, at an optional level.

With the worst abuses of LMS in the past, the value of accountability in raising standards in schools and departments could make the national curriculum a positive step, provided testing does not reduce learning and as long as the ambitious schools and teachers

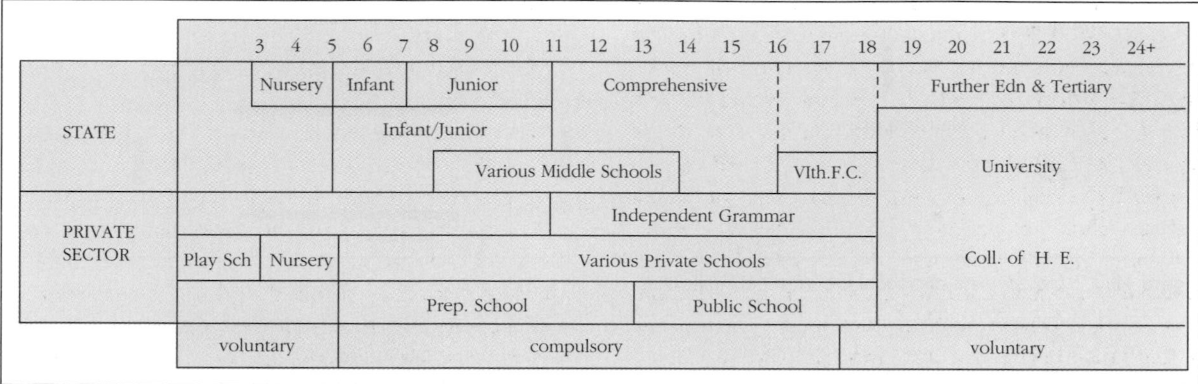

Figure 16.1 English and Welsh school system.

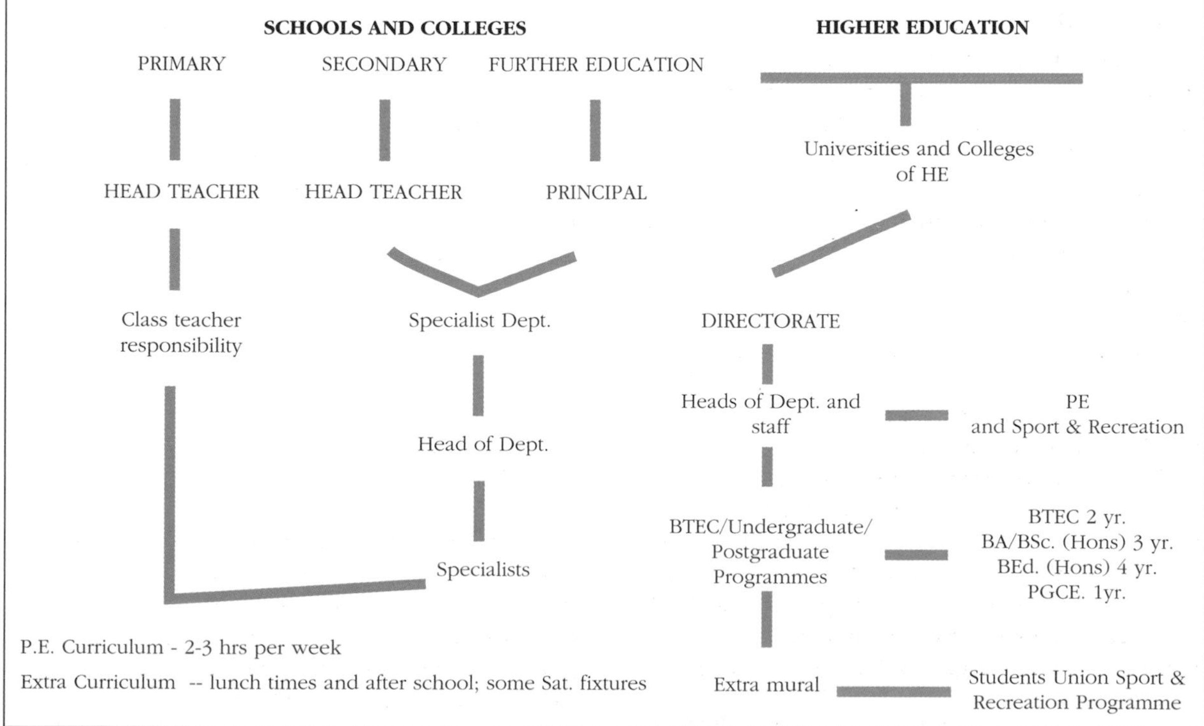

Figure 16.2 Institutions.

are free to do more than the national requirement. It would seem, however, that the ambitious content of the PE attainment tests will require either a policy of specialist PE teachers in the Primary Sector or increased professional training in PE for prospective general teachers.

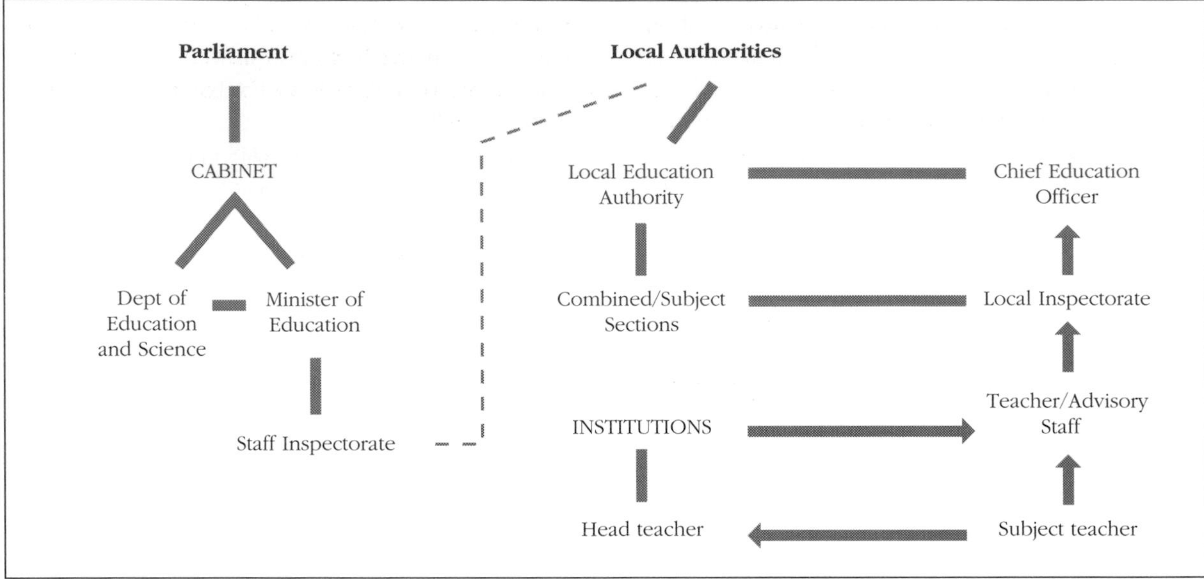

Figure 16.3 Government and Local Government Authorities.

Investigation 16.1

Trace the following three administrative processes from ministerial level to the child in the school:

a. A particular school is in need of a new swimming pool.
b. A parent asks a teacher about safety regulations in the gymnasium.
c. A pupil wants to do an 'A' level PE programme.

Having produced a structural framework for the administration of physical education in the United Kingdom, we now want you to examine the level at which it operates in your own school. Four research models are presented below and it is suggested that the class should be separated into four sets, with each set researching one model.

These exercises should help us to get a balanced picture of what is actually happening in our own institutions, but will also be useful when we try to look across at physical education in other societies.

If we visit a school we see a curriculum in action; if we read articles on curriculum theory, we begin to appreciate what the curriculum ought to consist of; but most important, we should be able to use our theoretical knowledge to get the most out of the limited provision in any given situation. Whitehead (1970) simplified this into a model which he called **the credibility gap** (Figure 16.4).

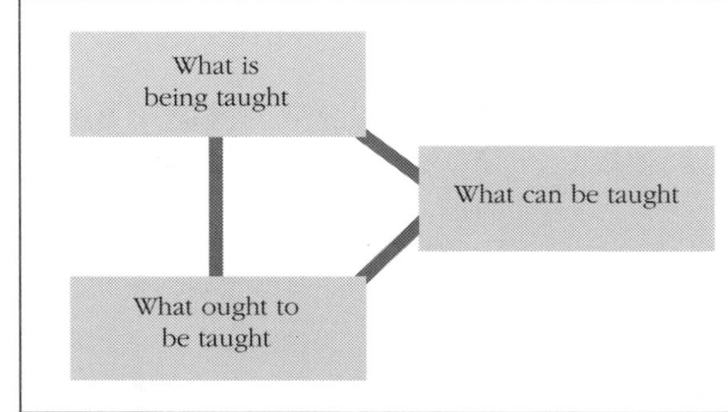

Figure 16.4 The credibility gap.

We can't always achieve what **ought** to happen, because of limitations in staff ability, provision, finance, children's attitudes, etc., but with effort we could probably improve what we are doing at the moment.

Investigation 16.2

You will have all played either basketball or hockey. You know quite a bit about how an ideal session should be organized.

You go to another school and you see 30 children being given a one hour lesson in basketball or hockey. Throughout the period they use only one ball in a game situation, with those not selected in the teams acting as spectators.

Suggest what limitations may have brought this situation about and then describe how you would use your knowledge of what **ought** to be happening to produce the best experience for the children that the limitations will allow.

If we are going to understand the British PE curriculum, it should be possible to produce a model which will act as a series of 'coat-pegs' for us to analyse what **is** happening, or what **might** happen in any given school. Almond (1975) suggested the model in Figure 16.5.

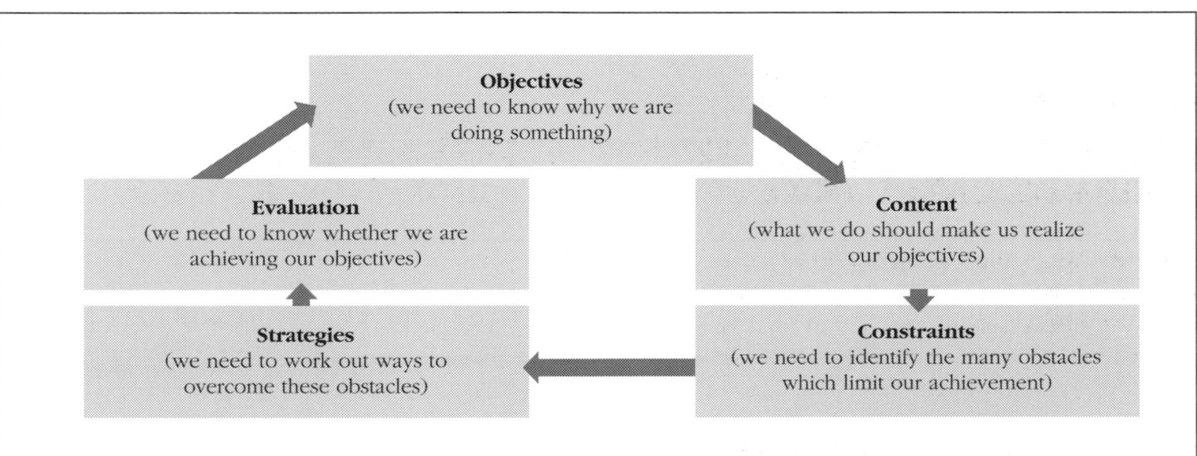

Figure 16.5

Investigation 16.3

Select an individual pursuit (athletics, swimming or gymnastics) and show how each of these conditions can be met in a half hour practical session.

In the early 1970s, the Schools Council researched the PE objectives favoured by teachers of secondary schoold boys and girls. They asked the teachers to rank order nine objectives and the results are listed in Table 59.

We are going back some 20 years for this information. Very few PE teachers were graduates in those days and most of the teacher-training programmes were practical in content. In addition, general attitudes have changed as regards the role of the female in society; and there has been an extensive campaign by the Sports Council in the shape of Sport for All.

Table 59 : Teachers' rank order of PE objectives

Boys	Girls
1. Motor Skills	1. Emotional Stability
2. Self-realization	2. Self-realization
3. Preparation for Leisure	3. Preparation for Leisure
4. Emotional Stability	4. Social Competence
5. Moral Development	5. Moral Development
6. Social Competence	6. Organic Development
7. Organic Development	7. Motor Skills
8. Cognitive Development	8. Aesthetic Appreciation
9. Aesthetic Appreciation	9. Cognitive Development

Investigation 16.4

i. Ask all the members of your PE staff to make their own rank order.
ii. Ask the group to rank order these objectives.
iii. See if you can account for changes over the 20 years as well as the differences you might find between the views of staff and students on the rank order of these objectives.

Finally, let's put all this together with a framework produced by Layson (1971).

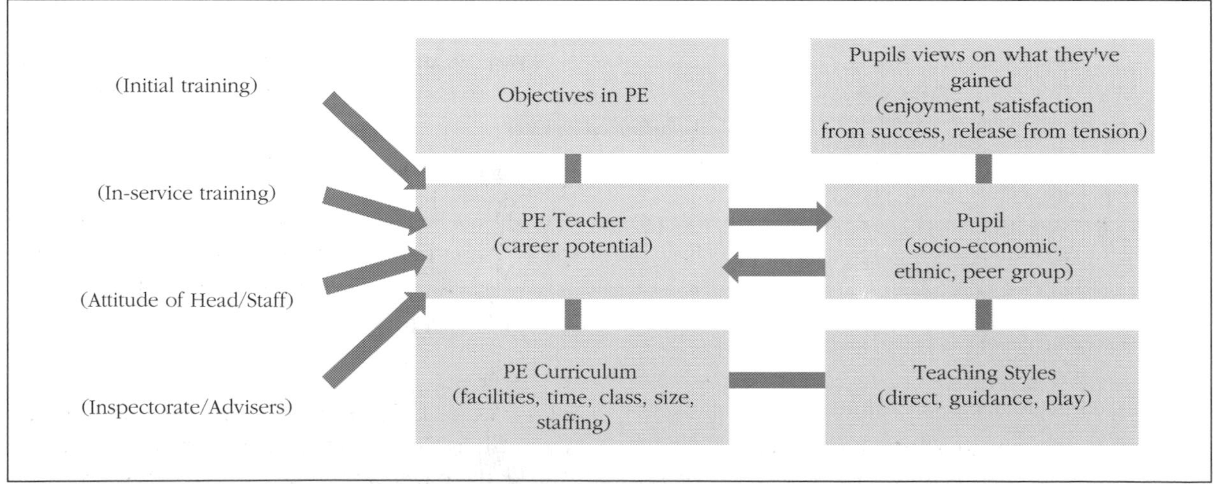

Figure 16.6

Investigation 16.5

With the help of the staff, see if you can gather the information to explain the relationships between objectives, programme and outcomes in the teaching of physical education in your school or one PE class in your school.

THINGS YOU OUGHT TO KNOW ABOUT BRITISH PHYSICAL EDUCATION

Local Authority

With senior advisers increasingly involved in the inspection of standards arising from the central directive on accountability, a number of advisory teachers have been appointed to retain the close liaison between the local authority and individual schools. Finance for courses and in-service has been distributed by local authorities, but is becoming the responsibility of individual schools.

Teachers

In-service is now a compulsory part of the teachers' contract.

There is concern at the degree of wastage, where a large proportion of PE teachers leave the profession.

There have been problems over a reduction in the birthrate which has led to a cut-back in the number of teachers being trained and also a number of redundancies and job-reallocation.

New contractual regulations for teachers are having a detrimental effect on extra-curricular activities.

Exams

The introduction of GCSE and 'A' level examinations in PE has led to more of the graduate knowledge being brought into play.

In-service

National in-service courses are held annually at Loughborough and Winchester on an optional basis, with financial aid from local authorities.

Increasingly, local authorities, colleges and schools are structuring in-service programmes at a local level.

Teacher training

Although physical education is a graduate profession, there are still a number of older teachers who are only certificated.

Undergraduate programmes have changed dramatically over the last ten years in terms of the increased proportion of theoretical study, and also in the delay of professional studies until the third or fourth year. It is felt in some quarters that this has had an adverse effect on teaching standards.

Extra curriculum

City schools have established league fixture programmes in most sports, whereas their rural counterparts tend to retain friendly fixtures with schools in the locality. The English Schools Sports Associations are very well organized and there is a creaming system in most games and sports from area level through to national representation in each of the four home countries.

Schools

The schools in the private sector still tend to give more credibility to PE and have PE lessons and games afternoons.

There remain but a small number of 'sports schools' in the UK. These include 'public schools' like Kelly College, Llandovery, Millfield and Gordonstoun, where scholarships or special arrangements are made for talented performers. Alternatively, governing bodies are setting up 'schools' in conjunction with local education authorities. The F.A. soccer school at Lilleshall is an example of a Governing Body establishing a selective school. It was opened in 1984 and 16 boys per year are selected to spend two years at this boarding institution, where they have special coaching facilities and complete their normal schooling in Telford.

To date this experiment has had only limited success and it may be that community ventures like the Manchester United Soccer School and the Aston Villa Community Project will more closely meet the needs of aspiring young footballers.

Dual use and joint provision of major facilities arebeing encouraged to increase participant use and to share costs.

Parents

Parents are being encouraged to play a more active part in school management. There is a long history of PTAs, but there are now elections for parent governors.

Curriculum

PE is one of ten core subjects on the recently instituted National Curriculum. It recommends a minimum of 10% of the timetable for PE and some LMS committees have opted for this minimum. Market forces, particularly examinations, may lead to many schools offering more than the statutory minimum.

Gymnastics tends to be taught in most primary schools as 'movement' rather than formal skill gymnastics and games teaching is following this pro-active teaching style through 'games making' and 'games for understanding' approaches.

FRANCE

The traditional structure of the French educational system is similar to the United Kingdom in that it has a private and state sector, where private schools have tended to attract a wealthier clientele. However, French private schools and colleges are largely Roman Catholic institutions, whereas in Britain—though many private schools have church associations—only a minority are directly managed by church bodies. A second similarity has been the gradual change in the state sector from a tripartite system, where the lycée (grammar school) had considerable status, to a predominantly comprehensive system. As in Britain, the private sector has been left relatively unchanged by successive governments and has retained the attraction of lycées in a society which values intellectualism.

The French educational system remains **centralized**, and as such it has a uniform, authoritarian basis which makes it totally different from the British model in decision-making terms. Any structural analysis, therefore, must start from the government and involves government-administered official instruction. The communication of these directives is carried out by regional authorities, but, unlike the British equivalent, policy is implemented and not initiated at this level.

The present organization of physical education dates from the 1967 Official Instructions, and in 1969 new provisions in respect of PE and sport in schools were made in a weekly timetable in primary and secondary schools. This is called the **programme** and is a syllabus equivalent. The credibility gap mentioned in the British situation is certainly operating in the presentation of this programme. Schools are required to teach it, but human resources, such as the quality of teaching, and physical resources, such as equipment, do not always allow this to happen.

Central Authority Structure

Unlike the British system of virtual headteacher autonomy, administration is directed through the following bureaucratic channels.

Unlike the British local inspectorate and advisers, the French regional director and his inspectors have little autonomy.

The most obvious example is in the *'tiers-temps pedagogique'*—primary instructions that six hours per week should be devoted to PE and sport. A practising French teacher from Brive suggested in 1987 that this was a 'beautiful dream'. However, he did say that the problem over physical resources was much less than in the 1970s. He claimed that 'infant school children' in the area had a bout six hours of PE a week; and primary school children between one and three hours. He suggested that the most interesting developments were occurring in extra-curricular sport in the primary schools. Formerly, about 25 per cent of the pupils took part in sport on a Wednesday afternoon, and about 30 per cent within the *tiers-temps* programme. By 1987, this had increased to 50 per cent during *tiers-temps* with only seven per cent on Wednesdays. It is important to note that primary school teachers assist programmes on a voluntary basis, and so there is a great range from one school to another. The *'tiers-temps'* programme is part of the teachers' paid commitment.

All these sporting activities are administered by an independent association (USEP), acknowledged by the Ministry of Education and reflecting the centralization policy. In addition, agreements are being reached where staff and coaches from individual sports federations are going in to schools to initiate interest in specific sports. In the Brive school this has so far involved rugby, riding, climbing and athletics federations.

France is even more 'examination conscious' than the UK and physical education is assessed formally at three levels: Brevet des Collèges—15-year-olds; Brevet d'Enseignement Professionel—17-year-olds; and Baccalaureat (Higher Education Entrance)—18+. In the Baccalaureat, besides the compulsory PE section, candidates who are specially gifted can take an optional complementary exam in a definite sport or activity, thus scoring extra marks which will be added to their overall mark. This also occurs in music, art, handicraft and languages. In each of the three PE examinations, there is a system of continuous assessment throughout the final year, which mainly concerns practical performance—but also includes marks for general attitude and behaviour, goodwill shown and effort made.

The unfortunate consequence of these tests is that they can dominate the PE curriculum and act as a focus of interest for the candidates to the extent that attempts to extend the physical education experience are frustrated. It is hoped that the GCSE and 'A' level programmes in Britain will have the opposite effect because they are given additional time and also include extensive theoretical components.

If the overall impression is that the French PE curriculum is stilted compared with the British equivalent, then the opposite would seem to be the case in the context of **extra-curricular** sporting activities.

Britain has a tradition of games afternoons and school fixtures from a public school and grammar school system, but over recent years political and financial constraints have reduced these activities in many of the state schools. The opposite is the case in

France. All French schools have had Saturday morning school and a games afternoon in the week as a long tradition. However, these sports afternoons, now normally a Wednesday, were optional and, therefore, extra-curricular, but instead of being administered by the individual schools they were controlled by a national sporting body called the ASSU (Association du Sport Scolaire et Universitaire)(1962–1978). More recently, the organization of school sport has been taken over by UNSS (Union National du Sport Scolaire). Once again this is part of a centralized policy which takes the organizational responsibility away from individual schools. Nevertheless it gives the children in poorly organized schools a better chance to participate, and ensures a pyramid structure for the promotion of talented performers.

One of the inherent problems of PE in schools was the lack of status of the PE teacher. Other teachers

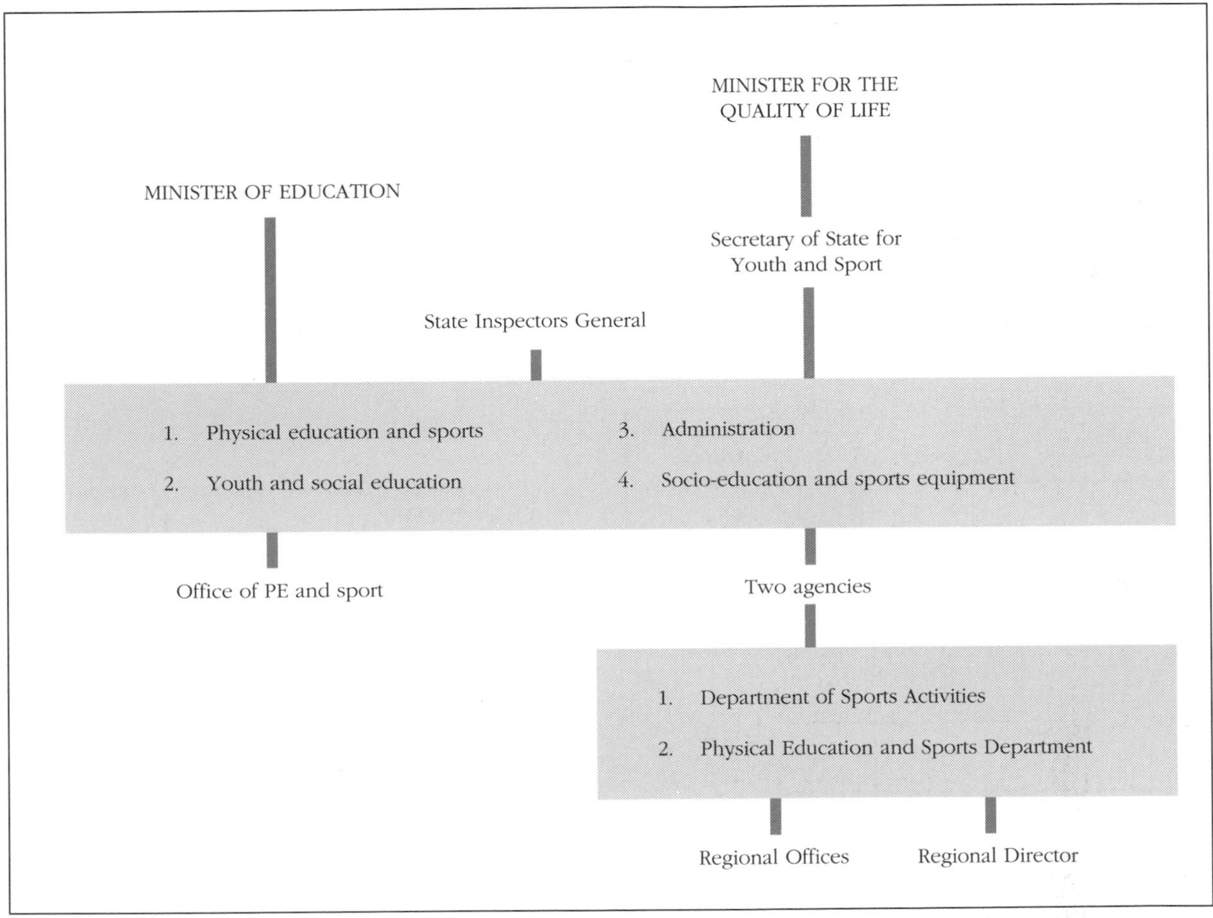

Figure 16.7 Central authority structure.

Note:

1. Unlike the British system of virtual headteacher autonomy, French authority is directed through central bureaucratic channels.
2. Similarly, the British local inspectrate and advisory teachers have more autonomy than the French regional directors and inspectors.
3. The greater the distance from Paris, the less notice is taken of government directives. It remains to be seen whether the same will apply with the national curriculum in Britain.
4. The key stage tests initially appear to be much more formal and ambitious than the 'brevets' in French PE.

The secondary PE curriculum retains a focus on 'la gym' as a part of a long tradition, but over the last ten years sport, in the sense of individual activities and games, has become an increasingly important part of the **programme**.

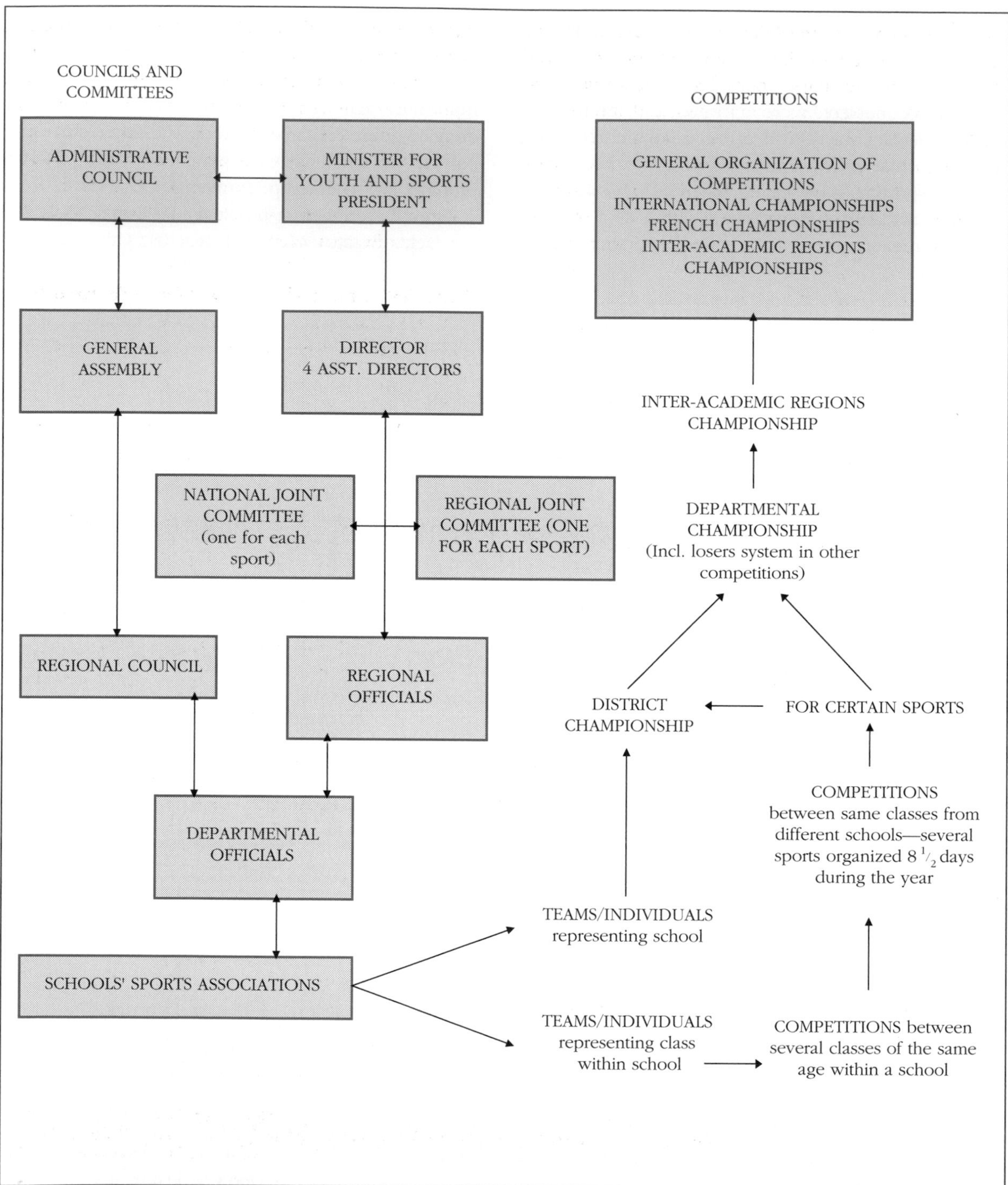

Figure 16.8 Structure of UNSS (formerly ASSU).

were answerable to the Ministry of Education, but PE teachers came under the Department for Youth and Sport. This was changed in 1982 and the status of the staff and the subject has increased since that time.

There had always been a very restricted allocation of places for specialist teachers of PE at a specialist college (ENSEP), but in 1982 the ENSEP stopped teacher training and became the National Institute of PE and Sport (INSEP). The ENSEP had had considerable influence on schools because it supplied all the specialist staff and was responsible for any new professional initiatives. The INSEP still influences the schools, but now has a broader impact on research and sporting development in general. PE teachers are trained at special units attached to universities (UEREPS).

The French equivalent to sports schools are called **sports study sections**. They consist of special classes for talented children, but they are not allowed to interfere with academic study. Schools specialize in certain sports and children are selected to attend them. Some centres cater for excellence in one sport, but others are multi-sport centres. Expert staff are appointed and facilities are well above average. These sections are on the increase and though they are regionally based they are centrally controlled.

The 1987 figures show that UNSS is flourishing:
890,000 licences and 1,200,000 participants;
90,000 sports associations (virutally one in each school);
2,500 school coaches;
250,000 qualified officials in 44 sports;
8,000 participants in the 1986 Jeux de l'UNSS.

Table 60 : The French School System

Age	Education	Establishment	Curriculum
2 to 5	Pre-School (non-compulsory)	Nursery School	All-round development, physical, motor skills, co-ordination of movement, special awareness
6 to 10	Primary	Primary School	Wide range of developmental possibilities (in theory)—many schools still concerned with social control through physical situation
11 to 16	Secondary—1st stage	Collège	
16 to 18	Secondary—2nd stage	Lycée	
18+	Higher	University 'Grandes Ecoles'	

Table 61 : Weekly hours of PE and Sport

	Primary	Secondary	
		Stage I	**Stage II**
PE & sport (compulsory)	1/3 teaching time 6 hours	PE & sport 3 hrs **SPORT** (CAS) 2 hrs	PE & sport 2 hrs **SPORT** (CAS) 3 hrs
Sport (optional)	USEP 1/2 day	1/2 day UNSS (formerly ASSU)	

UNITED STATES

American education and physical education is **decentralized**, but not to the same extent as in Britain.

It is very important for a European to recognize that each American state is comparable to a European country, and that Federal action by the American Government is rather like a confederation of European States agreeing with a unifying policy and constitutional foundations.

The size and population, together with a tradition of state autonomy, has resulted in each of the 50 states of America being responsible for the jurisdiction and general administration of their own education. However, the pluralistic, community-centred tradition means that control is administered at local board level.

Given these variables it is always dangerous to generalize. Certainly, each state is different and the relative affluence of a state determines the quality of its educational system. This also applies to the local school boards, some of which are in wealthy neighbourhoods while others are impoverished. In addition, some urban school boards are responsible for hundreds of schools, while some rural boards are responsible for just two or three.

American education has a private and a public sector, where the private sector is self-supporting and often associated with church groups. Though it tends to cater for a more affluent section of the community, this is more apparent at college level than in the schools.

If we look at the school as the primary unit, there is a very important difference between the American school and a British equivalent. The American teacher responsible for physical education in the school does not produce his/her own programme. This is presented by the superintendent employed by the school board for the area. The teacher simply works through this set programme, much as the French teacher has to do. The value of this approach is a guarantee of minimal content and planned progression; however, it tends to remove the elements of spontaneity and creativity evident among better teachers in the British sys-

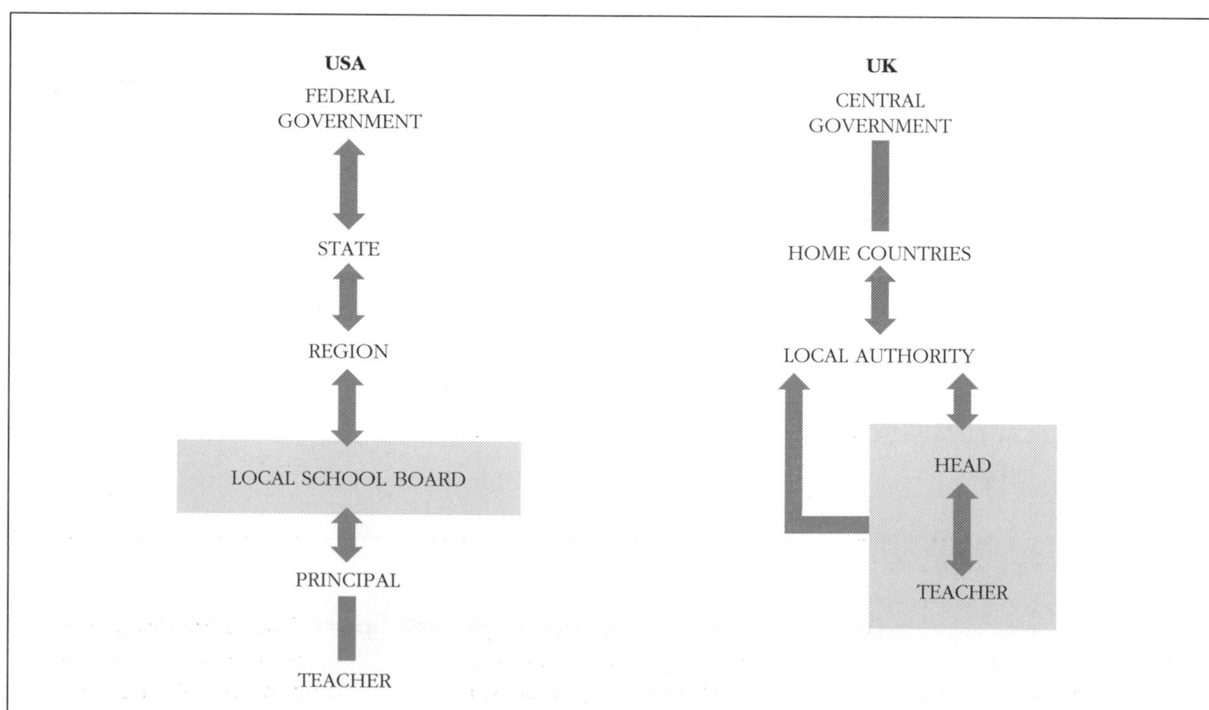

Figure 16.9 Diagrammatic comparison of decision-making.

tem. It would also seem to promote an instructional approach, in that the heuristic style identified in Movement Education (see below) is not easily written into a fixed programme. Given that most of the teaching content is in fitness programmes and direct skill learning, it is not possible to write a programme of progressions, and the American system is flexible enough to allow individual differences, human and physical, to be recognized. Unlike the French and English syllabuses, the American programmes are localized, allowing for community variables. Additionally, there are avenues for review, where teachers can approach the superintendent and work towards innovation.

A programme exists for elementary and high school children, and specialist teachers teach the subject at both levels. Elementary schools average three 50 minute periods each week, but the larger high schools often work on a tri-semester basis limited to five subjects per semester. In the event, physical education may be taught daily for two terms, but excluded from the third term.

It is also important to recognize that the top quality high school facilities are used extensively. An example of the use of an ice rink in Minneapolis high school is:
4.30am individual ice hockey coaching.
7.25am 6 one-hour PE lessons start.
2.30pm ice hockey coaching recommences.

In Minneapolis, for example, the school day and bus travel are closely inter-related. The early start at the high school reflects the fact that the oldest children catch the first bus, followed by the junior high and then the elementary age group. The seniors are picked up first, followed by the others, to give each type of school an equal-length day.

The advantage of the early finish in the senior high school is that it allows for the implementation of not only a major athletics programme, but also programmes in drama, dance and other subject areas.

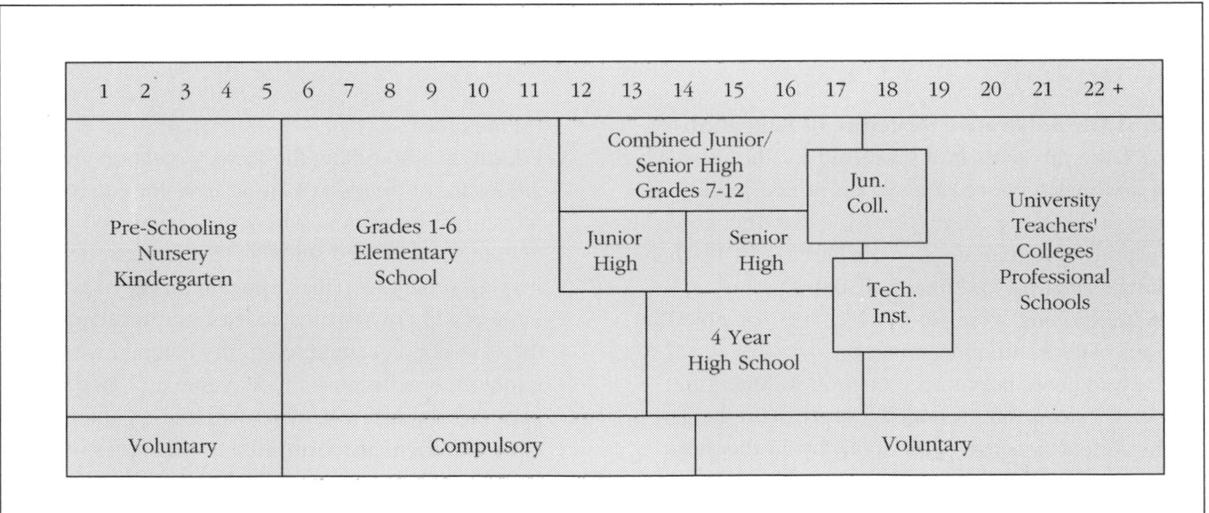

Figure 16.10 American school system.

1. Mainstream route is for children to attend pre-schooling.
2. All children attend elementary school, normally progressing from Grade 1 to 6.
3. Most children attend junior high school (equivalent to our middle school), followed by senior high school, graduating from Grade 12.
4. At 17, approximately one third leaves school; one third goes to junior college, with about half progressing to university; and one third goes straight to university.

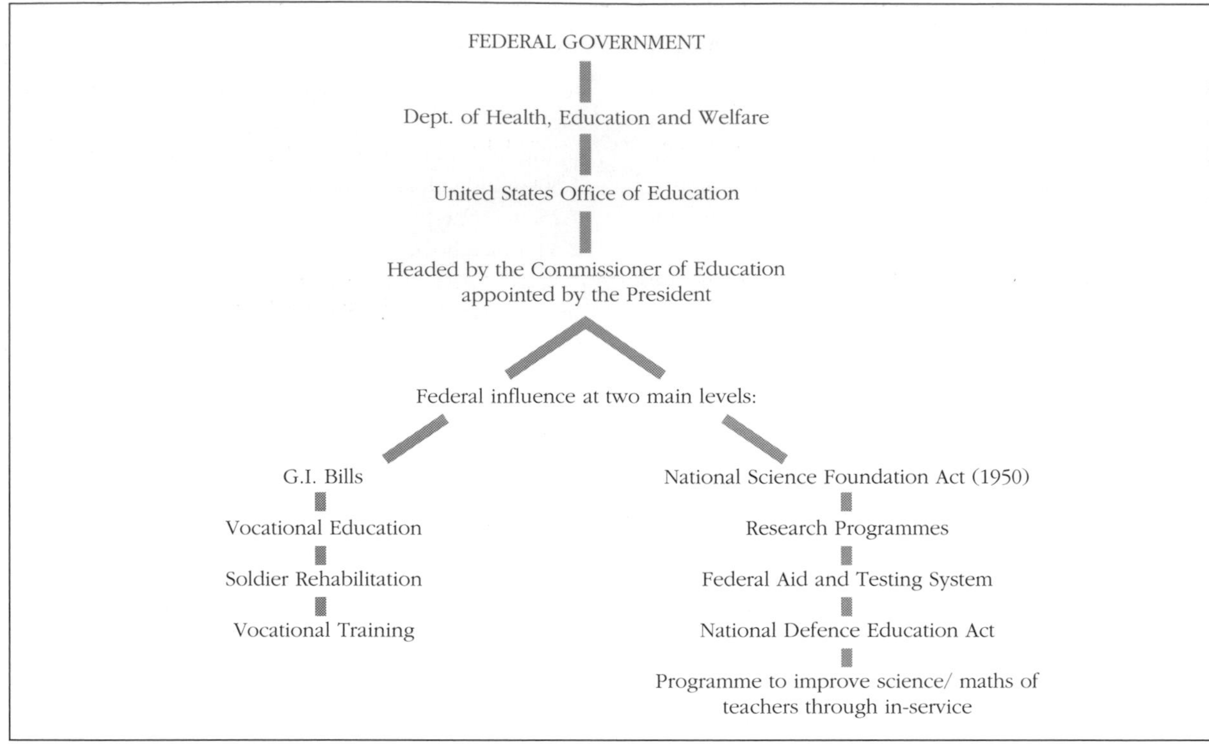

Figure 16.11 Federal administrative structure of education.

Federal Administrative Structure of Education

Each of the 50 states is responsible for the establishment and maintenance of a system of free public education. Each state is responsible for the general instructional programme; the certification of teachers; building standards; and financial support.

If we are looking for a set of objectives for American PE, four patterns are most common.

1. The traditional importance of sport in American society makes inter-scholastic athletics (in the general American sense of the term) by far the most powerful local objective, encouraged by ambitious parents and reflecting the commercial competitiveness of American society. This promotes skill-centred programmes, and may result in an elitist programme, where the physically able will have greater opportunities with better staff.
2. Certainly since the Kennedy administration, great importance has been placed on physical fitness and particularly its measurements. Once again, in a society where accountability is significant, physical educators look for a measurable facet of their subject. An awareness of health-related fitness is also very popular in Britain, but one must always consider the value of the experience on the one hand, and the time taken measuring temporary outcomes on the other.
3. Educators who follow the Dewey tradition and who are aware of trends in Europe have introduced Movement Education, where task-orientated programmes encourage students to engage in decision-making situations. This approach has been adopted more readily by females, at least partly because they are not as committed to the competitive sports tradition. It is because the Movement or Heuristic approach is seen to conflict with the competitive ethic that there are relatively few examples of this 'counter-culture' approach in boys' programmes, despite the number of books written on it.
4. The basis of American schooling is traditionally social education—the bringing together of pluralistic communities into harmonious, patriotic units. It also stresses the individuality of the American citizen, his/her ability to cope and his/her desire to make good. The more aggressive qualities fit well within the competitive sports concept, but many of the progress reports in high schools also include gradings for social attitudes such as co-operation, sportsmanship and leadership.

If we look at the specific objectives of certain schools, we can see the extent to which they identify with these suggested patterns.

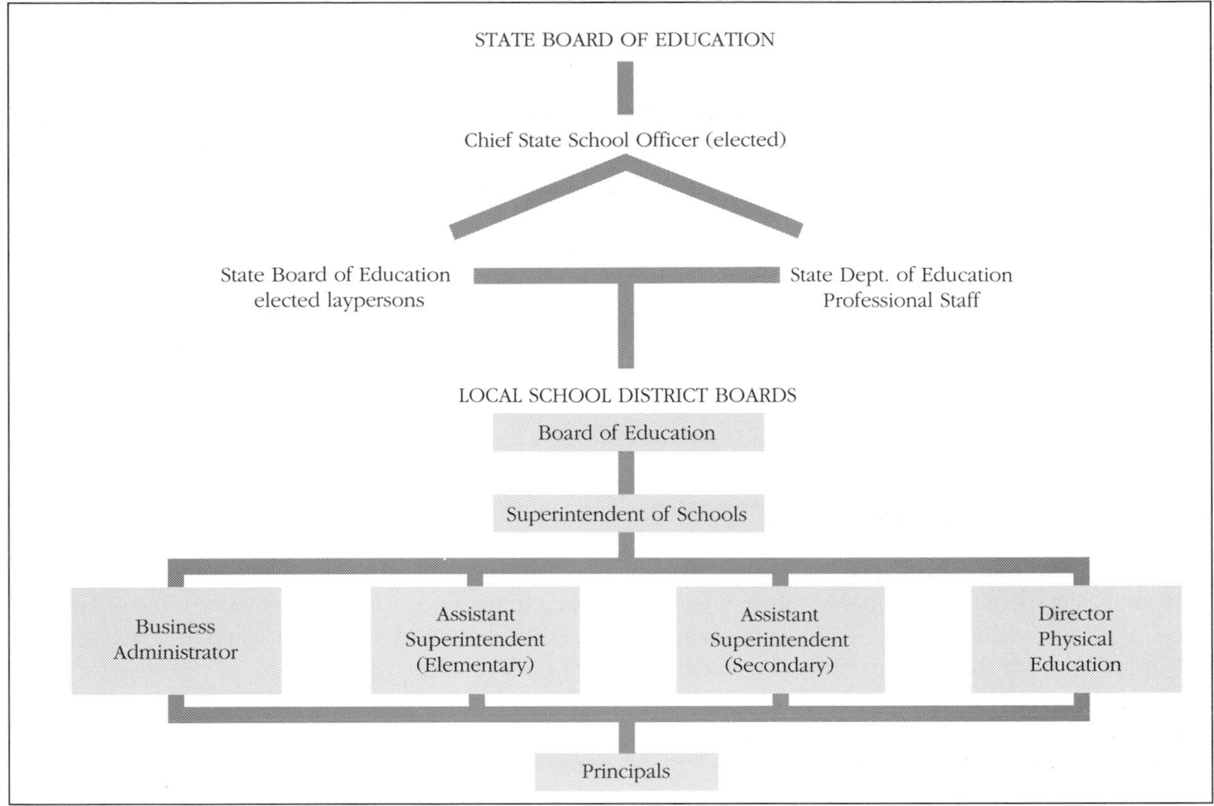

Figure 16.12 State administrative structure of education.

Elementary School (Grades 1–6)

a) Orange County School District (Benning, 1978)

Objectives of PE programme:

i) maximum motor development, commensurate with their physical abilities
ii) move with ease, confidence and a sense of well-being
iii) movement utilized as a means of self-expression
iv) develop and maintain a high level of physical fitness
v) desirable social growth and development
vi) utilize motor skills in worthwhile leisure activities

b) California State Board of Education (Benning, 1980)

PE goals

1. Motor skills 2. Physical fitness 3. Self-image 4. Social behaviour 5. Recreational interests

The importance of the extra-curricular athletics programme cannot be overstated. The boys aspire to make one of the inter-scholastic squads; children compete to be part of the cheerleader support group; the reputation of the school and community rests on athletic success; and parents, in addition to the kudos gained, realize that success can mean a sports scholarship place in higher education.

There is some conflict between feminists and the role of girls in the male athletics arena. Certainly, **Title IX** has dramatically increased the quantity and quality of girls' physical education and sport participation. Briefly, **Title IX** is legislation which requires state educational institutions receiving federal money to fund and staff boys' and girls' programmes equally.

In the context of girls and the athletics programme, there has been a tremendous increase in traditionally female sports, and the national reputation of women's athletics, swimming, basketball and volleyball has led to scholarship potential in higher education for girls as well as boys. However, in many senior high schools there is still a tremendous enthusiasm by girls to get onto one of the cheerleader teams rather than actually participate as performers in their own right. Certainly, cheerleaders work extremely hard, and the number of girls involved is considerable, given that each competitive team in the major sport has its own cheerleader group. It may well be that more girls should be actively involved in school athletics as performers on the field of play—rather than playing a supporting role as entertainers confined to the sidelines. However, the admittedly limited possibilities of creative dance in schools allow at least some girls expression at a performance level.

Physical education is required to be taught coeducationally, and while this prevents some of the more aggressive athletic sports being played on the curriculum, it tends to make instructional method even less suitable, given the diversity of the class.

A similar comment might be made about the **adaptive programme.** A great deal of money has been spent on the education of children with special needs. They are given special help, but every attempt is also made to integrate them in the class and in the community. While this objective is admirable, it is questionable whether an instructional approach from a formal programme with mixed groups is the most effective teaching style.

Europe has no equivalent to the American senior high school athletics programme. It makes a considerable amount of money from spectator support, which makes it self-sustaining. It pays for the building of outstanding facilities, which are also available for curriculum classes, and pays the salary of coaches in each of the major sports. The Director of Coaching has a highly responsible post and usually a far higher salary than the PE teachers in the school. He is responsible for his team of coaches and for the administration of public occasions, and may also teach PE part time. However, his appointment, as is the case with all the coaches, depends very much on results.

The advantages to physical education of the status of sport in the high school have already been outlined, but there are also disadvantages. Inevitably, the objectives and the programmes in PE tend to be obscured by the pressure to build successful squads in the leading inter-scholastic sports. This leads to a focus on physical objectives rather than humanistic ones. This may be one reason why **testing** and **measuring** play such a vital part in American PE.

Another problem which tends to reduce the significance of physical education, as Europeans perceive it, is the misfortune that the profession is an aging one, largely because a hugh enrollment programme after the Second World War has resulted in a large number of teachers of pensionable age, in a profession which is far less mobile than the British equivalent. Full pension rights require 30 years minimum in the same state; the more outgoing teachers make it in coaching; and teaching a fixed programme can inhibit job satisfaction.

It is also important to remember, however, that the Kennedy Administration promoted a major fitness programme and this was one of the few federal projects that directly influenced physical education. This includes programmes for children with special needs.

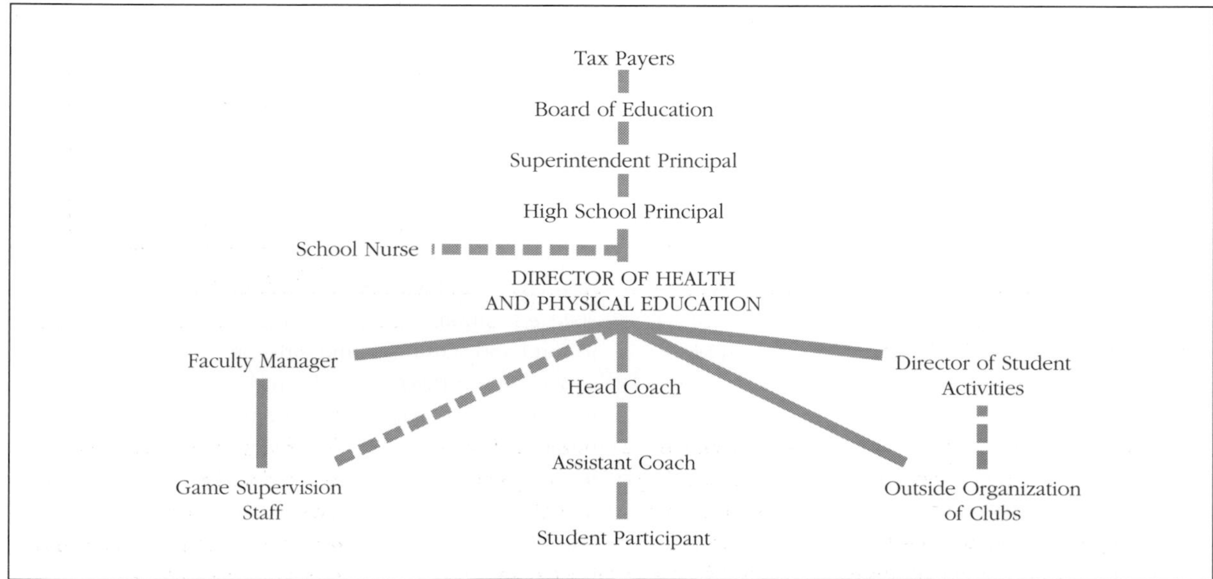

Figure 16.13 Organization of athletes. (Butcher, Koenig and Barnhard, 1970.)

SOVIET UNION AND POST-REFORM RUSSIA

Education has been free, universal and administered by the State since the 1917 Revolution. As a Union of so many different republics and cultures, and as a conformist, authoritarian society, the Soviet Union had a centralized system of education, where the school was regarded as one of the most important agencies for the retention and promotion of Marxism. The break-up of the Soviet Union has led to each republic becoming the highest level of government, but Russian education continues to be centralized and part of a 'socalist' if not a Marxist political regime.

Physical culture was considered to be of appreciable importance in a society which emphasized the role of the manual worker as against the part played by the intellectual. Physical education was both a small part of this broad concept and referred to directed activities on the school and university curriculum.

A shortage of schools and teachers to keep pace with the rising population has remained a problem in some republics and has resulted in a 'split-shift' system of schooling which has meant an early start for one group and an afternoon start for the other. This allowed widespread use of some of the palaces, clubs and sports schools for the other half of the day.

There has also been an important educational role for extramural establishments like **Young Pioneer Palaces**, schoolchildren's clubs and centres for young technicians, naturalists and tourists. In 1985 there were some 5,000 pioneer palaces and 6,700 children's sports schools (Malkova, 1985). The political and economic crisis has resulted in the palaces losing not only their political justification, but also their automatic state funding.

Physical education continues to be a compulsory subject with a stipulated two hours per week. The general Soviet philosophy of exercise breaks also applied to schools and on occasions short exercise sessions were held between lessons. Exercise breaks are also practised by the Japanese and so the political changes may not affect these programmes long term. In addition, an emergent Russia will probably give health as well as production a high profile, retaining the status of regular exercise. The Soviet schools worked to a general syllabus and this was also the case in physical education. Speak and Ambler (1976), after a visit to several schools, commented that the common syllabus was not only recommended but observed.

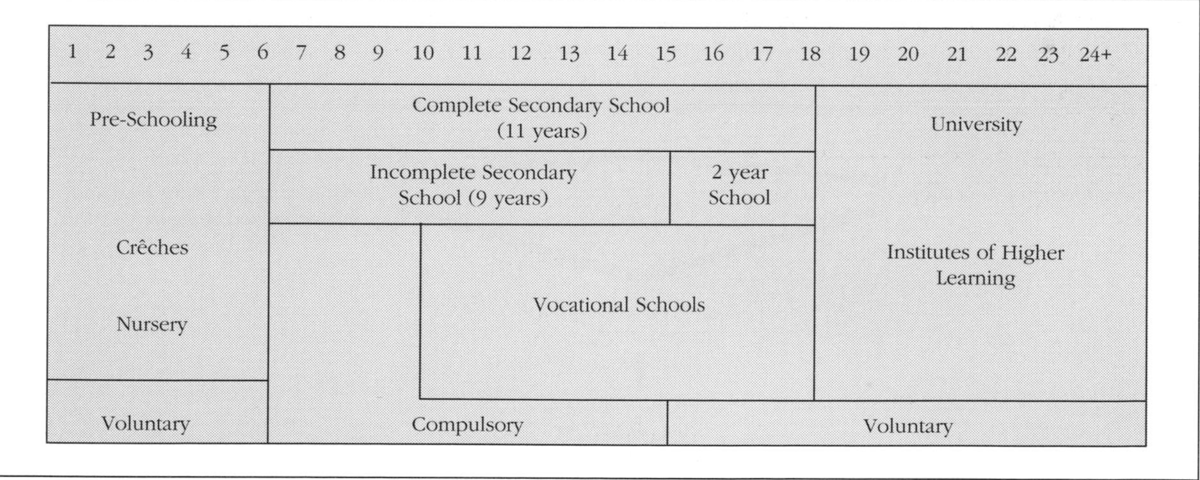

Figure 16.14 The Soviet school system.

Comments:

1. A primary objective of literacy; a fear of intellectualism; a need for economic advancement; and a desire to lead the world for the sake of communism, are intensions which do not easily coexist.
2. The intention continues to be to give free schooling for all through an egalitarian, polytechnical education.
3. Pre-schooling is still widespread, part of a policy to free both parents to work.
4. The last two years of schooling have been designed to link with industry and higher education.
5. Vocational schools continue to be of many kinds and include various types of sports schools.

A journal, *Physical Culture at School*, has been published monthly by the Ministry of Education and this has contained articles on methodology, skill learning analysis and lists of GTO standards around the country. Speak and Ambler (1976) were impressed with the quality of the articles and the value of the publication to practising teachers.

There continues to be a policy of coeducation, at least up to the age of 15, with male and female staff involvement. The content of the syllabuses has regional alternatives to account for climate, but in the main the term physical education refers to a wide variety of gymnastics, games and athletics.

As with France and America, the existence of a set of instructions tends to result in direct teaching of specific skills, but all the work has had an underlying political component. This political indoctrination is no longer a part of the educational system and it will take some time before a new set of values are established, but it is likely that in the forseeable future the major concern will continue to be with exercise and basic levels of fitness.

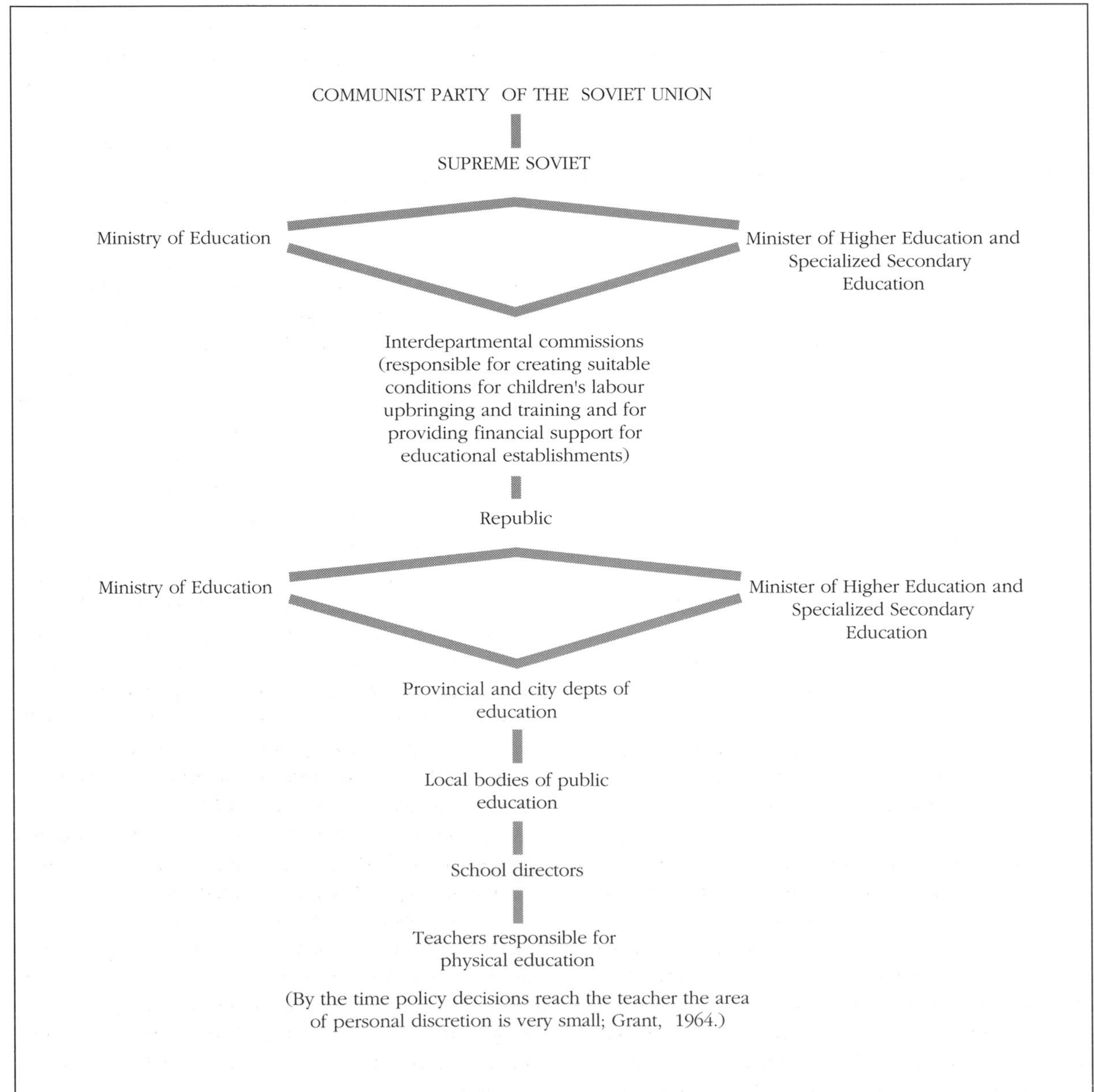

Figure 16.15 Soviet central administration.

The GTO Award System (Preparation for Labour and Defence)

This classification was centrally organized and given priority in all schools. It catered for the young, through to middle age, and it was meant to encourage mass participation and not just record-hunting. It was a graded system of physical exercise which promoted health, ensured medical supervision and provided a unified system (Sullivan, 1964). The tables (see Figure 16.15) were revised regularly and the content was changed to match changes in political attitudes.

Though it was designed and categorized for all age groups, there were three sections for children of school age: boys and girls 10–13; 14–15; and 16–18.

There was some criticism that the tests exercised a time-consuming constraint on actual teaching, a problem which exists in most countries where assessment becomes more important than learning. Information coming out of Russia in 1993 suggested that the GTO is no longer operating. It was always likely to be interpreted as 'political' by reformers and it may be some time before a substitute fitness programme is put into effect, and when this happens it is much more likely to be linked with fitness for sport.

In 1975, the quality of school facilities was poor, a criticism already levelled against French schools, but in the intervening years there may have been improvements. The reason for the limited school provision reflected the importance of sporting facilities in the factories and community, leaving PE as a minimal health and social control provision. Once again there are parallels here with America, but in the Soviet Union the extra-curricular programme was often away from the general school. This view was substantiated by Speak and Ambler (1976), who found hardly any inter-school sport, but some school teams working towards knock-out tournaments which would lead to **Spartakiads** at specific times of the year.

There was a major increase in the number of sports schools in the Soviet Union—figures for 1971 showed 4,079 junior sports schools, whereas it was claimed that there were 6,700 in 1985. Their function has been to search for and develop talent and they have been the key to Soviet athletic success. Administrators have referred to them as 'our Olympic reserve' (Sullivan, 1964). Their aim has been for pupils to obtain their school leaving certificate with proficiency to 'Master of Sport' level in their chosen sport.

The junior sports schools have normally recruited 11-year-olds, but the age has been lower in the case of some sports, e.g. swimming (7–8) and gymnastics (girls–9, and boys–10). There have also been youth sports schools with a four-year programme for 15–20-year-olds. While there has been specialization, a wide range of activities continued to be covered at a low level and academic schooling has not been interfered with.

Riordan (1975) refers to 'children's and young people's sports schools'. These would seem to be facilities which have been open to most enthusiastic children, maybe as part of a school, a factory provision or a pioneer palace, and making sports coaching available outside normal school. Different centres specialize, but they tend not to be exclusive. Riordan goes on to identify **sports proficiency schools** and **higher sports proficiency schools**. At these selective day schools talented children have been given the best coaching available.

Finally, there continues to be a large number of **special sports boarding schools**, where the very best young performers are given a special educational programme in ideal surroundings. There is little evidence of pressure being applied by the authorities to recruit. On the contrary, parents and children work hard for selection and while teachers and coaches gain recognition for finding talent, many are reluctant to part with their most promising athletes. There is likely to have been at least a temporary breakdown in local sports schools, although there is evidence that factories are sponsoring local sports facilities. It would also seem that the prestigious sports boarding schools are too good to be abandoned by a society used to picking up Olympic medals.

In higher education, there continue to be two separate but co-operating bodies: the **Faculty of Physical Culture and Sport**, with the objectives of preparing students for the GTO and promoting massovost sport; and the **Burevestnik**, or university students sports society, which caters for elite sport. With the GTO now defunct, it is likely that the Faculty of Physical Culture will focus on mass participation, similar to the intra-mural programmes in the USA.

The Moscow University Faculty of PC and Sport has around a hundred staff belonging to eight departments or commissions. Facilities include ten sports halls, a swimming bath, indoor athletics track, eight open-air basketball courts, eight volleyball courts, a special soccer pitch and two practice pitches.

The premier institute of physical culture is the Lesgaft Institute in Leningrad. It trains some 5,000 students in physical culture with a specialist staff of 325 lecturers.

'Handgrenadier'
Strength & Courage
for Youths & Girls 16-18 years

Requirements: (pass examination)

1. Knowledge about physical culture and sport in Soviet Union.
2. Knowledge & carrying out of rules of personal and public hygiene.
3. Master programme of elementary battle-training, including section on defence against weapons of mass-striking-power and to remain one hour in a gas-mask, or to take a course on programmes of training specialist in organisation - D O S A A F or to have one of the practical technical specialities (for youths). For girls, to know the basic rules of civil defence and stay in a gas-mask for one hour.
4. To be able to explain meaning of and carry out the set of exercises relating to morning hygienic gymnastics.

Exercises & Standards.

Kinds of Exercise	BOYS		GIRLS	
	for silver badge	for gold badge	for silver badge	for gold badge
1. Running 100 m (sec.)	14.2	13.5	16.2	15.4
2. Cross-country				
500 m (min. sec.)	-	-	2.00	1.50
1000 m (min. sec.)	3.30	3.20	-	-
OR				
3. Skating (ordinary skates) 500 m (min. sec.)	1.25	1.15	1.30	1.20
Long jump (cm)	440	480	340	375
OR				
High jump (cm)	125	135	105	115
4. Grenade throwing weight				
500 gram (m)	-	-	21	25
700 gram (m)	35	40	-	-
OR				
Putting the shot weight				
4 kg (m)	-	-	6.00	6.80
5 kg (m)	8	10	-	-
5. Ski racing 3 km (min.)	-	-	20	18
5 km (min.)	27	25		
OR				
10 km (min.)	57	52		

Kinds of Exercise	YOUTHS		GIRLS	
	for silver badge	for gold badge	for silver badge	for gold badge
In snowless regions				
Forced march 3 km (min.)	-	-	20	18
5 km (min.)	35	32		
OR				
Cross- country cycling				
10 km (min)	-	-	30	27
20 km (min)	50	46		
6. Swimming 100 m (min.sec)	2.00	1.45	2.15	2.00
or without timing (m)	200	-	100	-
7. Pulling-up on horizontal bar (no. of times)	8	12		
Lifting from a hand and holding by rolling* over or by strength. (*revolution)	3	4		
Arms supported on gym bench, bend and straighten (no. of times)	-	-	10	12
Shooting small calibre rifle at 25 m (points)	33	40	30	37
OR at 50 m (points)	30	37	27	34
Shooting with battle-weapons: elementary exercises according to programme of elementary military training on assessment	satis-factory	good	satis-factory	good
9. A hike and test of hiking skills and ability to find one's bearings	1 hike of 20 km or 2 hikes of 12 km	1 hike of 25 km or 2 hikes of 15 km	1 hike of 20 km or 2 hikes of 12 km	1 hike of 25km or 2 hikes of 15 km
10. Sport rating for: Motorcar, outboard motor, motorbike, glider, parachute,aeroplane, helicopter, under-water sport, all round sea-sport, modern pentathlon, machine-gun firing, radio, scouting (finding one's bearings), wrestling all kinds), boxing		III		III
11. Any other kind of sport		II		II

Figure 16.16 The GTO Awards, USSR—Ready for labour and defence: sample table.

Note:
For the gold badge it is essential to fulfil not less than 7 standards at the level established for the gold badge, including a temporary swimming standard and 2 standards at silver badge level (excluding the 10th standard). Girls having passed a course for 'combatant medical orderly' are considered to have passed a 10th standard gold badge test.

Figure 16.17 Vocational School No. 68 in Baku is frequently called a sports school. It has 12 sports clubs in which activities are run by volunteer trainers—instructors and foremen employed at the school. Future cooks, sale assistants and other specialists in the services sphere successfully participate in city competitions in various sports. (Sport in the USSR, 8/81.)

Figure 16.18 Indoor stadium.

Figure 16.19 Athletics facilities. How do there facilities compare with your school/college?

Summary

UK, PE:

1. **Decentralized administration; autonomous institutions;** the institution of a national curriculum with PE as a core subject, is intended to raise minimum standards and includes attainment tests to evaluate standards.
2. Credibility gap between **ought, is,** and **might be**.
3. Curriculum Theory based on **objectives, content, contraints, strategies** and **evaluation**.

France, PE:

1. **Centralized administration; fixed syllabus; examination based.**
2. *Tiers-temps* pedagogy in primary schools—six hours PE per week, but not always achieved.
3. UNSS a well organized sports programme for schools, one afternoon per week.

US, PE:

1. **Decentralized administration;** power with **local school boards.** Great variations between different states.
2. PE dominated by sport.
3. Title IX legislation aimed to give equality to girls' PE in schools receiving federal funds.
4. Emphasis on **health** and on **fitness testing.**
5. Major interest in adaptive PE.

USSR, PE:

1. Term **physical culture** widely used: more general than the term PE.
2. **Centralized administration** with polytechnical education.
3. **Fixed syllabus** with emphasis on the **GTO Award programme,** until the political reforms curtailed it.
4. Development of sport and sports schools to establish **massovost** and an **Olympic reserve**.

16.2 The Administration of Sport

UNITED KINGDOM

The Department of the Environment has been the government department primarily responsible for government policy regarding provision and public expenditure in the development of sport. Since 1962 there has been a **Minister *for* Sport**, with each of the Home Countries having their own Minister with responsibility for sport. It is important to note that they are not Ministers *of* Sport, having only an advisory role in Britain's decentralized organization of sport. In 1990 the Ministry was moved to the Department of Education and Science, but in 1992 it achieved Cabinet status as part of the responsibility of the **Secretary of State for the National Heritage**.

The Countryside Commission is an independent statutory body, which reviews matters relating to the conservation and enhancement of the landscape and the provision and improvement of facilities of the countryside for enjoyment, including the need to secure access for open-air recreation.

The Sports Council was established in 1965 and received its charter in 1972. It is an independent (autonomous) body with overall responsibility for British sport. It provides capital grants to governing bodies of sport; assesses the need and demand for facilities; and advises local authorities on the provision of facilities. It promotes courses for the preparation of coaches and co-ordinates training. The five **National Sports Centres** are the focus of these activities, but there are also regional sports centres run by individual Governing Bodies of Sport. The nine regional offices of the Sports Council have the responsibility of implementing its policies according to regional needs, interests and conditions, and these in turn have a network of local committees.

The Sport Aid Foundation is an autonomous fund raising body. It grants aid to individual established sportspeople for their financial needs in relation to training, preparations and medical treatment. It raises funds from commercial and industrial backing and distributes its grants through the governing bodies of sport. It aims to place Britain's talented performers on the same footing in relation to training and preparation as those in the USA and Eastern Europe. The S.A.F. has nine regional offices to raise funds locally and to help local competitors reach national standards.

The National Coaching Foundation is the education service for coaches in the UK. Based in Leeds, the network comprises sixteen **National Coaching Centres** in different higher education institutions in England (11), Scotland (2), Wales (2) and Northern Ireland (1). Its function is to improve the quality of coaching in this country by providing introductory packs; a programme of key courses for practising coaches; advanced workshops and a diploma for experienced coaches; and a documentary resource.

The Central Council of Physical Recreation (CCPR) is an independent national voluntary organization representing over 240 governing and representative bodies of sport and physical recreative activities. It is the 'collective voice' of British sport: a representative body which formulates and promotes measures to improve and develop sport and physical recreation in the United Kingdom; and a consultative body to the Sports Council. The CCPR receives financial support from the Sports Council by contract, in addition to its members' donations. The Council has introduced a Community Sports Leaders Award scheme to encourage young people to assist in coaching sports groups.

The British Olympic Committee enters competitors in the Olympic Games and the qualifying rounds. It is autonomous and must resist all political, religious and commercial pressures. It is also responsible for fund raising in conjunction with the governing bodies of sport.

The Governing Bodies of British Sport are completely autonomous. They are responsible for the organization and codification of their individual sport, and for financial solvancy.

National Sports Centres

There are five national residential sports centres managed and financed wholly or partly by the Sports Council. Priority of use is given to national team training, competition and the training of leaders and officials. When these needs have been met, however, the centres are available for general courses to improve personal performance and to introduce beginners to new activities. The centres are:

1. **Crystal Palace:** Established in 1964 in Norwood, London. Britain's first multi-sports centre built by the

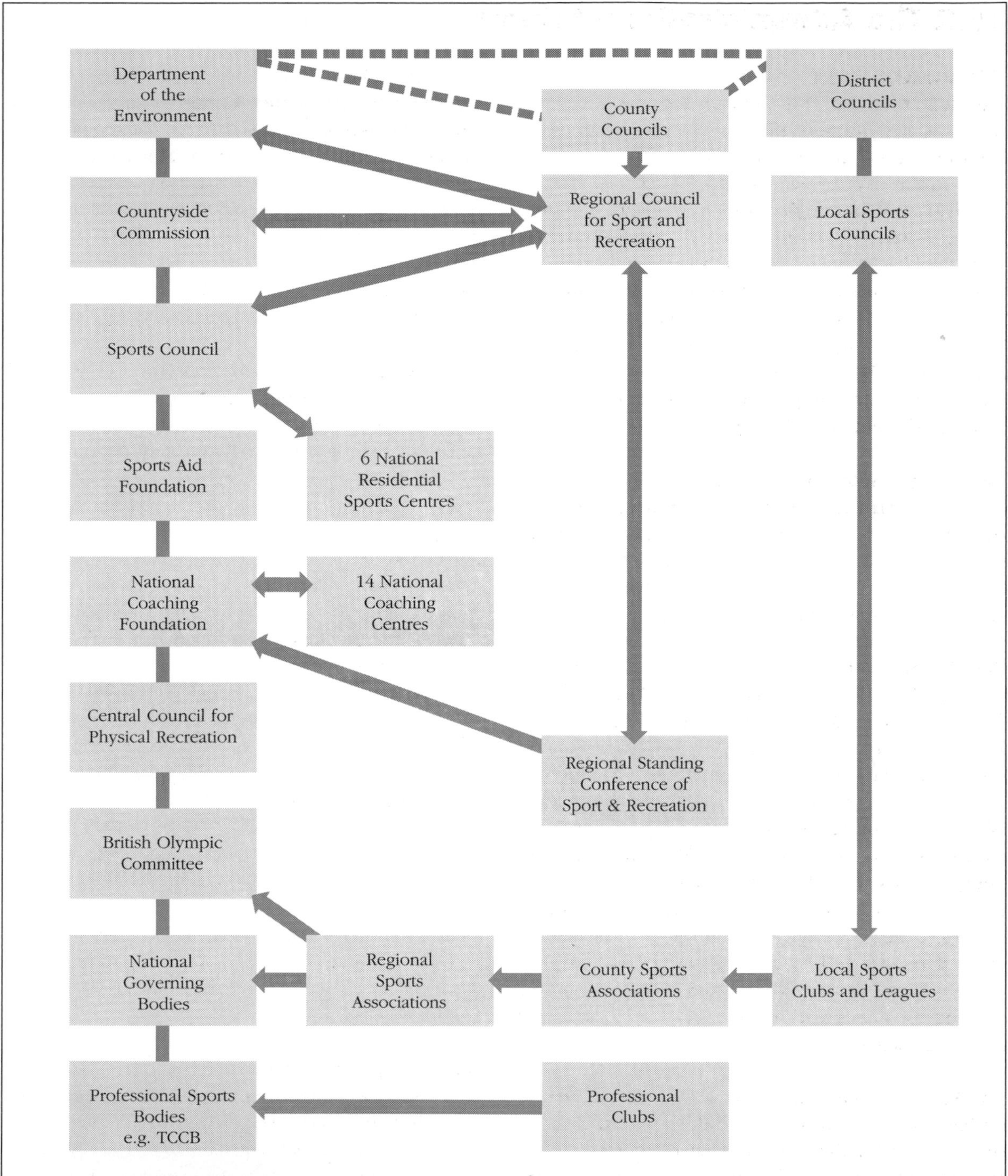

Figure 16.20 The administration of British sport.

Greater London Council and managed by the Sports Council. Facilities include swimming and diving pools to international standard, a separate teaching pool, a large indoor arena, cricket school, badminton courts, squash courts and a floodlit stadium with an international athletics track.

2. **Lilleshall Hall:** Established in 1951, near Newport, Salop. Set in secluded grounds, Lilleshall's facilities include a covered training track, a dance and gymnastics studio, squash courts, two indoor sports halls and outdoor pitches. In 1977 the Sports Council and the Football Association launched their development scheme to make Lilleshall the country's premier soccer school. There is also a sports injuries clinic.

3. **Bisham Abbey:** Established in 1946, near Marlow, Bucks. A 12th century abbey foundation adapted to the needs of 20th century sport. Facilities include an extensive sports workshop, providing indoor training and tactical play facilities for all major sports, and a range of outside facilities, pitches and tennis courts.

4. **Holme Pierrepont:** Established in 1973 in Nottingham. A national water sports centre developed on derelict land as a joint project with Nottinghamshire County Council. Extensive water areas include an international 2,000 metre rowing and canoeing course and separate lagoons for water-skiing and angling, all contained within a new country park. Lecture and conference facilities are also available.

5. **Plas y Brenin National Centre for Mountain Activities:** Established in 1955 at Capel Curig, North Wales. Provides an outlet for adventure through the mountains and outdoor activities. Personal performance courses in rock climbing, canoeing, camping, skiing, fly fishing and field studies. Mountain leadership certificate courses for leaders and instructors.

Cowes National Sailing Centre: Established 1968, Cowes, Isle of Wight. Used to be a national sports centre until it was sold in 1990. Now functions as a commercial sailing centre. There are plans to establish a new national centre in the Portland/Weymouth area.

REVIEW QUESTIONS

The Sports Council has published details on all governing bodies of sport, and the Palmer Report (1988) on **eligibility** is available from the CCPR.

See if you can use these publications to:

a) Build up an organizational structure for your own sport;
b) List the main regulations for amateur performers in your sport.

Future Developments

Subject to the resources being made available, the Sports Council will:

- Seek the development of the following facilities for high level training and performance:
  A national indoor velodrome.
  A national ice skating training centre.
  A national centre and arena for movement and dance.
  A national indoor athletics training centre.
  A national outdoor competition centre for bowls.
  Training facilities for judo, boxing, modern pentathlon, sailing, alpine skiing and hockey.
- Pursue in close co-operation with the governing bodies, the policy which it agreed early in 1987 for the future development, management and use of its national sports centres.

(Source: Into the 90s, 1988.)

Figure 16.21 Sport is all about getting it right on the day with a little help from others!

Figure 16.22 Holme Pierrepont National Water Sports Centre.

FRANCE

The sports movement is made up of two networks—**Federation** and **Olympic.**

The basic unit in French sport is the club and for the most part these are affiliated to federations. The point to be made is that this network has been built from the clubs up to the federations, very much as in Britain. These federations determine the technical and ethical rules in their respective sports. They are delegated by the Minister of Sport to organize competitions at which international, national and provincial titles are awarded. The federations issue licences to each registered performer. This makes it very much easier to obtain accurate statistics on regular participation.

There are four types of federation: **Sports Olympiques** (Olympic federations); **Non Olympiques** (non-Olympic federations); **Multisports** (associated federations); and **Scholaires & Universitaires** (school and university federations). These four bodies make up four 'collèges' within the French National Olympic and Sports Committee.

The Olympic network has been built the opposite way, that is from the top down, where the **National Olympic Committee** represents and promotes French sport and includes members from all the sports federations. This process of finding and promoting talented performers is achieved through **regional** and **county committees**.

Financial aid is controlled by the **French National Olympic and Sports Committee** in equal partnership with the State. This is divided into two sections, top class sport at national level and sport for all at regional level.

Sport currently comes under the **Ministry of Youth and Sport**. Regional and county directorates of youth and sport exist, but mainly to fulfil the objectives of the Ministry. A level of decentralization has been taking place since 1982, with the establishment of regional and general councils which have the power to finance local sports facilities. This suggests that there is an increasing similarity with the regional and local sports advisory committees in Britain.

The latest development is for the Government to set up three co-operative associations: the **National Council of Sport and Physical Activity;** a **National Committee for Research and Technology;** and a top class **Sports Commission.**

Table 62 : Percentage of French people who practised each sport at least once in 1981. (From Marmet, 1987.)

Sport	Total	Male	Female
Jogging	18.0	21.5	14.7
Swimming	14.7	15.2	14.2
Football	11.1	18.3	4.4
Gymnastics	10.0	6.8	13.3
Tennis	9.5	11.7	7.4
Cycling	7.8	9.1	6.6
Skiing	7.5	8.4	6.5
Sailing	2.9	4.0	1.9
Table tennis	2.5	4.1	0.9
Horse riding	1.8	2.0	1.5
Judo	1.4	2.2	0.6
Dance	0.9	0.1	1.6
Boules	0.8	1.6	0.1
Motorcycling	0.7	1.4	0.1
Shooting	0.4	0.6	0.2
Golf	0.2	0.3	0.1
Archery	0.1	—	0.1
Other	3.5	5.2	1.9

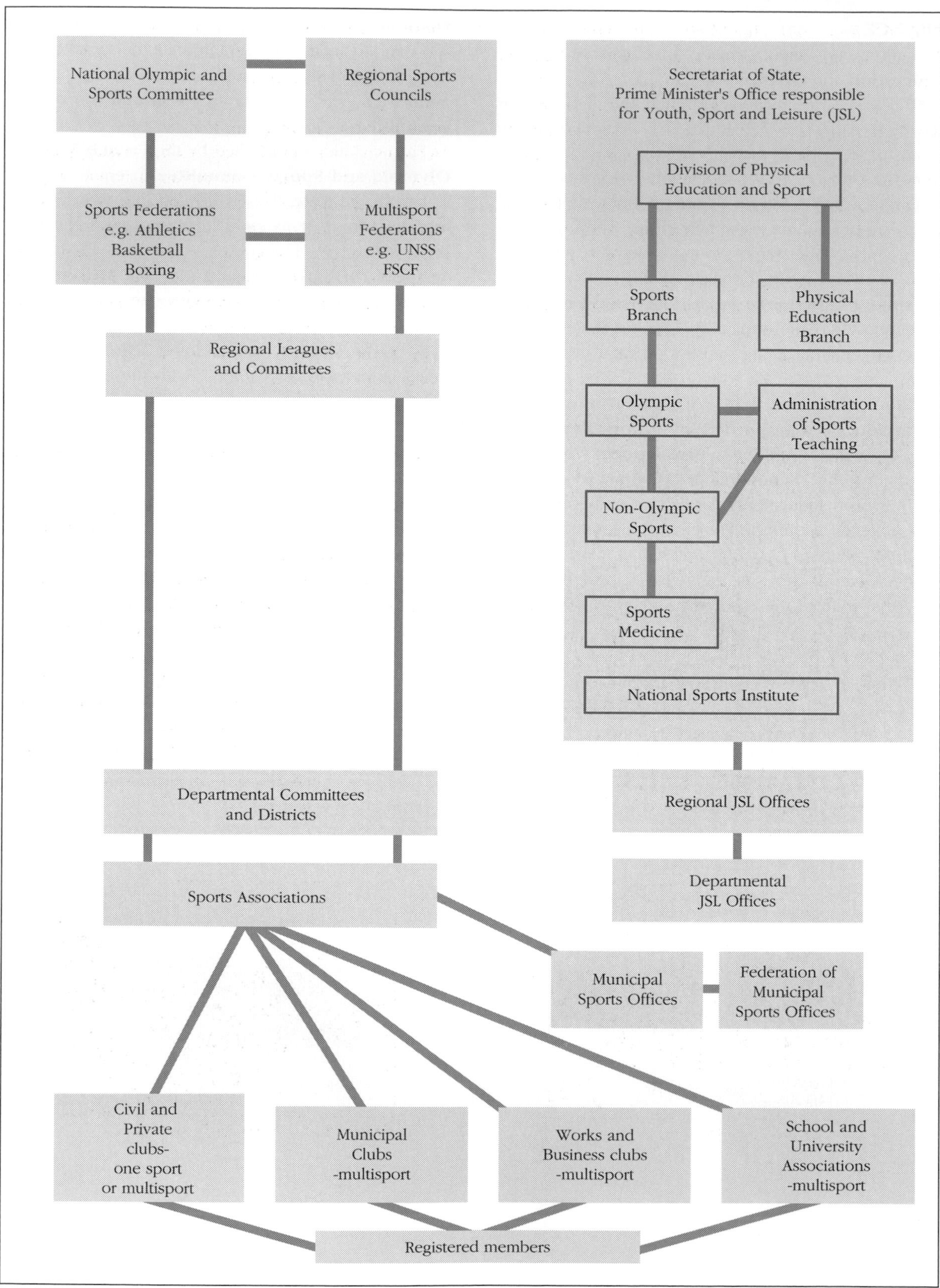

Figure 16.23 The structure of sport in France.

Table 62, from 1981, should give you some comparative insight into popularity variables with the United Kingdom. It is interesting, for example, to note that in 1981 golf had not become a popular game in France. This has changed dramatically over the last decade as a result of the high international media profile and its promotion as a commercial tourist attraction.

There are a number of national centres of excellence, such as the **National Institute of Sports and Physical Education (INSEP),** the **National Yachting School,** the **National Riding School** and the **Regional Sports and Physical Education Centres.** They all assist the Ministry in training officials and preparing athletes for top class competition.

Ethnic sports in the provinces are very popular. These range from a variety of folk activities in the Pays Basque to Breton wrestling and the ever popular street bowls (boules/petanque).

Qu'est-ce que 'Sport pour Tous'?

Within everyone's reach; need to be physically active; a noble life style; mass participation in a wide range of activities; encourage multisport development; socialization of the family and community through sport; instil a love of the open air; a new approach as an alternative to elitism; part of the new image of the sports federations; and spontaneity as against the constrictions of professional sports.

(free translation from *le Sport pour Tous. Une Dimension Nouvelle*, 1976.)

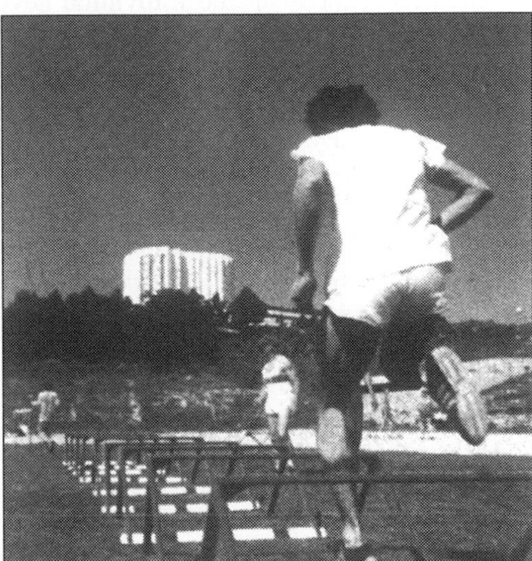

Figure 16.24 INSEP: lies in Vincennes Park on the outskirts of Paris; facilities include:

- Six covered tennis courts, two swimming pools, an outdoor track and field stadium, and two straight tracks and a sprinters' track, one cycling track, two gymnasiums, football and rugby pitches, two fencing halls and the biggest judo hall in Europe.
- Europe's biggest research laboratory specializing in various fields: physiology, biomechanics, measuring instruments for athropometrical tests, muscle building methods, computers to assist in training, and instruments to test and classify sports equipment.
- An audio-visual department and library containing video equipment and publications, some of which are in English, Spanish and Arabic.

Figure 16.25 Scieurs de Long.

Figure 16.26 Course au Sac en Relais.

UNITED STATES

Three ethics appear to co-exist in American sport.

The Lombardian Ethic: winning is everything. The end result justifies the means of achievement.

The Radical Ethic: the excellence of outcome is important, but more important is the way it is achieved.

The Counter-culture Ethic: The process is everything and the end product is unimportant. A strongly anti-competitive view.

Structure and function exist within these conflicting ethics and remain sufficiently fluid to accommodate them.

It is important to remember that **athletics** is a term used to describe high level sport in America and is often associated with professionalism and the Lombardian Ethic. The term **Lifetime Sport** is associated with the European 'Sport for All' concept and tends to reflect the Radical Ethic; it is regularly associated with the intra-mural sports scene in educational institutions. The term **Eco-sport** has been used to reflect sport which is healthy, fun and environmentally based, rather than competitive, and reflects the Counter-culture Ethic.

The structural basis of American competitive sport, athletics, lies in the specific club unit within an institution or a community. It is invariably private, in the sense that members subscribe to it, but at higher amateur and professional levels it is subsidized by sponsorship and gate money.

There are four main levels at which this administration functions:

The National Federation of State High School Athletic Associations is a national advisory body which has branches in each of the states and controls inter-scholastic competition. Very little federal money finds its way directly into sport. The exception is the sponsorship of the Olympic team. These individual organizations have met over a period of many years and produced associations which act as governing bodies to maintain rules, regulations and competitions.

At the collegiate and university level, there are two organizations in operation. **The National Collegiate Athletic Association (NCAA)** is responsible for the inter-scholastic athletic programmes at larger institutions, and the **National Association of Intercollegiate Athletics (NAIA)** controls the athletic competitions between smaller colleges.

The surge of feminism in American colleges and the increase in the number of women athletes as a result of Title IX would seem to have resulted in a counterproductive administrational move, where in 1981 the independent AIAW, which had been responsible for female athletic programmes, lost control and the male-dominated NCAA took over responsibility for all athletics. In addition to scholastic institutions, religious associations, like the YMCA, and larger industrial companies and trade unions, have had considerable influence in the promotion of sport.

At a third level, there are the **individual governing bodies** of American amateur sport.

As a result of the President's Commission on Olympic Sport (1977) and the subsequent Amateur Sports Act (1978), the powerful **Amateur Athletic Union (AAU)** was replaced by the creation of individual governing bodies of sport, for example **The Athletic Congress (TAC)** for track and field athletics, the **United States Gymnastic Federation (USGF)**, the **United States Amateur Swimming (USAS)**, etc.

The rivalry between the NCAA and the AAU has thus been removed by legislation.

At a fourth level there is the professional scene. Each major professional sport has a separate controlling body or bodies. Such is the place of sport in America that to achieve success as a professional sportsperson is to guarantee heroic and financial status for life.

Formation of the United States Olympic Committee (USOC), 1950

> *'The various Olympic developmental programmes—sports club based in Western Europe, sports school in Russia and Eastern Europe and armed services in developing countries—contrast sharply with the system of non-government involvement somewhat unique to the USA.'*
>
> Johnson, W. Secondary School Sports, in *Gymnasion* XI 1, 1974.

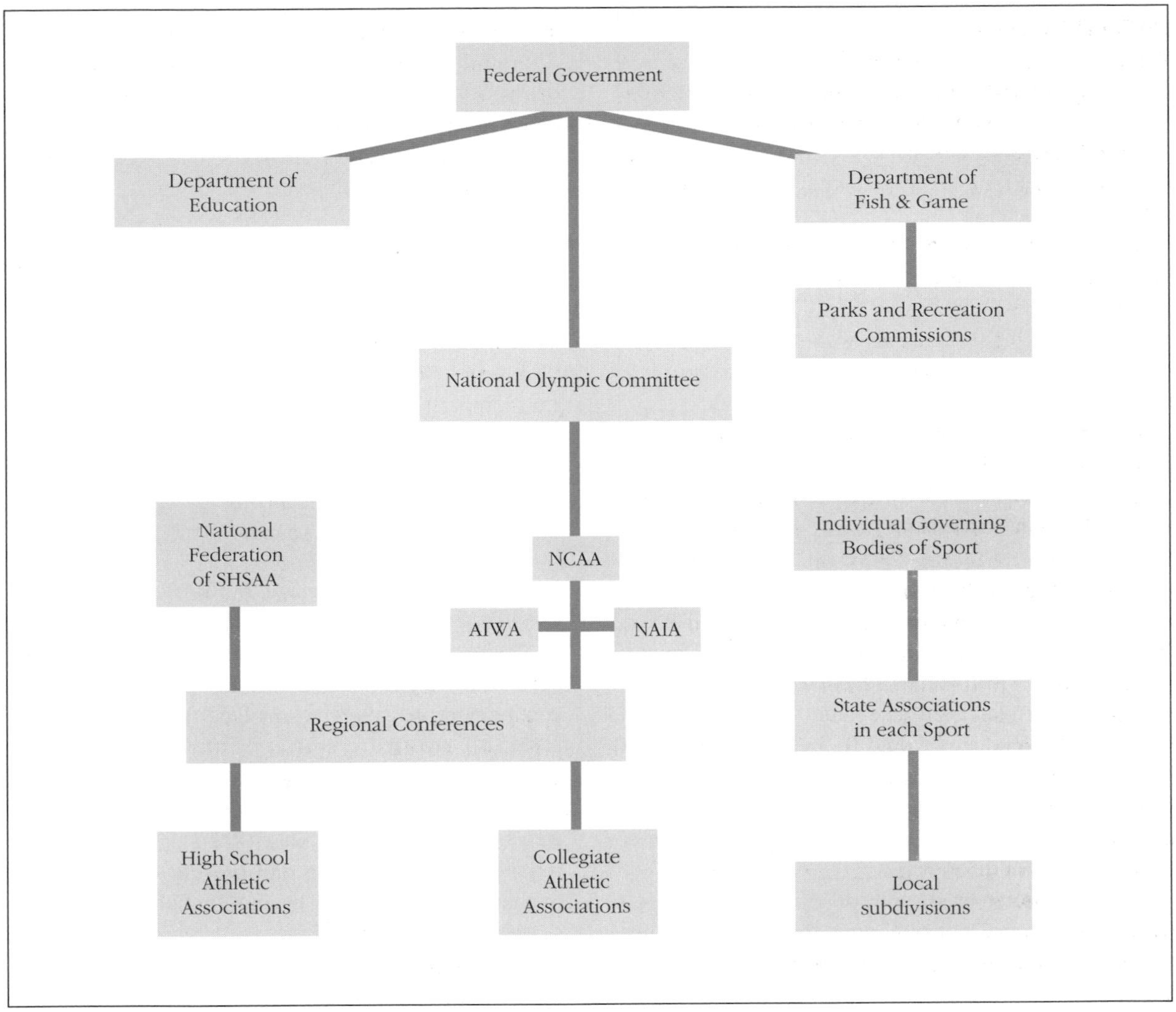

Federal Government
Department of Education
Department of Fish & Game
Parks and Recreation Commissions
National Olympic Committee
National Federation of SHSAA
NCAA
AIWA
NAIA
Individual Governing Bodies of Sport
Regional Conferences
State Associations in each Sport
High School Athletic Associations
Collegiate Athletic Associations
Local subdivisions

Figure 16.27 Administration of sport in the USA.

National Basketball Association
American Basketball Association
National Football League
American Football League
National Baseball League
American Baseball League
Divisions
Conferences
Leagues
Individual Clubs
Individual Clubs
Individual Clubs
Rose Bowl
Rose Bowl
Super Bowl
World Series

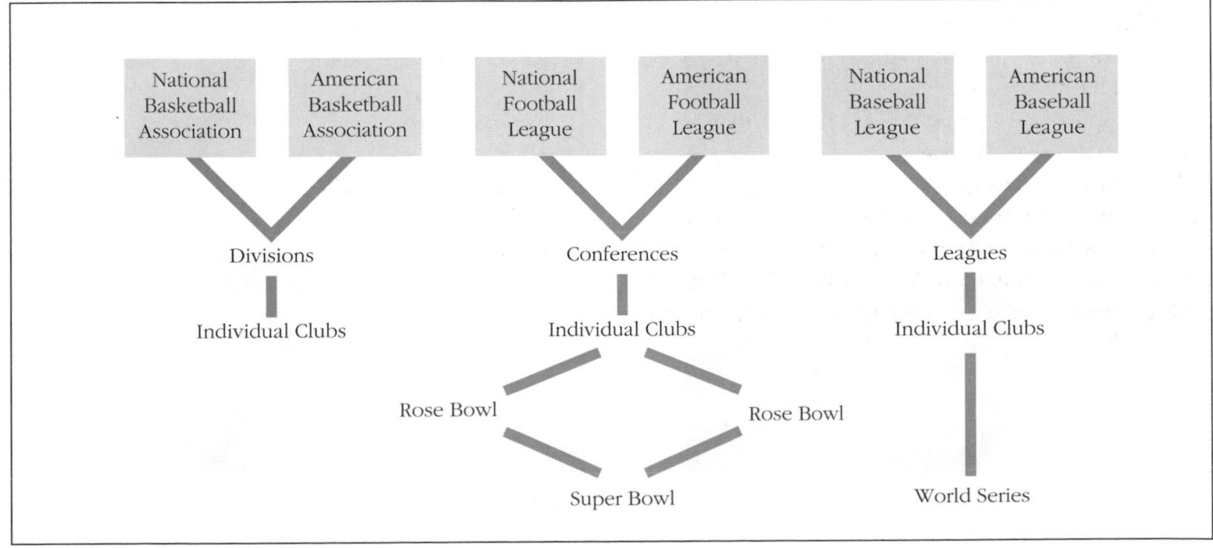

Figure 16.28 Professional Associations.

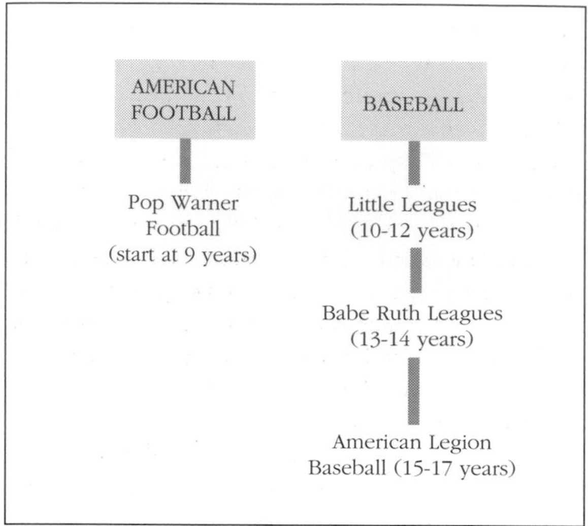

Figure 16.29 Children's sport.

Children's sport in the community exists very much on the same lines as English 'lad's and dad's' soccer. Parents and ex-players coach teams to play in leagues. The criticism is sometimes levelled that professional attitudes are encouraged at a time when recreational and educational values would be better. **Pop Warner Football** and **Little League Baseball** are the two best-known organizations, and to young Americans this may be the start of the glory trail to the Super Bowl or the World Series.

The huge commercial enterprise of collegiate football and basketball not only pays for the scholarships and seasonal costs of the whole athletic and intramural programmes, but also subsidizes other college projects. The American 'alumni' or 'old students' are a constant source of patronage, but it is often a successful athletic programme which motivates their generosity. There are criticisms at intervals from 'academics' against the 'jocks', but such is the public and alumni commitment that there seems little likelihood that this tradition could be seriously threatened by any counter-culture revolution. Sports scholarship students should not always be blamed for their apparent disinterest in academic studies. Often the commitment required by the coaching staff prevents even the well-intentioned athlete from having enough time to study as well as train.

The college athletes in the major sports have sports scholarships which give them a free higher education, as long as they fulfil the requirements of the coach in

Figure 16.30 Why are high scoring games attractive to the American public?

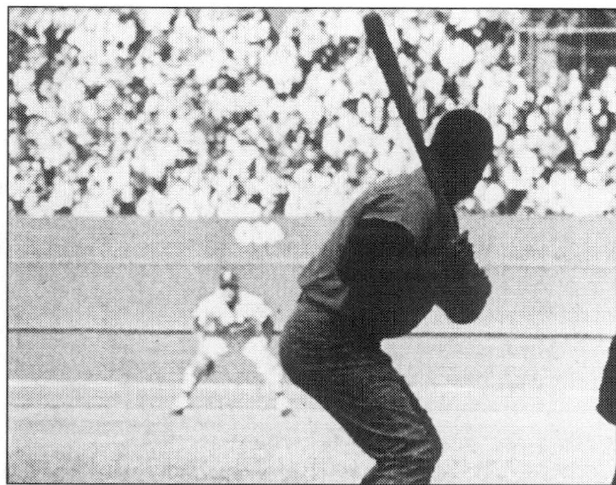

Figure 16.31 Why baseball and not cricket in America?

their particular sport. Baseball tends to be the exception here, in that it is very much the inner-city game, and numerous community leagues exist to act as a proving ground for those aspiring to reach the professional ranks.

At a professional level, by far the largest amount of money is made through television and, as with any advertising franchise, this income is a direct reflection of success. Huge crowds attend professional football games, but the facilities are of such a high standard that violence seldom breaks out. Baseball is an exception here. The crowd is more volatile and the players are given to occasional fist-fights, suggesting some parallels with European soccer. It is also important to recognize that the distances travelled for away games result in most American professional games being played in front of home crowds.

Such is the pressure on winning at collegiate and professional athletics that coaches have a highly paid, but a very insecure, job. Reference is often made to a 'hire and fire' policy. It means that, as with European soccer managers, you are retained only as long as you win regularly.

Amateur sport is very strong in the United States, possibly because of the status of professional sport, but also because to many Americans sport is the last frontier. The Americans consistantly furnish one of the largest Olympic teams and invariably finish in the top three medal winners. The strength of American amateur sport reflects the quality and variety of collegiate athletics. With around 50 per cent of 18-year-olds going into higher education and with a far higher proportion of promising athletes taking advantage of enthusiastic athletics departments, the American Olympic Committee has a ready-made selecting process. Such is the intensity of competition between universities that there are also numerous sports scholarship places for promising athletes from Europe and Africa to enable colleges to boast a winning team.

America differs markedly from Europe in that it does not have a strong private sports club system. This may be the result of the strong collegiate representation, which supplies quality athletes. However, this results in a rapid reduction in sports participation after college, except for the few who are good enough for the professional ranks.

The pro-draft system exists for football and basketball. Well over 700 college football players are drafted into the professional ranks each year. This still represents less than one in a thousand college players making the pro. game. The procedure is for the draft to be ranked and the lowest placed professional club has first choice. This system is not absolute, as wealthier clubs can break the draft by offering highly lucrative private deals with the clubs who have an early draft choice.

To some extent this frustrates the Sport for All idea, and even with exceptions like tennis and golf, many of the facilities for these two games are associated with country clubs where membership is very expensive. More recently, European soccer and rugby are becoming popular and clubs are springing up. It would be wrong to say that Americans have no sporting amenities for the less wealthy adult, but these tend to be recreationally based ice rinks and swimming pools.

Figure 16.32 Can you explain why American females appear to accept this role in sport?

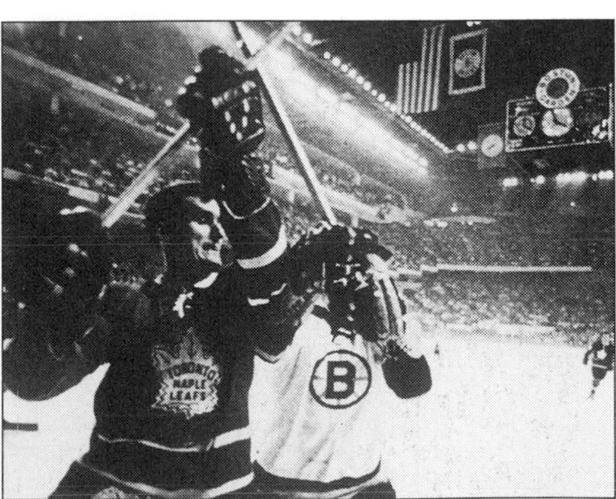

Figure 16.33 Can you account for the high level of violence in some American games, but the low level of spectator violence?

SOVIET UNION AND POST-REFORM RUSSIA

Nowhere has there been a better example of the so-called **sport pyramid** than in what was once the Soviet Union. The idea that the **participation** base and the **diversity** base should be **universal** is still at the **ought** stage, but it is well beyond the Sport for All campaigns in the western world. Our participation plans, though now well advanced as a result of improved facilities and marketing, could not cope if there was a sudden increase in participation percentages. We have now identified target groups who are not participating, but we are still faced with a variety of social constraints. We will not have the diversity in terms of opportunity in all sports until certain traditional social barriers are broken down.

The recent reforms in Russia may have an adverse effect on the status of sport and equal opportunity for sport in the different republics. Economic constraints and the emergence of a market economy may result in a re-emergence of social inequalities, but if the reforms are 'people-led' then there is the sporting infra-structure to retain the high status of sport.

The narrowing of the pyramid should be delayed as long as possible and marketing means keeping the public active in sport as long as possible. We have seen that the major sports in America are for the youthful and outstanding. Britain has many sports clubs which extend the period of participation, but the Soviet Union seems to have progressed further with the principal of sport for life by encouraging a range of strategies to keep the public interested.

The programmes which encouraged participation for life included the GTO scheme, which had classified fitness and achievement figures for male and female adults, which were also graduated according to age. There were also classified sports rankings which allowed athletes to set personal targets of achievement; and for the better performers, there were national awards of athletic proficiency, rising through Masters of Sport to the Order of Lenin for services to sport. Though the politically orientated GTO is now defunct, it is probable that the sports rankings will undergo only a temporary collapse as they are features of all top sporting countries. However, the reform movement will no doubt re-label the top awards, allowing role status and financial endorsement to replace political meritocracy.

The narrowing of the pyramid in the Soviet Union towards sporting excellence was not accidental but rather a carefully constructed stairway where every help was offered to allow athletes to achieve their optimum potential. Certainly, there was an ulterior political motive, but individual sportspersons gained from this State endorsement. Sporting excellence in a huge range of activities appears to have been promoted; a policy of delaying work commitments for the vital periods of

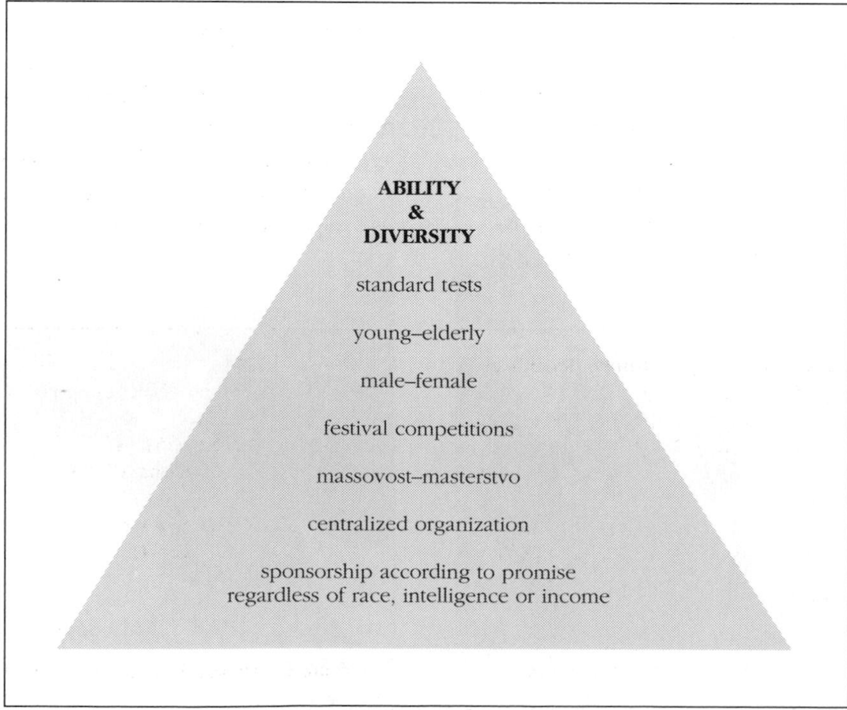

Figure 16.34 Sport pyramid.

training was established; and a circular process of development whereby achievement and knowledge were fed back into the sport programme was encouraged.

We are looking at a pyramid which still appears to be intact in most of the independent republics, where a base called **massovost** encourages all citizens to participate in sport, regardless of age, sex or race. With sport regarded as a purposeful institution in Soviet society, there is the organization—a wide range of sporting festivals and standardization programmes—to stimulate and maintain participatory interest. The point of the pyramid represents a 'creaming' process to produce excellence and is called **masterstvo.**

The opportunity to participate has been a key to all Sport for All campaigns. The frequency of provision varies from one republic to another, but the Supreme Soviet was committed to a policy of sponsorship. This could be seen in the number of factory sports units; the diversity of voluntary sports clubs; the availability of pioneer palaces; and the convenient placing of 'sandlot' facilities in built-up areas. All these facilities have been available to members of the public on the payment of a small annual subscription of 30 kopeks (less than a pound or a dollar). Although financial aid is no longer available from the Supreme Soviet, it is possible that, if a market economy is widely introduced, some republics will continue to give state aid—as in France—while others will look for a mixture of public and private funding.

Spartakiads or sports festivals have been held by all the voluntary clubs and urban units. They have brought competitors together in competition, but have also been structured on a knock-out basis, so that success can take an athlete to a higher level of competi-

Figure 16.35 Sport is popular at the Polytechnic Institute in the city of Frunze, Kirghiszia. The Polytechnic student sports club has a membership of over a thousand people, who work out in 30 groups—mountaineering, basketball, football, volleyball, pentathlon, to name but a few. Kirghizia's landscape and climate make it impossible to go in for conventional skiing. It is replaced by free-for-all events, in which almost all the institute's students and faculty take part. (Sport in the USSR, 4/82.)

Figure 16.36 The Olimp multi-purpose sports complex of the Trudoviye Rezervy Society was built 1,200 metres above sea level in the resort town of Kislovodsk. The complex also includes a rehabilitation centre, as well as diagnostics consulting rooms. Over 3,000 sportsmen—wrestlers, archers, boxers, and track and fielders—have already been in training there. (Sport in the USSR, 4/82.)

GTO Badge Holders	**Sports Rankings:**		**Titles**
1. Men, 40–60; Women 35–55;	I		Merited Master of Sport
	II	Adult Rankings	
2. Men, 19–39; Women 19–34;III	III		Master of Sport (International Class)
3. Boys and Girls, 16–18;			
			Master of Sport (of the USSR)
4. Boys and Girls, 14–15;	I	Junior Rankings (15–18 yrs)	
5. Boys and Girls; 10–13.	II		
	III		Candidate Master of Sport
			State Honorific Award: Order of Lenin.

Figure 16.37 The GTO award scheme, rankings and titles.

Figure 16.38 In Turkmenia 60 years ago, the words 'water' and 'life' were practically interchangeable. Today in the republic, a network of man-made canals and reservoirs have joined the landscape in a significant part of the territory which is desert. Water sports enthusiasts have not been forgotten either. A swimming pool and a new rowing centre on Lake Kurtslin, a short distance from Turkmenia's capital of Ashkhabad, have opened. They will be used by the republic's trade union sports society, Zakhmet, with its 120,000 youth membership for training swimmers and rowers. (Sport in the USSR, 4/82.)

tion. The ultimate Spartakiad has been the National Games, which were held annually. However, the break-up of the Union has meant that the highest internal competition are now the individual republican spartakiads, but, given peaceful co-existence in the future, many of the republics will still want to compete together to test their relative athletic strength.

The organizational structure of Soviet sport was **centralized** with administrative and financial control maintained by the **Supreme Soviet Sports Committee.**

At a second level, there was a tripartite control by three central committees: the **Union of Sports Societies and Organizations Committee;** the **Sports Federations Committee;** and the **Soviet Olympic Committee**.

At a third level, these committees had branches in each of the 15 republics. Within each of these republics, which after all have the size and population of most European countries, there were regional committees responsible for major cities and rural areas. There is no reason why the internal structure of republican sport should have changed, unless there are major financial problems to overcome.

Finally, there are the local organizations and clubs known as **kollectivs**. The majority of these were factory linked and sponsored by the trade unions. Their own working committees had lines of communication through to the central committees. Even if some of the republics remain 'socialist', it is unlikely that all funding will continue through the unions, although unions are likely to continue to support their own workers as they do in the West. However, there is already evidence that the management of various factories and businesses is channelling money into leisure provision to retain the quality of life for the community.

The importance of massovost and masterstvo in Soviet society was reflected in the amount of financial expenditure and the kudos of sport in the community and internationally, and also by the quality and availability of coaches to encourage standards of performance. The status of coach was always a very honoured one in Soviet society, the job often being awarded as a reward for services as a performer, and has proved an 'advantaged' career opportunity. With the Reforms, job security has disappeared from coaching and many have been attracted by good financial offers from abroad. Their expertise is acknowledged by leading athletic nations and so the best are in great demand. Though this is good for world standards, the exodus will eventually undermine performance in the ex-Soviet republics.

The Soviet sports scene was subdivided into four groups: **Olympic, Non-Olympic, Ethnic,** and **Technical.** Each fitted into seasonal and team/individual variables and some had climatic constraints operating.

The greatest effort was made in the Olympic activities, mainly because this was where success would get the most recognition, but also because it was the public arena where amateur competition could be promoted worldwide. It may be a coincidence, but the Reforms in the Soviet Union occurred at the same time as the Olympic Movement entered a phase where professional performers were allowed to compete. This suggests that the older Soviet motives of displaying amateur qualities as a political image now moves across to presenting a nationalistic and commercial image by producing Russian or Ukranian champions as the world's best performers.

The role of ethnic sport in a country which is so racially and culturally diverse is just as important in the separate republics as they are also multi-racial, and to prevent conflict it is important to encourage cultural activities which allow harmless tribal expression.

Non-Olympic activities continue to be encouraged because they extend the diversity of sporting experience. Rugby football is a typical activity in this context, and field sports, like hunting and shooting, are carried on without social exclusivity.

Finally, the technical activities like parachuting, biathlon, and motor racing were the least universal in

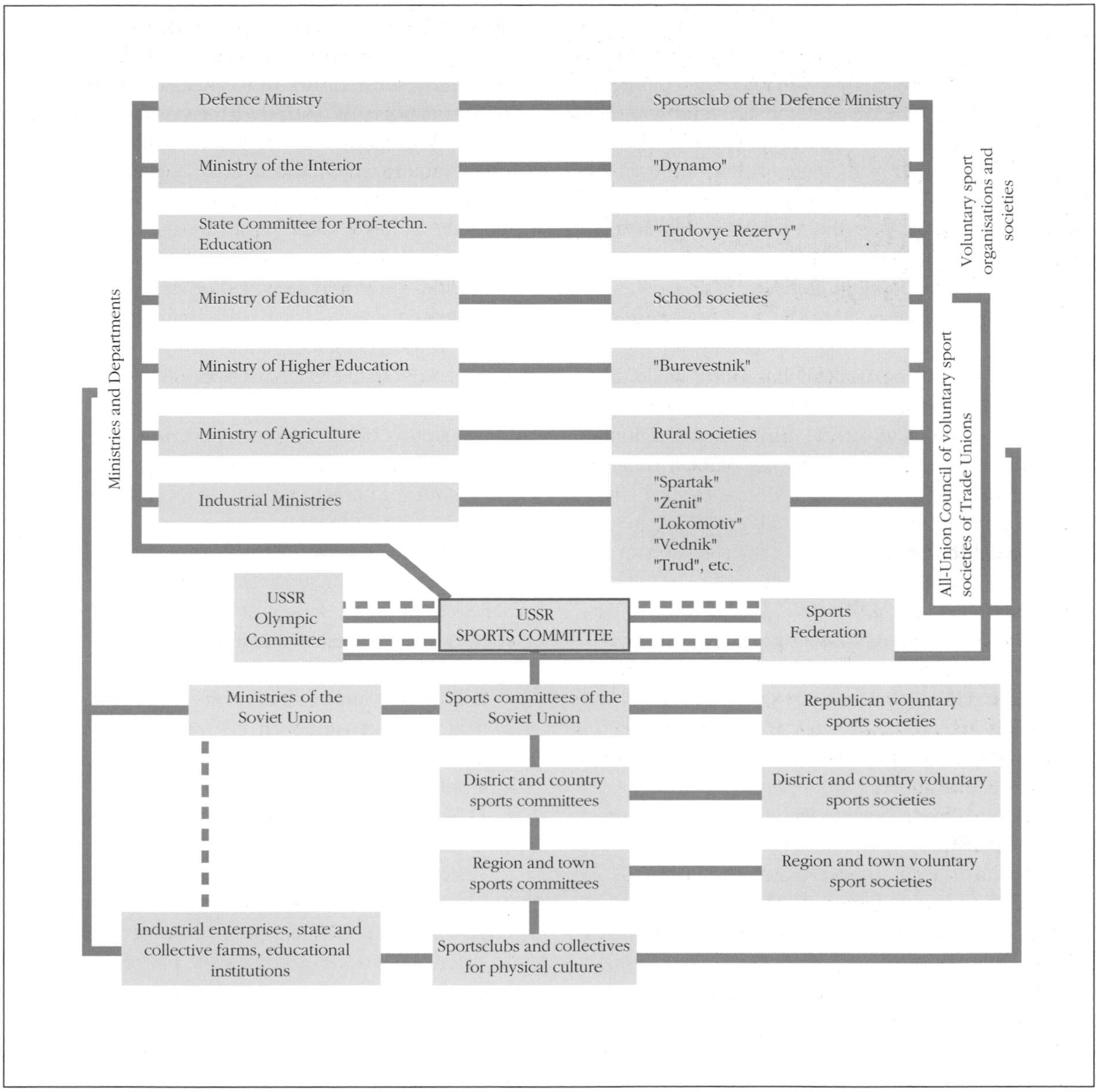

Ministries and Departments

Defence Ministry — Sportsclub of the Defence Ministry

Ministry of the Interior — "Dynamo"

State Committee for Prof-techn. Education — "Trudovye Rezervy"

Ministry of Education — School societies

Ministry of Higher Education — "Burevestnik"

Ministry of Agriculture — Rural societies

Industrial Ministries — "Spartak" "Zenit" "Lokomotiv" "Vednik" "Trud", etc.

Voluntary sport organisations and societies

All-Union Council of voluntary sport societies of Trade Unions

USSR Olympic Committee

USSR SPORTS COMMITTEE

Sports Federation

Ministries of the Soviet Union — Sports committees of the Soviet Union — Republican voluntary sports societies

District and country sports committees — District and country voluntary sports societies

Region and town sports committees — Region and town voluntary sport societies

Industrial enterprises, state and collective farms, educational institutions — Sportsclubs and collectives for physical culture

Figure 16.39 Organization and structure of sport in the Soviet Union. (Speak and Ambler, 1976.)

Figure 16.40 A lasso thrower catching reindeer at an area competition for reindeer drivers, hunters, fishermen and geologists in Naryan Mar, capital of the Jamalo-Nenets Autonomous Area. Other national sports, such as reindeer and dog-sled racing, jumping over sleighs and hatchet throwing, are also popular there. (Sport in the USSR, 4/82.)

the Soviet Union, tending to be the preserve of military personnel. If they are to continue then, given the new market economies, they will need the commercial sponsorship of international companies and will probably be the first activities to become exclusive.

The Soviet Union was contemplating the establishment of professional soccer teams to compete on equal terms with the rest of Europe and South America. This trend was overtaken by the Reforms and now all the major football clubs are being organized on a professional basis. With the authoritarian regime at an end, there is also the opportunity for the best players to join other European clubs, but, while this is very good for the players and their families, it may undermine the quality of the game in the republics. This is a complete break with the Marxist tradition, because the concept of professionalism in the gladiatorial sense of American football, and the 'opium of the masses' sense of British football, can hardly be justified in a 'socialist' society. It may well be that amateurism is moving so fast along the path of fully sponsored training and playing time, together with trust funds to ensure that recognition is given to success, that there is just as little future for the old concept of professionalism as there is for amateurism. With social inequalities ostensibly removed, it may be possible for all athletes to strive for world champion status and receive rewards commensurate with their ability. If this is the case, and there is an opportunity to excel, with a parallel career base for those who fail, together with an efficient feedback into the sport, we may be on the road to a far more socially desirable system.

Summary

UK SPORT:

1. Decentralized administration, but increasing central influence due to funding pressures. Minister for Sport with a voice at Cabinet level since 1992.
2. Autonomous Governing Bodies of Sport with a regional network linking up with local clubs. Many anomalies still exist between these bodies.
3. Sports Council, assisted by the CCPR, has nine regions and five national sports centres.
4. Sports Aid Foundation sponsors top performers through its governing bodies and has nine regional offices.
5. National Coaching Foundation, with Regional Centres, established to promote coaching at all levels and improve information services.

FRANCE SPORT:

1. Centralized joint control—**Federation** and **Olympic** networks.
2. All regular performers are registered (licensed).
3. Strong links between **youth** and **sport**.
4. State aid for all Olympic sports.
5. Professional sports are commercially based.
6. Ethnic sports tradition very strong in the provinces.

USA SPORT:

1. **Decentralized administration**, with **autonomous** governing bodies.
2. Powerful professional sports, with considerable public support.
3. Commercial sponsorship and major media influence.
4. Lombardian 'win-at-all-costs' ethic arising through professionalism and capitalism, but a strong counter-culture at an intellectual level, where excessive competitiveness is criticized.
5. College tradition acts as a sponsored nursery for professional and Olympic performers.

USSR AND RUSSIAN SPORT:

1. Centralized administration from the Supreme Soviet, with a major political influence and State funding, changing to organization by individual Republics—but still with a centralized administration.
2. Masterstvo... Communist World has changed only insofar as each Republic now has nationalistic ambitions.
3. Sport as a shop window was for communism; it is now part of each nation-building process, as each gets its economy in order and strives to build a reputation in the free world.
4. State-sponsored amateurism which taught the rest of the world so much about effective training, has now opened the doors to professionalism as the Olympic Movement embraces a new concept of eligibility.

16.3 The Organization of Outdoor Recreation and Outdoor Education

UNITED KINGDOM

Outdoor recreation is taken to mean recreational activities in the natural environment. While it is fundamentally concerned with enjoying and appreciating natural scenery, there is an element of escape in that many outdoor recreationists are getting away from the urban environment. There is also a concern for conservation, with environmentalists reminding us that abuse and excessive use of the countryside can lead to pollution and erosion.

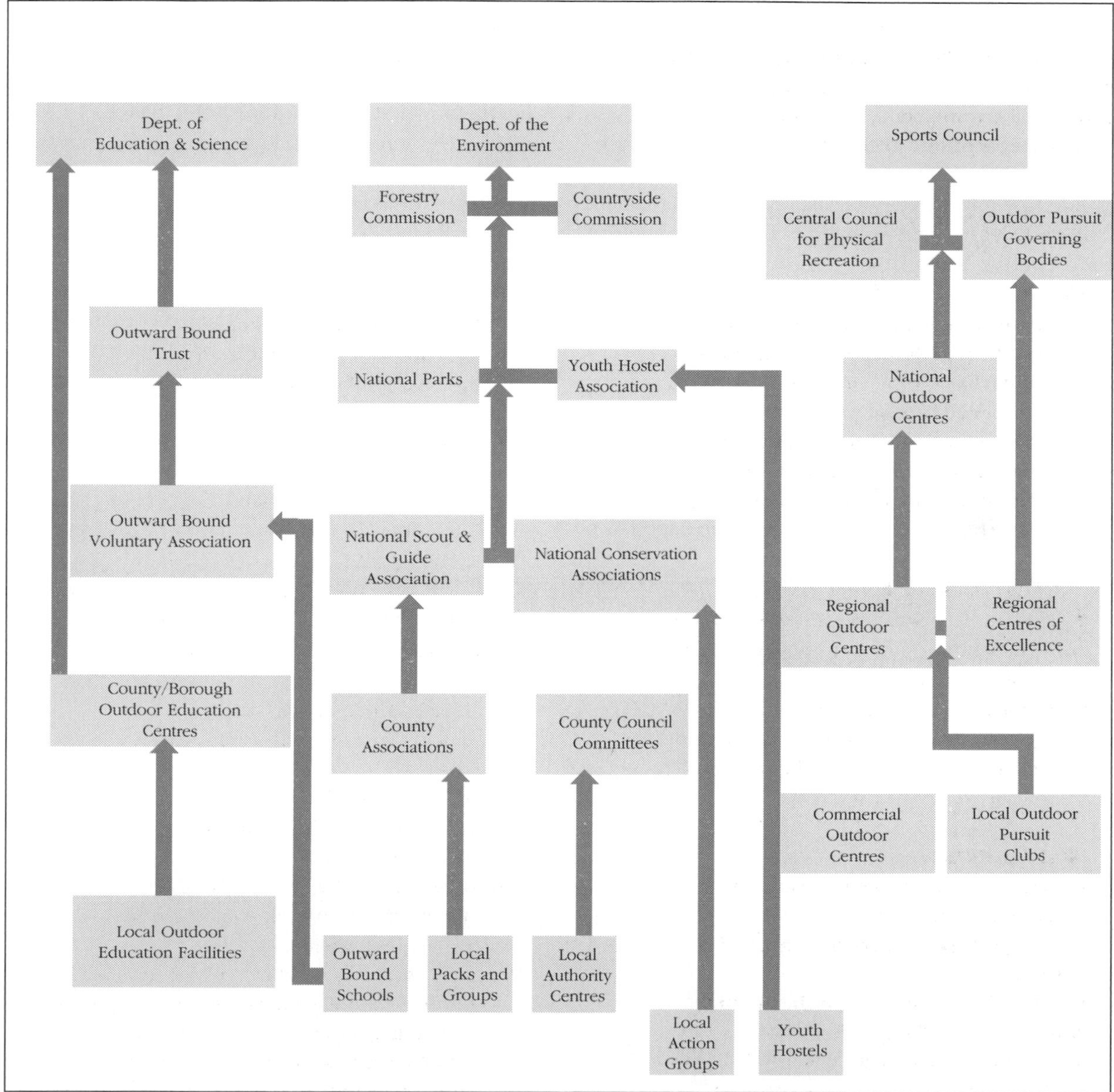

Figure 16.41 Structural framework of outdoor recreation and outdoor education in the UK.

When different ways of exploring the natural environment are considered, this takes us into the area of **outdoor pursuits.** At the most recreational level, this can simply be the use of skills like canoeing or climbing to travel and reach places; or it can mean engaging in the challenge of nature and the elements, through canoeing on wild water or attempting classified rock climbs; finally, there is the sporting dimension, evident in sailing and canoeing, where contests are held on fixed courses.

The use of the term **outdoor education** implies the inculcation of educational values in the natural environment and may involve physical, personal and social development, as well as learning more about the natural environment.

The **Department of the Environment** was established in 1970 and took over three existing ministries. It is led by the Secretary of State for the Environment and one area of responsibility is the conservation of the countryside and the provision and upkeep of amenities. In Wales, the **Welsh Office** deals with all services affecting the physical development of the country.

National parks

The ten national parks cover a total of 13,600 square kilometres, or more than nine per cent of the land area of England and Wales, much of it open countryside in the mountains or on the high moors. This is land considered to be of such great scenic importance that it has been given a special legal status to protect it against inappropriate development, but the fact that an area has been designated a 'national park' does not mean it is in public ownership. As in the rest of the country, all land in the national parks is owned, much of it privately, and farmed, forested or used in some other way, even on the moors. There is also no general right of public access simply because the land is within a national park and the normal rules about access to open land still apply.

Countryside Commission, 1987

Open country

'Open country' is what its name suggests. It is any area consisting wholly or mainly of mountain, moor, heath, down, cliff, sea foreshore, beach, or sand dunes. The term also includes woodland, as well as rivers and canals and their banks.

Although this is usually private land, local authorities are able to make access agreements or orders giving the public a legal right of access to it. Generally, access will be only on foot subject to certain restrictions. You may not be able to camp, for example, and you may have to keep a dog on a lead; and even where public access is guaranteed through an agreement or order, it may be suspended temporarily—for example, to reduce the risk of fire during very dry weather, especially in woodlands, or to prevent the spread of a livestock disease.

Table 63

Long-distance routes designated by the Countryside Commission	*Length (km)*	*(miles)*
Pennine Way	402	250
Cleveland Way	150	93
Pembrokeshire Coast Path	290	180
Offa's Dyke Path	270	168
South Downs Way	129	80
South-West Pennisula Coast Path:		
Somerset and North Devon	132	82
Cornwall	431	268
South Devon	150	93
Dorset	116	72
Ridgeway Path	137	85
North Downs Way	227	141
Wolds Way	127	79
Peddars Way and Norfolk Coast Path (opened 1986)	150	93
	2,711	**1,684**

The South Downs Way and parts of the Ridgeway and the North Downs Way are open to horse riders and cyclists as well as walkers.

Picnic sites and country parks

Throughout England and Wales there are hundreds of picnic sites, some opened with the support and collaboration of the Countryside Commission, others provided by the Forestry Commission or bodies such as the National Trust. Each occupies a few acres, with seats and tables with car parking nearby, and is chosen for the beauty of its surroundings.

There are about 170 country parks supported by the Countryside Commission, ranging in size from a few to several hundred acres. They cover a wide range of scenery, from open parkland and woodland to parks where abandoned industrial land or a worked-out quarry or gravel pit or even a disused reservoir has been transformed to create an attractive landscape. Depending on the site, it will have woods, streams and pools, good habitat for a variety of wildlife, and it may also include a golf course, enough open water for sailing, and space for horse riding. The Countryside Commission advises with the planning of country parks and awards grants to help pay for them. A few are owned and managed privately, some by the National Trust for example, but most belong to local authorities or other public bodies. Country parks exist for the enjoyment of the public and within them you may go where you choose, although occasionally small areas may be reserved for wildlife.

Countryside Commission, 1987

Although there are number of very influential national bodies, like the **National Trust**, the **Youth Hostel Association** and various outdoor pursuit **governing bodies**, the emphasis is on a decentralized organization, which is controlled at local authority level and exercised with a great deal of freedom for individuals, families and organized parties. County councils and urban councils have **Town and Country Planning Committees**, responsible for matters to do with public access to the countryside. As with all British leisure administration, there is a mixture of state and private provision for community and school use.

The Countryside Commission is an advisory and promotional body which aims to conserve the landscape beauty of the countryside; to develop and improve facilities for recreation and access in the countryside; and to advise government on countryside interests. There is a separate commission for each of the home countries.

The **National Trust** owns and protects 522,458 acres of Britain's finest countryside, 452 miles of unspoilt coastline and 276 houses which are open to the public. In 1987, the Trust had 1,193,946 members, who were entitled to free entry to its properties. Parks and areas open for rambling purposes may be privately owned, where access permission is needed, commercially based, or belong to the local authority.

The **Duke of Edinburgh's Award Scheme** is an attempt to help young people to make the best use of leisure time. Established in 1956, it involves boys and girls aged 14–20 in a series of challenging alternatives designed to help them with their personal development and their social awareness. There are bronze, silver and gold awards and they are valued by both participants and employers.

A wide range of **Outdoor Education Centres** is owned by Local Education Authorities (LEAs). The Centres are a fully subsidized part of the education system and the majority have residential facilities. The warden and staff receive children from the authority and the majority of state school children have an opportunity to attend at least one field week during their school career. Young children have programmes in environmental studies mixed with simple open country activities; older children have programmes in outdoor education involving outdoor activities; and youth groups have leadership courses involving outdoor pursuits.

In addition, college students and others attend award courses for proficiency and coaching, such as the **Mountain Leadership Certificate** and awards organized by the BCU and RYA.

The **Outward Bound Trust** is a registered charity whose patron is the Duke of Edinburgh. It was formed in 1946 to promote personal development training for young people, and today administers five Outward Bound centres in the United Kingdom and has inspired some 35 centres of a similar type overseas. The Trust is supported by 35 Outward Bound Associations which consist of groups of people voluntarily promoting the Trust and raising funds to assist deserving cases financially.

A wide range of courses include Outward Bound, Expedition and Outdoor Skill Courses; the DoE Award; City Challenge courses, an urban equivalent to Outward Bound; the Gateway and Senior Gateway courses, which are associated with business management skills; and Contract courses, which can be arranged by individual companies and organizations.

All the programmes are 'intensive experiences involving personal development experience, designed for young people to develop skills, judgement and confidence to meet the future with its problems, uncertainties and new responsibilities'.

FRANCE

The whole concept of French outdoor recreation is expressed in the phrase *Le Plein Air*. Historically linked with twin European traditions of the **'spa movement'** and **'naturalism'**, it has become a campaign to get the young away from the corrupting influence of the inner cities and to introduce them to the simple pleasures of life in the countryside. However, French administrators recognize that fresh air may not be enough and so they include physical exercise and strive to re-establish the '**rustic simplicity**' of being able to make the most of the natural environment.

A number of key variables need to be taken into account when looking at the French development of outdoor recreation.

The amount of open countryside and the range of climatic and topographical types give the French people greater opportunities than those available in Britain. They can ski in the Alps; walk in the Massif Central; bathe in the Mediterranean; fish and canoe on the many waterways; and sail on the extensive coastal waters.

The British have chosen to spread holidays over a three-month period to off set crowding, but the French still cling to traditional holiday periods, which means that in the first week of August, workers down tools and start a grand exodus to the countryside. Inevitably, this concentration causes crowding in the more popular areas, but, as with British excursion trips, many holiday makers appear to enjoy the bustle and social conviviality. At the centre of this ritual there is *le camping français*. Families swarm out of the cities and head for the sun, taking miniature homes along with them. Alternatively, the trains are filled to capacity twice a year to take skiers to the Alps at Easter and to get families to the sea in August where 'beaches boil with Gallic bodies'.

The French family has changed a great deal over the last 20 years. Mazeaud (1976) suggested that, with working wives and fewer children, spare time was becoming increasingly precious and parents were looking for more free time to pursue their own interests. This led local authorities and firms to sponsor holiday centres for children, **centres de vacances**. One example, the **colonie de vacances**, a rural institution, has the much in common with the American camp school. In addition to the function of freeing the parents, these 'colonies' are designed to take children out of the towns and, originally, many of the local authority centres made special efforts to cater for underprivileged children. Traditionally, wealthier children have tended to take private or commercial alternatives.

The programme in these residential centres includes educational, social and cultural elements as well as outdoor pursuits, with emphasis on promoting *le plein air*, a love of the open air. Children can stay at these residential centres for the whole summer holiday

Figure 16.42 Sea school in Brittany.
Why are water sports so popular in France?
(France Information, 1985.)

Figure 16.43 Snow school in Auvergne.
Why has the French Government poured money into snow schools?

and are then returned to their parents.

Although reference has been made to residential *colonies de vacances*, there are many different types of leisure centre frequented by young people, some small and local, others of national significance, where outdoor pursuits are taught to a high level. For example, **Le Centre National des Sports de Plein Air** at Vallon-Pont-D'Arc is equivalent to Britian's Plas y Brenin, and there is a famous mountain school at Chamonix.

Alternatively, in the Nantes district, for example, there are leisure centres available for children to use on Wednesday afternoons; there are ten or more local centres spread throughout the town for children aged 4–15 to use in the holidays; there are adventure playgrounds situated at various points; and, on a larger scale, there is a *village de vacances*, which is a permanent holiday complex for children and an urban equivalent of a *colonie de vacances*.

If these are holiday opportunities for French children, then the *classes* are outdoor experiences promoted as part of the school programme. As early as 1953 snow clases were started, where children were taken out of the towns to stay in the mountains for about a month under the supervision of their regular teachers, PE staff and qualified ski instructors. In addition to the snow classes, there are now classes in the countryside, also sea schools, and—as a result of government support and subsidies from Municipal and General councils—there has been a steady increase in the number of children involved. In 1984, for example, some 120,000 children attend a total of 4,600 classes.

Figure 16.44 Class de vert.
How does this compare with English environmental studies?

The full title of the programme is *les classes transplantées: la ville à la campagne*, and the key to understanding its intention lies in the word 'transplanting'. Children are taken from the town to a country location in another region. It is an attempt to broaden the child's experience and knowledge about the natural environment, but also to take him/her to another part of France where traditions and customs may be different. It is a formal educational experience as parents have to be convinced that academic standards and health will not suffer as a result of a month away from formal schooling.

It is important to recognize the difference between the holiday and the school programmes. There are critics who believe that much of *le plein air* concept is lost in the formality of the *classes*: that it can be truly expressed only through a family holiday or as a leisure experience at a *centre de vacances*. There are others who see the value of the *classes* as the richest school experience, pointing to the social awareness of being taught in the natural environment. In both cases it would seem that the British outdoor education programme does not match up to the opportunities available to the average French child.

UNITED STATES

The size and beauty of the United States' natural resources are sufficient in themselves to make outdoor recreation one of the most rewarding elements in American culture, but there is also the legacy of Theodore (Teddy) Roosevelt. Acknowledged to have been one of the country's greatest presidents, 'T.R.' established a tradition of conservation and national pride for America's unspoilt wilderness. By 1909 he had set aside some 230 million acres of national forest, more than 50 federal wildlife refuges, and doubled the number of national parks. Despite tragic economic setbacks like the 'Dustbowl' in the 1930s, this pride in the 'Great Outdoors' has remained part of the American Dream, nurtured no doubt by the heritage of the 'Frontier Spirit' which went with it.

In 1965, the Land and Water Conservation Fund Act ensured that the 'dream' could be a financial possibility, when the **Bureau of Outdoor Recreation**, as part of the **Department of the Interior**, was given the power to administer a fund for state, local and federal outdoor education purposes. As a result, all 50 states now have park systems and every **State Highways Department** has to maintain roads into recreational areas.

Given the status and scope of these natural parks, it has been necessary for the Bureau to produce a co-ordinated administration. It is difficult for Europeans to conceive wilderness areas so vast that, without a stringent organization, many hikers could get lost and die. Necessary regulations take away some of the freedom of action expected by hikers in Britain, but are essential to ensure safety standards. One method used to enlighten the public is through a classification of areas (See Figure 16.45).

Wilson (1977) suggested that in the 1970s there was a major expansion in what was called 'wilderness sport participation', and research indicated that the two main reasons were a desire to escape from the technology and urbanization of modern living; and a desire to achieve a greater sense of self-awareness. These related attitudes were shared by mountaineers, backpackers, cross-country skiers and bicyclists alike, and represented findings by the National Park and Forest Services as well as State Park Authorities.

Outdoor education has developed since the Second World War as part of an 'alternative' form of education. Very much in line with the philosophies of William James and John Dewey, it represented an experiential approach to learning and was readily associated with nature study and interdisciplinary study. Jenson and Briggs (1981) claimed that there were four main categories of outdoor education: personal growth programmes; interdisciplinary studies; socializing agencies; and recreational education.

In Britain, France and the United States there has been a desire to broaden the experience of urban children, but in America there is also a 'counter-culture' element operating, as an escape from the elitism and commercialism of the professional sports scene.

The **American Outward Bound Association** is an extension of the British Outward Bound Trust. It is a non-profit making educational organization and has the support of many senior high schools, where credit is given for attendance. Programmes range from standard 21–26 day experiences in the wilderness, to shorter intensive adventure experiences, and there are also courses in leadership skills and for potential business executives. These courses also include a variety of snow experiences, canoeing and backpacking, rock climbing and cycling, all with the intention of testing the resilience of the individual in an alien environment and group co-ordination in challenging situations. In 1981 there were seven centres: Dartmouth, Colorado,

Figure 16.45 Classification of areas.
Class I: Areas intensively developed near towns and designed for extensive use.
Class II: Areas wtih substantial development for a variety of recreational uses.
Class III: Areas which are suitable for recreational use in a natural environment, but within easy each of habitation.
Class IV: Areas of outstanding scenic beauty some distance from civilization.
Class V: Undisturbed roadless areas, characterized by natural, wild conditions, including 'wilderness areas'.
Class VI: Historic and cultural sites.

Hurricane Island, North Carolina, Northwest and Southwest. They are all situated in areas of natural beauty with wilderness characteristics.

In addition to outdoor education as a direct extension of schooling, and Outward Bound as an intensive adventure experience for those over 16, there is a wide-ranging provision of summer camps. As with the French system, it is important to differentiate between programmes with an educational basis and those with a recreational–vacational function. Examples of American children's camps go back to the 19th century and most of them were associated with taking impoverished children out of their depressed urban environment.

Since the Second World War camp schools have mushroomed in all the more scenic areas, particularly where there is a large supporting population within a convenient distance. These are essentially holiday experiences and there is a strong tradition of American children spending at least part of their long summer vacation in a residential camp school. These permanent institutions are run by a variety of groups and ownership tends to dictate the type of child involved. Many camps are run by the state or individual civic

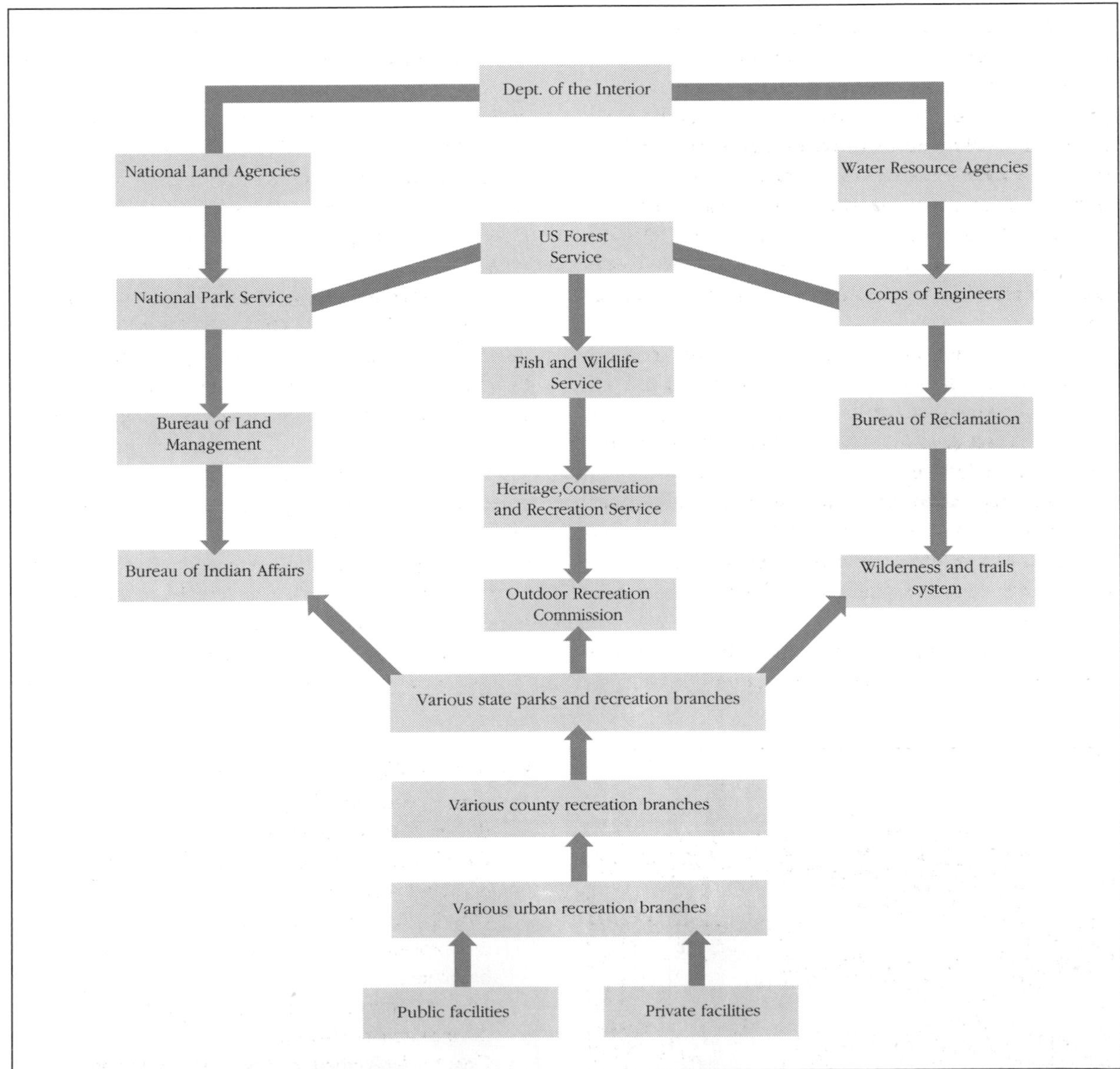

Figure 16.46 Agencies involved in outdoor recreation in the USA. (For detail see Weiskopf, 1982.)

authorities, and these tend to be heavily subsidized to allow poorer children to 'escape' to the countryside. Then, there are camp schools which are sponsored by firms, ethnic groups and religious bodies, and, finally, there are commercial camps, where the reputation of the centre tends to dictate cost and, consequently, the clientele. In all cases, the children are on holiday and every effort is made to give them a good time, but also a safe time.

Traditionally, there are numerous challenges designed to encourage personal growth, socialization, and a love of the natural environment, combined with 'camp fire' and patriotic ritual.

There is little doubt that, as in France, there is a tendency for American parents to go on separate holidays while the children are under careful supervision at camp school. From the children's point of view, many make lasting friendships, particularly when they return to the same camp year after year.

A number of organizations, like Camp America and BUNAC, have the franchise to appoint staff from various countries, and many British students work as counsellors over the 6–8 week period.

Figure 16.47 What characteristics of the Outward Bound Movement do these photographs illustrate?
Source: Colorado Outward Bound brochure, 1979.

a.

b.

Figure 16.48 What do these photographs tell you about an American camp school?
Source: Colorado Outward Bound brochure, 1979.

a.

b.

TOURISM IN THE SOVIET UNION AND POST REFORM RUSSIA

As the Soviet Union considered itself an emergent 'socialist' society, it is important to recognize that recreation had bourgeois connotations and consequently the term **tourism** was more regularly in use.

The struggle for literacy and military preparedness meant that more dynamic aspects of physical culture had priority in the early years and that tourism has been a priority only since 1968.

The term **tourism** implied a raising of the cultural and political awareness of the Soviet people. A major part of this cultural awareness concerned the natural environment but, with such a diverse and ancient country, there was also a considerable interest in the country's heritage. Pride in Mother Russia was framed in a political acknowledgement that, without communism, there would be no culture worth visiting. In the context of the Reforms it is difficult to justify the continued use of the term 'tourism' as it has had so many political connotations, but its broad basis remains conceptually attractive. However, it is likely that, if progress continues towards a market economy, the label and concept of 'recreation' will become a part of the new order, hopefully, without the negative characteristics of discrimination.

As a country which has been industrialized in the last 50 years, working-class free time has been many years behind the Western model. A five-day, 40-hour week has been broadly established only since 1972; and, up to 1968, 15 days' 'prescribed leave' was the annual holiday for the majority. In 1972, however, a legal minimum of 15 days was established, and an upper limit of 26 days. This led to a dramatic change in lifestyle, the weekend becoming a major leisure period, acheiving a significance not unlike that of European countries. There was an inevitable shift of interest from explosive sports and spectatorism in the cities to a pattern of weekend excursions, where rural centres with a variety of sporting facilities were built .

In terms of the natural environment, the 15 republics have the same diversity as the United States, but with at least twice the area of wilderness. However, its administration was totally different, with central control emanating from the **Supreme Soviet**, and policy exacted through a series of master plans. These were transmitted to the various republics; the regions within the republics; and down to individual districts. In addition, all Soviet republics had their own voluntary nature protection societies with a reputed membership of one in five of the population. With the republics now independent, it is unlikely that the administrative structure within each will have changed in the short term, but it is likely that national interests will be more adequately served—even though there may be a halt in the expansion of recreational programmes until the respective economies are on a more sound footing.

It would seem that national support for conservation will continue. The **State (National) Forestry Committee**, for example, not only is responsible for all logging and felling, but controls the woodworking industry as a whole and is responsible for the protection of forests. At a rough estimate, almost a third of the old Soviet Union is forested, with timber reserves put at 82,000 million cubic metres in 1977. Very much the same is true of nature reserves in terms of conservation, but also the provision of facilities and communications to encourage tourism, sport and camps.

Given the importance of sport and active leisure, every opportunity has been made to turn natural resources into outdoor pursuit facilities, and most of these have been administered and sponsored by individual factories. Parts of the old Soviet Union are naturally suited to specific outdoor pursuits: the Carpathian Mountains have numerous skiing centres; the Black Sea is famous for aquatics and sailing; and the Pamir Peaks are excellent for mountaineering and rock climbing.

The **tourism** aspect of **physical culture** made giant strides forward as a result of the National Economic Plan (1971–75), when children's **Excursion-Tourist Stations** were set up; tourist sections were encouraged in the various sports clubs; and tourist centres were built throughout the Soviet Union, rather than just in the traditional holiday centres of the Black Sea and the Caucasus.

Though well behind the United States in the development of National Parks, there is a trend in this direction as witnessed by the Armenian National Park.

Angling is very popular, as in all European countries, and major efforts have been made to reduce the levels of river pollution in industrialized areas.

Soviet holiday categories before the reforms.

1. The majority of workers applied to attend camps run by their factory trade union. Normally, with the larger firms and farm collectives, a trade union had access to a number of camps of varying standards and the selection process involved an assessment of the worker's contribution to the firm over the year. In this way, a pass to a Black Sea resort was used as a work incentive. It is probable that factories will continue to sponsor these holiday camps,

but it is more likely that the management or a joint committee will take on the funding. However, if the industries need money they might well sell these assests to entrepreneurs.

2. **Independent holidays** represent an increasing trend among the better-off urban white collar workers. Although it would seem to be a political contradiction, there has been a strong tradition of financially secure families having a holiday home or dacha, which would be visited at weekends and holidays. It would seem probable that with the increased freedom of perestroika more and more families will be hoping to organize their own holidays around hotels and *dachas*.
3. **The Communist Youth League (Komsomol)**—a political youth organization for 15- to 26-year-olds—organized holidays called **Operational Camps**. These involved a sizable group of student volunteers working on major projects during the summer vacation. The largest was to assist in the building of the Baikal-Amur Railway (BAH), resulting in an alternative route to Siberia being established which opened up huge areas for population expansion. The break-up of the Soviet Union resulted in the Communist Party, and its youth wing, the Komsomol, losing most of their influence. The principle of encouraging young people to help develop major projects is a sound one, however, but with the removal of authoritarianism any new programme is more likely to be on the lines of the Voluntary Overseas Service which operates in the Western world.
4. **Children's holidays**. As with the other countries in this section, there are two concepts operating—**outdoor education** and **holidays** in the outdoors. However, under the Soviet dictum of purposeful leisure, it was difficult to separate the two, all children's leisure having been to an extent educational, even if it was only a form of political education. Schools in the different republics have clubs, which they call circles, and some of these involve outdoor activities. The pioneer palaces, which are community facilities for children, also have circles.

It is important at this point to identify the main children's organizations operating before the 1992 Reforms. We have already mentioned the **Komsomol** which was a highly political youth group but now exercising little power. There were two younger groups. The **Pioneers** were boys and girls aged seven to 17, and the **Octobrists** (after the October Revolution) were under seven-years-old. These political youth groups are now in disarray with their funding cut off and their political function rejected. However, care for the wellbeing of children is deeply rooted in Russian society and so families will probably promote a 'scouting' equivalent in the near future.

The Pioneers were much more politically oriented than scouts or guides, but shared several common features. These included a desire to reinforce a strong moral code: encouraging a sound understanding of the natural environment; performing tasks for the community; and instilling a sense of national pride. They wore a uniform and had organized activities at school and in the community palaces. Though central-

Figure 16.49 Trade Union Central Council on Tourism Excursions. Why are the Soviets so anxious to link workers and tourism?
(*Sport in the USSR*, 8/81.)

Figure 16.50 Dilijan Nature Park, part of the Armenian National Park. (*Soviet Weekly*, 20.8.77.)

ized, their organization tended to work from the republic down, through regional committees to district level, and there was a direct link with political organizations at each level. Soviet children were not obliged to be Pioneers and many attended the pioneer palaces and camps without being members, suggesting that if a new source of funding could be found these excellent facilities could be utilized by the new outdoor education organizations.

Prior to the breakdown of the Soviet Union, the majority of Soviet children attended a summer camp which had a lot in common with the American camp school system. However, none of the Soviet examples were profit-making; they all had very close ties with the Komsomol and Pioneer organizations; they were run on much more authoritarian lines; and they were mainly sponsored and managed by trade union societies. Normally, parents had to pay about 30 per cent of the cost, with the trade union covering the balance. Camps lasted for six weeks during the long summer vacation and most catered for about 400 children. Quality varied and schools were able to recommend their best pupils as a rewards for effort. The most famous children's camp was probably Artek on the Black Sea.

The programme at the camp included some related school subjects, like environmental studies and some political lessons, but most of the time was spent exploring the natural scenery or engaging in other outdoor activities. As with the American camps, there was a lot of 'camp fire' ritual and numerous group challenges. However, much of the outdoor programme has been structured to achieve the **Young Tourist Award** (children aged 12-15) and the **Tourist of the USSR Award** (those aged 16+).

Finally, we must mention the historical features of tourism. Post-Revolution history was very important to the Soviet Union, particularly the Russians; children were constantly reminded of the way the country had to struggle to achieve its status, and of the bravery of its people, especially in the fight against Germany in the Second World War. With independence and glasnost the history books may be rewritten, allowing the development of a free pluralist society that can grow to appreciate the natural environment without any political overtones being included.

Figure 16.51 Operational Tourism. These youngsters spent their summer holidays helping archaeologists carry out excavations of ancient settlements.

1. A Pioneer loves his Motherland and the Communist Party of the Soviet Union.
2. A Pioneer prepares himself to enter the Komsomol organization.
3. A Pioneer honours the memory of those who gave their lives in the struggle for freedom and for the prosperity of the Soviet Motherland.
4. A Pioneer is friendly to the children of all countries.
5. A Pioneer learns well.
6. A Pioneer is polite and well disciplined.
7. A Pioneer loves labour and is careful of public property.
8. A Pioneer is a good comrade: he cares for the young and helps the old.
9. A Pioneer is brave and unafraid of difficulties.
10. A Pioneer is honourable and values the honour of his detachment.
11. A Pioneer hardens himself, does physical exercises every day, and loves nature.

Figure 16.52 Extract from the Pioneer Principles. How does this differ from the English Guide or Scout movement?

a.

b.

Figure 16.53 Artek pioneer camp on the Black Sea. Only children with outstanding 'merit marks' have a chance to attend this showpiece.

Summary

UK, OR:

1. **Outdoor education** is supervised in most schools.
2. **Outdoor pursuits** are controlled by governing bodies and individual enterprise.
3. **Outward Bound Trust:** residential schools to promote adventure and character building experiences.
4. **Countryside Commission** administers the **National Parks**, supported by the **National Trust.**
5. **Green Movement** on conservation is getting stronger.

France, OR:

1. ***Le plein air*** is an important concept.
2. Significance of ***les classes transplantees*** which take the children into the countryside and teach them sailing and skiing.
3. ***Colonies de vacances*** are residential holidays, often used by the local authorities to give underpriviledged children an extended open country experience.

US, OR:

1. **Federal** as well as **state** organization of **outdoor recreation**.
2. **Outward Bound Trust** also functions in the US.
3. **State** and **commercial camp schools** very popular, attracting a wide range of children through the summer months.

OR in the Soviet Union and Post Reform Russia:

1. Soviet **'Tourism'** included all branches of outdoor recreation. Very much a politically motivated organization.
2. **Octobrists, Pioneers** and **Komsomol** were the political child and youth bodies.
3. **Pioneer palaces** have been well equipped youth centres and **pioneer camps** have been residential camp schools.
4. Conservation also had strong political support, with an increasing number of national parks being opened. This should continue in the independent republics.

REFERENCES AND FURTHER READING

United Kingdom

Anthony D. *A Strategy for British Sport,* Hurst, 1980.

Armstrong N. (ed.) *New Directions in PE,* Human Kinetics, 1990.

Cashmore Ellis, *Making Sense of Sport,* Routledge, 1990.

CCPR The Howell Report, *Sports Sponsorship,* 1983.

CCPR, *Organization of Sport and Recreation in Britain,* CCPR, 1991.

CCPR *The Palmer Report. Amateur Status,* etc., 1988.

Coe S. et al. *More Than a Game,* BBC Books, 1992.

Coghlan J.F. *Sport and British Politics,* Falmer, 1990.

DES, *Physical Education in the Curriculum,* HMSO, 1992.

Hendry L.B. *Sport, School and Leisure,* Lepus, 1978.

Houlihan B. *The Government and Politics of Sport,* Routledge, 1992.

Macfarlane N. *Sport and Pollitics,* Collins and Willow, 1986.

McIntosh P.C. *Sport and Society,* West London Press, 1987.

Sports Council. *The Next Ten Years,* 1982.
Which Ways Forward, 1987.
Into the 90s, 1988.
Sport: A Guide to Governing Bodies, As Updated, New Horizons, 1994.

France:

French Embassy. Sports in France, *France Information,* 125, 1985.

Hantrais L. Leisure and the family in contemporary France, *Leisure Studies,* Vol. 1, (1), 1982.

Mairie de Paris, *La Direction de la Jeunese et des Sports en Chiffres,* 25, Boulevard Bourdon, Paris, 1992.

Mairie de Paris, *Sports et Jeunesse: 10 ans d'Action Municipale,* 1991.

Mermet G. *Francoscopie, Larousse,* 1987/88/90/91.

Platt J. The development of sport exchange, *Outdoors,* Vol. 3, No. 4, Nov. 1973.

Rigby F. The place of PE and sport in a centralized educational system—France, *PE Review,* Spring 1978.

United States:

Bucher C.A. et al. *Secondary School Physical Education,* Mosby, 1970.

Calhoun D.W. *Sport, Culture and Personality,* Human Kinetics, 1987.

Hellison D.R. *Goals and Strategies for Teaching P.E.,* Human Kinetics, 1985.

McPherson B.D. *et al. The Social Significance of Sport,* Human Kinetics, 1989.

Sage G.H. *Power and Ideology in American Sport,* Human Kinetics, 1990.

Soviet Union:

ISCPES. *Comparative P.E. and Sport,* Vols 3/4/5, Human Kinetics, 1986/7/8/

ISCPES. *Sport For All, Into The 90s,* Vol. 7, Meyer & Meyer Verlag, 1991.

Riordan J. *Sport in the Soviet Union,* CUP, 1977.

Speak M.A. and Ambler V.H. *PE, Recreation and Sport in the USSR,* Univ. of Lancaster, 1976.

Chapter 17
Sociological Considerations of Physical Education and Sport

17.1 Towards an Understanding of Sports Sociology

It is not intended to go into any detailed analysis of sociology as a discipline. The feeling is that in your reading you may need to be able to interpret certain sociological articles, and it will help you to understand some of the contemporary issues in our society, if you can use sociology as an analytical tool. Unfortunately, the lay person is sometimes frustrated by the technical language and meanings used by some sociologists and so it is hoped to make you conversant with the main terms and concepts as they concern physical education, sport and outdoor recreation.

Two sociologists were asked to define their discipline:

1. Sociology deals with the way individuals interact with one another to make up a social structure.

   (Given that there is a great deal of group action in sport, there should be plenty to interest a sociologist!)
2. Sociology is the scientific discipline that describes and explains human social organization. The size of the human group under study can range from two people wrestling, to a sports club, a governing body, the leisure pattern of a community, or the place of sport in a society. The sociologist is interested in the patterns that emerge whenever people interact over periods of time. Although groups may differ in size and purpose, there are similarities in structure and in the processes that create, sustain and transform the structure. In other words, although one group may be involved in aerobics while another is striving to win a football match, they will share many features. For example, they will have a **division of labour; a ranking structure; rules of procedure; punishments for rule breaking; special language and gestures;** and **co-operation to achieve group objectives.**

It is probable that most of you will want to adopt the first definition, and it you think the longer definition is rather repetitive and verbose, then you are probably right. However, if you take the second one step by step you will have a better working framework.

REVIEW QUESTION

Take the two activities mentioned in the second definition, aerobics and football, and explain how they might share those six common features.

A sociologist makes an objective evaluation of what exists. Developmental treatment of what is established is left to 'professional' groups to interpret. Much of what follows includes both stages insofar that we are using sociology only to help us recognize how to achieve desirable social objectives.

Some basic sociological theories

1. Relationships (Figure 17.1) are what happens in a group or between groups.

The study of **intrapersonal relationships** is a part of social psychology. It means looking at the interaction within a group and the resultant influence on individual members.

The study of **interpersonal relationships** tends to focus on the influence of one group on another.

2. Structure (Figure 17.2) is the organization of a group—*what* it is.

Function is the behaviour of the group—*how* it operates.

Deviance is what occurs when members, or the group as a whole, break with the accepted structure and function of a group to achieve alternative objectives.

In an **authoritarian** situation, **deviance** is automatically presumed to be **destructive.**

In an **open** situation, it might be termed **'divergent thinking'** and result in **creative possibilities.**

The **structure–function** model is useful when we classify the largest groups in a society down to the smallest.

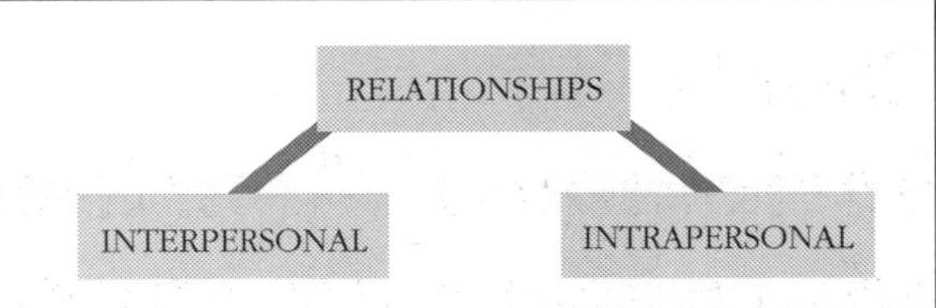

Figure 17.1

a. If you were observing your team in a basketball game, what intrapersonal features might be evident?

b. Explain what is happening when racist comments are made by sections of a home football crowd against a successful away team player.

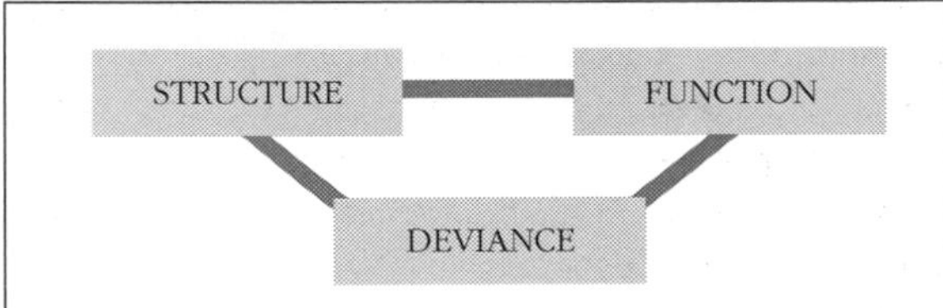

Figure 17.2

a. What is the structure of your school/college badminton club?

b. Suggest what might happen when one partner in a pair is playing badly in a key game watched by the rest of the club.

c. What illegal or unethical means might be used to win the particular key game already mentioned?

d. You have already identified the disruptive effects of deviance in a formal game of badminton. Suggest a situation in gymnastics or in an outdoor pursuit where deviance might have positive results.

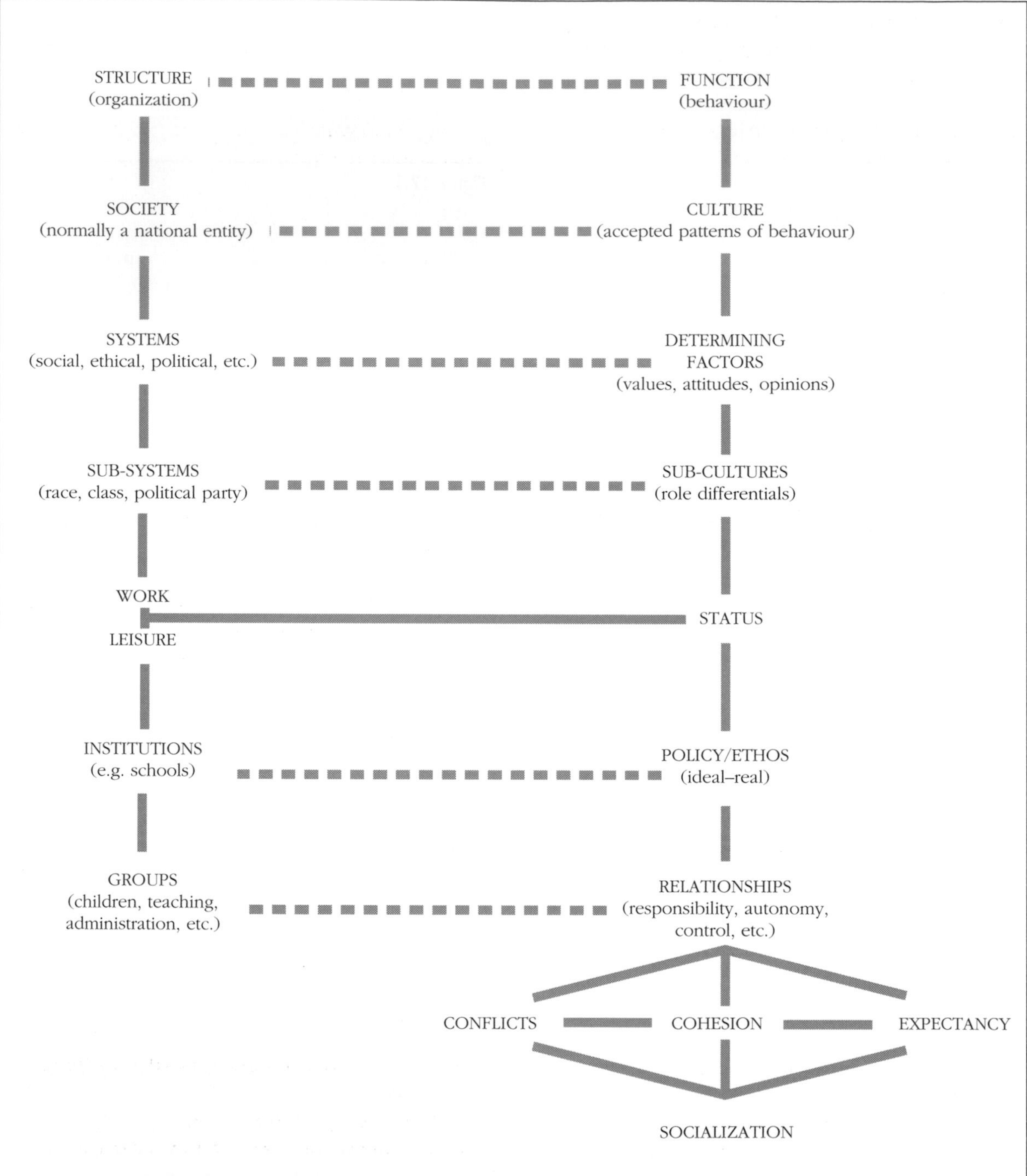

Figure 17.3 Structure function model

3. Role theory (Figure 17.4) suggests that people react to certain stimuli and adopt the role that circumstance dictates.

Action theory suggests that though the stimuli are received by a person, he/she has the capacity to make an individual interpretation.

a. What did the Romans have to gain by slaughtering the Christians in the gladiatorial games?

b. Why is it suggested that a boxer who loses his temper loses the fight?

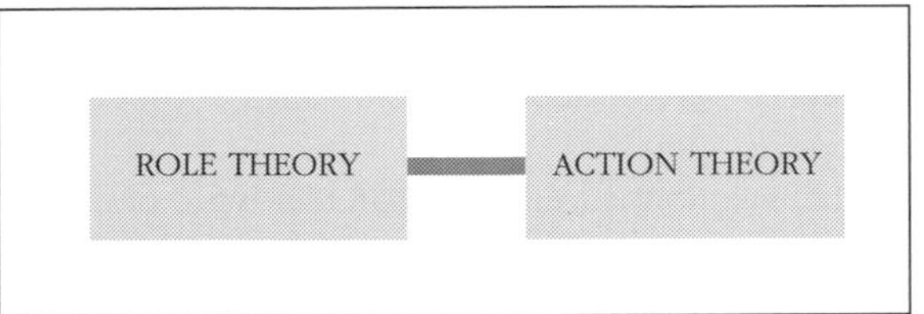

Figure 17.4

4. Conflict theory suggests that change and/or progress are made by one group at the *expense* of another.

Balanced tension theory suggests that a degree of stress can be productive if it is controlled and channelled.

a. Can you describe the action of a hockey umpire who sees an off-side? Is it predictable?

b. A climber has an injured friend several miles from civilization. What does the climber do?
If you decide that he/she has several alternatives, identify them and justify one.

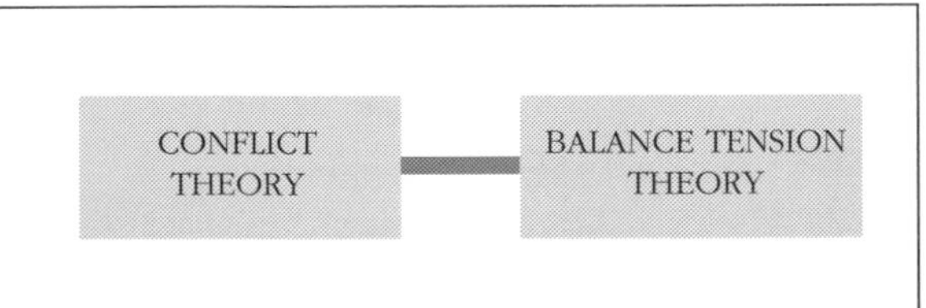

Figure 17.5

Summary

1. **Sociology** deals with the way people **interact.**
2. **Intrapersonal** and **interpersonal.**
3. **Structure—function—deviance.**
4. **Society—culture—systems—determining factors.**
5. **Role theory—action theory.**
6. **Conflict theory—channelled aggression.**

17.2 Society, Culture and Sport

You have been introduced to a number of sociological theories and each one has been examined in a sporting situation. We are now ready to look at a few of these in more detail.

We have decided that **society** is the structural composition of a community of people. We will be using it as a national identity, where this large group of people has an organization which is unique.

Secondly, we have decided that **culture** explains the way this society functions. It describes the unique patterns of a society, summarized in the term **lifestyle**. It reflects the customs, attitudes and values of the people and can be analysed at ethical, socio-economic and artistic levels.

Societies have **institutions** as organizations within their structure and these normally have a degree of autonomy with their own unique cultural interpretation.

Sport is one such institution. It has its own traditions and values, but these normally reflect the patterns in society at large. The same applies to physical education, but in this case we are concerned with a subject within a school institution, and so PE may be influenced by educational factors which do not directly apply to sport.

The intention is to look at different types of culture and to see how they affect organized physical activity. We haven't used the term 'sport' at this point because we might find that it is too sophisticated a notion to exist in some simple communal groups.

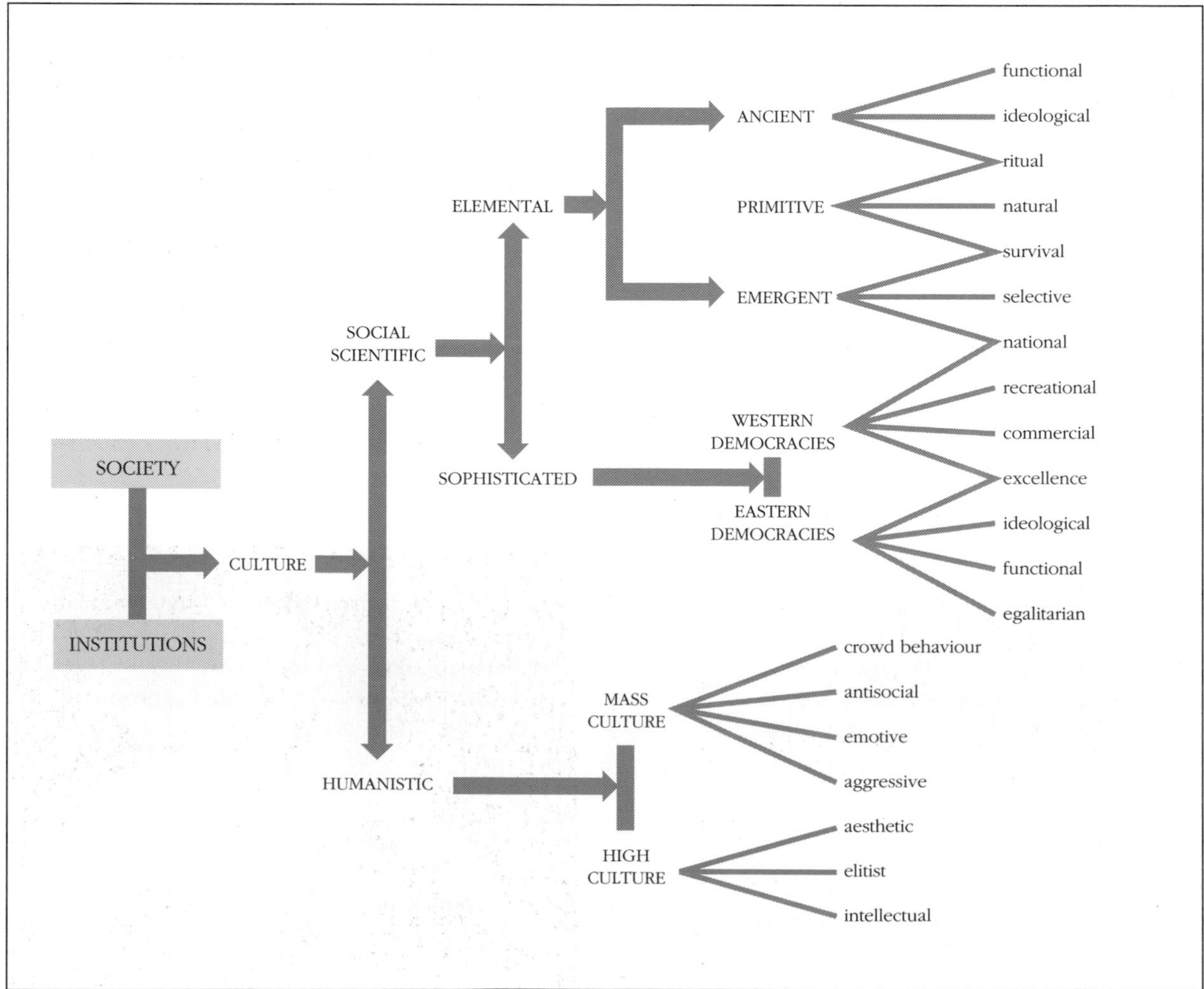

Figure 17.6

Investigation 17.1

See if you can work your way through Figure 17.6 from left to right. Look at the social scientific section first.

a. To what extent was the sport of the Ancient Romans functional, ideological and concerned with ritual?
b. How was physical activity in the life of the American Red Indian ritualized, natural and concerned with survival?
c. Look at an emergent country like Kenya and see if sport is linked with cultural survival and whether it is selective and nationalistic.
d. Take a western democracy, Britain if you like, and decide whether sport is based on recreation and excellence, and explain how this is linked with commercialism.
e. Test your knowledge of Soviet sport by assessing the importance of excellence in the context of political ideology and purposeful intention.

In Investigation 17.1 you should have thought about five different cultures, using the key words to trigger your response. You may have agreed with the suitability of these words or questioned them.

Most of your suggestions will have been **value judgements,** but you may have had some genuine evidence or obtained some information from a published article.

The important point to be made is that your own ideas are useful, but they do not represent social scientific evidence. A sociologist, archaeologist or anthropologist has systematically to collect and collate data and present them for public scrutiny. We need, therefore, to take this extra step and read what researchers have found. If we do this we are attempting to comment accurately on what is or was the situation in these cultures.

ANCIENT CULTURES, PHYSICAL ACTIVITY AND ARCHAEOLOGY

Minoan Crete: We have frescoes and vases which were retrieved from the ruins. They show acrobats in the art of bull leaping, a ritual to please the Minoan God Minos who was half bull, half man. This type of bull fighting combined piety and courage, and reflected an affluent society, which used captives to fight the bulls while the citizens enjoyed the festival.

Ancient Egypt: There is considerable evidence in the stone carvings on tombs. The best example is Beni Hasan's tomb (Figure 17.7) (2000–1500 BC), which shows the technical development of wrestling, and also boxing, fencing, swimming, rowing, running, archery and horse riding. These contests seem to have advanced beyond the level of religious ceremony to a

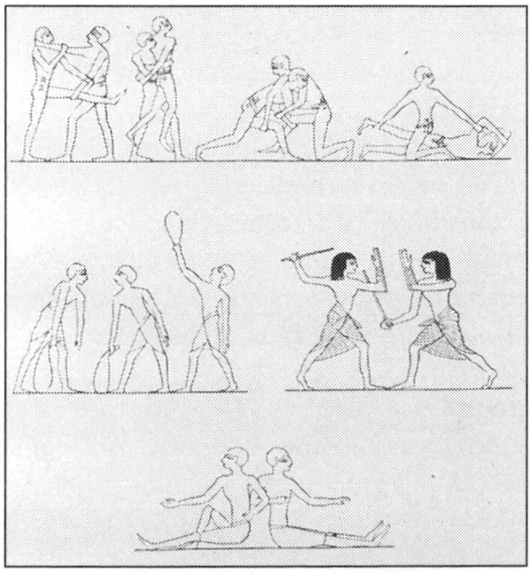

Figure 17.7 Ben Hasan's tomb, Ancient Egypt.

Figure 17.8 Sculpture of Ancient Greek wrestlers.

sporting experience. Perhaps more directly linked with ritual, there are frescoes which show women engaged in various partner activities.

Ancient Greece: The earliest evidence concerns the funeral games, contained in Homer's *Iliad* and *Odyssey*, books which were written around 800 BC. They are legendary and so not an accurate record, but athletic feats, violent contests and chariot racing were part of a need to maintain fighting fitness, appease the gods, and express the Greek ideology of 'Man of Action'. It is from these ancient myths and stories that the ancient Olympic Games derived as religious ceremonies connected with Zeus and lesser gods. Formal contests were held between city states despite the fact that they were constantly at war. Evidence of the diversity of activities and the athletic form which was idolized is to be seen on a wide range of frescoes, painted objects and sculptures (Figure 17.8).

Ancient Rome: Recorded in written form, sculpture, and as monuments like the Colosseum. Evidence suggests that the Ludi or Roman Games were spectacles of extreme brutality, serving to illustrate the status of the Patricians (ruling class) and the attempts to **appease** the Plebians (subject races). Affluence led the Romans away from vigorous participation to the spectator situation of the Games and the recreational pastimes of the thermae (baths).

PRIMITIVE SOCIETIES, PHYSICAL ACTIVITY AND THE SOCIAL ANTHROPOLOGIST

General

The suggestion that primitive societies had **functional** physical activities is supported by the popularity of competitive foot racing among the Sioux tribe in North America, where the ability to cover distances on the Plains was economically necessary. Log racing by the Timbira tribe in South America was not competitive, but assessed on team success to get logs down the river, another economic strategy. In terms of **ritual,** the ball symbolized the supernatural in the case of the Aztecs, the Arizona Indians, and in the old Celtic game of hurling. An extension of **ritual** into victory **ceremony** is demonstrated in the Red Indian game of baggataway, later refined into lacrosse. Similarly, Peruvian Indians played with a feathered object like a shuttlecock, in a simple version of badminton.

Samoans

Dunlap (1951) suggested that games were a central part of Samoan culture. In terms of the fulfilment of **social needs,** she identified social mixing; outlets for rivalry; opportunities for leadership; opportunities for prestige and honour to be won; and an outlet for excessive emotions connected with birth, marriage and death. As a fulfilment of religious **ritual needs**, she suggested that erotic dancing was intended to stimulate the gods; fertility festivals were linked with nature and the tribe; and the flow of blood served to demonstrate devotion to the gods. Finally, at the third level, she identified fulfilment of **militaristic needs** partly through skill with weapons, and partly with the physical strength essential for military preparedness. The significance of **outside influence** was also considered. **Missionaries** prevented the association of vigorous amusements with the old religion; certain sports like bonito fishing were denied their ritual and tribal status; and erotic dances and tumbling were banned. The **colonial** influences changed the method of warfare by introducing guns; reduced the freedom of travel between the islands; and introduced colonial games, some of which were eventually modified to meet local methods of play. The success of the Fijians and Western Somoans in rugby union, particularly at 7-a-side, is an interesting phenomenon. They have adopted the colonial game, but incorporated the aggression and flair of their culture to produce a unique variable of that game. The Haka is a typical re-emergence of ritual from a pre-colonial culture.

Polynesia

Jones (1967) looked at ten Polynesian cultures, including Hawaii, New Zealand, Fiji and Tonga. He observed their games, which consisted of canoeing, hide-and-seek, spear throwing, dart games, bandy (primitive hockey) and sham fights. They played string games, and hand clapping, kites and surfboard riding were all in evidence. He found that the social psychological need of group interaction was the major influence on the choice of activities; there were strong self-preservation and government control factors; very few family activities because of the Polynesian group culture; and a great deal of ritual significance.

Aborigines

Salter (1967) studied the Australian Aborigines. He suggested that group pastimes, like tribal dancing, were most popular, followed by group games, which included hide-and-seek, mock battles, throwing the boomerang, and plunging from a height. He felt that co-operational activities were much more common than competitions, because they were few in number and needed one another to survive. Weapons were also necessary for survival and the various ritual dances were intended to please the gods.

Pueblo Baseball

Fox (1969) noted that ancient Indian witchcraft was being mixed with a superimposed Catholicism to produce a non-competitive culture. With the importation of baseball, the competitive game conflicted with the culture and there was an emergence of witchcraft strategies within the game.

EMERGENT COUNTRIES AND SPORT AS A NATIONAL IDENTITY

All developing countries are in the process of **nation-building** and this normally entails the authoritarian **integration** of a variety of tribal groups to establish stability. In turn, this can be achieved only if the nation is healthy and strong, which leads to emphasis on the **health** of the people and their **military preparedness**. One outcome in the modern world is the recognition that **sport** is a competitive frontier which draws a nation together without bloodshed. However, technological and financial limitations mean that an **elitist** route is necessary, where focus has to be on a specific activity, which is straight forward to establish. Funding and effort are then **disproportionately** allocated to achieve **excellence** in this one area. The reward for international success is the production of a **role model**, which at once **inspires** and **appeases** less fortunate members of the society under one banner and gives the developing country international **exposure** and **recognition**.

This rationale has been developed by James Riordan in his article, State and Sport in Developing Societies (ISCPES, *Comparative PE and Sport*, Vol. 5, 1988).

Africa

The world prominence of middle-distance and long-distance runners in East Africa and boxers in West Africa is out of all proportion to the sporting population of these countries. Tribal traditions and altitude have made athletics a natural choice in the East and the heavier build of Ghanaians and Nigerians has made boxing a natural choice for them. There is no need for sophisticated coaching methods or technological infra-structure, and both athletics and boxing have the world stage—resulting in a few elite athletes stimulating tremendous national pride as well as international respect.

Far East

The colonial impact on the old British colonies has had a widespread influence on the development and choice of sports. Success in these activities reflects the success of the family as a relic of colonial superiority. Cricket, hockey, badminton, table tennis and squash are games which have considerable cultural importance. The impact of holding the Olympic Games in South Korea has yet to be fully assessed—but the expression of nationalism; the use of the sports arena to demonstrate a political identity; and, perhaps most significantly, the opportunity of showing the world the richness of Korean culture through a variety of artistic displays gave a small country the world stage.

South America

Here, the sport and culture link lies in the pre-eminence of football. Each of the South American countries uses the game to express its national identity; to allow its volatile emotions to be expressed; to appease the underprivileged; and to provide an escape route for a few of them to earn lasting fame and fortune.

The popularity and success of cricket in the West Indies is an excellent example of the association between the natural lifestyle of tropical island communities and the pursuit of a colonial game which was initially elistist, but has now become an expression of the people, played in a style which is uniquely their own.

ADVANCED WESTERN DEMOCRACIES AND SPORT

You will be realizing that the roots of many of our games and individual activities lie in the inventiveness of ancient and primitive cultures and, more importantly, that changes which have occurred to those games are the result of changes in society in general. Three revolutions have been at the heart of this change: the **agrarian,** the **industrial** and the **urban,** leading to the present social structure of a sophisticated technological administration, based on a high population.

A sociologist looking at sport in such a country would be likely to say that sport is a solution to the problem of leisure; a release of physical energy and aggression in a harmless way; a challenge which is artificially created to give an ensuing sense of achievement; and a part of institutionalized education through physical education. The more complex social structure leads to a more sophisticated sporting system, but—as Loy (1969) has pointed out—sport exists as a **social institution,** thereby having a considerable influence on society at large; and as a **social situation,** so helping in the socialization process in a group, community or society.

The complexity of an industrialized society results in a number of **primary** determinants, such as the mode of production; relationships between rural and urban society; the division of labour; and the distribution of power, in economic and political terms. It is also possible to produce a number of **consequential** determinants, such as the centralization of authority; the provision of communications; social-class and racial divisions; and the provision of specialized facilities, which are a necessary part of maintaining an advanced society. The tribal chief, elders and family could cope with all the social issues in a tribal community, but this level of administration would not work in the United Kingdom, France or the United States. Some sociologists might argue, however, that at a local level these simple, self-nurturing groups continue to operate even in an advanced society.

It is important to recognize the hypothesis by Luschen (1966) and others that, in a sophisticated society, sport has a codification of rules which may not be the same as the cultural values outside sport. Things are done legitimately on the football field which would be common assault on the street. Critics of sport are also saying that it is excessively achievement-oriented, a situation which is already too strongly identified in our materialistic society. Finally, this **dysfunctional** possibility is carried to an extreme in the behaviour of some sports crowds, where it is suggested that antisocial behaviour is promoted in the sports situation and overflows into society at large.

You should be able to attempt a question linking Western sport with a social influence, e.g. how does commercialism influence high level sport in the USA?

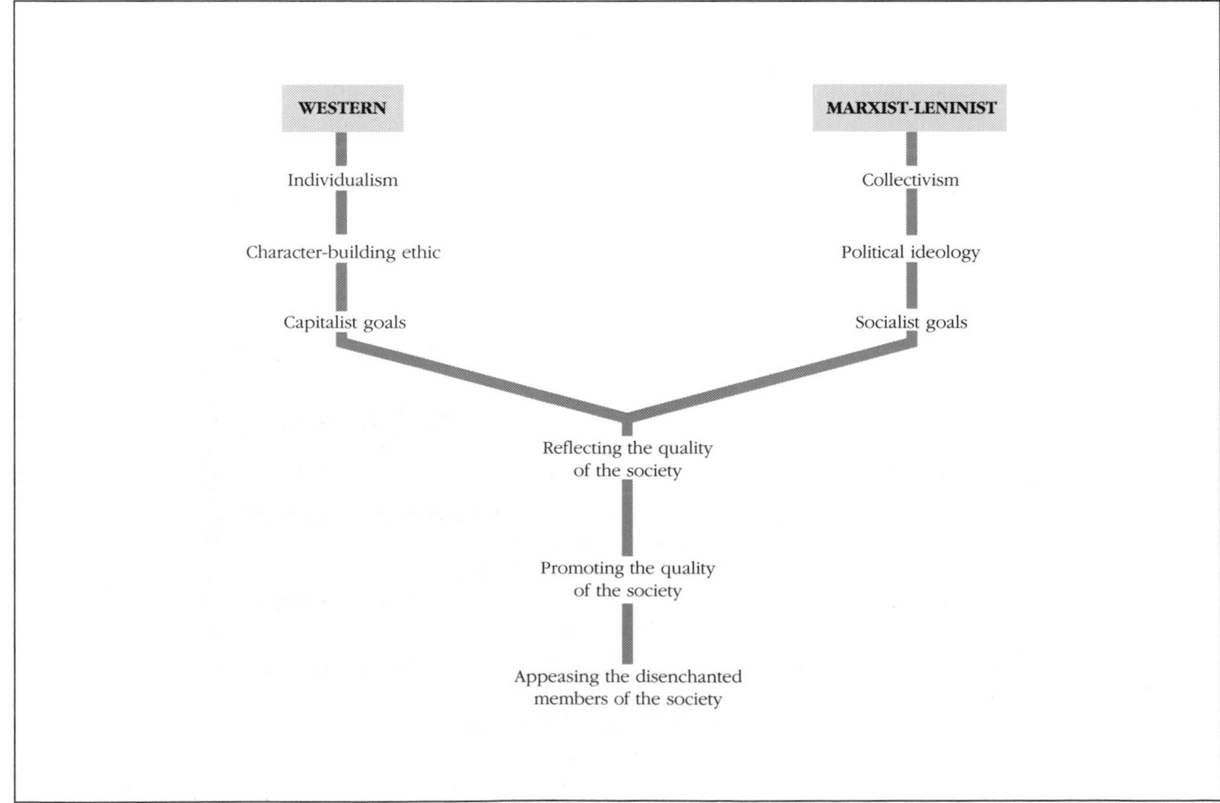

Figure 17.9 How West and East differ in ideological terms.

EAST EUROPEAN DEMOCRACIES AND FUNCTIONAL LEISURE

The Reforms in the Soviet Union do not mean an end to communist or 'socialist' influence in the world. China and Cuba still have communist political systems, even if they are increasingly adopting free market economics. Russia and the other old Soviet republics may yet revert to communist government or retain 'socialism' as a moderate version of stressing the community rather than the individual. It is also important to recognize that it might be single-party authoritarianism as against democracy which is critical, not right-wing or left-wing politics.

Today, we can see so much in common between the West and the East, but it is important to realize that the political principle of putting the individual or the community first can give rise to a different interpretation of the function of sport. Interestingly, Wohl (1966), a sociologist from Eastern Europe, came up with two cultural links similar to those identified by the American John Loy. He recognized **sport as a social influence,** stimulating social integration and overcoming cultural barriers; and **sport as a social process,** objectively improving work production, transportation and military needs. Yet the small print clearly establishes that the relative freedom of the individual to recreate in Western cultures differs from the more authoritarian association of the socially productive impact of physical activity as part of some grand ideological design.

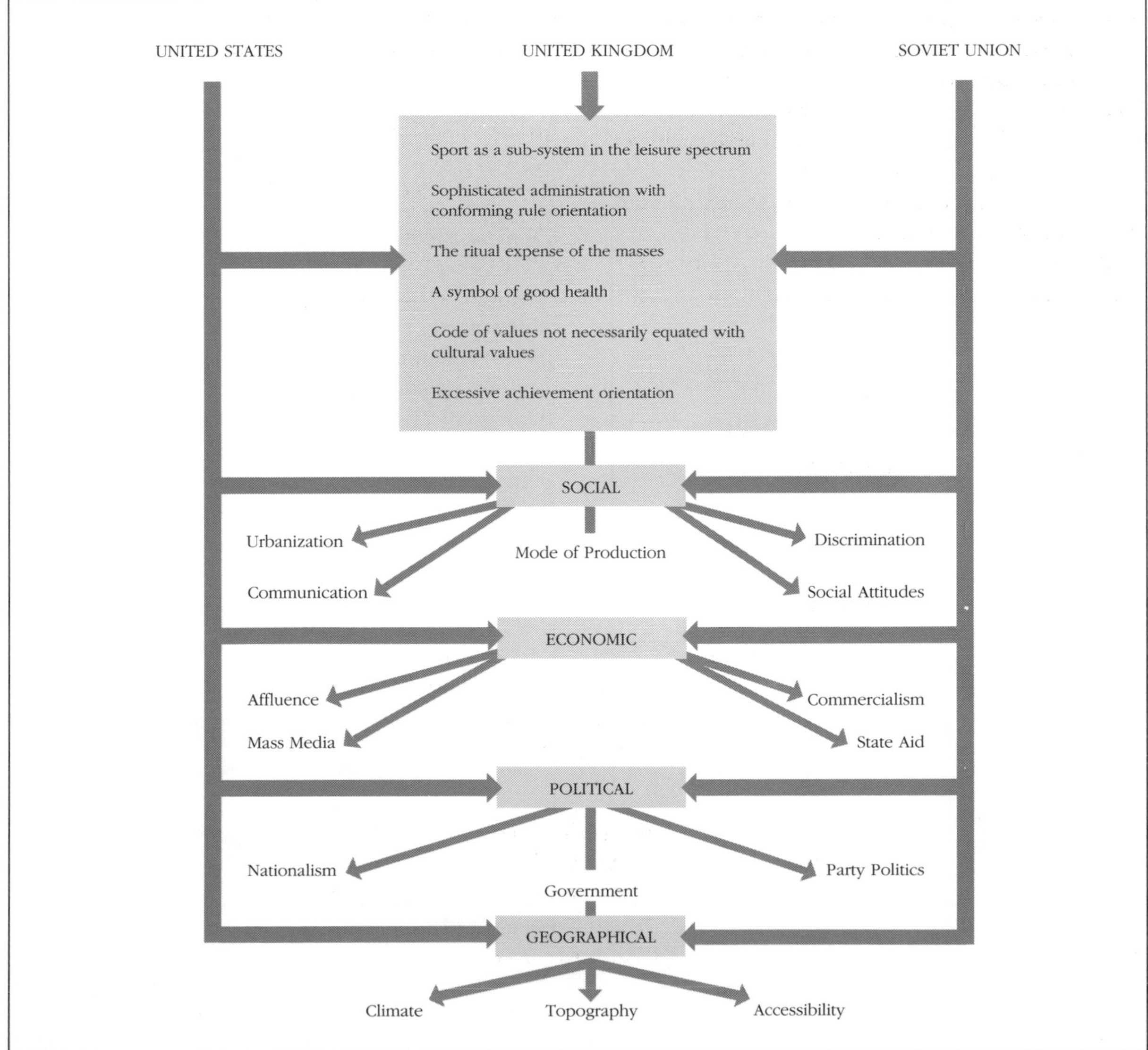

Figure 17.10 Try to put examples to each stage of this model.

REVIEW QUESTION

Explain why East European countries have used sporting success as a political agency.

SPORT AND LOW (MASS) CULTURE

An alternative way of studying sport and culture is to look at the behaviour of groups of people from a humanist viewpoint. Our basic model identified two polarized patterns of behaviour: mass culture and high culture.

Mass culture is normally associated with modern industrialized societies with large population groups. It suggests that these groups can have common unifying values which may not match up to those held by other groups in the community. They are bound by a code of behaviour and emotional sharing, where a sport might bring them together as a group and stimulate them to act collectively. The behaviour of such a group represents the standard of the lowest member of the group, in a gravitation of standards permitted by the diminished responsibility of an individual in a crowd. It is generally felt that membership leads to a coarsening of human expression.

In attempting to identify examples of mass culture operating in sport, you should be looking for situations with limited intellectual expression but considerable immediate excitement.

Certainly, the most common example of mass culture in British sport at the present time is hooligan behaviour by members of a soccer crowd.

A great deal has been written on this topic, where almost everyone points to a different set of causes. Some blame society; others criticize the way the game is played and the attitude of players; some suggest that the facilities are at fault; others blame media hype and commercialism while probably most point the finger at the excessive use of alcohol. The Harrington, Popplewell and Taylor Reports made a lot of recommendations, but the problem is still with us. We can argue it out with value judgements or we can attempt to produce a **sociogram** of the problem (Figure 17.12).

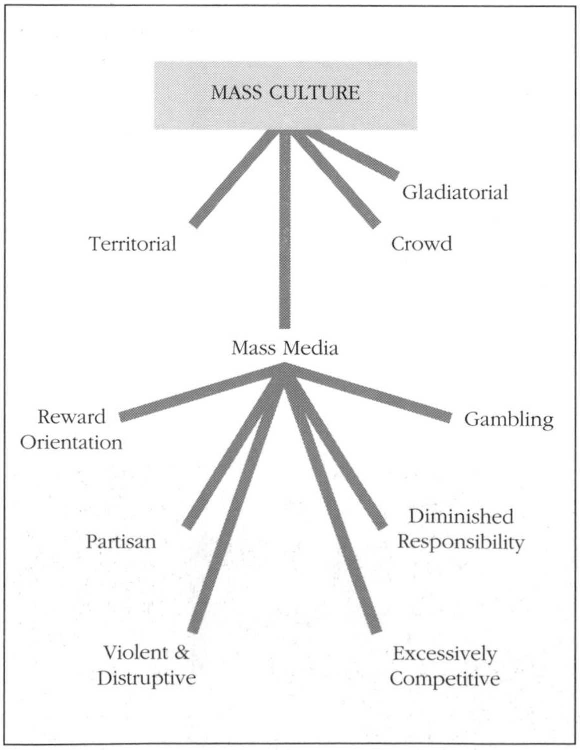

MASS CULTURE
Territorial
Gladiatorial
Crowd
Mass Media
Reward Orientation
Gambling
Partisan
Diminished Responsibility
Violent & Distruptive
Excessively Competitive

Figure 17.11

A mass culture sporting situation might be: a fight between players in a rugby league game, a tag-wrestling contest, or the football crowd at a local derby game.
Select one of these and use Figure 17.11 to establish any mass culture elements.
Link your 'popular sport' with the four basic interpretations and then continue the analysis of sport as a mass media.

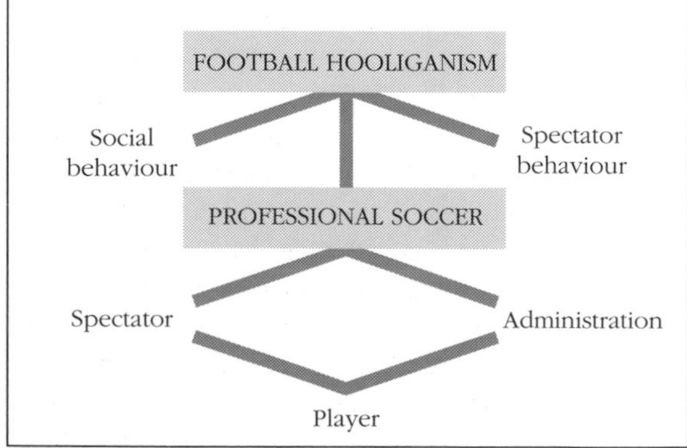

Figure 17.12

Investigation 17.2

You could visit a ground and assemble some data. Then, armed with some facts, we might have more than points of view to offer.

a) Does it fit a **mass culture** classification at my ground?

Does a faction in my club bring violence to the ground; does the game trigger violence; or is it a combination of the two?

b) Is there a domination of certain **sub-cultures** in the hooligan element? Can you identify a **youth cult;** a **class cult;** a **regional cult;** or/and a **religious cult?**

c) Is there an **interaction** of a **sub-system?**

Can you see the crowd being driven towards anti-social behaviour by the **code of the game;** by the **attitude of the players;** by the **condition of the facilities;** or by some other factor?

d) What are the **group dynamics** operating in the **crowd**. Can you pinpoint aggression, conflicting aspirations, collective bravado, and protective reaction?

e) Is there evidence as to what incidents cause excessive stimulation or frustration, and to what extent is this loss of control carried into the streets?

f) Can you point to similar examples of group misbehaviour in the community at large and, if so, what evidence have you that this is a law-and-order problem in your town?

g) Is this a **territorial** issue, resulting from away fans invading, and home fans protecting their territory?

SPORT AND HIGH CULTURE

High culture is the training, development and refinement of the mind, taste and manners in society. It identifies with the highest moral, social, intellectual and physical qualities of a culture.

In a society where there are differentials of class, gender or race, the underprivileged are unlikely to be included in the activities which make up this quality of life. It might be argued that such people have their own ethnic or communal qualities which off set this. Arguably, in a 'socialist' state, such as the old Soviet Unionclaimed to be, social discrimination cannot exist and so these activities must be available and sought after by the whole of society. However, high culture tends to be based on affluence and intellect, and it may be that the Soviet Union did not have sufficient resources to fulfil high culture right across society; it may be that intellectualism and the stain of Tsarist culture stood in the way of its full expression. It now seems likely that there was so much corruption taking place that major inequalities continued to exist in the Soviet Union, which may have been one of the causes for its decline. Similarly, if we look at the commercialism and the competitiveness of American culture and particularly sport, there is a brashness which makes high culture activities part of the counter-culture. It is in the older cultures of Britain and France that high culture is at its strongest and where sport has had difficulty in achieving acceptance as a subject for aesthetic expression or as an art form in its own right.

The biggest problem with sport being accepted as an art form has been the inability to capture it for public appraisal. In sport, the moment of beauty is transitory. Today, we have film and video to capture the moment and to relay it in slow motion, providing time for its moments of artistry to be appreciated and stand up to critical reflection.

REVIEW QUESTION

How does a gymnastics audience differ from a boxing crowd? Are they mutually exclusive?

Figure 17.13 'Children's Games' by P. Bruegel. How has the artist justified sport as an art subject?

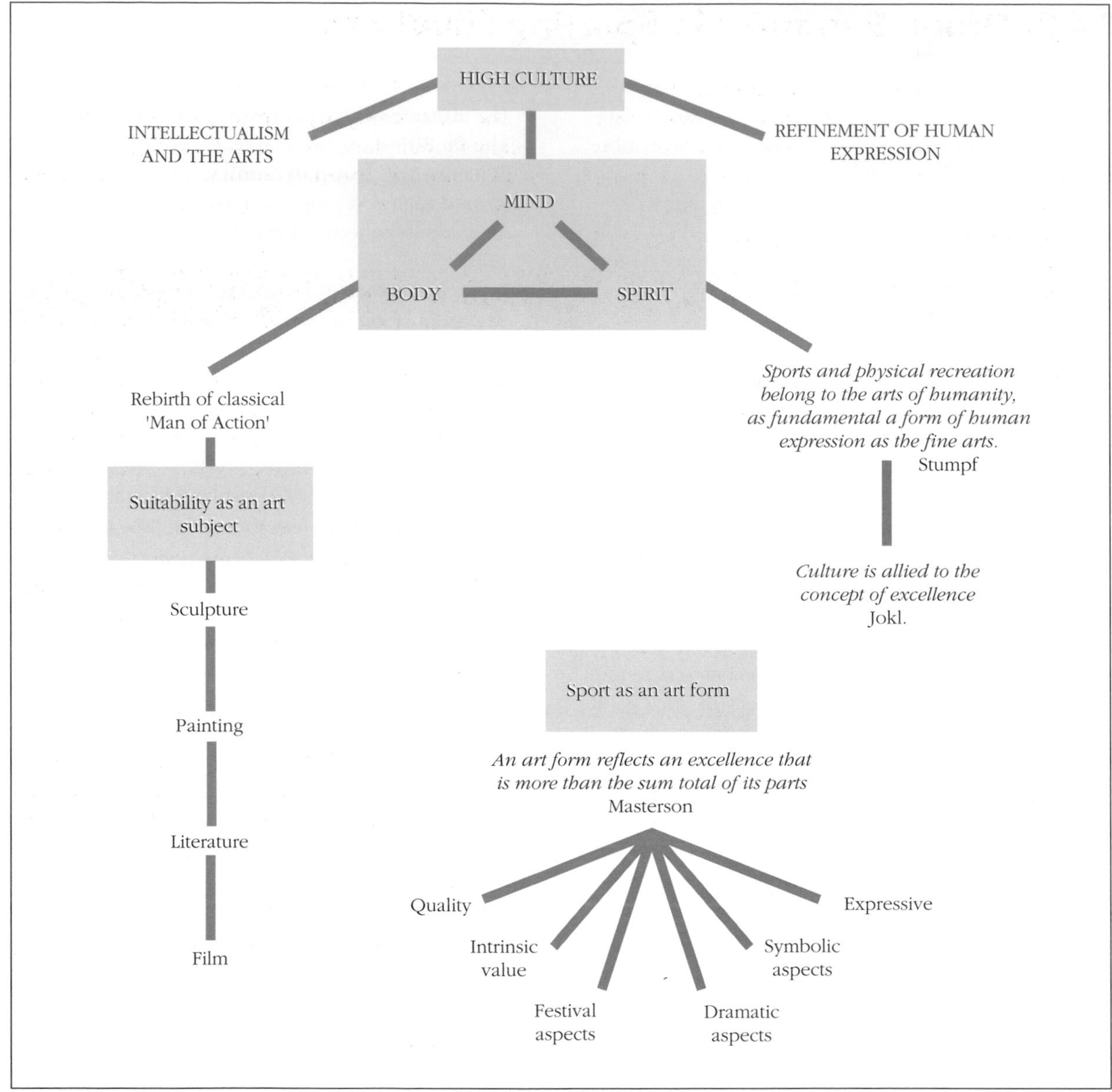

Figure 17.14

Summary

Sport & Culture:

1. **Social scientific** components: **elemental**—ancient, primitive and emergent; **sophisticated**—Western and Eastern industrialized societies.
2. **Humanistic: mass culture**—emotive crowd experiences with anti-social tendencies; **high culture**—aesthetic and elitist attitudes.

17.3. Group Dynamics in Sporting Situations

Now that we have examined the **interaction** between sporting groups and the social setting in which they exist, we need to look inside a sports group to see how it works. This may enable us to overcome problems which might arise from something going wrong at the **intrapersonal** level. You've probably all played in a team which has 'cracked up'.

The term **'group dynamics'** suggests simply that within a group there are constantly changing relationships which influence the outcome of what the group is trying to achieve.

Investigation 17.3

Get into sets of 4–5 people, decide on a sporting activity and play for a time. Don't just choose a game; include a contest and an individual activity too. Then decide:

a. What did we have to do to make this a group?
b. What are the main objectives of the group?
c. What strategies should we employ to achieve these objectives within the spirit and rules of the activity?

Let's see if you reached similar conclusions to leading theorists in this area.

Cratty (1973) has suggested that a group (sports group) is *a collection of people mutually interacting to solve a common problem or general type of problem.*

Were you mutually interactive? I mean everyone contributing!

Did your objectives tease out the problem(s)? Or didn't you even consider what you were playing for?

Will your strategies solve the problem(s) by helping you to work together to achieve your objectives? Albeit as a group playing basketball, fencing, or in a cross-country race?

You'll quickly become aware that a group in sport has a **structure,** which allows it to work successfully (Mason, 1966). This could involve fixture arrangements, playing positions, conventions or rules. Similarly, a group involves many **relationships,** which determine how well it works. Here we mean the sort of roles you might adopt playing the activity. These may make you a successful group or perhaps merely a contented one. In sport we have this very meaningful word **'team',** which describes group structure, and the expression **'team spirit',** which describes desirable group relationships.

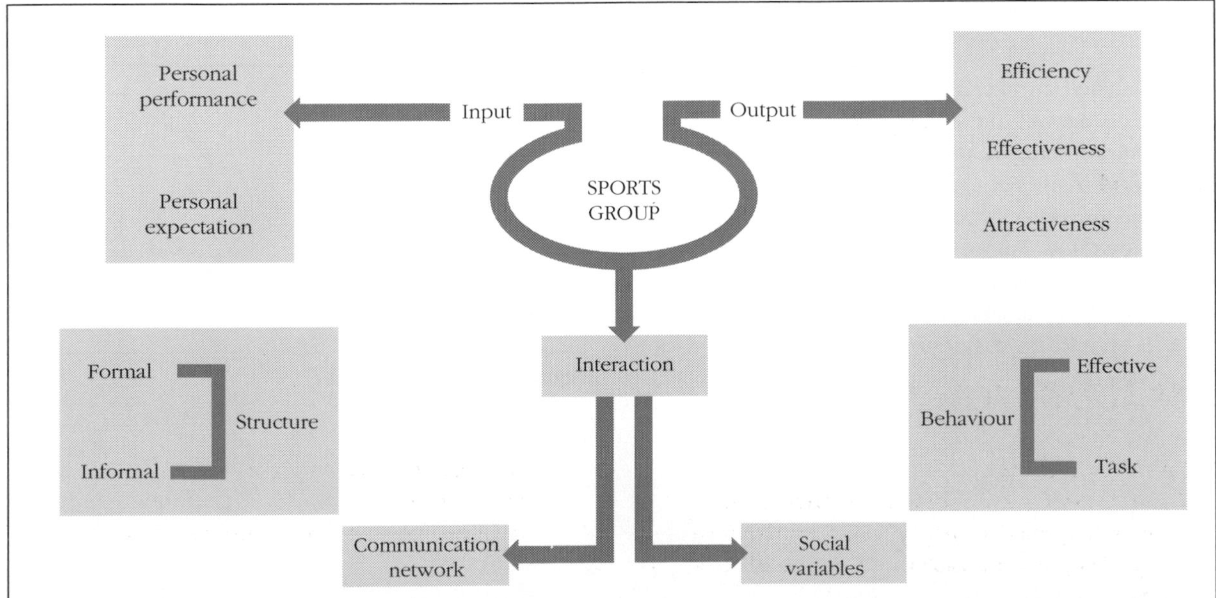

Figure 17.15 The dynamics of a sports group.

Figure 17.16 Things aren't always what they appear on the surface.

List what you consider to be the characteristics of a good team; and the qualities identifiable with team spirit. Then compare your ideas with other members of your work group.

The **input** of a group is all about **personal performance** and **personal expectation.** Here we have a mixture of ability and enthusiasm which will make you a worthwhile member. While the group is operating there is always **interaction** going on.

When you play a game of football or hockey, for example:

a. Is the structure **formal** or **informal?** (Are you playing in fixed positions or not?)
b. What is the **communication network** like? (Are you using an agreed code?)
c. Are you committed to **effective** or **task** behaviour? (Are you letting the run of the game decide or have you been given a fixed job to do?)
d. What **social variables** are operating on the group? (What are the pressures on winning? What are the rewards? What attitudes are acceptable within the group?)

If we watched an inter-school match, we would soon be able to answer these questions and it would be interesting to compare this interaction with the operation of a professional team. If we are going to understand the **output** of a group we need to look at its **efficiency** (How much does it achieve?); its **effectiveness** (How valuable is it to the group?); and its **attractiveness** (How valuable has it been to each individual?). It should be easy enough to sit down and do this after a match.

A physical performance group is almost invariably held together by the challenges it sets itself. This may be the competitive element in games; the contest of combat; the perfection-seeking of many individual activities or the adventure of outdoor recreation. Let's call this the **sporting situation.**

It is important to reassert that these challenges are self- or group-inspired and are couched in the experiential medium of play and self-realization. The deliberate infliction of injury, on oneself or others, is not compatible with the desired values of a sporting situation.

The survival of the group is very much dependent on the balanced satisfaction of the four group motives shown in Figure 17.17.

Sporting challenge and competition are contrived situations where cohesion, conflict and expectation are channelled to give a desirable outcome.

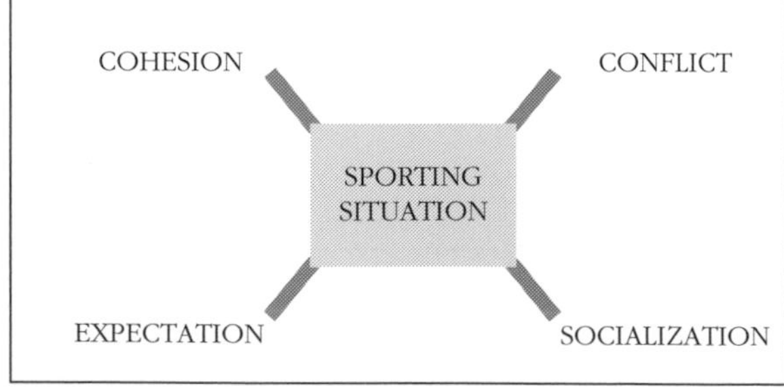

Figure 17.17 Group motives.

Cohesion

Cohesiveness of a group is the result of all the members wanting to remain in the group. It embodies an underlying sense of co-operation.

- It can be identified as the essence of team spirit, where there is an **attraction** in belonging to a group with high **morale** and **shared responsibility.**
- It almost always involves the development of **friendships**, many of which may be long-lasting through mutual interest, e.g. Dr Roger Bannister's famous phrase 'friendships forged in the fire of competition'.
- An individual member tends to follow the collective will of the group in a form of **mutual mimicry.**

Figure 17.18

1. What are the cohesive elements evident in Figure 17.18?

2. Engage in a game of basketball, making a mental note of cohesive elements and stopping at intervals for discussion; or play a game of volleyball with exaggerated elements of group reinforcement and cooperation, subsequently discussing advantages.

3. Select a sporting activity and explain the cohesive elements within it.

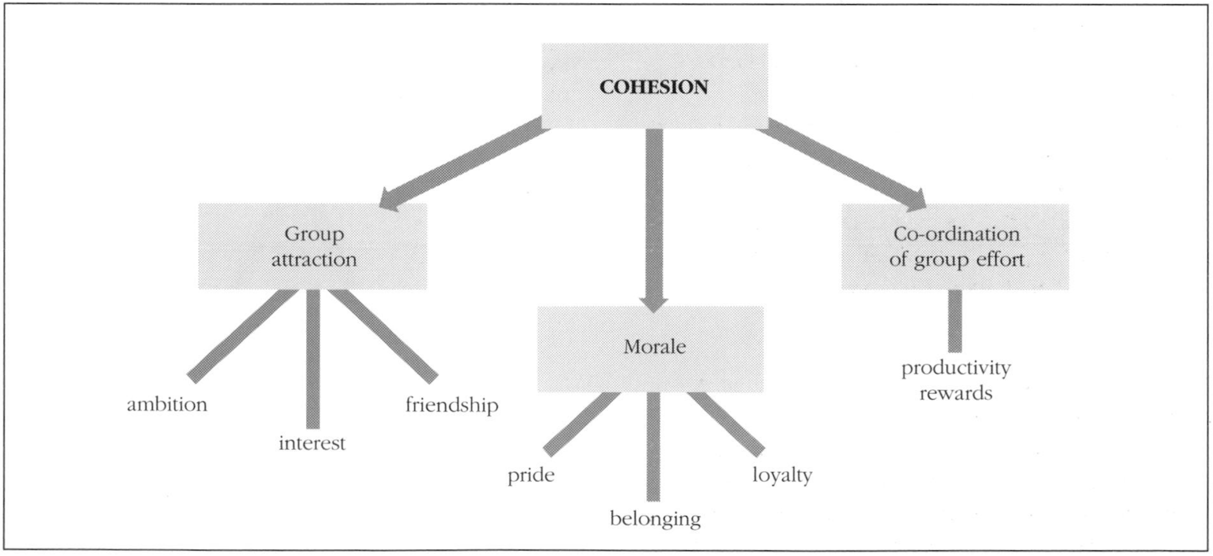

Figure 17.19

The basic cohesive ingredient of a **match** is the **contract** between two teams to engage in a fixture.

Given that the match always involves **opposition,** the team is drawn together by this outside threat. However, the opposition is required to **conform** to the same rules and this in itself is a cohesive element.

For the winning team there is the **shared reward** of victory and, in a well-oriented losing side, there is a tendency to **close ranks** and work for future success.

When the game ends with the final whistle, opposing sides should be **drawn together**, having put each other to the test. Similarly, the completed expedition, where risk and adventure is shared, results in the cementing of **life-long relationships**.

Conflict

Testing your mettle, temperamentally and physically, is the essence of physical performance. It is invariably a question of competing **against** self, others and/or nature.

The level of conflict varies in different types of activity and in different specific situations. In games it can be against another team; to win a place in your own team; and against match conditions. Individual activities like swimming and athletics also include rivalry and conditions, but are concerned mainly with pitting yourself against a previous best performance. In gymnastics, performance also includes subjective assessment and so the contest involves impressing the judges. Finally, the outdoor pursuit situation may involve competition against others and self but the emphasis is normally on the challenge of the environment.

REVIEW QUESTIONS

1. Discuss the specific conflict elements in: an athletics squad, a hockey team, a judo squad and an expedition party.
2. Look at Figure 17.20 and decide what the headings mean before allocating your different conflict elements to them.
3. Try to relate the following statements to Figure 17.20:
   a. The level of aggression should always be within the spirit and letter of the rules of play, but should also satisfy the needs of the occasion.
   b. The required aggression of a combat sport would be much greater than that needed for an afternoon sail on a lake.
   c. Winning a ball in hockey with the need for commitment against opposition, is very different from the personal discipline of refining a gymnastic routine.
   d. Surviving a difficult rapid in a canoe is real and unpredictable, as compared with the tension which exists in the controlled environment of target archery.

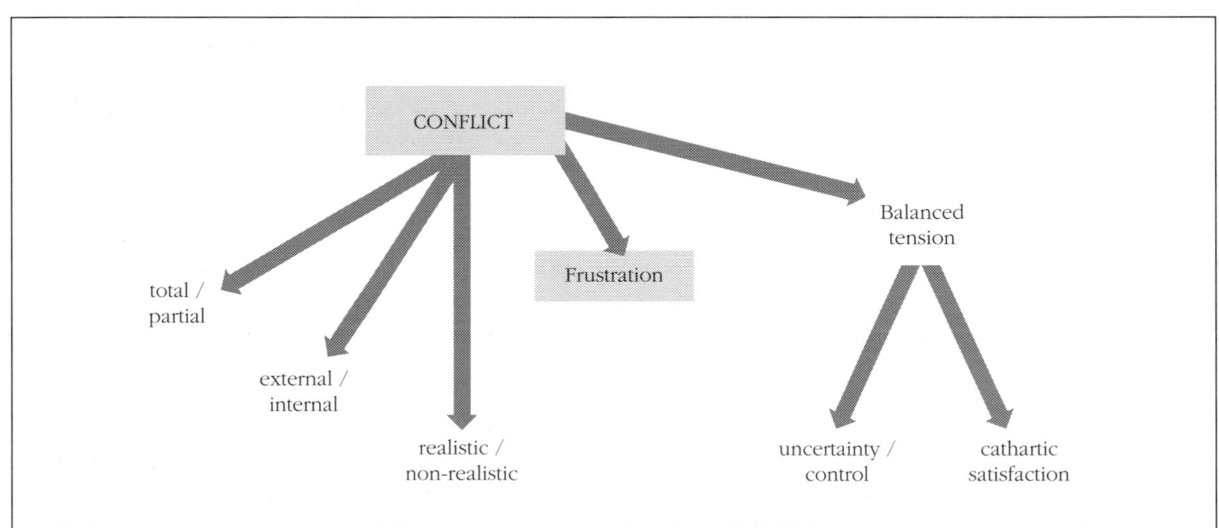

Figure 17.20

This is a good point at which to compare functional conflict with instances of outright aggression which lie outside the rules of play. Sport can claim to be culturally valuable only if it can be seen to give individuals and teams an opportunity to discipline themselves in the face of provocation.

This takes us into the conflict which occurs as a result of frustration. Here is a possible cause of instances of outright aggression. Fighting on the field and among spectators may reflect tensions which the game itself has promoted. Some educationists are concerned that sport stimulates aggression in a society which some claim is already excessively competitive.

Man is aggressive; the sporting activity requires commitment and effort; the heat of the moment and the desire to win test temperament control to the maximum. The key, therefore, is **channelled aggression** or **balanced tension.** The coach and athlete work to produce a top performance and this involves lawful strategies to make the most of that particular sporting situation.

If we learn to control aggression through sporting competition: if we satisfy the human need to be aggressive without overstimulation, educationists may begin to recognize the socialization potential of the sports group.

Set up some practical conflict role play situations and monitor the effects e.g.
a. an example of gamesmanship
b. weak refereeing
c. excluding a player from receiving passes
d. verbal criticism of team-mates.

Expectation or aspiration

The desire to succeed is fundamental to all sporting groups and to individuals within each group. Problems arise when the aspirations of an individual are not shared by the group.

We can be aware of how good we are and consequently what is feasible; alternatively, we can believe in our potential and speculate on our hopes. In both cases the significant factor is that the expectations should be realizable. Given the challenging motives underlying sport, however, it is important that these expectations should be at the limit of potential achievement in order to challenge the individual and the group.

Cratty (1973) suggested that *'an individual's aspiration level is related to his perceived standing in the group'*. If this is not the case, there is likely to be dissention. Frustration exists at an individual and group level when expectations are too high.

It is also important to recognize that an individual who lacks ambition is as counterproductive in a group as someone with unreasonable expectations. Expectation is conditioned by the degree of role freedom in the group. For example, in American football, with the exception perhaps of the quarter back, players have a very **closed** role.

It is necessary for the player to fulfil his role to the satisfaction of the coach, other players, supporters and himself.

Try to tease out expectations *in* this game and then expectations *from* this game.

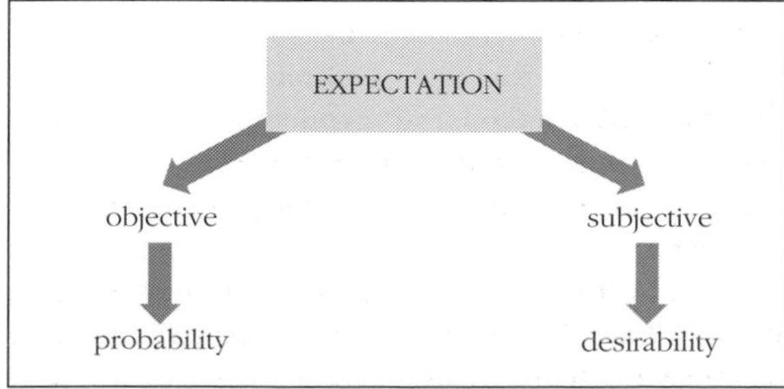

Figure 17.21

Netball is another example of individuals accepting specific roles, which may require them to condition their own ambitions.

Saunders (1977), in looking at rugby football, suggested that it has a closed structure in terms of rules, but an open system of relationships.

In British mini rugby a wide range of alternatives are **open** to the young person. He is free to explore various alternatives and other members of the group are likely to be extremely permissive.

Remember, a good team player subsumes personal aspirations for the advancement of the team; and a sound coach invariably promotes a variety of objectives along an achievement continuum to stimulate his/her squad with a succession of small victories on the way to a major challenge.

REVIEW QUESTION

If you want to explore 'expectation' in a practical way:
a. Set up players with unreasonable aspirations
b. Play people out of position
c. Introduce a selfish or apathetic player.

Always discuss the intention and outcomes of these role play situations afterwards.

Socialization

At a societal level, socialization is **man's adjustment to his culture.** At a more specific level, it follows that it is also the **sportsman's adjustment to sport as a sub-culture.** In relationship terms it would seem that **social adjustments in sport may influence behaviour in society at large.**

It is worth remembering that Lüschen (1967) points out that this might be a **functional** or **dysfunctional** process. We have the potential to produce heroes or villains!

In the field of physical education the teacher uses the sporting experience to inculcate socially desirable skills, norms and values, whereas sport tends to leave the ethics and rules to promote these indirectly.

The degree to which a group is **open** or **closed** decides the extent to which an individual can hope to inculcate social changes. The status of the individual is also significant, e.g. a captain would probably be able to influence the group; a talented player might be able to; but a newcomer would probably not.

At what levels might we presume socialization can take place in a sporting situation? Simply being accepted into a sports group is a social experience. The ethics and rules of the group, team or club require the individual to make a social adjustment.

In the competitive or challenging situation, the individual and the group are required to meet the requirements of the sport in skill and behaviour terms.

In playing together with others, the individual learns to submerge his/her own interests in favour of the group. Similarly, he/she has to accept the outcomes regardless of personal disappointments.

A sports group may include members from different racial or social class minorities where sport can help in the removal of discriminatory barriers. The sports group which is based on physical performance is a vehicle for social mobility where social constraints still operate in society at large.

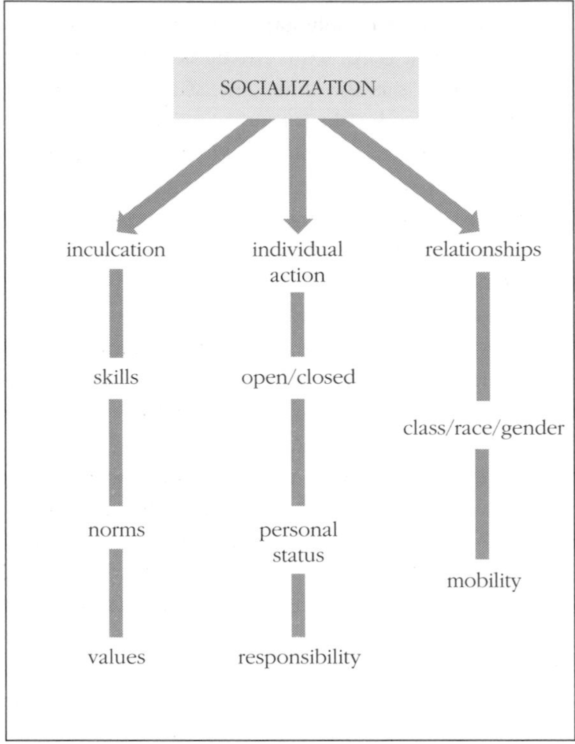

Figure 17.22

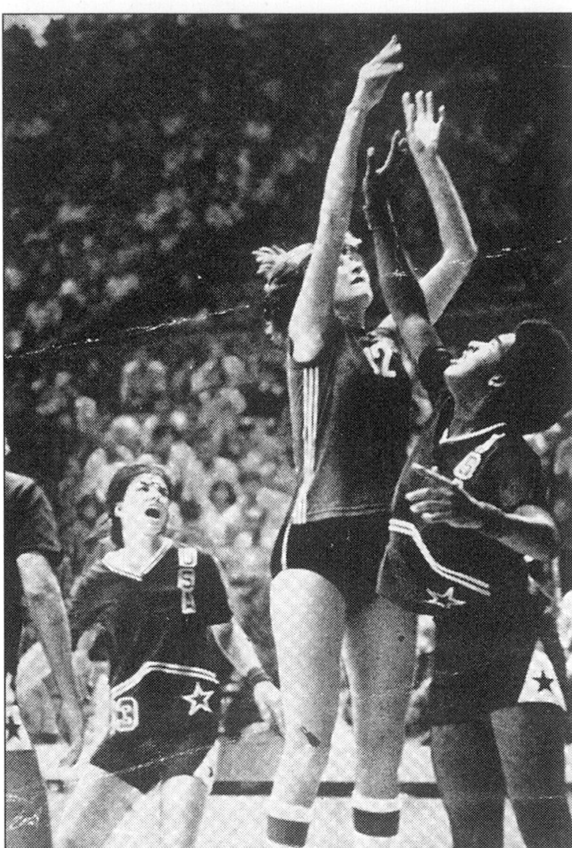

Figure 17.23 Why was it so important for the Soviets to beat the Americans at women's basketball?

Summary

Group dynamics:

1. **Input** into a group **personal performance and aspiration.**
2. **Interaction** in a group—**structure, communication, behaviour and social variables.**
3. **Output** from the group **efficiency, effectiveness and attractiveness.**
4. **Dynamics: cohesion**—attraction, morale, shared responsibility; **conflict**—test of temperament and physical **capacity, channelled aggression** and **balanced tension,** problems with **dysfunctional aggression** and **gamesmanship; socialization**—inculcation of values, development of friendships, opportunity for individual action; **aspiration**—objective probability or subjective desirability.

17.4. Roles in Sport and Physical Education

When people find themselves in a social situation they behave in a specific way: in other words, an individual has one or more roles to play in every sports group. There are a number of variables operating which decide what that role is and how it is determined.

Your **status** in the group is probably the most significant single factor; to quote Linton (1936), 'role represents the dynamic aspect of status'. This means simply that your standing in the group decides how you behave. You might be leader of an expedition; playing your first game in a hockey team; or coaching an Olympic athlete. How you act depends on your status in the relationship.

The second variable in role concerns your own **make-up** and, therefore, the way you like to behave with others. How you act depends very much on your personality, and while you can be 'someone else' for a time, this is difficult to maintain and there is usually a 'reversion to type'.

In addition to personal traits, there is the **impact** of the group on the individual or group make-up. How rigidly is your behaviour controlled by others in the group; by the dynamic of the game; or by the rules imposed by an authoritative body?

If you want to know more about these dimensions, then you can look into **autonomous** (self-directed) roles and **authoritarian** (imposed) roles (Calhoun, 1987).

If we stay within the spheres of play and games, then you will recall that children's play is very much a set of make-believe experiences, which may involve self-development as well as social development. If you look at games, you will recognize that we artificially restrict our actions to the needs of the team and the game's code: that, as with play, our experiences might lead to personal and social development.

The complexity of the game situation, according to Mead (1967), is that instead of just taking over the role of someone else, for example the striker in a soccer team, you also take on the role of the whole team: that is, you have to maintain your place in the fluid interaction of players and situations for the good of the team. If this is the case, then the value of group role play in a 'serious' sporting situation involves continuous judgements, and these experiences may overflow into a more effective life style.

An extension of this hypothesis takes you into the 'reality' of a role: the view that for roles to be effective they must be internalized. If we only 'play' a role, our commitment lacks the intensity required to fulfil it adequately. An American school for actors uses the technique of 'method acting'. They attempt to internalize the person totally—they become 'them'. In sport we talk about 'intensity of focus'; the performer closes the world down to the immediate objectives of the contest. Incidentally, some opponents use gamesmanship tactics to break down that concentration. When we think of great tennis players like Laver, Ashe and Borg, we realize that when their focus was complete the 'strategies' of Nastase and Connors, although also great players, did not succeed.

Because so much of a person's role is visual, the easiest way to establish it is by observation or by attempting to recreate situations. This is also the best way to understand what can appear to be complicated hypotheses.

Investigation 17.4

Case Study One

A PE teacher is teaching a group of children soccer. He/she is very keen to establish the spirit of the game as well as the rules, recognizing that the game, if played with a high moral content, might help to reinforce desirable values. The teacher knows that the game itself tests the self-control of the player; that in games against other schools there is the temptation to retaliate in reaction to fouls and gamesmanship; that the players have the professional game as their model and so may see their heroes practising gamesmanship.

1. Set up a role play situation where there is a teacher and a team of young players. The teacher explains why he/she intends to punish the players severely for any acts of gamesmanship or retaliation during a forthcoming game. Try to establish all the reasons why gamesmanship is counter-productive and anti-social, but encourage the players to voice their reasons for allowing it to take place.
2. Having done this, what would you say if one of the players claimed to have seen you, the PE teacher, playing in a club game on a Saturday afternoon, where you were sent off for a deliberate foul?

Case Study Two

A party of four are high on an isolated mountain in extreme winter conditions. The group has made camp in a snow hole to decide whether to make a final assault on the summit. The leader is very experienced, but willing to listen to the views of the others. The next most experienced person is a member of the opposite sex, suffering a little from mountain sickness. The third member of the party is young and aggressively headstrong. Throughout the climb he/she has been difficult, unwilling to accept group decisions or the authority of the leader. There is a particularly dangerous rivalry between this young person and the second-in-command. The fourth person is the least experienced, and it is his/her first time ever in such difficult conditions. The leader has had a lot of problems with this person, who is completely lacking in confidence and desperately afraid.

1. Set up the four roles and engage the team in a discussion on whether to go for the summit. Before you start, try to establish the individual status of each member; establish their personal feelings; and the levels of group responsibility felt by each one.
2. Let's presume the decision was to go for the top. Unfortunately, the experienced climber falls, breaks a leg and has internal bleeding. They manage to get back to the snow hole, but face a 12-hour journey, in white out conditions, to make it down. With only a day's emergency rations they have to decide what to do.

The leader listens to the arguments and decides. The alternatives would seem to be: all stay; one or two go for help (but who?); three go, presumably leaving the injured one; or all struggle down with the injured person.

Discuss these alternatives and the possible consequences of your decision.

Case Study Three

The coach of a mixed hockey squad is preparing his/her team for a major championship game. Together with two selectors, the coach watches a practice game and decides that the captain is so out of form that he/she will have to be dropped for the all-important game. The captain is recovering from injury, but has also suffered the anguish of a relative involved in a car crash. The members of the team have loyalties to their captain and their coach, but also a desire to win this championship game.

1. Set up a role play situation (see Figure 17.26).
2. When you have decided whether the captain should play or not, discuss the degree to which the coach's authority has been compromised if:
   a. the game is won: without the captain; with the captain;
   b. the game is lost: with the captain; without the captain.
   Select one of these and act it out.
3. As a result of this study of the coach, are you aware how many different roles he/she has to play in a situation like this? Each member of the group should take one of the roles shown in Figure 17.27 and explain how he/she would act given this problem with the captain.

The result of the two role play situations will be markedly different, depending on the role(s) the coach decides are most important for each occasion. The lesson to be learnt is that you may have many choices in the way you behave but, by internalizing and thinking through the consequences, your judgement can completely change the process and the product of any given sporting situation.

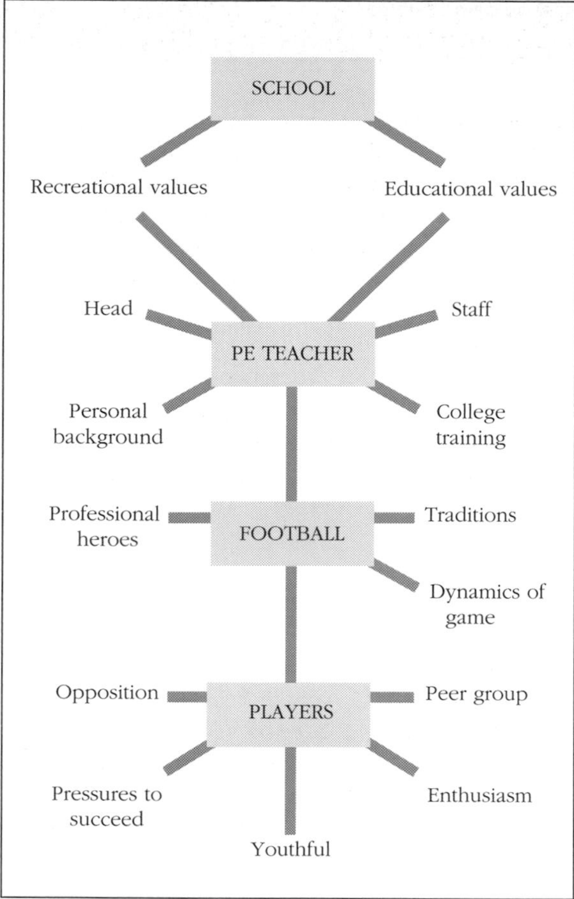

Figure 17.24 A sociogram for Case Study One.

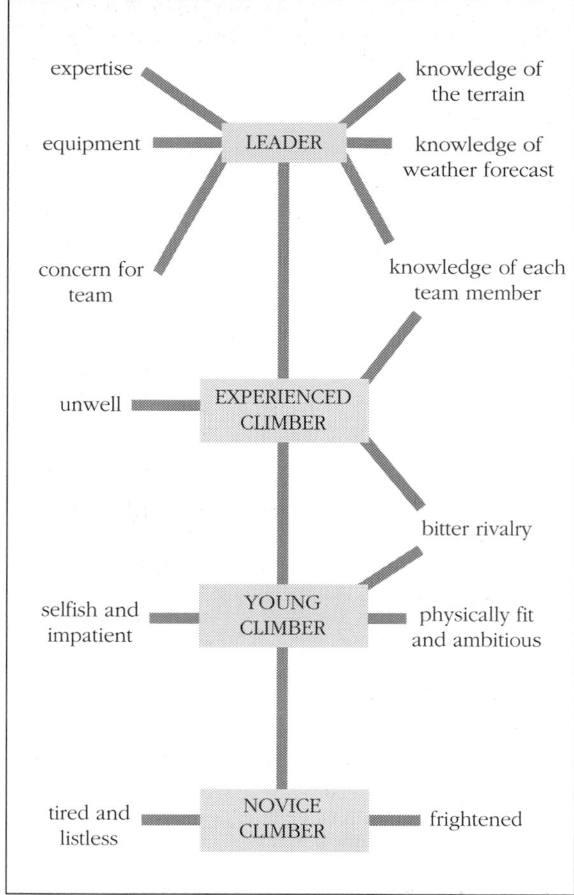

Figure 17.25 Sociogram for Case Study Two.

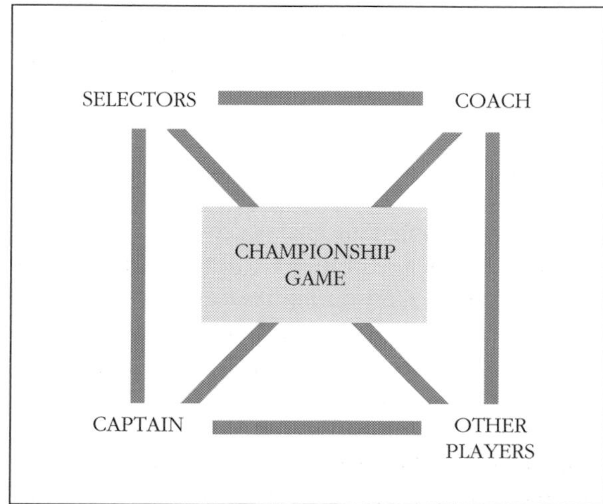

Figure 17.26

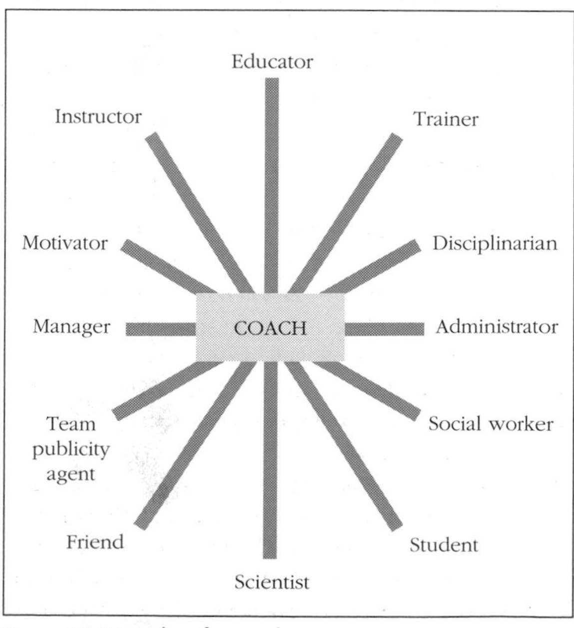

Figure 17.27 Roles of a coach.

Armstrong (1984) in writing the *Effective Coaching* booklet for the NCF Level 2 Programme, produced a series of role play situations which might serve to broaden the understanding of what might be expected of a coach in sport.

Coach and Chairperson of Selectors
Coach feels that she/he has too little say in selection, discussions, decisions, and that selectors do not really know what they are doing. History of poor communication between them.

Selector feels coach is too autocratic and not sufficiently dispassionate. Selector has years of experience.

Coach and Captain
Coach is worried that strong personality of captain is undermining his/her authority—captain talking of alternative strategies to players without acknowledging coach.

Captain feels that the coach's knowledge is inadequate in certain respects and that the players know best because they are the ones facing the challenges.

Coach and Physio
Coach concerned that performer is becoming psychologically dependent on the physio and treatment, and that his/her selection decisions are undermined by this.

Physio sticks to point of view that medical assessment comes first to safeguard the future health of athlete.

Coach and Performer
Coach wants a full squad to attend a residential training weekend to help develop team cohesion, even though it is expensive.

Player lives locally and can accommodate a couple of others, all on student grants, therefore does not see why they need to be resident.

Coach and Referee
Coach has been asked by squad to broach the subject of bias with one of the competition officials.

Official/referee defends position as objective arbiter of performance.

Summary

Role play in sport:

1. Alternatives of **Role Theory** or **Action Theory**
2. **Communication skills; sound knowledge skills; range of teaching styles; sensitivity** regarding the many roles required.

FURTHER READING

Armstrong M. *Effective Coaching*, Pack 13, NCF, 1984.
Baker W.J. *Sports in the Western World*, Rowman and Littlefield, 1982.
Calhoun D.W. *Sport, Culture and Personality*, Human Kinetics, 1987.
Coakley J.J. *Sport and Society: Issues and Controversies*, Mosby, 1982.
Dunning E. (ed.) *Sociology of Sport*, Frank Cass, 1970.
Edwards H. *Sociology of Sport*, Dorsey, 1973.
Gardiner E.N. *Greek Athletic Sports and Festivals*, Brown, 1970.
Gleeson G. *The Growing Child in Competitive Sport*, Hodder & Stoughton, 1986.
Hendry L.B. The role of the PE teacher, *Edn. Rev.* 17, 2, 1975. *School, Sport and Leisure*, Lepus, 1978.
Loy J. and Kenyon G. *Sport, Culture and Society*, Macmillan, 1969.
Rees C.R. and Mirade A.W. (eds) *Sport and Social Theory*, Human Kinetics, 1986.
Saunders E. and White G. *Social Investigations in PE & Sport*, Lepus, 1977.

Chapter 18 Some Contemporary Issues in Physical Education and Sport

The issues approach to the study of physical education and sport allows the student to use a range of disciplines to get to the root of a particular contested area. Having completed a contemporary analysis of any issue in our country, it is valuable to study it from the **historical** perspective, where focus would be on causation, or from the **comparative** perspective, where we might learn from studying other countries.

The suggested order of study is:

The Issue
The group needs to make a serious attempt to identify the different parameters of the problem.

Definitive
Analysis should start by establishing the meaning of the main words being used to describe the problem. In each of the three examples in this chapter, this definitive aspect is covered in some detail, but each group should discuss the accuracy of the definitions being offered.

Structural Framework
You need a series of headings to work under, which outline the structural basis of the study area. Only the framework is offered here and so it is necessary for each group to collect and collate data which are specific to the particular problem area. Some of the information has been included in earlier parts of this text, but additional specialized articles and books need to be studied. For this reason a specialized reading list is given with each topic; students should be encouraged to build files of contemporary articles; and the school should make use of the National Documentation Centre at Birmingham University.

Functional
The data you have collected should also help you to explain *how* the issue operates in this country and you may wish also to consider how it functions in a number of other countries.

Cultural Analysis
Regardless of whether you embark on this comparative analysis, it is essential that you put the problem in a social setting. The 'cultural determinant' framework is offered to help you to explain how certain cultural factors might influence the problem.

Reformative
Finally, it is important that you should be able to suggest a series of reform procedures. This may be reorganizing your own country's policy, provision and administration, or may involve the introduction of certain ideas used abroad. The important point here is to recognize the problems which might be associated with the recommended changes.

Issues would seem to exist at three main levels, **social, institutional** and **subcultural.** A sample issue in each of these has been selected for examination together with a list of alternative topics.

18.1 Societal: Excellence in Sport

THE ISSUE

There is a debate on the social ethics of elitism in sport: whether emphasis should be placed on the success of a few over participation by the majority. At an administrative level, the issue is whether a particular society has got it right or whether we can learn from the policies and procedures of other countries.

The structural dynamic of sport is shown in Figure 18.1.

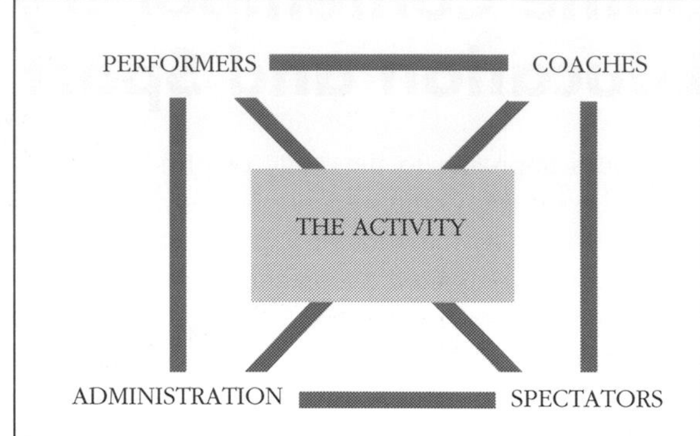

Figure 18.1

DEFINITIVE

For **excellence** to be achieved a high level of **commitment, resources**, and **expertise** is necessary from each group involved.

Excellence

This is the objective assessment of **quality**. Though in sport the end product is the level of performance in competition, it should not be separated from the support role played by coaches, supporters and administrators.

This can be **elitist** in the sense that certain privileged individuals are given opportunities not available to the majority. If the reward is sufficient, societies may accept this social inequality. If everyone has the opportunity in terms of selection, where the talented are given every opportunity to attain their optimum level of achievement, this is a form of meritocracy which is widely accepted. This justifies rewards given to a few as a result of open selection.

There is an alternative, personalized notion that any enthusiast who achieves his/her optimum level of performance is on an excellence continuum. Where this view is individualized we have a Western cultural analysis; where it is collectivized, as in communist cultures, the society is presumed to reap the reward.

Status

A great deal depends on the status of sport in a society. Where there is a recognition of the cultural importance of sport at national, political and commercial levels, the ideological and financial support will be greater.

The status of the performer is also important. In a country where professionalism exists with high financial rewards, and where the professionals are drawn from the middle class, there is high status. Where there is a strong amateur tradition involving the middle classes, the same may apply, but, in financial terms, the performers may be left to their own resources and prestige may exist only at a personal level. However, where amateurism is strongly reinforced by state aid and political significance, the status of the performer will be high.

Figure 18.2 Commitment and pain may be the price of success.

STRUCTURE

See Figure 18.3.

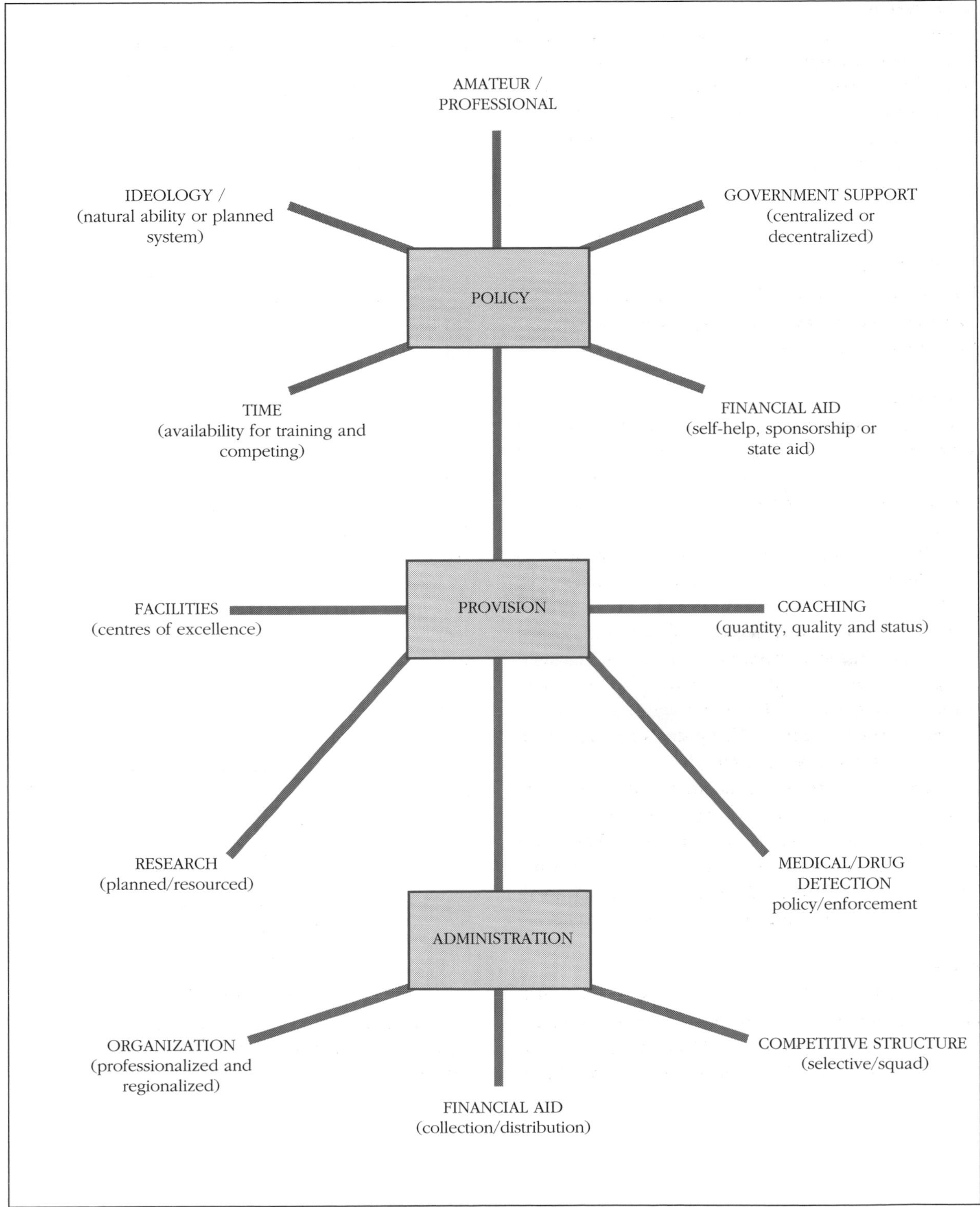
AMATEUR / PROFESSIONAL
IDEOLOGY / (natural ability or planned system)
GOVERNMENT SUPPORT (centralized or decentralized)
POLICY
TIME (availability for training and competing)
FINANCIAL AID (self-help, sponsorship or state aid)
FACILITIES (centres of excellence)
PROVISION
COACHING (quantity, quality and status)
RESEARCH (planned/resourced)
MEDICAL/DRUG DETECTION policy/enforcement
ADMINISTRATION
ORGANIZATION (professionalized and regionalized)
COMPETITIVE STRUCTURE (selective/squad)
FINANCIAL AID (collection/distribution)

Figure 18.3

FUNCTION

Policy and practice for children:
1. Preparation for excellence in curriculum PE.
2. Extracurricular programmes for excellence.
3. The sports school in operation.

Youth opportunities and the Olympic Reserve:
1. Club/community facilities for youth excellence.
2. Industrial provision for youth excellence.
3. Higher education and sporting excellence.

Organization and Sporting Excellence:
1. Efficiency of the administrative framework for selection.
2. Distribution of financial aid.
3. Equality and use of centres of excellence and other facilities.

Status and human factors:
1. Effects of status on development.
2. Level of opportunity and esteem for performers. The temptations of drug abuse.
3. Preparation and proliferation of coaches.

Here are three photographs reflecting excellence: the organization and performance standard of the Tour de France; the Astrodome as an outstanding facility; and a Soviet sports school. What is there in the United Kingdom to compare with these?

Figure 18.4 The Tour de France cycle race.

Figure 18.5 Astrodome in the United States.

Figure 18.6 A sports school in the Soviet Union.

CULTURAL DETERMINANTS

See Figure 18.7.

If ONE of these sub-systems is analysed, it will become clear how much additional knowledge is required to understand links between a problem in sport and the society in which it exists.

e.g. **Ranking Structure**

This refers to the status of specific groups of people in a society. Arguably, in the egalitarian Soviet society efforts were made to live up to a socialist philosophy by giving everyone equal opportunity, but history has shown us that the political ideal is not always achieved. In European countries like France and Britain, there is a very powerful democratic ideal, but tradition tends to give certain groups an advantage which they try to retain. Thirdly, it is important to recognize that in addition to some people starting off with an advantage, abilities and attitudes vary, and so, in a 'free' society, able people 'get on' better than those who are less able. In economic terms, a capitalist market economy encourages this and so status is fluid, reflecting the material success of an individual, and this brings them cultural as well as material advantages. American society does have strong 'ranking', explained in the initials W.A.S.P. (White Anglo-Saxon Protestant) and can be defined as 'hegonomous', but allows more opportunities for 'excellence' to be achieved through the ideological support given to opportunism, as they would say 'rags-to-riches'.

Social Ranking, therefore, is one of the major factors determining the opportunity to participate in sport; adequate access to provisions for sport; and sufficient self esteem and social acceptibility to enter fully into a high level sports programme.

The suggestion is that, in an unequal society, certain groups find it difficult to play a full part in sport: that society is **ranked** according to **status**. This may be the consequence of restrictions put on them by dominant groups or reflect a lack of confidence or affluence among the members of that minority group.

In Britain, there is the traditional influence of **social class** which lies at the root of most discrimination, but **gender** bias is also the result of values cemented in Victorian tradition.

Many Afro-Caribbeans and Asians have settled in Britain in the last 40 or so years, and have tended to move into an industrial working class social stratum, which combines the existing class discimination with the additional problems of class rivalry and racism. These negatives are made worse for females, because ethnic minorities tend to retain their own cultural taboos in an adopted social system which already discriminates against females. This is a particularly powerful factor when **religion** also plays a part in gender roles.

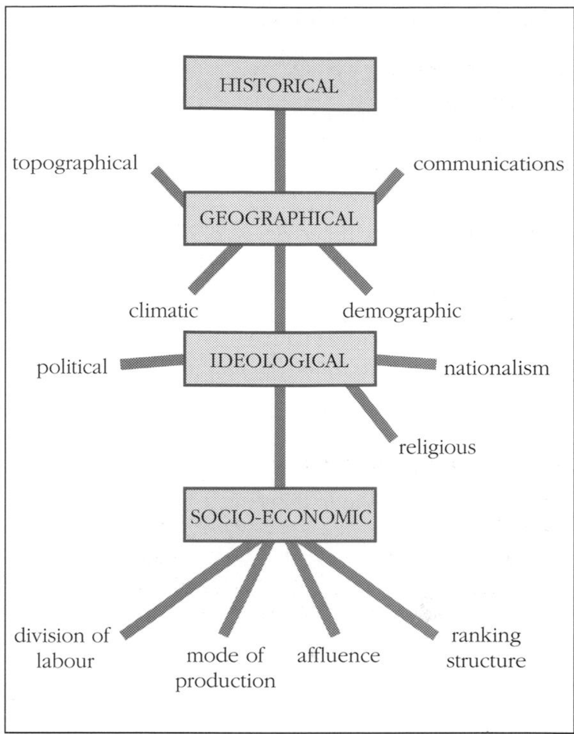

Figure 18.7

Sport, particularly high level sport, has always been dominated by the dynamic young adult and, consequently, **age**, particularly in the case of the very young and the elderly, has also been a target for discrimination. Young people are often exploited to achieve excellence or are excluded because adults find their presence disruptive. Older people suffer from the accusation of 'being over the top' and there are still only a few sports where 'veteran' events are actively encouraged. 'Lifetime Sport' is a concept which has still to be fully realised in Britain.

Finally, elite sport is normally focused on **physical ability**, resulting in anyone who is not able-bodied being discriminated against. The notion of 'a disabled person being handicapped by society' is one which suggests that discrimination is not limited to sport: that sport offers a solution to the problem of people being handicapped by a disability through contests where individuals are able to test themselves against their peers.

Class, gender, age and disability: these are the factors which our social system classifies and stratifies, ranking individuals and, in so doing, influencing their likelihood of achieving excellence in sport. It is equally important to recognize that the Sports Council's target groups also reflect this social ranking and as a result highlight the constraints operating against the successful implimentation of a Sport for All policy.

REFORMATIVE

Development potential

1. What might we usefully consider at school level?
2. What youth policies abroad could help in Britain?
3. What organizational and financial improvements might the British adopt?
4. How might we change things at a personal and status level?

Constraints which might operate

1. Cultural resistance to the imposition of foreign methods.
2. Unacceptable influence on the status quo.

FINAL COMMENTS

The international status and organization of sport make the adoption of successful ideas from abroad attractive. The significance of international sport is such that success has value well beyond the scope of sport itself.

The model used for this analysis should be adaptable for any major policy or campaign being operated by a society. Other recommended issues in this category are: **Sport for All, recreational provision;** and **outdoor recreation and tourism.**

Summary

Societal issues:

1. **Structure, function** and **cultural determinants.**
2. **Campaigns** and **Policies. Excellence** or **Sport for All.**
3. **Policy**—ideology, government stance, public attitude, financial aid, time availability.
4. **Provision**—facilities, coaching, research, medical back-up.
5. **Administration**—organization, financial distribution, competitions.

FURTHER READING

Anthony D. *A Strategy for British Sport,* Hurst, 1980.

Bennett B.L. *et al. Comparative PE & Sport,* Lea & Febiger, 1975.

Calhoun D.W. *Sport, Culture & Personality,* Human Kinetics, 1987.

Cashmore Ellis. *Making Sense of Sport,* Routledge, 1990.

Coakley J.J. *Sport in Society: Issues and Controversies,* Times Mirror/Mosby, 1986.

Dunstan J. *Paths to Excellence and the Soviet School,* NFER, 1978.

French Information. *125 Sports in France,* French Embassy, 1985.

Gardner P. *Nice Guys Finish Last,* Allen Lane, 1974.

Hargreaves J. *Sport, Power and Culture,* Polity Press, 1986.

Hemery D. *Sporting Excellence,* Willow, 1986.

Humphreys J.H.L. French sports hot house, *BJPE,* Vol. 10, No. 1,1979.

Lawton J. *The All American War Game,* Basil Blackwell, 1984.

Macfarlane N. *Sport and Politics,* Willow, 1986.

Nixon H.L. *Sport and the American Dream,* Leisure Press, 1984.

Parry S.J. *et al. The Pursuit of Excellence in Sport and Physical Education,* NAFTE, 1978.

Riordan J. *Sport in Soviet Society,* CUP, 1977.

Sage G.H. *Power and Ideology in American Sport,* Human Kinetics, 1990.

Sports Council:

The Next Ten Years, Sports Council, 1982.

Which Ways Forward, Sports Council, 1987.

Into the 90s, Sports Council, 1988.

18.2 Institutional: Outdoor Education

THE ISSUE

There is an accountability argument as to whether the expense and time needed for outdoor education are justified by the experience it offers. It might be suggested that the objectives would be better served through a recreational programme. At an administrative level, the issue is whether a particular society's outdoor education programme can be improved by looking at other systems.

DEFINITIVE

Formal education

This is an **institutional** focus. Concern is with what happens in a school or college. It may be part of the curriculum or part of the intramural/extracurricular activity of the institution.

Informal education

A broader concept of education acknowledges that there is a form of social education operating when recreational **institutions** exist to promote a particular life style, where the outcome may be a transmission of desirable cultural values.

Outdoor education

This is a means of approaching educational or cultural objectives through direct experiences in the natural environment, using its resources as learning materials.

Outdoor pursuits

These are physical activities in the natural environment which place the individual in decision-making adventure situations, and as such are a central part of outdoor education.

Vacation camps

Though recreational, these offer adventure situations in the natural environment and indirectly promote the same values as outdoor education centres.

Escape

There is a strong feeling of escape: from work, from urban existence, as a holiday; as a return to rural simplicity and basic survival; as a return to one's cultural roots; but also as romantic/religious awareness of natural beauty.

DESIRED VALUES

See Figure 18.8.

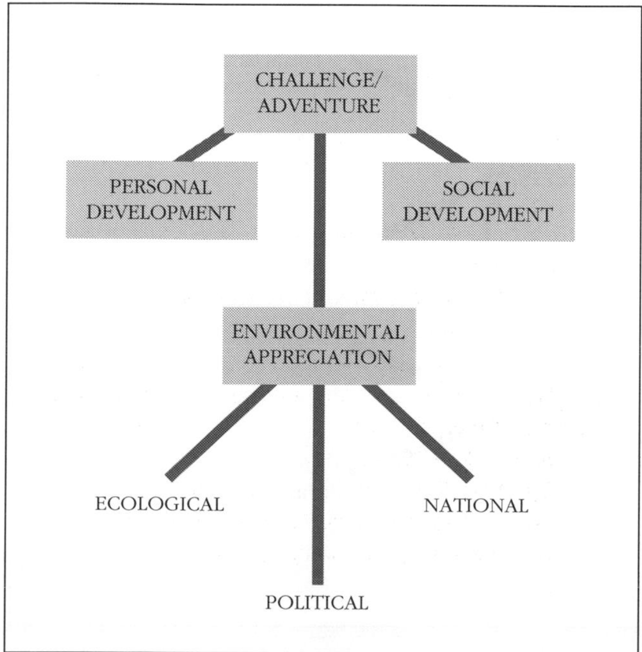

Figure 18.8

STRUCTURAL

See Figure 18.9.

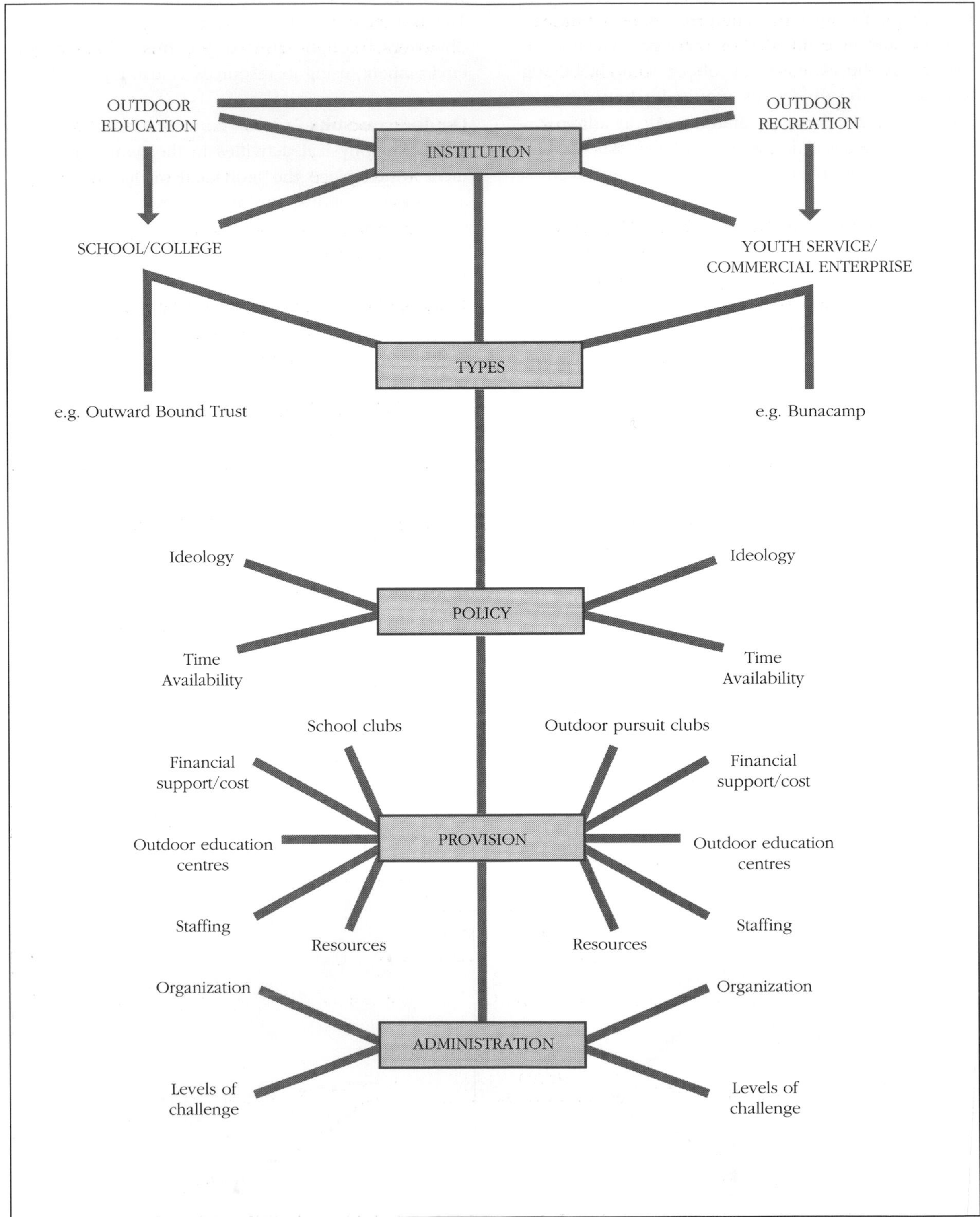

Figure 18.9

FUNCTION

Policy and practice in the schools:

1. Outdoor activity curriculum programmes in primary, secondary and higher departments.
2. Extracurricular/intramural clubs in outdoor activities.
3. Schools/colleges with special interests in outdoor activities, e.g. Gordonstoun and Charlotte Mason College.

Policy and practice in Outdoor Education Centres:

1. Outdoor centres belonging to specific schools.
2. Local government outdoor education centres.
3. National Outdoor Education Centres, e.g. Plas y Brenin and Holme Pierrepont.
4. Outward Bound Trust and other adventure schools.

Policy and practice of specific associations and schemes:

1. Youth associations and their facilities, e.g. scouts, pioneers, etc.
2. Adventure youth schemes, e.g. Duke of Edinburgh Award.

Organization of outdoor recreation holiday schemes:

1. State sponsored outdoor facilities, e.g. Pioneer Camps.
2. Commercially sponsored facilities, e.g. PGL, BUNACAMP, etc.

Organization of natural areas of beauty:

1. Administration of national and local parks.
2. Promotion of conservation.

CULTURAL DETERMINANTS

See Figure 18.10.

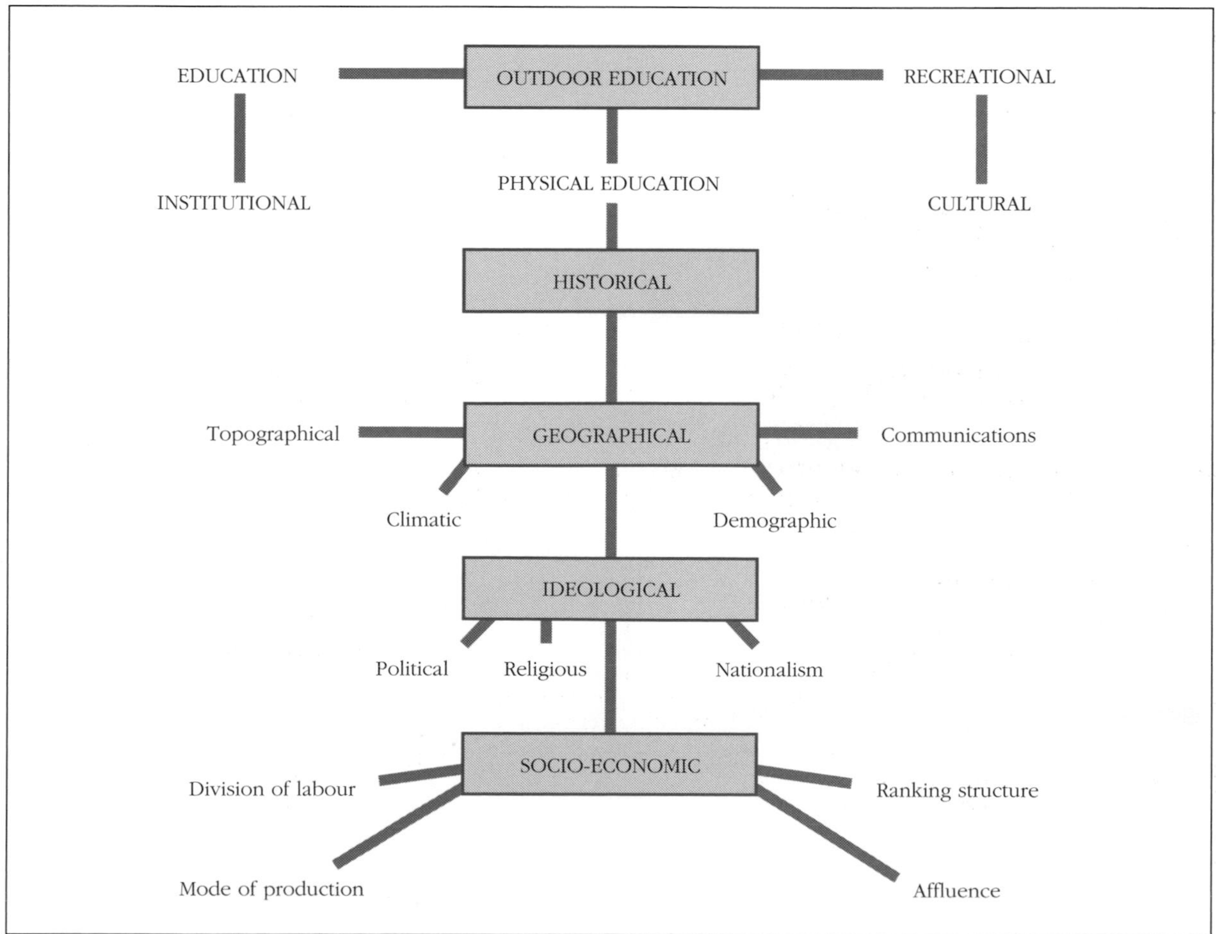

Figure 18.10

REFORMATIVE

Developmental potential

1. Can we improve the relationship between physical education and outdoor education?
2. How might we usefully improve outdoor education in and around the school?
3. How might the function of outdoor education centres be improved?
4. How might we extend special schools?
5. How might we broaden opportunities for summer camps and winter holidays for children?
6. How might we communicate the message of conservation more effectively?

What are the fundamental differences between a camp school and an Outward Bound School in the USA, and how did these compare with a Soviet pioneer camp?

Constraints which might operate

1. Limits imposed by our educational and physical educational philosophies and administrations.
2. Cultural resistance to the introduction of foreign methods.
3. Limits imposed by the geographical determinants.

FINAL COMMENTS

There appears to be a serious attempt to educate young people to respect and conserve the natural environment. This education is particularly necessary in a world which is becoming increasingly materialistic and where population expansion puts the natural environment at risk. In a world which is becoming increasingly urbanized and technological, there is a need for a renaissance of rusticity on the one hand and the opportunity for adventure on the other.

The model used for this analysis should be adaptable for any major institutional issue. It need not be limited to education, but could focus on industry or the armed forces, where one facet of an institution may have to operate alongside others. Other recommended issues in this category are: **competitive sport in school physical education; teacher training in physical education; industrial sports provision; sport in the Army,** etc.

Figure 18.11 An adventure situation on the Colorado.

Figure 18.12 Orlyonok Camp on the Black Sea.

Summary

Institutional issues:

1. **Concepts** of outdoor education–physical education; formal–informal education; sport—conservation—escapism.
2. **Variables** include: institutions, systems, policies, provision and administrations.
3. **Functional problems** include: cost and time.
4. **Cultural determinants** include: geographical factors, ideology and socio-economic variables.

FURTHER READING

Bacon W. (ed.) *Leisure and Learning in the 1980s,* LSA., 1981.

Bank J. Outdoor development, *Leadership & Organization Development Journal,* Vol. 4, No. 3, 1983.

DES. *Learning Out of Doors,* HMSO, 1983.

Gray D. Access to open country, *Sport & Recreation,* Vol. 18, No. 3, 1977.

Johnson A. School it isn't: education it is, *School Sport,* 4.4, 1979.

JOHPER (ed.) Intra murals, *JOHPER,* February 1983; Leisure & tourism, *JOHPER,* April 1983; Family recreation, *JOHPER,* October 1984; Leisure today, *JOHPER,* October 1988.

Lombardo M.S. and Groves D.L. Content and process for outdoor education, *JOHPER,* March 1978.

Mortlock C. *The Adventure Alternative,* Cicerone, 1984.

Parker T.M. and Meldrum K.I. *Outdoor Education,* Dent, 1973.

Rhudy E. An alternative to outward bound programmes, *JOHPER,* January 1979.

Smith J.W. Outdoor education, *AAHPER,* Omnibus, 1976.

RECOMMENDED PERIODICALS

Jeunesse au Plein Air.

JOHPER.

Outdoors. (PEA.)

Sport in the USSR.

18.3 Subcultural: Women in Sport

THE ISSUE

In many societies, women do not have an equal opportunity to participate in sport. It is necessary to tease out desired differences in role from culturally induced discrimination and look at other countries to see if we can learn from them.

DEFINITIVE

It is important to recognize that this is not fundamentally a sport issue, but a case of social inequality which also manifests itself in sport.

The physiological differences between males and females are the source of sexual stereotyping, but cultural traditions and trends distort and exaggerate the male/female roles in society to the extent that basic freedoms are denied.

Where social inequality exists, the forces of a democratic society can press for reform. However, an additional problem exists when social inequality is justified on biological grounds and a policy is enacted which presumes women's predisposition for certain sports.

In Britain for example, the resistance to women's soccer is based on traditional stereotyping, and the conservatism of the FA. This does not appear to be the case in the United States, where the game is played by both sexes largely because it is a recent innovation and does not rival the prestigious male preserve of grid iron football. In the Soviet Union, the 'official' view is that women's soccer is physiologically harmful and morally degrading, and every effort is made to discourage it. The view that certain sports undermine femininity is the most difficult to overcome, because it often has the support of many women.

The differentiation of sex roles in society stems from the traditional notion of family life. This tradition recognizes the role of the woman as a wife and mother, where her leisure time is committed to home and family. Though it was, originally, very much a middle-class concept, it became a feature of the respectable working class family, replacing the survival role of the wife as a bread-winner. The development of this stereotype coincided with the emergence of modern sport and this resulted in a dominance by men. However, we now have career women making the stereotype outmoded.

It is easy to see this as a female problem, but when sex discrimination operates, it can result in constraints on males as well as females, where certain sports are considered feminine and so unsuitable for men.

It is this feminine stereotype in sport and society at large which prevents freedom of the individual to operate and so 'Women in Sport' will remain an issue until every person is free to participate in a full range of sports with equal support from the community.

There are a number of routes which may be taken to increase female opportunity in sport. The right to participate could include the right to remain separate from mixed sport, but the choice must be available to the individual. The American Title IX legislation (1972) presumed that for children to get an equal opportunity in an unequal culture, physical education had to be coeducational. The problem with a categorical decision like this is that it stimulates a counteraction from male teachers, who see sports standards slipping. The fact that Title IX applies only to federally aided institutions also presents another anomaly.

There are a large number of myths about the capacity of women to cope in sport. Many of these are being refuted, as illustrated by the successful inclusion of a women's marathon in the 1988 Olympic Games, but it is a slow process of eroding traditional attitudes. In Britain, the Equal Pay Act (1970) and the Sex Discrimination Act (1975) now allow women in sport to go to court if their rights are abused, but it is important to recognize that sex discrimination in itself is not unlawful, only instances where discrimination creates financial consequences. In addition, Section 44 makes concessions in cases:

> *'Where the physical strength, stamina or physique of the average woman puts her at a disadvantage to the average man . . . as a competitor . . .'*

A clause which may have been designed to protect the female, but which can be used to exclude her. Similarly, Rule 29 of the Olympic Charter (1983) states that female competitors must be registered female. These so-called sex tests may have been designed to protect genuine female competitors but feminists might want to know why males should not also be tested.

Figure 18.13 Don't get carried away by all this. Women can use a hammer, but they are still not allowed to throw it!

STRUCTURE

See Figure 18.14.

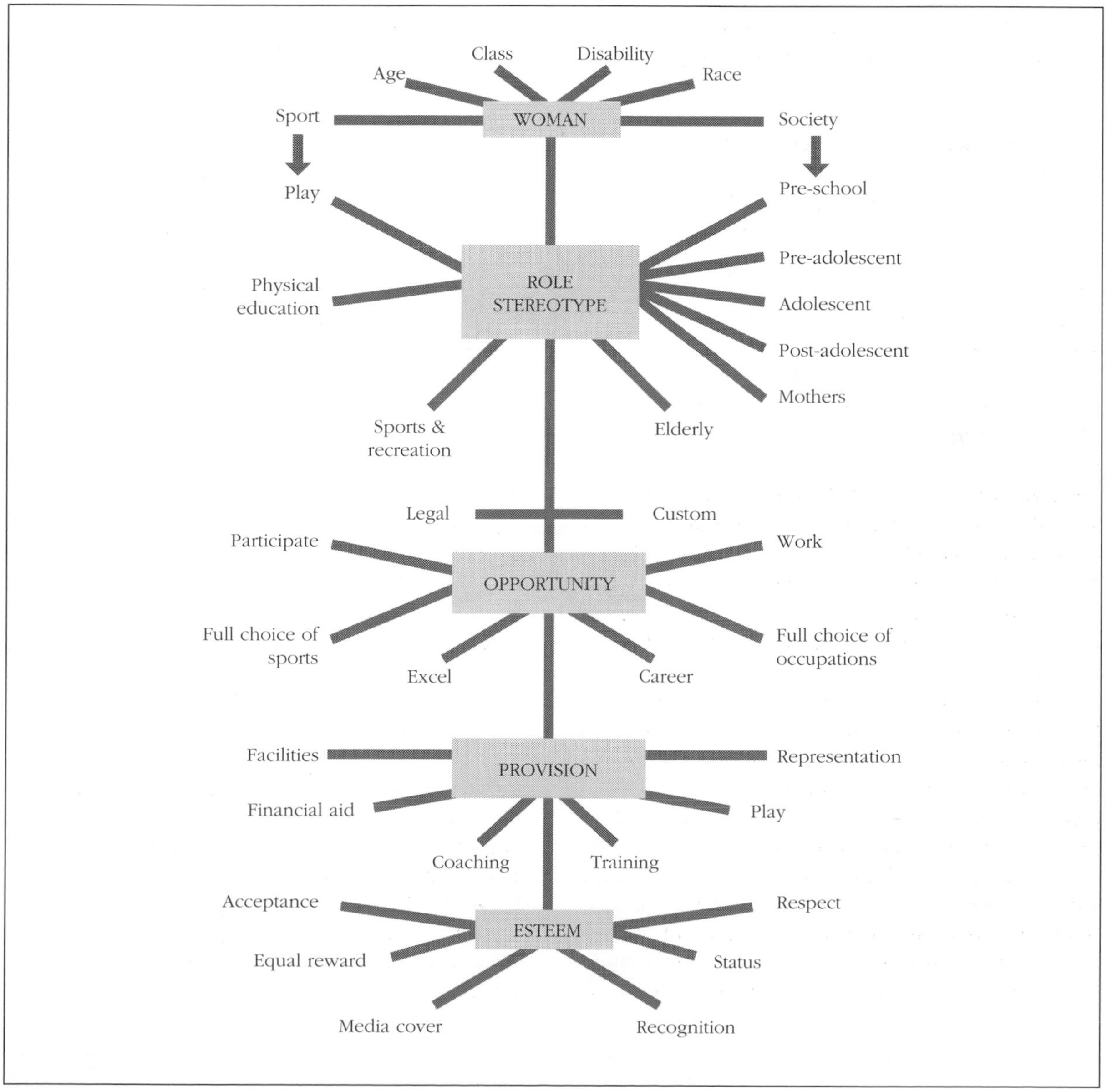

Class Disability
Age Race
Sport WOMAN Society
Play Pre-school
Physical education
ROLE STEREOTYPE
Pre-adolescent
Adolescent
Post-adolescent
Mothers
Sports & recreation
Elderly
Legal Custom
Participate Work
OPPORTUNITY
Full choice of sports
Full choice of occupations
Excel Career
Facilities Representation
PROVISION
Financial aid Play
Coaching Training
Acceptance Respect
ESTEEM
Equal reward Status
Media cover Recognition

Figure 18.14

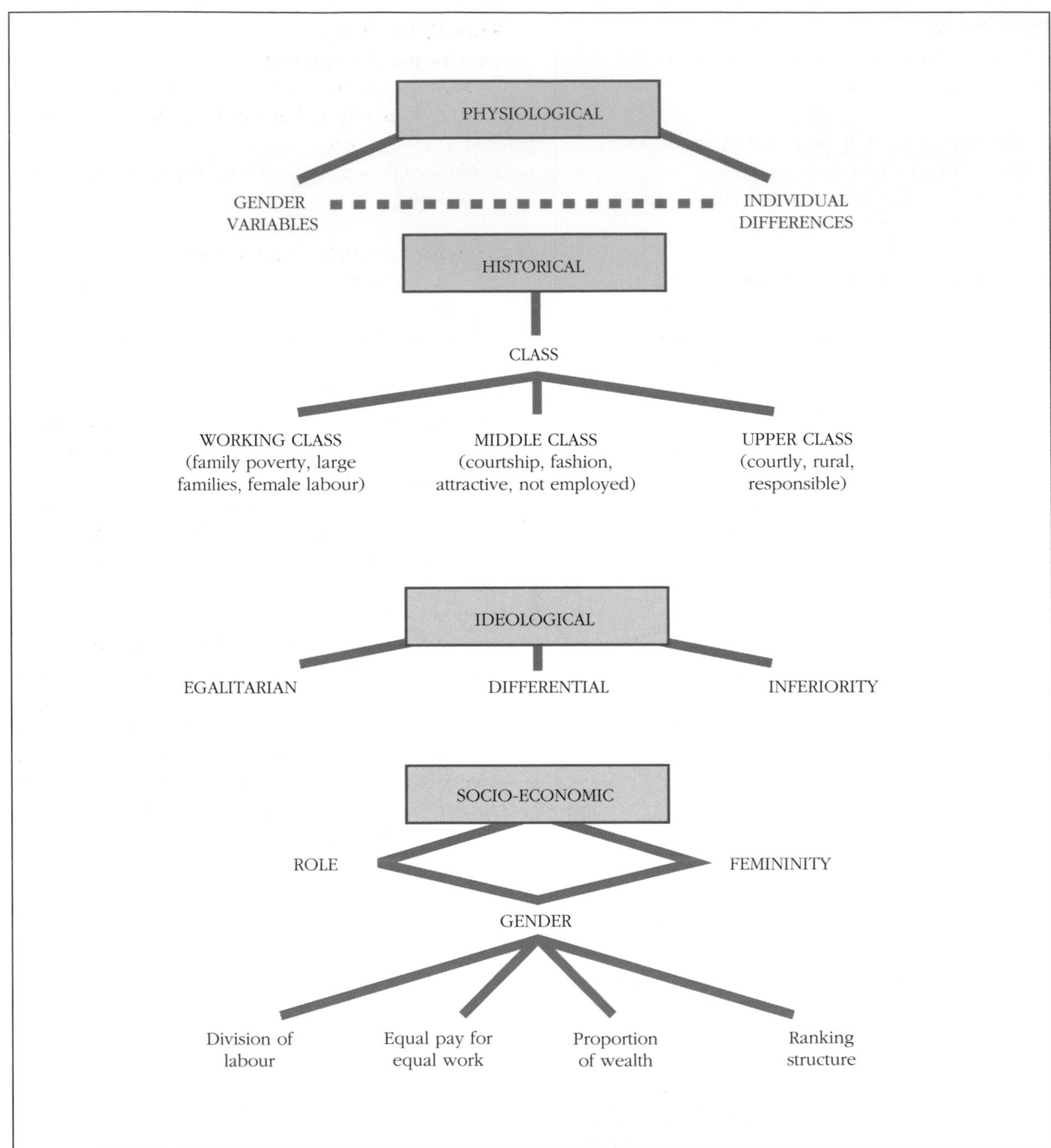
PHYSIOLOGICAL
GENDER VARIABLES
INDIVIDUAL DIFFERENCES
HISTORICAL
CLASS
WORKING CLASS (family poverty, large families, female labour)
MIDDLE CLASS (courtship, fashion, attractive, not employed)
UPPER CLASS (courtly, rural, responsible)
IDEOLOGICAL
EGALITARIAN
DIFFERENTIAL
INFERIORITY
SOCIO-ECONOMIC
ROLE
FEMININITY
GENDER
Division of labour
Equal pay for equal work
Proportion of wealth
Ranking structure

Figure 18.15

FUNCTION

UNITED KINGDOM—FRANCE—UNITED STATES—SOVIET UNION

Policy and practice in school PE programmes:
1. Inequalities in the PE curriculum.
2. Inequalities in extracurricular sport.
3. Inequalities in outdoor education.

Policy and practice in Sport for All programmes:
1. Differences in proportional involvement.
2. Differences in the availability of facilities.
3. Differences in the variety of activities.

Policy and practice in sports excellence programmes:
1. Variations in selection and coaching.
2. Variations in the distribution of financial aid and income.
3. Variations in career possibilities in sport.

Organizational inequalities:
1. Sporting activities not open to females.
2. Sporting activities where sexes are not mixed.
3. Sporting activities where female involvement is taboo.

CULTURAL DETERMINANTS

See Figure 18.15.

REFORMATIVE?

It takes a great deal of courage and independence to decide to design your own image instead of the one that society rewards, but it gets easier as you go along.

Germaine Greer,
The Female Eunuch,
1971.

REFORMATIVE

Developmental potential
1. What might we usefully change at school level?
2. What organizational and financial improvements might we adopt?
3. How might we change things at a personal and status level?

Constraints which might operate
1. Cultural resistance to the imposition of foreign methods.
2. Unacceptable influence on the status quo.

FINAL COMMENTS

The right of the individual to a free choice of legitimate activities or life styles is a cornerstone of a free society. As yet these rights are not being observed in the context of women in sport. Even if social attitudes are slow to change, there can be no excuse for administrational and financial discrimination to operate. The different contribution that men and women bring to sport enriches the total experience. What is at fault is the singular stereotype of what it is to be a sportsperson.

The model used for this analysis should be adaptable for any major area of discrimination in sport. Other recommended issues in this category are: **Racial Discrimination in Sport; Sport for People with Special Needs; Sport and the Unemployed; Social Class Discrimination in Sport; Sport for Young People and the Elderly,** etc.

Summary

Sub-cultural issues:

1. **Race, class, gender, special needs, age,** etc. may cause problems because of **discrimination**.
2. **Role stereotypes and variations in opportunity, provision and esteem** may cause **inequality**.
3. **Positive discrimination** might be a short-term possibility.

FURTHER READING

Blue A. *Grace under Pressure,* Sidgwick & Jackson, 1987.

Fletcher S. *Women First: The Female Tradition in English Physical Education, 1890-1990,* Athlone Press, 1984.

Geadelmann P.L. *Equality in Sport for Women,* AAHPER, 1977.

Gerber E.W. *et al. The American Woman in Sport,* Addison Wesley, 1974.

JOHPER (ed.) The role of women in sports, *JOHPER,* March 1986.

Lenskiyj H. *Out of Bounds. Women, Sport and Sexuality,* Toronto, The Women's Press, 1986.

Mangan J.A. and Park R.J. *From 'Fair Sex' to Feminism,* Frank Cass, 1987.

Oglesby C.A. *Women and Sport,* Lea & Febiger, 1978.

Pannick D. *Sex Discrimination in Sport,* Equal Opportunities Commission, 1983.

Perchenok Y. *Women in the USSR,* Novosti Press, 1985.

Riordan J. *Sport in Soviet Society,* CUP, 1977.

Sport & Leisure Supplement. *Women in Sport, People with Disabilities, Young People and Sport, (Policy and Frameworks for Action),* Sports Council, 1994.

Talbot M. *Women and Leisure,* Sports Council, 1982.

Twin S.L. *Out of the Bleachers,* NY, McGraw Hill, 1979.

Women in Sport, Women's Sports Foundation, 1980–1984.

Chapter 19
Historical Perspectives and Popular Recreation

19.1 Historical Perspectives

Figure 19.1 Looking at the past helps us to understand the present and to do something about the future.

Henry Ford suggested that all history is bunk, but then cars devalue more quickly than culture!

An approach to historical study

The study of sports' history can stand on its own as it increases the knowledge and understanding of people and situations in the past. It can be based on different sports or socially based on different sectors of society at a particular time. In each case the intention is to establish what happened as objectively as possible, attempting not to allow our present situation to affect our judgement.

We would like to suggest that history comes to life when we attempt to interpret the intentions and attitudes of people, as well as their recorded actions. However, we must be careful not to find **what we are looking for** rather than **what really happened**. Remember, we want to **understand** history, not **change** it. For example, it is thrilling to think that Webb Ellis picked up the ball and in so doing invented the game of rugby football . . . but it wasn't quite as simple as that!

The focus of this book is on **contemporary physical education and sport,** but we need to look at the past as part of a **continuum of change,** where understanding how things have developed may give us the **keys to the present.**

Figure 19.1 Looking at the past helps us to understand the **present** and to do something about the future.

So how can I become a historian?

The basic approach is to establish a **descriptive record** of events. Look through Wisden or some contemporary narrative accounts. The value of this knowledge lies entirely in its accuracy, but be careful—we know from modern reports that they can be biased.

The second level takes us into the **interpretation of relationships.**

You might want to know the links between games in the 19th-century public school and the authority of the headmaster; or between football in a community and the local factory. In this situation, the historian tries to build as complete a picture as possible, providing a greater understanding of the human experience in a social setting

The objective work of Joseph Strutt in *Sports and Pastimes of the People of England* (1802) helps us to understand what popular recreations were like before the 19th century.

Sometimes, even fiction can be helpful in this context. Thomas Hughes, in *Tom Brown's School Days,* may have exaggerated reality, but his romantic style has given us a valuable insight into public school life through a fictional adventure.

The historian is interested not only in one time and place, but in the **influence of one situation or experience on another.** Thomas Hughes's book may have been inaccurate, but it was believed by generations of schoolboys and almost certainly was the single greatest influence on trends in public school athleticism.

Thirdly, some historians think they can identify **causation factors.** I suppose I've just done it in the case of *Tom Brown's School Days.* They try to recognize patterns of development and identify the cultural determinants which influenced sport and reflected society. Bailey (1978) looked at sport and the middle classes; Cunningham (1980) studied the industrial working classes in the context of leisure; and Newsome (1961) attempted the even more difficult task of linking sport, education and religion. You need to read books like this!

How do I know certain things really happened?
Some historians put up hypotheses just like scientists, but the majority **ask questions** and **look for answers** in the **evidence** available. This leads to the tricky point that if you don't ask the right questions, you won't find out what really happened.

Equally important, if your evidence is inaccurate, your conclusions are worthless. Still, let's not give up but rather look at types of **evidence.**

Primary evidence is taken to be information reported by a person who was a witness to the event as a **direct experience,** and could be presented in **written** or **oral** form. Written material is more permanent, but changes everytime it is re-written, and oral evidence changes every time it is recalled or retold. For that reason, maps, pictures, authentic documents and supported testimonies are most valuable on accuracy grounds, and oral evidence tends to be suspect without support.

Once that evidence is copied or retold, it becomes **secondary evidence** and that much less reliable.

Try to go to a County Record Office or Local History Study Centre and look at some **primary evidence.** Most libraries have documents and photographs; they keep old papers and periodicals; and they have books written at the time of the event. Then you could re-approach your contemporary histories to confirm their level of accuracy. A good historian always looks for **cross-references.**

Finally, take your tape recorder to the oldest people you know and ask them to recall 'the old days'. They'll probably love to talk to you and what they get wrong will in many cases be more than compensated for by the insights they will give you into events which would otherwise never be recorded.

Investigation 19.1 : Let's test out some evidence

1. The painting in Figure 19.2 was exhibited at the Royal Academy in 1839.

a. Is this a primary or secondary source?
b. How would you justify the claim that this is a valid piece of evidence?
c. Interpret the structure of the game from this painting.
d. How does the painting reflect the society of the day?

Figure 19.2

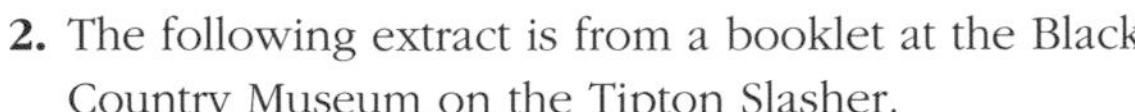

2. The following extract is from a booklet at the Black Country Museum on the Tipton Slasher.

Sayers was a small man, a middleweight, about 11 stone in weight and five feet eight inches tall. Perry announced that this fight was to be his last and the experts all agreed with him that Sayers would be slashed to ribbons within a few rounds.

Noah Hingley, who had been born a nailmaker, and in 1857 was a thriving industrialist with chain and cable works already established at Netherton, warned the Slasher not to risk his all on the fight.

'Yoh bay gettin' no younger,' he said. 'You're a fighter and yoh con lose—I'm a skamer (schemer) and I con win. Why doh you invest some money with me for a rainy day.'

The Slasher was a stubborn man and he thought he could not lose. Noah Hingley's advice was unheeded. His all was spread amongst the bookmakers at 2 to 1 on. £400 was deposited as stake money.

On the 16th June, 1857, the ring was pitched on the Isle of Grain. Tass Parker and Jack MacDonald, a hideously disfigured old pug who had been a chopping block for many better men, were the Slasher's seconds. Sayers' seconds were Bill Hayes and Nat Langham. Langham was a recently retired fighter, now publican, who had defeated Sayers some years earlier. Tom had been forced to retire blinded in this fight, but there had been no permanent damage to his sight.

This was indeed the Slasher's last fight. He entered the ring at the apparent peak of fitness for he had trained hard, and he left it a broken, half blind and mentally impaired man. Early in the fight Sayers struck the Slasher a violent blow on the temple. The Slasher went down like a load of wet cement and his seconds had to work very hard on him to bring him to the scratch.

I believe that the Slasher had a brain injury when he entered the ring and this chance blow activated it, for after this he fought a brainless battle. His skill and ring craft had gone and from the way in which he struck and missed he could not have been focussing properly. The contest lasted for one hour and forty-two minutes, and one of the rounds lasted fifty minutes, a record never likely to be surpassed.

Owen Swift, the Slasher's principal backer, was sickened by the slaughter and stopped the fight in favour of Sayers. The blinded Slasher, who would not surrender, was held down by the four seconds whilst the sponge was thrown in.

Twice during the contest his black eyes had been nicked and the blood sucked from them by Parker and MacDonald. This is an eye witness description of the Slasher at the end of the fight.

'Perry's face had long since lost its humanity. A hideous gash stretched from his lip to beneath his right eye. His right ear was hanging in ribbons and the blood fell copiously on to his chest. He was as mad as a baited bull. Striking the thin air where Sayers was not. For his eyes no longer saw. Where they should have been were two black swellings oozing blood.'

a. Is this fact or fiction?
What is the level of objectivity?
Is it primary or secondary evidence?
b. What phrases give you an insight into the prize ring?
c. What does it tell us about the attitudes and opinion of the people involved?
d. To what extent is this a commentary on Black Country Life?
e. Where might you go from here, if you were a social historian interested in this topic?

19.2 Factors Underlying the Origins of Sport

We need to know only a little about the origin of some of our older sports and the cultures they grew up in to set the scene.

Tribal

We have been invaded by numerous races in the distant past and each one has brought its own cultural activities with it. Some of our sports can be traced back to the Celts, Romans and, particularly, the Normans.

Ritual

Most sports and pastimes had religious and ceremonial associations, both pagan and Christian. These were joyful festival occasions held on special days. We only need to look at events associated with Shrove Tuesday and May Day to recognize this.

Survival

Many ancient sports have their origin in fitness to survive in dangerous surroundings; the ability to obtain food; and military efficiency with a weapon. Often there has been an interesting transition from functional to recreative in activities linked with survival.

Recreative

In all societies children copy adults in their play. Similarly, all civilizations seem to reach a point where the level of maturity is measured in the recreative pursuits of their leading citizens and the violent activities of the lower orders.

REVIEW QUESTION

Without presuming that an activity necessarily belongs in only one category, can you explain the placement of the following activities:
stag hunting, mob football, archery, pancake races and real tennis.

19.3 The Pattern of Popular Recreation in Great Britain

The term **popular recreation** is used to describe natural, often violent, sports and pastimes, which were part of an ancient feudal right to recreation, claimed by all branches of the rural community.

Try to explain the following precepts. This may require you to read extracts from Brailsford (1969), Ford (1977) or Malcolmson (1973).

Some **popular recreation** precepts:

- Feudal basis of the **courtly** and the **popular: courtly** with courtesy and high culture; **popular** with peasant vulgarity and low culture.
- Both an inherent part of the **Merrie England** concept.
- **Conservatism** of the **rural gentry** not wishing to change the natural order of country life, with the **escapism** of the **peasant class.**
- Attacked by the **clergy** as decadent and irreligious; by the **middle classes** because it offended their sense of decency; and by the **industrialists** because they needed a disciplined **workforce.**
- **Popular recreation** against the **Protestant work ethic.**

The second step is to link these **precepts** with the **social groups** and **activities** shown in Figure 19.4; and explain why certain **reforms** took place.

Some Landmarks you ought to know about.

You should be aware of the Tailteann Games. Watman (1968) tells us they originated around 2000 BC in County Meath, Eire, and continued until AD 1168 with the Norman Conquest of Ireland. It is probable that similar Celtic games existed in Britain at least until the Roman Conquest.

Now to the Romans. Read this extract to get a picture of Roman Britain:

It is unlikely that these sports ever included athletics meetings on the Greek pattern. The nearest point to Britain at which such meetings are known to have been held is Vienne, in the Rhône valley near Lyons. The athletics festivals in this city, established by a bequest in the will of a citizen, were abolished about AD 100 by a magistrate, and on appeal to the Emperor his decision was upheld. The reason for the abolition was that the meetings constituted a danger to the morals of the citizens; such was the reputation of Greek professional athletes in the Roman world at this time. If Greek sport was on the retreat in this way in a part of Gaul where, owing to the influence of the Greek cities of Marseilles, Nice and Antibes, it had earlier been strong, it is highly improbable that it would have crossed the Channel into Britain.

On the other hand, it is certain that the exhibitions of the arena were available in Britain. A dozen amphitheatres have been identified in the province. Two of them are well known, Maumbury Rings at Dorchester in Wessex and the arena of the legionary fortress at Caerleon. These do not compare in size with the vast structures on the Continent. The oval arena of each is roughly half the size of a soccer pitch; the amphitheatre of the small fort at Tomen-y-Mûr, beautifully situated among the hills of Merioneth, would hardly accommodate a tennis court. There is little direct evidence of the entertainment provided in these places, but there is no reason to suppose that in this respect Britain differed from other parts of the Empire. A vase in Colchester Museum depicts gladiators and bear-baiting; it was almost certainly made in East Anglia, and this suggests a familiarity with these subjects in the province. The smaller arenas may well have exhibited cock-fighting, a popular pursuit among the Romans.

Figure 19.3 Popular recreation: the right to participate regardless of personal risk.

The same degree of uncertainty hovers over the question whether the provincials of Roman Britain were able to enjoy chariot racing. A mosaic found in a Roman villa at Horkstow in Lincolnshire and now in the British Museum depicts a chariot race. This of course merely shows that the owner of the villa was interested in racing; it does not prove that the racing took place in Britain.

Source: Harris, 1975.

Compare this with the following extract which refers to the contribution made by the Saxons in sporting terms:

Indeed, it is not by any means surprising, under the Saxon government, when the times were generally very turbulent, and the existence of peace exceedingly precarious, and when the personal exertions of the opulent were so often necessary

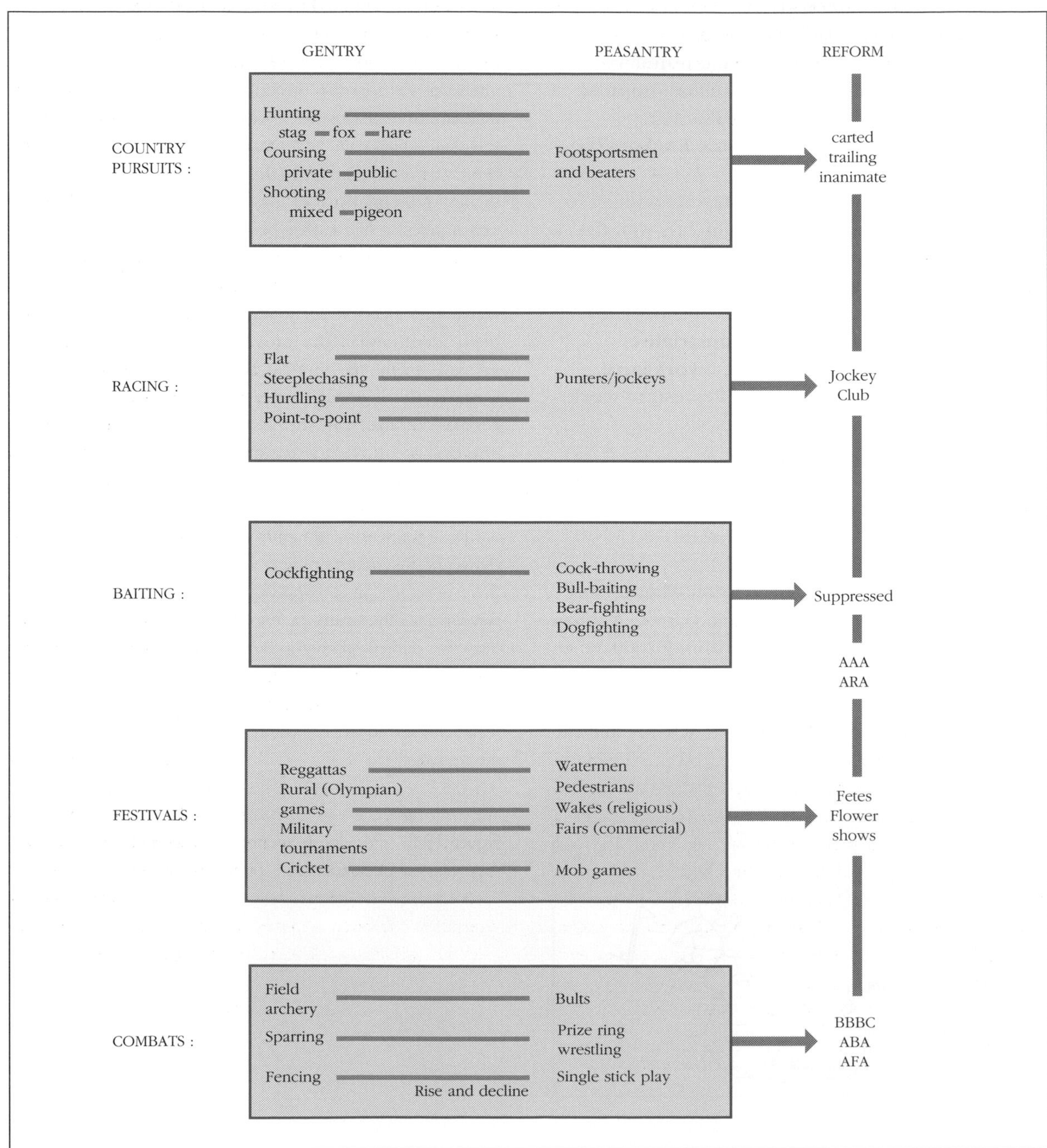

Figure 19.4

for the preservation of their lives and property, that such exercises as inured the body to fatigue, and biassed the mind to military pursuits, should have constituted the chief part of a young nobleman's education: accordingly, we find that hunting, hawking, leaping, running, wrestling, casting of darts, and other pastimes which necessarily required great exertions of bodily strength, were taught them in their adolescence. These amusements engrossed the whole of their attention, every one striving to excel his fellow; for hardiness, strength, and valour, out-balanced, in the public estimation, the accomplishments of the mind; and therefore literature, which flourishes best in tranquillity and retirement, was considered as a pursuit unworthy the notice of a soldier, and only requisite in the gloomy recesses of the cloister.

Among the vices of the Anglo-Saxons may be reckoned their propensity to gaming, and especially with the dice, which they derived from their ancestors.

Source: Strutt, 1801.

By the 15th century, pagan and Christian recreations were hopelessly intertwined within the concept of **Merrie England.** These extracts from Strutt (1801), Malcolmson (1973) and Brailsford (1969) should set the scene:

May Day Festivals

This custom, no doubt, is a relic of one more ancient, practised by the Heathens, who observed the last four days in April, and the first of May, in honour of the goddess Flora. An old Romish calendar, cited by Mr. Brand, says, on the 30th of April the boys go out to seek May-trees, 'Maii arbores a pueris exquirunter.' Some consider the May-pole as a relic of Druidism; but I cannot find any solid foundation for such an opinion.

It should be observed, that the May-games were not always celebrated upon the first day of the month; and to this we may add the following extract from Stow: 'In the month of May the citizens of London of all estates, generally in every parish, and in some instances two or three parishes joining together, had their several mayings, and did fetch their may-poles with divers warlike shows; with good archers, morrice-dancers, and other devices for pastime, all day long; and towards evening they had stage-plays and bonfires in the streets. These great mayings and may-games were made by the governors and masters of the city, together with the triumphant setting up of the great shaft or principal maypole in Cornhill.

Source: Strutt, 1801.

Bull-running in Stamford

Bull-running was a prominent diversion in Tutbury, Staffordshire, Stamford, Lincolnshire, and perhaps one or two other towns. The bull-running in Stamford, held on the 13th of November, was a major festive occasion for the town and its surrounding countryside which attracted each year hundreds of spectators and participants. The sport was essentially a free-for-all bull-fight without weapons, or at best with only sticks and heavy staffs; it seems to have been much like some of the bull-runnings recently (or still) found in parts of France and Spain, and it was characterized by a similar sort of carnival atmosphere. On the morning of the 13th the entrances to the main streets were barricaded, shops were shut up, and at eleven o'clock, with the bells of St Mary's tolling his arrival, a bull was released from a stable to the swarms of onlookers and participants (called 'bullards') who packed the street. The excitement was provided by the ensuing confusion and disorder, and by displays of daring in tormenting the bull—by throwing irritants at him, perhaps, or by baiting him with a red effigy and then manoeuvring out of his way. A talented bullard might pack himself in an open-ended barrel and roll it at the bull: the objective here was to provoke him to toss the barrel, and yet at the same time to avoid getting dislodged or mauled. 'If he be tame,' wrote a hostile observer in 1819, 'he is soon surrounded by the *canaille,* and *loaded,* as the bullards express it; that is, some have hold of his horns, and others his ears, some are beating his sides with bludgeons, and others are hanging at his tail.' A man in trouble would be aided by diversionary antics from his friends. Sometimes the bull was stormed by groups, and often he was simply chased through the streets. After an intermission for lunch the bull was again let loose, but this time he was driven towards the main bridge spanning the Welland River. The bullards surrounded him on the bridge and together lifted him over the parapet and into the water: this was known as 'brigging' the bull. He would shortly make his way to the adjacent meadow where a few dogs might be set upon him (though he was not tied down), and where bullards would give chase for a while around the muddy lowland. In late afternoon he was escorted back to town, frustrated and fatigued no doubt, but not usually mutilated. He was then slaughtered and sometimes the meat was sold cheaply to the poor or served up in the public houses. The odd bull which had refused to be 'brigged' was spared his life.

Source: Malcolmson, 1973.

Festival Wakes

The inhabitants of Stone, Staffordshire, where the church was dedicated to St. Michael and All Angels, celebrated their patronal festival with bull-baiting, bear-baiting, dog-fighting and cock-fighting.

Source: Brailsford, 1969.

a. Can you now describe the atmosphere at Stamford on 13 November 1819?
b. Can you explain what was meant by a Wake?
c. Do you understand the ritual associated with Medieval festivals?

We know that the Norman Conquest led to the establishment of our present nobility. It also led to the development of the **tournament** and the clear division of sports into **courtly** and **popular.**

Use Figure 19.5 to describe this class divide through an explanation of the **joust** as against the **quintain.**

You need to know something about the Tudor Dynasty and athleticism. Henry VIII was a champion of most sports, but he also restricted certain activities to the nobility. Figure 19.6 shows Henry throwing the hammer, but he was also a great horseman and a champion real tennis player.

The blackest time for sports in English history was during and after the Civil War (1649). The country was divided into two complex groups. The Royalists tended to be gentry, rural and High Church, while the Parliamentarians or Roundheads were largely merchant class, urban and Low Church. The success of Cromwell led to an imposition of a Puritan life style which continued as an ethic for the lower classes for many years after the Restoration.

Popular recreation was criticized on religious grounds as well as being identified with the King's Book of Sports.

Read the following extract and summarize the place of popular recreation before the Civil War:

And as for Our good people's lawfull Recreation, Our pleasure likewise is, That, after the end of Divine Service, Our good people be not disturbed, letted, or discouraged from any lawful recreation, Such as dancing, either of men or women, Archery for men, leaping, vaulting, or any other such harmless Recreation, nor from having of May Games, Whitson Ales, and Morris-dances, and the setting up of Maypoles, and other sports therewith used, so as the same be had in due and convenient time, without impediment or neglect of Divine Service: And that women shall have leave to carry rushes to the Church for the decoring of it, according to their old custom. But withal we doe here account still as prohibited all unlawful games to bee used upon Sundayes onely, as Beare and Bullbaitings, Interludes, and at all times, in the meaner sort of people, by law prohibited. Bowling: And likewise we barre from this benefit and liberty, all such knowne recusants, either men or women, as will abstaine from comming to Church or Divine Service, that will not first come to the Church and serve God: Prohibiting, in like sort, the said Recreations to any that, though conform in Religion, are not present in the Church at the Service of God, before their going to the said Recreations.

Source: Govett L.A. *King's Book of Sports,* 1890.

Figure 19.5 Jousting.

Figure 19.6 Henry VIII hammer throwing.

Figure 19.7 The Dover Games were revived after the Restoration of Charles II. The picture shows the types of activities which were re-introduced. Source: Whitfield C. *Robert Dover and the Cotswold Games, 1962.*

a. How many activities can you name?
b. To what extent were the old 'courtly' and 'popular' concepts revived too?

Some of the cruellest popular recreations were not revived. Cock-throwing, which involved throwing sticks or stones at a tethered cockerel, was banned, but cockfighting continued; and bear-baiting became less popular, even though bull-baiting continued.

A COUNTRY IN TRANSITION

The Puritan Ethic of the 17th century gave way to the Protestant Ethic in the 1700s, marking the birth of Britain as an industrial nation; as a world power; and as a centre of Evangelism. If these three forces were not enough, the conservatism of rural England was shaken by the emergence of a Regency clientele, where high living in fashionable spa surroundings; architectural genius; and the Fancy dominated upper-class life. The Fancy was a mixed group of 'sportsmen' who were preoccupied with horse-racing, cockfighting and the prize ring: totally consumed by the blood, sweat and wager of the contest.

The date which is often used to identify these seeds of change is 1760. Let's look in a little more detail at the three major 'revolutions'.

The **industrial revolution** began with the increased use of coal in smelting and led to factories and industrialists taking over from the ancient cottage industry controlled by independent craftsmen.

This machine age came to the countryside, reducing labour-intensity at the same time that enclosure marked a reduction in common land. This was an **agrarian revolution** which forced countless farm labourers to take their families to the towns in search of work. It is also important to recognize that the prospect of industrial wages attracted the more ambitious farm workers to the towns.

With machine-operated factories, an expanding capitalist economy and abundant cheap labour, the industrial towns expanded at a tremendous rate, a phenomenon which has been called an **urban revolution.** Though this is often identified as a working class population expansion, it also marked the emergence of a powerful, respectable, urban middle class.

In older towns, this led to many of the old slums being cleared and fashionable shopping centres being built. Each major town became a corporation and built its own town hall, free library, cottage hospital and public swimming baths.

In the heavily industrialized towns, factories and smoke replaced green fields, and tightly packed, back-to-back, terraced houses were built as near to the factory as possible. From 6 a.m. to 6 p.m. for six days a week, men, women and children worked in the 'satanic mills'.

We now need to consider the impact of these changes on popular recreation. Let's look at **country pursuits** first.

Despite the growth of towns, country life continued much as before, particularly as it concerned the **landed gentry.**

THE GROWTH OF FOX HUNTING

Figure 19.8 shows the older sport of **otter hunting.** Today, the otter is protected and most people regard it as a lovable creature. In the 19th century, it was hunted and killed mercilessly.

Figure 19.8 Otter hunting.

Try to explain the Victorian attitude to otter hunting and why we feel differently today.

THE SPORT OF GREYHOUND COURSING

This ancient sport was very popular in rural England throughout the 19th century. Hares were 'flushed' out of 'cover' and two greyhounds were 'unleashed' by the 'slipper', and the dog which made the 'pussy' deviate the most times won the 'course'.

Can you interpret this statement and also establish the attractions of such an event at that time?

Figure 19.10 Coursing.

Fox hunting, on the other hand, is still very popular in many parts of the country, although there is an increasingly vociferous lobby against it—manifested most vividly by the activities of the hunt saboteurs.

Figure 19.9 Fox hunting.

Can you identify the attractions of fox hunting to the landed gentry in the 19th century—taking as an example the athleticism required?

THE REFLECTIVE AND SPORTING PASTIME OF ANGLING

Izaak Walton identified a sport for every man, but 19th century work patterns and pollution resulted in a class divide for 'game' and 'coarse' fishing.

Explain this statement in the context of the 'revolutions' we considered earlier.

Figure 19.11 Fishing and fowling in a village.

FALCONRY AND THE ART OF SHOOTING

You may have seen the film *Kes*. It was about the relationship between a boy and a kestrel.

Can you examine this and other elements in the sport of **falconry**?

Figure 19.12 Falconry.

Mixed shooting also had a similar attachment, this time between a man and his gun-dog. Though falconry as a sport is no longer acceptable, pheasant and grouse shooting are.

How do you account for this? Is it social privilege, marksmanship, food for the table or something else?

Figure 19.13 Mixed shooting.

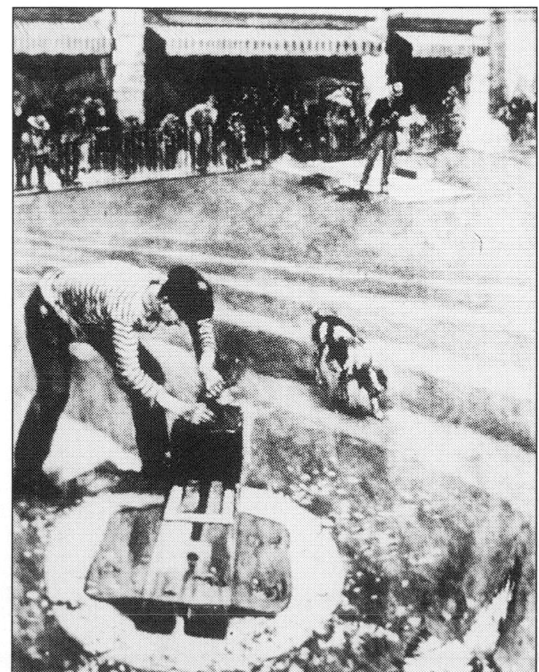

Figure 19.14 Pigeon shooting.

Pigeon shooting was equally popular, with birds sprung from traps for marksmen to shoot at, but now society has changed this to **clay pigeon shooting.**

Why should pigeon shooting have been curtailed, when mixed shooting survived?

HORSE RACING AND BLOOD SPORTS: THE TRADITIONAL FESTIVAL OCCASIONS

Horse racing is as old as horse riding. The nature of man is to make a contest in any unpredictable situation which allows him to wager his competence against another. Horse racing had two distinct phases of development. The first took place in the reign of Queen Anne when three arabian stallions started bloodstock breeding in Britain. The second came when the railways allowed horses and crowds access to different racing centres, resulting in a well organized **racing calendar.**

Figure 19.15 Horse racing.

Use this photograph of Epsom Races to explain the level of organization in flat racing at that time.

Figure 19.16 Steeplechasing.

This picture gives clues as to the development of steeplechasing. Use this visual evidence to explain what might have happened.

Blood sports were relics of an earlier period. They were extremely cruel, but arguably reflected a cruel society, where the function of animals was either to work or entertain.

Cockfighting went hand-in-glove with the **races.** **Bull-baiting** could always be guaranteed to attract a crowd.

Figure 19.17 Cockfighting.

This picture shows two fighting cocks, with an apparently respectable crowd. The birds will fight to the death; there will be blood and feathers everywhere; money will change hands, but not until a cock has crowed. Can you appreciate the attraction at a time when a person was hanged for stealing a sheep?

Figure 19.18 Bull-baiting.

Can you apply the attractions of the cockfight to bull-baiting, thus explaining its popularity at that time? Can you link this with refrigeration and beating a steak before cooking it? Can you explain why we no longer bait our bulls and yet bull fighting is still acceptable in some countries? Can you link this analysis with shooting, where the gun-dog has been replaced by a bull terrier, but man has a similar chance to test his training and breeding skills, and put his money on them?

POPULAR SPORTING FESTIVALS AND PEDESTRIANISM

The term **pedestrian** referred to a group of lower class individuals who earned part of their living by competing in certain sports for money. It was a fore-runner of the term **professional.** One of the earliest examples of this was in sculling. Thames watermen competed for the Doggett Coat and Badge on the 1st August annually from 1715. It arose from the idea of wager boats. Small boats ferried passengers across the Thames and wagers were struck to see who could get across first.

A similar situation existed on the roads, in that the upper class employed footmen on their coaches who took part in wager footraces. These developed to challenge events over long distances with wagers being made on the result or on the 'walker' completing his self-imposed task. One of the most famous occasions of this type occurred in 1800 when Captain Barclay completed 1,000 miles in 1,000 hours for 1,000 guineas.

These events became very popular, attracting huge crowds on the major horserace courses. The best-known competitors were the two Americans, Deerfoot who toured Britain in the 1860s, accepting challenges at all distances; and Weston, who walked 2,000 miles in 2,000 hours around Britain in the 1870s and gave a lecture on 'abstinence' each evening.

Figure 19.19 Doggett race.

Figure 19.20 Pedestrianism.

Here we have a 'ped' versus a 'gent'. Can you list their motives for competing?

Figure 19.21 Deerfoot, the great American pedestrian.

Use this picture to explain why Deerfoot was as much a show-man as a competitor.

Early **cricket professionals** fitted much the same mould. They were paid wages to keep the ground in order, coach gentlemen players and play when wager matches were arranged.

Figure 19.22 Hampshire cricket in the 18th century.

What aspects of this picture lead you to think it is an 18th-century example of cricket?

Figure 19.23 Hampshire v. Surrey.

Here is a women's county cricket match in 1835. Can you recognize similar characteristics to the men's game, and note the freedom of female opportunity prior to Victorian constraints?

THE SURVIVAL OF FOLK GAMES

Folk games were occasional contests between different groups in a community and often involved considerable violence. By the 19th century many of them had been suppressed, but some survived as an annual event in more isolated towns. You may have heard of the **Ashbourne Football,** the **Haxey Hood Game, Lutterworth Mob Hockey,** the **Hallaton Bottle Game,** and mob football at **Atherstone** and **Derby.**

Dunning and Sheard (1979) produced a framework to show the structural properties of these folk games (Figure 19.24).

Can you set up a mob game situation, like mat-bat and compare it with a modern game like volleyball, using a simplified version of the Dunning and Sheard framework.

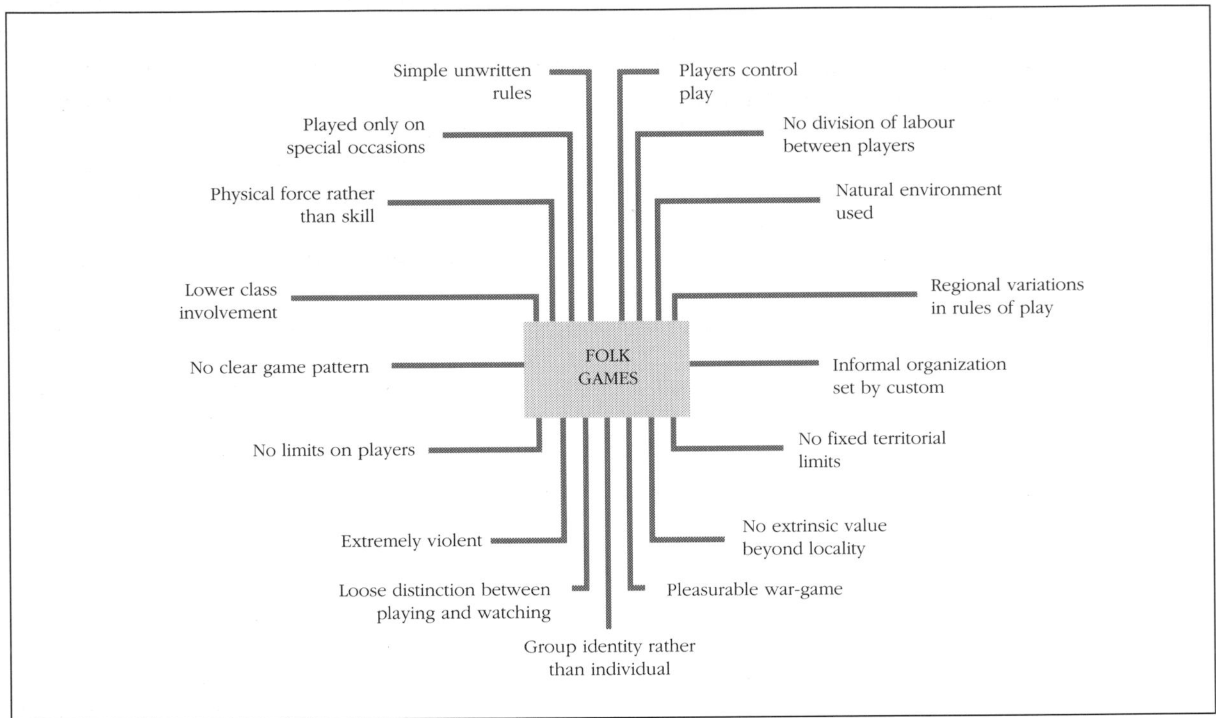
FOLK GAMES
Simple unwritten rules
Played only on special occasions
Physical force rather than skill
Lower class involvement
No clear game pattern
No limits on players
Extremely violent
Loose distinction between playing and watching
Group identity rather than individual
Players control play
No division of labour between players
Natural environment used
Regional variations in rules of play
Informal organization set by custom
No fixed territorial limits
No extrinsic value beyond locality
Pleasurable war-game

Figure 19.24 Structural properties of folk games.

Figure 19.25 Town mob football.

Figure 19.26 Rural mob football.

The following is the account of the Derby game given by Glover in his *History of Derbyshire*, published in 1829:

The contest lies between the parishes of St. Peter's and All Saints, and the goals to which the ball is taken are 'Nun's Mill' for the latter and the Gallows balk on the Normanton Road for the former. None of the other parishes in the borough take any direct part in the contest, but the inhabitants of all join in the sport, together with persons from all parts of the adjacent country. The players are young men from eighteen to thirty or upwards, married as well as single, and many veterans who retain a relish for the sport are occasionally seen in the very heat of the conflict. The game commences in the market-place, where the partisans of each parish are drawn up on each side, and about noon a large ball is tossed up in the midst of them. This is seized upon by some of the strongest and most active men of each party. The rest of the players immediately close in upon them and a solid mass is formed. It then becomes the object of each party to impel the course of the crowd towards their particular goal. The struggle to obtain the ball, which is carried in the arms of those who have possessed themselves of it, is then violent, and the motion of the human tide heaving to and fro without the least regard to consequences is tremendous. Broken shins, broken heads, torn coats, and lost hats are amongst the minor accidents of this fearful contest, and it frequently happens that persons fall owing to the intensity of the pressure, fainting and bleeding beneath the feet of the surrounding mob. But it would be difficult to give an adequate idea of this ruthless sport. A Frenchman passing through Derby remarked, that if Englishmen called this playing, it would be impossible to say what they would call fighting. Still the crowd is encouraged by respectable persons attached to each party, who take a surprising interest in the result of the day's sport, urging on the players with shouts, and even handing to those who are exhausted oranges and other refreshment. The object of the St. Peter's party is to get the ball into the water down the Morledge brook into the Derwent as soon as they can, while the All Saints party endeavour to prevent this and to urge the ball westward. The St. Peter players are considered to be equal to the best water spaniels, and it is certainly curious to see two or three hundred men up to their chins in the Derwent continually ducking each other. The numbers engaged on both sides exceed a thousand, and the streets are crowded with lookers-on. The shops are closed, and the town presents the aspect of a place suddenly taken by storm.

Source: Shearman M. *Athletics and Football.*

How does this description match up with the folk game framework?

Here is a modern description of the Haxey Hood Game:

There is, for instance the Haxey Hood Game in Leicestershire, in which tightly rolled lengths of sacking are used. There is, perhaps, something sinister about the ritualistic method of play, which it has been suggested could be symbolic of the struggle between winter and summer. However, the legend behind the game does not support this theory of the struggle between the seasons. It is said that sometime in the 13th century, while riding on the Isle of Axeholme, Lady Mowbray lost her hood. It was found and returned by 12 peasants from the village of Haxey. As a reward she gave to the village a piece of land, thence called the Hoodland, the rent from which had to be used to buy hoods each year to be played for by 12 villagers. The game is also thought to have been played at Epworth on the Isle of Axeholme.

On the Eve of St. John (23 June) each year at Haxey a committee is elected consisting of 12 *Boggons*—sometimes called *Boggans* or *Boggins*—one *King Boggon* and a fool.

On the following day at 2 pm, to the pealing of the church bells, the committee meet dressed in scarlet jerkins and tall hats, except for the Fool who wears a grotesque costume; he has his face blacked and smeared with red ochre and is dressed in trousers of sackcloth with coloured patches and a red shirt. On his head he wears a tall hat with a goose's wing and red flowers adorning it. He carries a short-stocked whip on the end of which is a sock filled with bran.

The boggons then go up to the top of Haxey Hill. There, on the village boundary, they form a circle with the King Boggon in the centre holding 13 hoods. The King Boggon throws a hood and if someone other than a Boggon catches it he tries to run to a nearby public house while the Boggons attempt to stop him. If he succeeds in reaching the pub he demands a shilling. If, on the other hand, he is caught by a Boggon, the hood is returned, to be thrown up again. On the 13th hood throwing, a part of the game known as the *sway* begins. Hundreds of people join in and attempt to force the hood into a public house. If successful, drinks on the house are called for and the hood is kept on the premises for the following year.

Source: Jewell, 1977.

The Haxey Game doesn't involve a ball and the Hallaton Game starts with a scramble for hare pies and concludes with a 'bottle' kicking game. Yes, and they are still being played today! Little wonder every attempt was made to stop these activities. In the Middle Ages various kings pronounced edicts; and later local corporations established by-laws banning street football. We should also recognize the changing times which produced more effective policing; a breakdown of the old rural traditions; and the growth of middle class respectability.

There were as many alternatives involving the use of a stick, each culture seeming to have its own version. The Scots played 'shinty', the Irish 'hurley', the Cornish 'hurling' and the English 'bandy', a game normally played on ice.

Figure 19.27 Shinty at Blackheath.

Can you pick out the characteristics of this game of shinty and find out why it was being played at Blackheath in London?

Figure 19.28 One of the most famous mob hockey games was held annually at Lutterworth in Leicestershire.

How many of the mob characteristics are evident from this picture?

Find out if your own local area had a mob game. It would be a worthwhile school project to produce a description of it. For example, if you find yourself in Gloucester Cathedral, look for the mob game carving on one of the misericords and a stainglass window of a 'golfer'.

The **sophisticated exclusivity** of **real tennis** was the exact opposite to the **rustic simplicity** of **folk games.** Here was a 'courtly' game borrowed from France and developed as a reflection of high culture in Tudor England.

By the 18th and 19th centuries, the game had become the exclusive property of the nobility, supported by a servant class of professionals in the cricket mould.

If we use the Dunning and Sheard framework we now have a completely different set of characteristics (Figure 19.29).

With the rise in popularity of rackets and lawn tennis, an exclusive clientele continued to regard real tennis as the ultimate game. The courts at Lords, Queen's Club, Hampton Court and Royal Leamington Spa served simply to reflect its 'Royal' status.

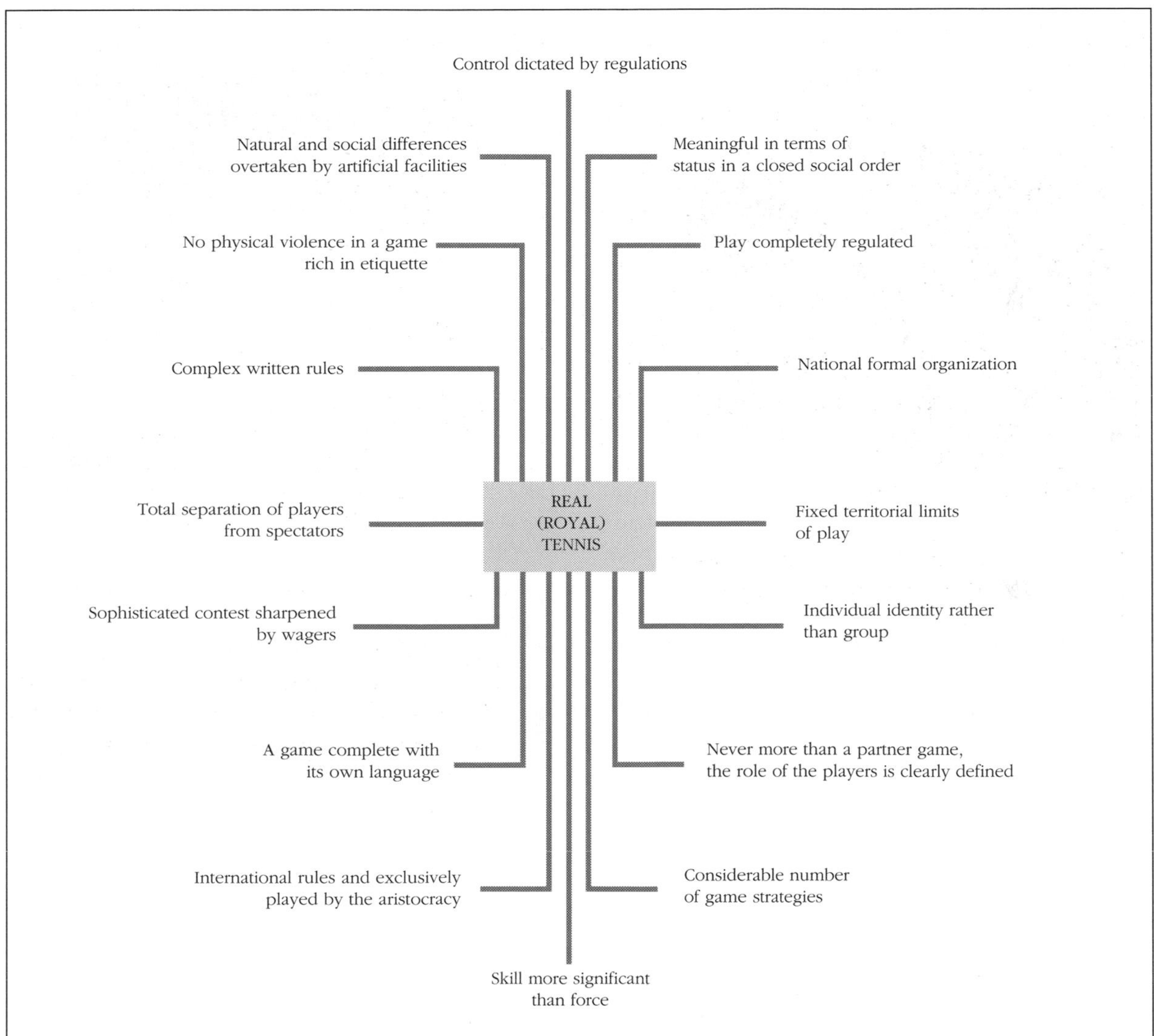

Figure 19.29 Structural properties of real tennis.

Figure 19.30 Even from this early picture of the game, you should be able to establish why it was so exclusive, but it is important to recognize what is happening outside the court of play.

Figure 19.31 This picture of the Honourable Arthur Lyttelton playing real tennis is another key to the continued status of the game. A member of the nobility and a famous diplomat, he was one of England's greatest 'Corinthians'. He was the amateur tennis champion; played cricket for England; was an outstanding soccer player, athlete and golfer; and was also a leading yachtsman.

THE RISE AND DECLINE OF CONTESTS

Archery and **fencing** share a similar history. They both involved weapons of war and so had great importance, until gunpowder made them obsolete. They would have completely disappeared but for a dedicated band of followers who first of all valued the ceremonial role of both activities and then built each into a sophisticated sport in its own right.

Figure 19.32 An early picture of archery in an English churchyard.

Figure 19.33 When archery was revived in the late eighteenth century it was part of the Regency movement, an expression of the most exclusive members of society.

How does this picture express this social elitism? Why was it acceptable for these females to participate?

a. Can you explain the transition of an activity from a military training exercise to a sport?
b. To what extent does the picture tell you whether this is military training or a sport?
c. Can you think of reasons why a churchyard might have been used for this occasion?

Unlike archery, swordplay cut across society. There was a lower class version of backswords or single sticks, and a 'courtly' version of fencing which owed its status to the duel.

Single stick play was very much part of the rural festival and the intention was to hold contests, where the winner was the first to draw blood.

Fencing, on the other hand, was retained after the sword had lost its military function, with the rapier being carried as a ceremonial weapon and used for duelling if a gentleman's honour was questioned.

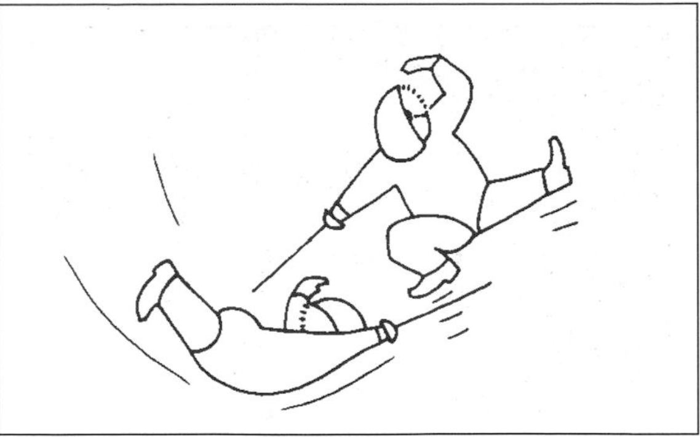

Figure 19.35 Military Sports: when does the idea of training for war change to training for sport?

Figure 19.34 Single sticks.

Figure 19.36 Fencing practice at Angelo's Academy in London. Once duelling was banned, fencing declined, only to re-emerge at the end of the 19th century as part of physical training (alongside gymnastics).

Prizefighting dates back to the 13th century when there were 'gladiatorial' schools preparing individuals to defend themselves and compete if they wished in 'sword and buckle' contests. In Henry VIII's time these so-called 'professors of defence' had formed a company entitled Masters of Defence. This was the cradle of the Noble Art of Self Defence which came to prominence in the 18th century, led by James Figg who opened the Academy of Boxing in London in 1718.

Figure 19.38 shows Figg being beaten by his pupil Jack Broughton. Broughton had already won the Doggett Coat and Badge and went on to become famous by changing the rules of the prize ring and establishing the birth of **pugilism.** He excluded weaponry and wrestling, limiting the contest to bare-knuckle punching and throws. The tradition of teaching the gentry to defend themselves continued, and it was as a result of 'sparring' that 'mufflers' were used—yes, boxing gloves!

Unfortunately, when Broughton unexpectedly lost to Jack Slack in 1750, the Duke of Cumberland, his patron, took it badly, largely because he lost a wager of £10,000, and used his influence to drive the prize ring underground. From this time the Fancy had to run the gauntlet of the police and magistrates, but when good champions came along they still attracted the crowds and huge sums of money changed hands.

Figure 19.37 Figg on the 'stage' ready to accept any challenger. As a Master of Defence he had to be able to defend himself against all-comers at swordplay, cudgels, quarterstaff or grappling. He was also employed as a tutor to 'fashionable dandies' who wished to test their skill and this occasionally included ladies.

Figure19.38 Figg and Broughton.

Figure 19.39 Cumberland wrestling.

When grappling was removed from the prize ring, **wrestling** lost much of its popularity. For many years it only survived in isolated areas, such as Cumberland and Devon, where individual styles were retained. This pattern changed when professional wrestling became part of the music hall, and when amateur wrestling was included in the revival of the Olympic Games.

Summary

Popular Recreation

1. Historical objectivity, causation and keys to the present.
2. Traditional activities of the common people. By right and by law.
3. Constraints by respectable citizens, church, law.
4. Natural, occasional—holy days, violent and riotous, sports and pastimes.
5. Romantic links with rural Merrie England.

FURTHER READING

Aberdare Lord. *The Story of Tennis,* Stanley Paul, 1959.

Bailey P. *Leisure and Class in Victorian England,* RKP, 1978.

Baker W.J. *Sports in the Western World,* Rowman & Littlefield, 1982.

Brailsford D. *Sport in Society,* RKP, 1969.

Cunningham H. *Leisure in the Industrial Society,* Croom Helm, 1980.

Dunning E. and Sheard K. *Barbarians, Gentlemen and Players,* NY, NYUP, 1979.

Ford J. *Prizefighting,* David & Charles, 1971.

Harris H.A. *Sport in Britain,* Stanley Paul, 1975.

Heath E.G. *A History of Target Archery,* David & Charles, 1973.

Jewell B. *Sports and Games,* Midas, 1977.

Kent G. *A Pictorial History of Wrestling,* Spring Books, 1968.

Lovesey P. *Kings of Distance,* Eyre & Spottiswoode, 1968.

Malcolmson R.W. *Popular Recreations in English Society,* CUP, 1973.

Strutt J. *Sports and Pastimes of the People of England,* 1801.

Vamplew W. *The Turf,* Allen Lane, 1976.

Watman M.F. *History of British Athletics,* Hale, 1968.

Wymer N. *Sport in England,* Harrap, 1949.

Young P.M. *History of British Football,* Stanley Paul, 1968.

Chapter 20
Athleticism in Nineteenth-Century English Public Schools

20.1 Background to Public School Development

In looking at popular recreation, we have mentioned the European Renaissance, which marked the rebirth of Greek 'idealism'. Our main interest lies in the re-emergence of Olympism and the associated importance of 'Man of Action' and the oft quoted phrase *'mens sana in corpore sano'* (a healthy mind in a healthy body). It is important to recognize that these values came to England at the time of the great Tudor Dynasty and so had all the more impact because Henry VIII championed athleticism as well as nationalism and intellectualism.

The education of the ruling class at this time was through tutors who imparted knowledge, but also leadership qualities as part of the education of an elite. The influence of Roger Ascham on the education of Queen Elizabeth I was considerable, particularly as it concerned his belief that archery reflected a model life style. It was at this time that the Age of Chivalry was changing to the Age of Courtesy, where men like Elyot suggested that sporting pastimes made man stronger and more valiant, without the need for life to be endangered.

Monastic Schools had existed prior to the Tudors, but the Reformation led to the dissolution of monastic churches, leaving an education void which was filled by the endowment of 'free' grammar schools by various monarchs (free in this context means free from church control). It was around this time that Mulcaster became Master of Merchant Taylors' School and recognized the value of healthy exercise for boys at the school. Unfortunately, these endowed grammar schools were very small, seldom having more than 30 boys; they were mainly local day schools; and most of the boys left school at sixteen. With such small schools, controlled by one 'Master' and consisting of just a schoolroom, there was little likelihood of anything more than mob games being played and even this was frowned upon by 'Masters' committed to the Puritan ethic.

If you want to know more about the roots of our education system, Brailsford (1969) is a very good source of information.

20.2 The Structural Basis of the English Public School System

Definitions

'An endowed place of education of old standing to which the sons of gentlemen resort in considerable numbers and where they reside from eight or nine to eighteen years of age. '

Sydney Smith, 1810.

The only important addition to this is the factor that the children tended to be 'non-local'.

It is a useful exercise for readers to find out what they can about one public school and then test their knowledge against the key definitive words identified in Figure 20.1.

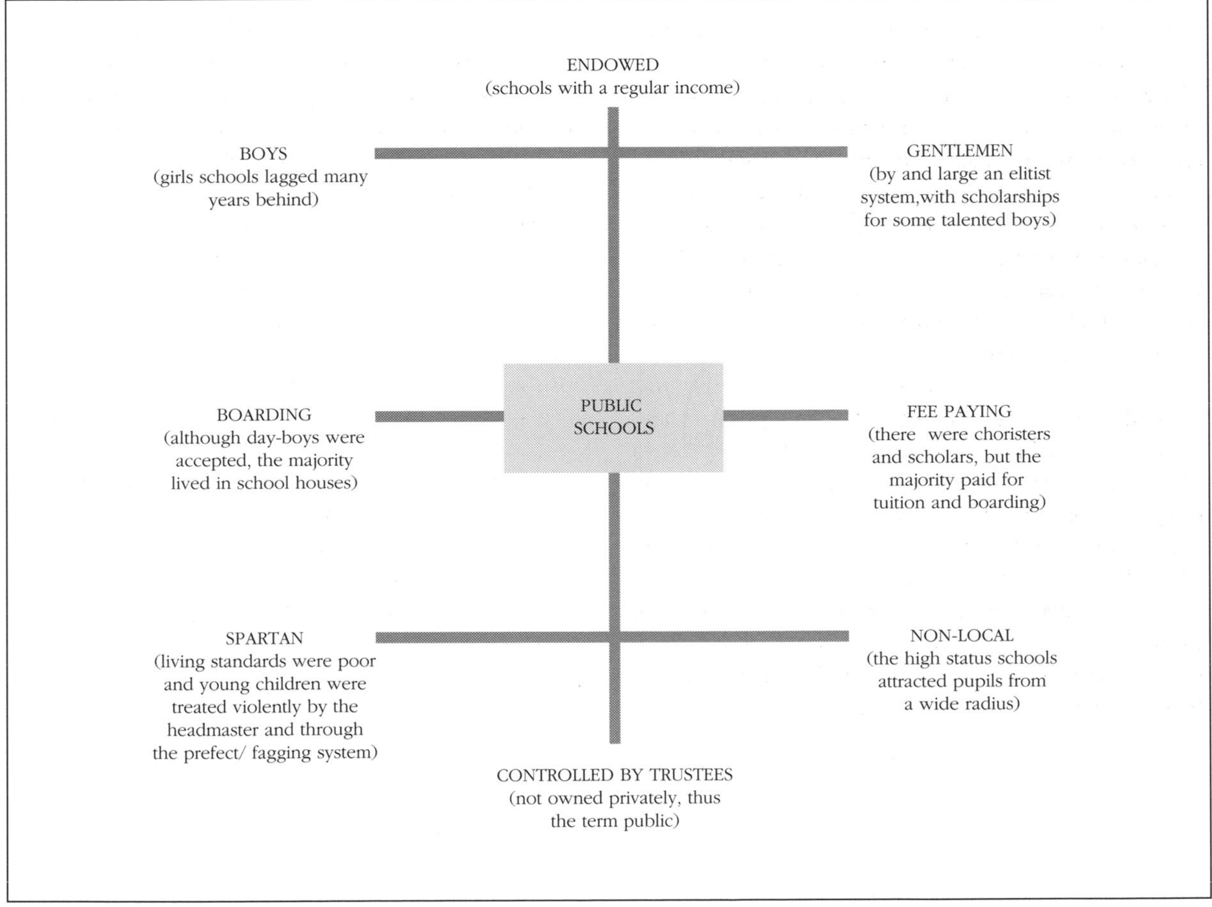

Figure 20.1

The word **athleticism** is less straightforward to define, because it was a developmental word and the full expression of public school athleticism was not achieved until the 1850s.

It had fundamental links with the:

Muscular Christian view of manliness

reflecting:

Physical endeavour and moral integrity.

It is important that you should be able to explain these values in the context of your favourite sport a hundred years ago and today.

If you feel you need to know more about the meaning of these terms in a nineteenth-century context, read some of Newsome (1961) or Percival (1973).

Figure 20.2 Athleticism: Playing according to the letter and spirit of the game.

From around 1860, a lot of changes occurred which led to an exploitation of the English gentleman's love of sport. In modern phrasiology, there was almost a 'sports school' situation. This led Smith (1974) to suggest that **athleticism** became 'the exaltation and disproportionate regard for games, which often resulted in the denigration of academic work and in anti-intellectualism.'

With so many old and new schools involved, the problem lies in deciding whether this **'cult of athleticism'** actually led to a lowering of academic standards. To assure yourselves, the group needs to study a number of different public schools to assess the extent to which this might have been the case.

TYPES OF PUBLIC SCHOOL IN THE NINETEENTH CENTURY

If you have managed to look at athletic developments in a number of public schools, you can categorize your examples using the following list and then look around for a local example of each type of school.

Clarendon Schools

Examined in the 1864 Clarendon Report, these were nine exclusive boys' schools. They were Eton, Harrow, Rugby, Shrewsbury, Charterhouse, Westminster, Winchester, St Paul's and Merchant Taylors. Each had expanded to take over 300 pupils at the end of the eighteenth century and the first seven were predominantly non-local and boarding. Matthew Arnold called them 'Barbarian' schools because they maintained the gentry tradition.

Ladies' Academies

Finishing schools for the daughters of the gentry, they were normally small and more concerned with elegance and etiquette than with academic learning.

Proprietary Colleges

These were middle class copies of the gentry schools. They were built with outstanding facilities to attract wealthy clients and eventually broke the monopoly held by the few elite schools. Cheltenham College (1841) was the first to be opened, with other famous colleges at Clifton, Marlborough and Malvern. Matthew Arnold called these proprietary schools 'Philistines' because he claimed they were simply materialistic copies of the traditional gentry schools.

Cheltenham Ladies' College (1854) was the first proprietary school for girls, but by the end of the century almost every major town had a middle-class girls' high school.

Denominational Schools

Cathedral Schools at such county towns as Canterbury, York and Worcester were ancient foundations which became Kings Schools after the Reformation, but they remained small until the 1870s.

Towards the end of the nineteenth century, the Church of England built some new boarding schools to educate **the sons** and daughters of the clergy. Lancing College is probably the most famous of these.

Endowed Grammar Schools

Almost every town in England had its own 'free' grammar school for boys, named after the king or queen who endowed it. Some of these schools built up a reputation in the mid-nineteenth century and became major public schools. The most famous of these are Uppingham, Repton and King Edward's, Birmingham. However, the majority remained small until the 1880s, when there was an expansion of secondary education for boys from the commercial classes.

In general, girls' grammar schools did not appear until the twentieth century.

PRIVATE SCHOOLS

These were owned by individuals or families. The quality of education varied considerably, but some of them, for example Malvern Girls' College, eventually became exclusive public schools. Many of these better schools had excellent sporting facilities to attract an upper-class clientele.

Figure 20.3 This view of Malvern College shows the impressive school buildings facing the playing fields.

Figure 20.4 Although this picture is called 'The Ladies' Cricket Club', it looks as if the club could be operating within a private girls' school.

20.3 The Technical Development of Sports in the Public Schools

Though this was a gradual development over a period of fifty years, it is easier to review it in three stages and limit comment to gentry schools for boys; middle-class schools for boys; and middle-class girls' schools.

STAGE ONE: SCHOOLBOYS AND POPULAR RECREATION

The traditional gentry schools expanded at the end of the eighteenth century, resulting in a considerable increase in income, which led to improved facilities and staffing. This started a spiral which in turn led to a small number of schools becoming exclusive and being able to charge higher fees.

Boarding gave the boys a great deal of time together outside the classroom, and in their free time they played the games they had learnt at home. They were entirely organized by the boys and ranged from the relative sedateness of cricket to the violence of mob football; from illegal poaching to organized hare and hounds; from casual boating to rackets in the 'quad'.

In *Tom Brown's School Days,* Thomas Hughes writes about the sports Tom experienced at home.

The great times for back-swording came round once a year in each village, at the feast. The Vale 'veasts' were not the common statute feasts, but much more ancient business. They are literally, so far as one can ascertain, feasts of the dedication, i.e. they were first established in the churchyard on the day on which the village church was opened for public worship, which was on the wake or festival of the patron Saint, and have been held on the same day in every year since that time.

In fact the only reason why this is not the case still, is that gentlefolk and farmers have taken to other amusements, and have, as usual, forgotten the poor. They don't attend the feasts themselves, and call them disreputable, whereupon the steadiest of the poor leave them also, and they become what they are called. Class amusements, be they for dukes or plough-boys, always become nuisances and curses to a country. The true charm of cricket and hunting is, that they are still more or less sociable and universal; there's a place for every man who will come and take his part.

Upper-class boys were taking these popular sports to the schools. How does Hughes offset the values of rural sports against the intolerance of authorities?

Some headmasters did their best to stop the more violent activities taking place in school. You will probably know the famous phrase by Butler of Shrewsbury 'Football is only suitable for butchers' boys', but at the same time he condoned cricket and was only critical of rowing because of the danger of drowning. Meanwhile, there seems to have been support for cricket and rowing at Eton and Westminster before the nineteenth century, and the Harrow authorities did not attempt to curtail arehery or rackets.

In reality, the early headmasters were powerless to stop any of these activities, particularly when they took place away from the school. Flogging was the normal punishment for any kind of disobedience, but, occasionally, there were cases of rioting in the schools and then it was necessary for the militia to be brought in.

Most of the problems arose when boys went into the town or travelled to other schools. There was invariably a great deal of drunkenness and riotous behaviour. Some of the rural sports carried with them a tradition of drinking and gambling, which the boys were only to keen to include in their school life.

A number of key features are associated with this initial phase of school sport. The boys brought the games into the schools and were responsible for their organization. They had the opportunity to play them regularly and so the occasional popular recreations became part of a continuous season of play, and this had a major impact on the regularization of rules. Some sports were already socially acceptable and these were encouraged by the school authorities and, with regular play possible, standards of performance improved dramatically.

Where the sports lacked existing rules, the facilities available at the school determined the developmental form of the activity. For example: the 'Close' at Rugby with its soft turf; the 'Quad' at Charterhouse, where the 'dribbling' game emerged; and the unique version of mob football found at Eton, where the 'wall game' was instituted.

Figure 20.5 Racket ball being played in the cloisters at Harrow School.

Figure 20.6 The Eton Wall Game.

Take any example of a primitive game in a public school and explain why it developed its unique qualities.

STAGE TWO: ARNOLDIAN INFLUENCE AND THE ROLE OF A CHRISTIAN GENTLEMAN

In 1828, Dr Thomas Arnold was appointed head of Rugby School and died in office fourteen years later. For well over a century he has been regarded as the father of public school athleticism, largely as a result of the impact of *Tom Brown's School Days* in 1857.

Many modern writers, including McIntosh (1952), Ogilvie (1957), Bamford (1967) and Percival (1973), recognized that Arnold was one of a number of progressive headmasters, who established an environment which eventually stimulated athleticism. It is important that you recognize the modern change of emphasis. For example; McIntosh suggested that:

> *'While it is probable that Arnold's reforms at Rugby indirectly encouraged the growth of athleticism, both there and in other schools, it is improbable that he was immediately responsible for the change of attitude or that he himself approved of athleticism. '*

Figure 20.7 Rugby at Rugby School. Dr Arnold was watching this game with a royal visitor. Something he would hardly have done if he had been against the game.

For example, it was Dr Thomas James (1778-1794), who initially expanded Rugby School and it is now felt that many of Arnold's ideas came from the reforms he had seen operating at Winchester School under Dr W.S. Goodall. It has been successfully argued that Arnold was much more concerned with moral reform—a desire to produce Christian Gentlemen—than to promote a Muscular Christian tradition. He believed in a form of 'manly piety' which was moral, intellectual and social rather than physical.

The safest analysis is to recognize that the athletic momentum came from the boys, and Arnold was astute enough to use this enthusiasm to achieve a range of moral reforms, which hinged on the boys being given responsibility. Even this level of intention was questioned by Bamford (1967) when he suggested that Arnold's reputation was the consequence of nostalgic staff loyalty; the enthusiasm of some old Rugbeians; and a 'train of fortuitous circumstances' of which the emergence of rugby football as a national game had particular relevance.

Having identified the supposed 'accident' of events, it is important to mention Wymer (1953) who had access to Arnold's family records. He suggests that Thomas Arnold loved cricket to the degree of having his children tutored in the game; that his life-long friendship with the Wordsworths reflected his love of the Lake District and mountain walking; and that his enjoyment of swimming, shooting, sailing and riding suggested that he had a high regard for healthy physical activity.

However, there was a direct conflict between Arnold's moral stance and some of the field sports pursued in the school. He was not prepared to allow poaching, fishing or any activity which involved trespass, on the grounds that it caused friction between the school and the community. On the other hand, he made no attempt to interfere with cricket or football.

Tom Brown's School Days may be romantic recollections of someone's childhood, but there is much to be learnt from reading some of the sporting incidents.

Read this extract on a cricket match and see if you can identify the values that the game is presumed to have had:

'Come, none of your irony, Brown,' answers the master. 'I'm beginning to understand the game scientifically. What a noble game it is, too!'

'Isn't it? But it's more than a game. It's an institution,' said Tom.

'Yes' said Arthur, 'the birthright of British boys old and young, as habeas corpus and trial by jury are of British men.'

'The discipline and reliance on one another which it teaches is so valuable, I think,' went on the master, 'it ought to be such an unselfish game. It merges the individual in the eleven; he doesn't play that he may win, but that his side may.'

'That's very true,' said Tom, 'and that's why football and cricket, now one comes to think of it, are such much better games than fives' or hare-and-hounds, or any others where the object is to come in first or to win for oneself, and not that one's side may win.'

'And then the Captain of the eleven!' said the master, 'what a post is his in our School-world! almost as hard as the Doctor's; requiring skill and gentleness and firmness, and I know not what other rare qualities.'. . .

'I am surprised to see Arthur in the eleven,' said the master, as they stood together in front of the dense crowd, which was now closing in round the ground.

'Well, I'm not quite sure that he ought to be in for his play,' said Tom, 'but I couldn't help putting him in. It will do him so much good, and you can't think what I owe him.'. . .

'I think I shall make a hand of him though,' said Tom, smiling, 'say what you will. There's something about him, every now and then, which shows me he's got pluck somewhere in him. That's the only thing after all that'll wash, ain't it....'

Finally, if Thomas Hughes is to be believed, there is a lot to be learnt about the Doctor and the role of the Sixth Form in the following extract about a fight.

What do you gather from this extract and what was to be gained from letting the fight continue?

Meantime East is freshing up Tom with the sponges for next round and has set two other boys to rub his hands.

'Tom, old boy,' whispers he, 'this may be fun for you, but it's death to me. He'll hit all the fight out of you in another five minutes, and then I shall go and drown myself in the island ditch. Feint him—use your legs! draw him about! he'll lose his wind then in no time, and you can go into him. Hit at his body too; we'll take care of his frontispiece by and by.'. . .

'Ha! Brooke. I am surprised to see you here. Don't you know that I expect the sixth to stop fighting?'

Brooke felt much more uncomfortable than he had expected, but he was rather a favourite with the Doctor for his openness and plainness of speech; so blurted out, as he walked by the Doctor's side, who had already turned back—

'Yes, sir, generally. But I thought you wished us to exercise a discretion in the matter too not to interfere too soon.'

'But they have been fighting this half-hour and more,' said the Doctor.

'Yes, sir; but neither was hurt. And they're the sort of boys who'll be all the better friends now, which they wouldn't have been if they had been stopped any earlier—before it was so equal.'

In addition to the two extracts about the cricket match against the M.C.C. and Tom's playground fight against Slogger, you should also try to read about Tom's adventures with the gamekeeper, when he goes fishing; the problems met by Tom, East and Arthur, when they try to enter the Hare and Hounds; and the famous description of the football match, where Tom decides that his help is needed to save the game.

In all five extracts, it is valuable to identify the technical changes which have occurred; to establish the different social relationships which exist; and to recognise the ethics which Thomas Hughes is promoting in this romantic portrait of public school life.

It would be wrong to assume that Thomas Arnold was alone in this process of educational reform. Kennedy of Shrewsbury; Moberly of Winchester; Wordsworth of Harrow; and Hawtry of Eton, were all 'new brooms' sweeping away a decadent system of thrashings and classics for a new wave of moral and social education, where athleticism was becoming an instrument for the promotion of a new set of values. In sporting terms, the technical changes which occurred between 1830 and 1850 hinged on the regularity of play and the responsibility of the Sixth Form to organize fixtures. In the later schools, the boarding house became an important social feature and one of the roles of the house master was to see that the boys were usefully organized, and this was often achieved through sporting competitions. The desire to get rid of antisocial elements like gambling, blood sports and poaching was commonplace, and this was achieved by attempting to limit activities to the playing fields.

Figure 20.8 The fight from Tom Brown's School Days.

Figure 20.9 This picture of Cheltenham College and its 'Playground' was typical of this second phase, where governors and trustees were now prepared to recognize the importance of sport in the life of the public schoolboy.

STAGE THREE: ATHLETICISM AND THE CORINTHIAN SPIRIT

The influence of the first generation of progressive headmasters on the pupils was so great that these young disciples carried their interpretation forward to Oxford and Cambridge. It was in the **'melting pot'** of these universities that athleticism became the all-important catalyst and the Oxford-Cambridge competitions in a wide range of sports served to identify the most talented performers. Many of these **'blues'** became assistant masters and not only coached the boys, but played for the school team when required.

It was in the twenty years following Arnold that most of the new proprietary colleges were opened and the headships were awarded to assistant masters from the gentry schools. Men like Cotton of Marlborough, Percival of Clifton and Jex-Blake of Cheltenham were typical of a new breed of headmasters who were enthusiastically in favour of athleticism as an educative medium. In human terms, therefore, the staff was now actively supporting sport in school rather than condoning it.

It was this second generation of teachers who carried athleticism into the 'Muscular Christian' era. Expansion in the size, significance and number of schools led to a massive building programme which invariably included a gymnasium and extensive playing fields. The school day included morning academic studies; afternoon games; and evenings involved in prep (homework) and House activities. The time spent on playing a particular game could be up to five hours a day, with **professional coaches** and **'blues'** producing a standard of play which raised the quality of amateur performance throughout the country.

It was in the public schools that the first football rules were written and it was the fixtures between these schools, and matches with gentlemen's clubs, which started regular organized **rational recreation.** Nor was it simply a technical development. The term rational recreation implies a moral component.

With some additional reading you should now be able to describe the technical changes which occurred in public school sport from 1800–70. The Clarendon Report (1864) gave considerable recognition to the development of athleticism in the nine elite gentry schools, and the Taunton Commission Report was published in 1868, having gathered information on 782 other public schools and colleges.

Cheltenham Ladies College was included in the Taunton Commission Report and by 1868 they had afternoon games and a wide programme, which included calisthenics, swimming and horse riding. Miss Beale, the headmistress, was not too keen on 'aggressive games' on the grounds that they were not lady-like, but she allowed tennis and rackets, and the School Council eventually persuaded her that a hockey field was also a necessity. A study of specific school histories will help you to see that despite initial opposition, all the girls' high schools had an extensive athletic programme by the turn of the century and were largely responsible for the growth of female athleticism in society at large.

Figure 20.10 Interschool rowing.

What moral elements might be promoted as a result of this rowing fixture between Eton and Westminster?

SOCIAL CONTROL THROUGH PHYSICAL ACTIVITY IN THE PUBLIC SCHOOLS

In looking at technical development, we have been concerned with **recreative and sporting** changes. A second level of analysis lies in the way various authorities used athleticism as a vehicle to control themselves and others.

Explain the changing role of the people in Figure 20.11, as school sport evolved. Comment on such things as individual and group status, discipline and leadership opportunities.

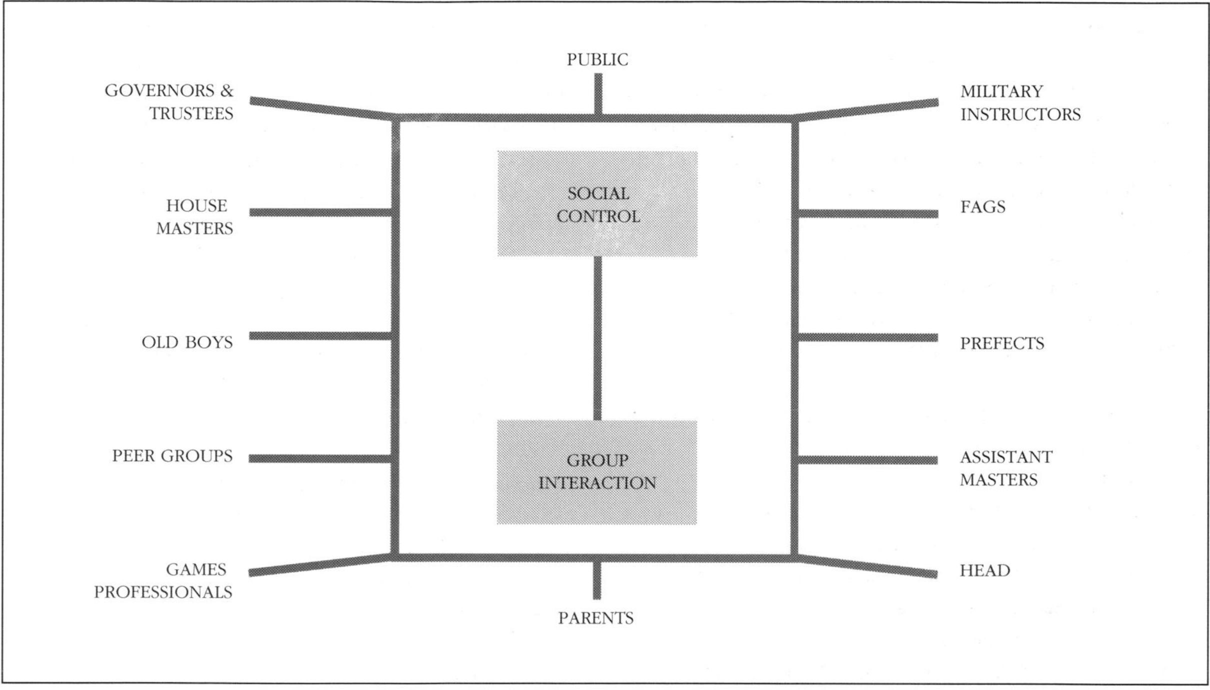

Figure 20.11

20.4 Athleticism and Character Development

Probably the most significant feature of public school athleticism was the belief that school sport was not only a vehicle for personal development, but was the essence of education, representing a model life style. It consisted of a fundamental link being made between **manliness** and **godliness** in what has been called **muscular christianity.** An educational experience involving **physical endeavour** and **moral integrity.**

You may have read Henry Newbolt's poem:

There's a breathless hush in the Close tonight
Ten to make and the match to win—
A bumping pitch and a blinding light,
An hour to play and the last man in.

The verse ends with the well known line:

Play up! Play up! and play the game.

It is easy for us to link this with a game we've played with all the tensions of a close finish, but the poet is writing about more than cricket here. He goes on to say:

The river of death has brimmed its banks
And England's far and Honour a name,
But the voice of a schoolboy rallies the ranks:
Play up! Play up! and play the game.

Can you see the importance of the game and the way you play it, if it is preparing you for life and the battlefield? In such a game, to win gracefully and to lose with honour is so much more meaningful; and to do your best could mean being willing to give your life. Honour, bravery, brotherhood, leadership—these are the values the public school saw in the games they played, and they believed that through them, these qualities became a permanent part of the player, and also of the person.

Fraser, in *The World of the Public School,* quoting Hon. R. Grimston (cricket teacher at Harrow for 50 years):

I claim for our cricket ground and football field a share, and a very considerable share too, in the formation of the character of an English gentleman. Our games require patience, good temper, perseverance, good pluck and, above all, implicit obedience. It is no bad training for the battle of life for a boy to be skinned at football, or given out wrongly at cricket, and to be able to take the affliction quietly, with good temper and in a gentlemanlike spirit.

Figure 20.14 shows an outline of the main values which the public schools linked with athleticism.

Figure 20.12 Tom's exploits at football.

Figure 20.13 Play up! Play up! And play the game!.

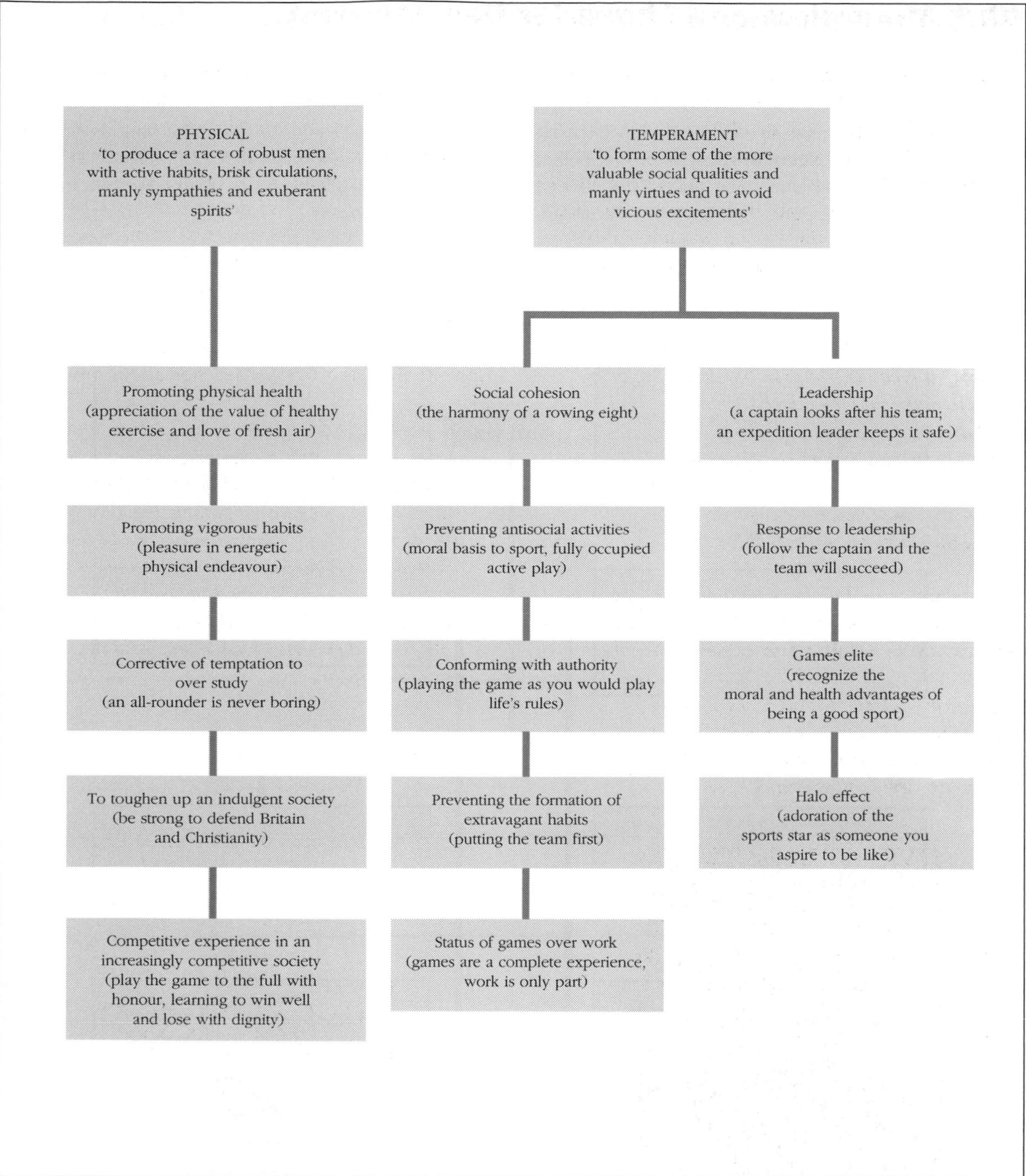

Figure 20.14 Main values linked with athleticism.

Comment on the relevance of each of these today, firstly in the context of physical eduction, and then on to the extent to which they exist in our professional sport.

20.5 The Influence of Public School Athleticism on Sport in Society

Popular recreation was in decline and was being replaced by **rational recreation.** It is probable that the development of athleticism in public schools had more influence on this trend than any other social factor. Figure 20.15 and 16 show the various ways this happened. It is important that you compare these with the present links between physical education in school and sport in society.

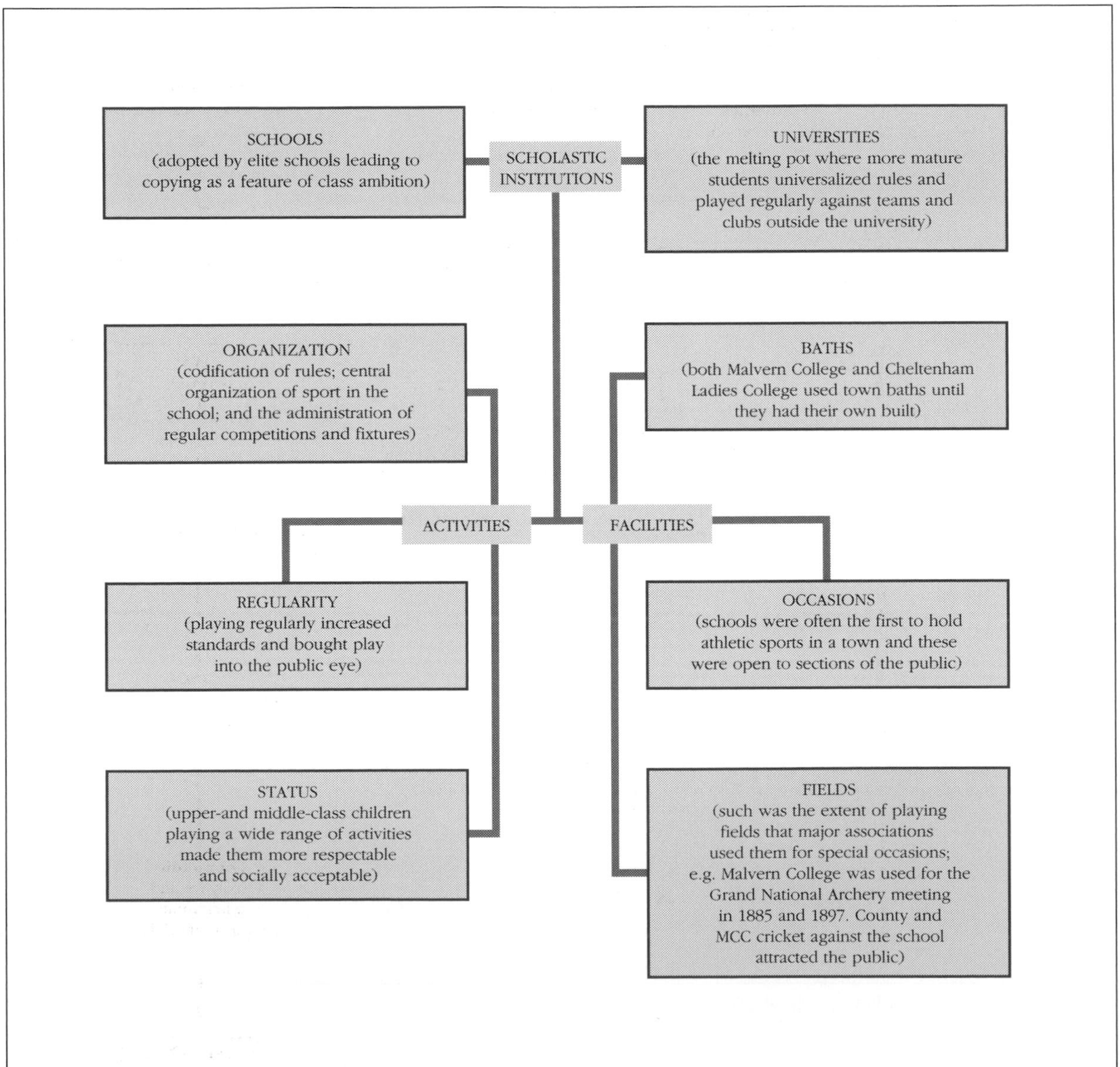

Figure 20.15 Provision.

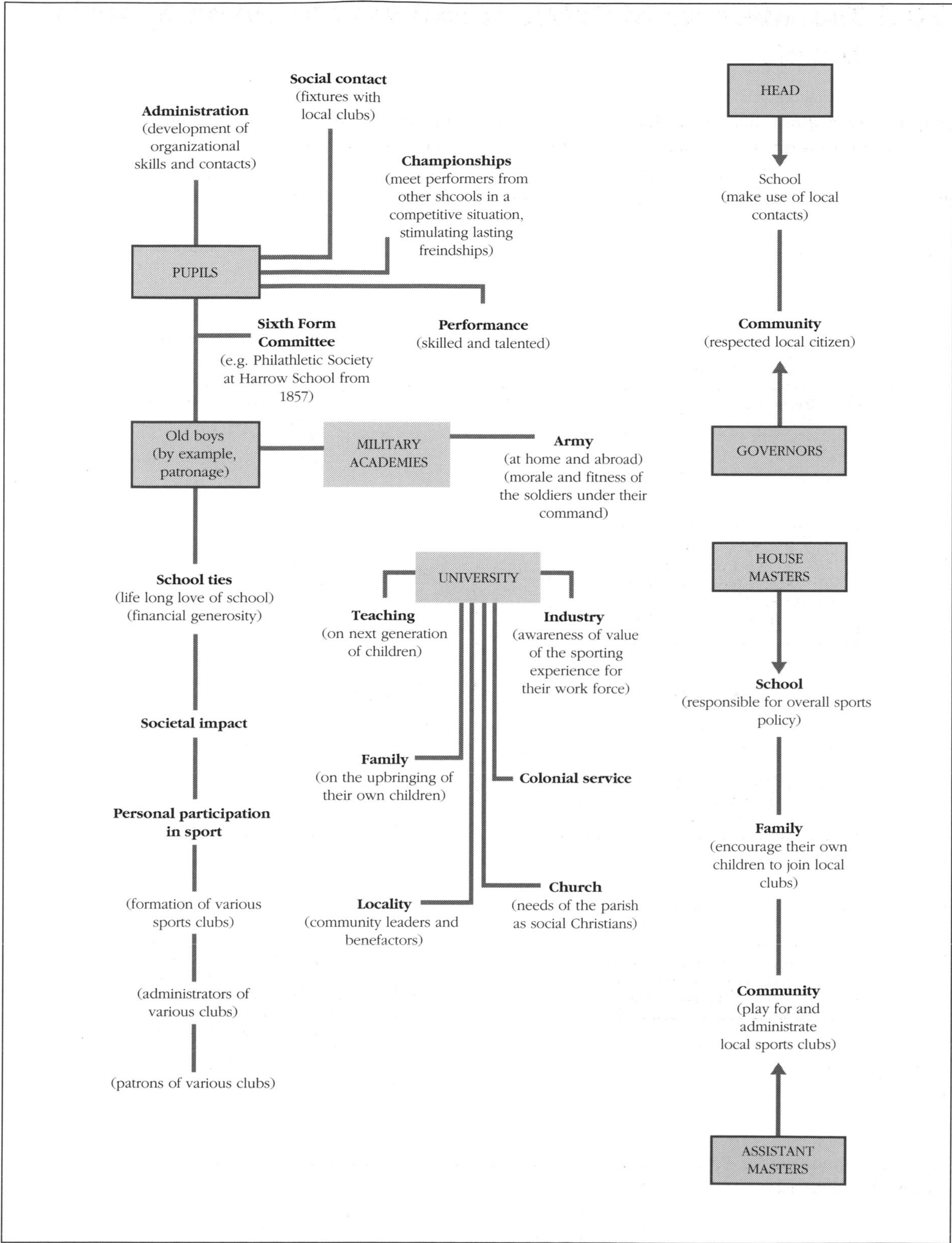

Figure 20.16 Interpersonal relationships.

REVIEW QUESTIONS

1. What were the technical developments which occurred?
2. How did social control vary in relation to athleticism?
3. What were the main values which the sporting experience was supposed to be giving young people?
4. What was the impact of certain headmasters and other staff on the development of athleticism?
5. Why did the Old Boys have such a large influence on the development of athleticism in their own schools and in society at large?

It would also be worth your while to get a detailed knowledge of one particular public school—there are history texts written on most of them; and also be able to take one of the major sets of activities—cricket, rowing, football, racket games, etc. through the technical changes.

Finally, though a great deal of reference has not been made to girls' public schools, it is important that you should read some of Mangan and Park (1987) and/or Fletcher (1984).

Summary

Summary
Public Schools:

1. Sons of gentlemen, boarding, fee paying, endowed, spartan, non-local controlled by trustees.
2. Clarendon, Gentry Schools; middle-class Proprietary Colleges Denominational Schools; Grammar Schools.
3. **Athleticism:** physical endeavour and moral integrity
4. Sport and character development in education.
5. Sport as an instrument for social control.
6. Educational reform and Arnold of Rugby.
7. Impact of public school athleticism on the development of rational recreation in British society.
8. Play up! Play up! And play the game!

FURTHER READING

Bamford T.W. *The Rise of the Public Schools,* Nelson, 1967.
Brailsford D. *Sport and Society,* RKP, 1969.
Clarke A.K. *A History of the Cheltenham Ladies College,* Faber & Faber, 1953.
Craze M. *King's School, Worcester 1541-1971,* Baylis, 1971.
Dunning E. and Sheard K. *Barbarians, Gentlemen and Players,* NYUP, 1979.
Hughes T. *Tom Brown's School Days* (various since 1857).
Fletcher S. *Women First: The Female Tradition in English Physical Education,* Athlone Press, 1984.
McIntosh P.C. *Physical Education in England since 1800,* Bell, 1952.
Mangan J.A. and Park R.J. *From 'Fair Sex' to Feminism,* Frank Cass, 1987.
Morgan M.C. *Cheltenham College,* Sadler, 1968.
Newsome D. *Godliness and Good Learning,* Murray, 1961.
Noake V. *The History of Alice Ottley School,* Worcester, Baylis, 1952.
Ogilvie V. *The English Public School,* Batsford, 1957.
Percival A.C. *Very Superior Men,* Knight, 1973.
Simon B. and Bradley I. *The Victorian Public School,* Gill & Macmillan,
Smith W.D. *Stretching their Bodies,* David & Charles, 1974.
Walvin J. *Leisure and Society,* Longman, 1978.
Webster F.A.M. *Our Great Public Schools,* Ward Lock, 1937.
Wymer N. *Dr Arnold of Rugby,* Hale, 1953.

N.B. Many of these books are out of print, but are obtainable through lending libraries.

Similarly, old schools and local archival centres have copies of school magazines which give some tremendous insights into the place of sport as far as the boys of the school were concerned.

Chapter 21
The Pattern of Rational Recreation in Nineteenth-Century Britain

A new form of physical recreation began to emerge in Britain around the 1850s. It consisted of a formal, morally based presentation of contests, individual activities, games and outdoor pursuits, by respectable members of the community, in a form which no longer contained the excesses evident in popular recreation. It stemmed from the gentry and gentry schools and was enthusiastically taken up by the middle classes and their schools. As a product of social Christianity and liberalism, these sporting opportunities were gradually made available to the working classes, together with a respectable form of professional sport to accommodate a new form of spectatorism.

Elias (1971) called this process the 'genesis of sport', suggesting that primitive sports associated with popular recreation had little or nothing in common with this **rational recreation** as a sophisticated reflection of an industrialized society: that sport as we know it was born in the mid-nineteenth century. This is an interesting theory, but it has loop-holes, some of which are explored by Cunningham (1980).

SOCIAL FACTORS INFLUENCING THE DEVELOPMENT OF RATIONAL RECREATION IN BRITAIN

Urbanization and Population Expansion

The size of town determined the recreative needs of a community. Old towns had medieval slums which were gradually cleared to make shopping and commercial centres. The larger the town, the greater the distance to the countryside and natural recreative provision. The rate of growth, particularly lower class, meant that population outstripped recreative provision. There was a gradual improvement in facilities towards the end of the nineteenth century with public parks being opened and public baths being built.

Communications and Travel

The distance an individual could travel was dependent on the free time available and the cost. An increase in the speed of transport allowed people to travel further in the same time.

Figure 21.1 Rational recreation: the test of temperament and physical competence.

Figure 21.2 An excursion trip to Epsom Downs.

Travel had two basic links with sport:

- as a means of getting to a sporting venue, in the transport sense
- the process itself was recreative or sporting.

It is possible to link river communications with angling, bathing, fowling and boating. With roads, there was the growth of pedestrianism, and walking race horses, followed later by the impact of the cycle. Finally, the railways opened up the countryside and the seaside resorts. They allowed fixtures to be made in different towns and stimulated spectatorism.

Communication and Literacy

The printed word was a positive influence on sport. The evolution of the free press; the promotion of literacy; the mechanization of the printing industry; cheaper production of weekly newspapers; and the publication of pocket editions led to an informed public. This permanent record was also achieved by artists who recorded major sporting events, and in the 1890s photography played a considerable part in promoting and reflecting sport, particularly when pictorial supplements were published by the weekly press.

Religious and Secular Institutions

You have already read about the negative influences of religion on popular recreation. The picture changed completely when Muscular Christianity and Rational Recreation came together. Young curates, fresh from public school and university, joined parishes and promoted athleticism for their parishioners. The YMCA in particular, became an athletic as well as a religious centre, and it encouraged young clerks to engage in a variety of rational sports.

Similarly, there were mechanics institutes and working men's clubs which tried to wean the lower-class male away from drink and popular recreation by offering him social amenities, literary classes and rational recreations.

The Working Classes and Industrial Provision

While the cottage industry existed, the workers were able to select their own time for recreation, but factories changed this. Machines determined working hours and pay reflected profits and sales. It was commonplace for men to be working for 72 hours **a week** for one pound.

A major break-through came with the **Saturday half-day.** Clerks and skilled workers achieved this by the 1870s; semi-skilled in the 1880s; and most labourers by the 1890s, resulting in most working-class males doing a 56 hour week by the end of the century.

Working-class opportunities for sport must be seen in the context of the squalor of the industrial slums; the poverty of those out of work; and low wages, which caused a family-man to work overtime.

The sons of industrialists brought athleticism to the factories and started sports clubs. Initially, this only involved the salaried staff, but gradually facilities were built for shop-floor workers in the belief that it would improve morale and loyalty. An older form of patronage continued to exist where an annual feast or excursion was paid for by the owners. With larger firms this involved a day trip to the sea-side, with all expenses paid.

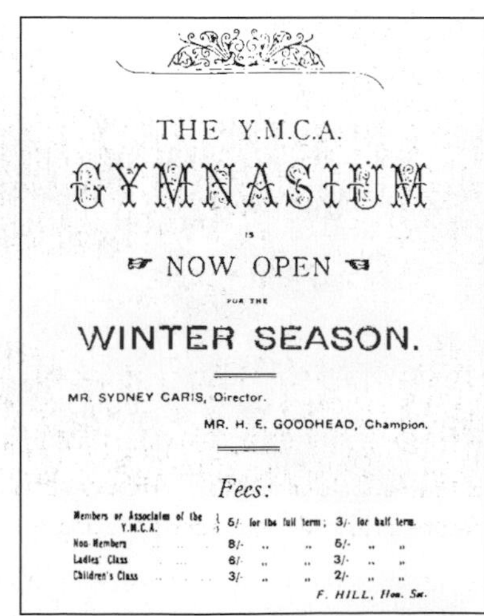

Figure 21.3 Source: Burton–upon–Trent YMCA, 1884-5.

Figure 21.4 Poverty on the streets.

THE RATIONAL DEVELOPMENT OF ACTIVITIES AND GAMES

Swimming and Bathing

Recreational bathing

When it was hot, the natural thing to do in river towns was to go bathing. The trouble was it was dangerous, and the sight of naked urchins upset respectable citizens. As a result, bathing stations were built on the river bank.

Spa and sea bathing

'Taking the waters' became a Regency fashion and led to spa towns being built with extensive bathing facilities. The fashion switched to the seaside and led to seaside bathing.

Public baths

The Wash-house Acts (1846) led to many industrial towns building public baths to clean up the labouring classes. They were called 'penny baths' because there was a fixed limit on charges for the second-class facilities.

Competitive swimming

Most of the middle-class swimming clubs were formed in the private Turkish baths. The first national championships were held in 1874 with the formation of the SAGB, and the ASA was formed in 1884: Water polo mainly developed in the public baths and was codified in 1885. The Amateur Diving Association was not formed until 1901.

Athletics and Cross-Country

University athletics

Public schools had sports days which formalized the old rural sports. The Old Boys took this idea to Oxford and Cambridge, with the Exeter College Autumn Meeting (1850) being the first amateur athletics meeting. It was run like a horse race meeting.

The Wenlock Olympian Games

Meanwhile, Dr Penny Brookes re-established an old rural sports at Much Wenlock in a rational form. In 1865 the National Olympian Association (NOA) was formed as a governing body and they defined amateurism.

Amateur athletics

The AAC (1866) was formed by ex-Oxbridge gentlemen athletes. They also defined amateurism but excluded the working class. They were rivals of the NOA and set up their own National Championships in 1866. In 1880, the AAA was formed and the 'exclusive' class was removed and 'no financial gain' became the central amateur criterion.

Cross-country running

Almost like the poor man's hunting, many Harrier Athletic Clubs were formed in the 1880s with 'hare and hound races' and 'paper chases'. These clubs also held summer sports meetings and led to our tradition of middle-distance running.

Figure 21.5 Bathing huts at the seaside.

What does this picture tell you about bathing and Victorian morality?

Figure 21.6 Athletic sports meeting.

Use this picture as a basis to explain the development of amateur athletic sports meetings.

Gymnastics

Archibold Maclaren, friend of Ruskin and Morris, was a versatile sportsman. An outstanding oarsman, he built a gymnasium at Oxford (1850) and one at Aldershot for the Army (1861). He published texts on gymnastics and the public schools and urban clubs used his approach rather than Continental methods.

Muscular Christianity and the YMCA

Gymnastics was recognized as a non-competitive instrument for increasing respect for the human body. Liverpool and Manchester YMCAs had a great influence on developments.

Figure 21.7 Maclaren's Gymnasium at Aldershot.

Describe English gymnastics from this picture.

INVASION GAMES

The classification of an **invasion game** in modern times is: a territorially fluid team game with goal targets and involving free play of the ball with variations of body contact.

In rational recreation terms, they were rule-based with a 'spirit' and 'letter' of play; they were highly organized with governing bodies and affiliated clubs; and played regularly with fixtures, officials, and club colours in fixed seasons.

Association Football

The public schools changed the mob games into respectable, regular games. Eton, Harrow and Charterhouse promoted a 'dribbling' game which was played under the Cambridge Rules from 1856. Old Boys Teams helped form the FA in 1863. There were ten clubs in 1867 rising to 50 by 1871. By 1905 there were 10,000 clubs with 272 in the FA Cup.

Professionalism was legalized in 1885 and the Football League was formed in 1888. At the opposite end of the scale the Corinthian Club had gentlemen as members and only played friendly games. The game spread to all sections of society with leading clubs being formed from:

Old Boys' teams, e.g. Leicester City/the Old Wyggestonians;
Street teams, e.g. Rotherham (1884) was formed under a street lamp;
Employees teams, e.g. Manchester City/the Lancs & Yorks Railway Club (1885);
Church teams, e.g. Everton (1878) was a Sunday School team;
and various other sources, e.g. Sheffield Wednesday was an Early Closers' team.

Figure 21.8 Association football.

Use this picture to show how the rational game differs from mob football.

Rugby Football

This code was initially limited to Old Rugbeians. They founded Guys Hospital Club (1843) and Blackheath (1862). In 1871, Blackheath and 20 other clubs formed the RFU, and in 1877 the game was restricted to 15-a-side.

The 'broken time' debate led to a split between southern and northern clubs in 1895 on the subject of professionalism, and this led to 22 clubs breaking away to form the Northern Union, which eventually became the Rugby League.

Hockey

There were initially two separate lines of development. Blackheath and Bristol rationalized the old mob game in a form which lasted until 1895.

Meanwhile, a number of cricket clubs in the Home Counties were experimenting with winter hockey. In 1871, there were clubs at Richmond, Teddington and Sutton. A Hockey Union was set up in 1876 to join the two codes, but they could not agree. In 1886 the Hockey Association was formed, based on the Teddington model, and the Blackheath game slowly disappeared.

Women's club hockey can be traced to an East Molesey Club in the 1880s. The Irish Ladies' Hockey Union was formed in 1894, and a year later the AEWHA was established to coincide with the first international fixture between Alexandra College, Dublin, and Newham and Girton Colleges, Cambridge.

Figure 21.9 Rugby football.

Use this picture to show how the rational game differs from mob football.

Figure 21.10 Hockey.

What qualities were the girls' schools trying to promote through hockey?

TARGET GAMES

The classification of a target game is: it involves a team or pair in a game which has targets such as wickets, skittles or holes. There is alternate play, which restricts body contact, and in team versions each team has a separate role to play, e.g. batting or fielding.

Many of the rational elements of these games developed much earlier because they were less violent. Strict rules of play, spirit and letter, were observed, and controlled by governing bodies. Though games tended to be on a friendly basis, championships involving amateurs and professionals had early developments.

Cricket

The tour of the All-England XI in the 1840s led to a growth of gentlemen's county cricket clubs. The old village clubs continued alongside these, while there was a massive growth in the number of urban middle-class clubs.

Croquet, rounders and baseball function within the same general classification.

Regular fixtures at all levels led to increased competition at county level and so more artisan professionals were employed and middle-class amateurs started to play county cricket.

Such was the belief in the value of cricket that church leaders, teachers and employers started to encourage the urban working class to play the game.

Women's cricket was limited by Victorian attitudes, but in the 1880s there was a revival of the 'ladies' game as the result of increased athleticism in the middle-class girls' schools.

Golf

This was always the Scottish equivalent of cricket. It suited a smaller population, with uneven terrain, and an inclement climate. It was also close to the other Scottish game of shinty.

Normally played on 'links' (seaside), St Andrews has always been the 'home' of the game. In Scotland, golf was a 'popular' game, but in England, wealthy Scots introduced it to the upper class and it remained an elite game throughout the nineteenth century. There was always an artisan version of the game, even in England, where a lower-class club had use of the course in return for keeping it in good condition. Ladies used the men's courses until their numbers grew sufficiently to open their own.

Figure 21.11 Cricket.

Identify the changes from the eighteenth-century game.

Figure 21.12 Golf.

Use your knowledge of female sport to establish why golf was acceptable for 'ladies'.

Bowls

Skittles, bowls and quoits belonged to a group of games, which were associated with taverns. This delayed their acceptability in respectable circles until middle-class clubs started to be formed and public parks started to provide greens for the lower classes.

The Yorks & Lancs Crown Green Association (1888) and the Flat Green Association (1895) were the two governing bodies which co-ordinated fixtures and championships.

Quoiting was very popular in rural areas in the last quarter of the nineteenth century, but has almost disappeared today.

Figure 21.13 Skittles.

Can you account for the advantages and disadvantages of skittles being associated with taverns?

COURT GAMES

The classification of these games is based on a court being used for play. There should be no body contact, with alternate play over a net or against a wall and points are scored in a singles or pairs situation.

The rational game goes back to real tennis, which, because of its exclusivity, was sophisticatedly codified from the sixteenth century. This game evolved into a variety of forms to suit different situations and conditions.

Rackets

Initially the poor man's version of real tennis, its popularity in public schools, alongside fives, led to clubs being set up throughout the country. The rational stage was achieved when 'open' courts with one wall were changed to indoor 'closed' courts. Prince's Club, and then Queen's from 1886, controlled the codification of the game. The 1880s also saw the introduction of a junior 'squashy' ball, which has led to the modern game of squash.

Badminton

This game had slightly different roots, because there was an ancient pastime called shuttlecock and battledore. This activity was still being played in gardens in the nineteenth century and legend has it that, on a wet day, the family at Badminton House (Duke of Beaufort) took the game indoors.

The first rules were written in 1877 by members of the British Army and Diplomatic Corps in India. The Badminton Association was formed in 1893 and the championships were held at Wimbledon, alongside lawn tennis and croquet.

Figure 21.14 Rackets.

Can you suggest some explanations for rackets being played in Fleet Prison?

Figure 21.15 Badminton.

Why do you think badminton did not have a governing body until the 1890s?

Lawn Tennis

The modern game has three main roots. Major Gem introduced a game at Leamington in 1866 and the Leamington Club had written rules by 1870; J.H. Hales introduced Germain Tennis in 1873; and Major Wingfield patented a game called 'Sphairistike' in the same year. The modern rules of lawn tennis were codified by the MCC in 1875, with the All England Croquet and Lawn Tennis Club being established at Wimbledon in 1876.

One reason why lawn tennis became so popular was the changing role of the middle-class female. In the privacy of their own gardens, it became acceptable for females to play athletic games.

Initially exclusive, early tournaments were associated with county cricket. These tended to be played behind closed doors and it wasn't until 1884 that public championships were held for 'ladies' at Wimbledon.

Figure 21.16 Lawn tennis.

Discuss the links between lawn tennis and athleticism.

AQUATIC ACTIVITIES

Rowing

So-called amateur regattas appeared around 1870. They tended to exclude the lower classes as they were run by clubs consisting of public school oarsmen.

The ARA controlled rowing on the Thames from 1879 and by 1885 became the national governing body. The 'exclusion clause' limited competitive rowing to public school boys. The NARA (1890) was a rival body which permitted broader participation.

Canoe touring was popular in the last half of the nineteenth century, largely due to the exploits of John MacGregor and his book A *Thousand Miles by Rob Roy Canoe.*

Sailing

Yachting was a sport of the aristocracy and the Royal Navy. The Duke of Cumberland Cup (1781) was the

Figure 21.17 Rowing.

Can you explain the main characteristics of Henley?

premier schooner race. Several clubs on the Isle of Wight were patronized by William IV and Queen Victoria.

The America's Cup was first held in 1851 as a challenge between British and American yachts. The winner chose the next venue and until recent times the Americans won every year.

Dinghy sailing started with the Solent Classes in 1870. Middle class clubs were formed at Southampton and Portsmouth and they promoted races for 21-, 25- and 30-foot craft.

Skating

There were three main lines of development on ice. The oldest were the ice fairs which were very similar to rural fairs.

Speed skating came from Holland and developed on the Fens. The National Skating Association (1879) controlled the amateur championships and there were also professional championships.

Figure skating developed with improved skates. The world centre was the Serpentine in London.

Difficulties were met when attempts were made to develop 'glacariums' and so roller skating rinks developed in the 1870s as an alternative.

Figure 21.18 Sailing.

How many reasons can you find to explain why Britain has never won the America's Cup?

Figure 21.19 Skating.

Use this picture to explain the many attractions of ice and roller skating.

CLIMBING AND CYCLING

Climbing

Life in the mountains initially hinged on shepherds and local people acting as guides. The Romantic Movement brought the gentry to the mountains, but it was the scenery rather than climbing which appealed to most of them. This love of mountain scenery extended to the Alps and snow climbing developed through the Alpine Club (1857). This led to the development of mountaineering—the art of reaching the summit.

Scientists looking for alpine plants opened up the Lake District and North Wales. W.P. Haskett-Smith at Wasdale Head and O.G. Jones at Pen-y-Gwryd were the most famous climbers. This led to rock climbing—the practice of finding the most difficult route up a crag. While mountaineering was very much an upper-class pursuit, rock climbing was taken up by the middle and working classes.

Cycling

An excellent sport to show social variables. It reflected the urban and industrial revolutions in that a machine was used as an urban substitute for a horse. It became the most common vehicle whereby people in towns managed to escape to the countryside. It was very much an urban, middle-class male preserve to begin with. The gentry despised it and the working class could not afford it. It started as a novelty fashion with the hobby horse and progressed. via France, to the boneshaker or velocipede. The inventiveness of English industrialists led to the Ordinary or Penny Farthing. The large wheel allowed increased speed and kept the person above the mud, but it was dangerous. A safer version, the tricycle, was developed, and this was largely used by females and the elderly until the Rover Safety and pneumatic tyres were invented.

There were three main branches of cycling. Track racing (BCU) was part of the athletic sports meeting; touring (CTC) became highly organized with consuls, guide books, repair shops and hotels; and, finally, there was the development of road racing. The problem with the latter was that mass starts were banned and so pursuit racing took its place in England. Mass starts were allowed on the Isle of Man and the Continent and this led to the Tour de France becoming the premier road racing event.

In terms of social class development, the gentry, particularly ladies, took up cycle touring, following the lead of Queen Victoria's daughters. At the same time the second-hand cycle trade allowed poorer people to buy bicycles. Middle-class females followed the lead of the upper class and fashion became an important feature, first with 'bloomers' and later the 'rational dress'.

Figure 21.20 Mountaineering.

Why were there very few limits on women climbers?

Figure 21.21 Penny Farthing riders.

Explain the influence of cycling on female sporting opportunities.

Summary

Rational Recreation:

1. **Respectable** sports promoted by the **gentry** and the **urban middle classes.** Instruments of **social reform** for the **lower classes.**
2. **Regular, codified, stringently organized, letter** and **spirit of play** emphasized.
3. **Clubs, governing bodies** and **championships** based on the concept of **amateurism.**

FURTHER READING:

Altham H.S. *A History of Cricket,* Vol. I, Allen & Unwin, 1962.

Bailey P. *Leisure and Class in Victorian England,* RKP, 1978.

Baker W.J. *Sports in the Western World,* University of Illinois, 1988.

Clark R. *Victorian Mountaineers,* Batsford, 1953.

Cleaver H. *A History of Rowing,* Herbert Jenkins, 1957.

Cunningham H. *Leisure in the Industrial Society,* Croom Helm, 1980.

Dunning E. and Sheard K. *Barbarians, Gentlemen and Players,* NYUP, 1979.

Ford J. *This Sporting Land,* New English Library, 1977.

Lovesey P. *Centenary History of the AAA,* Guinness Sup. ,1979.

Mason T. *Association Football and English Society,* Harvester, 1980.

Marples M. *Shank's Pony,* Dent, 1959.

Medleycott J. *100 Years of the Wimbledon Tennis Championships,* Hamlyn, 1977.

Meller H.E. *Leisure and the Changing City,* RKP, 1976.

Richie A. *King of the Road,* Wildwood House Ltd, 1975.

Titley U . A. and McWhirter A.R. *Centenary History of the RFU,* RFU, 1970.

Walvin J. *The People's Game,* Allen Lane, 1975.

Walvin J. *Leisure and Society,* Longman, 1978.

Watman M. *A History of British Athletics,* Robert Hale, 1968.

Wymer N. *Sport in England,* Harrap, 1949.

Young P.M. *A History of British Football,* Stanley Paul, 1968.

Chapter 22
Transitions in English Elementary Schools

22.1 Nineteenth-Century Drill and Gymnastics

J.C.F. Guts Muths (1749-1839) was the 'Father of European Gymnastics'. He published *Gymnastik fur die Jungend* and this was a source of subsequent developments in Sweden (P.H. Ling, 1776-1839); in Germany (F.L. Jahn, 1778-1852); in Denmark (F. Nachtegall, 1777-1847); and in Britain (A. Maclaren, 1820-1884).

Maclaren used continental developments, but felt that many features were unsuitable in England. He preferred apparatus work and a mixture of other activities, like walking and riding, swimming and country pursuits.

Dr. Mathias Roth was the leading supporter of the Swedish System in England and was a rival of Maclaren. He supported 'rational gymnastics' for medical and military reasons.

Elementary schooling prior to 1870 was dominated by two major organizations, the National Schools Society (1811), a Church of England association, and the British and Foreign Schools Society (1808), which was linked with non-conformism. Some of these schools had playgrounds and even playing fields, but many of those in the industrial towns had no playing facilities and could not cope with the massive population explosion, despite a great deal of absenteeism.

The 1870 Forster Education Act was an attempt to 'plug the gaps' in elementary schooling, and led to the establishment of Board Schools. The Act ignored Roth's efforts and the 1871 Code of Regulations only introduced 'permissive' legislation.

> *'Drill for boys only, if given under a competent instructor, for not more than two hours a week, and twenty weeks in the year, could be counted as school attendance. '*

It consisted of marching, posture exercises and dummy arms drill and was taught by Army NCOs for sixpence a day and a penny a mile for marching, using the *Army Field Exercise Book* (1870). Girls were included in 1873, but the content remained 'free standing' military drill.

Gymnastic apparatus was available in public schools and some open spaces, but the intention of the drill in these working class schools was to improve the fitness of Army recruits and to instil discipline.

In the 1890s the Education Department recommended the inclusion of some Swedish drill, largely as a result of Swedish-trained inspectors being appointed in London. There was also a trend for qualified teachers to take over the drill from the military instructors.

The Prize Day Programme for the Worcester Board Schools in 1894 (Fig. 22.1) reflects this broader approach.

Changing attitudes were also evident in a speech by the Rev. C.E. Hopton in Worcester in 1899:

> *'I hope that when the Transvaal War (Boer War) is over people will be able to say that those victories had been won on the playgrounds of the elementary schools of England. To teach boys to be brave, noble, honest and self-sacrificing, so that when they went out into the world, those characteristics would stick by them, and would fit them to be worthy citizens of this great country.'*

It would seem that at least one 'Muscular Christian' felt that the same qualities were possible for poor children as for the rich.

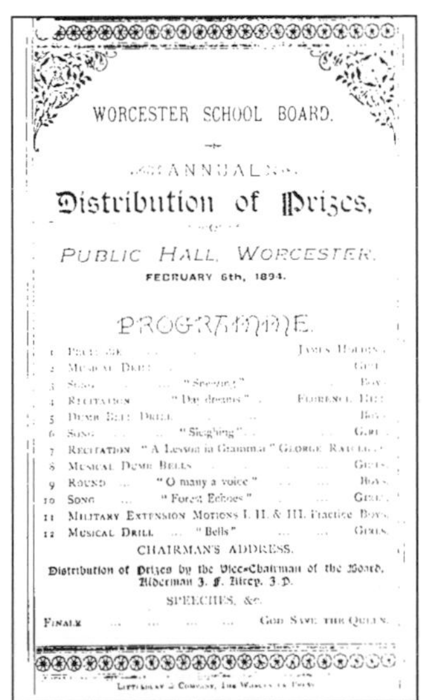

WORCESTER SCHOOL BOARD.

ANNUAL

Distribution of Prizes,

PUBLIC HALL, WORCESTER.

FEBRUARY 6th, 1894.

PROGRAMME.

1 [illegible]
2 [illegible]
3 [illegible]
4 Recitation "Day dreams" [illegible]
5 [illegible]
6 Song "Sleighing" [illegible]
7 Recitation "A Lesson in Grammar" [illegible]
8 Musical Dumb Bells [illegible]
9 Round "O many a voice" [illegible]
10 Song "Forest Echoes" [illegible]
11 Military Extension Motions I. II. & III. Practice Boys.
12 Musical Drill "Bells" Girls.

CHAIRMAN'S ADDRESS.

Distribution of Prizes by the Vice-Chairman of the Board, Alderman J. F. [illegible] J.P.

SPEECHES, &c.

Finale ... God Save the Queen.

Figure 22.1

22.2 The 1902 Model Course

The Boer War (1899-1902) was fought between the might of the British Empire and the Boers, South Africans of Dutch extraction. Great Britain lost a great deal of prestige because their large, but ponderous army found it very difficult to defeat a small force of mobile guerilla fighters.

Back in England, accusations were mainly that the working classes were unhealthy and ill-prepared to fight and, as a scapegoat, politicians blamed the Swedish drill being taught by teachers in the elementary schools. As a result the Model Course was imposed in 1902 in all these schools. It was produced by the War Office and controlled by Colonel Fox of the APTC. He was instructed to achieve two main objectives:

1. 'To increase fitness for military service through acquaintance with the discipline of military drill'.
2. To train children to, 'withstand the hardships of combat and have familiarity with weapons'.

There was a directive that these lessons should replace Swedish drill and military instructors should be used. Boys and girls were involved in this programme up to the age of twelve. but they were instructed as little soldiers, not children.

Investigation 22.1 : The 1902 Course

It is important that you should have some idea of the content of this syllabus and the method of instruction, and this is a very good opportunity for you to use role-play methods by going through a model lesson. Young people today are not used to the command-response of military drill and so you should find it an interesting experience.

Enact the following lesson, where teachers or students can take it in turns to act as instructors.

Note: ______ is a long cautionary word;
and ∪ is a short sharp executive command.

1. *Right marker; in two ranks, fall in; right form*
(this means falling in on the markers right, an arm's distance apart).

2. *Stand at ease; atten-tion.*
(Repeat this, looking for exact positions and moving together.)

a. Stand at ease.

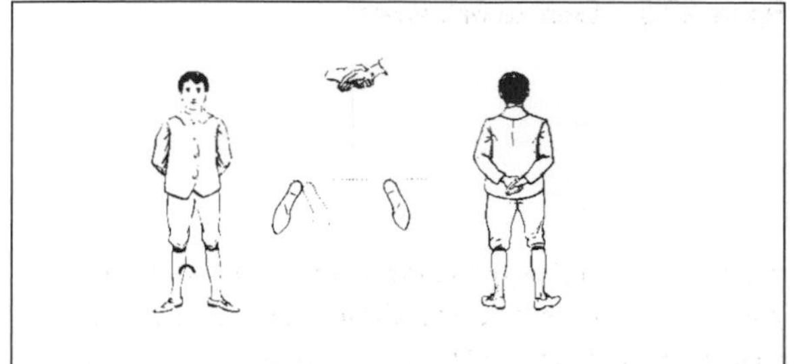

b. Attention.

Figure 22.2

3. *Right turn, one; two; by the left, quick march; left, right, left, right, etc. Squad halt; about turn; quick march; squad halt; right turn; stand at ease.*

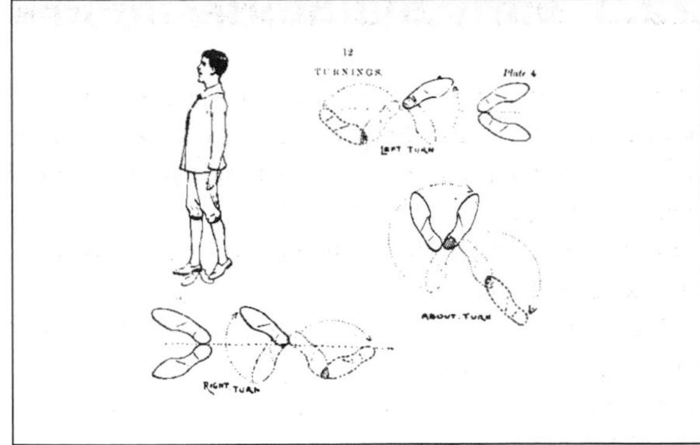

Figure 22.3 Turning.

4. *Atten-tion; arms bending and stretching, arms bend; out; bend; up; bend; down;* (repeat); *stand at ease.*

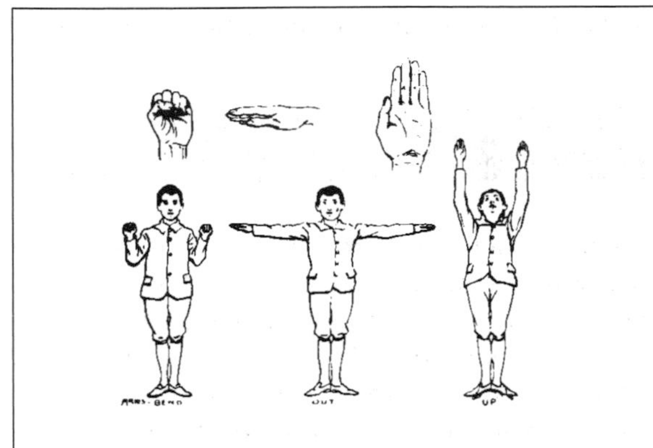

Figure 22.4 Arms bending and stretching.

5. Exercise with staves (corner poles),

atten-tion; ready; astride with cross stave ready; one; two; three; and up; and forward; one; two; three; and up; and forward; stave ready; atten-tion; stand at ease.

Figure 22.5 Exercise with staves.

6. *Deep breathing by numbers, in; out; in; and out.*

7. *Marching back to class, left turn one; two; quick march; squad halt; fall out (right turn).*

If you insist on this being done accurately and seriously, you will soon realize the difficulties of synchronized movement and you will be able to judge the degree of exercise you are getting. You should also question the level of activity, skill, and individuality.

22.3. Early Syllabuses of Physical Training

The Model Course came under constant attack from inspectors and teachers and in 1904, the Board of Education set up two **Interdepartmental Committees.**

One committee examined the Model Course and criticized it on the grounds that there was no apparent intent to equate physical exercise with general education; it had a specific military function; it failed to recognize the need to cater for different ages and sexes; and caused a reduction of subject status through the use of military personnel rather than qualified teachers. The formal recommendation was that a new syllabus be produced which recognized different ages and sexes.

The second committee looked specifically at the 'physical deterioration among the working classes' and recommended that the male adolescent population should undergo training that would 'befit them to bear arms'.

By separating elementary school physical training from military training, the cause had been won to reinstate Swedish 'therapeutic' exercises.

THE 1904 SYLLABUS

This was the first Board of Education Syllabus and it set out to satisfy the recommendations of the relevant Interdepartmental Committee.

Explain the meaning and intentions underlying the following recommendations:
1. 'exercises from many well-known systems'
2. 'suitable for children of school age'
3. 'without need of apparatus'
4. 'no exercises likely to prove injurious'
5. 'to be purposeful'
6. 'as a minimum of exercise'.

How the Syllabus covered these intentions.

At a **conceptual** level, it identified the **physical effect,** that is the intention to improve health and physique; and the **educational effect,** that is to develop qualities of alertness, decision-making and the control of the mind over the body. This was 1904, but if you took one of your modern PE lessons, you would quite probably have similar intentions.

Now **how** did they expect to put them into practice? Their view of our subject started from a medical (physiological) base. They wanted to present a system of physical exercises which would improve respiration and circulation; and stimulate nutrition. They envisaged things like play activities: the development of vital capacity through breathing exercises; corrective exercises to improve posture; exercises against resistance; and control exercises involving skill learning. Once again you might be surprised at the knowledge and 'vision'.

The problem lay in putting these theories into practice. They produced 109 tables, where each consisted of a series of activities designed to systematically exercise the whole body. The structure of each **table** consisted of such exercises as: arms; balance; shoulders; head and trunk; marching; jumping; and deep breathing.

A study of the Syllabus shows that not all the military features were removed, for example, they were still taught in lines with marching; commands were still formal; and 'attention' was still 'pigeon-chested'.

The authorities suggested that the class teacher should give two or three 20-minute lessons a week, but that there should also be daily 'recreative sessions to 'refresh the child for further study'.

Some of the **content** of the 1904 Syllabus is shown in Figure 22.7 and you should be able to compare this with the exercises in the defunct Model Course.

You may like to repeat the role-play exercise, emphasizing the changes. Remember, you will now have teachers with children, rather than NCOs with little soldiers; and there should be a more varied lesson, but still taught through action-response commands.

Figure 22.6 Drill or Physical Education? A healthy mind in a healthy body means keeping your eyes on the target.

I PLAY RUNNING OR MARCHING
Play or Running about. The children should, for a minute or two, be allowed to move about as they please.

II PRELIMINARY POSITIONS AND MOVEMENTS
Attention.
Standing at Ease.
Hips Firm.
Feet Close.
Neck Rest.
Feet Astride.
Foot Outward Place.
Foot Forward Place.
Stepping Sideways.
Heels Raising.
Right Turn and Right Half Turn.
Left Turn and Left Half Turn.

III ARM FLEXIONS AND EXTENSIONS
Arms Downward Stretching.
Arms Forward Stretching.
Arms Sideways Stretching.
Arms Upward Stretching.

IV BALANCE EXERCISES
Heels Raising.
Knees Bending and Stretching.
Preparation for Jumping.
Heels Raising (Neck Rest).
Heels Raising (Astride, Hips Firm).
Heels Raising (Astride, Neck Rest).
Head Turning in Knees Bend Position.
Knees Bending and Stretching (Astride).
Leg Sideways Raising with Arms Sideways Raising.
Knee Raising.

V SHOULDER EXERCISES AND LUNGES
Arms Forward Raising.
Arms Sideways Raising.
Hands Turning.
Arms Flinging.
Arms Forward and Upward Raising.
Arms Sideways and Upward Raising.

VI TRUNK FORWARD AND BACKWARD BENDING
Head Backward Bending.
Trunk Forward Bending.
Trunk Backward Bending.
Trunk Forward Bending (Astride) .
Trunk Backward Bending (Astride)
.
Note Exercises bracketed should be taken in succession.

VII TRUNK TURNING AND SIDEWAYS BENDING
Head Turning.
Trunk Turning.
Trunk Turning (Astride, Neck Rest).
Trunk Turning (Feet Close, Neck Rest).
Trunk Sideways Bending.
Trunk Sideways Bending (Feet Close, Hips Firm).
Trunk Sideways Bending (Feet Close. Neck Rest).

VIII MARCHING
Marking Time (From the Halt).
Turnings while Marking Time.
Quick March.
Marking Time (From the March).
Changing Direction.

IX JUMPING
Preparation for Jumping.
Note Work from this Column should be omitted until the above exercise has been taught under IV.

X BREATHING EXERCISES
Breathing Exercises without Arm Movements.
With Deep Breathing, Arms Sideways Raising.

Figure 22.7 1904 Syllabus, HMSO.

What may not have become apparent is that in recognizing age variations, the Syllabus separated **infants** into a different category and, for children under seven, play became an accepted part of the lesson. There was also considerable stress on the **open air** and the importance of having suitable clothing.

Major political and administrative changes occurred over the next few years. In 1906 the Education Act was particularly concerned with the welfare of working-class children, and the Open Spaces Act improved urban leisure provision with the development of more public parks. The following year. under the radical Liberal Government of Lloyd George, physical training was directly linked with the Medical Department of the Board of Education, with the appointment of Dr George Newman. An immediate administrative development was the appointment of Miss Rendal and Lt. Commander Grenfell as staff inspectors, both with backgrounds in Swedish drill. Meanwhile, Colonel Malcolm Fox was sent to Sweden to learn more about their approach. These events led to a revised and expanded syllabus being published in 1909.

THE 1909 SYLLABUS

In 1909 two new emphases occurred. The first was an increase in therapeutic elements, probably directly due to Dr George Newman.

The purpose of physical training is not to produce gymnasts, but to promote and encourage the health and development of the body.

The second reflected a change in social attitude.

The value of organized games as an adjunct to physical training is very great, though they should not take the place of the regular lessons of physical exercise.

Three of the male associations linked with gymnastics, objected to the first purpose and the Ling Association, largely representing female teachers. objected to the second, reflecting the gulf between men and women in the PE profession.

In terms of **content** the 1909 Syllabus had 71 tables instead of 109, suggesting that there was a tightening up of alternatives. The work remained 'free standing' with unison response to commands, but Danish rhythmic swinging exercises were also included.

THE 1919 SYLLABUS

This followed the First World War (1914–18). It is important to recognize the tragedy of this war with so much loss of life, particularly as it virtually wiped out a generation of public school boys. Less well known was the huge number of additional deaths which occurred in a 'flu' epidemic immediately after the war.

If there was a positive outcome it was the improved status of women as a result of their contribution in schools and factories during the war. Blame for the low level of fitness among the working classes was once again levelled at school physical training, but Dr George Newman cleverly deflected this, claiming that remedial exercises and morale boosting recreational activities in convalescent camps had helped to prepare the wounded for a full return to civilian life.

It was Newman's recognition of the 'recreational' which represented the most significant innovation in the 1919 Syllabus.

the formal nature of the lesson has been reduced to a minimum and every effort has been made to render them enjoyable and recreative.

It was suggested that half of every lesson should be devoted to 'active free movements, including games and dancing' and the tables were remodelled to:

place increased responsibility upon the class teacher and to allow scope for personal initiative, freedom and enterprise.

However, particularly in the case of lessons for older children, the tables allowed the old-fashioned teacher to continue to use the old restrictive exercises. The theory that there was a need to:

consider happiness and enjoyment while accustoming the body and mind to external suggestions and stimuli

was made possible for infant children by a complete restructuring of lessons for the under sevens. The more serious intention of therapeutic exercise remained central for the older children. The whole class was still expected to work in unison in response to direct commands.

If we look outside the classroom at society, this obedience training and therapeutic focus reflected the rigid social class demarcation before the Second World War, where those in power were anxious to retain a clean, disciplined working class, who worked hard and accepted their 'place' in society.

THE 1933 SYLLABUS

We have now reached a period in history which is within living memory of relatives and friends and so your first task should be to find out from them what life was like in the inter-war years and what they did in PE. They may remember the giddy years of the 1920s when the upper class 'flappers' had their last fling; they might recall the business influence of the urban middle class, which was literally taking over our society; or they might remember the harsh reality of post-war Britain, where soldiers and sailors were demobilized, many of them with injuries, without any planning, little financial support or prospect of work. Never was the social class system more clearly defined, but the compulsory school leaving age had risen to 14 and many secondary schools were being built for working-class children. All these new 'senior' and 'central' schools had playing fields and a gymnasium.

The industrial depression in the 1930s left the working class without jobs, but the crash of the stock exchange and the stagnation of industry also affected the middle classes. It was in the middle of this depression that the last Board of Education syllabus was produced, but it was a highly respected publication and 'has been recognized as the watershed between the best of the past and revolutionary developments yet to come.

The concept of therapeutic exercise to produce a sound physique remained, but the recognition of gymnastic and games skills was a major step forward, reflecting both the Reference Books published in 1927 for secondary schools. Children were still taught by direct method, but elements of play were carried through into the lessons for older children.

Probably the most revolutionary change was the introduction of group work All the other syllabuses had been class activities with everyone doing the same thing at the same time. The 1933 Syllabus included a final phase in each lessor where the class was divided into four or more sets or corners, where different activities were set for each group. This was the first vital step towards the decentralized lesson.

Figure 22.8 shows a table from the 1933 Syllabus. The teacher would select items from each of the six sections, but Part I and Part II would be of about equal length. Where other pages are listed, the Syllabus gave additional information on these pages. Look out for a copy of this Syllabus in second-hand bookshops, there are still plenty around.

PART ONE

1

Introductory Activity

1. **Free running, at signal, children run to 'homes' in teams.** (Four or more marked homes in corners of playground.) **All race round, passing outside all the homes, back to places and skip in team rings.**
2. **Free running, at signal all jump as high as possible and continue running. Brisk walking, finishing in open files, marking time with high knee raising.**
3. **Aeroplanes.** (Following the leaders in teams.)

Rhythmic Jump

1. **Skip jump on the spot, three low, three high** (continuously) *(Low, 2, 3,high,2,3,etc.)*
2. **Astride jump.** *Astride jumping— begin! 1, 2,1, 2, etc. stop!*
3. **Skip jump, four on the spot, four turning round about** (8 counts) **and repeat turning the opposite way** (8 counts)

2

a. **(Astride [Long sitting]) Trunk bending downward to grasp ankles. Unroll.** *(With a jump, feet astride—place! [with straight legs—sit.!] Grasp the ankles—down! With unrolling, trunk upward—stretch! With a jump, feet together—place!*

b. **(Astride [Astride long sitting]) Trunk bending downward to touch one foot with opposite hand.**

c. **(Feet close [Cross-legged sitting].) Head dropping forward and stretching upward.** *(Feet—close!) Head forward—drop! Head upward—stretch!*

(Crouch) Knee stretching and bending. ('Angry Cats') *(Crouch position—down!) Knees— stretch! bend! up! down! etc. stand—up!*

3

a. **As small as possible, as tall as possible.**
[(Crook sitting, Back to wall) Single arm swinging forward–upward to touch wall.]
[(Crook sitting) Drumming with the feet, loud and soft.]

b. **Single arm circling at a wall.** (Run and stand with side to wall, nearest hand supported against wall about shoulder height. Circling with free arm. Turn about and repeat.)

4

a. **Free running like a wooden man. Finish in open files in chain grasp.**
(One foot forward, heel level with the other toe) Knee full bending and stretching with knees forward. (Several times. Move the back foot forward and repeat.)
(Lean standing) Hug the knee.
[(Crook lying) Hug the knees. (Lower the feet quietly.)**]**

b. **Running in twos, change to skipping, finish in a double ring facing partner holding hands. Knees full bend. Knee springing. Hands on ground and jump up.**
Knees full bend ! Knee springing— begin! 1, 2,1, 2, etc. Stop! Placing the hands on the ground, with a jump stand—up!

c. **Form a ring. Gallop step left and right, at signal, run and stand with side to wall, nearest hand supported against wall** (the other arm sideways). **Kick the hand.** (Turn about, or run to opposite wall and repeat several times with each leg.)

(cont.)

Figure 22.8 A table from the 1933 Syllabus.

5

a. **Brisk walking anywhere, change to walking on heels or toes, at signal run to open files facing partners.**
(Feet-close, Arms forward, Fists touching.) Trunk turning with single elbow bending. (Elbow raised and pulled back. 'Drawing the bow.')
(Feet—close! With fists touching, arms forward—raise!) With the right arm, draw the bow—pull! Let go! With the left arm—pull! Let go! etc. Arms— lower!

b. **Race to a wall and back to centre line and join right hand across with partner.**
Tug of war with one hand.

c. **(Informal lunge with hand support.) Head and trunk turning with arm raising to point upward.**
(Left (right) foot forward with knee bent and left (right) hand on knee (informal lunge)—ready!) With arm raising to point upward, head and trunk to the right, (left)—turn! With arm lowering, forward—turn. (Repeat several times.) *With a jump, feet change!*

PART TWO

6

Class Activity

1. **Running, jumping over a series of low ropes.** (In ranks of six or eight in stream.)
2. **Frog jump anywhere.**
3. **Free running or skipping, tossing up a ball and catching it.** (A ball each. Who can make the greatest number of catches without missing.)

Group Practices

1. **Running or galloping with a skipping rope.** (A rope each.)
2. **Running Circle Catch, with a player in the centre, throwing, or bouncing and catching a ball.**
3. **Sideways jumping over a low rope, partner helping.** (Partner astride rope, performer holding partner's hands does several preparatory skip jumps on the spot and then a high jump over the rope landing with knees bent and standing up again.)
4. **In twos, crawling or crouch jump through a hoop, held by partner.**

Game

Odd Man.
Free Touch with 6 or 7 'He's.' ('He's' carry a coloured braid or bean bag as distinguishing mark.)
Tom Tiddler.

7

Free walking, practising good position, lead into school.

Figure 22.8 (Continued)

22.4 The Effects of the Second World War (1939-45)

The majority of male PE teachers were enlisted and many were engaged in training military personnel. This was an entirely different war from the previous one, in that there was a mobile rather than a static battle ground; civilians were much more at risk through bombing; and training strategies were concerned with individual initiative and survival rather than the stoic obedience training of old. Large numbers of soldiers were taken prisoner and it was realized that recreative activity helped to maintain morale in the prisoner-of-war camps.

Finally, the threat of air-raids led to the mass evacuation of children from industrial towns to the countryside, giving them a taste of rural life. The bombing itself with the inevitable tragic loss of life at least levelled many of the nineteenth-century slums and resulted in a massive rebuilding programme.

The 1944 Education Act was a progressive piece of legislation, which ensured every child a free education. The tripartite system of grammar, technical and modern schools tended to reflect the class system, but it was soon to be overtaken by a move towards comprehensive education.

These post-war years marked the emergence of a full expression of physical education. The theory behind the inter-war syllabuses had educative intentions, but the 'practical' was predominantly physical training. There were probably four major areas of influence from within the subject:

1. F.J.C. Marshall and E. Major lectured at Carnegie College before the war, publishing several books. Though they continued to accept the 'tables' approach, they were part of a move to increase the place of skill learning and the use of small apparatus. They were in the Services during the war, but wrote a number of progressive articles for the *Journal of PE* suggesting changes towards contests, self-testing and initiative programmes. Perhaps the most important transitional phrase used was the suggestion that, 'the child was more important than the system'.
2. Leading female physical educationists were also going into print. An article by Veronica Tyndale-Biscoe (1945) described the modern dance extension of Rudolf Laban's work, using phrases like 'the body as a medium of expression'. Similarly, Ruth Clark (1946) wrote about Austrian Gymnastics, referring to movement in an educational medium and suggesting that, 'working on apparatus at his own pace has particular value to the timid child, who gains courage through the discovery for himself of his own capabilities'.
3. **New apparatus:** C.E. Cooke, an organizer in Bristol, visited the Northern Command Physical Training School and saw commandos using scrambling nets and assault course equipment. She felt that young children would 'enjoy the skill and adventure provided by this apparatus' and published her adaptations. With the flush of post-war building, many local authorities introduced their own versions of frame and tubular apparatus in their primary schools, and even old schools were given 'apparatus stations'.

Figure 22.9

4. **The Halifax Experiment:** Miss Dudgeon was working in a children's rehabilitation clinic during the war. The corner-stone of physical training had always been that all children should respond to a set task. At Halifax the individual disabilities of handicapped children led Miss Dudgeon to encourage individual interpretation of open tasks, where children were left to decide rhythm, timing and work at their own level. After the war, this novel approach attracted most of the progressive physical educationists in the country and they noticed that the levels of child involvement, enjoyment, and personal skill achievement were unequalled elsewhere in the country.

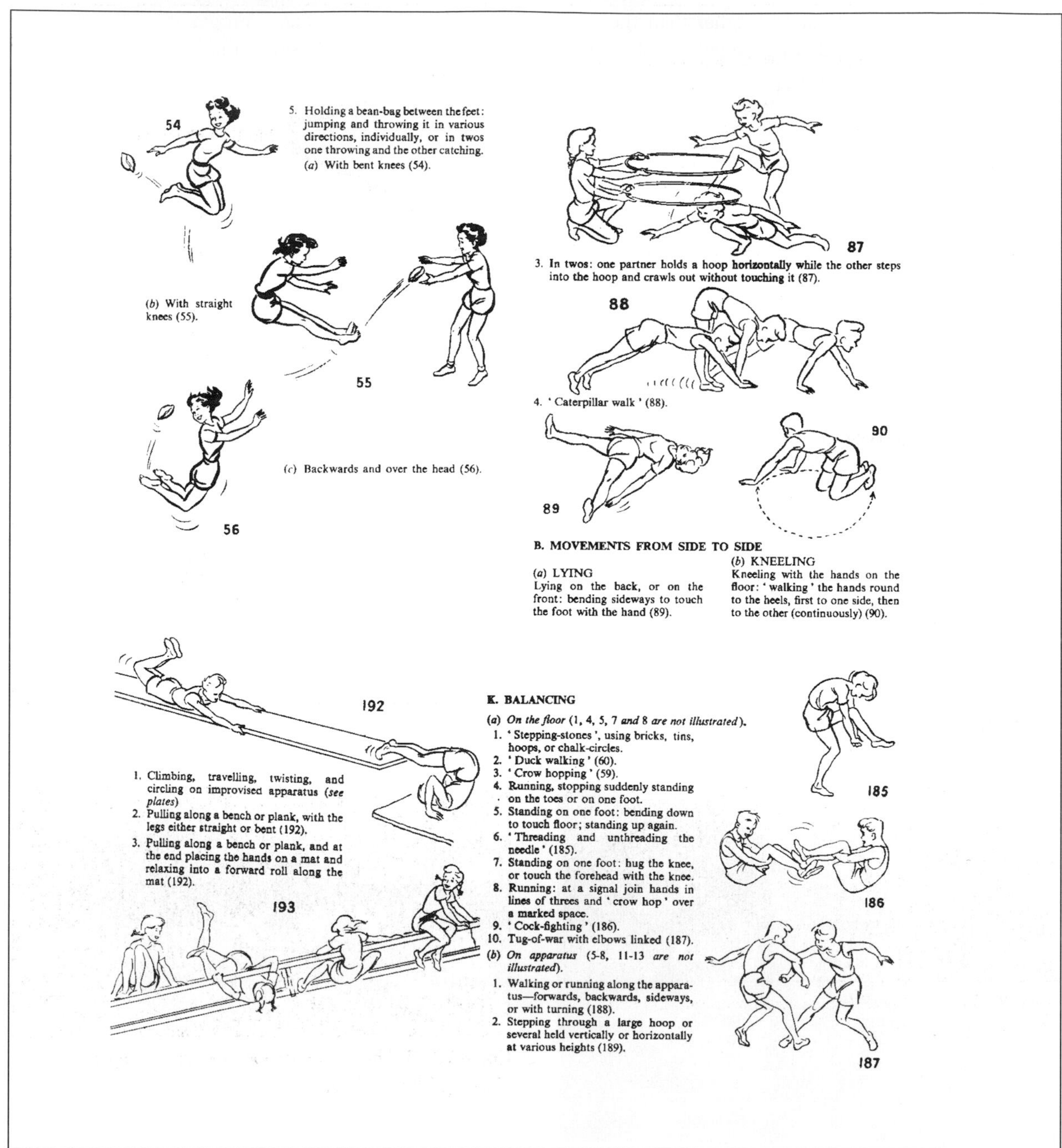

Figure 22.10 Source: Planning the Programme (HMSO, 1953).

The outcome of these progressive developments was the publication of *Moving and Growing* (1952) and *Planning the Programme* (1954). These 'revolutionary' books replaced the formal training syllabuses by introducing a child-centred approach to primary physical education. Both these publications are still to be found in bookshops. A small sample of the activities is included here, and it would be an excellent role play experience to use these or others from *Planning the Programme* to show how free and individualized physical education had become, compared with the initial Model Course.

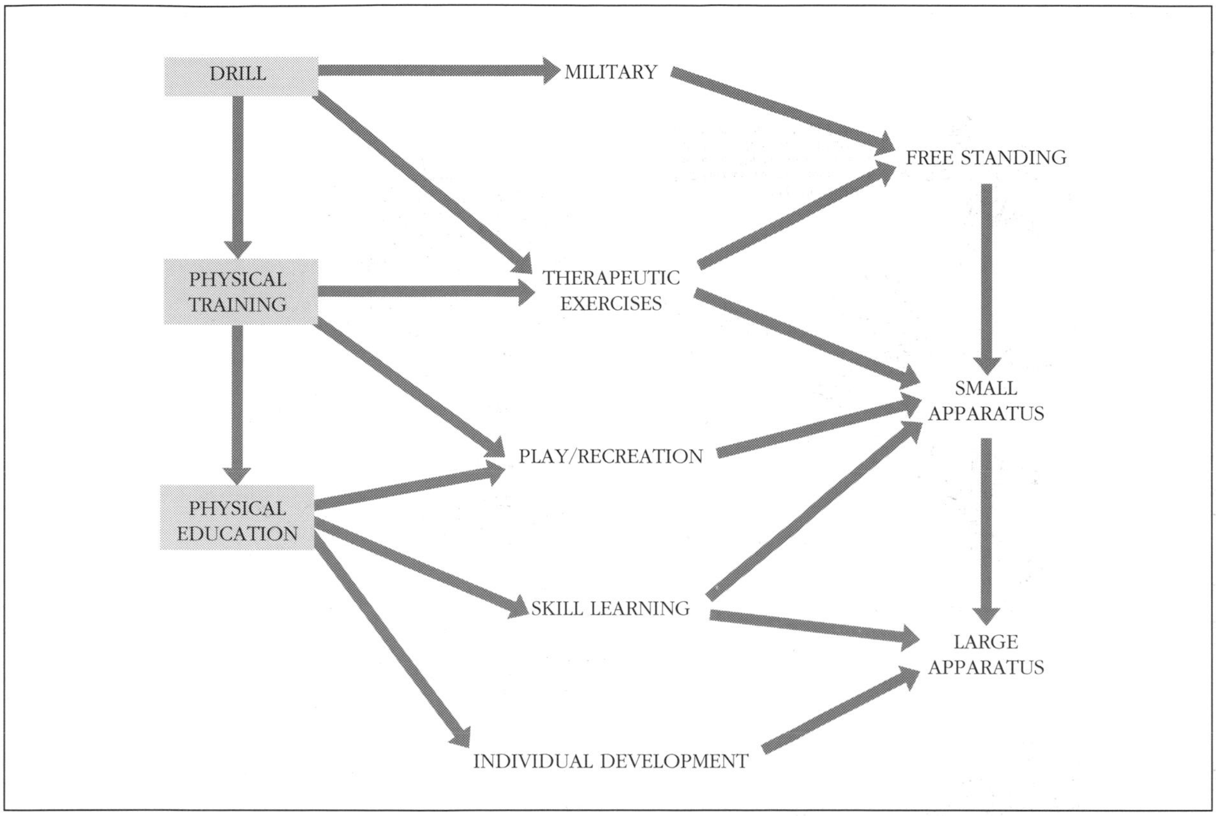

DRILL
MILITARY
FREE STANDING
PHYSICAL TRAINING
THERAPEUTIC EXERCISES
SMALL APPARATUS
PLAY/RECREATION
PHYSICAL EDUCATION
SKILL LEARNING
LARGE APPARATUS
INDIVIDUAL DEVELOPMENT

Figure 22.11

Figure 22.12 Drill and P.T. Source: *Moving and Growing* (HMSO, 1952).

Figure 22.13 Physical Education. Source: *Moving and Growing* (HMSO, 1952).

REVIEW QUESTIONS

1. Use Figure 22.11 to explain the major changes which occurred in junior schools between 1902 and 1954.

2. Compare the physical education envisaged for primary children in *Moving and Growing* with what you do in a secondary school today.

3. Use Figures 22.12 and 13 to explain the differences between drill and physical education.

Summary

Drill, PT, PE:

1. Founded on **Continental Gymnastics** and **Military Drill**.

2. Need for lower classes to be **Fit to Fight.**

3. **Model Course** followed by **Syllabuses.**

4. Trend from **Military Drill** to **Therapeutic Drill.**

5. **Physical Training**—a system of exercises to improve the health and posture of lower class children at elementary schools.

6. Introduction of **skills** and **group work** in 1933 led to birth of PE with **educational** and **physical values** being recognized.

7. **Moving** and **Growing** marking the post-Second World War progression in terms of **personal development** and **heuristic teaching method.**

FURTHER READING

Board of Edn. 1902 Model Course;
1904,1909,1919,1933 Syllabuses, HMSO.
Journal of PE Clark R., Nov. 1946.
Cooke C.E., March 1946.
Major E., Nov. 1943,1947.
Marshall F.J.C., March 1942,1944.
'Somerset Cage and Bars', Nov. 1947.
'Southampton Apparatus', Nov. 1947.
Tyndale-Biscoe V., March 1945.

Min. of Edn. *Moving and Growing,* HMSO, 1952.
Planning the Programme, HMSO, 1954.

McIntosh P.C. *Physical Education in England since 1800,* Bell, 1952.

Munden I. *Suggestions for Small Apparatus in PE,* Ling, 1947.

Smith W.D. *Stretching their Bodies,* David & Charles, 1974.

Index

Abduction 21
Ability 235
Acceleration 174
Acclimatization 137–138
Acetylcholine 43
Achievement motivation 307
  see also Motivation
Actin filaments 40
Actin–myosin bonds (cross bridges) 41
Action potential 42–43
Active mobility 151
Adaptation 129–132
Adduction 21
Adenosine diphosphate (ADP) 94
Adenosine triphosphate (ATP) 41, 44, 93–94, 100–101
Administration
  physical education 378–397
  sport 398–412
ADP (adenosine diphosphate) 94
Adrenaline 54, 112–113
Aerobic exercise 159
Aerobic power 105
Aerobic system 93–94, 96–97
Affective response 253, 311
Aggression 303–304
Agility 116
Agonist 31
Agonist/antagonist response 135
Aids to performance 139
Air resistance 175, 190–193
Alactacid oxygen debt component 101
Alactic anaerobic system 94
All or none law 42, 44
Altitude 137–138
Alveolar ducts 72
Alveolar macrophages 72
Alveolar oxygen tension 77–78
Alveoli 72, 77
Anaerobic capacity 108
Anaerobic power 93–94
Angina 163
Angular acceleration 220
Angular momentum 224
Angular velocity 216–218, 224
Anticipation 253
Anxiety 318–319
Aorta 75
Aponeuroses 30
Appendicular skeleton 8–18
Apprehension 302
Arousal 316
Arteriole 62
Arteriovenous oxygen difference 130
Artery 62
Articular (hyaline) cartilage 8, 14, 19–20, 131
Aspiration 443
Assertion 303
Association 271
Atangonist 31
Atherosclerosis 163
Athleticism 488–502
ATP (adenosine triphosphate) 41, 44, 93–94, 100-101
ATPase 37–39
Atrioventricular node 52
Atrioventricular valve 50
Atrium 51
Attitudes 304–305
Attribution 310–312
Audience 301
Audition 240
Autonomic nervous system 316
Axis of rotation 202

Balance 116
Ball and socket joint 20, 21
Ballistic mobility 153
Barometric pressure 137–138
Baroreceptors 54, 64, 75
Basal metabolic rate 113
Base of support 212
Bernoulli effect 195
Biofeedback 322
Blood
  circulation 30, 60–63
  constituents 59–60
  flow 64–69
  pressure 64, 66, 68
  viscosity 64
Body awareness 135
Body composition 116
Body image 293
Bone 9–13, 15–18
Bony features 12
Bradycardia 57, 131
Breathing 70–76
  at altitude 138
  quiet 73, 82
British Olympic Committee 398
Bronchi 70
Bronchioles 70–72
Bundle of His 51
Bursae 20

Calcium 41, 43
Cancellous bone 15
Capillaries 62
Capillarization 131
Capsule 20
Carbaminohaemoglobin 79
Carbohydrates 112
Carbon dioxide transport 77–79
Carbonic acid 79
Cardiac arrest 164
Cardiac centre 54
Cardiac cycle 52
Cardiac impulse 52
Cardiac muscle 49–50
Cardiac output 53
Cardiovascular disease 163–168
Carotid arteries 75
Cartilage 14, 19
Cartilaginous joint 19
Causal attribution 310
Central Council of Physical Recreation 398
Central nervous system 30, 42
Centre of gravity 208–209
Centre of mass 208–209
Cerebellum 46
Channel capacity 253
Character 287
  development 498–499
Chemical energy 91, 93
Chemoreceptors 75
Circuit training 148–150
Circulatory system 30, 60–63
Circumduction 21
Citric acid cycle 96
Closed loop control 257, 275
Closed skills 234
Co–operation 296–297
Co–ordination 42–47, 116, 263
  gross body 265
  problems 297
Coaches 448
Coactors 301
Cognitive stress management 323
Cohesion 298, 441
Collagen 15
Command style 280
Compact bone 15
Concentric muscle contraction 33–34, 41, 150
Conditioning 271–272
Condyloid joint 21
Conflict 442
Connective tissue 14–16, 131
Constituents of blood 59–60
Constitutional theory 288
Construct validation 125
Continuous skills 232
Continuous training 141
Controllability 310
Cool-down 137
Coronary heart disease 163–165
Coronary thrombosis 163–164
Corpuscles 59
Countryside Commission 398, 415
Couple 202
Coupled reaction 94
Cross bridges 41
Cultural determinants 453–454
Culture and sport 136, 430–438

Deceleration 174
Decision making 45, 248–253
Demonstration 282
Depolarization 42
Depressions, bony 12
Development 259
Diaphragm 73
Diaphysis 16
Diastole 52
Diastolic blood pressure 66
Diffusion
  capacity 78
  gradient 80
Direct energy measurement 92
Disabled people 375, 377
Disaccharides 112
Discrete skills 232
Discrimination 373–377
Distributed practice 284
Dorsiflexion 21
Drill 515
Drive reduction theory 271
Drive theory 303–304, 316
Driving pressure 78
Dynamic equilibrium 180
Dynamic flexibility 265
Dynamic muscle contraction 33
Dynamic precision 263
Dynamic strength 265

Eccentric muscle contraction 34, 41, 150
Efficiency 92
Effort 201
Electrocardiogram 54
Electromyography 323
Electron transport chain 96–97
Elementary schools 515–526
Elitism 450
Emotionality 290
Endocardium 50
Endochondral ossification 17
Endomysium 38
Endurance 115
  cardiovascular 115
  muscle 28, 115

Energy 88–99
  balance 160
  expenditure 92
  input 160
  metabolism 93, 113–114
  and motion 177
  muscle contraction 41
  output 160
Enzymes, muscle 37–39
Epiglottis 70
Epimysium 30, 37
Epiphyseal disc 17
Epiphysis 17
Epithelium, bronchial 70
Equilibrium 180, 211, 241
  gross body 265
Eustress 320–321
Evaluation apprehension 302
Eversion 21
Excellence 450
Executive programme 255
Exercise
  aerobic 159
  and coronary heart disease 165
  isokinetic 150
  isometric 150
  isotonic 150
Exhaled air 78
Expectancy 311, 443
Expiration 74
Expiratory capacity 82
Expiratory reserve volume (ERV) 82
Explosive strength 265
Extension 21, 31
Extensor muscles 31
Extent flexibility 265
External rotation 21
Externally–paced skills 233
Extrinsic motivation 306
Extrovert 290
Eysenck Personality Inventory/Questionnaire 287–290

Fascia 30, 37
Fasciculi 37
Fast twitch muscle fibre 24, 28
Fatigue index 105
Fats 112–113
Fatty acids 112
Feedback 254–257, 272–274
  negative feedback control 54
  sensory 45
Fibres of Purkinje 52
Fibrous (fixed) joint 19
Filaments, actin and myosin 40
Financial aid 370–372
First order factor 288
Fitness 115–125
Fixator 31
Fixed joints 19
Fixed practice 284
Flat bone 9
Flexibility 116, 210, 263
  extent flexibility 265
Flexion 21, 31
Flexor muscles 26, 31
Fluid friction 190–193
FOG (type IIa muscle fibres) 28
Force 174–175
  measurement 181
  moment of 202–203, 220
  net force 179, 209–210
  reaction 185–187
  resultant 174
  as vector 179–200
France
  geographical influences 360
  historical influences 362
  outdoor recreation 416–417
  physical education administration 384–387
  sports administration 366, 401–403
Frequency 126
Friction
  fluid 190–193
  forces 188–189
FTG (type IIb muscle fibres) 28
Fulcrum 202
Functional residual capacity (FRC) 82
Fundamental movement patterns 259–262
Fusiform muscle 24

Galvanic Skin Response 323
Gaseous exchange 68, 72, 77–81
General Adaptation Syndrome 320
General motor ability 235, 263–269
Geographical influences 359–361
Glandular malfunction 158
Gliding joint 21
Global self-esteem 294
Glottis 70
Glucagon 112–113
Glucose 54
Glycerol 112
Glycogen 94–96, 100–101, 113
Glycogen-loaded diet 103
Glycolysis 94, 96, 100
Goal-setting 323–324
Golgi tendon apparatus 45
Gradation of contraction 44
Gravitational field strength 182
Gravity
  centre of 208–209
  field 182
Gross body co–ordination 265
Gross body equilibrium 265

Gross motor abilities 263
Group dynamics 439–444
Group processes 296–298
Growth 259–260
 spurt 259
Guidance 282–283

Haemoglobin 78–79, 137
Haemoglobinic acid 80
Haversian systems 15
Heart 49–58
 attack (cardiac arrest) 163–164
 coronary heart disease 163–165
 rate 52, 54
 sounds 53
 see also cardiac *entries*
Height 13
Hering–Breuer reflex 75
Hierarchical organization 256
Hinge joint 21
Historical influences 362–365
Historical perspectives 465–487
Homeostasis 54, 132, 320
Huxley's theory of muscle contraction 40
Hyaline (articular) cartilage 8, 14, 19–20, 131
Hyperpolarization 43
Hypertension 163

Imagery relaxation 322
Impact 196–199
Impulse 196–199
Impulsion 263
Incentive 306–307
Indirect energy measurement 91
Inertia 183
 moment of 220–226
Information processing 237–258
Inhaled air 78
Inhibition 135
Injury 135
Insertion, muscle 30
Inspiration 74
Inspiratory capacity 82
Inspiratory reserve volume (IRV) 82
Instinct theories 303
Institutional issues 455–458
Insulin 112–113
Intensity 113
Interaction 297
Intercostal muscles 73
Intercostal nerves 73
Internal forces 201–213
Internal rotation 21
Internationalism 368
Interval training 142–147
Intramembranous ossification 18
Intrinsic motivation 306
Inversion 21
Inverted U Theory 317
Involuntary reflexes 46
Irregular bone 9
Isokinetic exercise 150
Isokinetic muscle contraction 33–34
Isometric exercise 150
Isometric muscle contraction 33, 41, 45
Isotonic exercise 150
Isotonic muscle contraction 33

Joints 8, 19–23
Joule 88

Kinaesthesis 241
Kinetic energy (motion energy) 177
Kinetic mobility 153
Kreb's cycle (citric acid cycle) 96

Lactacid oxygen debt component 101, 102–103
Lactate dehydrogenase
Lactic acid 103
 anaerobic system 94–96
 and oxygen debt 100–101
Laminar flow 193
Larynx 70
Leadership 299–301
Learned helplessness 312
Learning 231–232, 271–278
Leisure 333–338
Lever 202, 205–207
Ligaments 20, 30
Linear motion 170–178
Lipids (fats) 112–113
Load 201
Locus of causality 310
Long bone 9, 16
Long-term memory 246
Luck 310
Lungs 70–72
 gas exchange 68, 72, 77–81
 volumes 82–87
Lymph 68

Macrophages, alveolar 72
Magnus effect 195
Manual guidance 283
Mass 182
Maturation 136, 263
Mechanical guidance 283
Medulla oblongata 54, 73, 75
Memory 244–247
Menisci 20
Mental rehearsal 284, 323
Mesocycle 155
Metabolism 93, 113–114
Microcycle 154

Minerals 111
Minute ventilation 82
Mitochondria 37–39, 78, 96
Mitral valves 50
Mobility
  active 151
  passive 151
  training 150–153
Models 273, 294
Moderation 135
Modification of display 283
Moment of a force 202–203, 220
Moment of inertia 220–226
Momentum 198
Monosaccharides 112
Motivation 271, 273, 306–315
Motor
  ability 235, 263–269
  control 256–257, 275–276
  end–plates 42, 43
  fitness 115, 116, 124
  neurone pool 43
  neurones 42–45
  programme 255–256
  skill 230
  units 42–45
Movement
  fundamental patterns 259–262
  time 249
Muscle 24–32
  adaptation 131
  blood flow 64–69
  cardiac 49–50
  contraction 24, 28, 33–36, 40–41, 44–45
  enzymes 37–39
  fibres (muscle cells) 28–29, 37–39
    energy release 93–98
    gas diffusion 37, 39
    structure 39
  glycogen stores 103
  groups 24
  hypertrophy 131
  myoglobin 39, 78, 108
  pump 68
  soreness 103
  spindle apparatus 45
  structure 37–41
  twitch 44
  used in expiration 73
  used in inspiration 73
Musculoskeletal attachments 30
Myelin sheath 43
Myocardium 49–50
Myofibril 39
Myoglobin 39, 78, 102
Myosin filaments 40

Nasal cavity 70
National Coaching Foundation 398
National Curriculum 383
Nationalism 366–368
Need to achieve 307
Need to avoid failure 307
Negative energy balance 158, 159
Negative feedback control 54
Negative reinforcement 306
Negative transfer 276
Nervous impulse 42
Net force 179, 209–210
Net oxygen cost 92, 108
Neuroticism 290
Neutral energy balance 160
Neutral equilibrium 211
Newtons 181
Noise 243
Norepinephrine 54
Nutritional balance 111–114, 159

Obesity 157–162
Open loop control 256–257, 275
Open skills 234, 242
Operant conditioning 272
Organization 279
Origin, muscle 30
Ossification 17–18
Osteoblast 17–18
Osteoclast 18
Osteocyte 17
Outdoor recreation 343, 455–458
Outward Bound Trust 415
Overeating 158
Overload 126
  adaptation 129–132
Oxygen
  at altitude 137–138
  consumption 75, 91, 105–110
  debt (oxygen recovery) 75, 96, 100–104
  dissociation curve 77
  partial pressure 77
  transport 77
Oxygenated myoglobin 39
Oxyhaemoglobin 78–79

Pacemaker (sino–atrial node) 50–52
Pacing continuum 233
Pads of fat 20
Parasympathetic nervous system 54
Parietal membrane 70
Partial pressure of oxygen 77
Passive mobility 151
Peak anaerobic power 105
Pennate muscle 24
Perception 242–247
Perceptual ability 235

Perceptual-motor skill 230, 237–258
Performance 231
  aids 139
Pericardium 49
Perimysium 37
Period 136
Periosteum 16–18, 30
Peripheral resistance 64
Personality 287–291, 307–308
Pharynx 70
Phosphagen restoration 101
Phosphocreatine (PC) 94
Phrenic nerves 73
Physical education 329, 353–357
  administration 378–397
Physical fitness 115–116
Physical proficiency abilities 263
Physical recreation 329, 343–346
Physiological adaptation 133–136
Physique 287
Pivot joint 21
Plantar flexion 21
Plasma 59
Platelets 60
Play 329, 339–341
Pleural cavity 70
Pleural fluid 70
Plyometrics 34, 150
Pneumotaxic centre 75
Pocket valves 61
Politics 369–370
Polysaccharides 112
Popular recreation 469–487
Positive energy balance 158
Positive reinforcement 306
Positive transfer 276
Potassium/sodium pump 42–43
Potassium 42, 54
Power 91, 116
Precapillary sphincter 61
Principle of moments 202–203
Problem solving 280
Progression 135
Progressive part presentation 284
Progressive Relaxation Training 322
Pronation 21
Proprioceptors 45, 75, 239, 240
Proteins 111
Protrusions, bony 12
Psychological refractory period 251
Psychometric method 288
Psychomotor abilities 263–269
Public schools 488–502
Pulmonary arteries 51
Pulmonary blood pressure 78
Pulmonary circulatory system 60, 68
Pulmonary pleura 70
Pulmonary veins 51
Pulmonary ventilation 70, 77–81
Pulse 54
Pure part presentation 284
Purkinje fibres 52
Pyruvic acid 94

Queen's College Step Test 106
Quiet breathing 73, 82

Radial artery 54
Radian 215
Range of movement 21
Ratchet mechanism 41
Rational recreation 503–514
Reaction forces 185–187
Reaction time 116, 248–250
Reciprocal innervation 46
Reciprocal style 280
Recognition 242
Recovery (oxygen debt; oxygen recovery) 75, 96, 100–104
Recreation 342
  popular 469–487
  rational 503–514
Red blood cells 59
Red muscle 39
Reflex arc 46
Reflexes 46
Reflexive movement 46
Regression 132
Reinforcement 271, 273
  negative 306
  positive 306
Relationships 427, 439
Relaxation 322
Repetition 135
Repolarization 42–43
Residual volume 82
Resistance
  air 175, 190–193
  to blood flow 64
Respiration *see* Breathing
Respiratory bronchioles 70–72
Respiratory centre 75
Respiratory muscles 73
Respiratory pump 68
Response time 248–250
Resting potential 42–43
Resultant force 174
Reticular activating system 291
Risk taking 304
Role play 293
Roles in sport and physical education 445–448
Rotating systems 215–227
Rotation 21
Rotational energy 224

Saddle joint 21
Saltatory conduction 43
Sarcolemma 37–39
Sarcomere 39, 40
Sarcoplasm 37–39, 96
Sarcoplasmic reticulum 37–39
Scalar 176
SCAT 319
Schema theory 275–276
Second order factor 289
Selective attention 244–247
Self concept 292–295
Self-confidence 323
Self-directed relaxation 322
Self-efficacy 323
Self-esteem 292–295
Self-paced skills 233
Self-report questionnaire 288, 322
Semilunar valves 50
Sensory feedback 45
Sensory input 239–241
Sensory neurone 45
Serial skills 232
Set 142
Sharpey's fibres 30
Short bone 9
Short–term memory 244
Significant others 294
Simplification 282
Sino-atrial node 50–52
Sixteen Personality Factor Questionnaire 289
Skeletal muscle 30–32, 37
Skeleton 8–18
Skill 133, 230–236
Skill training 133, 154
Skinfold measurements 121
Slow twitch muscle fibres 24, 28
Smooth muscle 37
Social facilitation 301
Social learning theories 304
Social loafing 297
Socialization 443–444
Societal issues 450–454
Socio-economic factors 366–377
Sociology of sport 426–429
Sociometry 298
Sodium 42–43
Somatic stress management 322–323
Source trait 288
Soviet Union
  geographical influences 361
  historical influences 364–365
  outdoor recreation 421–424
  physical education administration 393–397
  sport administration 367–368, 408–412
Spaced practice 284
Spatial summation 44–45
Specificity 133
Speed 116, 173, 176, 263
Sphygmomanometer 66
Spins 219, 224, 226
Spirometer 82
Sport 329, 347–352
  administration 398–412
  sociology of 426–429
  women in 460–464
Sport for All 341, 351
Sports Aid Foundation 398
Sports Council 398
Stability 211–213
Stable equilibrium 211
Stage training 149
STAI 319
Stamina 166, 265
Starling's Law of the Heart 53–54
State anxiety 320
Static equilibrium 180
Static (isometric) muscle contraction 33, 150
Static precision 263
Static strength 265
Status 450
STEN score 289
Stimulus 243, 271–272
Streamlining 192–194
Strength 115
  explosive 265
  static 265
  training 129
Stress 126, 320–323
Stressor 320
Stretch reflexes 45
Striated muscle 37
Striped cardiac tissue 49–50
Striped muscle 37, 40
Stroke volume 53
Strokes 163
Sub-cultural issues 460–464
Subroutine 255–256
Supination 21
Surface trait 289
Sweating 112, 132
Syllabuses, early 518–522
Sympathetic nervous system 53, 54
Synapses 43
Synergist 31
Synovial fluid 20
Synovial joint 19, 21
Synovial membrane 20
Systemic circulatory system 60
Systole 52–53
Systolic blood pressure 66

Tangible rewards 306
Task complexity 281, 317–318

Teaching style 279–285
Temperament 287
Tendons 30, 131
Tetanic contraction 44
Thermoregulation 132
Threshold 130
Tidal volume 82
Tissue fluid 68
Tissue respiration 68, 77, 78–79, 93
Torque 202
Total lung capacity 82
Total metabolic rate 113
Touch 239
Trabeculae 15
Trachea 70
Training 126–156
  continuous 141
  fuel use 113
  individual response 136
  interval 142–147
  mobility 150–153
  stage 149
Trait anxiety 319–320
Trait theory 288
Transfer 135, 276–277
Triad vesicles 37
Tricuspid valves 50
Triglycerides 112
Trunk strength 265
Type I (slow twitch) muscle fibre 24, 28
Type II (fast twitch) muscle fibre 24, 28

United Kingdom
  geographical influences 359
  outdoor recreation 413–415
  physical education administration 378–383
  sport administration 366, 398–400
United States
  discrimination 374–375
  geographical influences 360
  historical influences 363
  outdoor recreation 418–420
  physical education administration 388–392
  sport administration 366–367, 404–407
Unstable equilibrium 211

Vagus nerve 54, 75
Validation 125
Variable practice 284
Variance 135
Vascular system 59–63
Vasoconstriction 64
Vasodilatation 64
Vasomotor control 62, 64
Vector 176, 179–200
Vein 62
Velocity 176
Vena cavae 62
Venomotor control 62, 64
Venous return 53, 68
Ventricle 51
Venule 62
Verbal guidance 283
Vertebral column 9, 11
Visceral membrane 70
Vision 240
Visual aids 282
Visual guidance 282
Visualization 322
Vital capacity 82
Vitamins 111–112
$\dot{V}O_2$max.105
Voluntary movement 46
Voluntary (skeletal) muscle 30–32, 37
Voluntary reflexes 46

Warm–up 137
Water 112
Watt 90
Wave summation 44
Weight 182–183
Weight control 159–161
White blood cells 60
White fibrocartilage 14, 19
White muscle 39
Whole method 281
Whole-part-whole method 281
Wingate anaerobic power test 108
Women in sport 460–464
Work 88–92

Yellow elastic cartilage 14